T0391440

THE LAW OF ENERGY FOR SUSTAINABLE DEVELOPMENT

This book is a compilation of articles by leading world energy experts on the laws for implementing energy programs to meet the economic development needs of developing countries by environmentally sustainable means. An introduction by United Nations Secretary-General Kofi Annan emphasizes the importance of this work – and the creation of the IUCN Academy on Environmental Law where the articles were presented – for addressing the energy aspects of alleviating world poverty, health, and gender challenges. The articles include lead pieces by Professor Jose Goldemberg of Brazil and Professor Thomas Johansson of Sweden, respectively editor and coordinator of the World Energy Assessment, and by Dr. Zhou Dadi, Director of the China Energy Research Institute. The articles address environmentally sound legislation for all energy media and the energy challenges of every region of the world by renowned regional authors.

Adrian J. Bradbrook is the Bonython Professor of Energy Law at the University of Adelaide, Australia, and the former Chair of the IUCN Commission on Environmental Law, Energy Law, and Climate Change Working Group. He is a Fellow of the Australian Institute of Energy and the International Energy Foundation. He is the author of the book *Solar Energy and the Law* (1984), and he has published numerous legal academic articles, primarily on environmental aspects of energy law, with particular emphasis on energy efficiency and renewable energy resources.

Rosemary Lyster is Senior Lecturer in the Faculty of Law, University of Sydney. She specializes in environmental law and administrative law. In environmental law, her primary areas of interest are energy law, water law, Asia-Pacific environmental law, and environmental dispute resolution. She is Director of the Australian Centre for Environmental Law (Sydney) and editor-in-chief of the *Asia Pacific Journal of Environmental Law*. She is a member of the IUCN/World Conservation Union's Commission on Environmental Law.

Richard L. Ottinger is Dean Emeritus and Professor of Law at Pace Law School in White Plains, New York, where he taught environmental law and was dean from 1994 to 1999. He is a member of the IUCN Commission on Environmental Law and Chair of its Climate and Energy Working Group. He served for 16 years in the U.S. Congress, chairing the House Subcommittee on Energy, Conservation and Power. He was a founding staff member of the U.S. Peace Corps and was an associate in the New York law firm of Clearly, Gottlieb, Friendly & Hamilton.

Dr. Wang Xi received his B.A. degree from Wuhan Normal College in 1981. He graduated from Wuhan University in 1984 (M.L.) and from Washington University in 1987 (M.J.S.). He concluded his Ph.D. at Wuhan University in 2000. He is currently Professor and Associate Dean of the School of Law, Shanghai Jiao Tong University, and Director of Environmental and Resources Law Institute at the same university. He is a member of the Academic Committee of Environmental Law under the Ministry of Education of China.

IUCN ACADEMY OF ENVIRONMENTAL LAW RESEARCH STUDIES

The Law of Energy for Sustainable Development

Edited by

ADRIAN J. BRADBROOK
University of Adelaide

ROSEMARY LYSTER
University of Sydney

RICHARD L. OTTINGER
Pace University

WANG XI
Shanghai Jiao Tong University

with a Message from Kofi A. Annan,
Secretary-General of the United Nations

CAMBRIDGE UNIVERSITY PRESS
Cambridge, New York, Melbourne, Madrid, Cape Town,
Singapore, São Paulo, Delhi, Mexico City

Cambridge University Press
The Edinburgh Building, Cambridge CB2 8RU, UK

Published in the United States of America by Cambridge University Press, New York

www.cambridge.org
Information on this title: www.cambridge.org/9781107407718

First published 2005
First paperback edition 2012

A catalogue record for this publication is available from the British Library

Library of Congress Cataloging in Publication Data

The law of energy for sustainable development / edited by
Adrian J. Bradbrook . . . [et al.].
   p.   cm.
Includes bibliographical references and index.
ISBN 0-521-84525-4
1. Power resources – Law and legislation.   2. Electric utilities – Law and
legislation.   3. Sustainable development.   4. Energy industries – Environmental
aspects.   I. Bradbrook, Adrian J.   II. IUCN Academy of Environmental Law.
K3978.L39   2005
346.04'679–dc22   2004050126

ISBN 978-0-521-84525-0 Hardback
ISBN 978-1-107-40771-8 Paperback

Contents

Acknowledgments

Preparation of this volume, encompassing the research papers presented at the first Colloquium of the IUCN Academy of Environmental Law, has been possible because of the contributions of many individuals and institutions. We are grateful to them all and wish to acknowledge their substantive support.

The Members and Council of the International Union for the Conservation of Nature and Natural Resources (IUCN) and IUCN Secretary General Achim Steiner made possible the launch of the IUCN Academy of Environmental Law. The Members of the IUCN Commission on Environmental Law (CEL) and the IUCN Environmental Law Centre worked diligently over a five-year period to lay the foundation for the new venture and research reflected in these pages. The expertise and financial support of CEL played an important role in the success of the first Colloquium. We thank the prior chairmen of CEL, Dr. Wolfgang E. Burhenne and Dr. Parvez Hassan, the Head of the IUCN Environmental Law Programme, John Scanlon, Esq., and Bhagwat Sing, representative of IUCN at the United Nations, for their strong encouragement and help in launching the Academy and this initial volume of research. The Colloquium and resulting publications could never have been such a success without the untiring and devoted efforts of Maria Sorcorro Manguiat, Legal Officer, and Katerina Sarafidou, CEL Liaison Officer of the Environmental Law Centre.

Shanghai Jiao Tong University, its President, Dr. Xie Shengwu, and its Vice President, Dr. Ye Quyuan, as well as the School of Law and its Environmental and Resources Law Institute (ERLI), provided a most gracious and efficient setting for the deliberations at the first Colloquium on November 4–6, 2003, in Shanghai, China. The leadership of the Director of ERLI, Prof. Dr. Wang Xi, was essential to the success of the Colloquium and production of this research volume. Prof. Feng Zhijun, Vice Chairman of the Committee on Environmental and Resources Protection of the National People's Congress, and Wang Yuqing, Vice Administrator of the PRC State Environmental Protection Administration, provided essential support and expertise to the Colloquium. The superb services of graduate student leaders from Shanghai Jiao Tong University, especially Ms. Dong Yan (Maggie Dong), are acknowledged with thanks.

We warmly thank United Nations Secretary-General Kofi A. Annan for his very gracious introduction to our publication. The United Nations Development Programme and the United Nations Environment Programme provided essential contributions of financial support and expertise for which we are most grateful. The endorsement of the United Nations Institute for Research and Training (UNITAR) also is greatly appreciated, as are the expertise and the wonderful support of the Asia Pacific Centre for Environmental Law of the National University of Singapore and its Director, Prof. Koh Kheng Lian.

We are especially grateful for the support of Pace University President Dr. David A. Caputo for his support and his address to the preparatory committee for the Academy and Colloquium. The financial and in-kind support provided by the Center for Environmental Legal Studies of Pace University School of Law (New York, USA), and its co-Directors, Professor Richard L. Ottinger and Nicholas A. Robinson, and Prof. Lee Paddock, Director of Pace's Environmental Law Programs, is warmly appreciated, as are the superb organizational and substantive assistance of Pace Law School graduate student Nancy Kong.

The support of the 60 universities from 42 nations that sent more than 150 professors to deliberate together at the Colloquium provided a wealth of intellectual talent that helped hone the research papers. We are grateful to Professor Alexandre Kiss whose remarkable lectures are included and to all the other scholars whose work is here published.

We are very grateful to Cambridge University Press and its representative, John Berger, for the timely publication of this initial scholarship of the IUCN Academy of Environmental Law.

Finally, thanks are due to the Chair of the IUCN Commission on Environmental Law, Professor Nicholas A. Robinson, who co-chaired this first Colloquium. His tireless endeavors have nurtured the IUCN Academy from the germ of an idea in 1996 to a present reality.

The Editors

UNITED NATIONS   NATIONS UNIES

THE SECRETARY-GENERAL
--
MESSAGE TO THE INAUGURATION OF THE IUCN
ACADEMY OF ENVIRONMENTAL LAW
Shanghai, 4 November 2003

Environmental law, both national and international, establishes the principles and rules that states have adopted in order to protect the precious ecosystems and resources upon which all life and progress depend. *Agenda 21* recommended strengthening the law for environment and development, and called on universities in particular to cooperate in building capacity in the realm of environmental law. That call was repeated last year in the Plan of Implementation adopted at the World Summit on Sustainable Development in Johannesburg.

It is therefore most welcome that the International Union for the Conservation of Nature and Natural Resources is establishing a new global network of university law departments dedicated to progress in this area. I would like to congratulate all academic leaders assembled at Shanghai Jiao Tong University for their role in making possible the launch of the *IUCN Academy of Environmental Law*. IUCN's Commission on Environmental Law has rendered an important service in implementing *Agenda 21*'s recommendations that academic institutions cooperate in the areas of curriculum planning, course development, and the dissemination of information on legal and regulatory innovations in the field of environment and development. It is heartening indeed to see the successful realization of the planning decisions taken at the Academy's Preparatory Meeting, which were reported to the Legal Counsel of the United Nations and others at UN headquarters on 16 April this year.

The United Nations looks forward to the teaching and research that the Academy will now undertake. And we welcome the academic contributions that law professors worldwide will make towards our common goal of sustainable development on our one and only planet.

Kofi A. Annan

A Global Learned Society to Address Earth's Evolution: The IUCN Academy of Environmental Law

Nicholas A. Robinson*

Law, as the manifestation of the human drive to live within an ordered society, has been at the center of life in all nations and in all civilization. Law always had a regard for nature, as the ancient Chinese pictogram for the law, FA, makes clear. However, until the late nineteenth century, law took nature for granted. As the industrial revolution emerged, as the scientific revolution brought to Earth the perspectives from space, and as human populations placed unprecedented demands on Earth's natural resources to meet human needs and wants, humans began to induce an evolution in the planet. Deserts have grown, the Aral Sea has dried up, species have become extinct, urban settlements have become vast conurbations producing ever greater demands for housing, food stuffs, jobs, potable water, and energy.

It is not only natural that the field of law should address these phenomena, as a matter of simple justice law it must. No international authority mandated that the field of environmental law should be established. The field emerged in the 1970s, and now exists in all nations and as a growing element of international law. As the norms of environmental law have made clear,[1] it also has become clear that much of the implementation of these norms remains unrealized. Much of this is due to the lack of trained personnel and deficiencies in the legislation comprising the first generation of environmental laws. To provide remedies for these deficiencies, the International Union for the Conservation of Nature and Natural Resources (IUCN), through its Commission on Environmental Law, called upon the university law faculties, law schools, and law departments of this Earth to establish a new learned society. In 2003, at Shanghai Jiao Tong University, over 150 professors from forty-two nations, representing some sixty universities, established the IUCN Academy of Environmental Law.[2]

The Academy is a learned society examining how law advances a just society that values and conserves nature. Its membership is open to those university law faculties, law schools, and departments that have invested sufficient resources to be able to join together into a consortium of learning, research and teaching. Every year, the Academy gathers in a Colloquium to share research on a given subject. The first such gathering has featured the role and reforms needed if energy law is to provide support for sustainable

---

[1] *See, e.g.* Philippe Sands, *Principles Of International Environmental Law* (2d Edition, Cambridge University Press, 2003).

[2] The documentation recording the decisions and deliberations that resulted in the establishment of the IUCN Academy of Environmental Law can be accessed at http://www.iucn.org/themes/law.

* The IUCN Academy of Environmental Law.

development, as the United Nations World Summit on Sustainable Development (Johannesburg, 2002), defines that term. Each year, also, the Academy invites a distinguished senior scholar of environmental law to share with the academic community her or his reflections on the field of environmental law. This learned synthesis affords perspective and guidance for those scholars critiquing and advancing aspects of environmental law.

THE ACADEMY'S ANNALS

This volume represents the first publication of the Colloquium research and the annual synthesis of the field, as the Annals of the IUCN Academy of Environmental Law. Dr. Charles-Alexandre Kiss organized and published the proceedings of one of the very first international colloquia on "The Protection of the Environment and International Law" in 1973.[3] It is fitting that he provides this inaugural set of lectures for the Annals.

Since the demand for energy has guided humans ever since the mastering of fire at an early stage of human evolution, it is also fitting that this inaugural Colloquium focuses on the law of energy for sustainable development. Without law reform to restructure how energy is produced and distributed and used, there will not be a just society and natural systems will be changed in ways unintended and often detrimental to ecology and to human health. The chapters in this volume set forth the case for law reform in the energy law sector.

The Academy is grateful to Shanghai Jiao Tong University, which hosted the inaugural first Colloquium and to the able editors of this volume, Prof. Adrian Bradbrook, Rosemary Lyster, Richard Ottinger, and Wang Xi. The Academy is also grateful to the University of Nairobi and its Faculty of Law and related Institute for Sustainable Development, and Prof. Charles Odidi Okidi and his colleagues, for undertaking to host the second Colloquium of the Academy on October 4–8, 2004, in Nairobi, Kenya. Subsequent annual colloquia are being hosted by the University of Auckland (New Zealand), Macquarie University (Sydney, Australia), Pace University (New York, USA), and a review of environmental law on the fifteenth anniversary of the Rio "Earth Summit" (UN Conference on Environment and Development, 1992) in Rio de Janeiro with the Association of Brazilian Environmental Law Professors and the Institute of Lawyers for a Green Planet. Finally, the Academy is most grateful to Gilbert Kerlin, a renown lawyer and conservationist, whose generous contribution to the Academy through the Pace University Center for Environmental Legal Studies, has underwritten much of the initial organizing for the launch of the Academy. Gil Kerlin was keenly devoted to building the rule of law and strengthening international cooperation, and he took delight in making support for the Academy one of his last constructive works of his own days on this Earth. He died on April 9, 2004.[4]

The Second Colloquium in 2004 will address land stewardship through the analytic lenses of comparative law techniques, and a wide range of other subjects. In closing

---

[3] Alexandre-Charles Kiss, Editor, *The Protection of the Environment and International Law* (Hague Academy of International Law, Sijthoff, Leiden, 1975).

[4] Stuart Lavietes, "Gilbert Kerlin, 94, Riverdale Conservator, Dies," *New York Times*, p. B7, col. 1 (April 12, 2004).

this introduction, it may be useful to provide a précis to introduce how the Academy intends to advance its mission.

PRÉCIS: THE IUCN ACADEMY OF ENVIRONMENTAL LAW

University law faculties have provided human society with the capacity to frame and be guided by the rule of law since at least the fifteenth century. In the annals of history, their capacity to endure must be accounted as robust. They address the enduring human thirst to frame just and consistent rules to guide our behavior. Each epoch has recast its rules to cope with the perceived needs of their societies. In doing so, law, akin to the Roman God Janus, has rewarded those who understand this mission with a view to the past, and those who conceive the challenge anew with a view for the future.

Among our society's many pressing challenges at the start of the twenty-first century, how society responds to the human induced alternation of Earth's natural systems surely ranks as the most profound in terms of its implication for the future of all life as we understand it. One cannot at once melt the glaciers and polar ice caps, alter the climate, raise the relative levels of the seas, cause extinction of a wide range of species, and watch the rapid growth of the human population in crowded human settlements around the globe, without asking some fundamental questions: How shall we cope? Our past accomplishments are no sure guide for this future, are they?

Since the late nineteenth century, a small cluster of scientists and civic leaders have presaged and worried about these developments. Through their effort, in 1948 a coalition of states, ministries, scientific and other learned societies and nongovernmental organizations established IUCN, the International Union for the Conservation of Nature and Natural Resources.[5] Since then, successive generations of environmental leaders have built IUCN to become the premier international organization devoted to nature conservation and sustainable development. Today, IUCN has more state members than any other international organization that is represented as an official Observer in the United Nations General Assembly, and IUCN is unique in that role in having also over 120 ministries and over 800 nongovernmental organizations among its members. IUCN's membership altogether eclipses the entire number of organizations in consultative status with ECOSOC, and these numbers are growing. IUCN has become the only *fully* global system of governments, learned societies, and civic associations united in a mission to "sustain a just society that values and respects nature."

It should therefore come as no surprise that professors from university law faculties have played key roles in the evolution of IUCN. As the twentieth century concluded, law professors, particularly in Asia and the Pacific, called for establishment of a new academic network through which to coordinate their legal studies to guide the legal foundations for sustainable development through the IUCN Commission on Environmental Law. This led IUCN's members at the Second World Conservation Congress (Amman, Jordan, 1999) to endorse Commission's proposal to create a new, international, autonomous, learned society, the "IUCN Academy of Environmental Law."

The Academy is the first global, learned society dedicated at once both to advancing knowledge of how law advances a just society that values and conserves nature, and to building the capacity of university law faculties to provide legal education to address

---

[5] *See* Martin Holdgate, *The Green Web* (Earthscan, 1999).

the environmental challenges of global change. It does so through three interrelated undertakings:

(a) Annually, through one or more of its member universities, the Academy hosts an annual Colloquium to synthesize advanced research on a significant theme of environmental law, and to engage a senior law professor to reflect on the discipline of this entire field of law. The Cambridge University Press publishes and disseminates these edited Annals of the IUCN Academy of Environmental Law. The Colloquium rotates to a different region of the Earth each year, facilitating participation by professors from universities located in the region. Because environmental law is still a young discipline, dating from around the time of the 1972 Stockholm Conference on the Human Environment, the professors at many law faculties, schools, and departments have not yet had an opportunity to meet with each other, or even get to know each other. Although there are some twenty national environmental law societies, until now there has been *no* academic environmental law network for law professors and their universities to work through. The Colloquia, and the publications of the Academy, will build this community of knowledge across all regions.

(b) When the professors gather together, they have the opportunity to further their individual collaboration on teaching and research in environmental law. Gathered during the Colloquia, the Academy encourages professors to collaborate on curriculum development and course texts, develop visitorships among universities, team teaching of courses, and distance learning.

(c) Through knowing the respective expertise and research interests of their member university law faculties, the Academy works to structure joint research into the legal aspects of significant environmental challenges, to build an understanding of how society may cope with them, and to develop new concepts about how law can assist society worldwide. This conceptual law development has been a hallmark of IUCN's Environmental Law Programme, producing in the past the original studies for the Convention on International Trade in Endangered Species (CITES, 1973), the UN World Charter for Nature (UN Res. 37/7, 1986), and the Convention on Biological Diversity (1992). Research for conceptual law development is undertaken in dialogue with IUCN, and the Academy's research recommendations are provided to IUCN for its Programme and its Members. The Academy's research has an immediate audience, beyond the community of academics around the world. IUCN's Environmental Law Programme, with the worldwide Commission on Environmental Law, the Union's global Environmental Law Centre located in Bonn, Germany, which is the hub for partner centers around the world, are positioned to respond to the Academy's recommendations and focus on their implementation. By the time researched proposals for conceptual law development are in print, responses to them will be under way. This link between research and action is important if states around the world are to be assisted in coping with the effects of the profound global changes reported by scientists in other disciplines.

The Academy's stimulated collaboration in teaching and research also builds the strength of universities around the world. Innovations in information technology and the Internet allow universities to share their resources in designing new, electronic "knowledge" bases. They can also combine the talents of individual professors to collaborate in new interregional research projects. This can link universities north/south/east/west. The Academy can help broker research partnerships among interested universities, thereby overcoming the regional or national isolation that too often exists. Some universities lack capacity to undertake fundraising needed to sustain research, while others lack the contacts to build the partnerships with universities in distant parts of the world that are essential to making effective use of capabilities provided by the revolution in information technology. University law faculties in developed states too often lack firsthand knowledge of even urgent sustainable development needs of developing states. In like vein, law faculties in states with economies in transition, as in many developing countries, often lack access to their colleagues from developed regions, who would have an interest in collaborating with them on issues such as how liberalized trade agreements impact on environmental management, or how zoonotic diseases can be better managed across regions to protect public health.

In short, while it works to build knowledge about how environmental law can better serve sustainable development and cope with global change, the IUCN Academy also strengthens the environmental law capacity within each university, and across universities. It adds value to the participating universities in multiple dimensions, and thereby helps to ensure that the historic mission of the law school is renewed in the coming years as the effects of global change are realized.

These Annals are a modest first step toward building the collaboration that this new learned society seeks. Those interested in participation in the work of the Academy can contact the Academy through the IUCN Centre for Environmental Law, in Bonn, Germany.

Public Lectures on International Environmental Law

Alexandre Kiss*

LECTURE 1: INTRODUCTION – THREE QUESTIONS

Allow me to tell you how much I appreciate and admire the organization of the present conference, the contribution of the Shanghai Jiao Tong University and the huge preparatory work done by Professor Wang Xi and his outstanding team. I am very grateful for having been invited.

It is a great honor for me to deliver the First Academy Public International Lecture of Environmental Law. While I am very proud of this distinction, I am even more pleased that IUCN and its Commission of Environmental Law were able to create that Academy. I know the considerable difficulties that the initiative of that creation had to overcome and the immense talent and energy which the President of that Commission, Professor Nicholas Robinson, invested in this enterprise.

The present conference concerns international environmental law. I propose to you to examine separately the three terms that figure in this phrase: "international," "environmental," and "law." I will, however, modify this order and start with "environment" and then discuss successively "law" and "international."

1 WHY DO WE SPEAK OF THE ENVIRONMENT?

The term "environment" can describe a limited area, the entire planet, or even include a part of the outer space that surrounds the Earth. The term "biosphere," used in particular by the United Nations Educational, Scientific, and Cultural Organization (UNESCO), is more precise, if still broad. It designates the totality of the human environment, the part of the universe where, according to present knowledge, all life is concentrated. In fact, the biosphere includes a very narrow stratum encircling the globe. It comprises the Earth and several thousand meters above and under the surface of the earth and oceans.

Although respect for the Earth and the benefits it offers to humankind is deeply rooted in different religions and philosophies, the awareness that we can severely harm it by destroying its components is relatively recent. Indeed, the term "environment" is new in many languages, at least as it is defined today. In French, its origins go back to the

---

* Professor of Law, University of Strasbourg, France; President of the European Council for Environmental Law.

medieval verb "environner," but the term has been regularly used only since the beginning of the 1960s. In other languages new words were created during the same decade to express the concept: "Umwelt" in German, "Milieu" in Dutch, "Medio ambiente" in Spanish, "Al.biah" in Arabic, "okruhauchhaia sreda" in Russian, "kankyo" in Japanese. These inventions indicate that less than forty years ago the world simultaneously discovered a new phenomenon that represented a major challenge to modern society and which had to be labeled and studied.

Let us recall two images or, rather, two representations of our planet, the Earth. The first is rather old and was much used at the beginning of the "ecological era," which started at the end of the 1960s. It has a specific current significance nowadays for China, after the remarkable achievement of the first Chinese cosmonaut. The Earth can be compared to an inhabited spaceship navigating in the outer space. The members of the crew know and must realize that they have a given amount of oxygen, water, and food for the whole journey and that they will have no more supply until they land. Our planet can be compared to a certain extent to that spaceship, but only to a certain extent because first, we do not know how long humanity will have to continue the journey and second, we, the occupants of our spaceship, become more and more numerous. During the last century our number was multiplied by three and according to UN estimations, the number of the inhabitants of the planet could increase in the coming decades by a third at least of the present six billion persons.

The second image is taken from a novel that had a great success several years ago and was made into an even more popular movie, *Jurassic Park* by Michael Crichton. The most interesting component of the book is not the description of the island where dinosaurs were recreated or that of the disastrous events that annihilated this Disney-like enterprise. A statement by a scientist in the course of a final discussion on the disaster gives us a precious second key for further thinking:

> Our planet is four and half billion years old. There has been life on this planet for nearly as long. Three point eight billion years. . . . . Great dynasties of creatures arising, flourishing, dying away. All this happening against a background of continuous and violent upheaval, mountain ranges thrust up and eroded away, cometary impacts, volcanic eruptions, oceans rising and falling, whole continents moving. . . . Endless, constant and violent change. . . . The planet has survived everything, in its time. It will certainly survive us. . . . Let's say we had a bad (radiation accident), and all the plants and animals died, and the earth was clicking hot for a hundred thousand years. Life would survive somewhere. . . . And after all those years, when the planet was no longer inhospitable, life would again spread over the planet. The evolutionary process would begin again. It might take a few billion years for life to regain its present variety; And of course, it would be very different from what it is now. But the earth would survive our folly. Only we . . . think it wouldn't. . . .
>
> My point is that life on Earth can take care of itself. . . . To the Earth a hundred years is nothing. A million years is nothing. This planet lives and breathes on a much vaster scale. . . . We have been residents here for the blink of an eye. If we are gone tomorrow, the Earth will not miss us. . . . Let's be clear. The planet is not in jeopardy. We are in jeopardy. We haven't got the power to destroy the planet – or to save it. But we might have the power to save ourselves.

This long quote is self-explanatory and answers the first question we asked: Why do we speak of the environment and of its protection?

2 WHY IS LAW NECESSARY TO PROTECT THE ENVIRONMENT?

Every human society elaborates norms that express and tend to protect the common concern ("common interest," "intérêt général") of the group or of the whole species. Other species develop instinctive traits that show similar concerns. The basic components of such concerns are the need to survive and the need to ensure the survival of the species or of the group. Despite their evolution and the sophisticated stage they reached, humans have the same basic needs, only transposed to more sophisticated forms.

In the first place, they should ensure their own survival, by avoiding trying to destroy each other, in other words, by trying to maintain peace. This was the primary aim of the UN Charter, in whose Preamble the peoples of the United Nations express their determination "to save succeeding generations from the scourge of war." Human beings also need to survive by having access to the necessities of life and those things required for a decent life. This leads to the guarantee of fundamental economic and social human rights. Such rights, when they are accepted as creating an obligation or, at least, a target, lead to development that should allow every human being to have food, shelter, health care, and education. Development must, however, be sustainable, which means that the resources of the planet are used and managed so that they will be sufficient for ensuring satisfaction of the needs of humanity not only now, but for an indefinite future. Clearly, the protection of the environment is a basic factor in such development. Finally, historic experience shows that all these requirements cannot be ensured in human societies without the respect of the fundamental rights and freedoms of the individuals, men and women, who compose the communities. Thus, peace, development, preservation of the environment, and respect for human rights are the fundamental and interdependent values on which societies must be built and managed. They constitute the main components of the common concern of humanity,

Coming back to the role of law, its first aim must be to express, impose, and protect the common concern of humanity. Specifically, as far as the environment is concerned, law has the privilege to ensure its respect and preservation by imposing mandatory norms which can be enforced by public authority. It must be stressed that law not only means regulations that must be obeyed. It also has the task to help build adequate institutions having the mandate to draft and adopt specific rules, to implement them, and to control whether such implementation is correctly ensured.

Of course, law is not the only tool necessary to preserve the environment. The very nature of the environment imposes that we know what it is, its nature, its state, how it is deteriorated, and how to remedy such deterioration. Without almost the whole range of scientific disciplines no answer can be given to such questions. We should also not forget scientific branches that focus not on natural data but on the state and the evolution of human societies or on economic mechanisms and their dynamism which may orient or even govern them. There is thus an entire interdisciplinary chain that has to care for the preservation of fundamental values identified and protected by law. Law is the last link of the chain, because it must know and often use the findings of all the other scientific branches.

Consider the following example. The people living in a village in the proximity of a river complain of diseases that they never had before. A young man who just came home after having studied in the school of a nearby town thinks that this might be caused by some poison contained in the water of the wells. He persuades the members of the city council to ask his former professor of science to come and make a test. The professor accepts and, after having examined the water, decides that an analysis is necessary. A chemical laboratory finds the presence of pesticides in the wells. The peasants of the region, however, do not use pesticides. The laboratory contacts the authorities of the region who charge a geologist to find out where is the source of the pollution. The geologist finds that the pesticides come from the underground water shed, connected to a river which is several kilometers away. The analysis of the water of the river is positive so that more investigation is needed. Geographers are asked to study the situation of the region. After having examined the agricultural lands along the river they find out that the upstream landowners do not use pesticides either, but there is a factory of chemicals near a smaller river that flows into the main river. Hydrologists establish the probability of pollution coming from that industry and estimate that rain water coming from that place makes new chemical analysis necessary. The analysis discovers that the waste dump of the factory contains an important amount of residues of pesticides. The regional authorities are asked to ensure the cleaning up of the dumping place. They have, however, no legislative instrument that could be used, since the factory has ceased its activities and nobody knows who owns the polluted piece of land and where the owner is. They submit the case to the national government which, after having consulted economists, decides to prepare a draft law to be introduced in the Parliament in order to modify the existing laws on environmental pollution so that the problem of pollution caused by waste dumped on land which was later abandoned would be solved. The necessary legal provisions are to empower the authorities to investigate industrial sites, to order their cleaning up, to use penal responsibility against the owner or whoever can be held responsible, and to make it possible for the victims of the pollution to ask for damages in civil courts.

This story is not entirely imaginary. It is based, at least partly, on the heavy pollution of the Rhine caused by an industrial accident in Switzerland in 1986 that also raised the problem of international cooperation between affected river states – Switzerland, Germany, and France.

The relationship between law and other branches of science is a major problem. Sciences such as geology, chemistry, physics, botany, zoology, and many other scientific branches play an important role as sources of knowledge in the formulation of legal norms. In concrete cases scientific expertise can also solve or help solve environmental problems. The level of scientific knowledge, however, presented as scientific certainty or uncertainty must be taken into account. This is one of the main elements of the precautionary approach formulated for the first time less than fifteen years ago.

Another important point to discuss is the relationship of economics with law, which needs to be clarified. After an initial focus on environmental regulation that dominated in the 1960s and 1970s, a reaction in certain countries condemned what it called the "command and control" system. Instead, it advocated restricting the role and the importance of law in favor of using economic instruments for the protection of the environment.

Two responses can be given to such criticism. First, as a rule economic activities need a legal framework. Absolute freedom of trade, industry, finance, does not, cannot exist. The experience of the European Common Market, which is based on the freedom of trade inside the Community, shows by its thousands of progressively adopted regulations, directives, and decisions, many of which are related to environmental protection, that such freedom is a daydream – and not even necessarily a dream. Second, the adoption of economic instruments, such as taxes, subsidies, permit trade, certification, auditing, and quotas, cannot be used outside regulatory, legislative, or other norms that must invest them with the necessary legality and even legitimacy and ensure the availability of judicial control.

The situation is similar when environmental policy is to be drafted and applied. In past decades the importance of environmental policy was often stressed. It should not be forgotten that the definition of policy goals and principles needs the social consecration that only law can confer, because it expresses and protects fundamental values and has a permanent character. At the end of the day, legal norms are equally needed to implement goals and provide the means to implement environmental policy. The social mechanism of environmental protection can thus be characterized by a three-stage approach:

- In the first stage, law – mainly national constitutions, broad environmental laws, and major international conventions or declarations – defines the environmental values to be protected.
- In the second stage, environmental policy determines the objectives and strategies that should be used in order to ensure respect for environmental values, taking into account the prevailing economic, social, and cultural situations.
- In the third stage, legal or other instruments are used or have to be adopted to reach the objectives fixed by the environmental policy. The content of such instruments can be economic, political, social, or educational, but the form will be legal. As a feedback, the implementation of such instruments often needs the support of public opinion, the consensus of which was the very basis for recognizing the environment as a fundamental value.

Finally, we must mention a concept that has been very often used in recent years: environmental governance. Its contents are not very clear, but we may define it as the method of organizing the activities of and cooperation between national and international authorities, actors, and stakeholders, in order to ensure the good management and preservation of the environment.[1] Very clearly, governance must also be built on and aim at the foundation of the value system expressed and enforced by law. In that perspective it must use the tools of social architecture such as the creation of institutions, of partnerships, capacity building, public information and participation, establishment of systems of remedies and reparation. At the end of the process here again legal norms have to determine the rights and the obligations of everybody, from the different authorities to the different components of civil society.

3 WHY DO WE NEED *INTERNATIONAL* ENVIRONMENTAL LAW?

Globalization, an understanding of the solidarity which links countries, regions, continents, and the entire world, developed progressively during the twentieth century. One of its main aspects was the protection of the environment, whose transboundary and later global dimensions were discovered incrementally. The development of law followed this evolution.

---

[1] *See* D. C. Esty and M.H Ivanova, eds. *Global Environmental Governance*, Yale School of Environmental Studies, 2000.

The international character of problems concerning certain natural resources was first understood as a consequence of the pollution of surface waters, rivers, and lakes shared by two or more countries. In the relations between neighboring states the necessity of a multistate approach to such problems emerged as early as the end of the nineteenth century. Practically from the beginning legal techniques were used to address the issue. International agreements like the 1909 Treaty between the United States and Canada Respecting Boundary Waters progressively paid more attention to the pollution of shared water resources.[2] The arbitral award between the United States and Canada, handed down in 1941 in the well-known *Trail Smelter* case, resolved a problem of transboundary air pollution and formulated a basic principle in this domain. It stated that "no [s]tate has the right to use or permit the use of its territory in such a manner as to cause injury by fumes in or to the territory of another or the properties or persons therein."

The principle was confirmed thirty years later by the Declaration of the Stockholm Conference of 1972, whose Principle 21 proclaims that states have the responsibility to ensure that activities within their jurisdiction or control do not cause harm to the environment of other states or of areas beyond the limits of national jurisdiction.[3]

An important step in the development of the international legal approach to environmental problems was the understanding that environmental problems are not limited to transfrontier pollution in the relations of two or more neighboring states. As mentioned earlier, the globalization started quite early in the field of the environment and led to worldwide cooperation in fields as diverse as the control of marine pollution, the protection of wild fauna and flora, and even long-range transboundary air pollution. The expansion of the need of action involving the cooperation of all countries continued with the discovery of the destruction by man-made substances of the stratospheric ozone layer that protects not only humans, but also other forms of life, the understanding of the threat that the international movements of dangerous substances or waste can represent, the danger of climate change and, last but not least, the depletion of biological diversity. In our days hundreds of international instruments, both treaties and formally nonbinding texts, are intended to respond to the necessity to prevent environmental degradation and to preserve our common heritage, the global environment. Even environmental problems mainly concerning one or several regions of the world, such as desertification, the protection of the polar regions, or the dangers to which migratory birds or other animals are exposed, are recognized as necessitating the cooperation of a large part of the world if not its totality.

Another important aspect of the globalization of environmental problems involves enhancing the development of poor countries. It will be discussed in another lecture, but let us already stress that it cannot be ignored nor separated from the problem of the wise use and management of the world's resources. This has been progressively recognized since the 1972 Stockholm Declaration. The 1992 Declaration of Rio de Janeiro on Environment and Development, adopted twenty years later, proclaimed that development must be sustainable, which means that it shall not exhaust the Earth's natural resources. The Political Declaration adopted in 2002 by the World Summit on

---

[2] Treaty Between the United States and Great Britain Respecting Boundary Waters Between the United States and Canada, Washington, 4 *American Journal of International Law*, 239 (1920 Supp).

[3] UN Doc. A/Conf.48/14/Rev.1.

Sustainable Development (WSSD) stressed the universal character of the obligation of sustainable development, proclaiming that the representatives of the peoples of the world assume "a collective responsibility to advance and strengthen the interdependent and mutually reinforcing pillars of sustainable development – economic development, social development and environmental protection – at local, national, regional and global levels."

One could ask, what is the place and the role of law in this context? Referring back to an earlier point, it is clear that no political or economic action and instrument can ignore the legal aspect of environmental protection. We may also quote here a paragraph of the draft Covenant on Environment and Development, an important step toward the codification of international environmental law. Begun in the late 1980s, its last version was adopted by an expert meeting of the Commission on Environmental Law of IUCN held in March 2003. The text insists on the need to "integrate environmental and developmental policies and laws in order to fulfill basic human needs, improve the quality of life, and ensure a more secure future for all." Clearly, after the initial bilateral approaches of environmental law, we have arrived at the global one.

Finally, it should be noted that the development of environmental law followed a parallel track in the different legal orders: national, regional (i.e., African, American, Asian, and European), and at the global level. During a first period that roughly corresponds to the 1970s and the beginning of the 1980s, environmental norms in the form of dozens of international treaties and national legal instruments were elaborated with the objective of protecting different sectors of the environment: the oceans, continental waters, the atmosphere, and wild fauna and flora. An important stage of the evolution was the adoption of worldwide instruments in all sectors that proclaimed general rules for each sector: the 1982 UN Convention on the Law of the Sea,[4] the 1997 Convention codifying the rules governing the non-navigational uses of international waters,[5] the Convention of 1992 aiming at the prevention of climate change[6] and the Convention on Biological Diversity[7] of 1992, which seeks to ensure the survival of all species, both wild and domesticated. This sectoral approach of environmental protection is always necessary and is continuing. Still, a new wave of normative activities emerged and developed, seeking to control the sources of pollution: chemical substances,[8] dangerous waste,[9] and radioactive material.[10] Here again, several global conventions parallel national and regional norms. Finally, there is a growing understanding that all human activity can harm the environment, so that environmental protection should control in fact most human activities. This trend, which emerged at regional levels,[11] is developing fast, but

---

[4] UN Doc.A/Conf.62/122

[5] Convention on the Non-Navigational Uses of International Watercourses, New York, May 21, 1997, International Environmental Law, Multilateral Treaties (EmuT, 997/39).

[6] Framework Convention on Climate Change, New York, May 9, 1992, EMuT, 992:35.

[7] Rio de Janeiro, June 5, 1992, EMuT, 992:42.

[8] *See, e.g.,* the Stockholm Convention on Persistent Organic Pollutants, May 22, 2001, EMuT, 001:39.

[9] *See, e.g.,* the Convention on the Control of Transboundary Movements of Hazardous Wastes and Their Disposal, Basel, March 22, 1989, EMuT, 989:22.

[10] *See* the Convention on Nuclear Safety, Vienna, September 20, 1994, EMuT, June 17, 1994, EMuT, 994:70.

[11] A path-breaking international regulation has been adopted for the region of the Alps in the framework of the Convention Concerning the Protection of the Alps (Salzburg, November 7, 1991), which was completed by successive protocols on Town and Country Planning, Mountain Agriculture, Nature

it will certainly reach planetary dimensions in order to solve global problems such as the climate change or the protection of the world's biological resources.

A look at international environmental law creates the feeling that we see the whole Earth and its problems at the same time from far, from another planet and under a microscope that shows the smallest details and the most intimate secrets and problems of life human, animal, and plant. This should lead every human to an intense feeling of responsibility, both as individuals and as members of a species that endangers its own survival.

LECTURE 2: SUSTAINABLE DEVELOPMENT

Environmental law today, whether international or domestic, must be integrated into sustainable development as affirmed and detailed at the World Summit on Sustainable Development (WSSD) held in August–September 2002 in Johannesburg.

How can the process of sustainable development be defined? A case illustrates the problem. According to scientists, the glaciers of the Andes are vanishing because of the global warming driven at least in part by pollution. Glaciers in Venezuela are nearly extinct and in Bolivia the mass of glaciers and snowcaps has shrunk by sixty percent since 1978, according to government estimates. In all, according to scientific studies led by the Byrd Polar Research Center at Ohio State University, Andean glaciers have retreated as much as twenty-five percent in the last thirty years. Their disappearance, scientists say, is nearly unavoidable. Shrinking glaciers are a planetary phenomenon, but the glaciers in the tropics – in particular the vast majority of glaciers in the Andes, stretching from Venezuela to Bolivia – are losing ground the fastest. They are smaller to begin with and they are located in a region that is more sensitive to climate change. This situation could lead to water shortages in places like Bolivia and Peru that depend on glaciers and the rain and snow that fall on the mountains. These ensure water for drinking, irrigating fields, and generating electricity. The most pressing concern, Bolivian officials said, is the possible shortage of water for the 1.5 million people of La Paz and the adjacent city of El Alto, especially because over the next decade, water use in the region is expected to increase by twenty percent.[12] Here we very clearly face problems of a deteriorating natural resource that affects agriculture, energy, health, poverty, in sum development, linked with environmental crisis and specifically with climate change. In other words, we face a problem of linkage between an environmental disaster and developmental needs.

Two approaches can be adopted in response. Since we speak of international environmental law, a first step could consist in trying to discover or elaborate the legal meaning of sustainable development and its main principles. This means identifying the general legal obligations flowing from sustainable development. It requires screening the principles of international environmental law as they appear or are expressed in the overall context of sustainable development. A second approach, which necessarily

Protection and Landscape Conservation, Mountain Forests, Soil Protection, Energy, Tourism, and Transport, EMuT, 991:83 and 991:83/A–I.

[12] "As Glaciers Shrink, Water Worries Grow," *New York Times*, December 1–2, 2002.

complements the first, is to find ways to insert existing norms of environmental protection into the process of sustainable development such as the different components of this process were defined at the WSSD.

1 THE CONTENT OF SUSTAINABLE DEVELOPMENT IN INTERNATIONAL ENVIRONMENTAL LAW

Sustainable development was first defined in 1989 by the World Commission on Environment and Development charged with the preparation of the 1992 Rio Conference on Environment and Development. According to its report, sustainable development is "development that meets the needs of the present without compromising the ability of future generations to meet their own needs."[13]

This definition contains two components: the basic needs of the world, in particular those of the poor, and the limitation of human activities on the use of the natural resources with a view of the needs of future generations. Two principles of the Declaration adopted in June 1992 at the Rio de Janeiro Conference on Development and Environment have further developed the concept. According to Principle 3:

> The right to development must be fulfilled so as to equitably meet the developmental and environmental needs of present and future generations.

Principle 4 of the Declaration adds that:

> In order to achieve sustainable development, environmental protection shall constitute an integral part of the development process and cannot be considered in isolation from it.

It is interesting to compare to these texts the corresponding provisions of the Draft Covenant on Environment and Development prepared by experts of the IUCN Commission on Environmental Law. The Draft constitutes an important attempt towards the codification of international environmental law.[14]

Two of its articles deserve special attention for our investigation:

> Article 8. Right to development
> The exercise of the right to development entails the obligation to meet the developmental and environmental needs of humanity in a sustainable and equitable manner.
> Article 9. Eradication of poverty
> The eradication of poverty, which in particular necessitates a global partnership, is an indispensable requirement for sustainable development.

Another important approach to the problem of sustainable development can be found in a judgment of the International Court of Justice. In the case of the *Gabcikovo-Nagymaros*

---

[13] World Commission on Environment and Development, Our Common Future, 1987 and U.N.G.A.Res. 44/228 of December 22, 1989.

[14] IUCN, Draft International Covenant on Environment and Development, Environmental Policy and Law Paper, No. 31, Rev, 2000.

Project (*Hungary v. Slovakia*), it gave if not a definition, at least an explanation of what is sustainable development:

> Throughout the ages, mankind has, for economic and other reasons, constantly interfered with nature. In the past, this was often done without consideration of the effects upon the environment. Owing to new scientific insights and to a growing awareness of the risks for mankind – for present and future generations – of pursuit of such interventions at an unconsidered and unabated pace, new norms and standards have been developed, set forth in a great number of instruments during the last two decades. Such new norms have to be taken into consideration, and such new standards given proper weight, not only when States contemplate new activities but also when continuing with activities begun in the past. This need to reconcile economic development with protection of the environment is aptly expressed in the concept of sustainable development.[15]

Thus sustainable development is qualified as a "concept." In his dissenting opinion, on the contrary, Judge Weeramantry presents sustainable development as a principle of international law. He recalls that after the early formulations of the concept of development, it was recognized that development cannot be pursued to such a point that substantial damage results to the environment within which it is to occur. Therefore, development can only be sought in harmony with the reasonable demands of environmental protection. He stresses that:

> It is thus the correct formulation of the right to development that that right does not exist in the absolute sense, but is relative always to its tolerance to the environment. The right to development as thus defined is clearly part of modern international law. It is compendiously referred to as "sustainable development."

Judge Weeramantry quotes a series of international instruments that support his opinion, beginning with the Stockholm Declaration and ending with the Rio Declaration. He shows not only its wide and general acceptance by the global community, but also that sustainable development constitutes an inescapable logical necessity. He adds that the general support of the international community does not of course mean that each and every state has given its express and specific support to the principle – but this is not a requirement for the establishment of a principle of customary law.[16]

We face here two different views concerning the nature of sustainable development. Is it a concept as the International Court of Justice qualified it or is it a principle?

We take the liberty to try and clarify the two notions. A "concept" is an abstract creation of human mind without having a material content. "Principles" are, on the contrary, fundamental norms for the orientation of persons, authorities, or others, materializing the content of legal, moral, or intellectual concepts, without necessarily being directly applicable. In this sense, the state is a concept, while its constitution proclaims principles in order to establish the fundamental rules of its functioning. In the application of such principles, specific laws are enacted to govern the functioning of the state's organs and the behavior of persons.

Thus, sustainable development should be considered as a concept while several principles have been proposed to establish its concrete content. The 2002 Johannesburg

[15] International Court of Justice, Judgment of September 25, 1997, No. 140.
[16] *Id.*, p. 92–5.

World Summit on Sustainable Development focused a large part of its work on sustainable development. Prior to that Conference, in April 2002, at its Conference held in New Delhi, the International Law Association adopted a Declaration on the principles of international law in the field of sustainable development.[17] The Declaration proposed seven basic principles followed by explanatory comments:

1. The duty of states to ensure sustainable use of natural resources. While, in accordance with international law, all states have the sovereign right to use their own natural resources pursuant to their own environmental and developmental policies, they are also under a duty to manage natural resources, including natural resources within their own territory or jurisdiction, in a rational, sustainable, and safe way so as to contribute to the development of their peoples and to the conservation and the protection of the environment, including ecosystems. States must take into account the needs of future generations. The Declaration stresses that all relevant actors, including states, industrial concerns, and other components of civil society are under a duty to avoid wasteful use of natural resources and promote waste minimization policies. One may add that the UN Convention on the Law of the Sea[18] already imposed on states "the obligation to protect and preserve the marine environment" (Art. 192) and the conservation of the living resources of the sea (Arts. 61–5, 117–20). The Declaration thus enlarges the obligation by affirming, in addition, that the protection, preservation, and enhancement of the natural environment, particularly the proper management of climate system, biological diversity, and fauna and flora of the Earth, are the common concern of humankind.

2. The principle of equity and the eradication of poverty. The New Delhi Declaration recalls that the principle of equity is central to the attainment of sustainable development. It refers to both intragenerational equity and intergenerational equity. The first means the right of all peoples within the current generation to fair access to the Earth's natural resources. The second imposes the duty on present humanity to take into account the long-term impact of its activities and to sustain the resource base and the global environment for the benefit of future generations. "Benefit" is to be understood in this context as including, inter alia, economic, environmental, social, and intrinsic benefit. From the recognition of the right to development flows the duty of states to cooperate for the eradication of poverty. While it is the primary responsibility of the state to aim for conditions of equity within its own population and to ensure, as a minimum, the eradication of poverty, all states that are in a position to do so have a further responsibility to assist other states to achieve this objective.

3. The principle of common but differentiated responsibilities. All states and other relevant actors, international organizations, corporations, nongovernmental organizations, and civil society should cooperate in the achievement of global sustainable

---

[17] According to its preamble, the Declaration is based on the Rio Declaration on Environment and Development, as well as the final documents resulting from the series of world conferences on social progress for development (Copenhagen, 1993), human rights (Vienna, 1993), population and development (Cairo, 1994), small island states and sustainable development (Barbados, 1994), women and development (Beijing, 1995), least-developed countries (Brussels, 2001), and financing for development (Monterrey, 2002) respectively.

[18] Montego Bay, December 10, 1982, UN Doc.A/Conf.62/122.

development and the protection of the environment. The special needs and interests of developing countries and of countries with economies in transition should be recognized. Developed countries bear a special burden of responsibility in reducing and eliminating unsustainable patterns of production and consumption and in contributing to capacity building in developing countries.[19]

4. The principle of the precautionary approach to fields such as health, natural resources, and ecosystems. According to the Declaration, a precautionary approach commits states, international organizations, and civil society, particularly the scientific and business communities, to avoid human activity that may cause significant harm to human health, natural resources, or ecosystems, including in the light of scientific uncertainty.[20] This approach should include accountability for harm caused, where appropriate, state responsibility, planning based on clear criteria and well defined goals, effective use of environmental impact assessments, and establishing an appropriate burden of proof on the person or persons carrying out or intending to carry out the activity.

5. The principle of public participation and access to information and justice. The Declaration stresses that public participation is essential to sustainable development and good governance. It is a condition for responsiveness, transparency, and accountability both for governments and civil society organizations, including industrial concerns and trade unions. The text adds that the vital role of women in sustainable development should be recognized. Public participation requires effective protection of the human right to hold and express opinions and to seek, receive, and impart ideas. It also requires a right of access to appropriate, comprehensible, and timely information held by governments and industrial concerns regarding the sustainable use of natural resources and the protection of the environment. Nondiscriminatory access to effective judicial or administrative procedures should be ensured in the state where the measure has been taken to challenge such measure and to claim compensation.[21]

6. The principle of good governance. The Declaration proclaims that civil society and nongovernmental organizations have a right to good governance by states and international organizations. This means the adoption of democratic and transparent decision making procedures and financial accountability, effective measures to combat corruption, the respect of the principle of due process, of rule of law and human rights, and the implementation of a public procurement approach. Good governance also calls for corporate social responsibility and socially responsible investments and a fair distribution of wealth among and within communities.

7. The principle of integration and interrelationship, in particular in relation to human rights and social, economic, and environmental objectives. This principle reflects the interdependence of social, economic, financial, environmental, and human rights aspects of principles and rules of international law relating to sustainable development as well as of the interdependence of the needs of current and future generations

---

[19] This principle was first formulated in the Declaration of the 1992 Conference of Rio de Janeiro on Environment and Development (Principle 7).
[20] This principle is discussed in question 2 of this lecture.
[21] Principle 10 of the Rio Declaration advocates public participation.

of humankind. According to the Declaration, states should strive to resolve apparent conflicts between competing economic, financial, social, and environmental considerations, whether through existing institutions or through the establishment of appropriate new institutions.

On the whole, these principles are rooted in the Declaration of the Conference of Rio de Janeiro and in Agenda 21 and can be considered as generally accepted, although their legal nature can be discussed. Several questions arise in this connection.

First we should ask the question: Who is the target of the principles of the New Delhi Declaration, to whom has it been addressed? For a large part they directly address non-state actors. In such conditions one may wonder whether they are still to be considered as norms of international law or whether the very nature of international environmental law and of development should be considered as being fundamentally different from that of general international law. The general rule of traditional international law remains that state authorities are automatically the compulsory intermediaries between international legal norms and their nationals. The compatibility of the concept of sustainable development – as it has been defined during the last decade – with international law in general can thus be questioned, unless explicit treaty provisions or even generally accepted customary law rules allow nonstate actors to intervene in the interstate field. As a matter of fact, the participation of civil society in the process of sustainable development is an elementary necessity. The fact has been strongly stressed at the World Summit on Sustainable Development and, indeed, international environmental law progressively opens the door for nonstate actors and does not ignore other stakeholders either. It should be recalled that law's role in the protection of the environment can be threefold:

- to regulate the use of natural resources;
- to implement scientific and technical standards; and
- to ensure by legal means the avoidance or settlement of conflicts over the use of natural resources.

In each of these fields such cooperation is not only possible, but can even make the action of law more effective. Such is also the conclusion that can be drawn from the texts adopted by the WSSD.

2 LEGAL ASPECTS OF SUSTAINABLE DEVELOPMENT AT THE WSSD

The Declaration adopted by the WSSD includes a series of elements that support the proposals of the New Delhi Declaration, beginning with a strong reaffirmation of the commitment of participating states to the Rio principles.

The Plan of Implementation[22] also expresses the resolution of the participating countries to undertake:

> concrete actions and measures at all levels and to (enhance) international cooperation, taking into account the Rio Principles, including, inter alia, the principle of common but differentiated responsibilities. . . . These efforts will also promote the integration of the three components of sustainable development – economic

---

[22] Doc.UN A/Conf.199/CRP7.

development, social development and environmental protection – as interdependent and mutually reinforcing pillars (No. 2).

Further, the Plan of Implementation declares that good governance within each country and at the international level is essential for sustainable development (No. 4) and proclaims that respect for human rights and fundamental freedoms, including the right to development, is essential for achieving sustainable development (No. 5).

The Plan also contains a whole chapter on poverty eradication (Nos. 6–12) and another on changing unsustainable patterns of consumption and production (Nos. 13–22).

Going into details, the following points of the Plan of Implementation can be stressed as being particularly important:

- adopting and implementing policies and measures aimed at promoting sustainable patterns of production and consumption, applying, inter alia, the polluter pays principle;

We have seen that policy needs legal concepts for its definition and legal regulations for its implementation. In addition, the polluter pays principle, although it mainly constitutes an economic directive for the internalization of environmental costs, certainly has a legal meaning and produces regulatory consequences.

- developing production and consumption policies while reducing environmental and health impacts;

Both consumption and production policies and the reduction of environmental and health impacts need the legal definition and adoption of standards in the form of regulations: standards of products, of emission of pollutants, and adequate standards for ensuring an acceptable quality of water and of air.

- developing and adopting, where appropriate, effective transparent, verifiable, non-misleading and nondiscriminatory consumer information tools to provide information relating to sustainable consumption and production;

It must be recalled here that a principle that progressively emerged in environmental law, the "right to environment," as a new human right includes in its present formulation public information on the state of the environment and of its deterioration (Rio Declaration, Principle 10). The international instrument that best developed Principle 10 of the Rio Declaration is the Aarhus Convention on access to Information, Public Participation in Decisionmaking and Access to Justice in Environmental Matters.[23]

- increasing investment in cleaner production and ecoefficiency in all countries through, inter alia, incentives and support schemes and policies directed at establishing appropriate regulatory, financial, and legal frameworks. This would include actions at all levels to establish and support cleaner production programmes and centers and more efficient production methods by providing, inter alia, incentives and capacity building to assist enterprises and particularly in developing countries, in improving productivity and sustainable development; investment in cleaner

---

[23] June 25, 1998, EMuT, 998:48.

production and ecoefficiency; information on cost-effective examples of cleaner production, ecoefficiency, and environmental management.

This paragraph openly speaks of an "appropriate regulatory, financial and legal framework." It is not quite clear how far the "regulatory" framework is different from the "legal" one, but, anyway, even the financial framework can need legal norms as far as it makes necessary the intervention of state bodies exercising budgetary functions, such as raising taxes or distributing subsidies.

- integrating the issue of production and consumption patterns into sustainable development policies, programs, and strategies.

Here again we may think of the relationship between policy and law.

- enhancing corporate environmental and social responsibility and accountability.

The meaning of "environmental and social responsibility" is not clear. While "accountability" is not a legal term, the two other words used, "environmental" and "responsibility," can include some legal elements.

- encouraging industry to improve social and environmental performance through voluntary initiatives, including environmental management systems, codes of conduct, certification, and public reporting on environmental issues.

Although codes of conduct are mainly nonlegally binding texts drafted by nonstate actors, such as corporations, and thus do not really represent a legal framework, law appears with the words "certification" and "public reporting" that may or may not involve public authorities.

- providing support for the development of sustainable development strategies and programs.

Such programs and strategies are policy instruments and thus involve law and especially environmental law.

- continuing to promote the use of economic instruments with due regard to the public interest and without distorting international trade and investment.

It is not necessary to develop here again the relationship that exists between economic instruments and their legal framework.

As the present conference concerns energy and environment, it may be useful to present some of the relevant results of the WSSD:

Energy
The Plan of Implementation refers to the relevant recommendations and conclusions of the UN Commission on Sustainable Development and advocates:

- integration of energy considerations, including energy efficiency, into socioeconomic programs, especially into policies of major energy-consuming sectors;
- development and dissemination of alternative energy technologies with the aim of giving a greater share of the energy mix to renewable energies;
- improvement of energy efficiency, and greater reliance on advanced energy technologies, including cleaner fossil fuel energies;

- increased use of renewable energy resources development, dissemination and deployment of affordable and cleaner energy efficiency, and energy conservation technologies;
- improvement of the functioning, transparency, and information about energy markets.[24]

Transport

The Plan of Implementation recommends increasing energy efficiency but also reducing pollution, especially greenhouse gas emissions, including through the development of better vehicle technologies that are environmentally sound.[25]

Water Resources

This lecture started with the short presentation of a concrete problem, that of the shrinking of the glaciers in the Andes and the disastrous consequences which it is likely to produce on the water supply of populations. It must be recalled that the problems of water resources were in the very heart of the Johannesburg Conference. The Plan of Implementation advocates integrated water resource management, the preservation or restoration of water ecosystems and their functions, in particular in fragile ecosystems with human, domestic, industrial, and agriculture needs, including safeguarding drinking water quality. It also calls for the development of programs to mitigate the effects of extreme water related events.[26]

Climate Change

Section 36 of the Plan of Implementation declares that change in the Earth's climate and its adverse effects are a common concern of mankind and that all countries, particularly developing countries including the least developed ones, face increased risks of negative impacts of climate change. It stresses that the problems of land degradation, access to water and food, and human health remain at the center of global attention. Small island developing states are especially mentioned. Another section which focuses on their problems proposes to assist them in mobilizing adequate resources and partnerships to aid their adaptation to the adverse effects of climate change, sea level rise and climate variability, consistent with the UN Framework Convention on Climate Change, where applicable (No. 52 j).

Section 36 of the Plan of Implementation stresses that the Framework Convention is the key instrument for addressing climate change and reaffirms the commitment of the states present in Johannesburg to achieving its ultimate objective of stabilization of greenhouse gas concentrations in the atmosphere at a level that would prevent dangerous anthropogenic interference with the climate system. This should happen within a time frame sufficient to allow ecosystems to adapt naturally to climate change, to ensure that food production is not threatened, and to enable economic development to proceed in a normal manner, in accordance with the principle of common but differentiated responsibilities and respective capabilities. It recalls the United Nations Millennium Declaration, in which heads of state and government resolved to make every effort

---

[24] Plan of Implementation, Nos. 8 and 19.   [25] *Id.*, No. 20.
[26] *Id.*, No. 25; *see also* No. 38.

to ensure the entry into force of the Kyoto Protocol[27] and to embark on the required reduction of emissions of greenhouse gases. States that have ratified the Kyoto Protocol strongly urge states that have not already done so to ratify the Kyoto Protocol in a timely manner.

The Plan of Implementation calls for action to:

- provide technical and financial assistance and capacity building to developing countries and countries with economies in transition, in accordance with the Marrakech Accords;
- develop and transfer technological solutions, disseminate innovative technologies in respect of key sectors of development, particularly energy;
- promote the systematic observation, enhance the implementation of strategies of the Earth's atmosphere, land, and oceans;
- support initiatives to assess the consequences of climate change, including the environmental, economic, and social impacts on local and indigenous communities; and
- enhance cooperation at the international, regional, and national levels to reduce air pollution, including transboundary air pollution, acid deposition, and ozone depletion.

3 CONCLUSION

One may wonder whether the objective of speaking of the relations between international environmental law and the promotion of sustainable development has been forgotten. The Implementation Plan of the WSSD, which seems to somewhat ignore law or legal rules, could be considered as particularly counterproductive in this regard.

It seems, however, that we come back to the relations between environmental policy and law. Earlier we recalled that policy measures are necessarily linked with law. At the highest level, law, as the expression of the common concern of a community, has to determine the values to be protected and, after defining and adopting the policies that serve that objective, needs to fulfill the proposed tasks. Almost every paragraph of the Implementation Plan contains the word "policy," which means that in reality its implementation involves legal measures. Further, when good governance is proposed, it also includes good institutions and good norms, which again mean law and mainly environmental law.

The following scheme can represent a conceptual approach to sustainable development:

Fundamental values of humanity; definition by global legal instruments:

- peace (UN Charter);
- human rights (UN Charter, Universal Declaration of Human Rights, Covenants on Civil, Political Rights and Economic, Social, and Cultural Rights);
- environment (Declarations of Stockholm and of Rio de Janeiro, WSSD Declaration, and Plan of Implementation).

---

[27] Kyoto Protocol to the United Nations Framework Convention on Climate Change, December 11, 1997, EMuT, 992:35/A.

Concept of sustainable development (Declaration of Rio de Janeiro); *principles flowing from the concept:*

- sustainable use of the environment;
- pollution control;
- equity and eradication of poverty;
- common but differentiated responsibility;
- prevention of harm and precautionary approach (health, natural resources, ecosystems);
- public information, participation and access to justice;
- good governance;
- integration and interrelationship in particular in relation to human rights and to social, economic, and environmental objectives.

Policies (Stockholm: Action Plan; Rio: Agenda 21; WSSD: Declaration and Plan of Implementation). They include in particular:

- land use planning;
- health care;
- habitat;
- energy;
- ecosystem management;
- soil protection;
- education, awareness raising, training, capacity building.

Legal tools implementing the policies adopted for enhancing sustainable development:

- international conventions;
- constitutional rules;
- framework laws;
- laws concerning basic services (water and sanitation, energy, transports, health care, town and country planning, etc.);
- laws concerning specific environmental sectors (water, sea, air, biodiversity) and sources of environmental deterioration (polluting substances, wastes, nuclear material, etc.);
- regulations adopted at different levels (national, regional, subregional in accordance with the principle of subsidiarity) implementing such laws or framing economic instruments;
- judicial decisions.

LECTURE 3: FUNDAMENTAL PRINCIPLES OF INTERNATIONAL ENVIRONMENTAL LAW

While international environmental law is mainly concerned with relations between neighboring countries, and in particular transfrontier pollution, the growing under-standing of environmental problems has helped the development and elaboration of general principles. We will discuss first these principles, then integrate them into the international rules that govern relations between states sharing a natural resource such as watercourses, ecosystems, and air space.

1 GENERAL PRINCIPLES

Four important principles have developed a precise legal content and are described below. Two other principles are not discussed: the "polluter pays principle" and "common but differentiated responsibility." The first is essentially a guideline for improving the economic accountancy for environmental harm. It does not answer questions that have a fundamental importance for law, such as the identification of the polluter: should the producer, the dealer, or the user of a product or substance be the one who pays ? In addition, it could be understood as prohibiting all possibility of subsidies, including financial assistance to developing countries that pollute the air, the sea, or rivers and lakes. The common but differentiated responsibility principle should not be understood in a legal sense either. It mainly has a moral and political significance and has not much to do with the international responsibility of states, which cannot be applied in different ways depending on the economic and social situation of different countries.

The four principles discussed here are: state sovereignty; the duty to prevent environmental harm; the precautionary principle; and the principle of information and assistance in environmental emergencies.

1.1 State Sovereignty

State sovereignty is one of the oldest principles of general international law. Its meaning is that a state has exclusive jurisdiction on its territory. In other words, the state is the only authority that can adopt legal rules for its territory, has executive power, and competence to judge litigation. This principle is applicable in environmental matters, but with certain restrictions concerning the preservation of the environment. Principle 21 of the Stockholm Declaration makes it explicit:

> States have, in accordance with the Charter of the United Nations and the principles of international law, the sovereign right to exploit their own resources pursuant to their own environmental policies.

The same formulation has been reproduced in different international instruments, both binding and nonbinding. Principle 2 of the Rio Declaration uses the same wording, but enlarges its scope by adding to "environmental policies" "environmental *and developmental* policies." This was in accordance with the purpose of the Rio Conference, which focused not only on environment, but also on development.

Sovereignty is, however, not unlimited. Limitations flow from international treaties duly accepted and general international legal norms for the protection of the environment that emerge continuously, partly in texts, partly in international practice. Principle 21 of the Stockholm Declaration and Principle 2 of the Rio Declaration recall the obligation of states not to harm the environment of other states or of areas which are not submitted to any State jurisdiction. General norms also appeared concerning the obligation of all states to conserve the environment and the earth's natural resources. Although all international instruments have this aim, clear statements of the duty are rare. Article 192 of the UN Convention on the Law of the Sea, adopted in 1982 in

Montego Bay, however, explicitly proclaims the duty of states to protect and preserve the marine environment. Article 20 of the 1997 UN Convention on the Nonnavigational Uses of International Watercourses affirms the same duty for international freshwaters. The 1992 Convention on Biological Diversity lists the measures that should be taken to ensure conservation and sustainable use of biological resources, while the 1992 Framework Convention on Climate Change declares in Article 3(1) that the parties should protect the climate system.

Another limit to absolute state sovereignty is the general obligation to cooperate with others in order to resolve problems that concern the international community. Such an obligation results from the very essence of general international law. The thousands of international treaties – including the hundreds of environmental treaties – are based on the recognition of the need to cooperate with other states at different levels: bilateral, regional, or worldwide. The creation of numerous international institutions also corresponded to the necessity of cooperation.

In the field of environmental protection, international cooperation is necessary to conserve the environment in its totality, as much for states within their territorial jurisdiction as for space outside all territorial limits, such as the high seas, Antarctica, or outer space.

Following Principle 24 of the Stockholm Declaration of 1972, which stresses the need for cooperation "by all countries, big and small, on an equal footing . . . through multilateral or bilateral arrangements or other appropriate means," Principle 7 of the 1992 Rio Declaration proclaimed that: "[s]tates shall cooperate in a spirit of global partnership to protect and restore the health and integrity of the Earth's ecosystem."

Ten years earlier, Article 197 of the UN Convention on the Law of the Sea had given some practical indications concerning the obligation to cooperate in that specific area:

> States shall cooperate on a global basis and, as appropriate, on a regional basis, directly or through competent international organizations, in formulating and elaborating international rules, standards and recommended practices and procedures consistent with the Convention, for the protection and preservation of the marine environment, taking into account characteristic regional features.

International cooperation for the protection of the environment can, however, lead to the recognition of a certain freedom of decision of states in the framework of general obligations imposed by treaties. One may think here of the rules concerning relocation and transfer to other states of any activities and substances that cause or risk to cause severe environmental degradation or are found to be harmful to human health (Rio Declaration, Principle 14). If a state chooses to ban or restrict the importation of hazardous substances or the relocation of hazardous activities, the ban or restriction has to be respected by other states. The best illustration of this principle is the Basel Convention on the Control of Transboundary Movements of Hazardous Wastes and their Disposal,[28] which submits such movements to the authorization given by the state of destination. This trend has been further developed in regional conventions concerning such transfers of hazardous wastes and reached a new stage in 1998, with the FAO sponsored adoption of the Rotterdam Convention on the Prior Informed Consent Procedure for Certain Hazardous Chemicals and Pesticides in International Trade (PIC

---

[28] March 22, 1989, EMuT, 989:22.

Convention).[29] The objective of the Convention, expressed in Article 1, is to promote shared responsibility and cooperative efforts among parties in the international trade of certain hazardous chemicals in order to protect human health and the environment from potential harm and to contribute to their environmentally sound use, by facilitating information exchange about their characteristics, by providing for a national decision making process on their import and export and by disseminating these decisions to parties. Thus the states parties are recognized by a sort of veto to the importation of dangerous substances, but it must be well understood that such right can be exercised only in the framework of their general obligation to protect the environment from the harmful effects of certain substances.

1.2 Prevention of Environmental Harm

Experience and scientific expertise demonstrate that prevention must be the Golden Rule for the environment, for both ecological and economic reasons. It is frequently impossible to remedy environmental injury: the extinction of a species of fauna or flora, erosion, or even the dumping of long life pollutants into the sea create irreversible situations. Even if the damage is reparable, the costs of rehabilitation are often prohibitive. The duty of prevention also clearly emerges from the international responsibility not to cause significant damage to the environment extraterritorially, but the preventive principle seeks to avoid harm irrespective of whether or not there are transboundary impacts.

The requirement of prevention is complex; it gives rise to a multitude of legal mechanisms, including prior assessment of environmental harm,[30] licensing or authorization that set out the conditions for operation and the consequences for violation of such conditions, including civil liability or penal responsibility. Emission limits and other product or process standards, the use of best available techniques and similar techniques can all be seen as applications of the principle of prevention. The preventive principle also can involve the elaboration and adoption of strategies and policies. An example is given by Article 206 of the Convention on the Law of the Sea:

> When States have reasonable grounds for believing that planned activities under their jurisdiction or control may cause substantial pollution of or significant and harmful changes to the marine environment, they shall, as far as possible, assess the potential effects of such activities on the marine environment and shall communicate reports of the results of such assessments.

The same requirement can also concern other domains, such as the introduction of exogenous species into an ecosystem. The 1976 Convention on Conservation of Nature in the South Pacific provides that the contracting parties must carefully examine the consequences of such introduction (Article 5(4)).[31]

The preventive approach requires each state to exercise due diligence, which means to act reasonably and in good faith and to regulate public and private activities subject to

---

[29] September 10, 1998, EMuT, 998:68.
[30] This duty is expressed in the Rio texts: Principle 17, Chapter 22 of Agenda 21, Art. 8(h) of the Statement on Forests, and Art. 14(1)(a) and (b) of the Biodiversity Convention treat both the national and international aspects of the issue.
[31] Apia, June 12, 1976, EMuT, 976:45.

its jurisdiction or control that are harmful to any part of the environment. The principle does not impose an absolute duty to prevent all harm, but rather an obligation on each state to prohibit activities that could cause significant harm to the environment – for instance the dumping of toxic waste into an international lake – and to minimize detrimental consequences of permissible activities through regulation – for instance by imposing limits on the discharges of sulphur dioxide (SO_2) in the atmosphere. The preventive approach can also involve the elaboration and adoption of strategies and policies as well as the utilization of specific legal procedures such as environmental impact assessment[32] or for the long term strategic planning.

In fact, the objective of almost all international instruments is to prevent environmental deterioration, whether they concern pollution of the sea, inland waters,[33] the atmosphere, or the protection of living resources.[34] Only a few international texts use other approaches, such as the traditional principle of state responsibility or direct compensation of the victims.

1.3 Precaution

Should we speak of the precautionary principle or of the precautionary approach? The first term is used in continental Europe, in domestic legislation as well as in the successive treaties related to the constitution of the European Union. It is a rather strong statement and excludes negotiation on the content of the precaution. The term "approach," current in English speaking countries, indicates a method rather than an obligation and seems thus more flexible. In fact, the term appeared first in German legislation. It was first used at an international level in a Declaration adopted by a conference on the North Sea in 1987 that understood that the impact on the marine environment of the dumping of dangerous wastes could not be established with certainty.[35]

Principle 15 of the Rio Declaration states:

> In order to protect the environment, the precautionary principle shall be widely applied by States according to their capabilities. Where there are threats of serious or irreversible damage, lack of full scientific certainty shall not be used as a reason for postponing cost-effective measures to prevent environmental degradation.

The precautionary principle is included in almost all the international instruments related to environmental protection adopted since the beginning of the 1990s.[36] It is

---

[32] The obligation to conduct environmental impact assessment is prescribed inter alia by the Espoo Convention on Environmental Impact Assessment in a Transboundary Context, February 25, 1991 (EMuT, 991:15) and by Article 8 and Annex I of the Protocol on Environmental Protection to the Antarctic Treaty, Madrid, October 4, 1991 (EMuT, 991:74).

[33] *See* Article 22 of the UN Convention on the Law of the Nonnavigational Uses of International Watercourses, New York, May 21, 1997, EMuT, 997:39.

[34] Apia, June 12, 1976.

[35] *See* D. Austin and A. Alberini, *An Analysis of the Preventive Effect of Environmental Liability: Environmental Liability, Location and Emissions Substitution: Evidence from the Toxic Release Inventory* (Resources for the Future, Washington DC, 2001).

[36] "In order to achieve sustainable development, policies must be based on the precautionary principle. Environmental measures must anticipate, prevent and attack the causes of environmental degradation. Where there are threats of serious or irreversible damage, lack of full scientific certainty should not be used as a reason for postponing measures to prevent environmental degradation." Bergen Declaration, Principle 7, May 15, 1990, 20 *Environmental Policy and Law* 200 (1990).

also one of the bases of the European Union's environmental policy under the 1992 Maastricht Treaty.[37] Concrete application of the precautionary principle is often found in treaties for management of living resources, especially those concerning fishing. The 1995 Agreement for the Implementation of the Provisions of the UN Convention on the Law of the Sea Relating to the Conservation and Management of Fish Stocks and Highly Migratory Fish Stocks is explicit on what it calls the precautionary approach. According to its Article 6, the principle includes such approach to conservation, management, and exploitation of straddling fish stocks and highly migratory fish stocks, inter alia, by improving decision making in this field, by taking into account uncertainties relating to the size and productivity of the stocks, by developing knowledge, by enhanced monitoring, and by adopting, if necessary, emergency measures.

The Cartagena Protocol on Biosafety to the Convention on Biological Diversity of January 29, 2000,[38] is based upon the precautionary principle. Its Article 10(6) provides that:

> lack of scientific certainty due to insufficient relevant information and knowledge regarding the extent of the potential adverse effects of a Living Modified Organism (LMO) shall not prevent the party from taking a decision in order to avoid or minimize such potential adverse effects.

Thus, a country may reject an import even in the absence of scientific certainty that it will potentially cause harm. These provisions are broader than Rio Principle 15, because they make no reference to "serious or irreversible damage" or to cost effectiveness.[39]

While prevention still remains the general basis for environmental protection measures, the precautionary principle can be considered as its most developed form. Both principles seek to avoid environmental harm, but precaution is to be applied when the consequences of nonaction can be particularly serious, such as large-scale degradation of the environment or the extinction of a species. However, such circumstances are difficult to define and so is scientific uncertainty, which means that the scientists do not agree among themselves or, at least, that there is no clear and stable majority for

---

[37] *See e.g.*, the Bamako Convention on the Ban of the Import of Hazardous Wastes into Africa and on the Control of their Transboundary Movements within Africa, January 29, 1991, Art. 4(3)(f), EMuT, 991:08; Convention on the Protection of the Marine Environment of the Baltic Sea, Art. 3(2), Helsinki, April 9, 1992, EMuT, 992:22; Framework Convention on Climate Change, Art. 4(1)(f), New York, May 9, 1992, EMuT, 992:35; Convention on Biological Diversity, Preamble, Rio de Janeiro, June 5, 1992, EMuT, 992:42; European Energy Charter Treaty, Art. 19(1), Lisbon, December 17, 1994, EMuT, 994:93 ; Amendments to the Protocol for the Protection of the Mediterranean Sea against Pollution from Land-Based Sources, Preamble, Syracuse, March 7, 1996, EMuT, 996:13/I; Protocol to the 1979 Convention on Long-Range Transboundary Air Pollution to Abate Acidification, Eutrophication and Ground-Level Ozone, Gothenburg, November 30, 1999, EMuT, 999:84/H; Cartagena Protocol on Biosafety, January 29, 2000, EMuT, 992:42/A; Convention on the Conservation and Management of Highly Migratory Fish Stocks in the Western and Central Pacific Ocean, Honolulu, September 5, 2000; Convention on the Conservation and Management of Fishery Resources in the South-East Atlantic Ocean, April 20, 2001; Stockholm Convention on Persistent Organic Pollutants, May 22, 2001, EMuT, 001:39; Agreement on the Conservation of Albatrosses and Petrels, Art. II(3), Cape Town, February 2, 2001, EMuT, 979:55/I; Convention for Cooperation in the Protection and Sustainable Development of the Marine and Coastal Environment of the Northeast Pacific, Antigua, February 18, 2002, EMuT, 002:14; ASEAN Agreement on Transboundary Haze Pollution, Kuala Lumpur, June 10, 2002, EMuT, 002:44.

[38] "Community policy on the environment shall aim at a high level of protection. . . . It shall be based on the precautionary principle and on the principles that preventive action should be taken, that environmental damage should as a priority be rectified at source . . ."

[39] EMuT, 992:42/A.

adopting certain conclusions. Thus the policymaker must consider the circumstances of a given situation and decide which scientific approach is based on the most credible evidence and most reliable scientific methodology. The final decision will inevitably give birth to a legal norm.[40]

1.4 Information and Assistance in Environmental Emergencies

Information
According to Principle 18 of the Rio Declaration:

> States shall immediately notify other States of any natural disasters or other emergencies that are likely to produce harmful effects on the environment of those States.

The foundation of the rule appears in general international law and is linked with humanitarian duties. The customary duty is spelled out more concretely in numerous international treaties. In this regard, the most important international instrument is the UN Convention on the Law of the Sea, whose Article 198 sums up the provisions contained in various conventions relating to marine pollution, both in general and in regard to regional seas:

> When a State becomes aware of cases in which the marine environment is in imminent danger of being damaged or has been damaged by pollution, it shall immediately notify other States it deems likely to be affected by such damage, as well as the competent international organization.

It is worth stressing that according to this text states that are aware of a danger are obliged to notify states likely to be affected by the emergency, whether the cause of the emergency appears in the territorial waters, the exclusive economic zone, or on the high seas. Instructions must thus be given to captains of ships and pilots of airplanes to signal any emergency.

The duty to give relevant information is particularly important in the case of nuclear accidents. The Chernobyl accident of April 26, 1986, underlined the importance of such notification. As a consequence of the failure of authorities of the Soviet Union to fulfill their obligation to timely notify other states of the radioactive cloud approaching their territory, the reactions of the international community resulted in the conclusion of a special Convention on Early Notification in the Case of Nuclear Accident or Radiological Emergency in an exceptionally short time, only five months after the accident.[41] This instrument requires each state on whose territory a nuclear accident occurs to notify the other states that are or could be physically affected by the accident, its nature, the moment when it occurred and its exact location, in order to limit as much as possible the radioactive consequences to the exposed state or states.

The response to environmental emergencies must be organized in order to ensure prompt and effective action, in which notification is only the first step. This is how the International Atomic Energy Agency and the World Health Organization announced on February 26, 1988, the development of a worldwide early warning network that would alert states of the possibility of pollution resulting from a nuclear power plant accident. In

---

[40] See D. Freestone and E. Hey (eds.), *The Precautionary Principle and International law – The Challenge of Implementation*, Kluwer Law International, 1996.
[41] Vienna, September 26, 1986, EMuT, 986:71.

a different field, that of marine pollution emergencies, the 1990 worldwide Convention on Oil Pollution Preparedness, Response and Cooperation provides for detailed rules on reporting procedures on emergencies to the competent national authority or, as the case may be, to the nearest coastal state.[42]

Assistance

The assistance to affected states in case of an environmental emergency raises numerous questions so that the Rio Declaration only says that: "every effort shall be made by the international community to help [s]tates so afflicted" (Principle 18). Article 199 of the UN Convention on the Law of the Sea adds that: "States shall jointly develop and promote contingency plans for responding to pollution incidents in the marine environment." Such plans should focus on the organization of assistance and the scope and division of authority. Material aspects must not be ignored, including arrangements for the financing of assistance and customs formalities concerning border passage for aid personnel and supplies.

In fact, a growing number of bilateral or regional contingency plans do exist, mainly on emergency assistance in connection with radiation accidents and marine pollution casualties, starting with the treaty systems relating to the protection of regional seas (Mediterranean,[43] Caribbean,[44] South Pacific,[45] etc.). The only global contingency plan is the 1990 London Convention on Oil Pollution Preparedness, Response and Cooperation, which includes an interesting provision relating to the costs of the assistance.[46] If the action was taken at the express request of another state, the requesting state shall reimburse to the assisting state the cost of its action. If, on the contrary, the action was taken by a state on its own initiative, this state shall bear the costs of its action.

A particularly interesting development in this field is the ASEAN Agreement on Transboundary Haze Pollution of June 10, 2002, which provides for international cooperation for preparedness and joint emergency response through the provision of assistance in the case of land and/or forest fire that causes deleterious effects of such a nature as to endanger human health, harm living resources and ecosystems and material property, and impair or interfere with amenities and other legitimate uses of the environment (Articles 12 and 1(6)).[47]

2 EQUITABLE USE OF SHARED RESOURCES

As mentioned in Section 1, transfrontier damage to the environment was the starting point of the development of international environmental law. The notification of imminent harm and assistance in emergencies were important aspects of the cooperation

---

[42] London, November 30, 1990, EMuT, 990:88.

[43] Protocol Concerning Cooperation in Combating Pollution of the Mediterranean Sea by Oil and Other Harmful Substances in Cases of Emergency, Barcelona, February 16, 1976, EMuT, 976:15.

[44] Protocol Concerning Cooperation in Combating Oil Spills in the Wider Caribbean Region, Cartagena de Indias, March 24, 1983, EMuT, 983:23.

[45] Protocol Concerning Cooperation in Combating Pollution Emergencies in the South Pacific Region, November 25, 1986, Noumea, EMuT, 983:23/A.

[46] Article 7 and Annex.   [47] Kuala Lumpur, June 10, 2002, EMuT, 002:44.

in such relations. Clearly, the other principles discussed in Section 1 must be applied to the cooperation among states that share a natural resource.

A more specific approach was progressively adopted under the influence of problems raised by international watercourses and developed the understanding that shared resources, which can also include air, marine areas, and ecosystems, should be protected and managed by the concerned states in cooperation on the basis of equity. In 1978 the United Nations Environment Program adopted in this regard a set of nonmandatory Principles of Conduct in the Field of the Environment for the Guidance of States in the Conservation and Harmonious Utilization of Natural Resources Shared by Two or More States,[48] which lists the principles recommended in this field, several of which are based on the general principles discussed in Section 1. Many points of these guidelines have been repeated and developed in later instruments, both obligatory and nonbinding.

A particularly important text is in this regard the UN Convention on the Law of the Nonnavigational Uses of International Watercourses, drafted by the UN Commission of International Law and adopted in New York, on May 21, 1997.[49] Although not yet in force, it can be considered as the codification of existing legal rules in the international field not only for watercourses but for shared resources in general. The Convention particularly insists on the equitable and reasonable utilization of such watercourses:

> In particular, an international watercourse shall be used and developed by watercourse States with a view to attaining optimal and sustainable utilization thereof and benefits there from, taking into account the interests of the watercourse States concerned, consistent with adequate protection of the watercourse (Article 5).

A distinction can be made among the rules related to equitable utilization of shared resources between two aspects which concern respectively interstate relations and relations of nonstate actors with foreign states:

1. prohibition of significant harm. In interstate relations equitable utilization includes the general obligation not to cause significant harm to the resource and to exchange data and information on its condition. Particular obligations arise when a state plans measures that may have a significant adverse effect on the condition of the resource. Principle 19 of the Rio Declaration summarizes them:

> States shall provide prior and timely notification and relevant information to potentially affected States on activities that may have a significant transboundary environmental adverse effect and shall consult with those states at an early stage and in good faith.

The Codification Convention of 1997 related to international watercourses brought important precisions in this regard. Before a state implements or permits the implementation of its plans, it shall provide the potentially affected states with timely notification and adequate information. The concerned states shall enter into consultations and, if necessary, negotiations with a view to arriving at an equitable resolution of the situation. The consultations and negotiations shall be conducted on the basis that each state must in good faith pay reasonable regard to the rights and legitimate interests of the other

---

[48] UN Doc.UNEP/IG 12/2 (1978).   [49] EMuT, 997:39.

State (Articles 11–17). Watercourse states shall also, at the request of any of them, enter into consultations concerning the management of an international watercourse, which may include the establishment of a joint management mechanism. This can mean the planning of the sustainable development of the watercourse providing for the implementation of any of the plans adopted and any other measure prompting the rational and optimal utilization, protection, and control of the watercourse (Article 24).

At a regional level, that of the UN Economic Commission for Europe, the Espoo Convention on Environmental Impact Assessment in a Transboundary Context, of February 25, 1991[50] describes in detail the EIA procedure "that permits public participation and preparation of the environmental assessment documentation" the content of which is detailed in Appendix II. Interestingly, the Espoo Convention also provides for a postproject analysis, the objectives of which include monitoring compliance with the conditions set out in the authorization or approval of the activity and the effectiveness of mitigation measures (Appendix V).

2. equality and nondiscrimination. The second aspect of cooperation for the equitable use of shared resources concerns nonstate actors who are residents of the affected countries and who may be affected by the measures planned. Following a Recommendation adopted by OECD on May 11, 1976,[51] the principles of equality of access and nondiscrimination emerged. The first principle means that if the activities taking place within the limits of jurisdiction or control of one state cause or threaten to cause deterioration of the environment of another state, the residents of the latter who are or risk to be affected should have access to administrative or judicial procedures in the state causing the environmental harm, under the same conditions as the residents of that state. Equality of access is recognized not only to the nationals of the state that is the victim of transfrontier pollution, but to all those inhabiting the territory, even if they possess another nationality. Concretely, the principle of equality of access contains four elements:

- informing nonresidents of the area that might be affected, including if possible nonprofit organizations aimed at protecting nature;
- allowing their participation in decision making procedures;
- permitting the possibility of appeal in case of inadequate application of relevant rules during the procedures; and
- providing remedies in case of damage.

These requirements coincide with the obligations flowing from the 1998 Aarhus Convention[52] applicable in many European countries, which provides for information, participation, and access to remedies in environmental matters without distinction of nationality or country of residence.

The second principle, that of nondiscrimination, means that in all respects the legislation of the polluting state must be applied in the same way to residents and nonresidents.

---

[50] EMuT, 991:15.
[51] Recommendation on Equal Right to Access in Relation to Transfrontier Pollution, C(76)55 (Final).
[52] Convention on Access to Information, Public Participation in Decision-Making and Access to Justice in Environmental Matters, June 25, 1998, EMuT, 998:48.

3 CONCLUSION

From this short review of several principles of international environmental law two facts emerge that have a fundamental importance for environmental protection in particular but also for law in general.

The first is the interpenetration of legal rules originating in different legal orders: national, regional, and universal. The principle of precaution is a particularly characteristic example: it migrated from domestic to international law and came back from that level to regional treaties such as those related to the European Union as well as to quite a few national laws.

A second important fact is the emergence of an international civil society, reflected by the growing place and role of nonstate actors. This recognizes reality, because in most cases the deterioration of the environment is not caused by states, but by individuals or enterprises: states have the obligation to exercise due diligence and to control their acts, according to their own legislation or to international commitment. On the other side, states have obligations toward persons who are not their residents but who are potential or real victims of acts planned on or originating from their territory.

Such facts are only the components of a long-term process that was not immediately recognized: the globalization of our planet. It means not only the emergence of planetary phenomena, social, cultural, economic, and political, but above all the universal awareness of such problems. Environmental problems, or to express it more correctly, the problems of the global environment, are primary aspects of the process. This should not be hidden by the initiatives tending to create a global free trade system.

BIBLIOGRAPHY

Boyle, A. and Freestone, D., eds., *International Law of Sustainable Development, Past Achievements and Future Challenges*, Oxford University Press, 1999.

Brans, E. H. P., *Liability for Damage to Public Natural Resources, Standing, Damage and Damage Assessment*, Kluwer, 2001.

Freestone, D. and Hey, E., eds., *The Precautionary Principle and International Law, the Challenge of Implementation*, Kluwer, 1996.

Kiss, A. and Shelton, D., *International Environmental Law*, 3rd ed. Transnational Publishers, 2004.

Kunugi, T. and Schwartz, M., eds., *Codes of Conduct for Partnership in Governance, Texts and Commentaries*, The United Nations University, 1999.

Morrison, F. D. and Wolfrum, R., eds., *International, Regional and National Environmental Law*, Kluwer, 2000.

Nollkaemper, A., *The Legal Regime for Transboundary Water Pollution: Between Discretion and Constraint*, Kluwer, 1993.

Picolotti, R. and Taillant, J. D., eds., *Linking Human Rights and the Environment*, The University of Arizona Press, 2003.

Raustila, K., Skolnikoff, E., and Victor, D., eds., *The Implementation and Effectiveness of International Environmental Commitments, Theory and Practice*, International Institute for Applied Systems Analysis, 1998.

Romano, C. P. R., *The Peaceful Settlement of International Environmental Disputes*, Kluwer, 2000.

Sadeleer, N. de, *Environmental Principles, From Political Slogans to Legal Rules*, Oxford University Press, 2002.

Schrijver, N., *Sovereignty over Natural Resources, Balancing Rights and Duties*, Cambridge University Press, 1997.

PART ONE

SUSTAINABLE DEVELOPMENT
AND THE ROLE OF ENERGY LAW

1 Development and Energy

Jose Goldemberg*

1 INTRODUCTION

While energy is a physical entity well understood and quantitatively defined, the concept of development is less well defined and there are different perceptions about its meaning. The World Bank measures development by the gross national product (GNP) and nations are classified in categories according to their GNP per capita.[1]

This monetization of the concept of development is not well understood, nor accepted by many, particularly in developing countries, where income per capita varies dramatically between the poor and the rich. This is not the case in the Organization for Economic Cooperation and Development (OECD) countries where there is a large middle class and variations in income are not very large.

What the poor in the developing countries aspire to – and they represent seventy percent of the world's population – is a "better life," meaning jobs, food, health services, housing (rural or urban), education, transportation, running water, sewage communication services, security of supply, and good environment. These things are usually measured in industrialized countries by monetary transactions, but not necessarily so in many others. Climate, abundant and easily available natural resources can lead to a better life without great monetary expenses. In some countries cultural values are such that some items are less desirable than in others. In others the political system privileges some solutions over others that cost much less. This is why to compare stages of development only by GDP per capita can be quite misleading.

Energy in its various forms (mechanical, chemical, electrical, heat, electromagnetic radiation) is essential for all aspirations listed above and thus energy is closely linked to a range of social issues. The relationship is a two-way street: the quality and quantity of energy services, and how they are achieved, have an effect on social issues as well.

The stages of human development from man (one million years ago) to today's technological society can be roughly correlated with energy consumption, as indicated in Figure 1.1, which shows daily consumption of energy per capita for six stages in human development.

- "Primitive man" (East Africa about one million years ago), without the use of fire, had only the energy of the food he ate (2000 kcal/day).

---

[1] High income: US$9,266 or more; middle income: US$756–$9265; low income: US$755 or less (dollars of 1999).

* Professor and Former Rector, University of Sao Paulo, Sao Paulo, Brazil.

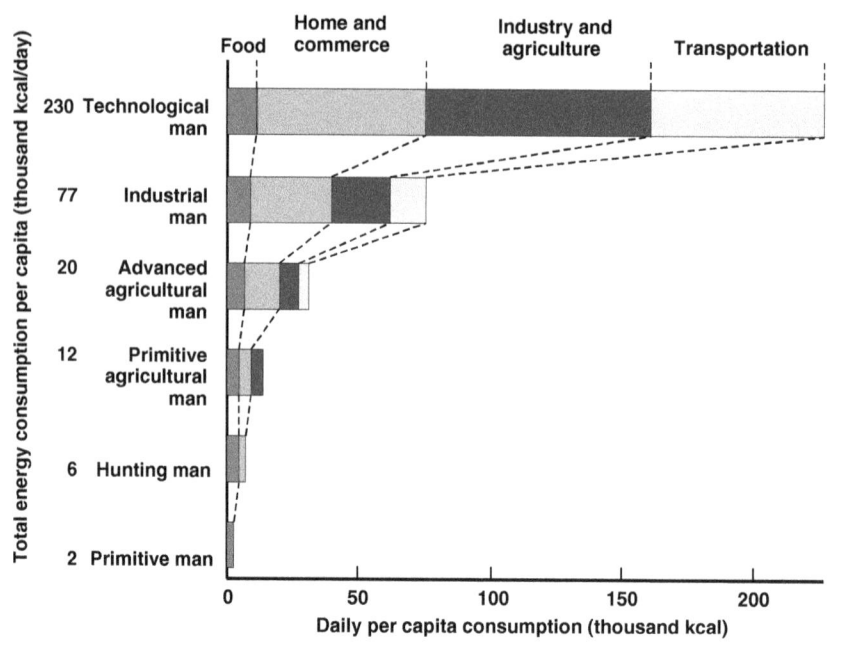

Figure 1.1 Stages of development and energy consumption. *Source:* Cook, E. *Man, Energy, Society*, W. H. Freeman and Co., San Francisco, US (1976)

- "Hunting man" (Europe about 100,000 years ago) had more food and also burned wood for heating and cooking.
- "Primitive agricultural man" (Fertile Crescent in 5000 BC) grew crops and used animal energy.
- "Advanced agricultural man" (Northeast Europe in 1400 AD) had coal for heating, water power, wind power, and animal transportation.
- "Industrial man" (United Kingdom in 1875) had the steam engine.
- "Technological man" (United States in 1970) consumed 230,000 kcal/day.

Starting with the very low energy consumption of 2000 kcal per day, which characterized primitive society, energy consumption grew, in one million years, to 230,000 kcal per day. This enormous growth of per capita energy consumption was only made possible by:

- Increased use of coal as a source of heat and power in the nineteenth century;
- Use of internal combustion engines, which led to the massive use of petroleum and its derivatives; and
- Electricity generated initially in hydroelectric sites and afterwards in thermoelectric plants.

Income per capita has also grown and one is thus tempted to find out if there is a clear correlation between energy consumption/capita and GNP/capita.

Figure 1.2 shows data for a number of countries. A linear relationship between energy consumption/capita and GDP/capita could be expected since higher income means more appliances, automobiles, larger homes, more travel, and many other activities but empirical evidence shows that is not the case. Clearly, there are many countries that do not fit into a linear relationship.

Table 1.1 Noncommercial energy in Africa		
Country	1973	1985
Uganda	83%	92%
Malawi	87%	94%
Guinea-Bissau	72%	67%
Gâmbia	89%	78%
Guinea	69%	72%
Burundi	97%	95%
Mali	90%	88%
Burkina Faso	96%	92%

Sources: World Resources, World Resources Institute 1998.

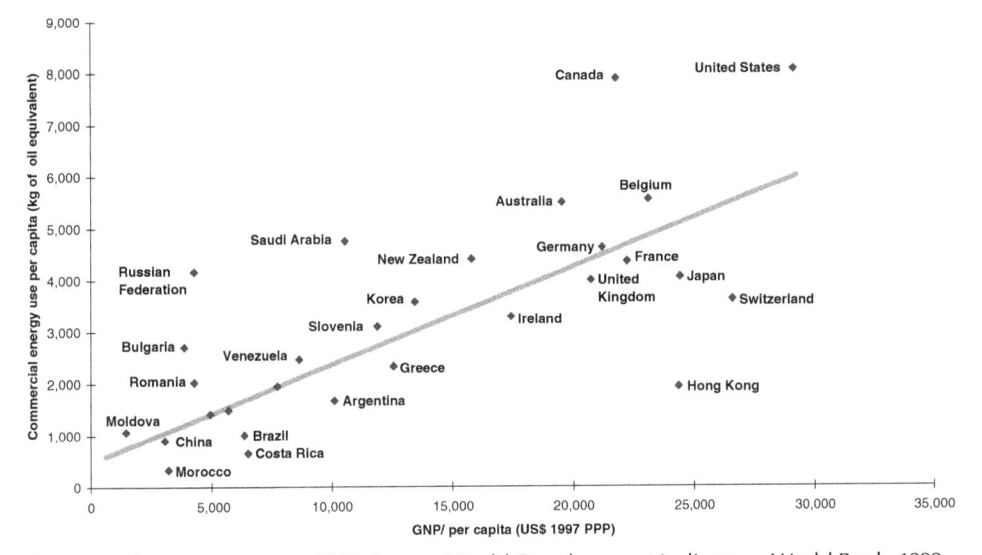

Figure 1.2 Energy use versus GNP. *Source:* World Development Indicators, World Bank, 1999

Moreover, some countries with the same GNP/capita can have very different energy consumption per capita, which is the case, for example, in Russia, China, and Morocco. Their GNP/capita is approximately the same but energy consumption in Russia is four times higher than in China and fifteen times higher than in Morocco.

2 THE IMPORTANCE OF NONCOMMERCIAL ENERGY

One problem with Figure 1.2, as far as the developing countries are concerned, is that the horizontal axis considers only commercial energy, which is the fraction of total energy consumption that can be quantified, since by definition it involves monetary transactions. In reality, in many areas noncommercial energy sources such as dung, agricultural residues, and firewood are used. In some countries it represents a large percentage of total consumption particularly for the poor. Table 1.1 shows the importance of noncommercial energy in a number of countries.

The importance of noncommercial energy is also clearly exemplified by the data in Figure 1.3, which shows the average energy demand by income segment in Brazil.

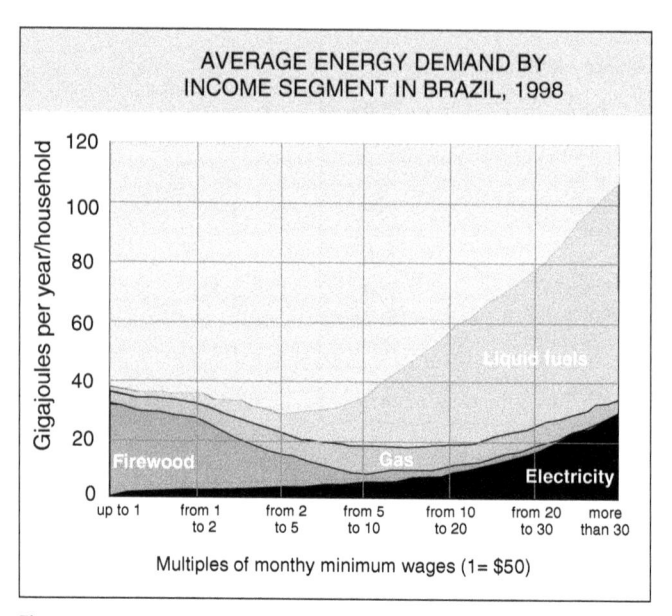

Figure 1.3 Average Energy Demand by Income Segment in Brazil, 1998. *Source:* Almeida, E. and Oliveira, A. "Brazilian Life Style and Energy Consumption" in *Energy Demand, Life Style Changes and Technology Development*, World Energy Council, London, 1995

For low-income households firewood (usually a noncommercial energy source) is the dominant fuel. At higher income levels firewood is replaced by commercial fuels and electricity, which offer much greater convenience, energy efficiency, and cleanliness. In most of Africa and India dung and agricultural residues are used in lieu of firewood.

3 THE ENERGY INTENSITY

Another reason for the lack of a linear relationship between energy and GNP per capita is that the amount of additional energy required to provide energy services depends on the efficiencies with which the energy is produced, delivered, and used. Energy intensity (the ratio of energy demand to GDP) often depends on a country's stage of development. In OECD countries, which enjoy abundant energy services, growth in energy demand is less tightly linked to economic productivity than it was in the past. (Figure 1.4).

The evolution of the energy intensity ($I = E/\text{GDP}$) over time reflects the combined effects of structural changes in the economy – built into the GNP – and changes in the mix of energy sources and the efficiency of energy use – built into the primary energy consumed E.

Although admittedly a very rough indicator, energy intensity has some attractive features: while E and GDP per capita vary by more than one order of magnitude between developing and developed countries, energy intensity does not change by more than a factor of two. This is due in part to common characteristics of the energy systems of industrialized and developing countries in the modern sector of the economy, and in part to the fact that in industrialized countries energy-intensive activities, such as jet travel, are increasingly offsetting efficiency gains in basic industries.

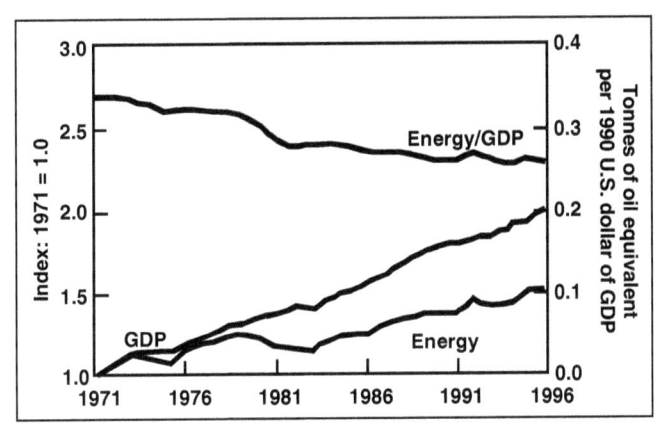

Figure 1.4 GDP and Primary Energy Consumption in OECD Countries, 1971–96. *Source:* "Energy Balances of OECD countries," IEA (International Energy Agency), Paris, 1999.

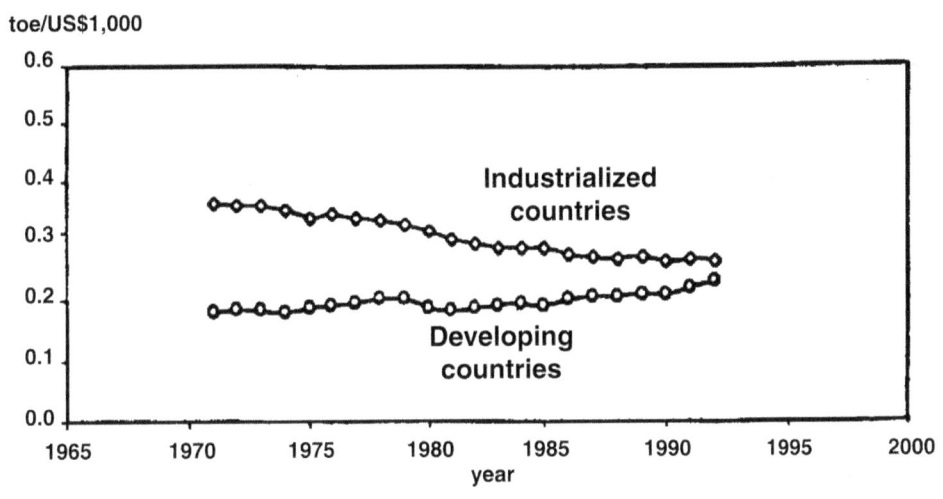

Figure 1.5 Energy Use/GDP–PPP (in 1992 US$). *Source:* Mielnik, O. and Goldemberg, J. "Converging to a common pattern of energy use in developing and industrialized countries," *Energy Policy* 28, pp. 503–8, 2000

Energy intensity (considering only commercial energy sources) declined in OECD countries in the period 1971–91 at a rate of roughly 1.4 percent per year. The main reasons for that movement were efficiency improvements, structural change, and fuel substitution. However, in the developing countries the pattern has been more varied.

A recent study indicates that the energy intensity in the period 1971–92 of developing and industrialized countries is converging to a common pattern of energy use. For each country, energy intensity was obtained as the ratio of commercial energy use to GDP converted in terms of purchasing power parity (PPP). The path of energy intensity of a country was given by the yearly sequence of energy intensity data over the period 1971–94. The same procedure was followed to have the energy intensity paths for a set of eighteen industrialized countries and for one of twenty-three developing countries. The energy intensity data for each of these subsets were given by the ratio of total commercial energy use to total PPP–converted GDP for each group of countries at each year of the period 1971–94 (Figure 1.5).

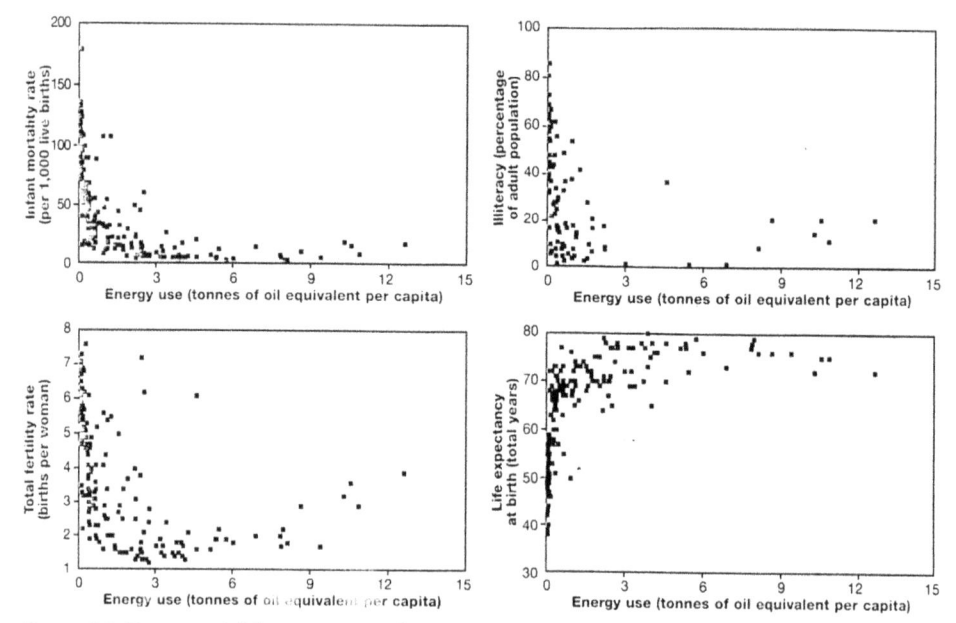

Figure 1.6 Commercial Energy Use and Infant Mortality, Illiteracy, Life Expectancy, and Fertility in Industrialised and Developing Countries. *Source:* World Energy Assessment, UNDP, DESA and WEC – Editor: Goldemberg, J., 2000

4 THE HUMAN DEVELOPMENT INDEX

Since a clear correlation between energy and income is difficult to establish one is tempted to look for other correlations between energy consumption and social indicators such as infant mortality, illiteracy, and fertility (Figure 1.6).

It is clear from such figures that energy use has great impacts on major social issues, which is not meant necessarily as a casual relationship between the parameters represented, but as a strong covariance.

Such behavior encouraged analysts to invent an indicator that would include not only GDP/capita but also take into account longevity and literacy.

The Human Development Index (HDI) developed by the United Nations Development Program (UNDP) is one way of measuring how well countries are meeting, not just the economic, but also the social needs of their people, that is, their quality of life. The HDI is calculated on the basis of a simple average of longevity, knowledge, and standard of living:

- longevity – measured by life expectancy;
- knowledge – measured by a combination of adult literacy (two-thirds weight) and mean years of schooling (one-third weight); and
- standard of living – measured by purchasing power, based on real GDP per capita adjusted for the local cost of living (purchasing power parity – PPP).

The HDI measures performance by expressing a value between zero (poorest performance) and one (ideal performance). Figure 1.7 shows HDI as a function of commercial energy consumption for a large number of countries.

The Table 1.2 lists the characteristics of a few countries, their HDI value, and HDI rank.

Table 1.2 HDI for a few countries

Country	Life expectancy at birth (years)	Adult literacy rate (% age 15 and above)	GNP per capita (PPR US$)	HDI	HDI rank
Russia	66.1	99.5	7,473	0,775	55
Brazil	67.5	84.9	7,037	0,75	69
Sri Lanka	71.9	91.4	3,279	0,735	81
China	70.2	83.5	3,617	0,718	87
Morocco	67.2	48.0	3,419	0,596	112
India	62.9	56.5	2,248	0,571	115

Source: Human Development Report UNDP, 2001

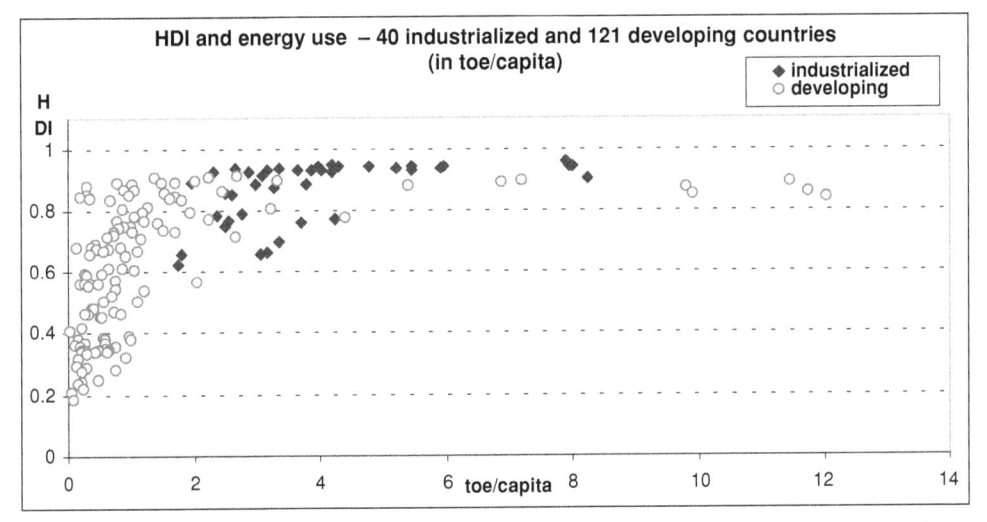

Figure 1.7 HDI and Energy Use. *Sources:* World Bank (1999 World Development Indicators for energy data), UNDP (Human Development Report 1998)

An analysis of this table indicates the importance of factors other than GNP/capita in determining the HDI rank of different countries. Just to give some examples, Russia and Brazil have approximately the same GNP/capita but adult literacy in Russia (99.5 percent) is much higher than in Brazil (84.9 percent), which puts the former in rank fifty-five against sixty-nine for Brazil. Sri Lanka and China have a GDP/capita approximately the same as Morocco, but the life expectancy and adult literacy of the former are much higher, which give Sri Lanka rank eighty-one, China eighty-seven and Morocco 112.

It is apparent from Figure 1.7 that, for an energy consumption above one ton of oil equivalent (toe)/capita per year, the value of HDI is higher than 0.8 and essentially constant for all countries. One toe/capita/year seems, therefore, the minimum energy needed to guarantee an acceptable level of living as measured by the HDI, despite many variations of consumption patterns and lifestyles across countries.

The relationship between HDI and energy has several important implications. The relationship can be considered to consist of two regions (Figure 1.8).

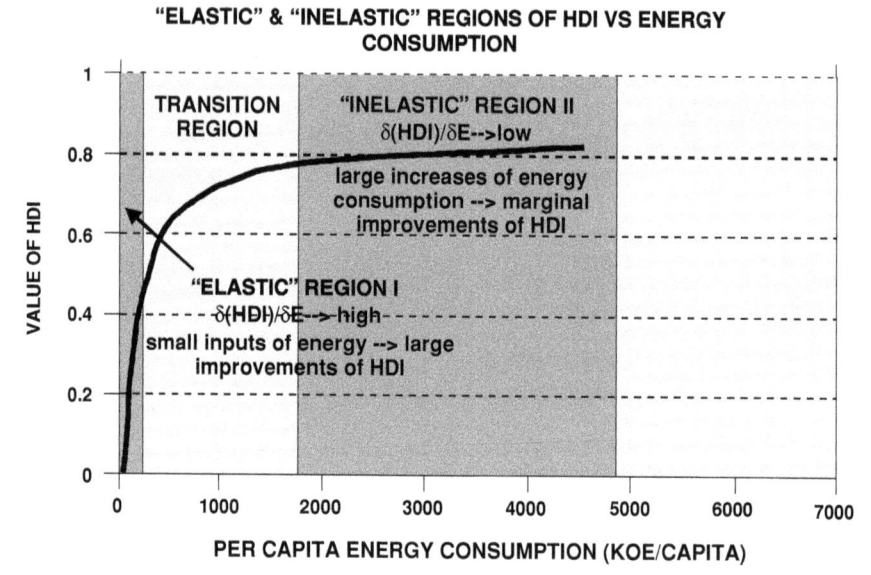

Figure 1.8 "Elastic" and "Inelastic" Regions. *Source:* Reddy, A. K. N. "Energy Technologies and Policies for Rural Development" in *Energy for Sustainable Development,* IIIEE and UNDP. Editors: Johansson, T. B. and Goldemberg, J., 2002

This Figure shows that in region I – the "elastic region" – the slope δ (HDI)/δ (E) of the HDI vs E curve is high. In region III – the "inelastic region" – the slope δ (HDI)/δ (E) of the HDI vs E curve is low; even large inputs of energy (large improvements of energy services) result only in marginal improvements in HDI, i.e., the HDI-energy (benefit-cost) ratio is very low. In the elastic region III, enhanced energy services lead directly to the improvement

Thus the implication of the elastic and inelastic regions is that in the elastic region increased energy services guarantee direct improvement of HDI, whereas improvement of HDI via income depends on what the income is used for.

5 GENERATION OF JOBS IN ENERGY PRODUCTION

There are estimates of the number of direct jobs generated in the production of energy from a variety of sources. We collected some of these estimates in Table 1.3.

These numbers were obtained from a variety of sources and include jobs involved in operating the generating stations, excluding jobs involved in producing and commisioning the equipment.

What is striking in the Table is the very large number of jobs generated by the truly decentralized options which are photovoltaics and ethanol from sugarcane.

Photovoltaics energy is usually generated (and used) in small modules of 100 watts and the generation of one TWh would require typically ten million modules to be installaded and mainted.

Ethanol from sugarcane in Brazil involves agricultural production in approximately four million hectares plus the industrial production in sugar-alcohol distilleries, which explains the large number of direct jobs generated.

There are also some rough estimates of the number of jobs generated by energy conservation. A study in Sacramento, California, shows that saving enough energy to

Table 1.3 Direct jobs in energy production

Sector	Jobs (person-years) Terawatt-hour
Petroleum[a]	260
Offshore oil[a]	265
Natural gas[a]	250
Coal[a]	370
Nuclear[a]	75
Wood energy[a]	1000
Hydro[b]	250
Minihydro[c]	120
Wind[c]	918
Photovoltaics[c]	7,600
Ethanol (from sugarcane)[b]	4,000

Sources:
[a] Grassi, G. "Potential Employement Impacts of Bioenergy Activity on Employment" Proceedings of the 9th European Bioenergy Conference Vol. I, pp. 419–423 Eds. – P. Chartier et al. Elsevier, Oxford (1996).
[b] Carvalho, L. C. and Szwarc, A. "Understanding the Impact of Externalities, Case Studies" Brazil International Development Seminar on Fuel Ethanol December 14, 2001 Washington D.C.
[c] Perez, E. M. "Energias Renovables, Sustentabilidad y Creacion de Enpleo: Una Economia Impulssionada por el Sol," pp. 270, 2001.
[4] Quoted in M. Renner, "Working for the Environment: a Growing Source of Jobs," Worldwatch Paper 152 (Sept. 2000) Worldwatch Institute.

avoid 100 megawatts worth of power plant capacity creates thirty-nine jobs, compared with the fifteen to twenty jobs required to operate the same amount of capacity at a modern coal- or gas-fired power plant.

6 CONCLUSIONS

The analysis presented shows clearly that energy has a determinant influence on the HDI, particularly in the early stages of development, in which the vast majority of the world's people, particularly women and children find themselves. It also shows that the influence of per capita energy consumption on the HDI begins to decline somewhere between 1,000 and 3,000 kilograms of oil equivalent (koe) per inhabitant. Thereafter, even with a tripling in energy consumption, the HDI does not increase. Thus, from approximately 1,000 koe per capita, the strong positive covariance of energy consumption with HDI starts to diminish.

More generally what we have shown is that what one understands by development, including the generation of jobs, depends on a number of factors and GNP/capita is not the only determinant. Furthermore, although an essential ingredient of development, energy is more important for low rather than high incomes.

2 The Imperatives of Energy for Sustainable Development

Thomas B. Johansson*

Many challenges threaten the movement toward sustainable development.[1] The most significant of these objectives include the simultaneous (i) social development and poverty alleviation, and (ii) economic growth, while (iii) protecting the environment. Past and present forms of economic growth have created a very uneven distribution of wealth between and within nations, and placed severe strains on the environment, resulting in urban air pollution, regional acidification, and global climate change, to name but a few.

Current trends in energy systems development, and several of the linkages between these systems and current unsustainable global socioeconomic development patterns shall be discussed here. The main finding is that strong links exist between sustainable development challenges and the energy systems in the world, and that major changes in energy systems are required to achieve sustainability at large.[2]

1 CURRENT ENERGY SUPPLY AND DEMAND

During the last century, the use of fossil fuel resources – oil, natural gas, and coal – dominated world primary energy. In 2001, fossil energy use made up seventy-nine percent of world primary energy consumption. In comparison, renewables (including large hydro, traditional biomass, and new renewable like solar, wind, geothermal) made up fourteen percent and nuclear seven percent of world primary energy use. Furthermore, demand for energy services continues to increase with growing economies and population size. For example, between 1960 and 1997 in the OECD countries, primary energy use and electricity use increased by a factor of 2 and 4.5 respectively, to support a three-fold increase in the economies and an increase in population size of fifty percent.

Regional differences in per capita energy use (commercial and noncommercial) are extreme. As of 2000, per capita energy use in OECD North America (420 million people)

---

[1] The concept of sustainable development was introduced by the United Nations Commission on Environment and Development (the Brundtland Commission) in the 1980s, founded on the three pillars of economic growth, social equity, and environmental quality.

[2] For a review of these issues, see the World Energy Assessment: *Energy and the Challenge of Sustainability;* http://www.undp.org/seed/eap/activities/wea/drafts-frame.html.

* Professor and Director, International Institute for Industrial Environmental Economics, University of Lund, P.O. Box 196, 221 00 Lund, Sweden. Email: thomas.b.johansson@iiiee.lu.se. This chapter is based on a presentation given at IUCN Academy of Environment Law Colloquium: The Law of Energy for Sustainable Development, Shanghai, P.R. China, November 4–6, 2003. The assistance of Martha Duenas and Alissa Boardley in converting the presentation into this paper is gratefully acknowledged.

amounted to 280 GJ, whereas per capita energy consumption in Asia[3] and Sub-Saharan Africa registered at just 25 GJ. In China, with the largest population in the world (1300 million people), per capita energy use registered 38 GJ.

2 ENERGY AND SOCIOECONOMIC DEVELOPMENT

The linkages between energy systems and economic growth are apparent and well understood. However, the relationship between energy systems on one hand and social development, health, and the environment on the other has attracted much less attention until recently.

The lack of access to modern energy carriers seriously constrains opportunities to earn incomes and lead healthy lives. Currently, almost 2 billion people have no access to electricity and an additional two billion people have access to unreliable electricity. Furthermore, more than two billion people cook using tradition fuels like wood, agricultural residues, and dung. Millions of women across the world spend hours a day carrying fuel and water. The use of these low quality fuels is particularly harmful to women and children. As women are also traditionally responsible for most cooking duties, they are often exposed to high levels of indoor air pollution from cooking. The World Health Organization estimates that indoor air pollution causes 2.7–3.0 million premature deaths a year, or 5–6 percent of global mortality.

The broader indicators of development, such as the Human Development Index (HDI),[4] and per capita energy use supports this picture. Countries with a HDI above 0.8 have per capita energy use of approx. 1.5 million ton of oil equivalent (Mtoe), and to reach above a HDI of 0.9, per capita energy use is above 3 Mtoe.

Development goals of the international community were identified in 2000 at the meeting of the United Nations General Assembly (the Millennium Assembly), and are known as the Millennium Development Goals (MDGs). Through these goals, the international community aims to achieve the following:

- eradicate extreme poverty and hunger;
- achieve universal primary education;
- promote gender equality and empower women;
- reduce child mortality;
- improve maternal health;
- combat HIV/AIDS, malaria, and other diseases; and
- ensure environmental sustainability.

With regard to this last goal, environmental sustainability is to be promoted by integrating the principles of sustainable development into national policies and programs. In addition, several concrete targets are identified. These include halving, by 2015, the proportion of people living on less than one dollar a day, the proportion of people without access to safe drinking water, and by 2020, to have achieved a significant improvement in the lives of at least 100 million slum dwellers. Despite increasing recognition of the importance of energy services in meeting development goals, improving access to safe,

---

[3] Asia here excludes the Middle East, China, and OECD countries.
[4] HDI is an indicator based on per capita income, life expectancy at birth, and literacy, annually published by UNDP (http://www.undp.org).

reliable and affordable energy services for the global population are not itself recognized as a goal of the international community. However, access to modern forms of energy remains a prerequisite for reaching the MDGs.

Without access to modern forms of energy it will be virtually impossible to reach any of these global development goals. Energy thus becomes an entry point to achieving broader societal objectives. Many objectives must therefore be met simultaneously in the pursuit of these targets.

Access to affordable, safe, and reliable energy services is increasingly being recognized as critical to social development and poverty alleviation. For example, at the Ninth Meeting of the UN Commission for Sustainable Development in 2001, access to affordable energy services was acknowledged as a prerequisite to meeting the international millennium development goal of halving the proportion of people living on less than US\$1 per day by 2015.

Energy was first acknowledged as a key part of the global political agenda in the process leading up to the World Summit for Sustainable Development (WSSD) held in Johannesburg, South Africa, in 2002. Energy, as outlined in the UN Secretary General Kofi Annan's WEHAB[5] agenda, was finally recognized as a necessary factor for sustainable development. By the end of the WSSD, an international appeal for improved access to energy, the sustainable use of biomass for energy, cleaner use of fossil fuels, reduced market distortions, and a substantial increase in the share of renewable energy "with a sense of urgency," had been launched. In addition, thirty-nine new partnerships on energy were formed, including the Global Network on Energy for Sustainable Development (GNESD), the Global Village Energy partnership (GVEP), an EU Energy Initiative (EUEI), a partnership for reduced Gas Flaring, a partnership for increasing the use of LPG for cooking, and another for the sustainable use of biomass for energy.

3 ENERGY AND SECURITY OF SUPPLY

Reliance on major oil imports raises questions about the security of supply, and leads to severe consequences for economic and social development if disruptions of supply occur. As for the OECD countries, in 1996, North America imported forty-five percent of its oil, Europe imported fifty-three percent and the Pacific[6] imported ninety percent of its oil. Reliance on imported oil is projected to increase by 2020, in North America to sixty-three percent, in Europe to eighty-five percent, and in the Pacific to ninety-six percent. The security of supply is already a major and growing concern of most governments.

Additionally, a large number of developing countries pay a very high price for these imports, using twenty to forty percent of their export earnings on fossil fuel imports. This means that poor countries spend their severely limited foreign exchange on energy imports that could be reduced with higher utilization of domestic energy and more efficient use of energy.

---

[5] The WEHAB agenda proposed the main priority areas for the summit: Water, Energy, Health, Agriculture, and Biodiversity.
[6] Australia, Japan, New Zealand, and South Korea (190 million people).

4 ENERGY AND ENVIRONMENTAL ISSUES

An awareness and understanding of the environmental consequences of past and present energy systems is also becoming more relevant and systematic. Energy use contributes to indoor and urban air pollution, acidification, and global warming. It is responsible for eighty-six percent of global anthropogenic emissions of sulphur dioxide, the main chemical responsible for environmental acidification that damages forests and lakes. As for global warming, the use of fossil fuels leads to major emissions of carbon dioxide and methane, the main greenhouse gases. Fossil fuel use contributes approximately seventy-eight percent of anthropogenic emissions of carbon dioxide and twenty-three percent of emissions of methane, as well as a significant fraction of emissions of long-lived small particulate matter, which poses significant risks to human health when inhaled.

The consequences of greenhouse gas emissions from fossil fuel use on global warming are particularly worrisome, and are of growing international concern. It is estimated that global emissions of GHG will have to be reduced by sixty percent or more to meet the objectives of the United Nations Framework Convention on Climate Change (UNFCCC). Achieving this while expanding economies now based on the use of fossil fuels is one of the major challenges facing the energy system.

5 REQUIREMENTS FOR CHANGE

The linkages between energy systems and economic development, social equity, and environmental protection described thus far indicate that a change in present energy system development is required if sustainable development pathways are to be realized. The magnitude of the change required is not small and the ultimate challenge will be finding ways forward that address all the issues simultaneously.

6 ENERGY RESOURCES

In spite of repeated statements to the contrary in the media, conventional oil and gas resources could last at least another 50–100 years, and total fossil fuel resources, including fuels locked away in tar sands and deep sea beds, are predicted to last at least several hundreds of years. This means that there will not be a resource constraint driven change of the world energy system for a long time to come. Thus, fossil fuel resource depletion will provide little incentive to change the current system. Accordingly, public policies will have to address the issues of the future energy system and put in place incentives in the marketplace that make market actors select options that not only provide profits but also support public objectives.

7 MAIN STRATEGIES FOR ENERGY SYSTEM CHANGE

In the pursuit of sustainable energy system pathways, three main strategies are identified. On the energy supply side, these include the exploration and adoption of more renewable energy sources such as biomass, wind, solar, hydro, and geothermal. Renewable energy flows on Earth are thousands times the current global energy use. The second strategy on the energy supply side involves the exploration and adoption of advanced energy technologies, including advanced fossil fuel technologies, with near zero emissions of greenhouse gases, and nuclear technologies if the issues associated with such technologies can be resolved.[7] On the energy demand side of the equation, strategies for improved energy efficiency at the point of end use in buildings, electric appliances, vehicles, and production processes must also be pursued to tap the very large economic (including an accounting for external health and environmental costs) potential for more efficient use of energy, thereby reducing the need for more supply.

As there are many combinations of technical options that would support sustainable development and the movement toward sustainable energy systems, the development of scenarios is a useful tool in the visualization of sustainable energy futures. Scenario development, often described as thought experiments, allow stakeholders to predict the benefits and/or consequences of different combinations of assumptions, including technologies, policies, and strategies. For example, in a scenario developed by the International Institute for Applied Systems Analysis (IIASA) and the World Energy Council (WEC) comparing a base energy technology future with a future including advanced technologies such as coal gasification and more renewables, coal use is significantly reduced in the advanced technology scenario. This is due to the adoption of more renewable technologies. A clear conclusion of scenario work is that an energy future that is compatible with sustainable development will not happen on its own. The creation of appropriate and effective policies is a prerequisite to the type of change required to bring about a sustainable energy future.

8 THE CASE OF CHINA

Over the last two decades, China has demonstrated a development strategy that has allowed for a significant decoupling of economic growth from energy use. The energy intensity of the Chinese economy has been reduced by approximately fifty percent during the last twenty years, thereby significantly reducing costs, imports, and environmental degradation. Large opportunities to continue to improve energy intensity exist. The current development strategy of China is known as the "3E strategy" and promotes:

- Economic development: provide energy services for a fourfold expansion of the economy by 2020;
- Energy security: avoid becoming overly dependent on oil and gas imports; and
- Environmental protection: protect public health, ecosystems, and limit climate change

Fortunately, there appears to be feasible options for meeting these challenges in China.[8] A main element is the concept of leapfrogging that is to make use of the most efficient technologies in new investments. There is a long way to go in all countries in the world, including China, to make use of the existing technologies to deliver the same energy services at a much lower resource use and environmental degradation. The rapid construction of commercial and residential buildings dominates growth of electricity

---

[7] For nuclear energy these include cost, reactor safety, radioactive waste containment, and linkages to nuclear weapons proliferation, see the World Energy Assessment.

[8] N. Weidou and T. B. Johansson, "Energy for sustainable development in China," *Energy Policy* (in press), available at http://www.elsevier.com/wps/find/journaldescription.cws_/home/30414/description #description, and a special issue on energy for sustainable development in China: http://www.ieiglobal.org/vol7/_issue4.html.

demand in China, and not making buildings and equipment more energy efficient means that a large future need for resources is generated. The expansion of the automobile fleet using relatively high mileage automobile technologies establishes a higher need for oil and thereby higher imports. These challenges could in principle be much reduced through the use of more energy efficient technologies and practices.

On the supply side, the next generation technologies for using coal, based on oxygen-blown gasification followed by conversion to liquid and gaseous fuels, heat, and electricity, suggests ways forward to continue to use coal while protecting the environment, and mitigate climate change through carbon dioxide sequestration. In addition, China has vast largely untapped renewable energy resources that are becoming increasingly attractive. These resources can be used to keep oil imports at the limited level in line with the objectives of the government.

9 POLICY MATTERS

As nations, regions, and cities struggle to transfer the calls for action made at the WSSD into policies, they will inevitably face many challenges. Sectoral approaches will be unlikely to deliver complete solutions, thereby requiring more integrated approaches. Emphasis on innovative system designs and guided investments is needed. Energy must be thought of as an instrument for sustainable development, rather than a separate entity driving gross domestic product (GDP) growth. Thinking and discussions around these issues over the years has already led to the identification of a number of policy areas that must be incorporated in addressing these challenges. These areas include, but are not limited to the following:[9]

- make markets work better, including mobilizing investments and improving energy efficiency –
  - ➢ remove subsidies to conventional energy forms, globally now on the order of $250 billion per year,
  - ➢ reflect external costs in the prices, rules and regulations in the marketplace,
- address the innovation chain, from research and development,[10] demonstration projects, investments to buy-down costs of new technologies, and wide dissemination, to develop an bring more sustainable technologies into use,[11]
- reform the power sector to enhance access to electricity, supply security, and environmental protection,
- build capacity to support policy and institution building, education and training, and transfer of technology,
- increase public awareness and participation.

---

[9] *See* T. B. Johansson and J. Goldemberg (eds.), *Energy for Sustainable Development – A Policy Agenda*, UNDP, 2002, available at http://www.undp.org/seed/eap/html/publications/2002/2002a.htm.

[10] Member states of the International Energy Agency have reduced their spending on energy R&D by 50% since the early 1980s, and at present 8% is allocated for renewable energy and 12% to energy efficiency.

[11] Two policy measures have proven effective for these two last objectives: Feed-in tariffs (used in Germany, Spain, and Denmark) that guarantee secure access to the market at known and favorable prices, and green certificate markets (used in, e.g., Sweden, United Kingdom, and Texas), where governments have set minimum quantities of green electricity and allowed for trading between those that have obligations to demonstrate the required quantity of green electricity.

The challenges of transforming the energy systems of the world to support sustainable development are very large indeed. The good news is that resources and technologies exist that can meet these challenges. However, it will take a concerted effort to formulate and implement the necessary policies at national and international levels to make sufficient use of them.

10 CONCLUSION

There are strategic advantages in adopting policies and institutional measures toward a framework for energy for sustainable development. Energy can be used as an instrument to promote poverty alleviation and sustainable socioeconomic development. Using energy for sustainable development approaches would promote growth while limiting environmental impacts, including climate change, and enhancing security. This is paramount in the ongoing process towards sustainable development at large.

3 2020 Energy Demand of China and Energy Conservation

Zhou Dadi*

Chinese energy strategy must begin with an analysis of the county's current and future demand for energy. A rapid rise in energy demand is the key driving force for the development of an energy strategy. There is not only one possible future for China. The goal is to keep energy elasticity at 0.5 for the next twenty years. But is it possible to achieve this target?

Table 3.1 shows the year 2000 China energy demand by resource and the projected demand for years 2010 and 2020.

The range of energy demand in China in 2020 by resource is: coal, about 18.5 to 28.5 million tons; oil, 400 to 520 million tons; natural gas, 120 to 200 billion cubic meters; primary electricity (hydro, nuclear, renewables), 1080 to 1400 twh; hydropower, 220 to 240 gw; nuclear, 30 to 40 gw; and wind, 15 to 30 gw.

Keeping low energy elasticity is possible. Total energy demand is projected at 2.4 to 3.1 billion tce, but it is not certain that it will stay lower than 3.1 billion. There is a strong need for energy conservation, a high-quality energy mix, strict environmental policy, and effective enforcement. There needs to be significant change in the mix of energy, for example, coal from seventy to fifty-five percent, natural gas from five to ten percent, and primary electricity from six to ten percent. There will be an increase in need for imported oil and gas. If total energy demand increases greatly, the demand for coal will rise. Replacing coal will result in higher efficiency and lowered emissions. Supply from hydro, nuclear, and wind resources must speed up.

Table 3.2 shows China's energy supply capacity in 2000 and the supply capacity forecast for the years 2010 and 2020.

There are a number of significant constraints to the increased production and use of coal. There are resource limitations on increased mechanical extraction of coal. Production and use of coal have severe environmental problems, including damage to water resources, the sinking of land, and pollution causing health and bad working conditions. Labor safety problems are serious. The production of coal causes social burdens on mining cities and towns. These constraints make it difficult to significantly increase coal production in the future.

There are also constraints on the increased use of alternative energies, however. Hydro soon will reach its resource limitation. Nuclear energy needs long lead times and big investments. Wind power can only comprise a small share of rising energy needs.

* Director General, Energy Research Institute, National Development and Reform Commission, PRC.

Table 3.1

Scenario	Types of Energy	2000[a]	2010	2020
1	Coal (million ton)	12.5	20.8	28.5
	Oil (10,000 ton)	2.24	3.1	5.2
	Natural gas (100 million cubic meter)	245	620	1,200
	One-time electricity capacity (100 million kilowatts)	2,392	7,078	10,791
2	Coal (million ton)	12.5	19.3	23.8
	Oil (10,000 ton)	2.24	3.0	4.8
	Natural gas (100 million cubic meter)	245	820	1,700
	One-time electricity capacity (100 million kilowatts)	2,392	7231	11,913
3	Coal (million ton)	12.5	17.0	18.5
	Oil (10,000 ton)	2.24	2.8	4.0
	Natural gas (100 million cubic meter)	245	980	2,000
	One-time electricity capacity (100 million kilowatts)	2,392	7,709	13,931

[a] Year 2000 Energy consumption has been adjusted accordingly with actual data.

Table 3.2

		2010		2020	
	2000	Low	High	Low	High
Coal (million ton)	1000	1600	N/A	2100	N/A
Oil (10,000 ton)	163	17,000	19,000	17,500	20,000
Gas (100 million cubic meter)	272	800	1,000	1,300	1,500
Hydrogen Electricity (million kilowatts)	79.3	185	195	240	300
Nuclear Electricity (million kilowatts)	2.1		25		50
New Energy (million ton standard coal)	1		N/A		N/A

Other renewable resources can make only a limited contribution to China's energy needs by 2020.

Therefore, the necessity for a large expansion of energy efficiency measures is clear. There is a need to keep a better balance between energy demand and supply. It is imperative to improve energy and economic security. To do so, improved market competition is essential. At the same time, there is the need to address pollution problems and prepare a response to climate change. Expanded energy efficiency has a great potential for lowering energy requirements, improving energy and economic security, and reducing environmental degradation.

The elements for achieving energy conservation targets, taking into consideration China's economic growth rate, include: providing for economic structural changes to make efficiency measures more attractive investments; exploring new models of sustainable consumption; promoting new technology developments for energy efficiency; and adopting strong governmental policy support measures.

The rate of economic growth may increase significantly. Is a 7.2 percent growth rate for next twenty years possible, or even higher? The focus remains on industrialization, which speeds urbanization and drives increasing requirements for employment. Coordinative development is essential to meet urban and rural needs, address the regional differences between east and west, meet economic and social goals, and achieve a balance between energy, societal, and environmental goals. Key challenges to achieving economic structural change include: addressing elements of energy consumption; lowering energy intensity; reducing pollution; and implementing higher added value structures to promote these changes. There remains high energy intensity and demand for raw materials in industries like steel, cement, etc. With significant change in the last twenty years, the high energy intensity sector is developing rapidly. Where will the market lead? There is a need to establish social consumption model accounts.

China needs to explore sustainable models of consumption. It is not realistic for China to copy current consumption models of developed countries. China faces the challenges of all developing countries: population increase, resources depletion, and environmental problems. China's problems are also a challenge for the rest of the world. China still needs to explore and learn the best practices for promoting energy efficiency that have been adopted in other countries.

There needs to be government intervention to promote technology development of energy efficiency measures. There is great potential for improvement of energy efficiency in China. However, the basis of market forces alone is far from sufficient for achieving energy efficiency goals. There needs to be consensus, policy intervention and promotion, and modification of China's current Energy Conservation Law. China must improve its energy standards and enforcement and promote more technology research and development (R&D). The government needs to apply economic leverage measures to the market to better provide for adoption of energy efficiency measures.

4 Sustainable Development and the Marrakech Accords

1 INTRODUCTION

Global warming is a paradigmatic sustainable development challenge. Greenhouse gases (GHGs) are emitted by a vast array of human activities that range from burning fossil fuels for electricity, heat, transportation, cooking, industrial, commercial, and governmental activities, to raising cows for meat and dairy products, growing rice, transporting natural gas, mining coal, and using fertilizer to grow the food we eat. The cumulative effect of the increased atmospheric concentration of GHGs is that more heat from the sun is trapped in the atmosphere, thereby warming the earth and modifying its climate. The climate change resulting from anthropogenic GHG emissions will adversely affect, among other things, public health, agriculture, weather patterns, water supplies, sea levels, the habitability of the coastal regions of the world, ecosystem health, and biodiversity; and could result in catastrophic effects such as the disappearance of the Gulf Stream, and alterations of other ocean currents. Adaptation to the climate change will be hugely expensive, to the extent adaptation is possible. Reduction of GHG emissions to mitigate the degree and speed of warming will require modifying the way we produce and use energy, grow our food, and changing the underlying price and market assumptions that organize our economic and social lives.

Sustainable development, although a concept difficult to define precisely,[1] seeks economic development that is ecologically sound, equitable as to both present and future generations, and promotes social welfare. Operationally, sustainable development requires a governance structure that integrates economic and environmental concerns into all decisions, promotes sustainable consumption and population levels, intergenerational equity, public participation, and imposes this common responsibility on all nations, although with the responsibility differentiated between developed and developing nations.[2]

In this sense, the United Nations Framework Convention on Climate Change (UNFCCC), at present the world's only binding international law on global warming, is better understood as a sustainable development treaty than as merely an environmental

---

[1] *See* David R. Hodas, "The Role of Law in Defining Sustainable Development: NEPA Reconsidered," 3 *Widener L. Symp. J.* 1 (1998).

[2] John C. Dernbach, "Sustainable Development: Now More Than Ever," in *Stumbling Towards Sustainability* (John C. Dernbach, ed., Environmental Law Inst., 2002).

[*] Professor of Law, Widener University School of Law, Wilmington, Delaware, USA.

treaty.[3] The treaty confirms this repeatedly by:

> *Recognizing* that all countries, especially developing countries, need access to resources required to achieve sustainable social and economic development and that, in order for developing countries to progress towards that goal, their energy consumption will need to grow taking into account the possibilities for achieving greater energy efficiency and for controlling greenhouse gas emissions in general, including through the application of new technologies on terms which make such an application economically and socially beneficial;
>
> *Determined* to protect the climate system for present and future generations.[4]

by defining its objective in terms of sustainability,[5] and by adopting as principles that:

> 1. The Parties should protect the climate system for the benefit of present and future generations of humankind, on the basis of equity and in accordance with their common but differentiated responsibilities and respective capabilities; and . . .
>
> 4. The Parties have right to, and should, promote sustainable development.[6]

Furthermore, among the treaty commitments is the requirement that all parties shall:

> (d) Promote sustainable management, and promote and cooperate in the conservation and enhancement, as appropriate, of sinks and reservoirs of all greenhouse gases not controlled by the Montreal Protocol, including biomass, forests and oceans as well as other terrestrial, coastal and marine ecosystems; and . . .
>
> (f) Take climate change considerations into account, to the extent feasible, in their relevant social, economic and environmental policies, and actions, and employ appropriate methods, for example impact assessments, formulated and determined nationally, with a view to minimizing adverse effects on the economy, on public health and on the quality of the environment, of projects or measures undertaken by them to mitigate or adapt to climate change.

The targets and timetables for GHG emission reductions established in the Kyoto Protocol to the UNFCCC still await the ratification of either the Russian Federation or the United States for the Kyoto Protocol to enter into force as international law. Nevertheless, the nations that have ratified Kyoto are working hard to lay the legal and institutional foundation for implementing Kyoto, particularly with respect to market-based mechanisms, as soon as it enters into force.

Progress on the adoption of a binding legal regime to govern GHG emissions is stalled as the world waits for Russia's final decision on the Kyoto Protocol to the United Nations Framework Convention on Environmental Law, and ponders how to proceed in the face of U.S. opposition to the Kyoto Protocol. Unfortunately, the world's stumbling stops toward agreement on a legal regime does not change the science of global warming,[7] reduce GHG emissions, or even slow the warming momentum built into our

---

[3] *See* Phillippe Sands, "International Law in the Field of Sustainable Development," 1994 *Brit. Yb. Intl. L.* 303, 331.

[4] United Nations Framework Convention on Climate Change, 1771 U.N.T.S. 108, *reprinted in* 31 I.L.M. 849 (1992) (concluded at Rio de Janeiro, May 29, 1992, entered into force, March 21, 1994) Preamble.

[5] UNFCCC, Art. 2.   [6] *Id.*, Art. 3, ¶¶ 1, 4.

[7] From a scientific perspective, the human fingerprint driving global warming is clearly discernible. *See* Intergovernmental Panel on Climate Change (IPCC) Third Assessment Report (Science) (2001). U.S.

climate system. But at levels just below the surface of international diplomatic relations, work is rapidly proceeding to develop a real market-based approach to GHG emissions reduction and mitigation.

This market-based approach, which I will refer to generally as "GHG emissions trading," is emerging in a variety of forms, at a variety of governmental levels, engages both the public and private sectors in innovative partnerships, and will ultimately involve both emissions reductions and the capture and storage of GHGs in so-called carbon sinks. If successful, GHG emissions trading may significantly reduce the cost of emission reductions, encourage new, more efficient technology, and unleash considerable capital for energy investments in the developing and developed world.[8] Derived from the lessons of the very successful sulfur dioxide (SO_2) allowance trading program created in the United States by the 1990 Clean Air Act Amendments[9] to promote market-based trading in SO_2 emission reductions from electric power plants, the concept first appeared in the GHG context in the late 1980s.[10] What was only the germ of an idea in 1990 is now, particularly with the recent push of the EU, a burgeoning field ready to blossom into a full-fledged international market. It is encouraging to imagine that when international law and politics catches up with the science, emissions trading will have matured to the point where it will be immediately available as a large-scale, least-cost, emissions reduction mechanism.[11] However, it is still unclear whether emissions trading will promote or thwart sustainable development.

Now is the time to examine whether emerging GHG emissions trading schemes will be consistent with principles of sustainable development. Five to ten years ago, GHG market trading was so conceptual that concrete analysis with respect to sustainability would only produce general policy debates of limited utility. If we wait another ten years, our analysis probably will be an after-the-fact exercise too late to influence policy direction or undo significant capital and resource commitments. This chapter will outline the present institutional structure of the emerging trading regimes, describe the range of projects that have been approved and are under consideration, and consider the sustainability implications of the emerging decision making structure that will govern GHG emissions trading. In particular, this chapter will look at two issues central to evaluating and approving Clean Development Mechanism projects for

---

National Academy of Sciences, in response to queries from a skeptical President Bush, affirmed the essential findings of the IPCC. The only recent debate has centered on a few articles by one group of authors that reported, based on satellite microwave data, that mid-level atmospheric temperature changes during the 1990s were less than global warming models predicted. However, the most recent study reports that when measurement biases and other inaccuracies in the satellite data are accounted for, the mid-level atmospheric temperature trends are entirely consistent with surface temperature increases and with global climate modeling: K. Y. Vinnikov and N. C. Grody, "Global Warming Trend of Mean Tropospheric Temperature Observed by Satellites," 302 *Science* 269 (10 Oct. 2003).

[8] Even though the Kyoto Protocol has not yet entered into force, GHG emission reduction credits are now trading at about 10 ($11.66) per ton of CO_2 equivalent. October 2003 *Joint Implementation Quarterly* 1.

[9] 42 U.S.C. §§ 7651–7651o.

[10] *See* Richard L Ottinger et al. (eds.), *Environmental Costs of Electricity* (Oceana Pub. 1990) 165–183 (analyzing several proposed pilot forestry based carbon sequestration projects for offsetting carbon dioxide emissions from coal-fired electric power plants).

[11] GHG emissions trading is only one of many policy instruments to regulate GHG emissions. It cannot be the sole approach, nor is it without its own problems and limitations. The literature on this topic is extensive; *see, e.g.*, Jonathon Baert Weiner, "Global Environmental Regulation: Instrument Choice in Legal Context," 100 *Yale L. J.* 677 (1999); and David M. Dreisen, "Free Lunch or Cheap Fix? The Emissions Trading Idea and the Climate Change Convention," 26 *B.C. Envtl. Aff. L. Rev.* 1 (1998).

emissions credits: (1) how should project baselines and additionality be defined; and (2) will principles of sustainable development be integrated into the review process, and, if so, how? How these questions are answered will have a profound effect on whether emission credits represent real emission reductions, from projects that promote sustainable development, or whether emission credits are just paper entries whose sole purpose is to generate private profits.

In addressing these issues, this chapter can neither be comprehensive, nor intensely focused. Rather, it is intended to introduce energy and environmental lawyers and policy analysts to the critical issues involved, so that they can become engaged in the challenging project of helping to make this system efficient, efficacious, and one that promises to sustain the development. The stakes are very high – if GHG emissions trading becomes merely accounting entries that support financial interests, and does not produce significant, real GHG emissions reductions, then the world may well be worse off following this path than if some more traditional means of regulating GHG emissions had been chosen.

2 THE GLOBAL WARMING PROBLEM

We begin with a brief introduction to the global warming problem. From a sustainable energy perspective, the consequences of attempting to limit global warming and of adapting to the adverse effects of global warming will be profound. The predominant GHGs are carbon dioxide (CO_2), methane (CH_4), and nitrous oxide (N_2O). Most of the increase in atmospheric concentration of CO_2 comes from the combustion of fossil fuels. Methane is released from leaky natural gas pipelines, coal mines, and oil production and refining facilities. Methane also is emitted by cattle and rice paddies. N_2O is predominantly emitted from agricultural activities. Thus, to reduce GHG emissions, we must change the way we heat, feed, and transport ourselves. If we do not learn to use energy more sustainedly, the consequences of climate change from global warming could be enormous.

From a scientific perspective, the human fingerprint driving global warming is clearly discernible. In 2001, the Intergovernmental Panel on Climate Change (IPCC) Third Assessment found the metaphoric human fingerprint on global warming: "[I]n the light of new evidence and taking into account the remaining uncertainties, most of the observed warming over the last 50 years is likely to have been due to the increase in greenhouse gas concentrations."[12] Later that year, the U.S. National Academy of Sciences responded to queries from a skeptical President Bush by "generally agree[ing] with the assessment of human caused climate change presented by the IPCC...scientific report."[13] The

---

[12] *Intergovernmental Panel on Climate Change, Climate Change 2001: The Scientific Basis* (J. T. Houghton et al., eds., Cambridge University Press, 2001) 60, 728 ("Results from optimal fingerprint methods indicate a discernible human influence on climate in temperature observations at the surface and aloft and over a range of applications").

[13] Committee on the Science of Climate Change, National Research Council, *Climate Change Science: An Analysis of Some Key Questions* 1 (2001). ("GHGs are accumulating in Earth's atmosphere as a result of human activities, causing surface air temperature and subsurface temperatures to rise. Temperatures are, in fact, rising. The changes observed over the last several decades are likely mostly due to human activities, but we cannot rule out that some significant part of these changes are also a reflection of natural variability. Human induced warming and associated sea level rises are expected to continue through the 21st century.")

sole surviving point of scientific debate on the presence of the human fingerprint on global warming has narrowly centered on reports by one group of scientists of mid-level atmospheric temperature changes based on satellite microwave data that indicated much less warming in the atmosphere than on the surface, a finding that would be inconsistent with global climate model simulations and with earlier satellite data studies that found atmospheric temperature to be rising faster than surface temperature. However, this apparent inconsistency has been resolved by a recent major reanalysis of the data that identified and then corrected for inaccuracies in satellite data that the few contrary reports had failed to do (particularly, instrumental biases and different observation times of satellites). When these biases were accounted for, the mid-level atmospheric temperature trends were entirely consistent with the warming trend established by surface temperature measurements, and, importantly, with the earth's global warming behavior predicted by climate models.[14] In fact, the corrected data reveals a long-tem warming trend in the troposphere that is as great, and possibly greater, than surface warming trends.

Thus, at the scientific level, there is no data that contradicts the IPCC findings that anthropogenic increases in GHGs have caused global temperatures to rise by $0.6°$ C $\pm 0.2°$ C since the late nineteenth century.[15] According to the IPCC, accumulated and future emissions will (depending on the emissions scenario the world follows), by the end of this century, warm the earth $1.4°$ to $5.8°C$ above 1990 temperatures. This prediction assumes that no large-scale singularities (nonlinear responses due to unanticipated feedback loops) will appear that could trigger runaway warming or other catastrophic problems.[16]

Other evidence of warming keeps appearing. The year 2001 was the second hottest year on record, nine of the ten warmest years since 1860 have occurred since 1990, global temperatures are now rising three times as fast as they were in 1900, and the year 2001 will be the twenty-third consecutive year with the global mean surface temperature above the 1961–90 average.[17] Global ocean heat content has increased significantly since the late 1950s. Warmer weather in Alaska has allowed beetle growth rates to soar, so that vast stretches of Alaska spruce forest have been destroyed.[18] Arctic permafrost is retreating as warming is increasing. Tropical mosquitoes are moving to higher latitudes. Worldwide precipitation has increased over the last century as warmer air simultaneously increases evaporation from the earth's sources of water and also enhances the air's capacity to hold moisture. One hundred year extreme weather events, and the catastrophic costs associated with them, are no longer the rarity that they should be. In 2002, the world

---

[14] Konstantin Y. Vinnikov and Norman C. Brody, *Global Warming Trend of Mean Tropspheric Temperature Observed by Satellites*, 302 Science 269 (Oct. 10, 2003) ("Our analysis shows that traditional averaging algorithms that ignore gaps in the data produced significantly biased estimates of global averages, with artificial trends related to changes in the altitude of the satellites." *Id.* at 272. The authors' analysis of satellite date demonstrates "good agreement between the surface and satellite observed warming trends." *Id.*)

[15] IPCC (Science) at 2.

[16] *Id.*, at 69; and IPCC, *Climate Change 2001: Impacts, Adaptations, and Vulnerability* (James J. McCarthy et al., eds., Cambridge University Press, 2001).

[17] World Meteorological Organization, *WMO Statement on the Status of the Global Climate in 2001* (2001) available at http://www.wmo.ch/web/Press/Press670.html.

[18] IPCC, *Climate Change 2001: Impacts, Adaptations, and Vulnerability* (2001) (IPCC (Impacts 2001)) 824–826.

simultaneously experienced 100 year droughts in the eastern United States and Australia, and the worst flooding in Europe in the last 150 years.[19]

The range and intensity of the potential consequences to human society and the world's ecosystems is both broad and great. Although computer models are unable to narrow the predictions to small areas or regions, they do broadly project the dangers inherent in the warming trend.[20] Coastal regions will face rising sea levels, increased storms, and increased salinity of rivers, estuaries, and related ground water. Increased disease from heat stress and reappearance of disease vectors, e.g., malaria carrying mosquitoes, will increase morbidity and mortality, burden human productivity, and stress public health resources. Precipitation changes will cause increased flooding, more profound droughts, and the more frequent occurrence, with greater intensity, of extreme weather events. Sea levels will rise, glaciers are melting and may disappear (and with them, important sources of freshwater in South America), droughts may become more persistent,[21] forests may die off, habitat essential to biodiversity will be modified or disappear, and agriculture will be profoundly affected by local and regional climate changes. The IPCC and others have described these and many other effects of global warming at great length. This brief list is sufficient to make the point that rapid warming predicted by the models should be avoided at all costs.[22]

3 THE FRAMEWORK CONVENTION ON CLIMATE CHANGE AND THE COP PROCESS

In 1992, before the IPCC identified the human fingerprint on global warming, the world was already "concerned that human activities . . . enhance the natural greenhouse effect and that this will result . . . in additional warming of the earth's surface and atmosphere and may adversely affect natural ecosystems and humankind" and "determined to protect the climate system for present and future generations."[23] In response to this challenge, the UNFCCC was entered into to:

> Achieve . . . stabilization of greenhouse gas concentrations in the atmosphere at a level that would prevent dangerous anthropogenic interference with the climate system. Such a level should be achieved within a time frame sufficient to allow

[19] U.N. Environment Programme, *2002: Natural Disasters Set to Cost Over $70 Billion* (Oct. 29, 2002) available at www.enn.com/extras/; *see also* WMO, *WMO Statement on the Status of the Global Climate in 2001* (2001) available at http://www.wmo.ch/web/Press/Press670.html (reporting on record floods and other natural weather related disasters in 2001), and John Shaw, *The New York Times*, Nov. 24, 2002, at 12.

[20] Improved supercomputer technology now being used in global climate modeling, and ever increasing improvements in the climate models, will produce more detailed predictions soon, as well as a better sense of the possibility of catastrophic consequences.

[21] Two recent studies have found that the drought across sub-Saharan Africa is driven by warming of the Indian Ocean and not local land use patterns; droughts in North America, Europe, and central-southwest Asia have been linked to surface temperature changes in the tropical Pacific Ocean. Richard B. Kerr, "Warming Indian Ocean Wringing Moisture From the Sahel," 302 *Science* 210 (Oct. 10, 2003); *see also* A. Gianni et al., *Oceanic Forcing of Sahel Rainfall on Interannual to Interdecadal Time Scales*, http://www.sciencexpress.org/9october2003/page1/10.1126/science.1089357.

[22] It is the speed and size of the warming that is problematic. If this warming were to gradually occur over a hundred thousand or million years, ecosystems and human society would be blind to the changes since climate would change much more slowly than human society and ecosystems change on their own.

[23] UNFCCC, Preamble.

ecosystems to adapt naturally to climate change, to ensure that food production is not threatened, and to enable economic development to proceed in a sustainable manner.[24]

In 1992, when the treaty was negotiated and signed, the science of global warming was less certain, and the fear of possible significant economic consequences of creating new, binding legal obligations confined international consensus to recognition that a global threat existed, that more research and information was needed, and that only general, substantive goals could be declared. Thus, instead of committing to binding targets for GHG emissions or atmospheric concentrations, the industrial nations agreed to "tak[e] the lead in modifying long-term trends in anthropogenic emissions" by taking steps to reduce GHGs "with the aim of returning... to their 1990 levels of... anthropogenic emissions of carbon dioxide and other greenhouse gases" by the year 2000.[25] Following the FCCC's principle of "common but differentiated responsibilities," the industrialized nations (designated as Annex 1 countries) agreed to take the lead in reducing emissions, assist in technology transfer, and follow the "financial additionality" concept with respect to involving developing nations.[26]

The FCCC, being a framework convention, envisioned the need for protocols to establish future targets, timetables, commitments, and rules, and so set up the procedural mechanisms for a continuing international effort to address climate change.[27] In particular, the Conference of the Parties (COP) was created as the institutional entity that would conduct future negotiations at regular meetings; the efforts of the COP and FCCC would be supported by a secretariat, headquartered in Geneva, and other subsidiary bodies assigned particular topics by the COP.[28]

Parallel to the FCCC and COP process, the World Meteorological Organization (WMO) and the United Nations Environment Programme (UNEP) established the Intergovernmental Panel on Climate Change (IPCC) to review, assess, and report on the current state of knowledge concerning climate change issues.[29] The IPCC is divided into three working groups. The mandate of Working Group I was to prepare a "comprehensive and up-to-date scientific assessment of past, present and future climate change" that will be "the standard scientific reference for all those concerned with climate change and its consequences" from scientists to policymakers in government and industry.[30] Working Group II was charged with preparing a comprehensive

---

[24] *Id.*, Art. 2.   [25] *Id.*, Art. 4 ¶ 2(a) and (b).

[26] *Id.*, Art. 4 ¶ 3. (For purposes of the UNFCCC, "additionality" is expressed as an obligation of the industrialized world to "provide new and additional financial resources" to developing countries to meet their "full incremental costs of implementing" measures under the FCCC. This species of additionality will be referred to as "financial additionality" as opposed to the CDM concept of emission reduction additionality, which will be discussed in Sections 5–7.)

[27] *Id.*, Art. 12–18.

[28] The Secretariat Internet web site is http://www.fccc.int.

[29] The WMO and the UNEP established the IPCC in 1988. It is open to all member nations of the UNEP and WMO. The IPCC is "to assess the scientific, technical and socio-economic information relevant for the understanding of the risk of human-induced climate change. It does not carry out research nor does it monitor climate related data or other relevant parameters. It bases its assessment mainly on peer reviewed and published scientific/technical literature." The IPCC Web site is http://www.ipcc.ch.

[30] IPCC, *Working Group I, Climate Change 2001: The Scientific Basis.* (J. T. Houghton, et al., eds., Cambridge University Press, 2001) (cover page). In addition to the hard copy version published by Cambridge University Press, the reports are also available in PDF form on the IPCC Web site at http:www.ipcc.ch.pub.

analysis of the potential consequences of and adaptation responses to climate change.[31] Working Group III's charge was to prepare a scientific, technical, and economic assessment of climate change mitigation options.[32] Each report also contains a definitive Summary for Policymakers, which were each fully reviewed and approved by IPCC member governments.[33] The most recent IPCC Working Group I, II, and III reports, commonly referred to collectively as the IPCC Third Assessment Report, was issued in 2001.[34]

The COP, at its first meeting (COP-1 in 1995), concluded that the FCCC's nonbinding approach was not going to achieve GHG reductions, and began years of intense negotiations that led to the drafting of the Kyoto Protocol[35] to the FCCC, at COP-3 in Kyoto in 1997.[36] The key element of the Kyoto Protocol was the creation of binding national targets for Annex 1 nations (developed countries and countries in transition to a market economy) to reduce their overall emissions of greenhouse gases at least five percent below 1990 levels[37] by 2008–12, the first commitment period.[38] To achieve total reduction of five percent, each Annex 1 nation agreed to reduce its own "aggregate anthropogenic carbon dioxide equivalent emissions of greenhouse gases listed in Annex A,"[39] according to a schedule of GHG reductions indexed to achieving a GHG emissions levels some six to eight percent below that country's level in 1990.[40] These

---

[31] IPCC, *Working Group II, Climate Change 2001: Impacts, Adaptations and Vulnerabilities* (J. J. McCarthy, et al., eds., Cambridge University Press, 2001).

[32] IPCC, *Working Group III, Climate Change 2001: Mitigation* (B. Metz et al., eds., Cambridge University Press 2001).

[33] The Working Group I (Science) Summary for Policymakers was prepared by 122 lead authors, 515 contributing authors, 21 review editors, and 420 expert reviewers, and was formally accepted by the 99 IPCC member countries at the 8th session of Working Group I in Shanghai Jan. 17–20, 2001. Working Group II's (Adaptation) Summary for Policymakers was approved in detail at the 6th Session of IPCC Working Group II in Geneva, Feb. 13–16, 2001. The Working Group III (Mitigation) Summary for Policymakers was approved in detail at the 6th Session of IPCC Working Group III in Accra Ghana, Feb. 28–Mar. 3, 2001.

[34] In July 2002, the IPCC agreed to start the process of preparing its fourth assessment, which it plans to release in 2007.

[35] Kyoto Protocol to the United Nations Framework Convention on Climate Change, U.N. Doc. FCCC/CP/1997/L.7/Add.1, *reprinted in* 37 I.L.M. 22 (1998) (signed Dec. 11, 1997) (not yet entered into force).

[36] As of October 16, 2002, 96 nations have ratified the Protocol, and the ratifications represent 37.4% of Annex 1 1990 emissions of carbon dioxide. Thus, Kyoto will enter into force when Annex 1 nations representing an additional 17.6% of 1990 emissions ratify. This could happen, even if the United States (36.1%) does not ratify, if Russia (17.4%) and any country or combination of Annex 1 nations accounting for 0.2% ratify, such as Canada (3.3%), Poland (3.0%), Australia (2.1%), Switzerland (0.3%), or New Zealand (0.2%). The status of the Kyoto Protocol can be checked at http://unfccc.int/resource/kpthermo.html.

[37] Unfortunately, the goal of the Kyoto Protocol is only to return the industrial world's emissions to about 8% below the 1990 level by 2008–12, which will only modestly slow the rate of increase of GHG concentration in the atmosphere, and will still result in significant additional global warming.

[38] Kyoto Protocol, Art. 3.

[39] The Kyoto Annex A GHGs are carbon dioxide (CO_2), methane (CH_4), nitrous oxide (N_2O), hydrofluorocarbons (HFCs), perfluorocarbons (PFCs), and sulfur hexafluoride (SF_6). Compliance flexibility was also promoted by the adoptions of a "comprehension" approach to all GHGs of concern. Each GHG's "global warming potential," as determined scientifically by the IPCC, would be scaled to CO_2 as 1, so that all GHG reductions could be calculated and expressed in the common currency of tons of CO_2 equivalent. *Id.*, Art. 5, ¶ 3.

[40] Annex B targets, as a percentage of 1990 emissions are: Australia 108, Austria 92, Belgium 92, Bulgaria* 92, Canada 94, Croatia* 95, Czech Republic* 92, Denmark 92, Estonia* 92, European Community 92, Finland 92, France 92, Germany 92, Greece 92, Hungary* 94, Iceland 110, Ireland 92, Italy 92, Japan 94, Latvia* 92, Liechtenstein 92, Lithuania* 92, Luxembourg 92, Monaco 92, Netherlands 92, New Zealand

emission reductions could be achieved directly or by earning credits for verifiably creating carbon sinks that remove and store carbon from the atmosphere.[41] Each nation, or the European Union as a group, would be allowed to develop its own mix of implementation policies, which could range from command and control to market based options or taxes, so long as the target was met within the commitment period 2008–12. However, to promote economic efficiency, the Kyoto Protocol, at the insistence of the United States, established a variety of flexible, international, market-based mechanisms to promote reductions: emissions trading,[42] joint implementation of GHG emission reductions between Annex 1 nations and countries in transition to a market economy,[43] and a Clean Development Mechanism (CDM), which would allow Annex 1 nations to invest in a fund that would finance emission reduction projects in developing nations and receive a credit for the certified emission reductions accruing from the project.[44]

The Kyoto Protocol created binding targets and envisioned flexible, market-based implementation. But the operating rules and definitions needed to measure, validate, and verify the reduction credits were the subject of contentious and frustrating negotiations that dragged on for years, through many COPs and an almost unending series of international meetings. While modest progress was being achieved in the COPs, emissions steadily increased. Ironically, when President George W. Bush rejected the Kyoto Protocol in March 2001,[45] the withdrawal by the United States, the world's greatest GHG emitter, seemed to galvanize the rest of the world. In July 2001, major political and policy issues were resolved at the Bonn COP meeting (the Bonn Agreements),[46] which allowed the Marrakech COP in November 2001 to

---

100, Norway 101, Poland* 94, Portugal 92, Romania* 92, Russian Federation* 100, Slovakia* 92, Slovenia* 92, Spain 92, Sweden 92, Switzerland 92, Ukraine* 100, United Kingdom of Great Britain and Northern Ireland 92, and United States of America 93. (* indicates countries that are undergoing the process of transition to a market economy.)

[41] Kyoto Protocol, Art. 3, ¶ 3.   [42] *Id.*, Art. 6.

[43] *Id.*, Art. 4. Joint implementation (JI) refers to "a market based implementation mechanism defined in Article 6 of the Kyoto Protocol, allowing Annex I countries or companies to implement projects jointly that limit or reduce emissions, or enhance sinks, and share the emission reduction units. JI activity is also permitted in Article 4.2(a) of the U.N. FCCC." IPCC (Mitigation 2001) 715. The FCCC also established a pilot phase for activities jointly implemented for projects among developed countries (and their companies) and between developed and developing nations (and their companies). At present, these activities do not receive any emission reduction credits, but may in the future, but are encouraged as first steps in creating a market in tradable permits for GHG emission reductions and sink enhancements. *Id.* at 427–429, 708.

[44] *Id.*, Art. 12. The Kyoto Protocol also expects Annex 1 nations to "provide new and additional financial resources" to institutions such as the Global Environmental Facility to fund the developing countries' cost of implementation of their FCCC obligations, and to cover the incremental costs of technology transferred to developing countries to reduce GHG emissions. Art. 11.

[45] The United States, under the Bush Administration, has refused to adhere to its proposed Kyoto reductions. Instead it proposes to slightly increase the efficiency of the U.S. economy so that the emissions per dollar of GDP are reduced by about 1% per year. However, this rate of efficiency occurs naturally in the economy, so the "new" idea is actually a "business as usual" proposal that will only lead to increased levels of GHG emissions.

[46] *See* Bonn Agreements for the Implementation of the Buenos Aires Plan of Action, UN Doc. FCCC/CP/2001/L.7 (2001). COP-4, Buenos Aires 1998, could not reach any substantive agreements on operational details to implement Kyoto and as a default it issued the Buenos Aires Plan of Action, which identified the issues on which rules were needed to implement Kyoto, and self-imposed a deadline of COP-6 for reaching agreement.

craft the detailed rules for emissions trading and control measures (the Marrakech Accords).[47]

4 THE BONN AGREEMENTS AND MARRAKECH ACCORDS

The Bonn Agreements and Marrakech Accords comprise hundreds of pages of language that attempt to resolve, first at a political level in the Bonn Agreements, and then at the detailed rule level in the Marrakech Accords, most of the many contentious issues at stake in the overall climate change negotiations. Generally speaking, they establish the operational guidelines for creating a transparent market in credible emission reductions. The Accords address so-called flexibility mechanisms, sinks (also referred to under the awkward title of "Land Use, Land Use Change and Forestry"), monitoring, reporting, review, compliance and enforcement, and funding for developing countries.

The key provisions of the Marrakech Accords concern the establishment of concrete rules and guidelines to support a market-based approach to GHG emission reductions and sink enhancements.[48] To do this, the Accords create a trading vehicle in the form of the emission reduction unit (ERU). Each ERU is equal to one ton of carbon dioxide equivalent (calculated using IPCC global warming potentials), is transferable and bankable (subject to certain banking limitations), and can be used to meet a Kyoto Party's emission reduction targets.[49] A supervisory committee of ten members of the Parties to the Kyoto Protocol or independent entities accredited by the supervisory committee must verify all ERUs generated by GHG reduction projects. To participate in a project and be allowed to earn and trade ERUs, a nation must be a Party to the Kyoto Protocol and have in place a national system of GHG emission measurements that meet IPCC best practice guidelines. Projects must first be approved after undergoing review in a transparent process that includes establishing baselines for measurement. Once implemented, projects must also be verified by a certified independent entity. The same process must be followed for credits under the CDM and other flexible mechanisms under Kyoto. All credits will be issued and transferred by the supervisory committee, which will be compensated for its administrative expenses by receiving a share of the project credits. Compliance and enforcement provisions were also included in the Accords.

It appears that the Accords create all the necessary elements for a global market in GHG emission reduction credits and sink enhancements. Such a system, if implemented effectively, could unleash an enormous demand for renewable energy technology and energy efficient supply side and demand side technology. Taken together, the texts from the FCCC to the Marrakech Accords comprise an emerging international legal structure to control GHG emissions. The next difficult step, however, is to make them operational. Institutions must be created to draft and implement rules and procedures. Policy choices

---

[47] The Marrakech Accords, UN Doc. FCCC/CP/2001/13/Add.1–4 (2002).

[48] For analysis of the Marrakech Accords, *see* Matthew Vespa, "Climate Change 2001: Kyoto at Bonn and Marrakech," 29 *Ecology L.Q.* 395 (2002); and David A. Wirth, "The Sixth Session (Part Two) and Seventh Session of the Conference of the Parties to the Framework Convention on Climate Change," *American J. of International Law* (July 2002).

[49] Marrakech Accords, Add. 2, Annex. Related tradable units also were created: "certified emission reduction," (the tradable unit for purposes of the Clean Development Mechanism) and "removal unit" (allowing trading in sink enhancement).

must be made as to baseline determinations, additionality, verification, monitoring, enforcement, transparency of process, and whether these initiatives will promote or discourage energy for sustainable development. As is true with most implementation of socially desirable goals, the devil is in the details.

5 FLEXIBLE MECHANISMS UNDER THE KYOTO PROTOCOL

The Kyoto Protocol creates three[50] market-based vehicles (flexible mechanisms) industrialized countries (Annex I Parties) may use, in addition to other policy measures they may adopt,[51] to meet their Kyoto targets: the Clean Development Mechanism (CDM), Joint Implementation (JI), and Emissions Trading. The centerpiece of each mechanism is the creation of a tradable and bankable (subject to certain limitations) emission reduction credit. These mechanisms will enable Kyoto Parties, and approved private or public sector entities, to reduce GHG emissions at the lowest price available anywhere in the world, and thereby reduce the costs of meeting their emission targets.

The CDM allows developed and developing countries to enter into agreements for emission reduction (or carbon sequestration) projects in developing countries.[52] Under the Marrakech Accords approved projects would generate transferable certified emission reductions (CERs) for use by the investor. Of the three mechanisms, CDM has advanced the furthest institutionally, and will be the focus of the thematic discussion below. The CDM is administered by the Executive Board of the Clean Development Mechanism (EB), which has already adopted rules of procedure, made policy decisions, and accepted and acted on applications for CDM methodology approval (the first step in the verification process).[53] Although the mechanisms differ in some technical details, several overarching issues apply to all the mechanisms.

JI allows Annex I countries to claim credit for emission reductions from investment in other industrialized countries.[54] Kyoto requires that the project be approved by the Parties involved, and must be in addition to any net GHG reduction that would otherwise have occurred. Kyoto allowed the EU to adopted an EU-wide JI scheme under which no one country need achieve its eight percent Kyoto reduction target, so long as the EU as a whole achieves the eight percent reduction target. On July 23, 2003, the EU proposed to link JI and CDM credits to its emission trading program, the EU Emissions Trading

---

[50] Depending how one counts, there may actually be five different mechanisms: International Emissions Trading, JI track 1, JI track 2, large-scale CDM projects, and small-scale CDM projects. Small-scale CDM projects can be (a) renewable energy projects with a maximum output of 15 MW; (b) supply or demand side energy efficiency projects that reduce electricity consumption by up to 15 Gwh per year; and (c) other projects that reduce GHG emissions and directly emit less that 15 kilotons of carbon dioxide equivalents annually. Small-scale projects will be subject to a simplified approval process designed to minimize transaction costs. *See* Executive Board of the Clean Development Mechanism, Dec. 21/CP.8, FCCC/CP/2002/7/Add. 3 Annex II.

[51] No one approach will be sufficient to meet even the modest reductions required by Kyoto. Other policies could include, but are not limited to, carbon taxes, carbon permits, demand and supply side strategies, education, labeling programs, subsidies, and incentives, direct regulation, government procurement policies, and sector-based approaches. *See, e.g.,* John P. Wyant, *An Introduction to the Economics of Climate Change Policy* (2000) (available at www.pewclimate.org), and Richard L. Ottinger and Fred Zalcman, "Legal Measures to Promote Renewable and Energy Efficient Resources," in *Energy Law and Sustainable Development* (Adrian J. Bradbrook and Richard L. Ottinger, eds., IUCN 2003) 79–113.

[52] Kyoto Protocol, Art. 12.

[53] All this material is available at the UNFCCC CMD Web site, http://cdm.unfccc.int/.

[54] Kyoto Protocol, Art. 6.

Scheme.[55] Under the Marrakech Accords, approved JI projects will create transferable ERUs for reductions made after January 1, 2008.[56]

Emissions Trading allows an Annex I nation to obtain credits towards its Kyoto targets by reducing GHG emissions in another Annex I country.[57] The Marrakech Accords designate these reductions from a nation's allowed emissions (its Kyoto targets) as assigned amount units (AAUs).

6 THEMATIC ISSUES

If these market-based mechanisms are to work as a real method of mitigating global warming, they must actually result in at least the reduction of emissions the projects claim. If projects increase emissions, yet generate emission reduction credits that will offset other emissions, then the world will have wasted precious capital, time, and human resources only to end up further behind in fighting global warming than when we began. Moreover, for these reductions to be durable, they must be consistent with sustainable development principles, for otherwise the adverse environmental, social, or economic effects of the projects may result in a net loss to society. Thus, we must consider how the applicable standards address these central concerns.

The EB, which operates under the UNFCCC, has developed a set of standards called the Clean Development Mechanism Project Design Document.[58] However, since the CDM is a creature of the Kyoto Protocol, which has not yet gone into effect, the EB modalities are only recommendations of the UNFCC COP to the first Kyoto Meeting of the Parties.[59] Thus, they remain a work in progress. Thus far, the EB approach has

---

[55] *See* Commission of the European Communities, *Proposal for a Directive of the European Parliament and of the Council amending the Directive establishing a scheme for greenhouse gas emission allowance trading, in respect of the Kyoto Protocol project mechanisms* (Com (2003) 403).

[56] JI will be administered by a Supervisory Committee to be elected at the first Meeting of the Parties after Kyoto goes into effect. The Supervisory Committee will establish rules and procedures for JI approval and verification, and will accredit independent entities that will validate Track 2 JI projects. JI Track 1 applies to projects in a host country that meets all JI country eligibility requirements. Track 1 countries will verify emission reductions under their own procedures and will issue ERUs directly. Track 2 applies to projects in a host country that meet only the first three country requirements (is an Annex 1 Party and a Party to the Kyoto Protocol, has an assigned amount calculated and recorded, and has a national registry). Track 2 projects must be approved under the Supervisory Committee's procedures (which probably will be similar to the CDM procedures) and be verified by an accredited independent entity.

[57] Kyoto Protocol, Art. 17.

[58] A CDM application requires:

General description of project activity
Baseline methodology
Duration of the project activity / Crediting period
Monitoring methodology and plan
Calculations of GHG emissions by sources
Environmental impacts
Stakeholders comments
Annex 1: Information on participants in the project activity
Annex 2: Information regarding public funding
Annex 3: New baseline methodology
Annex 4: New monitoring methodology
Annex 5: Table: Baseline data

[59] UNFCCC COP8, Decision 15/CP.7 (Nov. 10, 2001).

centered on detailed, individualized analysis of a proposed project's methodology for determining the baseline against which the project's additionality is to be measured.[60]

An alternative standard, called "Probase" (Procedures for Accounting and Baselines for JI and CDM Projects) has been proposed by the EU Fifth Framework Programme: Energy, Environment and Sustainable Development.[61] This project seeks to minimize emissions trading transaction costs by developing uniform procedures, parameters, and emission benchmarks by energy sector, region and country that would be a cookbook with clear, fixed steps project applicants and others can follow.[62] Probase would streamline the baseline and additionality process, which could reduce transactions costs to a level that would not be "too high for economically valid investments."[63] However, Probase is essentially silent as to sustainable development.

Concerned, among other things, that sustainable development goals were being ignored by the EB Project Design Document, the World Wildlife Fund (WWF) has proposed its own standard: "Gold Standard: Quality Standards for CDN and the JI."[64] The WWF Gold Standard proposes three criteria to supplement the CM Project Design Document. First, WWF proposes to limit CDM projects to renewable energy and demand side energy efficiency projects because these technologies carry inherently low environmental risks."[65] Second, WWF would "screen out projects that would have happened without the CDM." Third, WWF proposes using a matrix of environmental and social indicators to determine if the project advances sustainable development goals.

The critical issues for CDM (and inevitably, JI and emissions trading) fall into several categories. The first involves emission baselines and the concept of project additionality. The second involves whether project approval will consider sustainable development as a decision making factor, and if so how. The third issue is the degree of transparency the process will have, the opportunity for the public to comment or otherwise participate in the decision making process, and whether there will be any mechanism for independent review of EB decisions that may grossly depart from the CDM rules, procedures, or substantive standards of UNFCCC or Kyoto. The final issue is whether project monitoring will be adequate and accurate to support the emission credits sought for the project. In this regard, there is the significant issue of whether and how inadequate (or false) post project verifications can be challenged.

Baselines and additionality are critical, interrelated concepts. The CDM requires that a project applicant describe and justify the methodology it will be using to establish its GHG emissions baseline and the methodology it proposes to use to monitor the emissions. In its first review of applications in May 2003, the CDM EB rejected eight proposed baseline methodologies, placed five proposed methodologies in the "B"

---

[60] *See* recommendations of the CDM EB Methodologies Panel, available on the Internet at cdm.unfcc.int. For a review of the first round of recommendations, see "The MethPanel Evaluation – How to Get It Right?," Oct. 2003 *Joint Implementation Quarterly* 2–4.

[61] EU Fifth Framework Programme: Energy, Environment and Sustainable Development, Final Report (Jan. 28, 2003).

[62] *Id.*, at 12–13.

[63] Dr. Henning Rentz, Interview, Oct. 2003 *Joint Implementation Quarterly* 3 (worrying that the "emerging 'zoo' of different types of CO_2 credits is . . . from a business point of view simply unacceptable").

[64] The proposed standard, draft technical appendices and related documents are available at http://www.panda.org/news'facts/publications/climate'change/index.cfm.

[65] WWF, The Gold Standard Background Document (Oct. 2002).

category (i.e., they can be approved if EB required changes are made) and approved just one baseline methodology. However, that project (HFC Decomposition project in South Korea) was also marked as "B" because of inadequacies in the monitoring methodology. As of October 26, 2003, the EB approved only two methodologies (the Korean HFC project and a landfill gas capture and flare project in Brazil), twenty-eight projects are pending in "B – methodologies under consideration," and eight projects have been relegated to "C – not approved."[66]

The application must then demonstrate how the project is additional. The meaning of additionality within the CDM context has been controversial.[67] Many project applicants argue that projects need only establish "environmental additionality." Under this view, whenever a baseline is higher than the project's emissions, the project automatically meets the additionality criteria. In contrast, others argue that "project additionality" must be shown to meet the additionality requirement. For instance, the WWF Gold Standard requires the project both to "have occurred in the absence of the CDM" and to reduce emissions "below the level that would have occurred in the absence of the project."

Unfortunately, although the Marrakech Accords include additionality as an explicit CDM requirement, it does not define the term. In July 2003, the CDM EB clarified that "the methodology must demonstrate that a project is additional and therefore not the baseline scenario."[68] Even though demonstrating this proposition is ultimately a counterfactual exercise, to the extent that project additionality can be established then business-as-usual projects will not be the baseline for CDM projects. Unless reductions are additional to the no project scenario, GHG will increase. By using project additionality it will be possible to make progress in the direction of reduced emissions.

Proving project additionality may be tricky. The CDM EB suggests as example methods: (a) flow-chart or a series of questions that that lead to a narrowing of potential baseline options; (b) assessment of potential options to demonstrate why the nonproject option is more likely; (c) demonstration of barriers that obstruct the proposed project; and/or (d) that "the project is not common practice in the area" and not mandated by the party's laws.[69] Thus, as a practical matter, establishing project additionality under the CDM approach may be a complex, expensive task. It certainly will increase transaction costs.

Probase takes a different approach. It identifies five methods for answering the counterfactual problem:[70]

1. *Policy additionality*, which is "an assessment of whether a particular project would have been carried out anyway as a result of polices that are active in or relevant for the particular country or sector in which the project is developed"; in other words, are there legal mandates for the particular project (an easy case) or are there policies in place that provide incentives to encourage projects of this sort. This test will be hard to apply. Policies may be ambiguous, inadequate to make the project happen, or too general to justify an additionality determination.

---

[66] http://cdm.unfccc.int/methodologies (visited Oct. 26, 2003).
[67] At least 10 methodologies not approved had failed to address additionality adequately.
[68] CDM Executive Board, EB 10 Report Annex 1 (Aug. 1, 2003 version).
[69] *Id.*   [70] Probase at 137–140.

2. *Investment additionality using investment criteria* "attempts to reveal the economics of a JI/CDM project in order to find out whether it would have been carried out without the revenues from the GHG credits." This relatively straightforward approach is attractive in theory, but very difficult to implement. Investors will generally not divulge their confidential financial data, which is crucial to the analysis. It may be hard to determine "the critical rate of return below which the project would not have been implemented without the credits/incentives." Investor profit expectations will vary across regions and sectors, and from company to company.

3. The *combined barriers approach* "tries to identify possible barriers that might have prevented the project from being business as usual." Barriers might be technological, legal, institutional, financial, market-based, or social or even environmental. Ultimately, a combined barriers approach is qualitative and highly subjective.

4. *A priori* additionality is "a multi-project test, which would be applied to project types that are not being implemented on a large scale in potential JI and CDM host countries, such as *e.g.* renewable energy projects." This test is easy to apply, but conceptually weak. The lack of other projects of that type is only circumstantial evidence that the project would not otherwise have been implemented, especially since many technologies are only just beginning to penetrate many markets. On the other hand, because it is simple to observe whether a project of this type is in place or not, the transaction costs are very low. For this reason the CDM EB has adopted this method of additionality analysis for small-scale projects.

5. *Emissions benchmark additionality tests* assume "that non-additional projects (free riders) are cheaper and have less technical performance than projects, which are additional to what would have happened in the absence of the project." However, this approach might screen out valuable CDM opportunities, would require development of performance benchmarks for every project category even though there may be no data available, and "gaming can occur in the process of setting the level of the benchmark (e.g., by the government of the host country) but not in its application."

Thus, Probase does not reduce the project additionality complexity or associated transaction costs.

The WWF Gold Standard proposes to reduce complexity and transaction costs by both limiting CDM projects to renewable energy and end use energy efficiency and by applying to those project types an a priori approach modified by concrete assumptions and terms that attempt to broadly satisfy the environmental and developmental goals of the project additionality requirement. Under the Gold Standard, projects must show that:

1. No similar projects in terms of technology, fuel size, site, and process have been commercially implemented, without carbon finance, in the region in the previous five years.

2. The project cannot have been publicly announced prior to its development as a CDM project, unless formally cancelled, with a clear explanation why.

3. Barriers to finance or broader implementation – such as institutional blockages and lack of finance – are being removed.

4. The baseline is either watertight or the most conservative applicable.

5. ODA is not used to purchase CERs.

These simple tests can be easily proven, at relatively low cost. Essentially, by requiring that the project go beyond "commercially viable projects or normal practice," WWF requires technology additionality. A project would be "commercially viable" if the technology is currently in use at a commercial (not a pilot) scale, has received financing from commercial lenders, and "is financially viable without research or technology support grants;" and "normal practice" exists if "more than five similar projects have been implemented in the region (a project dependent concept) in the last five years."[71] Projects must also satisfy a second additionality screen. To do this, the project proponent must demonstrate that the project is additional for one of seven reasons, each of which is a type of barrier that would block the project but for the CDM credit support.[72] WWF has identified the test to be applied to each reason and a verifiable indicator different than the test.

The WWF Gold Standard seems consistent in goals with the guidance developed by the CDM EB. Unlike the CDM Project Design Document, WWF is more concrete. By defining additionality in a precise manner, the WWF approach reduces complexity and uncertainty, which will translate into reduced transaction costs for investors. This will both remove the GHG credit zoo that investors see on the horizon if the CDM continues to apply its baseline and additionality methodology tests in an unpredictable manner. Moreover, the WWF approach will enhance transparency dramatically by simplifying the information and analytical complexity required by CDM to establish project additionality. This will enable the public and investors to more easily analyze the proposal, to more effectively comment, and more easily determine if the project, as approved, actually provides additionality.

7 SUSTAINABLE DEVELOPMENT SCREEN

The WWF Gold Standard is particularly innovative in its requirement that projects pass a sustainable development screen consisting of environmental impact analysis, public participation requirements, and a normative sustainability matrix.[73] To pass the sustainable development screen, a proposed CDM project must conduct a "best practice environmental impact assessment" with local stakeholder input, based on explicit and transparent public participation procedure, in addition to input from project proponents and host governments, and satisfy the WWF Gold Standard "sustainability matrix." The best practice environmental impact assessment must be conducted in addition to any environmental impact assessment requirements that the host country, the CDM EB, or other authority requires. Moreover, a full EIA will be required if the project is to be located in a critical environment or region, exceeds the size limitations for small-scale projects, will use technology likely to cause an adverse environmental or

---

[71] World Wildlife Fund, *The Gold Standard: Quality Standards for CDM and JI Projects Draft Technical Appendices* (Dec. 2002).

[72] *Id.* at 6. The reasons a project is additional is that CDM status is necessary (a) to offset country risk; (b) to offer more competitive pricing; (c) to improve project economics to meet internal hurdle rates; (d) to improve project economics where there is a lack of local credit; (e) to improve project economics where market distortions exist; (f) to overcome internal institutional barriers; or (g) other verifiable barriers to the investment that the carbon finance will be used to overcome.

[73] The description of the sustainability screen is from WWF Gold Standard: Quality Standards for CDM and JI Projects, Draft Technical Appendices (Dec. 2002).

social impact, if the input from public participation processes indicates that a full EIA is needed, or if public participation procedures have not been followed.

The sustainability matrix includes local and global environmental sustainability, social sustainability, and economic development criteria. The approach is to identify key indicators of sustainability for each category of concern, and then to rate the project on a qualitative scale ranging from +3 (very positive) to −3 (very negative) on each indicator. The score is determined by answering how much better or worse that criteria will be after the project as compared to the project's baseline. To meet the standard a project's overall score must be positive and each of the three general component categories must be either neutral or positive overall, although on any single criteria the score may be negative. The environmental sustainability criteria are how the project contributes to water availability, water quality, air quality, soil conditions, and biodiversity. The social sustainability and development criteria are the proposed project's effect on employment, livelihoods of the poor, equal distribution and additional opportunity for disadvantaged sectors, access to essential services (water, health, education, etc.), and access to affordable energy services. The third component of the sustainability screen assesses the project's contribution to economic and technological development in employment (number of jobs), sustainability of balance of payments, hard currency expenditures on technology, replicability, and contribution to technological self-reliance.

The CDM EB project design document does not include any sustainable development screen, does not require data to be collected to answer questions about the project's contribution to sustainable development, does not require that there be local or regional experts involved in project monitoring, does not require analysis of whether the project proponent must perform any environmental impact assessment, guidelines for when or how such an assessment must be performed, nor does the CDM EB require that where the project may impose significant adverse impacts, that the project proponent develop credible mitigation and, where necessary, compensation measures. The CDM EB does not set minimum stakeholder hearings and consultation requirements; the EB requires that public comments, if any, be submitted within fifteen days. In contrast, the WWF Gold Standard requires all these inputs, and provides a detailed checklist of common concerns the project proponent must answer in consultation with the local stakeholders. Thus, it seems clear that the CDM EB Project Design Document does not address the sustainability mandate contained in the UNFCCC.

In contrast, the WWF standard, which is a supplement to the basic EB requirements, is an excellent framework for integrating sustainable development into CDM decisions.[74] It is straightforward, transparent, and specific in its criteria. It may add some additional effort in data collection, but some of that extra effort is offset by the clarity of its project additionality screen, and the sustainable development data it collects

---

[74] Other indicators may work better, or other scales may be better. As a first cut, the WWF Gold Standard attempts to address the central concerns of sustainable development. However, this chapter will not attempt to substantively critique whether the WWF sustainable development indicators are themselves the best, most valid, and reliable criteria to assess a project's sustainability. The framework appears to be conceptually sound, and not unreasonably burdensome in terms of costs and effort. Over time, project feedback will enhance learning about sustainable development. With this improved understanding, the criteria can be reviewed to improve the set of indicators that best represent sustainable development values, improve the measures used for each criterion, improve monitoring techniques for each criterion, and adjust the relative weight each criterion and measurement should be allocated.

at the beginning of the project design process. Thus, by the time the application is ready, approval should be relatively certain. For investors, the WWF Gold Standard should reduce both transaction costs and project uncertainty, both of which will be much higher under the CDM EB approach. By including local stakeholders from the beginning, project proponents can get stakeholder buy in before they go to the CDM EB for approval. In contrast, under the present approach, the public is notified late in the process, so objections and comments are made late in the process. There inevitably will be increased contentiousness since project financing and related commitments may be relatively firm by then, and the stakeholders may feel ignored or excluded. At that point, experience teaches that even if the EB approves, protests from angry stakeholders will often delay or kill projects. In the long run, predictability, certainty, and project success will be greatly enhanced by following a standard such as the WWF proposes.

8 CONCLUSION

The consequences of global warming on hopes for sustainable development are profound. In a world where, according to the United States, adaptation will be essential, those countries most vulnerable to climate change are also the countries with the fewest resources to spend on adaptation. They will suffer the most. They will be least able to weather the onslaught of drought, flood, heat, agricultural shifts, saltwater intrusion, coastal storms, greater levels of pest-borne disease, and ecosystem collapse.

To avoid dangerous climate change the world must significantly reduce greenhouse gas emissions. To do this will require legal and capital commitments to invest in new generations of technologies that will use energy more efficiently, cleanly, and renewably. These investments will not only help the world limit the pain and expense of adapting to rapid climate change, but will also advance the developing world's development goals sustainably. Joint implementation, greenhouse gas emission reduction, sink enhancement trading and Clean Development Mechanism investments will provide vehicles for investment in clean, sustainable, efficient, and low-cost energy for sustainable industrial, commercial, and residential development. For example, simply replacing existing dirty coal plants in the developing world with gas-fired plants and renewable sources of electricity will not only reduce greenhouse gas emissions, but will also reduce ambient SO_2 pollution and related mortality and morbidity. Each new capital investment in the developing world provides an opportunity to both enhance prosperity and reduce greenhouse gas emissions.

Each missed opportunity only accelerates the arrival of dangerous climate changes, to which the developing world is already unable to adapt. Each real GHG emission credit ultimately represents the supply of energy services more efficiently. Improved efficiency reduces the cost per unit of energy (or energy services), freeing up unused money for other human needs, and freeing up the wasted energy to be saved for future generations to use. This efficiency can translate into reduced poverty, improved environmental quality, improved access to clean water, and increased human health and productivity. The failure of the United States and other nations to participate in the Kyoto Protocol, and of all nations to insist that it be implemented in a manner that promotes sustainable development ensures that many opportunities to promote sustainable development will be missed.

5 Ethical Implications

Klaus Bosselmann*

1 INTRODUCTION

In 1999, the UNESCO World Commission on the Ethics of Scientific Knowledge and Technology (COMEST) set up a Subcommission on the Ethics of Energy. One year later, the Subcommission presented its first report.[1] The report begins with the following sentence:[2]

> Sustainable development, meaning the use of our planetary resources for the well-being of all its present and future inhabitants, has become the concept which must guide both individual and collective action at every level and national and international policies.

This is a remarkable statement as it contains the three key ethical challenges of energy for sustainable development:

1. The concept of sustainable development is to guide energy decision making at all levels, personal and collective, national and international. This calls for a broadening of our ethical concerns for energy. Energy is no longer a matter of maximizing supplies for more and more people, it is also a matter of social, environmental, and future equity.
2. Sustainable development is concerned with the well-being of all, not just human inhabitants of the planet. The inclusion of nonhuman beings poses important ethical challenges to the concept of sustainable development.
3. The guidance of sustainable development is seen as a must, not a mere consideration for our actions. This raises the question of ethical guidance for energy policy and law.

This chapter will focus on the second and third of these challenges. The first challenge can be neglected here, partly, as our Colloquium assumes the importance of sustainable development for energy, but also as the mentioned report clearly distinguishes the ethics for "sustainable" energy from mere "energy ethics" as a general concern for efficiency and access. Only a few remarks may be needed here, before discussing the wider concept of ethics for sustainable development and its significance for energy policy and law.

---

[1] World Commission on the Ethics of Scientific Knowledge and Technology (COMEST) Subcommission on "The Ethics of Energy," UNESCO Headquarters, Report, Nov. 2–3, 2000.
[2] *Id.*, 1.

* Associate Professor of Law, University of Auckland, New Zealand.

2 THE DIFFERENCE BETWEEN ENERGY ETHICS AND ETHICS OF SUSTAINABLE ENERGY

The report of the COMEST Subcommission gives an excellent introduction to energy ethics in the age of sustainable development. In comparison to the general and fairly well-established field of energy ethics,[3] sustainable energy ethics is relatively new and more focused.

In the age of industrialism, energy has been promoted as a prerequisite for development: the more energy, the more economic prosperity. The various forms of energy were assessed in terms of their short-term, not long-term, efficiency and largely dictated by available technologies. Long-term environmental effects were either ignored altogether or dealt with in separate environmental policies and laws.

A reflection of this focus on short-term efficiency is energy law's emphasis on ensuring adequate supply. Energy law has developed fairly isolated from environmental concerns. Until today, energy law appeared as an addendum to public administrative law with little regard to the principles that have shaped environmental law.[4] In a similar way, energy ethics has been concerned with social justice issues, such as access to, and fair distribution of, energy. Environmental concerns were of little importance.[5] A typical question of this nature was whether the government or the corporate sector is better equipped to meet ever growing energy demands.

The 1987 WCED Report and the 1992 Rio Summit have shifted the environment from the periphery closer to the center of economic development. With this shift the links between energy and greenhouse gases were disclosed. In the light of climate change, some forms of energy production appear favorable over others.[6] There is now an ethical divide between objectionable forms (coal, oil, and natural gas) and desirable forms of energy (solar, wind) with some indifference on nuclear and hydropower.[7] At the same time, the importance of energy conservation and efficient use is without any dispute.

In the age of sustainable development, energy becomes accountable to economic, social, and environmental objectives. That makes ethical considerations a lot more complex and, in a true sense, political. Should energy equally meet economic, social, and environmental needs, or are there certain hierarchies? Is, for example, economic prosperity a prerequisite for environmental protection or, the other way round, is the environment the basis of all human (i.e., economic and social) activities?

The COMEST report does not attempt to define these relationships, but makes some recommendations that can help clarify them. An important starting point is the introductory remarks of the Subcommission's Chair, Professor Hamish

---

[3] Addressing issues of fair access to, and distribution of, energy.

[4] Nicholas Robinson, "Foreword," In: Adrian J. Bradbrook and Richard L. Ottinger (eds.), *Energy Law and Sustainable Development*, IUCN, Gland, Switzerland and Cambridge, UK, 2003, at vii.

[5] The antinuclear movement of the 1960s to 1980s was hardly an exception as it signalled concerns for human safety (in terms of accidents and military use). The moral concern for long-term effects (of environmental contamination and, in particular, nuclear waste) is more recent.

[6] David Hodas, "Energy, Climate Change and Sustainable Development," in Bradbrook and Ottinger (eds.), *supra* note 4, at 11.

[7] Reflected, for example, in the COMEST report which contains general support for renewable energy sources, but also some indifference as for the acceptance of fossil, nuclear, and hydro sources. Overall, the report recommends "a balanced approach to the issue of renewable and non-renewable energy sources . . . taking into account subsidies and external costs, as well as environmental and social costs." *Id.*, note 1, at 15.

Kimmins.[8] When considering ethical approaches to energy, we must not deal with them in isolation, but realize that all human activities are linked with energy. This calls for a boarder approach based on relevant space and time factors. Considering that sustainable development requires the broadening of space (to include global dimensions) and time (to include future generations) in decision making, energy ethics need to address issues of ecological justice as well as social justice. As an ethical concept, sustainable development raises questions beyond inequalities in access to affordable energy. The new and more fundamental questions concern inequalities in environmental security and the perpetuation of human life.[9] Now the planet's ecology becomes our home and not just the country we happen to live in.

Ethical considerations of this nature require a new approach. Simply adding environmental concerns to the list of economic and social concerns of energy supply would not be enough. A short list of today's supply problems shows us why:

- there is a huge degree of inequality in the distribution of energy, with about 4 billion people in the world having no access or very limited access to electricity;[10]
- by contrast, the richest countries use nearly 25 times as much energy per capita as the poorest countries, with demand steadily increasing;[11]
- certain sources of energy are facing imminent rarefaction and exhaustion;[12] and
- more than half of greenhouse gas emissions are generated from the use of fossil fuels.[13]

All these problems are inconsistent with sustainable development and none of them can be solved without fundamentally addressing issues of how we organize our lives, especially in the rich countries. The framework for dealing with these issues is the ethics of sustainable development.

The COMEST report identifies a number of principles that are part of this new framework. Among these are:[14]

- *Sustainability and intergenerational equity*
  Energy sources should be sustainable, thus equitably meeting the needs of the present without impairing the ability of future generations to meet their own foreseeable needs. In this regard, energy sources should ideally be risk and pollution free and available in perpetuity;
- *Environmental responsibility*
  Active measures should be taken to reduce the environmental impact of energy production and use. This involves reductions in the negative environmental consequences of energy exploration, production, storage, and distribution. In the short run, particular emphasis should be put on:
  - the establishment of an effective global framework to limit the release of gases into the atmosphere, inducing the greenhouse effect, in recognition of the dangers associated with global warming;

---

[8] *Id.*, note 1, at 2.

[9] *Id.*, at 13.

[10] WEHAB Working Group, *A Framework for Action on Energy*, 2002, pg. 7 (WEHAB is an initiative of the UN Secretary General and stands for Water, Energy, Health, Agriculture and Biodiversity).

[11] *Id.*

[12] Jean Audouze, *The Ethics of Energy*, UNESCO, World Commission on the Ethics of Scientific Knowledge and Technology, Paris, 1997, at 6.

[13] *Supra* note 10, at 7.   [14] *Supra* note 1, at 17.

- the problem of storage of nuclear waste products; and
- the environmental impact of unmanaged and iunsustainable biomass energy use.

While these principles and recommendations are relevant to the promotion of sustainable energy, they cannot substitute a much wider investigation into the ethics of sustainable development. The report itself says "it is disappointing and alarming" how little progress has been made since the 1992 Rio Earth Summit "on issues fundamental to human safety, environmental quality and the future of humanity. Perhaps the most tangible indication of this neglect is the increasing global climate change (. . .)."[15] Such criticism hints to the systemic failure underpinning current energy policies.

An ethic of sustainable energy cannot be dealt with in isolation from its wider context. Recommendations to move toward sustainable forms of energy are meaningless if the causes for current unsustainable forms are not addressed. These causes lie in the way the economy works and in the way people define their needs and aspirations.

To start with, energy has no intrinsic value. It is a mere means to satisfy certain needs. Such needs may include heating and cooling, lighting, transportation, and other goods and services. None of these needs are so fundamental as, for example, food or water. And while they may be important, they have to be put into the context of concerns for justice and fairness.

For example, how can energy intensive cooling systems and car driving in rich countries be justified while so many people in poor countries have no access to food and water? As energy has a determinant influence on the quality of life,[16] energy for the poor becomes an urgent matter of global justice. And how can dams for hydroelectricity be justified when they have such devastating effects on river flows and flooding of natural habitats? Together with the indirect impacts of energy development on biodiversity (mainly through climate change), the world's 45,000 large dams contribute directly and significantly to the loss of biodiversity.[17] This raises the issue of justice in relation to the nonhuman world.

Examples like these highlight the complexity of justice issues associated with energy. Each form of energy use poses challenges for justice and fairness, both at national and international levels.

There are four levels of fair distribution:[18]

- among nations;
- within nations;
- between generations; and
- between human needs and the environment per se.

Addressing such multifaceted issues of justice is only possible within a broader ethical framework that captures all human activities. Such a framework can be found in the ethics of sustainable development.

---

[15] *Id.* at 14.

[16] Jose Goldemberg, "Development and Energy," in Bradbrook and Ottinger (eds.), *supra* note 4, at 1.

[17] Jeffrey A. McNeely, "Energy and Biodiversity: Understanding Complex Relationships," in Bradbrook and Ottinger (eds.), *supra* note 4, at 31. *See also* Achim Steiner and Lawrence J. M. Haas, "The Report of the World Commission on Dams: Some Implications for Energy Law," *Id.*, at 139.

[18] Nicholas Ashford, "Introductory Remarks on Ethics and Energy," UNESCO, World Commission on the Ethics of Scientific Knowledge and Technology, *Proceedings, First Session*, Oslo, April 28–30, 1999, 129.

3 THE ETHICS OF SUSTAINABLE DEVELOPMENT

The 2002 World Summit on Sustainable Development (WSSD) focused on energy as one of the key areas for sustainable development. The importance of access to energy for human dignity was noted in the Johannesburg Declaration[19] and further explained in the Johannesburg Plan of Implementation.[20] The Plan of Implementation details eight recommendations for improved access to energy services and resources, cleaner use of fossil fuels, and the development of regulatory and institutional frameworks. However, it says very little about the principles to guide these issues.

On the other hand, the entire Plan of Implementation is based on the concept of sustainable development. It is significant, therefore, that Article 5 bis acknowledges the importance of ethics for sustainable development.[21] This is the first time that states express their commitment to ethics for the implementation of sustainable development. Given the fact that sustainable development is essentially an ethical concept, this late commitment could be read as an admission of failure. However, it also reflects renewed ethical awareness among states.

The practical importance of Article 5 bis has yet to be seen. Much will depend on whether there is, in fact, a genuine desire among states to address the basic ethical issues. It is clear, however, that any such desire can rely on a body of principles that already exists in international and municipal law.

Some basic principles for sustainable development and sustainable energy are readily available. They are part of international environmental law. Among the principles relevant here are:

- the precautionary approach;[22]
- the "polluter-pays" principle;[23]
- the principle of common but differentiated responsibility;[24] and
- the principle of public participation.[25]

In addition to these general legal principles, there are further concepts that make up the framework of international environmental law. Among such concepts are:

- common heritage of humanity;[26]
- common concern of humanity;[27] and
- sustainable development.[28]

---

[19] Paragraph 18 of the Johannesburg Declaration on Sustainable Development, UN Doc. A/CONF. 199/L.6/Rev. 3 (2002).

[20] Paragraph 8 of the Johannesburg Plan of Implementation, UN Doc. A/CONF.199/20 (2002).

[21] "We acknowledge the importance of ethics for sustainable development, and therefore we emphasize the need to consider ethics in the implementation of Agenda 21."

[22] Proclaimed in Principle 15 of the Rio Declaration on Environment and Development (1992), 31 *ILM* 874.

[23] Principle 16 of the Rio Declaration.   [24] Principle 7 of the Rio Declaration.

[25] Principle 10 of the Rio Declaration.

[26] Legally implemented, e.g., in Articles 136 and 137 of the 1982 Convention on the Law of the Seas and indirectly referred to in Articles 6 to 10 of the 1992 Convention on Biological Diversity.

[27] Preamble of 1992 Convention on Biological Diversity and Preamble of 1992 Framework Convention on Climate Change.

[28] Informing much of the Rio Declaration, Agenda 21, the Biodiversity Convention, the Framework Convention on Climate Change, the Johannesburg Declaration, and the Johannesburg Plan of Implementation.

While the concept of sustainable development forms part of international law, it is not merely a component of it. On the one hand, the lack of consensus on the meaning of sustainable development has prevented it from becoming a general legal principle.[29] On the other hand, the scope, content, and recognition of the concept of sustainable development are much wider than any of the existing legal principles.

There is a compelling reason why the concept of sustainable development cannot be broken down to existing principles of international law: it is the very basis of legal principles and not just an addition to them. Sustainable development sets the tone for interpreting, applying, and developing the law,[30] is a key benchmark for all nations[31] and the fabric for "weaving the rules for our common future."[32]

Such fundamental importance clearly points to the need of defining sustainable development in line with and beyond the principles and concepts already mentioned. As Article 5 bis of the Johannesburg Plan of Implementation implies, there is now a need to identify the ethics underlying sustainable development.

The most popular approach to capture the essence of sustainable development is the idea of integrating environmental protection and socioeconomic development. This integrative approach was proclaimed in Article 4 of the Rio Declaration[33] and has been promoted in national and regional strategies for sustainable development around the world. It is perceived as bringing environmental protection and socioeconomic development in line with each other. But is this really the essence? The assumption of states and some doctrines[34] seems to be that integrating existing policies is all that is needed to achieve sustainable development. If that were true, we could just as well hope for world peace on the basis of integrating the nations' domestic and foreign policies. Obviously, further guidance is needed to define purpose and content of such policy integration.

It does not help to describe the three social, economic, and environmental policies as being of equal importance. The assumption of equal importance (commonly expressed as "three pillars" or "triple-bottom line") may be politically convenient, but is neither supported by international law[35] nor reflective of the ethical debate surrounding sustainable development. The key issue is one of priority: on what basis should conflicts between the three policy areas be solved?

---

[29] Patricia Birnie and Alan Boyle, *International Law and the Environment*, Oxford University Press, 2nd ed. 2002, at 95; Alexandre Kiss and Dinah Shelton, *International Environmental Law*, Transnational Publishers, Ardsley, New York, 2d ed. 2000, at 248.

[30] *See* Birnie and Boyle, *Id.*, at 96, who point out that this is perhaps the most important lesson to be drawn from the *Gabckovo-Nagymaros Case* (ICJ Rep. (1997)), 7 and the WTO Appellate Body's decision in the *Shrimp-Turtle Case* (WTO Appellate Body (1998) WT/DS58/AB/R).

[31] Separate Opinion of Vice President Weeramantry in the *Gabckovo-Nagymaros Project Case* (*Id.*).

[32] Marie-Claire Cordonier Segger, Ashfaq Khalfan, and Salim A. Nakhjavani, *Weaving the Rules for Our Common Future: Principles, Practice and Prospects for International Sustainable Development Law*, Centre for International Sustainable Development Law, Montreal, 2002.

[33] "In order to achieve sustainable development, environmental protection shall constitute an integral part of the development process and cannot be considered in isolation from it."

[34] See, for example, *Weaving the Rules, supra* note 32, where "the foundations" and "origins" (at 10) of sustainable development are described as integrating social development, economic progress, and environmental protection (10–33). As a consequence "international sustainable development law" appears as merely integrating the "three pillars" (at 10), i.e., international environmental law, international economic law, and international social law (171–213).

[35] Treaty law and soft law are simply silent on this issue.

3.1 Recognition of Ecological Sustainability in International Documents

From an ethical perspective, there has never been a suggestion to consider social, economic, and environmental issues as equally important. Rather, the debate has surrounded the question of whether ecological sustainability ought to guide human (i.e., social and economic) development or whether ecological sustainability and human development need to be balanced against each other. The challenge is, therefore, to positively define what makes development "sustainable" as opposed to "unsustainable."

At the level of international law, this issue was first addressed in the World Conservation Strategy (1980) prepared by IUCN, UNEP and WWW.[36] Ecological sustainability is defined there as a precondition to development. Two years later, the UN World Charter for Nature set out the principles "by which human conduct affecting nature is to be guided and judged."[37] Although the Charter does not specifically refer to sustainable development, it defines nature conservation as a prerequisite for all forms of resource use and development planning. Notably, the Charter describes humanity as "part of nature" and states: "Every form of life is unique, warranting respect regardless of its worth to man."[38] The World Conservation Strategy was revised in 1991 under the title "Caring for the Earth: A Strategy for Sustainable Living" to further define sustainable development. Its essence is described as improving the quality of human life while living within the carrying capacity of the Earth's ecosystems.[39] Its two principles are the commitment to a new ethic based on respect and care for each other and the Earth, and the integration of conservation and development.[40]

All these documents promote ecological sustainability as the prerequisite for development and the ecocentric ethic of respect for the earth (or life) as a whole.

By comparison, the famous definition of the World Commission on Environment and Development (WCED) is less outspoken by merely referring to "development that meets the needs of the present without compromising the ability of future generations to meet their own needs."[41] The WCED then gives an explanation to this definition: "It contains within it two key concepts: the concept of 'needs,' in particular the essential needs of the world's poor, to which the overriding priority should be given, and the idea of limitations imposed by the state of technology and social organisation on the environment's ability to meet present and future needs." The two key concepts became known as the principle of intragenerational justice and the principle of intergenerational justice. It is notable, however, that hidden between these principles is the reference to the "environment's ability" requiring limitations to technology and social organization. Essentially, this contains a call for self-restrictions within the limits of the planet's ecosystem.

Against the background of international documents existing at the time, the 1992 Rio Declaration on Environment and Development marked a significant step backward. Its idea of sustainable development took a reductionist approach to environmental values.

---

[36] IUCN/UNEP/WWF, *World Conservation Strategy: living resource conservation for sustainable development* (1980).

[37] Preamble of the *World Charter for Nature* (1983) 22 ILM 455.

[38] *Id.*

[39] IUCN/UNEP/WWF, *Summary – Caring for the Earth* (1991), 3 and 4.

[40] *Id.*, at 5; *see also* B. Boer, "Implementation of International Sustainability at a National Level" in K. Ginther et al. (eds.), *Sustainable Development and Good Governance* (1995), 111 at 113.

[41] WCED, *Our Common Future*, Oxford University Press, 1987, at 43.

Principle 1 states that "human beings are in the center of concerns for sustainable development," and the following twenty-six Principles express a strictly utilitarian view of environmental protection. Ever since the Rio Declaration the public image – not necessarily content – of sustainable development reinforced the idea that what needs to be sustained is human use, especially agricultural use and industrial production. Such reductionism is incapable of perceiving the environment as anything different from traditional instrumental values. What is more, it is inconsistent with the vast literature on sustainability ethics and its reflection in the international documents preceding Rio.

The critique of the Rio Declaration was already prominent during the Rio Summit. In direct response to the Rio Declaration, the Global Forum of NGOs negotiated an Earth Charter that rejected the Declaration's human centered concept and placed ecological sustainability into the center of development.[42]

The only two other international documents on the concept of sustainable development that have been produced since Rio, both follow the same spirit.

The 1995 IUCN Draft Covenant on Environment and Development sets out "an integral legal framework, comparable to those existing in other fields of international law, such as the law of the sea and the international protection of human rights."[43] In doing so the Draft Covenant "provides ecological and ethical guidance" in addition to legal norms.[44] This guidance is expressed in Articles 2 to 10 with its nine "fundamental principles"[45] for decision making based on the objective to achieve environmental obligations and sustainable development (Article 1). The ecocentric ethic expressed in Article 2 is commented on as "a reaction to former utilitarian approaches which limited legal protection to forms of life perceived to be immediately useful to economic interests, ignoring the functions of different species in ecosystems and even their future or potential usefulness."[46]

The 2000 Earth Charter is closely related to the Draft Covenant, both in terms of its origins and content. However, the Earth Charter deserves special recognition for two reasons. First, no other international document has been drafted in such a comprehensive and inclusive manner. It is the result of a decade long, worldwide, multicultural, multisectoral consultation process reflecting the "emergence of a global civil society."[47] Second, it is specifically designed as a "declaration of fundamental principles for building a just, sustainable and peaceful global society."[48] The process and content of the Earth Charter make it the most suitable document to date to identify the ethics of sustainable development.

[42] For a synopsis of the 1992 Rio Declaration and the 1992 Earth Charter, *see* Prue Taylor, *An Ecological Approach to International Law*, Routledge, London, 1998, at 324–7 and 379–81.
[43] IUCN Commission on Environmental Law (1995), *Draft International Covenant on Environment and Development*, prepared in cooperation with the International Council of Environmental Law, IUCN, Gland and Cambridge, 1995, at 30.
[44] *Id.*
[45] Articles 2 (Respect for All Life Forms), 3 (Common Concern of Humanity), 4 (Interdependent Values), 5 (Inter-Generational Equity), 6 (Prevention), 7 (Precaution), 8 (Right to Development), 9 (Eradication of Poverty), and 10 (Consumption Patterns and Demographic Policies).
[46] *Supra* note 42, at 32–32.
[47] Earth Charter Commission, *Earth Charter: Values and Principles for a Sustainable Future*, 1992, Brochure, Preamble. Also available at http://www.earthcharter.org.
[48] *Id.*, at "What is the Earth Charter?"

3.2 The Earth Charter as the Defining Framework

Like the Draft Covenant, the Earth Charter does not define sustainable development, but rather assumes the validity of the WCED definition. The Earth Charter aims, however, for a more complete elaboration on the guiding ethical principles.

The key is Principle 1 ("Respect Earth and life in all its diversity") with its definition for respect for life: "Recognize that all beings are interdependent and every form of life has value regardless of its worth to human beings." The principle of respect for life (in all its forms) is diametrically opposed to utilitarian, anthropocentric ethics of sustainable development. In the center of development is ecological sustainability described as the "community of life."

The WCED definition contains two ethical elements that are widely accepted as being essential to the idea of sustainable development: However, these two elements leave us with a "missing link": (1) Concern for the poor (intragenerational justice or equity) and (2) Concern for the future (intergenerational justice or equity). What do they mean with respect to the planetary ecosystem? If we are to share environmental goods and burdens fairly among those living today and also with future generations, what do we have to leave? The integrity of the planetary ecosystem, that is, "the natural stock" or our knowledge to control it, i.e., the "capital stock"?

As we are unable to determine the needs of future generations, the reasonable choice would be a duty to pass on the integrity of the planetary ecosystem as we have inherited it. Uncertainty requires precaution, and there seems no better choice than assuming that future generations would like the planetary ecosystem as bountiful as we have found it.

And yet, such an obvious duty is neither suggested by the WCED definition nor favored by governments. As the dominant morality of the industrialized world is confined to social ethics, the importance of an environmental ethic to incorporate nature is widely ignored. Instead, the standard view is that society, economy, and environment are of equal importance. As a result, sustainable development is perceived as a balancing act between economic, social, and environmental goals with trade-offs as a necessary outcome. There is no guidance that could ensure, for example, a preference for ecological sustainability or the needs of future generations. Without such guidance, policies may become more integrated, but they will not make a difference to existing unsustainable patterns of production and consumption.

This business-as-usual approach is commonly known as "weak sustainability."[49] If associated with moral obligations to the future, weak sustainability policies consider it our sovereign decision what kind of assets, "stock" or legacy we wish to leave for future generations. It could be the "natural stock," but it also could be the technology base altering the natural stock, for example, through excessive use of fossil fuels or climate change.

To preserve the integrity of the planetary ecosystem is the only reliable alternative and may, in fact, be a desirable goal for most people. However, only if we give this goal moral significance will we have the guidance needed for a policy of sustainable development. Only then will the weak will become the strong and the missing link in

---

[49] Klaus Bosselmann, "The Concept of Sustainable Development," in Klaus Bosselmann and David Grinlinton (eds.), *Environmental Law for a Sustainable Society*, NZCEL, Auckland, New Zealand, 2002, 81 at 90.

the WCED definition is found. A third element, therefore, needs to be added to the two mentioned above:[50] concern for the planetary ecosystem (interspecies justice or equity).

The Earth Charter reflects this element with the first set of Principles I:1 to 4 on "respect and care for the community of life," and Principles II:5 to 8, "ecological integrity." They outline the environmental ethic that has, so far, been missing in the states' discourse on sustainable development.[51]

The essence of sustainability ethics is to see the "community of life" in the center of concerns for sustainable development, as Principle I of the Earth Charter states, and not just "human beings," as Principle 1 of the Rio Declaration proclaimed.

From a legal perspective the Earth Charter's three ethical principles of sustainable development appear as aspects of ecological justice[52] with its three elements intragenerational, intergenerational and interspecies justice. While the first two elements are fairly established in international and national jurisdictions,[53] the notion of "interspecies justice" is less familiar. The ethical debate surrounding "justice for the nonhuman world"[54] and interspecies justice[55] has not yet entered the legal debate. Fundamentally, we have to ask whether the nonhuman world can be part of the *justitia communis* or whether is it bound to stay excluded?

Obviously, this question goes to the heart of how we perceive justice and fairness. Western legal tradition has always maintained its anthropocentric stance. The leading theorist of justice, John Rawls, has been quite clear about the exclusion of the nonhuman world from the *justitia communis*: "[the] status of the natural world and our proper relation to it is not a constitutional essential or a basic question of justice."[56] While Rawls acknowledges duties in this regard, he describes them as "duties of compassion and humanity" rather than duties of justice. Any "considered beliefs" to morally include the nonhuman world "are outside the scope of the theory of justice."[57] His original position cannot assume such a morality.

Contemporary Western legal theories of justice all suffer from avoiding the moral debate. That is why no legal theory has ever addressed ecological justice. And yet, the ethics of sustainable development demand no less than the recognition that the environment is of intrinsic value. Only then will thinking about justice and the law be informed by ecological ethics. It remains an open question whether international and domestic law will progress in this respect.

International law theory may be at a crossroads now. Either it reinforces the state-centered model of international law assuming that each international agreement limits

---

[50] Klaus Bosselmann, "A Legal Framework for Sustainable Development," *Id.*, 145, at 147; Klaus Bosselmann, "Justice and the Environment: Building Blocks for a Theory on Ecological Justice" in Klaus Bosselmann and Benjamin J. Richardson (eds.), *Environmental Justice and Market Mechanisms*, Kluwer Law International, London, 1999, at 30; Tim Hayward, "Interspecies Solidarity," in Tim Hayward and Jim O'Neill (eds.), *Justice, Property and the Environment*, Aldershot, Ashgate, 1997; Brenda Almond, "Rights and Justice in the Environmental Debate," in David Cooper and John Palmer (eds.), *Just Environments. Intergenerational, international and interspecies justice*, Routledge, London, 1995, at 15.

[51] Only thereafter, Principles 9 to 12, ("social and economic justice,") and 13 to 16, ("democracy, nonviolence, and peace,") describe the social ethics more familiar to the general sustainable development discourse.

[52] Bosselmann, *supra* note 50, at 30.

[53] Bosselmann, *supra* note 49, at 95; Birnie and Boyle, *supra* note 29, at 89–92.

[54] Almond, *supra* note 50, at 18.   [55] *Id.*, at 15.

[56] John Rawls, *Political Liberalism*, Oxford University Press, New York, 1993, at 246.

[57] John Rawls, *A Theory of Justice*, rev. ed., Oxford University Press, New York, 1993, at 448.

state sovereignty. Or it deliberately follows a community based model of international law made up by both states and global civil society. Such a broader approach is visible in the moves toward new world order,[58] a fundamental obligation of cooperation[59] and strengthening the role of nonstate actors.[60] However, underlying these moves is the awareness of globalization. In a globalized world values and ethics are no longer a national affair.

It seems appropriate, therefore, to take the search for globally shared ethics very seriously.[61] And while the search for a universally shared set of values and principles may be difficult, it cannot be left to states and governments alone. They are likely to reinforce their own paradigm of state sovereignty. There is no reason why the emerging global civil society should not be able to identify universally shared ethics.

With respect to sustainable development, the relevant principles and values can reliably be found in the Earth Charter.[62] The importance of the Earth Charter for international law and policy can hardly be underestimated. At the beginning of last year's World Summit in Johannesburg, President Mbeki cited the Earth Charter as a significant expression of "human solidarity" and as part of "the solid base from which the Johannesburg World Summit must proceed." In the closing days of the Summit, the first draft of the Johannesburg Declaration on Sustainable Development included in Paragraph 13, recognition of "the relevance of the challenges posed in the Earth Charter."[63] On the last day of the Summit, in closed door negotiations, the reference to the Earth Charter was deleted from the Political Declaration; however, the final version of the Political Declaration included, in Paragraph 6, wording almost identical to the concluding words of the first paragraph of the Earth Charter Preamble, which states that "it is imperative that we, the peoples of Earth, declare our responsibility to one another, to the greater community of life, and to future generations."[64] Furthermore, Article 5 bis of the Plan of Implementation is a reflection of the Summit's appreciation of the Earth Charter.

Recently the UNESCO General Conference adopted a Resolution to "recognize the Earth Charter as an important ethical framework for sustainable development, and acknowledge its ethical principles, its objectives and its contents, as an expression that coincides with the vision that UNESCO has with regard to their new Medium-Term Strategy for 2002–2007."[65] The Resolution calls on Member States to utilize the Charter for their education for sustainable development.

---

[58] *See* Richard Falk, *A Study of Future Worlds*, 1975, at 2–4.

[59] Kiss and Shelton, *supra* note 29, at 259; *see also* Alexandre Kiss, "International Trade and the Common Concern of Mankind," in Bosselmann and Richardson (eds.), *supra* note 50, Ch. 8.

[60] F. X. Perrez, *Cooperative Sovereignty: From Independence to Interdependence in the Structure of International Environmental Law* (2000); Joyeeta Gupta, "The Role of Non-State Actors in International Environmental Affairs" (2003) 63 *Zeitschrift für auslndisches ffentliches Recht und Vlkerrecht (Heidelberg Journal of International Law)* 459.

[61] Prue Taylor, "The Global Perspective: Convergence of International and Municipal Law," in Bosselmann and Grinlinton, *supra* note 50, 123 at 134; Prue Taylor, *An Ecological Aproach to International Law*, Routledge, London, 1998, generally.

[62] Taylor, *supra* note 61, at 136.

[63] *See* Stephen Rockefeller, *The Earth Charter and Johannesburg* (2002), at 2.

[64] Paragraph 6 of the Johannesburg Declaration, *supra* note 19.

[65] UNESCO Resolution adopted at General Conference Plenary Session, Oct. 16, 2003, Item 5.32; based on the Draft Resolution 32 C/COM.III/DR.1.

In 2003, the IUCN Council resolved to present the Earth Charter to the World Conservation Congress in Bangkok, November 2004, for endorsement as a guide to policy and program. Such an endorsement would be a further significant step toward recognition in international law.

Since the 1980s international documents have consistently promoted an ethic that puts ecological sustainability into the center of sustainable development.[66] The Earth Charter is a culmination of this process as it describes the entire ethical framework for sustainable development around respect and responsibility for the community of life. At the same time, the Charter represents a consensus of emerging global civil society. With the increasing acceptance of the Earth Charter by international organizations and individual states, the ethical framework for sustainable development can now be seen as forming part of international law.

4 ETHICAL GUIDANCE FOR SUSTAINABLE ENERGY LAW AND POLICY

The ethical principles for sustainable energy are now before us. They can be described within a framework of three guiding principles (in 4.1 below). Finally, their relevance for the development of national and international energy, law will be shown (in 4.2 below).

4.1 The Ethical Framework for Sustainable Energy

It should not cause much difficulty to define ethics for sustainable energy as reflecting ethics for sustainable development. If sustainable development is the overarching concept for future energy policies, both need to be guided by the same ethical framework. Thus, the ethics of sustainable development provide the ethical framework for sustainable energy.[67] All ethical considerations on energy should start from there.

A first task for these considerations is to explore the ethical contents of sustainable development. They can be found in a multitude of books, reports, and articles, but most reliably so in documents reflecting a certain degree of international consensus.

While there is no consensus in all respects of sustainable development, two core elements can be relied on: concern for equity among the people living today (intragenerational justice) and concern for equity between present and future generations (intergenerational justice). Manifestations of these two elements are, for example, equitable access and affordability of energy, conservation of energy, and the precautionary approach to energy policy and law.[68]

A third core element of sustainable development is the concern for equity toward the nonhuman, natural world (interspecies justice). This element is not recognized in international law. Promoted by global civil society and supported by international documents, states have yet to acknowledge the central role of ecological sustainability.

---

[66] The 1992 Rio Declaration is the notable exception.

[67] The World Commission on the Ethics of Scientific Knowledge and Technology (COMEST) and its Subcommission on the Ethics of Energy are not entirely clear in this regard. While both Commissions acknowledge the overall guidance of sustainable development, the actual thirteen "principles and recommendations" (Report, *supra* note 1, at 16 to 18) reflect a more narrow approach to sustainable energy addressing some, but not all aspects of sustainable development.

[68] See COMEST report, *supra* note 1, at 16–17.

They tend to overlook the simple truth that economic systems depend on the functioning of ecological systems, not the other way round.

International organizations such as the IUCN, the Earth Council, and UNESCO have accepted this ecological wisdom. With respect to energy ethics, this can be demonstrated in UNESCO's approach to defining the role of science and education. UNESCO is a task manager in the United Nations system of Chapters 15 (Science) and 36 (Education) of Agenda 21. The Subcommittee on the Ethics of Energy of UNESCO's World Commission on the Ethics of Scientific Knowledge and Technology describes its ethical considerations as follows:[69]

> The preservation of the environment is a key condition for the perpetuation and prosperity of human life. If this environment is to continue to provide what is needed for sustaining and developing the human species, it is imperative to fully understand the importance of preserving and improving its ecological functions at local, regional and global levels.

Quoting the World Energy Council, the Subcommission's report states that over the past forty years there has been an increase of 300 percent in global energy consumption with a further increase of between 50 to 225 percent predicted for the next forty years. For this reason, the way in which energy demands are satisfied needs to be modified. Referring, in particular, to global climate change as an environmental problem largely generated by fossil fuel consumption, the report expresses deep concerns for the environment to sustain itself.

With the recent adoption of the Earth Charter, UNESCO has stepped up its recognition of ecological sustainability as the key prerequisite for sustainable development. Principle II:5 of the Earth Charter reads: "Protect and restore the integrity of Earth's ecological systems, with special concern for biological diversity and the natural processes that sustain life." Subprinciple 5e calls for the management of the use of renewable resources within the capacity of ecosystems and subprinciple 5f calls for the management of extraction and use of nonrenewable resources such as fossil fuels in ways that minimize harm to the environment. These, and a number of other principles and subprinciples related to energy all assume the overarching importance of ecological sustainability.[70]

If UNESCO's activities can be seen as supporting the case for strong sustainability, they are in line with the relevant literature and some key international documents advocating that "the natural sphere is paramount and cannot be compromised."[71]

---

[69] *Id.*, at 14–15.

[70] Expressed as "resepct and care for the community of life" (Principle I) and "ecological integrity" (Principle II).

[71] Klaus Bosselmann, "Rio+10: Any Closer to Sustainable Development?" (2002) 6 *New Zealand Journal of Environmental Law* 297 at 302. Ulrich Beyerlin and Martin Reichard, "The Johannesburg Summit: Outcome and Overall Assessment," *Zeitschrift für Auslaendisches Oeffentliches Recht und Voelkerrecht (Heidelberg Journal of International Law)* 213, at 236, reason that this statement "mirrors a position that to date only a minority of international environmentalists have taken." This may be debatable, but does nothing to help understand the controversy between weak and strong sustainability. Broadly speaking, the division is between governments and big business, on the one hand, and civil society including small business, on the other. *See e.g.*, Robyn Eckersley, *Environmental and Political Theory: Toward an Ecocentric Approach* (1992); Andrew Dobson, *Justice and the Environment. Conceptions of Environmental Sustainability and Dimensions of Social Justice* (1998). Richard Falk has summed up the problem correctly: "There may be concealed fissures in the edifices of authority that create now unknown opportunities for reform and transformation. To take advantage of such fissures, to the extent that they exist, it is important

Essentially this would mean that energy must be generated and used in a way that does not compromise ecological integrity.

The three ethical principles for sustainable energy are, therefore:

The principle of ecological sustainability (or interspecies justice):
Energy must be generated and used in a way that does not compromise the integrity of the Earth's ecological systems.

The principle of social and economic equity (or intragenerational justice):
Energy must be available to individuals on an equitable basis and at an adequate level, allowing them to meet their needs.

The principle of responsibility for future generations (or intergenerational justice):
Energy must be generated and used in a way that does not compromise the ability of future generations to meet their own needs.

The first of these principles distinguishes strong sustainability from weak sustainability. It ensures that all human needs, present and future, can only be met within the limits of ecological systems. Principle 1 guides both following principles and is, in this sense, superior to them.

It should be recognized that a strict application of Principle 1 is difficult to achieve. As long as there are inequalities between nations as well as within nations, a total ban of fossil fuels, for example, could create new inequalities, thus violating Principle 2. So there needs to be room for flexibility to meet the requirements of Principle 2. That does, however, not diminish the importance of preserving the natural capital as a prime goal. The ecological focus of sustainable development is the only way to prevent excessive use of natural resources. Without it, trade-offs would be inevitable and business-as-usual policies likely.[72]

As noted in Section 3 of this chapter, there is a range of legal principles and concepts supporting these ethical principles for sustainable energy. The application of the precautionary principle, for example, helps to implement the principle of ecological sustainability as well as the principle of responsibility for future generations. Quite obviously, sustainable energy policies must take a precautionary approach.

It is also possible to formulate a number of more specific requirements for sustainable energy derived from existing legal principles and the ethics of sustainable development. Such requirements could, for example, include:

- protection of the natural environment without compromise, including the avoidance of irreversible impacts on the ecosystem and the maintenance of biodiversity;
- minimization, or preferably avoidance, of greenhouse gas emissions and other contaminants to the environment;
- use of all energy from all sources as efficiently as possible;
- maximum possible use of renewable energy sources within the capacity of the ecosystem to allow natural regeneration;

---

to remain alert for such possibilities. Anything less amounts to a submission to the existing order of governance that seems incapable of meeting the environmental challenge in humane and effective ways." ("Humane Governance and the Environment," in Brendan Gleeson and Nicholas Low (eds.), *Governing for the Environment* (2001), 221 at 236.

[72] Klaus Bosselmann, "Strong and Weak Sustainable Development: Making the Difference in the Design of Law," World Summit 2002 Conference Environmental Law Foundations for Sustainable Development, UNEP, IUCN Commission on Environmental Law, Pietermaritzburg, South Africa, Aug. 20–22, 2002.

- investment in, and research into, energy issues, including methods to improve energy efficiency and new sources of energy, particularly renewable sources;
- responsibility of all members of society to conserve energy and use it in an efficient way;
- provision of ambitious and binding targets alongside the provision of incentives to meet such targets; and
- promotion of public awareness of and involvement in energy issues.

These or similar requirements can be found in energy policies of countries implementing the Kyoto Protocol.

It is crucial, however, to not overlook the basic ethics of sustainable development. The ethics of sustainable energy reach wider than any existing principles of environmental law. They are more fundamental and should be expressed accordingly.

4.2 Expressions in National and International Energy Law

New Zealand

Examples for this broader expression can be found in the environmental legislation of New Zealand. The Resource Management Act 1991 (RMA) is guided by the principle of "sustainable management," which is not identical with sustainable development, but nevertheless related to it.[73] Section 5(2) of the RMA reads:

> Sustainable management means managing the use, development and protection of natural and physical resources in a way, or at a rate, which enables people and communities to provide for their social, economic and cultural well being and for their health and safety while:
> a. Sustaining the potential of national and physical resources to meet the reasonably foreseeable needs of future generations; and
> b. Safeguarding the life-supporting capacity of air, water, soil, and ecosystems; and
> c. Avoiding, remedying or integrating any adverse effects of activities on the environment.

The elements of this definition are compatible with the three ethical principles of sustainable development. The principle of intragenerational justice is expressed in the first part of the definition: "in a way and at a rate that enables people and communities to provide for their social, economic and cultural well being." The second principle of intergenerational justice is expressed in the second part: "while a. sustaining the potential ... to meet ... needs of future generations." The third principle of ecological sustainability is addressed in paragraphs (b) and (c) of section 5(2) of the RMA and further in Sections 6 to 8 of the Act with notions of "kiatiakitanga"[74] and "intrinsic values of ecosystems."[75] The recognition of intrinsic values and the reference to the ethic of guardianship are consistent with the legal principle of interspecies justice.

---

[73] David Grinlinton, "Contemporary Environmental Law in New Zealand," in Bosselmann and Grinlinton, *supra* note 49, 19, at 26–31.

[74] A Maori concept that is defined in the Act as expressing the ethic of guardianship.

[75] For a discussion of the ecocentric ethics underpinning the RMA, *see* Klaus Bosselmann and Prue Taylor, The New Zealand Law and Conservation, *Pacific Conservation Biology*, 1995, 114.

The approach of the RMA has, however, not yet been translated into energy policies based on strong sustainability. In January 2003, the Government issued a document called "Sustainable Development for New Zealand: Programme of Action."[76] Its "over-arching goal" for energy is "to ensure the delivery of energy services to all classes of consumer in an efficient, fair, reliable and sustainable manner."[77] To achieve this the Programme then lists three desired outcomes:

- Energy use in New Zealand becomes progressively more efficient and less wasteful;
- Renewable sources of energy are developed and maximised; and
- New Zealand consumers have a secure supply of electricity.

The second chapter of the Programme is entitled "Sustainable Development In Policy and Decision Making." It gives a list of principles for policy and decision making. Some of those principles suggest a move toward strong sustainability, including the following:

- Considering the long-term implications of decisions;
- Seeking innovative solutions that are mutually reinforcing, rather than accepting that gain in one area will necessarily be achieved at the expense of another; and
- Addressing risks and uncertainty when making choices and taking a precautionary approach when making decisions that may cause serious or irreversible damage.

This Programme now awaits implementation. New Zealand's current energy law and policy is based on weak sustainability but subject to criticism within government and civil society.[78] The Parliamentary Commissioner for the Environment, in particular, has repeatedly called for a strong sustainability approach to energy.[79] An example is this definition:[80] "A sustainable energy system, like a natural ecosystem, is characterised by its ability to deliver required energy services within available resource and waste sink constraints."

Germany

Looking at Germany's energy law, a similar picture emerges. The German Energy Report 2001 states the three objectives (or pillars) of sustainable energy as follows:[81] "Energy is sustainable when it meets the equal goals of supply security, economy and environmental protection."

The three pillar concept underlies Germany's current energy laws[82] such as Energy Industry Act 1998 (Energiewirtschaftsgesetz), the Law of the Feeding in of Electricity

---

[76] Department of Prime Minister and Cabinet, "Sustainable Development for New Zealand: Programme of Action," 2003.

[77] *Id.*, at 16

[78] Asher Davidson, *Sustainable Energy in New Zealand: A Call for a Guiding Ethic*, unpublished dissertation, University of Auckland, 2003.

[79] Office of the Parliamentary Commissioner for the Environment, *Creating our Future Sustainable Development for New Zealand* (2002); Office of the Parliamentary Commissioner for the Environment, *Framing the Environment's Future Focus*, Report from the Strategic Planning Workshops October–December 2002; Parliamentary Commissioner for the Environment, *Electricity, Energy and Environment* (2003).

[80] Parliamentary Commissioner for the Environment (2003), Part A, at 37.

[81] Federal Ministry of Economics, *Energy Report, Sustainable Energy Policy to Meet the Needs of the Future* (English version), 2001, Introduction.

[82] Carsten Corino, *Energy Law in Germany*, Beck, Munich, 2003, at 13–14.

1991 (Stromeinspeisungsgesetz), the Renewable Energy Sources Act 2000 and the recent Act for the Retention, Modernisation and Expansion of Combined Heat and Power 2002 (Kraft-Waerme-Kopplungsgesetz).

However, the current review of energy law to meet the Kyoto targets is surrounded by the controversy between strong and weak sustainability. While most Federal ministries prefer the three pillar approach, the Federal Environmental ministry favors a strong sustainability model.[83] The National Sustainability Council (Nationaler Nachhaltigkeitsrat) and independent Environmental Advisory Council (Sachverstaendigenrat für Umweltfragen-SRU) have also pleaded for the adoption of a stronger, more ecologically focused concept of sustainable energy:[84]

> Although it has to be acknowledged that a strict concept of strong sustainability is difficult to realize, the principle, to keep the natural capital constant over time, should be the guideline for the interpretation of sustainability.

European Union

At the level of the European Union, the EU Strategy for Sustainable Development contains a number of energy-related measures including a phaseout of subsidies for fossil fuel production and consumption by 2010.[85] There is a plethora of Directives regulating electricity and gas, energy efficiency, renewable energy, and energy taxes.[86] However, the overall approach is based on weak sustainability.[87] Calls for a strong sustainability approach came, in particular, from the European Environmental Agency and the European Consultative Forum on Environment and Development.[88]

China

With respect to current energy policies in China, Professor Yonglong Lu has commented on ethical challenges. He states that "China is now on the track of Rule by Law" with over thirty laws and regulations being adopted.[89] While he sees the emphasis still on

---

[83] *See* Martin Jnicke, et al., *Governance for Sustainable Development in Germany: Institutions and Policy Making*, OECD, 2001, at para. 24.

[84] Sachverstaendigenrat für Umweltfragen – SRU, *Umweltgutachten*, 2002, available at www.umweltrat.de; *see also* Konrad Ott, *Strong Sustainability and Environmental Policy: Justification and Implementation*, paper presented to the Global Ethics Conference in Urbino, June 2003; Ott is a member of the SRU. For a general discussion on sustainability as the guiding principle for environmental law in Germany, *see* Klaus Bosselmann and Michael Schrter, *Umwelt und Gerechtigkeit: Leitlinien einer kologischen Gesetzgebung*, Nomos, Baden-Baden, 2001.

[85] Communication from the Commission, *A Sustainable Europe for a Better World: A European Union Strategy for Sustainable Development* COM (2001) 264 final, at 10.

[86] Amanda Brown, *Energy Law and the Environment in the European Union*, unpublished dissertation, University of Auckland, 2003, at 26–32.

[87] The three pillar model is, for example, recorded in Article 3 of the new Electricity and Gas Directives; Directive 96/92/EC (1997) OJ L 27/20; Directive 98/30 (1998) OJ L 204/1. See further R. Wegenbaur and R. Wainwright, "European Community Energy and Environmental Policy" (1996), 16 *Yearbook of European Law* 59.

[88] Klaus Bosselmann, "The European Reform of Environmental Governance: Any Closer to Sustainable Dervelopment?" (2003) 9 *South African Journal of Environmental Law* 105 at 112 and 115; European Consultative Forum on the Environment and Sustainable Development, *Sustainable Governance: Institutional and Procedural Aspects of Sustainability* (2000).

[89] Yonglong Lu, "The Ethics of Energy: Case Studies in China," in World Commission on the Ethics of Scientific Knowledge and Technology (COMEST), *Proceedings, First Session*, Oslo, Norway, April 28–30, 1999, 149 at 151.

supply and distribution, he also notes "a change from reliance on non-renewable fossil fuels to renewable oriented energy"[90] and calls for a "long-term public participatory process"[91] including the business sector. "Without the participation of business circles, the ethics of energy will still be a word on paper."[92]

International Law

Perhaps the best way to advance strong sustainable energy ethics is to promote them at the level of international law. So far, international energy law has not been guided by sustainability ethics despite the fact that most international agreements since the 1992 Rio Summit aim for contributions to sustainable development. Nicholas Robinson makes the point, for example, "that the objectives of the 1992 United Nations Framework Convention on Climate Change could not be achieved without building the sustainability policies adopted at the UN Conference on Environment and Development (UNCED) in 1992 into the energy laws of each nation."[93] These sustainability policies have been developed through the UN Commission on Sustainable Development,[94] the energy-related paragraph 8 of the WSSD Plan of Implementation, and the various activities of international agencies.[95] The core of such sustainability policies, however, has yet to be discovered. If policies are not informed by ethical principles they are in danger of reinforcing business-as-usual.

An example of this is the Energy Charter Treaty (ECT)[96] and its accompanying Energy Charter Protocol on Energy Efficiency and Related Environmental Aspects (Protocol).[97] Article 19 (Environmental Aspects) of the ECT requires each contracting party,

> in pursuit of sustainable development and taking into account its obligations under those international agreements concerning the environment to which it is party . . . to strive to minimize in an economically efficient manner harmful environmental impacts occurring either within or outside the Area from all operations within the energy cycle in its area taking proper account of safety.

Such vagueness still allows for a priority of economic concerns over environmental concerns, and thus does not even meet the minimum standards for sustainable development.[98] The Protocol could, therefore, have been expected to give some further guidance. Instead, the Protocol provides a menu of good practices that may be good enough for states with transitional economies,[99] but merely reflect OECD practices. It

---

[90] *Id.*

[91] *Id.,* at 152.

[92] *Id.,* at 153.

[93] Robinson, *supra* note 4, at x.

[94] Including contributions from IUCN and the International Council of Scientific Unions (ICSU); IUCN-ICSU CSD-9 Dialogue paper (2000).

[95] *See* Thomas W. Wilde, "The Role of Selected International Agencies in the Formation of International Energy Law and Policy Towards Sustainable Development," in Bradbrook and Ottinger, *supra* note 4, at 171.

[96] (1995) 34 *ILM* 360.

[97] (1995) 34 *ILM* 446.

[98] With this environmental provision it is hard to see how the ETC could have a role in reducing barriers to energy sustainability as Barry Barton (2003) claims ("Does Electricity Market Liberalization Contribute Energy to Energy Sustainability?," in Bradbrook and Ottinger, *supra* note 4, 217 at 218).

[99] Craig Bamberger, Jan Linehan, and Thomas Wilde, "The Energy Charter in 2000," in Martha M. Roggenkamp (ed.), *Energy Law in Europe*, Oxford University Press, III.4, also available at http://www.Dundee.ac.uk/cepmlp/journal/html/article7#1.html.

certainly does not add to the understanding of sustainable development and its importance for energy law and policy.[100]

Existing treaty law offers little ethical guidance for sustainable energy, but then, it cannot really be expected to. As has been assumed throughout this chapter, ethical guidance can only develop in a bottom up approach. If civil society leads, states will follow.

Most promising are efforts that formulate an international consensus and translate it to codes of conduct, guidelines, or similar documents of "soft international law."[101] Soft law allows states to take an interest without having to commit. It makes a lot of sense, therefore, to promote a "statement of principles for a global consensus on sustainable energy production and consumption," as drafted by Adrian Bradbrook and Ralph Wahnschafft.[102] The purpose of such a statement on sustainable energy principles is to reinforce established principles and develop new ones. This way existing international law, whether "hard" or "soft," can be taken a step further to the next level.

5 CONCLUSION

The ethical principles underlying sustainable energy may be new in the sense of not being recognized by international law. However, they have been identified in the IUCN Draft Convention and the Earth Charter and can be seen as manifestations of a very fundamental principle: the principle of respect for life in all its forms.[103]

International law has only recognized one aspect of this principle, i.e., respect for human life. It first appeared in the Universal Declaration of Human Rights and manifested itself in many treaties negotiated since. Availability and affordability of energy should always be seen as an expression of respect for human life. But energy does more; it can also pose risks to future generations and to the environment. Therefore, we should also be able to see production and use of energy as a potential risk to future generations and life as a whole.

Reflecting the fundamental principle of respect for life in all its forms, the three ethical principles for sustainable energy can be, and have been, formulated. Politically, they describe the concept of strong sustainability. Legally, they describe ecological justice. But ultimately, they should be seen as merely reflecting common sense.

---

[100] For a critical view on the underlying concepts and effects of the ECT, *see* Bernard Mommer, *Grafting Liberal Governance on Oil-Exporting Countries*, Paper presented to the International Studies Association, 42nd Annual Convention, Chicago, IL, Feb. 20–24, 2001; available at http://www.isnet.org/archive/mommer.html.

[101] Adrian J. Bradbrook and Ralph D. Wahnschafft, "The Contribution of International Law to Achieving Global Sustainable Energy Production and Consumption," in Bradbrook and Ottinger, *supra* note 4, at 153.

[102] *Id.*, at 165–169.

[103] *See* Articles 2–10 of the IUCN Draft Covennant and Principles I:1–4 of the Earth Charter.

6 Technological Implications

William Chandler*

The most significant achievements over the past two decades in sustainable energy development have stemmed from creating appropriate market conditions. Yet, sustainable development will be unachievable without agreement on setting appropriate boundaries on energy markets. Without aggressive efforts to deploy emissions mitigation technology over the next ten to twenty years, the atmospheric concentration of greenhouse gas emissions will double, compared to preindustrial levels (see Figure 6.1). This chapter summarizes the impact of establishing appropriate market conditions on energy use and greenhouse gas emissions in selected nations, and discusses supplemental policies, investments, and cooperation needed to achieve both development and environmental protection.

1 EMISSIONS MITIGATION AND MARKET CONDITIONS

A review of recent history in transition and developing nations reveals significant progress in establishing the conditions necessary for sustainable energy development.[1] In countries as varied as Brazil, China, and Poland, growth in energy-related pollution has been slowed, usually for reasons having more to do with development than environment. But this record shows the importance of establishing appropriate market conditions. The record also shows just how much more emissions will grow without setting constraints on the market that are based in environmental science, particularly atmospheric sciences. The development of legal and regulatory mechanisms is essential for sustainable energy development. Economists generally agree that the role of the government is to shape or set boundaries for markets for energy technologies. This

---

[1] William Chandler, et al., *Climate Change Mitigation in Developing Countries*, Pew Center on Climate, 2002. *See* http://www.pnl.gov/aisu/pubs/CCMitDevCo.pdf.

* Senior Staff Scientist, Director, Advanced International Studies, Battelle Memorial Institute, Pacific Northwest National Laboratory. The author would like to note that this paper draws very heavily on previous publications, especially William Chandler, Roberto Schaeffer, Dadi Zhou, P. R. Shukla, Professor, Fernando Tudela, Professor, Ogunlade Davidson, and Sema Alpan-Atamer, *Climate Change Mitigation in Developing Countries*, Pew Center on Climate, 2002. *See* http://www.pnl.gov/aisu/pubs/CCMitDevCo. pdf. The contribution to this paper of the writing of the coauthors of that report is explicitly acknowledged. *See also* William Chandler, *Energy and Environment in the Transition Economies* (Boulder: Westview Press, 2000). The focus on the developing countries in this paper stems from the recognition that development priorities are, by definition, higher in developing countries than in nations such as the United States – the author's nation, but also that emissions mitigation successes in developing countries have been greater than the literature has recognized.

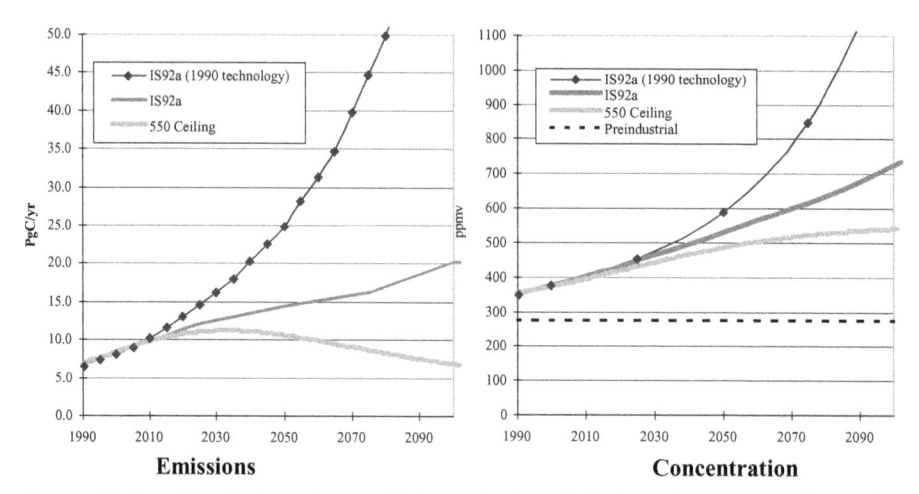

Figure 6.1 Need for Early Action to Mitigate Carbon Emissions. *Source:* Jae Edmonds, Joint Global Change Research Institute

role includes sponsoring science and technology development and technology transfer to the market. But increasingly we find that governments make a profound difference when setting goals for economic development, environmental protection, national security, and establishing laws that provide the foundation for the market and ensure fair competition. This role also involves setting standards to reduce energy demand growth, imposing taxes to reduce energy imports, and providing funds to research and develop new energy technologies.

1.1 Transition Economies

Market mechanisms can have both positive and negative impacts on the environmental sustainability of economic development. Often, market reforms can promote sustainability. The experience of energy sector reform in transition economies provides a case study of this issue.

The formerly planned economies of Central Europe and the former Soviet Union were very energy intensive before the revolutions of 1989–91. Their energy intensity was caused by four main economic factors of central planning. First, industry dominated Stalinist economies, and heavy industry such as steel making required more energy per unit of value added than light manufacturing or services, which have a higher ratio of labor cost.[2] Second, central planning grossly distorted price signals. Energy pricing under communism was just a way of keeping score. Prices had nothing to do with cost and were rarely adjusted. To their credit, most transition economies have endured great pain to impose more realistic energy prices. Third, soft budget constraints, as described by Hungarian economist Janos Kornai, help explain the inefficient economic behavior induced by central planning.[3] In plain language, soft budget constraints meant that

---

[2] William Chandler, Alexei Makarov, and Zhou Dadi, "Energy for the Soviet Union, Eastern Europe, and China," *Scientific American*, September 1990; William Chandler, *The Changing Role of the Market in the World's Economies* (Washington, D.C.: Worldwatch Institute, 1986).

[3] Janos Kornai, *Contradictions and Dilemmas* (Cambridge, Mass.: The MIT Press, 1986); *see also* Chandler, *supra* note 2, at 17.

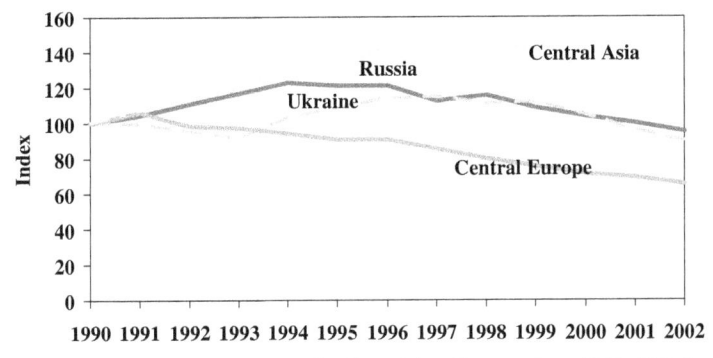

Figure 6.2 Energy Intensity in the Transition Economies, 1990–2002 *Source:* William Chandler, *Energy and Environment in the Transition Economies* (Boulder: Westview Press, second edition forthcoming)

production cost did not matter, or, perversely, the higher the better. Enterprise budgets for labor, capital, and energy were allocated based on planned quotas, and bankruptcy for inefficiency and waste was nearly impossible. The "opportunity cost" of capital, labor, and resources was not a concern for enterprise managers, whose opportunity cost was in not consuming planned allocations because that meant less allocation next year and less profit overall. Josef Bognar, also a Hungarian economist, called this system "cost-plus pricing." If enterprise managers could negotiate a budget with the central planners in which they used twice as much steel and twice as much energy as was physically required, they would get more profit for bonuses, internal projects, or expanding their little empires. And fourth, technological development was stifled. While the Soviet system trained and educated more scientists and engineers than the West, and while these experts developed advanced technologies, the market did not demand and develop them. Price incentives and hard budget constraints in the West drive technological development as a way of cutting costs. Competition among suppliers drives technology for improving quality and adding new services. Incentives and competition, of course, have only recently been introduced. Each of these four factors were prominent elements of the Chinese economy until recently, and they account in large part for the high energy intensity of Chinese society despite low per capita consumption levels.

Fortunately, reform in Central European nations – as in China – has resulted in dramatically improved energy efficiency, at least as measured in terms of energy intensity per unit of GDP (see Figure 6.2). Energy intensity has dropped by one-fifth in the countries of Eastern Europe, which are the most advanced in reform.[4] Conversely, in nations in which reform has lagged, energy intensity has increased. Energy per unit of GDP went up significantly in Ukraine and Central Asia over the last decade.

1.2 Developing Nations

Developing country carbon emissions will likely surpass those from developed countries within the first half of this century, highlighting the need for developing country participation in an international effort to reduce the risk of climate change. While developing nations have been reluctant to accept binding emissions targets, negotiating for richer

[4] William Chandler, *Energy and Environment in the Transition Economies* (Boulder: Westview Press, 2000).

nations to take action first to reduce emissions, they have nevertheless undertaken measures to mitigate economic and local environmental problems. These measures have significantly reduced emissions of greenhouse gases in Brazil, China, India, Mexico, and to a lesser degree in South Africa. Their examples inform policy making related to mitigation opportunities in these key and other developing nations.

Brazilian emissions are much lower than they would have been had the nation not implemented measures motivated by a desire to reduce energy imports and to diversify energy supplies. Brazil today produces energy-related carbon dioxide emissions totaling about 91 million tons of carbon, or about one-half ton of carbon per capita. Its current emissions are 20 million tons lower than had the nation not aggressively promoted biofuels and energy efficiency, a reduction of more than twenty percent. A tax incentive for buyers of low-powered engines appears to have been the single most effective carbon mitigation measure undertaken by that country, and it was adopted to make transportation more affordable for the middle class. If alcohol fuels, renewable electricity, cogeneration, and energy efficiency are encouraged in the future, year 2020 carbon emissions growth could be further cut in Brazil by an estimated 45 million tons. Deforestation, however, produces almost twice as much carbon dioxide as Brazil's energy sector, and in this sector government policy, with a few exceptions, only encourages emissions.

China has, through energy reform, made unprecedented progress in energy intensity reduction. For two decades the world's second largest energy consumer has reduced its energy intensity faster than any developing nation in history. China's growth in greenhouse gas emissions, is an unprecedented achievement for a developing country, has slowed to half the economic growth rate through energy efficiency improvements, fuel switching from coal to natural gas, afforestation, and population planning. Though these mitigating measures were undertaken for reasons different from climate change, they reduced growth in Chinese carbon dioxide emissions by an estimated 250 million tons of carbon per year, about one-third of China's current emissions. The main question regarding the future of Chinese emissions is whether the nation can sustain its policies for reform, efficiency, and environmental protection as it makes the transition to a more fully market-based economy. This remarkable result demonstrates that economic and energy demand growth can be decoupled to a large degree.[5]

Cumulative growth of energy-related carbon dioxide emissions in India was reduced over the last decade by an estimated 111 million tons. The key factors in these reductions have been economic restructuring, local environmental protection, and technological change. These drivers have been mediated through economic reform, enforcement of existing clean air laws by the nation's highest court, and renewable energy incentives and development programs funded by the national government and foreign donors. In 2000 alone, energy policy initiatives reduced carbon emissions by 14 million tons, over five percent of India's gross carbon emissions. Indian analysts suggest that India continues to offer a wide range of emissions reductions opportunities in the near term, with a substantial portion available at a very low cost. Some 120 million tons of additional carbon emissions mitigation could be achieved over the next decade at a cost ranging

---

[5] *From Plan to Market: World Development Report 1996* (New York: Oxford University Press, 1996); Mark D. Levine, "Presentations on Industry for PCAST Task Force on Energy Demand," Lawrence Berkeley National Laboratory, San Francisco, 1999.

from zero to $15 per ton. Major opportunities include technical efficiency measures in both energy supply and demand, fuel switching from coal to gas, power transmission improvements, and afforestation.

Mexico was the first large oil producing nation to ratify the Kyoto Protocol. The main processes affecting Mexican greenhouse gas emissions are population growth, economic development, social equity, energy supply growth, technological change, and land use change. Mexico has begun to reduce deforestation rates, switch to natural gas and save energy, already mitigating annual emissions over the last decade by five percent, or 50 million tons of carbon per year. The most significant Mexican emission reduction results have derived from improved energy efficiency and fuel quality. Mexican carbon dioxide emissions are projected to grow sixty-nine percent by 2010, but identified strategies have the potential to cut this growth by forty-five percent.

South Africa's experience underscores fundamental challenges developing countries face in addressing climate change. Policy priority is placed emphatically on development and on meeting the needs of very poor persons – one-third of the nation's households are not even connected to a power grid. Yet, South African experts indicate that a three to four percent downward deflection could be made in the South African emissions growth trajectory by 2010 by taking steps to reform the economy and improve energy efficiency. The government has already taken the significant step of phasing out subsidies to its unusual, carbon intensive coal liquefaction industry. Coal liquids are being replaced by opening the country to natural gas imports. The lifting of the international embargo imposed on Apartheid South Africa permitted the nation to pursue external energy sources. A revealing feature of South Africa's political economy is the absence of any publicly available futures studies of energy use and greenhouse gas emissions. Such forecasts are the fundamental basis for energy and climate policy discussions, and the absence of such tools in any major developing nation is an obstacle to progress in climate policy.

Each of these nations has made significant reductions in greenhouse gas emissions from a status quo ante baseline, that is, compared to emissions that would have occurred without enlightened, self-interested policies. These reductions range from a few percent to even tens of percentage points below what might have been expected. Because these nations represent over forty percent of the world's population, this fact is significant, particularly if the reductions can be sustained. Every country report contained in the study suggests that major reductions from expected growth can be captured for reasons supportive of economic development, local environmental protection, and business interests.

An encouraging aspect of this experience lies in the practicality of the measures it reveals have already been undertaken, and in their usefulness for emissions mitigation. These nations have already reduced emissions by almost 300 million tons per year below expected levels, an amount approaching the year 2010 Kyoto Protocol goal both in percentage and absolute terms (see Figure 6.3). While the developing countries made these reductions from a growing base, they have already made or continue to make them in the present, in contrast to the future horizon of 2008–12 when the Kyoto Protocol takes effect. Three main policy drivers – development, environment, and security – can be combined with sustainable domestic development strategies, using international collaboration, for climate policy purposes. Complementarity with climate change policy is quite logical: energy use is the primary source of greenhouse gas emissions growth

> **Ongoing measures have reduced the collective greenhouse gas emissions of Brazil, China, India, Mexico, South Africa, and Turkey by almost 300 million tons of carbon per year.**
>
> **Without these efforts, these nations' emissions would be 19 percent higher.**
>
> *For perspective, under the Kyoto Protocol, developed countries would have to reduce emissions by 392 million tons of carbon from projected levels in 2010.*

Figure 6.3 Battelle-Pew Developing Countries Emissions Mitigation Study, 2002. *Source:* William Chandler, Roberto Schaeffer, Dadi Zhou, P. R. Shukla, Professor, Fernando Tudela, Professor, Ogunlade Davidson, and Sema Alpan-Atamer, "Climate Change Mitigation in Developing Countries," Pew Center on Climate, 2002. *See* http://www.pnl.gov/aisu/pubs/CCMitDevCo.pdf

in the world, and energy use is tightly linked to economic, environmental, and security interests. These processes recognize and utilize technological change, which penetrates developing country markets as a result of investment. Action has come about as the result of self-interested policies intended to accelerate development and reduce local health impacts.

2 BARRIERS TO SUSTAINABLE DEVELOPMENT IN THE MARKETPLACE

Several market problems may frustrate efforts to continue the successes described in Section 1, especially lack of information, human capacity, investment, and technology. A major challenge for all developing nations is the lack of sufficient information. Only Mexico among the nations described here has consistently produced emissions inventories and national communications to the Framework Convention on Climate Change. At a much more fundamental level is the need for basic information about investment opportunities, including transparency for investors and the rule of law. These are basic development needs that happen to be amplified for climate change. This problem is being modestly addressed by bilateral programs of cooperation, but is far too modest in comparison with need.

Human capacity, investment, and technology all roll together as a major hurdle. Lack of personnel experienced in workable policies impede governments' ability to restructure and reform their economies, thus creating a serious impediment to investment. Lack of personnel experienced in developing investment projects prevents otherwise willing investors from engaging in projects that would improve productivity and reduce emissions. This latter problem is especially acute when there is a perceived risk associated with relatively new technology, such as the energy efficiency and clean energy systems used elsewhere in the world but not yet deeply penetrated in developing markets. The policies may be like those described in Section 1, involving price reform, privatization, introduction of hard budget constraints, and competition. The investments may also be similar to those detailed above, ranging from efficiency in steel and cement making to natural gas or biomass utilization or emissions control. Specific interventions that have most successfully helped respond to these barriers include programs that help organize financing to investing in technology transfer for cleaner energy and more energy efficient equipment, organize and lead environmental policy measures, and develop and apply new technologies. High priority programs might include increasing support for clean and efficient energy technologies from the multilateral banks or through bilateral mechanisms such as the trade development agencies and aid organizations.

Efforts to organize investment financing for energy innovation can multiply the effectiveness of government funds. The Clean Development Mechanism (CDM) of the Kyoto Protocol is one major program that could generate such investment. The price of carbon credits is unlikely to cover much more than the transactions costs of greenhouse gas emissions mitigation projects, but that may be all that is required to generate enthusiasm for that set of projects repeatedly found to make economic sense anyway. A large payoff comes especially by helping provide the conditions sufficient to attract international investors. Lack of credit, collateral, or funds to prepare business plans are the biggest barriers to energy efficiency and fuel switching in many economies. Financial programs can help overcome barriers to the deployment of small-scale clean and efficient energy technologies in transition and developing economies. Supporting and shaping energy sector reform accelerates financial performance and helps retain incentives for energy technology innovation. Bilateral programs can mobilize private and public sector experts to provide technical and policy advice, particularly for price reform and imposition of hard budget constraints. Organizing private sector investment for energy efficient and clean energy systems produces results far in excess of the money spent by public agencies. The leverage – dollar of investment per dollar of public expenditure – can average as high as fifty to one.

Environmental problems are now well recognized in all the countries mentioned here. Policy options assessed in this study include development of clean energy systems that match well with the targets described in national plans. Such solutions require a combination of policy initiative and technology introduction. In that regard, capacity building and investment project development of the types described above work well. But information, demonstration, and deployment measures are also needed.

A stronger effort to reduce the risk of climate change could promote international collaboration for sharing clean technology, strengthening the CDM and matching domestic economic instruments to climate change. Unfortunately, there is very little real cooperation of this type. Only the Global Environment Facility, the United Nations Development Program (UNDP), bilateral programs like that of the Dutch government, and a few foundations such as the United Nations Foundation make serious efforts of this nature. The United States and China, for example, have no major funding mechanism to cooperate on measures of this type. Mechanisms for capturing the opportunities presented above could include the creation of special funds or financial arrangements for investment, concessional trading conditions for clean technology, cooperative technology development, domestic capacity building, and cooperation on policy measures for economic restructuring, energy efficiency, and clean energy development. Prominent studies suggest several plausible actions, including promoting low energy consumption, introducing advanced technologies, and leveraging domestic sustainable development strategy. The reviews here and other major studies suggest that certain types of interventions work best to accomplish these actions. These include capacity building for market reform and restructuring, local environmental protection, and technology transfer through private investment, organized and facilitated by motivated public agencies.

3 ENERGY LAW AND TECHNOLOGY DEPLOYMENT

Market economies have not fully exploited the potential for clean energy technology. A variety of policy interventions can help overcome barriers to sustainable energy development, but there is no single solution to them. Current practice uses energy perhaps only one-tenth as efficiently as is technically possible over the long term.[6] But technical development and market deployment of energy end use efficiency and clean energy supply technologies are limited by market barriers, market distortions, and technology. A question for energy policy makers is how to assess the value of such opportunities and to promote them in a market economy. Examples of policies that are used extensively internationally include:

1. Appliance efficiency standards
2. Appliance labeling programs
3. Government procurement policy
4. Loans and tax incentives
5. Demand side management utility programs
6. Emissions taxes and standards
7. Building efficiency standards.

Energy efficiency policies such as standards, incentives, and information programs are applied by every major developed market economy.[7] Energy efficiency standards, for example, are used to establish minimum energy performance levels for manufactured equipment and new buildings. Similarly, tax and financial incentives are used to make clean energy investments more attractive to investors. Information, labeling, training, and certification programs can educate consumers and encourage efficiency levels exceeding minimum codes.

Governments everywhere have implemented – and have missed – opportunities to improve their energy systems and, in so doing, facilitate reform, promote economic growth, and reduce environmental pollution.

---

[6] R. U. Ayres, *Energy Efficiency in the U.S. Economy: A New Case for Conservation*, RR-89-12, International Institute for Applied Systems Analysis, Laxenburg, Austria, 1989; John H. Gibbons and William U. Chandler, *Energy: The Conservation Revolution* (New York: Plenum Press, 1981).

[7] International Energy Agency, "United States Energy Efficiency Policy," Paris: Organization for Economic Cooperation and Development, 1999; International Energy Agency, "Netherlands Energy Efficiency Policy," Paris: Organization for Economic Cooperation and Development, 1999; International Energy Agency, "United Kingdom Energy Efficiency Policy," Paris: Organization for Economic Cooperation and Development, 2000; International Energy Agency, "Japan Energy Efficiency Policy," Paris: Organization for Economic Cooperation and Development, 2001; International Energy Agency, "Italy Energy Efficiency Policy," Paris: Organization for Economic Cooperation and Development, 2001; International Energy Agency, "France Energy Efficiency Policy," Paris: Organization for Economic Cooperation and Development, 2001.

PART TWO

LEGAL ISSUES IN CONTEMPORARY ENERGY LAW

7 Legal Frameworks for Energy for Sustainable Development

Richard L. Ottinger*

Traditional energy production, dependent largely on the burning of biomass in rural areas and the burning of fossil fuels in industrialized areas, poses threats of economic, environmental, and social hardship for the world through global warming and for developing countries through exhaustion on energy-related imports of hard currency resources that are desperately needed for education, sanitation, health care, and other vital human needs.

There are proven cleaner and more affordable alternatives, including ways to use fossil fuel resources much more efficiently. Many of them are analyzed in The World Energy Assessment (WEA), sponsored by the UN Development Program (UNDP), the UN Department of Economic and Social Affairs (DESA), and the World Energy Council (WEC). The WEA, http://www.undp.org/seed/eap/activities/wea/, is an invaluable tool for countries to apply to resolve their energy challenges and resultant energy-related economic and environmental problems.

To effectuate these alternatives, legal structures to promote them are indispensable. Much attention has been given to new energy technologies and the means of technology transfer and capacity building. Very little attention has been given to the legal frameworks essential to their implementation. This chapter addresses these legal frameworks.

1 GENERAL MEASURES

1.1 Subsidy Removal

Among the legal measures to promote energy for sustainable development, by far the most significant is legislation to remove fossil fuel and nuclear subsidies. Subsidy removal not only is a costless measure, but by definition, it is a certain revenue enhancing one. As market mechanisms increasingly are being used instead of command and control measures to promote sound energy policies, creating a level playing field for resources in the marketplace is essential.

In many countries fossil fuel subsidies amount to tens or more millions of dollars. Global annual energy subsidies are estimated at about $250–300 billion in the mid-1990s, and that does not count the huge U.S. subsidies required to secure the supply of oil imports that has been estimated to produce a true oil cost of over

* Dean Emeritus, Pace Law School, New York, USA; Chair, IUCN CEL Specialist Working Group on Climate and Energy Law.

$100 per barrel.[1] Revenues saved from subsidy removal can be used to promote clean energy alternatives internally. The problem in achieving subsidy removal is political – recipients of subsidies get addicted to them and the subsidies tend to benefit the rich, powerful, and politically influential. But these subsidies both encourage increased use of fossil fuels and discourage the use of clean alternatives by making them less economically competitive.

The political difficulties of eliminating subsidies and the transition problems for local economies in fossil producing countries cannot be minimized. Nevertheless, countries such as Brazil, China, the Czech Republic, India, The Netherlands, Poland, the United Kingdom, and Russia have reduced or eliminated fossil subsidies successfully.[2]

Subsidies are usually granted by governments under the pretext of protecting domestic jobs, promoting use of domestic resources, and protecting the poor from high energy prices. In fact, subsidies are enacted under pressure from the wealthiest elements of society to increase their profits. In most developing countries, the poor do not even have electricity or automobiles and thus receive virtually no benefit from the subsidies. In many countries, fossil fuels are imported at great cost, displacing the ability to invest in basic needs such as education, health care, and the environment. In those countries that have domestic fossil resources, more beneficial use can be made of the subsidy funds to retrain and place workers and acquire clean energy resources, which also can be domestically produced.

Developing countries like China are eliminating coal subsidies, downsizing coal production, and creating major renewable energy industries that can be exported worldwide. China's actions are particularly remarkable. Between 1990 and 1997, annual fossil fuel subsidies in China fell from $24.5 billion to $10 billion. Coal subsidy rates fell from 61% in 1984 to 37% in 1990 to 29% in 1995, and further since then. Petroleum subsidies fell from 55% in 1990 to 2% in 1995. In 1999, 26,000 coal mines were to be closed out of the 75,000 mines remaining.[3]

Poland has decreased its fossil fuel subsidies by $3 billion per year, resulting in an overall 30% decrease in the amount of coal used between 1987 and 1994. Since 1990, Russia has lowered fuel subsidies by more than 50%, decreasing its carbon emissions beyond 30%. The United Kingdom decreased coal subsidies from $7 billion in 1989 to zero in 1995.[4]

1.2 Externalities

A legislative or regulatory requirement for consideration of externality costs can materially promote clean energy use. When the costs of fossil fuel use are compared to the costs of clean energy resources, the costs to society from fossil fuel emissions are generally ignored, thus effectively placing a zero value on these costs. Numerous studies have now shown that these external costs are substantial, especially with respect to the

---

[1] A. and L. H. Lovins *Making Sense and Making Money*, Rocky Mountain Institute (1997) at 19; A. K. N. Reddy et al., *Energy After Rio: Prospects and Challenges*, United Nations Development Program ISBN 92-1-12670-1 (New York, 1997).

[2] *Id.*

[3] C. Flavin and S. Dunn, *Rising Sun, Gathering Winds: Policies to Stabilize the Climate and Strengthen Economies*, Worldwatch Paper No. 138, Worldwatch Institute (Washington, DC, 1997).

[4] *Id.*

increased incidence of human health problems and early mortality. Some of these studies calculate that the externality costs of burning coal for electricity can be greater than the generation costs. No accurate assessment can be made of the comparative costs of clean energy without inclusion of externality costs.[5]

1.3 Life Cycle Costing

Another economic measure important for promoting clean energy is the use of life cycle costing. The costs of introducing clean energy resources often entail substantial first cost investments, but the savings over the life of these resources make them cheaper than fossil fuel alternatives over time. This phenomenon is particularly evident with efficiency measures and with solar, hydroelectric, and wind energy resources. The first cost of equipment acquisition for these resources can be considerable, but the total absence of fuel costs and very low maintenance costs result in their being much more economically competitive with fossil fuels over the anticipated life of their use. The costs of fossil fuels should always be compared to efficiency and renewable resource costs on a life cycle basis.

1.4 Pollution Taxes

Taxing pollutants or polluting fuels can be an effective way of raising the funding required for clean energy resources while promoting emission reductions in the marketplace. Such taxes make the polluters pay the externality costs of the damages to society from their pollution. They raise the price of emissions intensive goods and lower profits for fossil fuel use, thus allowing market forces to reduce emissions.

Taxation of carbon dioxide emissions or polluting fuels is one of the most direct ways of addressing global warming and raising revenues for clean energy. Carbon taxes have been imposed in Brazil, Denmark, Finland, Italy, Latvia/Lithuania, and Sweden.[6] Pollution taxes are politically difficult since inevitably some energy-intensive industries and jobs are affected and adverse competitive effects are feared. However, if the pollution taxes are offset by reductions in other business taxes, they can produce a net economic benefit. The competitive effects of carbon taxes can be ameliorated with border tariffs and rebates.[7]

1.5 Emissions Trading

An interesting innovation in reducing the costs of sulfur dioxide and nitric oxide emissions in the United States has been to provide for emission trading rights. Polluters may accumulate trading rights by reducing their emissions below adopted limits and then sell these rights to other polluters for whom pollution reduction is more expensive. The advantage of emission trading rights over pollution tax is that the pollution cap underlying trading rights assures specified pollutant emission reductions, whereas the

---

[5] R. Ottinger, et al., *Environmental Costs of Electricity*, Oceana Publications, Inc. (New York, 1991).

[6] Major international agency study pending publication.

[7] S. Bernow et al., *Carbon Taxes with Tax Reduction in New York State*, Tellus Institute (Boston, MA, 1997).

emissions reductions from taxes are somewhat speculative. The Norwegian government therefore has just decided to consider replacing its carbon tax, which has not resulted in sufficient carbon reduction to meet its goals, with an emissions cap and emission trading rights.[8] Some environmental groups object to the grant of a legal right to pollute. International emission trading rights for carbon dioxide are authorized in the Kyoto Protocol. The details of creating this market-based system are now being worked out as a means of reducing the costs of climate change measures in the Kyoto Protocol Conferences of the Parties' implementation negotiations.

1.6 Temporary Incentives

Enactment of temporary incentives to introduce new technologies into the marketplace has been used effectively in many countries. While long-term subsidization of any fuel, technology or product distorts the market and is therefore theoretically undesirable, temporary subsidies to bring new technologies into the marketplace can be effective, useful, and often essential to accelerate their market acceptance. Also, where fossil fuel subsidies persist, nonfossil fuel subsidies are justifiable to level the playing field for them.

A good example of effective use of such temporary incentives is found in Denmark's introduction of wind power. From the start of its wind power program in 1976 through 1996, the Danish government spent $75 million on wind turbine R&D. The government then provided subsidies for up to thirty percent of the investment costs of a turbine in 1980, which was reduced to fifteen percent in 1984 and repealed in 1989 as the market accepted the new technology. The government now requires Danish power companies to pay eighty-five percent of the retail electricity price of wind energy, paid for by carbon taxes on fossil fuels. Consumers now pay less for wind power than for power from coal. As a result of this program, Denmark now has over half of the world sales of wind turbines. Its turbine production now provides about sixty percent of new wind turbines installed throughout the world, produces revenues of nearly $1 billion a year, and has provided over 16,000 jobs. Today, 100,000 Danish families own wind turbines or shares in wind cooperatives.[9]

1.7 Environmental Impact Assessments

One of the most effective measures to promote energy for sustainable development is the environmental impact assessment or statement (EIS) such as required for all major "federal actions significantly affecting the quality of the human environment" by the U.S. National Environmental Policy Act of 1969.[10] The EISs must detail the environmental impacts of any proposed action, any unavoidable adverse environmental effects, alternatives to the proposed action, mitigation measures that could alleviate impacts, short- vs. long-term effects, and any irreversible commitments of resources. Assessments that do not conform to the Act can be challenged in court, a measure that has

---

[8] http://odin.dep.no/md/publ/1999/climatechange.
[9] C. Moore and J. Ihle, *Renewable Energy Policy Outside the United States*, Renewable Energy Policy Project Issue Brief No. 14 (Washington, DC, 1999).
[10] 42 U.S.C.A. §§ 4321–4379 (1969), particularly § 4332 (C).

been very effective in assuring that the consequences of proposed actions be considered before they are implemented. The environmental impact assessment offers an immediate legal method of identifying and remedying adverse impacts of energy projects. More than 175 countries have enacted their own environmental impact legislation.[11] Assessments have been required in a number of international environmental treaties such as Article 206 of the UN Convention on the Law of the Sea. The World Bank and other multilateral banks require such assessments under their administrative procedures.[12]

1.8 Disclosure

Laws requiring environmental disclosure by utilities of their emissions and power generation sources are very helpful in allowing consumers to select clean energy options in deregulated markets. A number of U.S. states have required disclosure by their utilities of their emissions and the sources of their power generation. Information required typically includes the reporting of generation sources, fuel mix, fuel emissions, kWh price, price volatility, and contract terms.[13] Market studies and polls consistently show that consumers want clean energy resources. In competitive retail markets, this disclosure requirement enables consumers to make informed decisions about the environmental consequences of their choice among suppliers.

2 STANDARDS

Standards are a particularly effective and low cost way of promoting use of energy efficient equipment and assuring that emission reductions will be achieved. Standards for minimum efficiency performance of products like appliances, light fixtures, ballasts, motors, and the like, are effective in removing from the marketplace the least efficient products.

2.1 Pollution Standards

Legislated standards for air polluting emissions from power plants and tailpipe emissions from vehicles are economic and can be very effective in promoting clean energy. The United States (through its Clean Air Act[14]), most European countries, and many developing countries have adopted such standards. Legislated pollution standards for stationary sources and vehicle pollution standards place numerical limits on plant and tailpipe emissions. These standards help to account for environmental externalities. By making it more expensive to use fossil fuels, they encourage the use of cleaner alternatives. Of course, the standards also reduce the health, mortality, and environmental

---

[11] N. Robinson, *Environmental Law Systems for Sustainable Energy*, Proceedings of the CleanEnergy2000 Conference, Geneva, Switzerland (January 24–28, 2000).

[12] *Id.*

[13] M. Kushler, *An Updated Status Report of Public Benefit Programs in an Evolving Electric Utility Industry*, American Council for an Energy-Efficient Economy (Washington, DC, 1998) at p. 12. States with disclosure requirements by law or commission order include California, Connecticut, Illinois, Maine, Massachusetts, Michigan, Montana, Nevada, New Hampshire, New Jersey, Pennsylvania, Rhode Island, and Vermont.

[14] 42 U.S.C.A. §§ 7401–7671.

effects of air pollutants, so there is a double dividend. The costs in terms of more expensive electricity or vehicles have been slight.

2.2 Building Codes and Standards

Most countries have adopted standards for the construction of new buildings. Many have now included energy requirements in these building standards. All the International Energy Agency (IEA) countries have energy requirements as a part of their building codes and many recently are strengthening them. For example, France is adopting more stringent thermal regulations for new residential and commercial buildings with the aim of improving energy efficiency by twenty-five percent.[15] Building energy standards usually require all new residential, commercial, and industrial construction to be built to a minimum energy efficiency level that is cost effective and technically feasible. In the United States, "good practice" residential energy codes, as defined by the 1992 Model Energy Code (now known as the International Energy Conservation Code),[16] have been adopted by thirty-two states, and good practice commercial energy codes, as defined by the ASHRAE 90.1–1989 model standard, have been adopted by twenty-nine states.[17] The Energy Policy Act of 1992 (EPAct)[18] requires all states to adopt this commercial building code standard and to consider upgrading their residential codes to meet or exceed the 1992 Model Code, but this legislative requirement has not been well enforced. Experience in the United States has shown building codes can reduce space conditioning energy use in new buildings by twenty-five percent or more.[19]

Emissions from existing buildings, which account for approximately two-thirds of the energy used in the buildings sector, also can be substantially reduced through cost-effective retrofits. Retrofits of fifteen office buildings as a part of EPA's ENERGY STAR Showcase Buildings Partnership reduced energy consumption by thirty percent on average. The technologies that can be used to upgrade efficiency include adding insulation to walls and attics, replacing standard single pane windows with energy efficient windows, sealing leaky heating and cooling air ducts, sealing air leaks in the building envelope, upgrading heating and cooling systems, replacing inefficient lighting, and installing energy use control systems.[20]

One measure worth pursuing is a law, adopted in some U.S. states, requiring that homes or commercial buildings be inspected at the time of resale, with a retrofit requirement for buildings that are found not to be up to standards.

2.3 Appliance Efficiency Standards

Legislated standards for appliance efficiency are particularly useful because most appliances are bought, not by bill payers, but by landlords, home builders, and public

---

[15] *See* http://www.iea.org/pubs/newslett/eneef/intro.htm.

[16] *Status of State Energy Codes*, Building Codes Assistance Project, Washington, DC (1999).

[17] H. Geller and S. Nadel, et al., *Approaching the Kyoto Targets: Five Key Strategies for the United States*, American Council for an Energy-Efficient Economy (Washington, DC, 1998), at 5.

[18] Pub. L.102–486, Title (October 24, 1992), 106 Stat. 2776.

[19] H. Geller, S. Bernow, and W. Dougherty, *Meeting America's Kyoto Target: Policies and Impacts*, American Council for an Energy-Efficient Economy (Washington, DC, 1999), at 5.

[20] *Id.*

housing authorities who have no economic interest in saving energy in selecting them; quite to the contrary, they are more likely to select for purchase those appliances which have the lowest first cost regardless of energy consumption. While incentives and appliance labeling for energy efficiency can be helpful in exceeding standards, only standards can assure that at least the most inefficient models will be removed from the market. The United States has adopted a broad range of appliance efficiency standards, estimated cumulatively to reduce electricity use by 2.7 percent in 2000 and 6 percent by 2015.[21]

Residential and commercial buildings currently account for 36.5 percent of national energy use in the United States, mostly consumed by heating and cooling equipment and electric appliances. Approximately 85 percent of residential energy is consumed in furnaces, boilers, air conditioners, heat pumps, refrigerators, water heaters, clothes washers and dryers, ranges, and dishwashers. Sixty-five percent of commercial energy consumption occurs in heating, cooling, lighting, water heating, refrigeration, and office equipment. In industry, lighting equipment and electric motors account for more than seventy-five percent of electricity consumption.[22] The United States has adopted a broad range of appliance efficiency standards starting in 1987, on fluorescent ballasts in 1988, and on a variety of commercial and industrial equipment in 1992. It is estimated that the U.S. standards cumulatively reduced electricity use in the U.S. by 2.7 percent in 2000 and will do so by 6 percent by 2015.[23]

A number of other countries have adopted appliance efficiency standards. For example, The European Union has adopted directives for its members to create energy efficiency standards for hot water heaters and boilers, refrigerators, freezers, washing machines, and tumble dryers. Argentina has adopted home electrical appliance efficiency standards for refrigerators and freezers, with labeling commencing by mid-2000, with standards and labeling for washing machines in progress.[24]

The European Commission also developed efficiency targets to reduce standby power consumption for TVs and VCRs. In implementing these targets, the Swiss Federal Office of Energy, pursuant to a Swiss statute, provided that if the industry fails to meet the target values by a specified date, it would set mandatory minimum efficiency standards for these appliances; it also provides for mandatory labeling of these products and a stiff reporting requirement. The results of the report for 1994 to 1996 show that TV and VCR sales for models with standby power of five watts or less increased from

---

[21] There are several reasons that the marketplace can and does not by itself attract the sale of the most efficient appliances. Lack of knowledge is a major factor, particularly in the residential sector. In the commercial and industrial sectors, purchasing decisions are often made by purchasing or maintenance staff who have little knowledge about or interest in the efficiency of the equipment they order. They tend to purchase the equipment that is lowest first cost, regardless of the cost of the energy used by the equipment, and they are judged by their superiors accordingly. Even if they were to purchase efficient equipment, the savings would not accrue to their departments. Furthermore, efficient equipment is often not stocked sufficiently by suppliers because of inadequate demand, thus requiring special orders and long lead times for delivery of the equipment. Developers and landlords have little interest in buying efficient equipment where they do not pay the energy bills. These are substantial barriers to the introduction of efficient equipment in the marketplace and a principal reason for the need for appliance efficiency standards. Incentives can be used to go beyond the standards. Lovins, *Supra* note 1 at 5–6.

[22] H. Geller et al., *Approaching the Kyoto Targets: Five Key Strategies for the United States*, American Council for an Energy-Efficient Economy (Washington, DC, August 1998), at 5.

[23] *Id.*, at 7.

[24] *See* http://www.iea.org/pubs/newslett/eneeff/intro.htm.

36 to 44 percent, while appliances using more than ten watts in standby power dropped from nineteen to eight percent.[25]

Over time, these standards result in considerable economic savings for consumers and society. While the first cost of the efficient appliances often is slightly more than inefficient models, the economic savings over the life of the appliance can be very significant and the savings to society from reduction of energy demand also are great, resulting in decreased use of polluting fossil fuels and thus promoting cleaner and more affordable energy.

2.4 Renewable Portfolio Standards

In the United States and other countries, renewable portfolio standards have been adopted or are being considered. These standards require electric utilities to purchase a certain percentage of their power from renewable resources. If such standards were to be widely adopted, they would allow mass production of renewable energy generation equipment, substantially reducing their costs. An international Renewable Portfolio Standard was debated but not adopted at the World Summit on Sustainable Development (WSSD), instead opting for an obligation for a "substantial increase" in use of renewable resources.

The United Kingdom has enacted a Non-Fossil Fuel Obligation (NFFO). After the UK's deregulation of its electric utility industry in 1989, it created Regional Electricity Companies (RECs) that in 1992 were required to purchase 1,500 MW of non-fossil generated power by the year 2000 in a series of auctions, five of which have now taken place. These auctions were so successful that 3,271 MW of non-fossil power has been purchased at the auctions, far in excess of the 1,500 MW requirement. The program's fifteen-year contracts with five-year repayment grace periods permit reasonable financing of projects. The auction device has driven renewable prices down to about 4.3 cents/kWh (very close to the electricity pool price of 4.2 cents). On the other hand, the intense competition arising from the auction process has favored large, deep pocket companies and has discouraged small investors, independent developers, and the domestic renewable energy manufacturing industry. Subsidies to pay the RECs for excess costs of non-fossil resources are paid from a tax on all electricity.[26]

Argentina, Denmark, and Germany also have adopted utility renewable requirements. The Netherlands mandates renewable purchases where utilities purchase excess power to cover avoided fuel and capacity costs. Denmark, in addition to pollution taxes and incentives for renewables purchases, has adopted a renewable portfolio standard under which a target for renewables is set legislatively and utilities are required to meet these targets. The utilities may either develop renewable resources themselves or purchase credits from other renewable generators. The extra costs of renewable purchases are handed down to all of the utility's customers.[27]

Japan adopted a "Project Sunshine" under which the government subsidizes photovoltaic purchases by utilities to meet a "Ten Thousand Roofs" goal, and in 1997 enacted

---

[25] Lovins, *supra* note 1 at 16.
[26] C. Moore and J. Ihle, *Renewable Policy Outside the United States*, Renewable Energy Policy Project Issue Brief No. 14 (Washington, DC, 1999), at 12–15.
[27] *Id.*, at 4.

a New Energy Law establishing a goal to provide 3.1% of primary energy from renewable resources by 2010 (vs. 2.1% in 1996). While there is no purchase requirement, the government's requests to suppliers are the effective equivalent of a required standard under the Japanese system.[28]

2.5 Vehicle Standards

Legislation regulating the vehicle miles per gallon standards for all vehicles sold can also make a big impact on pollution reduction, thus promoting cleaner energy policies. The U.S. Congress enacted Corporate Average Fuel Economy (CAFE) standards during the energy crisis in 1975, and Canada adopted a similar Motor Vehicle Fuel Efficiency Program with voluntary standards.[29] The U.S. CAFE standards provide that the passenger automobiles produced by each manufacturer must average a prescribed miles per gallon, with a lesser standard for light trucks. As a result, the average miles per gallon of the U.S. passenger automobile fleet was increased from 17 mpg in the 1970s to a high of 25.9 mpg in 1988, now reduced to 23.8 mpg because of the popularity of large, inefficient sport utility vehicles (SUVs).[30]

In other countries, similar programs have been adopted in the form of negotiated agreements between governments and the auto industry. Australia, for example, entered an agreement to reduce national average fuel consumption for new cars and required the use of a mandatory fuel efficiency label. The German auto industry is committed to a twenty-five percent reduction in cars built and sold between 1990 and 2005. Italy and Japan have similar programs. In Switzerland, a voluntary program was enacted calling for a fifteen percent fuel consumption reduction between 1996 and 2001, with the authority to adopt mandatory regulations if this target is not reached.[31]

Other vehicle measures adopted include multiple occupancy vehicle lanes on highways and car pooling incentives, including company provided vanpools, elimination of free parking by business establishments, and parking fees. These measures have been adopted in a good number of U.S. states.[32] France and Italy even have gone so far as to limit city parking to alternate days for odd and even license numbers and create "No Car Days."[33] The UK has instituted a regimen of taxes on cars that enter the downtown London area.

2.6 Enforcement

Effective enforcement is critical to the success of any standards program. In practice, governments and regulatory agencies often come to identify with the industries or

---

[28] *Id.,* at 9.

[29] 42 USC §§6231 et seq.; re Canada, *see* http://www.iea.org/pubs/newslett/eneeff/intro.htm.

[30] Geller, *supra* note 19 at 9.

[31] *See* http://www.iea.org/pubs/newslett/eneeff/intro.htm.

[32] A 1997 U.S. legal innovation permitted employers to cash out employee parking spaces, charging fair market value for each space and paying each employee a commuter allowance of equal after tax value, typically reducing demand for parking spaces which often cost $10,000–$30,000 each. Singapore charges drivers automatically registered toll fees designed to make them pay the social costs of driving and invests the proceeds in public transit and coordinated land use, with the result that it is virtually congestion free. Lovins, *supra* note 1 at 16.

[33] *See* http://www.iea.org/pubs/newslett/eneeff/intro.htm.

companies that they regulate. Also, political pressures often prevent effective government enforcement. Citizen enforcement, adopted in the United States in the Clean Air Act[34] and other environmental statutes, has been found to be a most effective enforcement mechanism. Nongovernmental organizations (NGOs) in the United States are able to hold regulators' feet to the fire very effectively by filing suit to enforce standards, with the award of attorney's fees for such litigation; the very presence of citizen suit provisions enables the NGOs to influence government enforcement policies.

3 UTILITY PROGRAMS AND REGULATORY REQUIREMENTS

Utilities in many U.S. states have been required by regulatory commissions to undertake integrated resource planning (IRP), including energy efficiency "demand-side management" (DSM) and renewable resources. They were required to provide incentives to their customers to purchase energy efficient lighting and appliances and to provide free or low cost energy audits to residential, commercial, and industrial customers to help them identify efficiency opportunities. These utility incentives were very effective in a regulated environment, but with the prospect of deregulation, the utilities have been allowed to cut back on these incentive programs for fear that their costs would make the utilities uncompetitive with those without incentive requirements – even though efficiency investments were made profitable for the utilities by the regulators[35] and the fact that efficiency investments save energy at a cost far less than new power plant construction. Utility spending on energy efficiency programs has declined from about $1.4 billion in 1992 to about $1.2 billion in 1996, with continuing declines to date and projected, despite the fact that only a handful of states have passed restructuring legislation.[36]

Other countries have been more aggressive in their utility regulation to promote efficiency. In Brazil, for example, a new federal utility regulatory agency in July 1998 required all distribution utilities to spend at least one percent of their revenues on energy efficiency improvements, with at least one quarter of this amount (about $50 million per year) to be spent on end-use efficiency projects.[37] Utilities in Australia, Austria, Belgium, Canada, Germany, and Ireland also have IRP and DSM requirements.[38] Ontario Hydro of Canada placed its primary emphasis on end-use efficiency and distribution planning to displace building transmission and generating capacity. Its first three experimental programs cut its investment needs by up to ninety percent, saving it $600 million.[39] Brazil has an extensive metering program run by PROCEL, a national electricity conservation program, and its national utility.[40]

---

[34] 42 U.S.C.A. §§7401–7671.

[35] These states simply decoupled utility profits from sales, letting utilities keep as extra profit part of the savings from energy efficiency measures they financed. Lovins, *supra* note 1 at 15.

[36] J. Eto et al., *Ratepayer-Funded Energy-Efficiency Programs in a Restructured Electricity Industry: Issues and Options for Regulators and Legislators*, American Council for an Energy-Efficient Economy (Washington, DC, May 1998).

[37] H. Geller et al., *Update on Brazil's National Electricity Conservation Program (PROCEL)*, American Council for an Energy-Efficient Economy (Washington, DC, June 1999).

[38] *See* http://www.iea.org/pubs/newslett/eneeff/intro.htm.

[39] Lovins, *supra* note 1 at 14.   [40] Geller et. al., *supra* note 37 at 1.

Application of utility incentives to rental apartment buildings can be a problem. The tenants have no incentive to install measures that will benefit the landlord and the landlord has little incentive to invest in measures that primarily will benefit the tenants. Some state utility regulators have addressed this problem by giving larger incentives to the landlords. To induce tenant cooperation, it is important that apartments be individually metered for electricity and gas consumption.

In the U.S. states that have deregulated their utility generation, environmental advocates have been quite successful in getting utility regulators or legislators to impose a "systems benefit charge" on the distribution utility, which remains a regulated monopoly, to fund efficiency, renewable, low income, and other public benefit investments; the revenues from these charges often are placed in independently administered public benefit funds. As of July 1999, fifteen U.S. states had adopted utility system benefit charges and benefit funds.[41]

Similarly, other countries have established a variety of public benefit arrangements to fill the gap for energy efficiency funding after deregulation. The United Kingdom established an Energy Savings Trust as a private limited company, funded by a small charge on distribution services, to promote energy efficiency for small customers. Norway adopted a small transmission tax earmarked for energy efficiency information, and it created and funded independent regional conservation centers to provide energy efficiency services. New Zealand set up an "Energy Saver Fund" as a part of its restructuring legislation to support residential programs funded by an $18 million appropriation for an initial three-year period.[42]

A new entrepreneurship of Energy Service Companies (ESCOs) has emerged to perform energy efficiency retrofits for homes and businesses as a profitable enterprise, but they have so far only penetrated niche markets for large customers in the United States.[43] Also, under deregulation, performance-based regulation (PBR) is replacing rate of return regulation for the monopoly distribution company. PBR can encourage distribution companies to provide electricity efficiently, rewarding performance measured against specific benchmarks.[44] Some commissions have placed a price cap on utility charges, giving the utilities an incentive to keep costs low; a revenue cap is far superior, however, since a price cap provides strong incentives for utilities to increase sales and thus discourages efficiency and renewable investments.[45]

3.1 Green Marketing

A number of U.S. commissions have required utilities to offer an option to customers to purchase a package of green generation products at a slight premium in cost. The programs are too new to have a good assessment of their effectiveness in reducing

---

[41] State restructuring funds are being used to finance energy R&D, energy efficiency programs, renewable energy programs, and low income programs. For a good discussion of these state programs, *see* M. Kushler, *An Updated Status Report of Public Benefit Programs in an Evolving Electricity Utility Industry*, American Council for an Energy-Efficient Economy (Washington, DC, 1998). And for a good discussion of the policy considerations involved in establishing such funds, *see* J. Eto et al., *supra* note 36.

[42] *Id.*   [43] *Id.*, at 14.

[44] J. Goldemberg and W. Reid (eds.), *Promoting Development While Limiting Greenhouse Gas Emissions: Trends and Baselines*, UNDP/Word Resources Institute (New York, 1999).

[45] Eto et al., *supra* note 36.

carbon dioxide and other pollutants. Other countries, such as The Netherlands, have created a green pricing program permitting consumers to purchase renewables at a small premium.[46]

A particularly ingenious and promising "Green Power for a Green LA" program was announced in 1999 by the Los Angeles, California municipal utility. It commits to customers that choose a six percent rate increase (about $3 per month on average) to use the entire rate increase proceeds to invest in new renewable generation sources, combined with a commitment to install free energy efficiency measures for subscribers, assuring that participating customer bills will as a result experience a net decrease in their bills – a strong incentive for participation. The utility president, David Freeman, one of the world's clean energy pioneers, has thus found a way to finance new renewable resources in a way which demonstrably will be at no cost to the customers, creating a unique win-win financing arrangement.[47]

4 GOVERNMENT PROCUREMENT

All governments are major energy users. Legislation or regulation to require purchase by federal, state, and/or municipal governments of clean energy products and processes can do much to promote cleaner and more affordable use of energy. Government procurements of green products also create markets to bring down their prices and set an example of the feasibility of their use for the private sector.

In the United States, the government is the world's largest single buyer of energy-using products, accounting for over $10 billion of such purchases each year.[48] The U.S. government, through legislation and executive orders, has required that all U.S. federal agencies must use thirty percent less energy per square foot in their buildings in 2005 than they consumed in 1985 and thirty-five percent less in 2010. In implementing these requirements, the Federal Energy Management Program (FEMP) requires the use of energy efficient lights and appliances in all its buildings and has adopted strict energy efficiency requirements for the construction of its buildings.[49] All federal agencies are required to purchase only products that qualify for the ENERGY STAR label, or, where there is no label, are among the twenty-five percent most efficient products on the market. Renewable resources must be acquired wherever cost effective.[50]

The program has saved the government agencies, and thus taxpayers, hundreds of millions of dollars in energy and pollution quantities and costs. The U.S. government also is including energy efficiency specifications in its contracting guide specifications used for construction and renovation projects. For example, by adopting efficiency criteria, the U.S. Navy in just one year (1998) saved an estimated $1.2 million per year in reduced electricity use by 500,000 efficient (T-8) fluorescent lamps, 200,000 electronic ballasts, and 20,000 light-emitting diode (LED) exit signs.[51] And, as a part

---

[46] Moore, *supra* note 9 at 4.
[47] Los Angeles Daily News, *L.A. leads way in developing true "Green Power"* (June 2, 1999).
[48] A. K. McCane and J. Harris, *Changing Government Purchasing Practices: Promoting Energy Efficiency on a Budget*, Proceedings of the ACEEE Summer Study (Asilomar, CA, 1996).
[49] Executive Orders 13123 and 12902; *see* http://www.nara.gov/fedreg/eo.html.
[50] *Id.*
[51] *See* http://www.epa.gov/appdstar/purchasing; http://www.eren.doe.gov./femp/procurement. An example of a state government agency efficiency success story: the Environmental Services Department (ESD)

of a massive renovation program, the Departments of Defense and Energy recently installed photovoltaic panels on the Pentagon.[52]

Government procurement programs of renewables involve payment of a premium up front, but result in very substantial long-term savings. Governments can also require the purchase for their vehicle fleets of clean and efficient vehicles. Many municipalities in the United States are now purchasing electric and natural gas turbine buses. The City of Los Angeles, California, has purchased a fleet of electric cars for municipal use and has installed recharging stations for the public throughout the city. California also adopted a law requiring "zero emission vehicles" and several other states have adopted the California standard.[53]

In the United States, city governments have been very aggressive about reducing their energy usage as a part of programs to decrease carbon dioxide emissions. Over 100 cities, representing ten percent of global emissions, have joined the Cities for Climate Protection program to reduce these emissions by investing in public transportation, building efficiency measures, planting trees, and installing solar collectors. Cities in other countries have taken similar action. Thus, Toronto, the first city to announce a climate plan, has undertaken to reduce its emissions by twenty percent. Saarbrucken in southern Germany has already cut its emissions by fifteen percent by measures including energy efficiency and public education.[54]

Similar efforts are being made in other countries. For example: Australia utilizes best practices in government procurement through performance contracting; Finland has adopted a target to reduce heating energy and electricity consumption in its government operations; Ireland has a program to reduce energy consumption in all state buildings; and the United Kingdom has a five-year program for reducing energy in government facilities. Canada, through a Federal Building Initiative, has been successful in achieving energy savings by contracting with ESCOs.[55]

A program sponsored by the Danish Electricity Savings Trust builds energy savings around a labeling requirement. The Trust organized a group of large institutional buyers, including housing companies and local governments, to jointly procure at a very favorable bulk-purchase price up to 10,000 energy efficient refrigerators that qualify for the top European Union efficiency label rating.[56]

Government procurement actions to stimulate development of improved energy efficient technology can also include the conduct of competitions to produce equipment with superior energy savings. A successful example was the U.S. government's

---

of San Diego decreased its energy consumption by 70% when energy efficient measures were implemented in its office building. The 73,000-sq.-ft. building received a new high-efficiency heating, ventilation, and air conditioning (HVAC) system; high-efficiency window films; fluorescent lamps and fixtures; and daylight and occupancy sensors. These improvements helped the building surpass California's Title 24 building code by more than 50%. Actual savings for ESD have been approximately $80,000 per year ($1.10/square foot). The building went from operating at 21–22kWh/square foot to 7–8kWh/square foot. J. Romm, *Cool Companies*, Island Press (Washington, DC, 1999).

52 FEMP Focus, U.S. Department of Energy (September/October 1999).

53 *See* http://www5.oadwp.com/services/electran/vehicles.htm.

54 C. Flavin, *Last Tango in Buenos Aires*, Worldwatch, vol. 11, No. 6, Worldwatch Institute (Washington, DC, November/December 1998), at 17.

55 *See* http://www.iea.org/pubs/newslett/eneeff/intro.htm.

56 P. Karbo, *Denmark Launches a Procurement Programme*, and *Danish Procurement Pays Dividends*, Appliance Efficiency Newsletter of the International Network for Domestic Energy-Efficient Appliances, 3:2 and 3:3 (Stockholm, 1999).

"Golden Carrot" Super-Efficient Refrigerator Program under which a consortium of government, utilities, and NGOs organized a competition to award a total of $30 million to the manufacturer offering the best new refrigerator that exceeded prevailing efficiency standards by at least thirty percent. The goal was met and many participating utilities also offered additional consumer rebates for it.[57] Sweden has a similar, very ingenious program under which purchasing offices issue requests for proposals guaranteeing to buy a large number of devices at specified prices if they meet technical standards for energy efficiency and customer savings.[58]

Governments also can aggregate procurements to make the production of energy superior equipment economic for manufacturers. Technology procurement for energy efficient products, pioneered in Sweden, subsequently has been used in the United States, The Netherlands, and Finland. Sweden's initial effort recruited housing cooperatives for a 1992 procurement creating a market for super-efficient windows that saved sixty percent more energy than standard Swedish triple-glazed windows. In 1995, the New York Power Authority and the New York City Housing Authority created a technology procurement project for new refrigerators that used thirty percent less electricity than those then on the market. And the IEA has sponsored a number of technology procurement projects for electric motors, heat pump dryers, LED traffic signals, and digital multifunction office copiers.[59]

The U.S. government has a Reporting of Greenhouse Gas Program through which energy efficiency and renewable measures are incentivized.[60] Under this program U.S. companies and organizations must report to the Energy Information Agency their programs and achievements in reducing greenhouse gas emissions. This program is useful in allowing companies to obtain recognition for their accomplishments and to establish a record of what they have done for eventual crediting against U.S. emission reduction requirements under the Kyoto Protocol.

5 TECHNOLOGY SOLUTIONS AND R&D

New energy efficiency and renewable energy technologies can materially advance the implementation of cleaner and more affordable energy solutions. Research and development (R&D) efforts have been instrumental in bringing to the market technologies that both improve performance and reduce the costs of such technologies. Governments have sponsored many of these developments.

A few examples of the results of recent government-sponsored R&D successes include the development of combined cycle natural gas power plants with double the efficiency and one-fourth the carbon intensity of coal-fired power plants.[61] These plants are being widely adopted in the United States and around the world in countries with

---

[57] M. Ledbetter et al., *US Energy-Efficient Technology Procurement Projects: Evaluation and Lessons Learned*, Pacific Northwest National Laboratory Report PNNL-12118 (Richland, Washington, 1999).

[58] Lovins, *supra* note 1 at 17.

[59] *Id.*; H. Wrestling, Co-operative Procurement: Market Acceptance for Innovative Energy Efficient Technologies, NUTEK Report B-1996–3 (Stockholm, 1996).

[60] The Reporting Program is required by §1605(b) of the Energy Policy Act of 1992, Pub.L.102–486, Title VII (October 24, 1992), 106 Stat. 2776.

[61] Lovins, *supra* note 1 at 8. An increase of average coal-fired power plant efficiency of 1% reduces carbon dioxide emissions by 2.5%. Energy Efficiency Report of IEA Greenhouse Gas R&D Programme, http://www.ieagreen.org.uk/efficiency.htm.

natural gas resources. Other relevant government-sponsored R&D successes include: the development of variable speed drive electric motors that produce the same work for less than half the use of electricity as conventional motors; the development of compact fluorescent light bulbs which last four times longer and use less than half the electricity of incandescent bulbs; and efficient wind machines that have drastically cut their costs. Much successful R&D has been done in the area of building efficiency, with the development of better insulation materials, double- or triple-glazed windows designed to utilize the sun's heat or protect from it, and many other innovations.

For the developing countries, technology transfer is a critical factor in enabling them to take advantage of energy efficiency and renewable technologies used in industrialized countries. Technical assistance and education of key energy players is essential to success. There are many such efforts being conducted around the world sponsored by governments and international agencies.

Improved technology offers great potential for developing countries to leapfrog to cleaner energy solutions. They can adopt the cleaner technologies from the start, avoiding the economic and pollution costs of using less efficient technologies and then having to replace or upgrade them, as has been done in the industrialized countries. One example is China's CFC-free Energy-Efficient Refrigerator Project begun in 1989 to develop an energy efficient CFC-free refrigerator. The final model, completed in 1996, demonstrated a forty-five percent reduction in energy use. The Global Environmental Facility Project Development Funding then funded studies with several manufacturers for large-scale production and distribution of the new refrigerator, demonstrating that even a twenty percent market penetration after ten years would reduce China's carbon dioxide emissions by over 100 million tons over the life of these refrigerators. The UNDP provided a $1 million technical assistance grant. The program thus leapfrogs to modern efficient refrigerator technology, providing China with major industrial opportunity with attendant jobs, consumer savings, power load reductions, and significant reduction of pollutants.[62]

There are numerous other government programs around the world to introduce energy efficient technologies into the marketplace. One of note is the Philippine Technology Transfer for Energy Management program that provided energy audits, technical assistance, and below market loans to more than 120 companies for adoption of energy-saving technologies, funded by $4.6 million from the U.S. Agency for International Development in 1985. The centerpiece was a Demonstration Loan Fund to demonstrate efficiency technologies and practices not widely used in the Philippines. Nearly 1,100 participants from the public and private sectors attended twenty-five seminars that were conducted nationwide under the program. Sixteen projects completed had an average internal rate of return of forty-one percent, with very significant cost and pollution savings.[63]

Some examples of government-sponsored technology R&D currently under way that could drastically reduce carbon dioxide emissions include: development of hydrogen fuel cells utilizable in both power plants and vehicles; the refinement and reduction of the

[62] H. A. Fine et al., *Sino-US CFC-Free Super Efficient Refrigerator Project Progress Report: Prototype Development and Testing*, U.S. Environmental Protection Agency (Washington, DC, 1997). *See also* http://eetd.lbl.gov/EA/partnership/China/refpubs.html.

[63] P. Rumsey and T. Flanigan, *Asian Energy Efficiency Success Stories*, International Institute for Energy Conservation (Washington, DC, 1995).

costs of photovoltaic cell manufacture and of various kinds of central station solar power stations; the manufacture of more affordable and efficient electric or hybrid vehicles and lighter weight, more efficient batteries; coal gasification; a new generation of advanced reciprocal engine or micro-turbine engine, particularly well suited for combined heat and power applications; and the development of carbon dioxide separation processes for hydrogen production and carbon dioxide sinks for storage and reuse.[64] A super-insulated car has been researched that will reduce heating and cooling loads by eighty and seventy-five percent respectively, saving fuel and improving safety by reduced glare and heat.[65]

Unfortunately, with the advent of increased global commercial competition and increasing privatization around the world, corporations have significantly decreased their long-term R&D expenditures. Utility spending on efficiency R&D also has drastically declined, by thirty-three percent from 1993 to 1996, from $708 million to $476 million.[66] As a result, if the benefits of new technology are to be achieved, governments will have to conduct the requisite R&D themselves or legislate the funding of R&D efforts; they could also mandate that a percent of sales be devoted by private entities to R&D or enter into partnerships with private companies to develop technologies that will improve technology performance and lower its costs.

6 RECYCLING PROGRAMS

Many countries today have laws providing for the recycling of their waste paper, glass, and metal products. For example, in Denmark, half of all waste is recycled and eighty percent of new paper is made from used paper.[67] Almost every city in the United States has legislated a recycling program for paper, glass, plastic, and metal wastes, with either curbside pickup or establishment of a central recycling municipal facility.

7 EDUCATION PROGRAMS

Education of the public is vital to let the people know the importance to them of taking the measures necessary to increase energy efficiency, to build the political support necessary for enactment of appropriate legislative measures, and to inform them of the options available to them.

Education is particularly important for architects, engineers, builders, commercial enterprise managers, tradespeople, and government officials at all levels, to inform them of the requirements of laws that have been adopted to promote energy efficiency and the costs and benefits of the measures they can take either voluntarily or

---

[64] *See* M. Brown and M. Levine, *Scenarios of U.S. Carbon Reductions: Potential Impacts of Energy Technologies by 2010 and Beyond*, Interlaboratory Working Group on Energy-Efficient and Low Carbon Technologies, Lawrence Berkeley National Laboratory, LBNL 40533 (Berkeley, California, 1997). Other promising R&D efforts include new kinds of heat exchangers and motors, membrane separators, sensors and controls, rapid prototyping and ultra precision fabrication, and processes using enzymes, bacteria, and biological designs: *id.* and Lovins, *supra* note 1 at 7.

[65] J. Kahn, *First Insulated Auto Enhances Comfort, Reduces Energy Use,* Sciencebeat, Lawrence Berkeley National Laboratory (Berkeley, CA, 1999); http://www.lbl.gov/Science Articles/Archive/insulated-auto.html.

[66] Eto, *supra* note 36.

[67] *Denmark Moves Ahead in Wind Power, The New York Times*, International Section (October 9, 1999).

pursuant to legal requirements.[68] It is important that retail sales staff, contractor installers, and maintenance/service personnel understand the benefits of efficient products and processes and can personally benefit from promoting these products to end users.

Much of this education must be conducted or contracted by governments, creating a legislative basis for this task and appropriating the funds for appropriate staff to do mailings, conduct workshops and conferences, and do media education work.

7.1 Labeling Programs

One effective educational measure has been the adoption by countries and municipalities of energy efficiency product labeling requirements. Labeling is an inexpensive educational tool. The United States, many of its states and cities, and many countries and their municipalities have adopted such labeling requirements. Appliance labeling has often been an effective precursor for the adoption of efficiency standards. New buildings can also be the subject of energy efficiency labeling requirements, as is required through building certification programs in Denmark and Canada. The United States and some other countries have a miles per gallon labeling requirement for all vehicles sold.

7.2 Ratings

Ratings of companies on the greenness of their products also can be an effective educational tool. For example, the major U.S. environmental organizations, together with consumer and industry participants and the NGO Center for Resource Solutions, have established a "Green-e" clean electricity certification program. This program permits display of the Green-e logo if power providers meet very rigorous "green" conditions: fifty percent plus renewables; for the remaining fifty percent, non-renewables with low emissions; full disclosure of electricity sources; no nuclear power generation; one year after deregulation, at least five percent new renewables, increasing five percent per year until twenty-five percent is reached. Also required is a commitment to biannual reviews of truth in advertising and annual independent audits of renewable offerings. The ratings are designed to inform electricity consumers of assured superior green power offerings.[69] With the advent of deregulation in the United States, a "Power Scorecard" also has been developed to rate the greenness of power plants, permitting informed consumer choice, being considered by the regulatory authorities for requirement by a number of states.[70]

7.3 Awards

Lastly, many governments and private organizations have established award programs to recognize companies, private organizations, and products that accomplish outstanding

---

[68] The usual means of compensating architects and engineers worldwide, as a percentage of building and equipment costs, has the perverse incentive of discouraging least cost solutions. It has been estimated that this incentive design has led the United States to misallocate about $1 trillion in air conditioning equipment and the energy needed to operate it than had the buildings been optimally designed to produce the same or better comfort at least cost. Lovins, *supra* note 1 at 18.

[69] *See* http://www.igc.org/crs2/details.html.

[70] Pace Energy Project, Pace Law School (White Plains, NY, 1999).

energy efficiency or renewable achievements. There also are a number of government information programs. For example, in the United States the Federal Trade Commission has issued "Energy Guide" labels and the EPA has its ENERGY STAR program.[71]

8 GOVERNMENT-SPONSORED VOLUNTARY PROGRAMS

The U.S. government has relied heavily on voluntary programs and partnerships with industrial companies to achieve energy efficiencies that will reduce pollutants and carbon dioxide emissions. Notable is its 1991 "Green Lights" program, under which companies agree to capture cost-effective lighting energy saving and in turn are allowed to advertise participation in the program. Since green products are popular with consumers, this certification is of value to the companies. The program also gives informational, technical, and trade ally support. As of 1997, the program involved more than 2,300 organizations and its retrofits were saving over half the lighting energy with thirty percent return on investment; the national potential for this effort alone has been estimated to be $16 billion annual savings with a twelve percent reduction in utility carbon and other emissions.[72]

Other countries have emulated this program. For example, in 1996, China began a China Green Lights Program in cooperation with the U.S.-sponsored Beijing Energy-Efficiency Center and a committee of outside experts, with the on-target goal of increasing the use of high efficiency lights to 300 million units by 2000, resulting in electricity savings of 26.8 TWh and peak load savings of 7.2 GW, along with large avoided costs for new electricity power plants. Pollution savings were estimated at 200,000 metric tons of sulfur and 7.4 million tons of avoided carbon emissions annually by the Year 2000.[73]

The U.S. government also has initiated the ENERGY STAR program that gives technical assistance and recognition to companies that market very efficient equipment. This program has been highly successful in promoting market transformation measures, which establish new energy efficient products in the marketplace. For example, the ENERGY STAR office equipment program convinced most manufacturers to produce only copiers, computers, etc., that automatically switch to a low energy consumption mode when not in use. And an ENERGY STAR program is successfully advancing horizontal-axis clothes washers, familiar in Europe but only recently introduced in the United States, that use half the water and one-third the energy of conventional U.S. models.[74] The program was saving half a billion dollars per year in 1997 and was estimated to save nearly double that by 2000 with a profitable 10 million ton per year carbon saving by 2005.[75] The program also encourages industry to convert to energy efficient motors and the EPA is considering the adoption of motor standards.

---

[71] Geller, *supra* note 19 at 7.

[72] *Id.*, at 16; *see also*, *Introducing the Green Lights Program*, EPA 430-F-93-050, U.S. Environmental Protection Agency (Washington, DC, 1993); http://www.EPA.gov/appdstar.green.glb-home.html.

[73] D. Zou et al., *Climate Change Mitigation: Case Studies from China*, Report to the U.S. Environmental Protection Agency, Battelle Pacific Northwest National Laboratories, Advanced International Studies Unit (Washington, DC, October 1997). *See* http://www.pnl.gov/aisu/pubs/noregchn.pdf.

[74] S. Nadel and L. Latham, *The Role of Market Transformation Strategies in Achieving a More Sustainable Future*, American Council for an Energy-Efficient Economy (Washington, DC, 1998), at 23–24.

[75] Lovins, *supra* note 1 at 16.

Canada started a Voluntary Challenge and Registry (VCR) program as a part of its National Action Program on Climate Change in 1995, which became an independent private/public partnership in 1997. Its purpose is to spur voluntary actions on climate change and publicize them. Two-thirds of its funding is from the private sector, the rest from the federal and provincial governments. In its first three years, Canada's VCR program registered about 700 companies and organizations. Resulting carbon dioxide emission reductions totaling just over nine metric tons of carbon were reported, about 6.5 percent of Canada's fossil fuel carbon emissions in 1998.[76]

Agreements between government and industry have resulted in substantial energy intensity reductions in European countries such as Germany, which committed in March 1996 to reduce carbon dioxide emissions by twenty percent between 1990 and 2005, The Netherlands, and Denmark. Belgium, France, Spain, and Norway are in the process of negotiating voluntary agreements with their principal energy intensive industries.[77]

9 LEGISLATIVE FINANCING MECHANISMS

9.1 Internal Resources

As indicated previously, there are a number of financial resources that can be generated internally by any government. The largest of these in most countries is the removal of fossil fuel subsidies. Many of the energy efficiency measures described above achieve large savings over time that provide very substantial revenue resources. Taxes on pollutants and fossil fuels have been used in many countries to help finance energy consumption reductions with large savings. Emission trading rights have been utilized to lower the costs of pollution reduction measures. Governments have used general tax revenues to support efficiency and renewable programs with considerable cost reductions and R&D for new technologies. They also have initiated programs to require the purchase of energy efficient appliances, lighting, and buildings for their own use. And they have required their electric utilities to do integrated resource planning and promote DSM and renewable resources.

9.2 Aggregated Loans

One way to overcome the problems with small loans for distributed resources is to aggregate the loans in various ways.

Installment Loans

An innovative credit arrangement to overcome these problems has been adopted by several countries, to make loans to creditworthy institutions like local utilities which

---

[76] *See* http://www.iea.org/pubs/newslett/eneeff/intro.htm.

[77] Geller, *supra* note 19 at 13. Two major types of industry agreement programs are frequent: (1) Target-Based Agreements include negotiated legally binding requirements, targets that preempt future regulatory requirements, or targets tied to a strong regulatory threat: for example, The Netherlands Long-Term Agreements involve about 1,200 industrial companies with over 90% coverage of industrial primary energy consumption; and (2) Performance-Based Agreements based on negotiated performance goals that are not legally binding such as The Canadian Industry Programme for Energy Conservation and the Norwegian Industrial Energy Efficiency Network. *See* http://www.iea.org/pubs/newslett/eneeff/intro.htm.

set up revolving funds to manage installment loans to individuals and small businesses on relatively attractive terms. Such arrangements have been adopted in Indonesia for its Solar Home Systems Project, in India for a solar photovoltaic program, in Kenya for its wood stove upgrading program and for off-grid photovoltaic systems, and in Bangladesh, the Dominican Republic, and Honduras.

Micro Utilities

Another innovative mechanism is financing service providers with the creation of renewable energy micro utilities which sell energy services, permitting financing to be aggregated to the service provider, the end-user being required to make payments based on the level of energy services received. This approach has been successfully demonstrated in the Dominican Republic and is now being implemented in a 10,000 solar home system program by a rural electric cooperative in Bolivia; and mortgage financing, allowing homeowners to incorporate the costs of installing renewable systems into the overall costs of their homes through mortgage financing. This approach is being tested in a rural housing/electrification program in South Africa.

Grameen Bank

A particularly fascinating development is the creation of micro lending organizations in some of the poorest countries for their most impoverished populations. Thus, Grameen Bank ("village bank") in Bangladesh has started a lending program for people earning on average less than $1 a day. Today, Grameen is established in nearly 39,000 villages in Bangladesh, lending to approximately 2.4 million borrowers. Established in 1986, it reached its first $1 billion cumulative loans in 1995. It took only two more years to reach $2 billion. The repayment rate hovers between ninety-six and 100 percent. In a typical year, five percent of Grameen borrowers, representing 125,000 families, rise above the poverty level. The Grameen model has now been applied in forty countries. In all, about twenty-two million poor people around the world now have access to small loans. Grameen has now established more than a dozen enterprises, often in partnership with other entrepreneurs. One such enterprise is Grameen Skakti (Energy), which has been helping to install solar energy systems into village households.

9.3 Other Legislative Financing Measures

Other useful internal financing mechanisms include: leasing clean energy equipment or services, thus avoiding for the user the necessity to raise purchase capital; vendor financing, which has been undertaken by some equipment suppliers to promote sales of their products; and performance contracting by ESCOs, under which the ESCO gets paid out of savings achieved and again, the user avoids capital financing.

10 CONCLUSION

There are abundant examples in both developed and developing countries of the successful adoption of cost-effective measures to reduce energy consumption, lower energy costs and reduce emissions. A wide variety of legislative and regulatory programs have been undertaken and the legal and financial mechanisms for doing so are also many and varied. These measures can be advanced on a basis of long-term profitability; indeed, many energy efficiency savings are so compelling that they should be undertaken just to save money. But achieving these goals will take determined action and political will among all the governments and international institutions of the world.

8 Air Pollution Control Laws: Common but Differentiated Responsibilities for Managing the Atmosphere

Nicholas A. Robinson*

1 INTRODUCTION

Energy law does not function in a vacuum. All energy production entails environmental impacts. The burning of carbon fuels and biomass produces greenhouse gases, with their attendant global implications for climate change, and at the same time produces air pollution, which harms the health of persons locally and contributes to tranboundary air pollution problems such as "acid rain" or the "atmospheric brown cloud" (ABC) phenomena. Although national governments currently only make halting progress at best when addressing emission of greenhouse gases, their national laws to control air pollution are marked with some success. Experience with successful air pollution control systems in some nations provides guidance for how all nations can meet their common responsibility to protect the public health from poisonous air pollution.

While addressing their duty to abate air pollution, nations also can make a major and common contribution to reducing greenhouse gas emissions. Despite contemporary political stalemates over the adherence by the Russian Federation or the United States of America to the Kyoto Protocol, much progress on reducing carbon dioxide emissions can be made in the course of enhancing the effectiveness of air pollution laws. Those who debate climate change have tended to devote rather too little attention to how the experience gained in abating pollution of the atmosphere can be applied to reducing greenhouse gas emissions.

Air pollution is a significant health hazard in most large cities around the world. This documented fact, however, provides scientific knowledge that is a necessary, but not sufficient, basis for controlling and then eliminating the worldwide scourge of air pollution. Environmental law provides tools to use the scientific knowledge and produce cleaner air. If all states are to restore air that is wholly beneficial to breathe, then all societies will need to pursue this common objective by undertaking focused and energetic measures appropriate to their own air pollution problems.

* Gilbert & Sarah Kerlin Distinguished Professor of Environmental Law, Pace University School of Law (New York), and Chair, Commission on Environmental Law, International Union for the Conservation of Nature and Natural Resources; A.B. Brown University (1967); J.D. Columbia University (1970); Professor Robinson served as the Deputy Commissioner and General Counsel of the New York State Department of Environmental Conservation, 1982–83, with responsibility for New York's State Implementation Plan under the U.S. Clean Air Act.

2 THE COMMON DUTY TO ABATE AIR POLLUTION

Under the Charter of the United Nations, states have the duty to cooperate together to cope with problems such as air pollution. National laws, and cooperation through the World Health Organization (WHO) or the United Nations Environment Programme (UNEP), or the International Union for the Conservation of Nature and Natural Resources (IUCN), offer concrete evidence that the duty to cooperate is understood and is being implemented. Within each nation, the differentiated characteristics of its air pollution control regimes constitute each nation's acknowledgment of their common responsibility toward mitigating transboundary and global effects. A state practice has emerged in which most nations acknowledge a legal duty to secure clean air for their people to breath, and to prevent air pollution from their territory spreading to harm people in other jurisdictions.

Each state's duties to abate air pollution are obligations binding on States.[1] At the same time, the duty to abate air pollution is recognized as both a legal and a moral obligation binding on individuals.[2] There are compelling reasons to acknowledge that the right to breathe is within the acknowledged right to life itself, and is a human right.[3] It is estimated that an individual breathes some 3,400 gallons of air each day, and none would deny another the right and opportunity to do so.

However, notwithstanding the recognition that we all have a birth right, defined by the functions of our lungs from the moment we leave the womb, to breathe,[4] we face a world in which urban air pollution is growing, exposure to rural air pollution from burning biomass adversely affects ever larger numbers of people, and this pollution harmfully crosses from one state into other states. Such contributions to worldwide patterns of environmental degradation induce change in the atmosphere and affect all living systems. It avails us little to debate the religious, philosophical, or jurisprudential bases for the duty to end air pollution, if we lack the means to do so.

Fortunately, the means, both legal and technical, to abate air pollution and to begin to manage the atmosphere exist. There are well-demonstrated examples of how states and cities have successful deployed these means. It is useful to survey the legal regimes that have been adopted to abate air pollution, and indicate where the legal tools have worked well, and where their implementation has been frustrated. It will suggest how the legal

---

[1] A general principle of public international law, restated as Principle 21 of the Stockholm Declaration, and as Principle 2 of the Rio Declaration on Environment and Development, provides that states have a duty to ensure that use of their own resources does not harm the resources or people of other states. *See The Trail Smelter Arbitration* (US and Canada), 3 R.I.A.A. 1938 (March 11, 1941).

[2] Many constitutions now provide a public right to a healthy environment (e.g., Brazil, India, or The Philippines), and a correlative duty on the part of the individual to protect the environment. The Earth Charter, endorsed by UNESCO, delineates an ethical framework within which the individual's duty to safeguard the environmental is delineated. *See also* the UN World Charter for Nature, adopted by the UN General Assembly. UNGA Res. 37/7.

[3] *Oposa v. Factoran*, GR No 101083 (July 30, 1993): "The right to a balanced and healthy environment . . . belongs to a different category of rights [beyond civil and political rights enumerated in a bill of rights] for it concerns nothing less than self-preservation and self perpetuation . . . , the advancement of which may even be said to predate all governments and constitutions. As a matter of fact, these basic rights need not even be written in the Constitution for they are assumed to exist from the inception of humankind."

[4] In ancient Rome, this was self-evident. In Justinian's Institutes it is provided that the air, like the running waters, is a part of the public trust doctrine. While access to waters is still enforced in the courts, access to the air has not yet been afforded comparable judicial protection.

system of environmental impact assessment can be used as a tool for the stewardship of the atmosphere. These legal means and tools have been developed within the young field of environmental law. They regulate most facilities that generate electricity from burning fossil fuels. Since in many places air quality is deteriorating, it is essential that these environmental legal tools be deployed to protect the public health. Indeed, the fact that environmental laws are not well implemented today is a direct result of the shallow understanding of their provisions on the part of administrators and political leaders in all regions, which in turn leads to the consequent lack of political will to implement their provisions. States and international organizations need to expand their capacity building measures to address such deficits in knowledge.[5]

3 THE EVOLVING LEGAL FRAMEWORK FOR AIR POLLUTION CONTROL

Isolated examples of laws to abate local air pollution can be traced to ancient Rome or ancient China. Governments have taken legal action to abate air pollution where it was a nuisance or frustrated other social goals. The first "modern" laws to cope with industrial air pollution were the Alkali Acts in England, adopted in the nineteenth century. Since then, and particularly in the second half of the twentieth century, the now familiar pattern of air pollution control laws has been implemented.

Contemporary "clean air laws" typically have several common characteristics. They usually define the required level of air quality desired,[6] specify the geographic region in which air quality has been measured as suffering from pollution, identify the sources of the air pollutants of concern to the legislators (principally only industrial, electrical generating, or motor vehicle sources), and then set forth selected legal controls deemed appropriate to monitor and abate the emission of such pollutants (frequently permits or design and operation standards). Framework laws governing air pollution control exist in most developed states, and many developing states.

However, as overall population growth and the migration into cities stimulate growth in larger urban conurbations, and as emissions of air pollutants increase with economic development, the air pollution in major cities has increased dramatically, as is recognized, for example, by authorities in China, in Mexico, and in Thailand. The rapid development of urban centers such as the growing cities in The Gulf shows the first trends in increasing air emissions and the resultant pollution levels.[7] Increasing air pollution causes marked deterioration of local public health conditions, especially during acute pollution episodes where local climate conditions (such as temperature inversions) often aggravate breathing problems for persons with asthma, emphysema, or other lung ailments, or for the very young and old. Many such sensitive persons die because of the unhealthy air during these episodes.

---

[5] Agenda 21, adopted in 1992, calls on states to do so, as the Johannesburg Plan of Implementation reiterated in 2002.

[6] These can be fairly rudimentary, such as use of the Ringleman chart to define and then set limits on emissions of smoke, or quite advanced and based on medical knowledge, such as the primary air quality control standards adopted under Section 109 of the Clean Air Act of 1970 in the United States, or the European Unions Council Directive (87/203/EEC of 7 March 1985) on air quality standards for nitrogen dioxide.

[7] *See, e.g.,* Annual Report 2002 on U.A.E. Abu Dhabi Municipality & Town Planning (September 2003), Ambient Air Quality Monitoring Network, Environment Protection Section, Public Health and Environment Administration.

When air pollutants leave one nation and cause acid precipitation elsewhere, international law provides only a rather weak regime. The UN Economic Commission for Europe has sponsored the 1979 Convention on Long-Range Transboundary Air Pollution, and its 1985 and 1994 Protocol on Further Reductions of Sulfur Emissions, together with Decisions on the Structure and Function of the Implementing Committee,[8] and the 1988 Nitrogen Oxides Protocol,[9] have contributed to a reduction in emissions that are precursors to acid rain in West and East Europe. This regime does not address acid rain in all other parts of the world, and the atmospheric brown cloud, or ABC, constitutes a vast redistribution of acid rain from East and Southeast Asia to South Asia. Despite regional efforts to abate acid rain in North America,[10] increasingly severe effects of acid rain are reported.[11] The UN ECE, through the 1979 Geneva Convention, also addresses emissions of volatile organic compounds that contribute to tropospheric ozone (smog), through adopting a 1991 Protocol on Volatile Organic Compounds (VOX),[12] which has had only limited success to date. Canada and the United States also have agreements on emissions of nitric oxides (NOX) and volatile organic compounds (VOX),[13] to combat transboundary ozone smog. The boundary agreement between Mexico and the United States also addresses cooperation to abate all air pollution.[14] The Commission on Environmental Cooperation, a Canadian-Mexican-U.S. agency established under the environmental side accord to the North American Free Trade Agreement (NAFTA) also is addressing ways to abate air pollution.[15] In Asia, it is said that China's greatest volume of exports to Japan is acid rain. The Association of Southeast Asian Nations (ASEAN) has a cooperative program to abate transboundary air pollution from biomass burning, the "Haze," which is still in the earliest stages of its potential effectiveness.[16]

Airborne transport of other chemicals hostile to human health and nature has become a subject of public international law. The Stockholm Convention on Persistent Organic Pollutants (POPs), bans the manufacture and use of chemicals that are transported far from their place of manufacture or use, enter the food chain, and endanger life.[17] The POPs agreement recognized the global and interrelated aspects of the biosphere as a basis for regulating national conduct. While still at an early phase of implementation, it provides a sound jurisprudential basis for addressing common but differentiated responsibilities for the atmosphere.

---

[8] 27 I.L.M. 707; 33 I.L.M. 1540 (June 14, 1994).   [9] 22 I.L.M. 212.

[10] 1991 U.S.-Canada Air Quality Agreement, 30 I.L.M. 676 (1991).

[11] Dr. Gene Likens, and others, continue to document the effects of acid rain at Hubbard Brook. The baseline for determining levels of acid rain in North America effectively is the report, Acid Deposition: State of Science and Technology: Summary Report of the U.S. National Acid Deposition Assessment Program (NAPAP), 1991.

[12] 31 I.L.M. 568.

[13] 2001 amendment to 1991 Protocol, *supra* note 8; *see* http://www.epa.gov/airmarkets/usca/.

[14] 1983 Agreement to Cooperate in the Solution of Environmental Problems in the Border Area ("La Paz Agreement"), 22 I.L.M. 1025. In September 2002, a plan to meet primary ambient air quality standards in the border area by 2012 was announced. *See* U.S. EPA, Border 2012: U.S.-Mexico Environmental Program (U.S. EPA Doc. 160-3-02-001).

[15] CEC, Montreal, Report (October 2003). *See* EcoAméricas, at 6–9 (January 2004).

[16] *See* N. A. Robinson, "Forest Fires as a Common International Concern: Precedents for the Progressive Development of International Environmental Law," 18 *Pace Environmental Law Review* 459 (2001).

[17] For a detailed analysis of the Stockholm Convention, *see* Marco Olson, *POPs Convention* (Oceana Publications, Dobbs Ferry, NY, 2003).

Despite recommendations of the WHO regarding abatement of air pollution, most states have yet to embrace clean air goals as a fundamental duty. The result is that the atmosphere continues to be used as a shared, mobile dump for gaseous wastes. Since effects of air pollution in the biosphere are not seen in the capitals of nations, they are a low priority. A higher priority arises from the distress over urban smog, and the attendant costs of health care, and the human losses due to morbitity and mortality.

The need to restore and sustain the public health in most urban settings stimulates a growing recognition of the increasingly urgent need to deploy these traditional legal systems for air pollution control with greater efficacy.

At the same time, the renewed interest in adopting stronger national air pollution laws and in securing their more effective observance and compliance, is being matched with a new concern that is not a part of these laws today. This is the rapidly emerging concern of many states to curb or eliminate the emissions of greenhouse gases that contribute to global climate change. Many air pollutants are also greenhouse gases. Air pollution also may mitigate some global warming by reflecting solar energy back away from the atmosphere. As protection of the stratospheric ozone became a priority in the 1970s, the Vienna Convention to Protect the Stratospheric Ozone Layer was negotiated, followed by the Montreal Protocol and London and related agreements, dramatically reducing emissions of the chlorofluorocarbons (CFCs). Each CFC molecule is on the magnitude of twenty times more effective as a gas retraining solar heat, as is a molecule of CO_2, and thus the stewardship regime for the stratospheric ozone is often also cited as a means to cut back on climate change emissions. The rapid adoption and ratification of the Montreal Protocol led to its rapid implementation; for instance, the U.S. Congress adopted the CFC cutbacks in its 1990 amendments to the Clean Air Act, even before ratification.

The negotiation of the Kyoto Protocol to the 1992 UN Framework Convention on Climate Change (UNFCCC) led many to envision a strict cutback of CO_2 emissions to the 1990 levels as a way to stabilize anthropogenic climate change. However, the refusal of the Bush Administration in the United States, and then the Putin Administration in Russia, to ratify the Kyoto Protocol, has prevented these cutbacks from becoming legally binding in international law. Whatever the timing of an eventual international agreement on how to abate CO_2 emissions, it is clear that individual nations are adopting and implementing measures to curb CO_2 emissions within their own territories, in explicit recognition of their common but differentiated responsibilities to do so. This has reenforced the interest in looking at air pollution laws, since the reduction in pollutants or CO_2 tends to be assigned to the same ministries and employ similar legal means.

Public policy concerns for global warming and climate change, therefore, have complicated the traditional air pollution legal regimes. National air pollution law is increasingly in transition. This gives rise to a challenge: How might review of air pollution laws be employed to both secure public health in the short term, and to mitigate climate change in the long term by reducing greenhouse gas emissions?

4 REASSESSING LAWS FOR ATMOSPHERIC STEWARDSHIP

Despite half a century of experience with contemporary air pollution, the legal regimes have yet to protect the air as effectively as hoped. Not all nations have enacted the national air pollution laws appropriate to their problems. Most nations have not adopted laws and treaties to eliminate unlawful transboundary air pollution, and relatively few nations are active participants in the decisions of the international organizations that address air pollution issues. States still allow their enterprises to dump wastes into the air, with the result that what is "out of sight is out of mind." Until a nation recognized that acid rain harms its forests and agriculture, melts alike its cultural heritage and its bridges and outdoor infrastructure, it cares little about where the winds may blow its gases. Until a nation sees the perverse effects on climate resulting from emissions of greenhouse gases, it ascribes a low priority to those issues. What each state cannot ignore, however, is the public health crisis that air pollution causes in its urban centers, many of which are its capital cities where national leaders breathe the same air as everyone else.

The effectiveness of the Clean Air Act in the United States[18] can be attributed to decisions taken by the U.S. Congress and President Richard Nixon to reverse two decades of increasingly dirty air in American cities. The lessons learned in implementing the 1970 amendments to the Clean Air Act[19] offer guidance for those who would clean the air in other cities around the world.

Air pollution laws in many major cities in the United States have significantly reduced air pollution since 1970. The Clean Air Act is a framework law that sets national standards but relies on states to carry a major role in implementing the standards. In states such as New York or California, strong state implementation has resulted in major strides in curbing air pollution. In states with weak implementation, such as Texas, air pollution has become worse in some cities. Examination of the legal features in the states with successful air pollution controls can provide a foundation for other states, which strive for greater effectiveness in abating air pollution, and also can guide the development of new laws to contain CO_2 and other greenhouse gases. Since commercial enterprises that emit air pollutants benefit economically by avoiding the costs of averting or controlling the gaseous wastes they emit, they and their trade associations often oppose air pollution regulation. The adoption and implementation of air pollution control laws are the result of hard fought debates and decisions.

A brief review of seven legal different issues that have emerged from implementing the U.S. Clean Air Act can help point to elements of effectiveness or ineffectiveness of certain legal tools.

First, perhaps the most fundamental attribute of the Act is its requirement to "restore and enhance" the air quality in the United States.[20] These words have been interpreted to prevent any deterioration of air quality. Congress clarified this duty in 1977 to require "prevention of significant deterioration" in designated clean air regions; new development there can only be allowed under strict standards, including closing older existing enterprises that pollute.[21] Once gains have been made, they may not be allowed to lapse.

Second, the Act requires the U.S. Environmental Protection Agency (EPA) to determine "primary air quality control standards" that protect the public health "allowing an adequate margin of safety."[22] Medical and other scientific analysis of what constitutes the health of an individual sets a clear standard that may not be manipulated by expedient economic or political ends. The courts have ruled that economic burdens

[18] 42 U.S.C. §§ 7401, et seq.
[20] Clean Air Act § 101.
[22] *Id.* § 109.
[19] Pub. L. 91-604; 84 Stat. 1676 (Dec. 31, 1970).
[21] *Id.* §§ 107, 160–169.

cannot be used as a basis for objecting to these health standards.[23] To be sure, delays in implementing more stringent standards can be identified, but in the end the scientific standard cannot be gainsaid and has prevailed.[24] The Clean Air Act also assumed that there might be standards for secondary air ambient air quality control standards, which would be needed to protect the public welfare in ways unrelated to meeting the basic public health standard. In practice, it is increasingly clear that there is no threshold beyond which a person can breathe the air safely, with consequences that might need regulating to protect economic or social or cultural ends (although acid rain precursor emissions or carbon dioxide emissions may be characterized in this way, political compromises have so far precluded this from happening).

The EPA has set health standards for carbon monoxide, particulate matter, sulfur oxides, nitrogen oxides,[25] hydrocarbon (which mix with nitrogen oxides in the presence of sunlight to form tropospheric ozone, or "smog"),[26] and a set of air toxics including lead. These too have been based on scientific findings, and been sustained and refined over time.

Third, the EPA has also set technology standards, which every industry across all states has to employ. This provides for a common technological and economic foundation for the manufacturing sector. Reasonably available control technology (RACT) must be employed by all,[27] and Best Achievable Control Technology (BACT), and in areas where the air is clear, Lowest Achievable Control Technologies (LAER),[28] and in the case of hazardous air pollutants ("air toxics"), Maximum Achievable Control Technology (MACT),[29] which as a practical matter usually is zero emissions. All these technological assessments are available to the public.

Fourth, the Clean Air Act expressly addresses the design standards for motor vehicles and for fuels. Because automobiles are manufactured or imported and sold on a nation-wide basis, Congress directed the EPA to regulate design and performance standards for motor vehicles. The automobile manufacturing industry has sued to delay implementation of design and performance and fuel efficiency standards.[30] These repeated suits have slowed, but not deterred the reformulation of gasoline in areas that do not attain the primary standards, and gradually manufacturers have acknowledged the need to design hybrid vehicles using electricity or natural gas, with on board generators.

Fifth, and perhaps most significantly, the Clean Air Act requires that every state has a duty to adopt a State Implementation Plan (SIP) designed to bring all the air within that

---

[23] *See, e.g., Lead Industries Association v. EPA* (D.C. Cir Ct. of Appeals, 1980).

[24] In 2001, EPA Administrator Ann Gorsuch insisted that the George W. Bush Administration retain the Particular Matter standards promulgated by the Clinton EPA, over heavy opposition from economic interests and politicians. In 1990, Congress finally overrode eight years of objections by the Reagan Administration and enacted amendments to the Clean Air Act, which President George H. Bush signed into law.

[25] In the case of sulfur dioxide, nitrogen oxides, and particulates, Congress reduced the emissions regulated in 1977 to a percentage of what hey would be without the technical controls, but in 1990 Congress replaced this with a system of sulfur dioxide allowances. The political pressure on Congress has delayed and weakened the measures required to attain the primary health standard, but has not annulled the standard itself. *See, e.g., Sierra Club v. Costle*, (D.C. Cir Ct. of Appeals, 1981).

[26] In 1982, the EPA withdrew the hydrocarbon standards as unnecessary, since the smog could be addressed through its precursors.

[27] Clean Air Act § 172.   [28] *Id.* § 171.

[29] *Id.* § 112.

[30] *See, e.g., International Harvester v. Ruckelshaus* (D.C. Cir Ct. of Appeals, 1981).

state into attainment with the national primary ambient air quality standards.[31] The elements of the Plan are specified in federal law, and include requiring that each state have adequate monitoring and assessment programs, and adequately staff and fund all its programs. If a state fails to promulgate an effective SIP, the EPA can impose a Federal Implementation Plan. The SIP is enforceable in federal or state court,[32] and citizens can sue to secure a court order to compel compliance if the federal or state authorities do not take such action.[33] Some states, such as California and New York, have adopted rigorous SIPs, requiring permits for the siting, construction, and operation of new stationary sources of air pollution, transportation controls for operation of motor vehicles, and emissions from new sources to match or reduce pollution through offsets of up to twenty percent of former air emissions.

A sixth aspect of the Clean Air Act is to insist on states meeting the primary ambient air quality standard to protect the public health even if it means inventing new technological systems to do so, or to shut down the polluting sources. This has come to be known as "technology forcing."[34] When Missouri adopted an SIP ordering electrical generating facilities to meet the new primary health standards or close down, the industry sought relief in the courts. The U.S. Supreme Court, however, upheld the EPA and the state. Mr. Justice Marshall ruled that technological and scientific infeasibility could not be used as a reason to frustrate the SIP requirement to ensure healthy air for its people.[35] This process of "technology forcing" has been one of the great innovations of environmental law. Industry eventually studied its engineering systems and found ways to comply. The same technology forcing was used when Congress enacted the ban on CFCs in the 1990 amendments to the Clean Air Act, forcing the industry to come up with alternatives to the use of the chemicals that deplete the stratospheric ozone layer.

Seventh, the Clean Air Act has authorized use of economic instruments, both incentives and disincentives, to facilitate how companies adapt and adjust to reduced emission limitations. For instance, in California, the SIP has established perhaps the only truly effective system to cap emissions on a scale that requires their reduction. The Southern California Air Quality Control Board has enacted a process for the Los Angeles Basin in which all emissions from all stationary sources are registered and subject to permit. No new stationary source can be opened until it buys the emission volumes it needs, plus twenty percent more, which are retired, from an administrative bank into which all the emissions from businesses that close or move have been deposited. This means each new business has reduced emissions associated with its operation by twenty percent. Economic growth has continued to be robust in Los Angeles, and air pollution has been reduced. In 1990, Congress required the use of such offsets nationwide, in every city where healthy air is not attained; Congress left it up to the states to either use the Los Angeles approach, or to use a strict permit system, or other techniques to achieve the offsets. For every new emission source, up to twenty percent of its estimated emissions must be eliminated.[36]

---

[31] Clean Air Act § 110.   [32] *Id.* § 113.

[33] *Id.* § 304.

[34] *See generally*, John Bonine, "The Evolution of Technology-Forcing In The Clean Air Act," 6 *Env't Rep.* (Bureau of National Affairs), Monograph No. 21 (July 25, 1975); La Pierre, "Technology-Forcing and Federal Environmental Protection Statutes," 62 *Iowa Law Review* 771 (1977).

[35] *Union Electric Co. v. EPA* (S. Ct. 1976).   [36] Clean Air Act § 172.

To ease the impact of compliance on a factory, Congress has allowed all the factory's emissions to be considered one source, with an imaginary "bubble" over the entire plan. This lets the company reduce emissions from parts of the factory that are economically easier for it.[37]

In one economic system to cap and trade emissions, the U.S. Clean Air Act has not been entirely successful. This is the provision for the acid deposition "trading" system.[38] It is relatively easy to document the total emissions from fossil fuel burning to produce electricity. Congress actually listed all the electrical generation facilities in the United States in the Clean Air Act, and then allowed them to sell emission rights. Companies in the East and Northeast sold their emission rights to companies with aging factories in the Midwest. This meant that these factories acquired an administrative "right to pollute," and did not have to cut back on their emissions of precursors of acid rain beyond a modest cap provided in the Act. This has frozen acid rain reduction and continues to cause deterioration of forests, historic, cultural, and other structures in the Northeast of the United States and Canada. In their enthusiasm to create an innovative economic model of an air emissions trading system, the economists failed to build the correct ecological model for the trading, and have produced a system that permits a harmful level of acid deposition as legally acceptable "externalities." This sours the public of the Northeast on any further trading as a matter of policy, and shows that this economic tool must be firmly grounded in science if it is to be effective in economics. Nature is the world in which the economy operates, not the other way around.

The air in most of the United States has gradually been cleaned up, while the economic growth of the nation has continued. By obliging enterprises to develop new, cleaner technologies, the United States has seen its industry innovate and compete more effectively with its renewed technological base.[39] The Directives and Regulations of the European Community have induced a similar Pan-European system of air pollution controls at the national level. Rigorous air pollution control systems in Germany and other states have achieved abatement of pollutants in ways that are analogous to those in the United States. There has been much slower air pollution control in Mexico and in many other regions of the world. It is time for states to adopt one international standard approach to air pollution to secure breathable air for their citizens. The elements of such as standard approach can be outlined briefly.

5 ELEMENTS OF AN EFFECTIVE AIR POLLUTION REGIME

Every legal system has within its fundamental principles a basis for protecting the air. This is true of the Islamic tradition, based on the Holy Qu'ran. It is so in the civil law and in the common law. It exists in socialist law fundamentals and even in the customary law. From these common yet diverse legal roots, a common approach to air pollution has been emerging. The industrial sources of air pollution are similar in all nations, and arise from comparable human activities and uses of the same technologies. The chemicals, human health impacts, and adverse effects on nature are the same in each nation.

---

[37] Id. § 173. *See Chevron v. NRDC*, (D.C. Cir Ct. of Appeals, 1984).
[38] Clean Air Act §§ 401 et seq. added in 1990 by Public Law 101–549.
[39] Kennedy, *The Wealth of Nations*, argues that Congress' measures to "force" industry to retool are one of the reasons why the industrial foundation of the United States is more robust than other regions where industry has not had to reinvent its systems of manufacturing.

Abatement of air pollution, like the practice of medicine, must be addressed based on the same knowledge and techniques in each country. There is neither a north/south divide nor a developed/developing nation divide on these issues; there is only the question of whether each nation takes the requisite measures to secure clean air for its people and its neighboring states. States can do this most efficiently by embracing a common approach to build interrelated and comparable administrative law systems.

Each nation's administrative law needs to address essentially six aspects of air pollution. Air pollution monitoring and assessment is needed in order to determine how widespread and severe are the adverse impacts of health from gaseous emissions from different sources. In order to assess the nature of its air quality problems, each nation must establish and maintain a comprehensive system of air pollution sampling and monitoring and assessment facilities. Each nation also needs to share this data internationally. Beyond these common, scientific activities, each nation then needs to determine how its own differentiated air pollution conditions can be most effectively addressed with the governmental and scientific resources at hand. These national responses constitute the common but differentiated responsibilities each state has to meet to combat air pollution.

Although the remedies for controlling each source of air pollution may tend to be different in different places, there are nonetheless some general approaches that can be briefly noted. Air pollution control regimes should commonly address these issues:

Electrical generating facilities. Cost-effective use of all electricity energy efficiency standards for the design and use of appliances, building standards for the construction and retrofitting of all structures, and energy conservation through pricing mechanisms, need to be a part of all national regimes for energy.[40] The Johannesburg Plan of Implementation, adopted at the UN World Summit for Sustainable Development, has called upon all governments to integrate energy efficiency considerations into all aspects of energy supply and demand, including the "planning, operation and maintenance of long-lived energy consuming infrastructures."[41] States need to enact legislation to manage the demand for electricity, and to ensure that it is used efficiently. This is called "demand side management" (DSM). Most nations do not have laws for DSM at present, and address solely the production of electricity. Both supply and demand must be managed if air pollution is to be abated.

Uses of hydroelectric and geothermal energy sources produce little air pollution. Use of nuclear energy produces air pollution in the fuel cycle of mining and processing uranium. The major sources of air pollution from generation of electricity come from burning coal, oil, and natural gas. Natural gas is increasingly used as a fuel for motor vehicles, to secure cleaner urban air conditions, and needs to be conserved for that purpose, and for generating electricity in and around urban concentrations where cleaner air and electricity are needed. While oil is abundant at present, in the future it too will need to be conserved – rather than burned – for use in petrochemical industries. Coal, while abundant, has been long recognized as a major source of air pollution, and a source of greenhouse gases when burned. Use of oil and coal must be accompanied by technologies to remove the sulfur and other polluting substances.

---

[40] *See* Richard L. Ottinger et al., *The Environmental Costs of Electricity* (Oceana Publications, Dobbs Ferry, NY).

[41] UN Johannesburg Plan of Implementation, Paragraph 20, UN Doc A/CONF.199/20.

The environmental laws for such facilities require use of an environmental impact assessment (EIA) for the siting of new facilities and their distribution grids, construction permits to ensure that the plants are built in such a way as to minimize air pollution, and operating permits to ensure that the plants do operate as intended. Operating permits need to be renewed periodically, with a full reassessment of their air pollution impacts and identification of ways to enhance prevention of air pollution. Energy waste needs to be avoided through the use of advanced industrial ecology designs, recycling, and reusing waste heat. The choice of fuels must minimize air pollution impacts, and process design or end of pipe technologies that eliminate air pollution need to be mandated for each fuel used. Nations need to strengthen their EIA laws to address how electricity is produced, distributed, and used. Since most nations have enacted laws for EIA, they should apply these laws to explore and develop their demand side management systems.

Industrial Fuels. The same regimes for electrical generating facilities need to be applied to factories. Industrial technologies exist for identifying and abating most sources of industrial pollution. The U.S. Clean Air Act required the Environmental Protection Agency to determine the applicable state of the air pollution control technologies for every type of manufacturing sector and to set a technology standard for new sources of air pollution. These technological assessments are public documents and could be used in every nation to ensure that the public is protected by the readily available technologies.[42] The use of these systems saves energy, in the long run saves expenses, and helps to modernize a nation's manufacturing sector making it more competitive. Nations need to adopt the prevailing advanced legal requirements, usually European Union or U.S. Clean Air Act standards, rather than waiting to "reinvent the wheel" by coming up with their own standards independently.

Motor Vehicle Pollution. Trucks, automobiles, aircraft, railroad engines, and ships contribute a vast amount of air pollution. They require technological improvements in their design, an induced retirement and recycling of polluting vehicles, and regulations governing use in order to ensure that they do not exacerbate urban air pollution.

Technology forcing will be needed, both within nations and internationally, to promote the use of alternative fuel vehicles. In urban centers, laws already require the purchasing of buses, refuse trucks, taxis, and other fleets of vehicles to burn natural gas. Use of diesel vehicles are being phased out. Older, more polluting vehicles are being retired and recycled. These sorts of measures need to be expanded.

Design and use criteria need to be applied to ships and railroads. Ship engines can be regulated to minimize their burning of fuel while in port. Redesign of engines in newer ships will need to be specified.

The 1990 amendments to the U.S. Clean Air Act required federal agencies to develop low or no emission technology, such as motor vehicles powered by hydrogen fuel cells.[43] Progress has been made toward developing a "mass-producible, cost-effective hydrogen fuel cell vehicle," as the Act requires. This progress has been promoted also by the Energy Policy Act of 1992,[44] which requires the government to buy for fleets of motor vehicles some fueled by alternative fuels other than gasoline. The Hydrogen Research Act of

---

[42] New Source Performance Standards, 1970 Clean Air Act § 111.
[43] §§ 241, 807. The clear alternative fuels are defined to include hydrogen.
[44] 42 U.S.C. § 13,201; Pub. L. 102–486, 106 Stat. 2276 (1992).

1990[45] and the Hydrogen Future Act of 1996,[46] have also accelerated development of fuel cell technology for motor vehicles. BP now has a demonstration in four nations to show how hydrogen fuel cell vehicles can be serviced and supported; as the systems for producing hydrogen fuels for serving motor vehicles are installed, major efficiencies in both air pollution and the elimination of greenhouse gas emissions can be achieved.[47] In order to take advantage of this new technology, nations other than the United States will need to amend their laws to require the early retirement of polluting vehicles and mandate use of these new clean vehicles. Too often, developing nations allow imports of obsolete technology (used cars) instead of requiring dealers in motor vehicles to provide these state of the art systems.

Natural Resource Extraction. Mining and oil and gas extraction from the Earth have attendant pollution. Much of it can be easily eliminated, such as recapturing and selling the natural gas that is now flared. Mining of gravel and cement can cause substantial dust, and needs to be undertaken with mitigating technologies in full use.

Agriculture production can use energy in polluting ways, as in the production of fertilizers and their uses. Dust generation and other potential air pollution problems require use of best management practices, training to promote their use, and economic incentives to promote their implementation. These sorts of reforms are needed for all other areas of natural resource use. Each can incrementally contribute to air pollution.

Biomass Burning. Natural biomass burning, such as forest fires caused by lightning, is being overwhelmed by human-induced burning. This includes the clearing of forests by farmers in Meso America and southern Africa, by palm oil plantation entrepreneurs in Indonesia, and by carelessness in human-made forest fires in all regions. Forest fire monitoring and assessment systems are needed in much of the world; fire fighting systems need to be developed and deployed, with agreements to share expertise and fire fighting services across nations in different regions. Mutual aid is an important dimension of combating fires, and agreements to that end need to be undertaken among nations.

Deliberate burning of biomass for fuel needs to be carefully regulated to avoid or avert pollution. Burning of waste needs to be replaced by recycling and reuse systems, often economically subsidized initially to convert wasteful social patterns into routine recycling systems. Legal frameworks to facilitate the use of economic incentives are important in this regard.

Indoor Air Pollution. The WHO's campaign to end smoking of tobacco needs to be fully embraced. Because "secondhand smoke" has health effects in nonsmokers, the prohibition of smoking in restaurants and other public places is important. The venting of this smoke, from transitional areas where smoking is still allowed, into the ambient environment is becoming a source of air pollution, albeit on a small scale. The use of polluting indoor heating fuels can have acute health impacts, and these fuels need to be replaced with nonpolluting energy systems for household use. Improvement of indoor

---

[45] 42 U.S.C. § 12,401; Pub. L. 101–566; 104 Stat. 2797 (1990).

[46] 42 U.S.C. § 7238; Pub. L. 104–271; 110 Stat. 3304 (1996).

[47] *See* "The Future of DOE's Automotive Research Programs," Hearings Before the Committee on Science, U.S. House of Representatives," available at www.house.gov/science; "The Drive for a Cleaner Car," (California Air Resources Board and Detroit News Research), *The Detroit News*, Autos Insider, January 6, 2003, available at http://www.detnews.com/2003/autosinsider/0301/06/do6-52378.htm.

air is also important symbolically to show that the air pollution controls cover the whole of the society, and are not limited to select sectors.

6 THE COMMON BUT DIFFERENTIATED RESPONSES OF THE LAW

If a nation is to be deemed to be observant of its duties under international law to protect the air quality found within its territory, then at a minimum its legal and administrative framework should address several common elements. How each nation does so will be differentiated by its geographic location, the types of fuels produced or consumed, and the ambient environmental conditions. The following characteristics should be found in each nation if it is to be deemed to be coping with its air pollution challenges:

Framework Law. A nation needs to set forth a basic "umbrella" law for restoring and maintaining healthy air. It needs to set the basic policies for the state, and to link the several sectors that are important in combating air pollution.[48] This law needs to adopt health-based standards for defining the quality of air. It needs to promote energy efficiency, and implement the Johannesburg Plan of Implementation's recommendation "to develop and disseminate alternative energy technologies with the aim of giving a greater share of the energy mix to renewable energies, improving energy efficiency and greater reliance on advanced energy technologies, including cleaner fossil fuel technologies."[49]

EIA. Over 120 States have already adopted environmental impact assessment, and the UN Rio Declaration has called for its use in all nations.[50] Since air pollution comes from many sources, and the conditions for the siting of new developments are key to avoiding new air pollution, it is necessary to use EIA. Only by examining in each and every development decision how to avoid exacerbating the release of greenhouse gases can emissions be controlled. The EIA system is the only comprehensive legal tool with the flexibility to examine all decision making. Only EIA can look at cumulative and induced impacts of an action on air pollution or climate change. EIA needs to be used far more extensively and effectively than at present, and this requires capacity building and training of personnel on how to use EIA. Too often economic development interests seek to avoid EIA.

Technology Forcing. There is a lag in the transfer of advanced pollution control technology from one nation to another. Many multinational companies already harmonize their conduct by using systems that avoid air pollution, but regional and local companies will do so only when required. States need to identify the publicly available state-of-the-art technologies and require their use by all private and government facilities. Technology forcing can be used locally in this way, as well as inducing creation of new and innovative technologies locally that can be of value more broadly. At a minimum, nations should use as a default system the more advanced technology standards in place in states such as California or nations such as The Netherlands.

Regional Cooperation Mechanisms. Air pollution is not an isolated, national legal undertaking, as the air is mobile and biospheric. Air must be regarded as a shared

---

[48] The EU and U.S. health standards are being generically reviewed by the WHO to prepare a global set of standards. In the meantime, the U.S. primary ambient air quality standards or the WHO Air Quality Guidelines for Europe may be used in other regions.

[49] UN Johannesburg Plan of Implementation, Paragraph 20(c), UN DOC. A/CONF.199/20.

[50] Principle 17, Declaration of Rio de Janeiro on Environment and Development, 1992.

resource. This means that nations must establish intermunicipal cooperation within nations, and interregional cooperation among nations, to combat air pollution. Active participation in the international organizations that combat air pollution, such as WHO and UNEP, is essential, and this can often be done through regional networks of states and their air pollution control agencies.

Continuing Review and Assessment. Executive and legislative systems need to provide support for monitoring and exchange of information on ambient air pollution conditions, and to provide for continuous training and education. This is a requirement in the U.S. Clean Air Act for each State Implementation Plan (SIP),[51] and should be standard operating procedure worldwide. Too often, this basic requirement is overlooked.

Support for the Judiciary. Nations must provide adequate resources to their courts and a legal foundation for the courts to ensure that air pollution laws are treated as a fundamental duty within each nation. Where the rule of law is weak, there will be a weak observance of air pollution laws. States need to recognize that access to justice is essential for environmental protection.

7 CONCLUSIONS

Air pollution is a serious and present threat to human health, as well as to economic and social development. No society can sustain its economic and social advances if its people are sick from air pollution–induced health problems. Laws for controlling air pollution also provide perhaps the most immediately effective means available for combating the greenhouse gas emissions that cause climate change on a global basis.

Because air pollution is not under control in many nations, the current phase of national and international air pollution law must be deemed to be still in its infancy, or at most adolescence. Legal responses remain fragmented and inadequate. Nations need to harmonize their approaches to the control of polluting technological systems and apply common management tools. The sooner states devote educational, managerial, scientific, and legal resources to this coming legal evolution, the sooner we shall pass from a world that suffers air pollution to a world than contains or averts it. The national air pollution control laws are a foundation for sustainable development and a necessary premise for securing the public health and the individual's right to breathe fresh air. Because nations have at least some experience in combating harmful emissions into the atmosphere, the world's air pollution laws also provide a way forward toward implementing ways to reduce greenhouse gas emissions. For this reason, properly conceived, air pollution laws are one foundation for an effective and sustainable energy law regime.

---

[51] Clean Air Act § 110.

9 Green Pricing and Green Power Marketing: Demand-Side Mechanisms for Promoting "Green Power" in Deregulated Electricity Markets

Alexandra S. Wawryk*

1 INTRODUCTION

The production and use of electricity generated by fossil fuels is one of the most environmentally damaging human activities on this planet. It is generally acknowledged that increasing the share of electricity generated by renewable energy is vital for reducing the environmental impacts of electricity generated by fossil fuels and achieving sustainable development. Protection of the environment is a key reason for the introduction of government policies encouraging the development of renewable energy through mechanisms such as tax and other financial incentives and the mandatory purchasing by electric utilities of electricity generated from renewable energy sources in developed countries since the 1970s.

More recently, the deregulation and/or privatization of energy markets in many countries, including the United States, United Kingdom, Canada, Australia, various European countries, and the countries of Latin America, has led to concerns about the future of renewable energy resources in the generation of electricity. As utilities in competitive electricity markets become more efficient, reduce costs, and charge lower electricity prices, it is feared that renewable energy sources, which are generally higher cost options for producing electricity, will find it increasingly difficult to penetrate electric power markets.

While proponents of renewable energy have pressed for government support of renewable energy to continue in competitive electricity markets, the suitability of applying policies for promoting renewables in regulated electricity markets to deregulated markets has been questioned.[1] As a result, governments have turned their attention to the most appropriate methods for promoting the supply of electricity from renewable energy sources or "green power" in competitive electricity markets. A number of mechanisms have been proposed and/or adopted, including both "supply-side" and "demand-side" mechanisms.

Supply-side mechanisms target the producers or generators of green power. The most popular type of supply-side mechanism is the renewable portfolio standard operating in conjunction with tradeable green certificates, whereby electricity wholesalers and/or retailers meet government requirements to acquire a certain amount or percentage of their

[1] Energy Information Administration, *Challenges of Electric Power Restructuring for Fuel Suppliers*, September 1998, http://www.eia.doe.gov.

* Lecturer in Law, University of Adelaide, Australia.

electricity from green power by generating or purchasing green power, or by purchasing green certificates issued by renewable energy generators. In contrast, demand-side mechanisms aim to increase the uptake of green power through increasing consumer demand for green power products. The demand-side mechanisms that have been most enthusiastically adopted by electricity companies are green pricing schemes and green power marketing schemes, and it is these mechanisms that are the subject of this chapter.

The structure of this chapter is as follows. Section 2 defines the key terms and concepts of green power, green pricing, and green power marketing. Section 3 describes the main features of green pricing and green power marketing mechanisms adopted in various jurisdictions that have deregulated their electricity industries, namely California in the United States, Alberta in Canada, and Australia, and the key legislation relating to these schemes. Section 4 summarizes the strengths and limitations of green pricing and green power marketing schemes, while Section 5 addresses the role of the law and sets out minimum legislative requirements for the successful operation of these schemes.

2 GREEN POWER, GREEN PRICING, AND GREEN POWER MARKETING

2.1 Green Power

Green power is "electricity generated from renewable energy sources, that mitigates climate change by producing few or no greenhouse gas emissions."[2] While there is no standard classification of the "renewable energy sources" that are green power sources, the generation of electricity is generally required to have a minimal impact on: local and regional air quality; water quality; watersheds, river systems and fisheries; flora and fauna; geophysical features; noise; visual aesthetics; and any additional buildup of hazardous or toxic waste. Some definitions of green power require specific environmental performance criteria such as pollutant emission limits to be met before the electricity product is certified as green power, for example the revised Canadian Environmental Choice Program guidelines, but others do not.

Examples of specific technologies and resources that are generally classified as green power sources include: solar energy (photovoltaics and thermal electric generators); wind energy; small hydroelectric facilities, such as run-of-the-river hydro facilities; biomass; geothermal heat and power; wave and freestream tidal power stations and water velocity turbines; and other technologies that use media such as hydrogen, compressed air or fuel cells to control, store, and/or convert renewable energy sources.

The production of power from large-scale hydroelectric power plants and nuclear plants is not considered to be green power, as these energy sources create significant environmental problems elsewhere in the ecosystem. Power produced from fossil fuels is generally not considered to be green power, although "superefficient" technologies such as fuel cells, which can be seen as clean power sources, have been classified as a

---

[2] M. Raynolds and A. Pape, *The Pembina Institute Green Power Guidelines for Canada*, Pembina Institute for Appropriate Development, July 2000, http://www.pembina.org at 4.

source of green power. Electricity sourced from natural gas cogeneration is not classified as green power.

2.2 Green Pricing

Green pricing is an optional utility service that enables customers to support a greater level of utility investment in renewable energy technologies. Under green pricing programs, consumers voluntarily choose to pay a premium above the "normal" price for electricity, which is used by their supplier toward the additional costs of investing in renewable energy technologies. As of January 2002, more than sixty-four utilities in the United States had developed or announced intentions to develop green pricing programs, with customer participation in the programs resulting in an installation of nearly 220 MW of new renewable resources and plans for installing another 110 MW.[3] Green pricing is also available in the deregulated electricity industries in the UK, the province of Alberta in Canada, and in Australia.

There is no definitive classification of the existing types of green pricing programs. Wiser, Bolinger, and Holt identify four general types of programs, which differ in the ability of customers to substitute an amount of green power for a utility's standard resource mix.[4] The first of these are *contribution programs* or *renewable energy contribution funds*, under which customers contribute to a utility-managed fund for renewable project development, but do not receive any part of their electricity directly as green power. The second type is an *energy tariff*, where the electricity supplier charges a c/KWh premium based on a specific amount of energy delivered to the grid. These may be sold in energy blocks (e.g., 100kWh of wind energy) or as a percentage of customer use (e.g., fifty percent renewable energy).

The third type of green pricing scheme is a *capacity tariff*, whereby utilities fund the development of a specific amount of installed renewable capacity by charging consumers a premium based on the number of capacity blocks they wish to reserve. This type of scheme has also been described as a "tailored renewable energy project," where a utility identifies a particular renewables project for which it solicits contributions and, after receiving a minimum number of subscriptions, the utility builds the project with the subscribers receiving energy from the new facility.[5] Fourth, *finance programs* involve the payment of monthly payments by consumers to lease or finance and install customer-sited photovoltaic systems.

While there are a number of different green pricing schemes, an essential and common element of all these programs is the existence of nonmandatory and/or legislative certification or eco-labeling schemes to protect electricity consumers from fraudulent suppliers who offer electricity that is described as green, but which is in fact sourced from fossil fuels. As will be seen in Section 3, consumer protection mechanisms are a vital part of green pricing schemes in all countries.

---

[3] L. Bird and B. Swezey, "Estimates of Renewable Energy Developed to Serve Green Power Markets," National Renewable Energy Laboratory, January 2002, http://www.eren.doe.gov/greenpower/new/gp/cap.shtml.

[4] R. Wiser, M. Bolinger, and E. Holt, *Customer Choice and Green Power Marketing: A Critical Review and Analysis of Experience to Date*, prepared for the ACEE Summer Study on Energy Efficiency in Buildings, August 2000, www.eren.doe.gov at 5.367–5.368.

[5] B. Swezey, "Utility Green Pricing Programs: Market Evolution or Devolution?" *Solar Today*, January/February 1997 at 22.

2.3 Green Power Marketing

Green power marketing is the sale of green power directly to customers in competitive markets with multiple suppliers and service offerings. Green power marketing enables electricity suppliers in competitive markets to differentiate their service, as retail customers can choose their electricity supplier and therefore switch to suppliers that make green power available directly to them. As of June 2002, retail customers in the United States could purchase competitively marketed green power in the District of Columbia, Illinois, Maryland, New Jersey, New York, Pennsylvania, Texas, and Virginia.

3 EXAMPLES OF GREEN PRICING AND GREEN POWER MARKETING SCHEMES BY COUNTRY

3.1 United States – California Case Study

One of the key elements of reforming the electricity industry in the United States has been the introduction of competition into the retail sector of the electricity industry. As of August 2002, twenty-five states and the District of Columbia had passed laws or regulatory orders to implement retail competition. Of these twenty-five states, six have experienced a delay in the restructuring process, while in September 2001 California suspended its laws allowing consumers direct retail access following the energy crisis in that state. Twenty-six states are not undertaking restructuring activities.[6]

Because green pricing and green marketing programs operate at the retail level, state governments are responsible for promoting the consumption of green power through these schemes. In states where electricity markets have been deregulated, governments and electricity suppliers have generally embraced green pricing and green power marketing schemes as a low-cost mechanism for promoting renewable energy. There is also evidence that consumers are supporting green pricing and green power marketing programs in the United States. As of January 2002, across the United States, 650 MW of new renewable capacity had been installed to meet demand for green power, of which 220 MW was installed to meet utility green pricing programs and 430 MW to meet demand for green power under competitive green power marketing schemes. Plans to install a further 440 MW were either under way or had been formally announced, of which 110 MW is to be installed to meet utility green pricing programs and 330 MW is planned for installation under competitive green power marketing schemes.[7]

As it is beyond the scope of this chapter to compare the laws for the promotion of green power that have been adopted in all the states that have deregulated their electricity markets, we will examine the laws of California to provide an example of the legislation that has been introduced. California has been the leader in both electricity industry restructuring and also, historically, in the implementation of policies promoting renewable energy. In 1996, prior to deregulation of the state's electricity industry, California produced by far the largest share of nonutility renewable energy generation

---

[6] Energy Information Administration, *Status of State Electricity Industry Restructuring Activity as of August 2002*, http://www.eia.doe.gov/cneaf/electricity/chg str/regmap.html.

[7] Bird and Swezey, *supra* note 3.

in the US, accounting for 23% of all US nonutility renewable electricity produced in 1996, followed by New York with 5.1 percent.[8] Also, although green power marketing in California has collapsed since the summer of 2000, largely because of structural problems relating to electricity deregulation, some legislation enacted to deal with specific aspects of green power marketing and green pricing, such as consumer protection laws, provide useful examples of legislative approaches to green power.

On September 23, 1996, the Governor of California signed Assembly Bill 1890 into law, thereby establishing a four-year transition period to make the state's electricity industry competitive. On March 31, 1998, California became the first state to open its retail electricity market to competition. Multiple electricity suppliers, including privately owned utilities, cooperatively owned utilities, state publicly owned utilities, and independent power producers provide multiple service offerings.

After the implementation of retail competition, customers of the utilities switched to alternative suppliers marketing green energy. As of August 2000, a total of twenty-three companies had registered with the California Energy Commission as renewable electric service providers. Swezey and Bird report that after two years of competition, 2.2 percent of all eligible utility customers had actually switched electricity suppliers, comprising 1.8 percent of the utilities' residential customers, 4.1 percent of commercial customers, and about 20 percent of industrial customers. Of the 160,000 residential customers that changed suppliers, virtually all received green power.[9] The green power products offered by the marketers varied. Some companies offered multiple products containing anywhere between fifty to one hundred percent of "eligible" renewable energy content (as defined in §383.5 of the Public Utilities Code), as well as power from large hydro and natural gas. In 1998, the price premium charged by green power marketers ranged from 1.1¢/kWh to 2.5¢/kWh, although in 1999 state credits of 1.0¢/kWh reduced the price to consumers.[10]

Following the electricity shortage in the summer of 2000 and spiraling electricity prices, green power marketing collapsed in California, forcing residential consumers to switch back to utilities as their service providers. As five percent of the state's peak electricity load is under direct access contracts, mainly with industrial customers, in September 2001 the California Public Utilities Commission suspended direct retail access as a means of alleviating the electricity shortage. Green power marketers will continue to provide green power to their customers under contracts made prior to September 2001, until the contracts expire.[11]

Although direct access to green power retailers has been suspended, electricity consumers are able to purchase green power through the green pricing programs offered by utilities. As of July 2002, seven public utilities offered green pricing programs to their customers, sourcing electricity from various renewable energy facilities including

---

[8] Energy Information Administration, *supra* note 1 at 70–72.

[9] B. Swezey and L. Bird, *Green Power Marketing in the United States: A Status Report* (National Renewable Energy Laboratory, Colorado, 5th ed., August 2000), http://www.nrel.gov/analysis/emaa/brief_5.html, p. 9.

[10] *Id.*

[11] California Public Utilities Commission, *Interim Order Suspending Direct Access*, D0109060, September 20, 2001, as modified by D0110036, October 10, 2001; and *Opinion Rejecting an Earlier Date Than Sept. 20, 2001, for the Suspension of Direct Access, and Implementing the Suspension, as adopted In D.01-09-060, as Modified by D.01-10-036*, D0203055, March 21, 2002. CPUC Internet site, Official Documents, http://www.cpuc.ca.gov/static/official+ docs/index.htm.

geothermal, biomass, wind, landfill gas, small hydro and rooftop photovoltaic installa-tions, and charging price premiums ranging from 1¢/kWh to 3.0¢/kWh.[12]

The California government has instituted financial and legal mechanisms to support green power. First, the Consumer Credit Account, created by the government in 1997, is a financial mechanism by which the California government supports green power marketing.[13] It contains $75.6 million to be used for customer rebates for the purchase of electricity produced by renewable energy (Public Utilities Code §383.5(e)(1)). Eligible consumers of electricity automatically receive a credit of up to 1.0¢kWh on their electricity bill for renewable electricity consumed. To be eligible for the credit, consumers must have switched from the utilities California Edison, Pacific Gas and Electric Company, San Diego Gas and Electric, or the Bear Valley Electric Company to a renewable energy provider that has been registered by the California Energy Commission (CEC). The renewable energy must be produced in California and not be utility-owned. Customers switching to registered providers receive the electric service from the utility, but the payments spent on electricity supported the energy sources of the customer's choice.

Second, in order to minimize the possibility of fraudulent claims by green marketers and other electricity suppliers regarding the supply of green power, in September 1997 the Californian legislature enacted Senate Bill 1305 to amend the Public Utilities Code to require retail suppliers of electricity to disclose the sources of generation to customers. Section 398.4 of the Public Utilities Code requires every retail supplier that makes an offering to sell electricity that is consumed in California to disclose its electricity sources to potential end-use consumers in all product-specific written promotional materials distributed to customers by printed or electronic means, excepting advertisements and notices in general circulation media. Electric service providers must also provide quarterly disclosure statements to their end-use customers who have purchased electricity (§398.4(c)).

The legislation distinguishes between "net system power," the source of which may not be traceable to individual generating facilities, as it is supplied to consumers from the power exchange or power pool, and "specific purchases," which refer to purchases of electricity that are traceable by an "auditable contract trail" to specific generation plants. Under the legislation, electric service providers must claim their electricity source to be either net system power or specific purchases. Section 398.4(g) requires electric service providers to disclose their net system power and specific purchases to end-use customers, expressed as a percentage of annual sales. For each of these two categories, electric service providers must further disclose, as a percentage of annual sales, the electricity that is derived from the following sources: coal, large hydroelectric, natural gas, nuclear, and eligible renewables. The information concerning renewables must be further classified into the percentage of annual sales derived from biomass and waste, geothermal, small hydroelectric, solar, and wind power (§398.4(h)). Retail suppliers must also disclose their projected specific purchases for the current year (§398.5(a)).

---

[12] The Green Power Network, "Summary of Green Power Programs," United States Department of Energy http://www.eren.doe/ greenpower/summary.shtml, July 2002.

[13] Assembly Bill 1890 of September 1996 amended the Public Utilities Code to establish a $540 million public benefits fund for renewable energy technologies, to be collected over 4 years. Senate Bill 90 of 1997 provides administrative guidelines for the fund. The program has since been extended through to January 1, 2012 (SB 1194 and AB 995).

For renewables, this may be expressed as the total eligible renewables and not broken down into subcategories.

Section 398.3 requires generators that report meter data to a system operator to report quarterly to the system operator on the amount of electricity generated in kWh, the fuel type(s) and fuel consumption by fuel by month. The system operator will make the information available to the CEC. Generators that do not report to system operators but claim specific purchases must report this information directly to the CEC. The legislation also requires retail suppliers that disclose specific purchases to annually report the following information to the CEC: the kWh purchased, by generator and fuel type during the previous calendar year, consistent with the meter data, including losses, reported to the system operator; the kWh sold at retail for each electricity offering; and, for each electricity offering, the disclosures made to consumers pursuant to §398.4 (§398.5). The information obtained by the Energy Commission is used to verify information disclosed to consumers and to calculate net system power.

SB 1305 required the CEC to specify guidelines for the format and means of disclosure to consumers under the Public Utilities Code. The Energy Commission has developed a Power Content Label as the mechanism for disclosure. The Label lists the different energy sources that can be used to generate electricity, shows the retail supplier's expected percentage of annual electricity sales derived from each energy source, and compares this with the power mix from the power exchange.

In addition to the legislative requirements, in November 1997 a nonprofit organization called the Center for Resource Solutions (CRS) established a voluntary certification procedure in California, called the "Green-e Renewable Electricity Certification Program." Various criteria must be fulfilled in order for an electric service provider to use the trademarked Green-e logo.[14] First, the electricity product offered by the supplier must meet various criteria, including the following: at least fifty percent of the electricity supply for the product must be generated from renewable energy resources (solar, hydro, wind, biomass, and geothermal); the fossil fuel portion, if any, of the product must have equal or lower air emissions than an equivalent amount of system power; and one year after deregulation of a state's electricity industry, the product must contain at least five percent "new" renewable electricity, a percentage which increases each year until twenty-five percent of the product content is from new renewable sources.

Second, companies must undertake certain activities to obtain Green-e certification. Companies participating in the program must: sign an application including a six-page contract containing a Code of Conduct and a legal affidavit on the resource mix of the electricity product for which certification is sought; provide all potential customers with a one-page summary of the contract information using a standardised Green-e format; provide a disclosure statement to potential customers listing the resources from which the green power is generated, using a standardised Green-e label; and provide customers with an annual disclosure of the fuel mix used in the past year to generate the electricity purchased by the customer.

Companies must also undergo, at their own expense, annual third party verification of contracts, meter data, billing statements, and any other records necessary to substantiate the electricity mix and air emission content required for certification. Finally,

---

[14] Center for Resource Solutions, "Introduction to Green-e," "Information for Power Providers" and "Certification Requirements," http://www.green-e.org.

companies must agree to abide by the Green-e Code of Conduct, which contains general ethical guidelines that must be obeyed by the company. Companies undergo a biannual review by CRS staff to ensure they are abiding by the Code of Conduct. Members that do not adhere to the Code lose the right to use the logo for eighteen months on any of their products.

3.2 Alberta, Canada

Under Canada's Constitution, electricity is primarily within the jurisdiction of the provinces, with the bulk of generation, transmission, and distribution provided by a few dominant utilities. While several provinces are now beginning to deregulate their electricity sectors, Alberta has been the leader in electricity industry restructuring in Canada. The deregulation and privatization of Alberta's electricity industry has occurred pursuant to the Electric Utilities Act of 1995 and the Electric Utilities Amendment Act of 1998. On January 1, 2001, Alberta became the first Canadian province to open its retail electricity market to competition and allow consumers to choose their electricity supplier.

Retailers in Alberta began offering green power packages to consumers in the year 2000. Of those companies providing retail services, EPCOR (retail affiliate of the City of Edmonton) and ENMAX Corporation (retail affiliate of the City of Calgary) are leaders in the provision of green power products to electricity consumers. The two main green power offerings are ENMAX's product "Greenmax" and EPCOR's product "Eco-Packs."[15]

ENMAX began offering Greenmax in 1998. The primary source of green energy supplied under Greenmax is wind energy, purchased from wind energy supplier Vision Quest Windelectric Inc. Residential consumers may choose a monthly premium of $5, $10, or $15 to purchase electricity produced from wind energy. Customers with average monthly energy consumption paying $15 per month would receive about forty-two percent of their power from wind energy. In November 2000, after energy from an initial two wind turbines had become fully subscribed, Enmax contracted with Vision Quest to install two more wind turbines. In May 2000 Enmax contracted with Vision Quest to install sixteen, 660-kW wind turbines by October 2001, to secure an additional 30,000 MW of electricity.

EPCOR began offering its EcoPack in July 1999. Renewable sources include biomass, run-of-the-river hydro, solar photovoltaics, and wind energy. Customers can choose to purchase ten, twenty, fifty, or one hundred percent of their power from renewable sources. Price premiums range from an extra C$5 per month for the ten percent option, to C$40 (approximately US$26.00) per month for the one hundred percent option (or approximately US$3.20 to US$26.00, based on an exchange rate of C$1 = US$0.641891). Based on an average use of 550 kWh per month, this translates to a premium of about C9¢/kWh (US5.7¢/kWh) per month under the ten percent option, and C7¢/kWh (US4.4¢/kWh) per month under the one hundred percent option.

In Alberta, green pricing premiums serve two uses. First, the premium ensures that electricity produced from renewable sources is purchased and dispatched to the Alberta

---

[15] Information on ENMAX's Greenmax product and EPCOR's Eco-Pack offering is available from the companies' Web sites, http://www.enmax.com and http://www.epcor-group.com.

Power Pool. Second, in Canada, the premiums also buy green power customers greenhouse gas "emission reduction credits" (ERCs). When green power customers demand electricity from renewable energy sources, this displaces electricity produced from fossil fuels, thereby reducing air pollution. ERCs, which are measured in terms of kilograms or tonnes of carbon dioxide equivalent, are used by consumers of electricity to offset their own carbon dioxide emissions from industrial plants, automobiles, and household use. In Canada, ERCs are reported in annual updates to the Voluntary Challenge Registry, which forms part of the country's national strategy for reducing greenhouse gases.

Green power schemes in Alberta are monitored by the national organization Environment Canada. Environment Canada's Environmental Choice ^{M} Program (ECP), established in 1988, is a national eco-labeling program for a range of products and services. The ECP has provided a certification process for distributors and generators of electricity, with the official symbol of certification known as the EcoLogo ^{M}, since 1996. Certification is based on compliance with environmental criteria established by Environment Canada. To obtain certification, companies must submit to independent third party verification of the company's compliance with the established environmental criteria. Auditing and verification for the scheme is conducted by TerraChoice Environmental Services Inc, an environmental program and consulting services firm.

With respect to electricity products, the ECP certifies "alternative source electricity distribution and generation."[16] As regards alternative source electricity generation, the ECP has established general certification criteria that apply to all relevant renewable energy facilities (solar, wind, hydro, biomass, biogas, and geothermal technologies) as well as environmental criteria specific to generation from each particular renewable energy type. The general criteria are:

- the facility must be operating, reliable, nontemporary and practical;
- during project planning and development, appropriate consultation with communities and stakeholders must have occurred, and prior or conflicting land use, biodiversity losses, and scenic, recreational, and cultural values must have been addressed;
- no adverse impacts can be created for any species recognized as endangered or threatened;
- supplementary nonrenewable fuels must not be used in more than two percent of the fuel heat input required for generation; and
- sales levels of ECP-certified electricity must not exceed production/supply levels.

The technology specific criteria for generation obviously vary between technologies, but include, for example, the proper disposal or recycling of cadmium wastes for solar energy producers, the protection of birds for wind energy producers, and maximum levels of air emissions for producers of energy from biomass.

Certification for alternative source electricity distribution requires the following conditions to be met: only components of a multisourced power product that fully satisfy all pertinent ECP criteria for generators can be identified as ECP-certified; sales levels of ECP-certified electricity must not exceed production/supply levels; and a criteria statement must appear with the EcoLogo. As of August 2002, thirty-one companies generating electricity and five companies providing electricity distribution services in

---

[16] Environment Canada Environmental Choice Program, "Browse a Product Category – Alternative Source Electricity and Generation," http://www.environmentalchoice.com/index_main.cfm.

Canada were listed on the ECP Internet site as offering certified products. In Alberta, both ENMAX's Greenmax product and EPCOR's Eco-Packs are certified as alternative source electricity distribution products under the ECP scheme, with their energy suppliers such as Vision Quest Windelectric Inc. being certified generators under the scheme.

Additional protection against fraudulent suppliers is supplied by legislation. The Electricity Marketing Regulation (AR 109/2000), made under the Fair Trading Act 1999 (FTA), requires retailers who offer electricity services to home, farm and smaller industrial and commercial consumers to hold a "marketing of electricity business licence" in order to engage in the marketing of electricity. As well as licensing requirements for electricity marketers, the Regulations: lay down duties with respect to documentation; set out requirements with respect to the terms of contracts between retailers and consumers; set out requirements for the provision of disclosure statements to consumers that must be signed before the consumer enters a contract; and contain a code of conduct for retailers. While the Regulations do not contain any provisions specifically aimed at preventing fraud with respect to the provision of green power, the code of conduct for retailers in Regulation 13 covers this type of behavior. Some parts of the code that may be relevant to misrepresentations about green power supply include the following provisions of Regulation 13(2):

(b) a marketer must not abuse the trust of a consumer or exploit any fear or lack of experience or knowledge of a consumer;

(d) a marketer must not make any representation or statement or give any answer or take any measure that is not true or is likely to mislead a consumer;

(g) a marketer must ensure that all descriptions and promises made in promotional material are in accordance with actual conditions, situations and circumstances existing at the time the description or promise is made;

(h) a marketer must ensure that all data the marketer refers to is properly established and reliable and supports any claim for which the data is cited;

(k) a marketer must not make any representation that savings, price benefits or advantages exist if they do not exist or if there is no evidence to substantiate the representation.

Regulation 13(3) provides that the code is breached if the breach occurs "in the course of inducing a person to enter into a marketing contract, even though the marketing contract is not entered into or is not completed." A contravention of Regulation 13 is an offense for the purpose of §162 of the Fair Trading Act (Regulation 15). Section 164 of the FTA sets out the penalty for convention of an offense, which is: a fine of not more than $100 000, or three times the amount obtained by the defendant as a result of the offense, whichever is greater; or imprisonment for not more than two years; or both.

Unlike California, there is no legislative provision that makes specific provision for the supply of information regarding renewable energy sources to consumers. The Electric Utilities Act §31.992(2)(a) provides that after December 31, 2000, retailers must maintain records and accounts relating to customers of the retailer respecting the provision of electricity services. Under Regulation 16(2)(a) of the Roles, Relationship and Responsibilities Regulation (AR 86/2000) the duty to maintain records and accounts extends to billing. Although Regulation 4 of the Billing Regulation (AR 290/99) sets out certain specified information that must be included in an account, this does not include separate details about the green pricing or green marketing programs.

However, Regulation 16(4) of the Roles, Relationship and Responsibilities Regulation (AR 86/2000) states that retailers must provide: (a) to the Minister, or (b) to the person holding the office of Executive Director of the Electricity Branch of the Department of Resource Development or a successor office, the information requested by that individual. In practice, this means that all retailers must register with Alberta Energy to enable Alberta Energy to monitor the development of the market and ensure that retailer information is posted on a "Customer Choice" Internet site (http://www.customerchoice.gov.ab.ca), which provides consumers with information about the electricity industry and retail suppliers.

3.3 Australia

In Australia, regulation of the retail sector of the electricity industry in each state is within the jurisdiction of the state governments, which have been keen to adopt green power policies to stimulate the growth of the renewable energy industry. Green pricing programs are available in all the Australian states and territories, although the price premiums for green pricing programs and the renewables mix differ between states and companies. In South Australia, the electricity retailer AGL offers a green power product called "AGL Green Energy." As of August 20, 2002, the product was based on biomass (89.7%), wind (6.8%), and solar (3.5%), and price premiums were: 0.55¢kWh for 10% Green Energy; 1.1¢/kWh for 25% Green Energy; 2.2¢/kWh for 50% Green Energy; and 4.4 ¢/kWh for 100% Green Energy.[17]

There is evidence that Australian consumers are supporting green pricing programs. As of June 30, 2002, there were sixteen retailers offering accredited products to ninety-six percent of all Australian residents, and about 67,000 customers had signed up to a green power product.[18] Total green power sales increased from 290,355 MWh in 1999/2000 to 454,505MWh in 2000/2001. Over the period 2000–2001, seventy-two percent of energy sold under the Green Power Program came from newly constructed generators.[19]

A major contribution toward the success of green power schemes by the governments of South Australia, New South Wales, Victoria, Queensland, and the ACT has been the establishment and operation of a joint accreditation program, called the "National Green Power Accreditation Program," which sets standards for green power and audits electricity retailers to ensure they are purchasing sufficient quantities of Green Power. In May 2000, the NSW Sustainable Energy Development Authority was appointed as the central program manager of the accreditation program and the Green Power Accreditation Steering Group was officially established.

For a company to sell an accredited Green Power product, it must satisfy a number of requirements outlined in the "Green Power Guarantee." The accreditation program

[17] AGL, "Green Energy," http://www.agl.com.au/AGL/Your+Home/ SA/Green+energy/default.htm.
[18] *National Green Power Accreditation Program, Quarterly Status Report – June 2002*, http://www. greenpower.com.au/go/download/1016407966 at 4.
[19] Sustainable Energy Development Authority, *National Green Power Audit* (March 2002), http://www. greenpower.com.au/go/download/1016407966 at 2.5 and 2.7.

uses a "government approved" green logo to certify that a retailer's green power product has met these requirements. To use the logo, an electricity company must:[20]

- use energy sources that are based primarily on a renewable energy resource and that result in greenhouse gas emissions reduction and net environmental benefit;
- source sixty percent of their green power from new renewable generators, defined as generators commissioned after January 1, 1997 – a percentage that increased to seventy in 2001 and eighty in 2002;
- submit monthly, quarterly, and annual reports to ensure that sufficient approved renewable energy is purchased to meet customer needs;
- place revenue from selling green power into a separate account that is independently audited;
- use green power account funds for the purchase of energy from renewable sources; and
- purchase green power themselves for their own electricity needs.

Regular reporting by energy suppliers allows SEDA to verify the compliance of green power products with the accreditation criteria. The monthly reports contain information on new, lost and current green power customers. Quarterly status reports provide a description of each green power product and customer numbers. Green energy purchases are given according to the type of renewable resource used, for both new and existing generators. The annual audit reports are technical and financial statements, which have been independently audited and then verified by SEDA. These provide detailed yearly summaries of green power product purchases, sales, customer numbers, and newly installed renewable generators.

Unlike California, in Australia there is no legislation addressing fraudulent claims by green power marketers, nor are there any legislative requirements regarding the disclosure of information regarding the electricity source mix to consumers. Similar to Alberta, each Australian state in the National Electricity Market has a retail code that regulates the sale and marketing of electricity to consumers but does not specifically address green power. However, the consumer protection provisions of the Trade Practices Act (Cth) 1974 will apply to contracts between electricity corporations and consumers. The Act provides remedies for misleading and deceptive conduct that will apply to representations made by green power marketers or utilities to consumers in order to obtain contracts for the supply of green power.

In South Australia, where AGL is the only retailer of green power products, the Industry Regulator has published a special Guideline regarding green power and consumer protection and information.[21] The Guideline, which applies only to the sale of green power products to consumers who cannot choose their retailer, requires AGL to accredit its green power products under the national accreditation program (§3.1.1.2) and to set a fair and reasonable price for green power (§3.1.2.2). It also: prohibits misleading and deceptive conduct, requiring AGL to ensure all representations are factually correct and to comply with the Trade Practices Act and other consumer protection

---

[20] Sustainable Energy Authority Victoria, *National Accreditation*, http://www.seav.gov.au/greenpower/accred.htm.

[21] South Australian Industry Regulator, *Consumer Information and Protection: Green Power*, Electricity Industry Guideline No. 7, November 2000, made under the *Independent Industry Regulator Act* 1999 (SA).

legislation (§3.1.3.2); and lays down requirements for billing practices (§3.2.1.3), complaints and dispute resolution (§3.2.1.4) and compliance reporting to the Industry Regulator (§3.3.1). The Guideline will remain in force until full retail competition is introduced in 2003.

4 STRENGTHS AND LIMITATIONS OF GREEN PRICING AND GREEN POWER MARKETING SCHEMES

Green pricing programs and green power marketing schemes are market-based mechanisms that are used to increase demand by consumers for electricity produced from renewable energy sources. These programs are voluntary and depend upon the willingness of consumers to pay a price premium for the supply of green power to them directly or the investment by a utility in developing renewable energy technologies. As market-based mechanisms, green pricing programs offer a number of benefits but are also subject to a number of limitations.

4.1 Green Pricing

The advantages of green pricing programs are that the schemes: enhance information and customer choice with a minimum of regulation; allow suppliers to encourage renewables development at no competitive cost to themselves or to customers interested in renewables; and provide a mechanism for promoting renewable energy that enhances individual freedom and economic efficiency.[22] Another benefit is that the schemes are not dependent on government support, in particular financial support, for their success.

Despite these benefits, green pricing programs are subject to a number of criticisms. First, green pricing schemes do not correct the market failure associated with the use of fossil fuels and do not allocate the cost of providing green power, a public good, across society. The costs of pollution associated with the production of electricity from fossil fuels are not taken into account in the pricing of electricity, thus the low electricity prices that render renewables uncompetitive in a competitive market do not reflect the true environmental cost of using fossil fuels. In economic terms, the marginal private cost to electricity companies of generating electricity from fossil fuels does not reflect the marginal social cost of electricity production. There is an externality or market failure associated with the production of electricity from fossil fuels. In contrast, the supply of electricity from renewable energy sources is a public good. Critics of green pricing schemes argue that as green power provides a public benefit to society, all electricity consumers should pay for green power. By asking a subset of consumers to fund a public good through voluntary contributions, green pricing transfers the costs for environmental benefits from the general public to a select group and enables utilities to avoid responsibility for environmental costs and perpetuate the market failure associated with the use of fossil fuels.[23]

---

[22] F. Sissine, "Renewable Energy and Electricity Restructuring," National Council for Science and the Environment, Congressional Research Service Issue Brief for Congress, RS 20270, July 20, 1999, http://cnie.org/NLE/CRSreports/energy/eng-56.cfm.

[23] R. Wiser, S. Pickle, and C. Goldman, "Renewable Energy Policy and Electricity Restructuring" (1998) 26 *Energy Policy* 465 at 466.

Other critics argue that while green pricing schemes have a useful role to play in supplementing supply side mechanisms, they should not be relied on as the sole method of promoting green power. The main reason for this is the problem of free riding. Because green pricing programs are voluntary, consumers have the incentive to buy the cheapest electricity available while hoping that others will buy more expensive green power.[24] It has also been argued that utilities with a large existing base of nonrenewable energy sources, such as coal and nuclear power, may fear that future sales of their electricity will be undermined by green pricing initiatives, and have no incentive to offer successful green pricing programs.[25] For these reasons, green pricing schemes alone are generally regarded as insufficient to ensure that green power will comprise an adequate proportion of total electricity generated in a deregulated market.

Finally, green pricing schemes have been criticised as promoting the perception that renewables are uneconomic at a time when many renewables are approaching, or have already achieved, cost-effectiveness.

4.2 Green Power Marketing

From the perspective of green power marketers and generators, experience to date in California, Pennsylvania, New Jersey, and Massachusetts indicates that green power marketing has proven to be a successful method of differentiating generation supplies. However, the percentage of residential customers who have switched suppliers is, on average, only about one percent. Studies of the electricity markets in California, Pennsylvania, New Jersey, and Massachusetts have identified a number of barriers to the success of green power marketing.

First, the cost of attracting and signing up new customers, particularly smaller customers, has been prohibitive for some green marketers. Demand for green power must be created through intensive marketing and by educating customers about the availability and benefits of green pricing schemes, which is a very costly undertaking. As the costs of acquiring new customers are raised, the profitability and attractiveness of the market are reduced. Wiser et al. have found that high start-up and customer acquisition costs in the early days of the California market "overwhelmed" profit margins from power sales, forcing some marketers to abandon the residential market.[26]

Second, the size of the "default service price" in deregulated markets is a key component to the success of green marketing schemes. The default service price is the price at which customers who do not switch suppliers or into new contracts will be supplied power after deregulation. Through a comparison of the markets in California, Pennsylvania, New Jersey, and Massachusetts, market researchers have found that the single most important factor affecting the success of green power markets is the default service price relative to the wholesale market price, as the difference between the two determines the ability of suppliers to earn profit margins and/or offer consumers discounts from current rates. A low default service price relative to the wholesale market price leaves green marketers little opportunity to earn profit margins and/or offer price savings to consumers, thereby providing little incentive either for marketers to enter the

---

[24] R. Fouquet, "The United Kingdom Demand for Renewable Electricity in a Liberalised Market" (1998) 26 *Energy Policy* 281, at 284.

[25] Swezey, *supra* note 5, at 23.　　　　　　　　　[26] Wiser, et al., *supra* note 4.

market and offer supply choices, or for consumers to spend time comparing electricity offers and switch suppliers.

The emergence of a successful market for green power depends on the existence of either a high default service price (e.g., Pennsylvania) relative to the wholesale market price or, where there is a low default service price, the introduction of a sizeable subsidy for green power customers, for example in California, where the consumer credit offsets a low default service price.[27] Even the existence of the consumer credit was unable to save green power marketers in California in the face of severe electricity shortages, when extremely high wholesale power prices, combined with retail electricity price caps of 6.5¢/kWh (operating retrospectively from June 1, 2000, to December 31, 2003) meant that green power marketers could not earn sufficient profit margins to survive.[28]

Third, false claims by green marketers in early markets have deterred some consumers from switching suppliers. In New England, during two retail competition pilot programs, green power producers made false claims about the "greenness" of their products.[29] The success of green pricing schemes and green power marketing relies on the provision of good quality green power products. As it is not possible for consumers themselves to ensure the veracity of claims made by suppliers about their green power products, consumer protection mechanisms such as disclosure and certification requirements play a crucial role in establishing successful markets for green power.

Despite the need for consumer protection mechanisms, these mechanisms may raise costs for green marketers and deter entry into the market. Reed and Houston cite the example of U.S. green marketer GreenMountain.com which, with a sizeable presence in Pennsylvania, refused to enter the New Jersey market until the state amended or abolished the rule requiring a customer's signature to be affixed to any agreement to switch generation suppliers (the "wet signature" rule). GreenMountain.com, which targets residential and smaller commercial customers, has relied heavily on telephone and Internet recruitment. The requirement that customers must ultimately mail or fax an agreement with a signature affixed was seen as a significant barrier to entry.[30]

Fourth, the requirement that the green power be sourced from new as opposed to existing facilities may deter marketers from entering the market. Using preexisting renewables capacity rather than new capacity limits the uptake of new renewables, and most certification programs require a certain percentage of green power to be sourced from new renewables. However, when green power markets are in their infancy, marketers do not have captive customer bases while they procure new sources of renewables. In new markets, it is less risky for green power marketers to use existing renewable resources as these are usually cheaper and contract terms are more favorable. In those areas without an established existing renewables sector, green marketers, who must procure more new generation in the early stages of the market when demand and consumer confidence are not yet established, face higher risk levels. Some marketers may not be willing to take the risk in the early stages of the market.

[27] G. Reed and A. Houston, "Status of the U.S. Market for Green Power," Prepared for the ACEE Summer Study on Energy Efficiency in Buildings, August 2000, http://www.nrel.gov/analysis/emaa/ brief/5.pdf.
[28] Retail price caps were introduced by AB 265 of September 7, 2000 (Stats. 2000, ch. 328).
[29] Wiser, et al., *supra* note 4.   [30] Reed and Houston, *supra* note 27, at 5.282.

Fifth, the utilities can act in a manner that impedes competition. For example, in California, the utilities made it more difficult for green power marketers to operate competitively by: making it impossible for green power marketers to offer products such as consolidated billing; refusing to allow customers to choose their green power provider at the time of first contact with the utility after deregulation; failing to explain adequately or accurately about how utility and green pricing worked to consumers; and, in the case of San Diego Gas and Electric, imposing price caps during the electricity crisis for all customers except those who had switched to a green power provider.[31]

5 THE ROLE OF THE LAW

Market research in the United States shows that while a majority of electricity consumers has expressed a willingness to pay higher prices for renewable energy, this has not yet translated into a large-scale change in consumer behavior. The majority of consumers only purchase green products when they are competitively priced and where there is no reduction in quality or convenience. This, combined with problems such as free riding, has resulted in electricity from renewables purchased under these schemes forming only a small percentage of all electricity purchased. Thus "while a niche market for green power clearly exists . . . full reliance on the green power market to meet national renewable energy objectives would be premature: traditional forms of public policy support will continue to be needed for the commercialization and maturation of the renewables industries."[32]

The limitations of green pricing and green power marketing schemes are recognized in most developed countries, where these voluntary schemes operate concurrently with mandatory supply-side mechanisms such as renewable portfolio standards. These include the Mandatory Renewable Energy Target in Australia and the Renewables Obligation in the UK, while the U.S. federal government is considering the introduction of a renewable portfolio standard to replace the mandatory purchasing provisions of the Public Utilities Regulatory Policies Act of 1978. An exception is Alberta, where there is no renewable energy portfolio scheme operating at the provincial or federal level. It is the policy of the Albertan government to encourage renewable power in the electricity market through open, nondiscriminatory access to the Power Pool of Alberta and consumer support of voluntary green power schemes. The provincial government has explicitly stated that the success of renewable energy projects "depends on how much value consumers put on supporting green power" and "not on a regulatory hearing or a government decision."[33]

Green pricing and green power marketing schemes provide a useful but small contribution to the uptake of renewable energy, and should operate in conjunction with mandatory supply-side mechanisms. Given that mandatory supply-side mechanisms are introduced, green pricing and green power marketing schemes as demand-side mechanisms should remain voluntary, thereby taking advantage of the existing benefits of the schemes, and a relatively light-handed approach toward the regulation of these

[31] Center for Resource Solutions, *Ten Factors That Affected California's Retail Green Power Market*, http://www.green-e.org/pdf/ topten.pdf.
[32] Reed and Houston, *supra* note 27, at 5.377.
[33] Alberta Resource Development, *Power of Competition: A Guide to Alberta's New Competitive Electric Industry Structure* (March 2000).

schemes is appropriate. The role of the government and law should be that of providing a level playing field in the deregulated electricity market for renewables producers, and providing education, information, and protection to consumers. In particular, governments through legislation should address the following issues.

In order to support green power marketing, governments should address the level of the default service price relative to the wholesale price. Upon deregulation of the electricity industry, the default service price is usually set out in the legislation restructuring the industry. Governments must ensure that the default service price is sufficiently high relative to the wholesale price so that consumers are encouraged to switch between suppliers. Alternatively, if the default service price is relatively low to the wholesale price, governments should offer a financial incentive to consumers that will encourage switching between suppliers, as in California.

Governments should play a role in educating the population about the environmental harm caused by electricity generated from fossil fuels, and the environmental benefits of green power. Government participation in the provision of education will reduce the costs to green power marketers and utilities offering green pricing schemes, enhancing the profitability and attractiveness of the market.

Governments also have a crucial role to play in consumer protection. False claims from some green marketers about the "greenness" of their product damages the credibility of the entire market for green energy. It is absolutely crucial that mechanisms are established to minimize the possibility of fraudulent claims by green marketers and other electricity suppliers regarding the supply of green power. The case studies of California, Alberta, and Australia demonstrate a number of ways in which consumer protection mechanism may be implemented.

Alberta relies on the voluntary certification scheme administered by the Canadian Environmental Choice Program for quality guarantee, with no government administered scheme laying down specific requirements for disclosure of information to consumers about the content of green power products. However, the government has enacted the Electricity Marketing Regulations, which specifically prohibit fraudulent behavior by electricity marketers. In Australia, the state governments have established a joint accreditation scheme for green power, administered by SEDA. While retail codes regulate the sale of electricity to consumers, there are no specific legislative disclosure requirements regarding green power such as those in California. The general consumer protection laws contained in the Trade Practices Act govern fraudulent behavior by green power marketers.

California has the most comprehensive mix of legislative and voluntary mechanisms for consumer protection. Legislation makes it mandatory for retail suppliers and electric service providers to disclose information to end-use customers through the Power Content Label, the eco-labeling scheme that is administered by the government through the California Energy Commission. Legislation also makes it mandatory for certain generators and retail suppliers to report to the CEC to enable the Commission to verify that information provided to electricity consumers is correct. The voluntary Green-e accreditation scheme run by the Center for Resource Solutions, a nonprofit organization, provides a further guarantee for consumers.

Laws containing mandatory disclosure and reporting requirements modeled on the California eco-labeling system, combined with laws specifically prohibiting fraudulent behavior by electricity marketers and laying down penalties for fraudulent claims, such as the provisions of the Albertan Electricity Regulations, should be enacted to provide a comprehensive system for consumer protection. Voluntary accreditation schemes such as that run by the Canadian Environmental Choice Program[M], which provide for independent third party monitoring and auditing of facilities, and set out stringent requirements for electricity to be classed as "green" power, will also benefit consumers, but should exist as voluntary schemes in addition to government regulation.

These recommendations are made on the assumption that green pricing and green power marketing schemes will operate in conjunction with mandatory supply-side mechanisms such as a renewables portfolio standard. Where a mandatory renewables portfolio standard is in place, all electricity suppliers will be contributing to the supply of green power, either by paying directly for extra generation from renewable energy sources or by trading in green certificates. However, in the case of countries that do not establish supply-side mechanisms but rely solely on green pricing and green power marketing to encourage renewable energy, such as Alberta, offering green pricing programs should be compulsory for all utilities. Utilities with a large existing base of nonrenewable energy sources may fear that future sales of their electricity will be undermined by green pricing initiatives, and have no incentive to offer genuine programs. In this situation, utilities must be forced to offer some green power product to electricity consumers, or stated support for renewable energy will be only illusory.

10 Agricultural Renewable Energy and Its Management in China

Zhu Jian-guo*

1 INTRODUCTION

This chapter will achieve the following: first, put forward and define the new concept of "agricultural renewable energy"; second, discuss the differences and similarities between "agricultural renewable energy" and "rural renewable energy," as well as consider the attributes of "agricultural renewable energy substances" as resources; third, analyze foreseeable problems in relation to the utilization and management of agricultural renewable energy in China, as well as efforts by the Chinese government in relation to the development of agricultural renewable energy and related administrative policies, plans, and achievements; and fourth, systematically consider the content of both national and local laws and regulations concerning the management of agricultural renewable energy, analyze current limitations in the management of agricultural renewable energy, including the incompleteness of the current legislative framework, and the lack of understanding of agricultural wastes as having similar attributes to conventional energy resources; and finally, discuss the legal responsibilities and obligations of governments at all levels for the management of agricultural renewable energy in China.

As the global economy continued to develop since the mid-twentieth-century, in tandem with continuous annual growth in global consumption of fossil fuels–based energy, an international energy crisis developed, such that it now impedes the sustainable development of the global economy, and threatens local peace. In the meantime, pollution and environmental harms all over the world, caused by current energy use patterns, which are based on the overconsumption of fossil fuels, are also serious concerns limiting the achievement of sustainable development. Beginning in the late twentieth century, the development of alternative energies, clean energy, and renewable energies has become a common objective for all countries, as part of their energy and environmental development strategies.

China has been the focus of global attention due to the speed of its economic and social development ever since the late 1970s. However, the overconsumption and irrational consumption of energy, as well as the resulting environmental pollution, has restricted the sustainable development of China's economy. The Chinese government has now begun efforts to enhance research and development in relation to new energies, alternative energies, or clean energy, while also developing new technologies

* Associate Research Fellow and a standing member of Environment and Resources Law Society of China Law Society (ERSCLS), Institute of Natural Resources & Agricultural Planning of CAAS, Beijing.

for better energy utilization and environmental protection. The development of renewable energies and relevant renewable energies infrastructure has been identified in China's governmental strategies on energy and environmental development, and also in Chinese legislation concerning the management of energy resources. The development of renewable energies has also been included in the legislative plan of the National People's Congress for the near future.

However, taking a comprehensive view of current research and China's existing legislation on the utilization and management of renewable energies, there are few provisions in relation to the development of agricultural renewable energy. China is a large country with a high percentage of the population engaged in extensive agricultural production. Therefore, the integrated utilization and management of agricultural renewable energy is important for the development of energy infrastructure, and also for environmental protection in rural areas.

This chapter will attempt to consider systematically the governmental framework for managing agricultural renewable energy in China.

2 THE CONCEPT OF AGRICULTURAL RENEWABLE ENERGY

The term "agricultural renewable energy" does not appear in dictionaries or thesauruses, nor is it defined in major academic publications. Although the term appears in several documents, it is still confused with the concept of "rural renewable energy." Therefore, before considering how "agricultural renewable energy" should best be developed and managed by governments, it is necessary to properly define the concept of agricultural renewable energy.

2.1 Definition of Agricultural Renewable Energy

For the purposes of this chapter, agricultural renewable energy combines the concepts of "agriculture" and "renewable energy." According to the Dictionary of Agriculture, "agriculture" is a human productive activity combining "natural reproduction" and "economic reproduction" for the purpose of obtaining the material goods needed for living and production, through the production of products involving plants, animals, and microorganisms, taking living animals and plants as the main objects of labor, and arable lands as the basic means of such production.[1]

According to the Huaxia Concise Encyclopedia, "renewable energy" is "recycled energy that has the ability of natural self-recovery in the ecological system and will not be lessened gradually through natural processes or human utilization including solar energy, hydro energy, wind energy, biological energy, tidal energy, wave power and geothermal energy etc."[2]

The concept of "biomass energy," in the context of "renewable energy," is defined in the Encyclopedia of China (Agriculture Volume) and the Encyclopedia of China (Succinct Edition) as energy generated from firewood, straw, carbohydrate-bearing

---

[1] Editorial Board of Dictionary of Agriculture, *Dictionary of Agriculture*, China Agriculture Press (Beijing, 1998) at 1190.

[2] Editorial Board of Huaxia Concise Encyclopedia, *Huaxia Concise Encyclopedia (Volume III)*, Huaxia Publishing House, (Beijing, 1998), at 749.

crops, oil crops, hydrophytes, farming wastes, and animal excrement formed through direct burning, or after being processed into gaseous, liquid, or solid fuel.[3] On the basis of these established definitions, the following characteristics can be identified for the purposes of defining and understanding the concepts of agriculture, renewable energy, and biomass energy:

1. agriculture is a human productive activity combining "natural reproduction" and "economic reproduction";
2. products generated or obtained from the act of agricultural production are biological products;
3. biological products obtained from agricultural production are used as the basis of human economic production and people's livelihoods;
4. renewable energy regenerates itself and so can be reused;
5. renewable energy will not exhaust itself through natural processes or human utilization;
6. biomass energy is a type of renewable energy;
7. biomass energy refers to biomass that can be directly or indirectly used as fuel; and
8. biomass energy mainly refers to wastes and processed products of wastes generated during the production and processing of agricultural, forest, and livestock products.

In this context, "agricultural renewable energy" can be defined as energy produced from biological substances, such as crop straw, firewood, agricultural wastes, or animal excrement, that are generated or obtained during agricultural production, such as planting, breeding, and reaping, which can be used as fuel directly or after processing. The focus of this chapter is on the integrated utilization and management of "agricultural wastes" and "subsidiary agricultural products" in agricultural biological substances. Therefore, "carbohydrate-bearing crops" and "oil crops," as defined in the Encyclopedia of China (Succinct Edition) are not included within the scope of this chapter.

2.2 Differences between the Concepts of Agricultural Renewable Energy and Rural Renewable Energy

Before considering the differences between the concepts of agricultural renewable energy and rural renewable energy, it is necessary first to define "agricultural energy." According to the Dictionary of Agriculture and Encyclopedia of China (Agriculture Volume) it is:

> energy developed and used in rural areas in accordance with local conditions including both *renewable energies*, such as firewood, straw, excrement, small hydropower schemes, solar energy, wind energy and geothermal energy, as well as *nonrenewable energies*, such as small coal mines[4]

and

> those natural resources located and consumed within rural areas to produce mechanical energy, heat energy, light energy, electromagnetic energy and chemical energy which are required for economic production and life in rural areas, and are produced

---

[3] General Editorial Board of Encyclopedia of China, *Encyclopedia of China (Agriculture Volume II)*, Encyclopedia of China Publishing House (Beijing, 1994) at 1021.

[4] *Supra* note 1, at 1176.

from energy sources such as animal power, biomass energy, hydro energy, mineral energy, solar energy, wind energy, geothermal energy and tidal energy.[5]

Rural energy has the following characteristics:

1. rural energy is a concept defined on the basis of geographical regions rather than on a particular mode of economic production, such as industrial production;
2. rural energy includes not only renewable energies (such as straw, excrement, solar energy, and wind energy), but also nonrenewable energies (such as mineral energy or fossil fuel energy); and
3. rural energy covers all types of known energies, with the exception of nuclear energy.

In light of this understanding of rural energy, it is clear that the term "rural renewable energy" refers to renewable energies obtained and used in the economic production processes and lifestyles of people living in rural areas. Such renewable energies are not limited to energy sources generated in the course of agricultural production, such as some biomass energy, but refers to all renewable energies, such as solar energy, wind energy, hydro energy, and geothermal energy.

Thus, it can be seen that the differences between agricultural renewable energy and rural renewable energy are:

1. in terms of what they connote, agricultural renewable energy is connected with the course of agricultural production and, accordingly, is a concept defined on the basis of a particular mode of economic production. Rural renewable energy, however, is a concept connected with rural geographic regions and is defined on this basis; and
2. in terms of what they denote, rural renewable energy is broader in scope than agricultural renewable energy, as agricultural renewable energy refers only to certain biomass energies generated or obtained in the course of agricultural production. Rural renewable energy not only includes energy sources that would fall within the definition of agricultural renewable energy, but also includes various types of nonbiomass energies that can be found in rural areas.

This chapter has pursued detailed definitions of these concepts and focused on the differences between the concepts of agricultural renewable energy and rural renewable energy to facilitate the more detailed consideration, which follows, of agriculture renewable energy and appropriate ways of developing and managing such energy. The definitions also clearly establish the scope of this chapter.

2.3 Dual Nature of Agricultural Renewable Energy Substances as Energies and Resources

Agricultural renewable energy refers to certain biological substances generated in the course of agricultural production or labor, including rural firewood, crop straw, animal excrement, and waste residues of agricultural products. They provide energy for economic production and household uses. Rural firewood includes reeds, Mao bamboo, shrubs, weeds, and tree branches. Crop straw includes the stem, leaf, vine, root, core,

---

[5] General Editorial Board of Encyclopedia of China, *Encyclopedia of China (Agriculture Volume I)*, Encyclopedia of China Publishing House (Beijing, 1994) at 737.

and bran of grain crops, such as wheat, paddy rice, corn, sorghum, cotton, and soybean. Animal excrement includes the excrement of livestock and poultry, whether or not they are fed in pens, as well as sludge in aquaculture ponds. Waste residues of agricultural products include the waste residues from industrial processing of grain crops, oil crops, and sugar crops, such as distillers' grains, bean cakes, and bagasse.

Biomass energy, produced using traditional and modern methods, can be used as fuel in rural China for the daily ordinary activities of rural people. Firewood, straw, and animal excrement could be used directly for such activities. Alternatively, renewable energy substances could be used indirectly as fuels in the context of activities of urban and rural people after being processed into marsh gas, liquefied gas, or solid fuels. For instance, substances such as straw, animal excrement, and waste residues of agricultural products could be processed into refined fuels. Further, such renewable energy substances could be made into building materials or feedstuffs after industrial processing with fiber, proteins, or other useful components of wastes in agricultural production.

Since biomass energy can be used directly for fuel, or be processed into fuel, agricultural renewable energy substances can be classified not only as "energy," but also as "resources."

Substances used to generate agricultural renewable energy can be also used as a resource in the following areas:

1. for paper making, for example, wheat straw, rice straw, reeds, and Mao bamboo can be used to produce paper pulp, paper board, packing cases, and packing boxes;
2. as building materials, for example, cotton straw and tree branches can be used to produce density board and fiberboard, while reeds, wheat straw, and rice straw can be woven into reed mats, straw curtains, and hay bands;
3. as feed, for example, agricultural wastes such as crop straw can be used as livestock feed directly or after being disposed of through silage or ammonization, while the waste liquid and residues of carbohydrate-bearing crops, oil crops, or sugar crops after brewing and pressing can be also used as livestock feed directly or after reprocessing;
4. as fertilizer, for example, crop straw, animal excrement, and sludge in aquaculture ponds can be used as agricultural fertilizers or be used to produce organic fertilizer products, such as bacterial manure and microelement fertilizers, for special use through innocuous and industrialized processing;
5. in art wares, for example, straw, reeds, cattail leaves, and corn peels can be used to weave or to make various kinds of art wares and daily household goods, such as straw hats, straw shoes, straw raincoats, curtains, portiere, and kang mats; and
6. for integrated utilization, to use all agricultural wastes according to its highest utilization efficiency, adopting scientific utilization techniques and a friendly ecological environment, so that the utilization potential of resources can be enhanced and exploited and pollution, caused by such wastes, can be reduced.

Understanding the dual nature of agricultural renewable energy as both energy and a resource is important for the following reasons:

1. in a broad sense, both managers and users of agricultural renewable energy substances should understand the dual nature of agricultural renewable energy so that they can pay attention to both these elements, when deciding how best to utilize

such substances. In this way, the irrational utilization of energies and resources can be avoided and the sustainable development of agriculture and the environment can be promoted; and

2. in a narrow sense, such analysis establishes a premise for researchers, managers, and law makers to scientifically and objectively discuss the management of, and enactment of legislation in relation to, agricultural renewable energy. This should prevent the development of flawed methods or laws and regulations. This is because all relevant parties understand the concept of agricultural renewable energy.

3 PROBLEMS CONCERNING THE UTILIZATION OF AGRICULTURAL RENEWABLE ENERGY IN CHINA

China is a great country with a large agrarian population and significant power to produce agricultural products, which has grown with China's economic expansion in the 1980s. China does not only produce large quantities of agricultural products to meet the needs of its domestic market, but also exports significant quantities of agricultural products. During the period from 1991 to 2000, comparing the first five years and the second five years, the output of agricultural products in China, such as grains, oil plants, sugar plants, fruits, meat, and aquatic products, grew respectively by 10.48%, 31.26%, 8.40%, 80.28%, 36.41%, and 104.42%. The number of pigs and sheep bred for slaughter also grew respectively by 23.11% and 15.97%,[6] which indicates that throughout this decade, the production of agricultural products in China maintained a trend of steady growth.

As the output of agricultural products grew considerably, the output of organic wastes used directly or used after treatment as "energy" substances or "resource" substances, such as straw, animal excrement, residues of crops after treatment, also grew significantly. China has abundant biomass resources, for example, the annual output of animal excrement is about 2 billion tonnes, and the output of crop straws and other agricultural wastes also reaches 0.7 billion tonnes.[7] Using units of standard coal as the basis for calculation, the resource content of agricultural wastes such as crop straw, is the equivalent of approximately 0.31 billion tonnes of standard coal and firewood resources are the equivalent of approximately 0.13 billion tonnes of standard coal.[8] The annual resource content of both agricultural wastes and firewood totals 0.44 billion tonnes of standard coal, equal to more than one-third of China's average annual output (approximately 1.25 billion tonnes of standard coal[9]) of raw coal, crude oil, natural gas, water, and electricity as at the end of the 1990s (1996–1999). This demonstrates the abundance of China's agricultural renewable resources and the potential significance of agricultural renewable energy in China's energy production.

---

[6] Online National Bureau of Statistics of China, "Result of calculation in accordance with the annual agricultural statistical data (1991–2000)," *see* http://www.stats.gov.cn/tjsj/ndsj/index.htm.

[7] Xiao Yang, "Development and Utilization Status of China's Renewable Energy and Resources" (2001) 1 *Rural Energy* 29.

[8] Chen Jiabin, "Research on Foreground for Renewable Energy as an Industry in our Country" (2003) 3 *Renewable Energy* 10–12.

[9] Zhan Hua and Yao Shihong, "Some Speculation about General Status of Energy and Development in China" (2003) 3 *Energy Engineering* 1–4.

Currently, approximately eighty percent of China's population still lives in rural areas. The annual energy consumption of rural populations in China is the equivalent of more than 0.6 billion tonnes of standard coal, most of which is sourced from biomass energy substances, such as trees, firewood, and straw.[10] In geographically remote rural areas, with underdeveloped economies that also lack mineral energy resources, energy for daily household and farm activities is mostly generated through directly burning straw (as occurs frequently in rural areas), cropping off or digging up trees and burning firewood (for instance, as occurs in remote mountainous areas), or even through burning animal excrement (such as in pasturing areas). China is the world's largest consumer of biomass energy and the volume of biomass energy consumed each year accounts for approximately twenty percent of total annual global consumption.[11] The utilization of agricultural renewable energy is influenced by levels of economic development, levels of technical knowledge, development and expertise, traditions, and the persistence of outdated approaches to energy consumption. Accordingly, there are still problems that require attention particularly in terms of the utilization of agricultural renewable energy in China.

3.1 Low Utilization Rate of Resources and Improper Treatment of Wastes Lead to Not only Resource Waste but also Environmental Pollution

Although China is the world's largest consumer of biomass energy, the utilization of crop straw in China by the end of the 1990s was still just fifty percent,[12] while the remainder was entirely unused for energy production. In keeping with the traditional lifestyles of many rural people, and the outdated means of production in many areas, many crop straw or other wastes are abandoned as they are considered improper, inconvenient, or unworthy for use. Such agricultural wastes are piled up at the edge of fields, sides of roads, sides of channels, and grain yards to decompose naturally or are burned in piles in fields and on roadsides as wastes. Furthermore, approximately 3.5 billion tonnes of straw each year cannot be used effectively, of which 2.5 billion tonnes are burned or wasted.[13] The abandonment or random burning of crop straw can lead not only to the wastage of substances of agricultural renewable energy, but also to the eutrophication of water resources when rotten straw leaks into surface water. The burning of crop straws also causes air quality to deteriorate in urban and rural areas, resulting in the sharp growth of potential safety hazards, including road and air traffic accidents.

Some large husbandry and agriculture enterprises not only fail to adopt effective strategies for turning waste into energy, but instead discharge them into natural water resources nearby, further exacerbating problems of eutrophication of surface and underground water. This water cannot be used for drinking, irrigation, or cultivation and local alternative water resources, such as reservoirs and water tanks, are lacking. As a result of this direct discharge of animal excrement, the potential biomass energy carried in animal excrement is wasted. The harmful bacteria and viruses carried in

[10] *Id.*   [11] *Id.*

[12] Zhang Shurong, "Current Status and Trend of Development and Utilization of China's Renewable Energy" (1999) 3 *Energy Technology* 8–11.

[13] Lu Fuming, "Shandong Province Solves the Problem of Straw Burning," *see* www.scnu.edu.cn/edu/jykx10/0711.htm. Note, the data provided in this document is different from related data provided by most other documents, so this author estimates that in this document, "straw" does not refer to dry matter.

animal excrement also breed in large numbers and, once released into the surrounding environment, have adverse effects on the health and safety of the environment in rural areas. For example, of approximately 33,000 large and medium-sized animal production farms all over China, more than ninety percent are not equipped with facilities for the integrated use of animal excrement and for the treatment of excrement, urine, and sewage. Animal excrement and sewage are directly discharged into nearby waters without any treatment,[14] which aggravates the eutrophication of such waters, including rivers, lakes, and the sea and also leads to the concentration of viruses and germs. In some areas, the discharge volume of animal excrement even exceeds human discharge volumes and industrial discharge volumes in urban areas. This is the first source of pollution and severely pollutes the waters in urban and rural areas.[15]

3.2 The Simple, Integrated, and Efficient Utilization of Energy and Resources Is Not Achieved

Through the gasification treatment of crop straw, thermal efficiency in the context of direct burning of such straw can be enhanced from twenty percent to more than sixty percent.[16] If all of the approximately 0.4 billion tonnes of animal excrement (dry matter) generated each year in rural and urban areas was processed into marsh gas, the annual output of marsh gas would reach 9 billion m^3.[17] The thermal efficiency of firewood is only approximately ten percent if traditional stoves are used, but if firewood-saving stoves are used, then thermal efficiency can be enhanced to twenty to thirty percent.[18]

Utilizing modern technology for the integrated utilization of biomass resources, crop straw can be used not only in paper making, the production of building materials and art wares, and used directly as feed and fertilizers, but can also be used to produce gaseous and liquid clean fuels, pellet feed, bacterial manures, a base stock of edible fungus, and green packaging materials. Animal excrement can be used not only directly as an organic source of manure, after being fermented and thoroughly decomposed, but can also be processed into bacterial manure and marsh gas for use in rural areas. Some animal excrement can even be used directly in, or processed into, livestock feed and for aquaculture. The integrated utilization of biomass resources can not only enhance the utilization efficiency of agricultural renewable energy, but can also be favorable for the protection of rural and urban environments, and the sustainable and healthy development of China's agricultural economy.

However, the utilization rate of agricultural renewable energy in China remains very low, particularly in most rural areas across China. Even towns, particularly in the underdeveloped regions of Central and West China, which are economically underdeveloped, lack the capital, technology, and equipment to make use of traditional approaches. Of the crop straw that is used to produce energy, most is used to generate energy for

---

[14] Jiang Shaohui, "Xinyi Bureau of Environmental Protection Promotes Multiple Modes for Animal Husbandry," *China Environment News*, January 21, 2003.

[15] Guan Ruijie, "Summary to the Status of China's Agricultural Environment," *see* http://www.rcre.org.cn/dyfx/zgncyj200121.htm.

[16] Wang Dashan, "To Develop Biological Gasification; To Utilize Renewable Energy, Energy Saving in Beijing," No.6 (1998) at 81.

[17] Wang Qingyi, "Current Status of China's Renewable Energy and Existing Obstacles and Countermeasures" (2002) 7 *Energy of China* 39.

[18] Wang Changgui, "Classification of New Energy and Renewable Energy" (2003) 1 *Solar Energy* 14–15.

ordinary household activities in rural areas and are used as a one-off fuel source. In relation to animal excrement, aside from being directly discharged into nearby waters, it is mostly used directly as fertilizer without treatment or integrated utilization. Furthermore, due to the unpopularity of firewood-saving stoves in rural areas, the thermal efficiency of crop straw and firewood is not effectively realized. The utilization efficiency of agricultural renewable energy substances is obviously low, which leads to substantial waste of rural energy and resources.

3.3 Natural Vegetation Is Still the Main Fuel Source in Areas that Lack Energy Resources

Some rural areas in China have a lack of mineral energy resources, low living standards and less developed systems of agricultural production. People in these areas cannot afford coal, natural gas, or solar energy equipment and do not have enough crop straw to develop marsh gas or to use crop straw as a source of fuel for their household needs. So they collect branches, chop down bushes, collect and cut weeds, and use them as fuel. The rational annual yield from firewood felling is approximately 158 million tonnes, but due to some irrational utilization phenomena, such as overfelling, the actual quantity of firewood used exceeds the rational yield by fifteen percent, that is, by 182 million tonnes.[19]

Soil erosion in the upper reaches of the Yangtze River and mid to upper reaches of the Yellow River, as well as desertification and grassland degradation in arid and semi-arid regions of Northwest China, have occurred as a result of the development of China's regional economies. However, the ecological safety of local regions, lower reaches, and surrounding areas has been seriously harmed. Ecological deterioration in these areas is not limited to deforestation and exploitation of rural grasslands, but is also closely related to the destruction of local vegetation by local people who, for a long period of time, have been using local plants to obtain cheap energy for their daily activities.

3.4 The Integrated Utilization of Biomass Energy Is Limited by Technological Problems

Currently, the main technological approaches adopted in rural areas for utilizing crop straw include straw gasification, straw silage, straw ammoniation, paper making, and the transformation of straw into manure. However, having regard to technical maturity and investment in equipment, the adoption of these approaches actually restricts the efficiency of crop straw utilization. For instance:[20]

1. If straw is changed into manure just after being smashed, the macro aggregates of straws in the soil will not be totally rotten until three to five years later. Before this, the existence of straw in the soil will lead to an unfavorable soil structure and also work against the preservation of moisture in farmland soil. This may, however, increase the content of organic matters in the soil;

2. Although the production of fuel gas through straw gasification equipment increases the utilization efficiency of thermal energy produced from crop straw, the technique

---

19 State Commission of Economy and Trade, "Key Points of 2000–2015 Development Program on New Energy and Renewable Energy Industry" (2000) 21 *China Economic and Trade Guide* 25–28.

20 Huang Yong, "To Change Straws to Manure in Form of Animal Excrement: An Effective Prescription to Ex terminate the Phenomenon of Burning," *see* http://www.cenews.com.cn/news/2002-10-22/20240.php.

is still not mature. The costs to develop the technology are so high that it cannot be widely popularized in the short term;

3. The use of crop straw for paper making is not ideal in terms of the utilization of such straw. First, the quality of the raw materials is usually poor. Second, most paper which is made is just used as packaging materials. Third, serious pollution is caused through such processes and the treatment of such pollution is difficult; and

4. Currently, the technique of straw ammoniation for animal husbandry is commonly used in rural areas.[21] Although through ammoniation, the digestion coefficient of crop straw can be increased by approximately ten percent, at the same time approximately seventy percent of ammonia sources will be wasted. So on the basis of a simple economic calculation of costs and benefits, such an approach is not quite rational.

All the four approaches to straw utilization mentioned above can achieve a certain level of consumption of straw, but they still cannot entirely solve the problem of ensuring the full and effective utilization of straw resources.

Furthermore, the use of animal excrement for the processing of biological fertilizer or feed requires advanced processing techniques, equipment, and investment. It also demands that the scale of centralized production of excrement and the design capability of processing equipment should be matched. However, given the current status of separated cultivation of livestock in China's rural areas, current industrial processing techniques are not appropriate for adoption. Although in many rural areas integrated utilization technology to produce marsh gas from human and animal excrement and crop straw by means of centralized production or family production is highly promoted, this is not always ideal. This is because of the differences of latitude, longitude, and altitude, and differences of climate and heat quantity across China, especially in those areas where the temperature is rather low in winter. Obviously, before the problem of the integrated utilization and treatment of animal excrement is resolved, environmental pollution caused by animal excrement is inevitable.

The integrated utilization of China's agricultural renewable energy substances is not only concerned with saving agricultural natural resources to the maximum extent possible and the enhancement of the utilization efficiency of agricultural renewable energy, it is also related to the protection of ecological environments in rural areas in China as well as the sustainable development of agriculture. Therefore, it is important that researchers and managers take into account this discussion about the management of agricultural renewable energy.

4 THE CHINESE GOVERNMENT'S EFFORTS IN THE MANAGEMENT OF AGRICULTURAL RENEWABLE ENERGY

Despite the problems mentioned in Section 2, Chinese governments at all levels since 1990 have established policies and plans, built legal capacity and frameworks, encouraged technical development, and supported projects relating to the management of agricultural renewable energy.

---

[21] Kang Ren, "Prohibition Mechanism of Straw Burning Should Be Put in Order," *China Environment Online, see* http://www.cenews.com.cn/news/2002-09-24/19714.php.

4.1 Related Authorities Establish Development Schemes, Action Plans and Development Programs for Agricultural Renewable Energy

Since the Chinese government formulated China's Agenda 21 – White Paper of China's Population, Environment and Development in 21st Century (China's Agenda 21) in 1994, related authorities under the State Council established future development schemes, action plans, or near-term and long- and mid-term development programs related to the integrated utilization and technical development of agricultural renewable energy.

In China's Agenda 21, government proposals "to hasten construction of rural energy and to improve the deterioration of the ecological environment caused by over consumption of biological energy" are set out in Objective 13.12. Actions 13.20 and 13.57(b) provide for government actions "to develop techniques that use biomass energy to produce clean liquid fuel and to firmly promote applied techniques of marsh gas."[22] In the Priority Program for China's Agenda 21, the development, utilization, and demonstration of biomass energy were listed as priority projects. Development objectives were also put forward to establish state development programs for biomass energy, to develop new techniques for the utilization of biomass energy, and to establish demonstration projects for the development and utilization of biomass energy in the period from 1994 to 2000.[23]

The Development Program of New Energy and Renewable Energy (1996–2010) established by the State Development Planning Commission in January 1995, prescribed energy development objectives, including hastening technical improvements in utilization techniques for rural biomass energy; the development of woodfuel forests and firewood-saving stoves; and the comprehensive utilization of waste residues of crop processing and wastes from animal husbandry.[24]

The Scheme of China's Policies on Energy Saving Technology – established by the State Development Planning Commission in May 1996 – set out the need to vigorously develop techniques in relation to the transformation and integrated utilization of biomass energy, such as gasification, liquefaction, and charring, and also the need to use agricultural organic wastes in rural areas to produce clean fuels, for example, marsh gas.[25]

In the Ninth Five-Year Work Plan for Resources Saving and Integrated Utilization established in July 1996, the State Economic and Trade Commission provided that preferential policies, such as tax adjustment, financial subsidies, and discounted government loans, should be enforced in connection with the integrated utilization of energy and improving renewable energy techniques.[26] The Key Points of Development of New Energy and Renewable Energy Industry in 2000–2015, established in August 2003, set out the objectives and tasks of "completing supporting technical service systems of renewable energy industry in 2006–2010," as well as "promoting construction of

---

[22] China's Agenda 21, *see* http://www.acca21.org.cn/cchnwp13.html.

[23] Priority Program for China's Agenda 21, *see* www.acca21.org.cn/pc4-5c.html.

[24] State Development Planning Commission, Development Program of New Energy and Renewable Energy (1996–2010), *see* http://www.ccchina.gov.cn/source/ca/ca2002122601.htm.

[25] State Development Planning Commission, Scheme of China's Policies on Energy Saving Technology, May 13, 1996, Great Collections of China Laws and Regulations (State Collections).

[26] Ninth Five-Year Work Plan for Resources Saving and Integrated Utilization, *see* china-window.com.cn/Anhui_w/gb/smjl/zcfg/04/011.htm.

large- and medium-scale marsh gas projects and developing equipment that can effectively utilize biomass energy."[27] The Tenth Five-Year Plan on Energy Saving and Integrated Utilization of Resources, established in October 2001, prescribed the objectives of studying and establishing "incentive policies that can adapt to the requirements of the market economy and promote energy saving and the integrated utilization of resources," including the "transfer of tax and tax burdens," "public financial support," and "privileges in relation to loans."[28]

The State Environmental Protection Administration of China has identified the need to vigorously develop renewable energy techniques, to reduce the damage to vegetation caused by logging, to actively develop straw feed, and to prohibit the random collection and digging of native flora. In the Scheme for National Protection of the Ecological Environment,[29] and in the Tenth Five-Year Plan on State Environmental Protection, the Administration determined the need "to popularize techniques for the integrated utilization and treatment of animal excrement"; "to vigorously promote integrated utilization approaches, such as the transformation of crop straw into manure and straw gasification; to develop new methods of industrial utilization of crop straw"; and "to develop new energy and new energy-saving technologies, such as marsh gas and energy-saving stoves." The stated objective of the Tenth Five-Year Plan was that the integrated utilization rate of straw all over China reach eighty percent and that the rate of animal excrement transformed into an energy resource reach seventy percent.[30]

In July 1996, in the Development Scheme of the State Project to Change Straw to Manure by Feeding it to Animals (1996–2000), the Chinese Ministry of Agriculture put forward policy approaches for the rational utilization of crop straw, for instance, the development of a comprehensive state plan for agriculture "to feed crop straw to livestock and to change straw to manure in the form of animal excrement." Furthermore, it was provided that the "Ministry of Agriculture and peoples' governments at all levels should establish medium- and long-term programmes and annual implementation plans regarding the project to feed crop straw to livestock and to return straw to farmland in the form of animal excrement"; "authorities should strengthen support for straw cultivation for livestock and financial authorities should arrange agricultural policy loans and support the development of straw feed"; "basic research and applied technological research on straw feed should be developed further"; the "Ministry of Agriculture and National Agriculture Integrated Development Office should formulate and complete methods and detailed implementation rules on the project to change straw to manure by feeding it to animals"; and "the development of strategic programmes for changing straw to manure by feeding it to animals all over China by the end of the 20th century."[31] Further, in China's Agenda 21 – Action Plan of Agriculture established by the Ministry

[27] State Economic and Trade Commission, Key Points of Development of New Energy and Renewable Energy Industry in 2000–2015, *see* http://www.china5e.com/laws/newenergy/newenergy-02.php.

[28] State Economic and Trade Commission, Tenth Five-Year Plan on Energy Saving and Integrated Utilization of Resources, *see* http://www.gzii.gov.cn/right/zwxx/nydl/nydt/1230a.htm.

[29] "Scheme of National Protection of Ecological Environment," *People's Daily*, Edition 5, December 22, 2000.

[30] State Environmental Protection Administration of China, Tenth Five-Year Plan on State Environmental Protection, *see* http://dp.cei.gov.cn/lszl/hygh_1/hb1001.htm.

[31] Ministry of Agriculture, Development Scheme of the State Project to Change Straw to Manure by Feeding it to Animals (1996–2000), *see* http://scmysp.net/zcfg/qgfg/zh/qgzhfg027.htm.

of Agriculture in January 1999, the action plan to rationally utilize straw resources, to develop straw feed, and to promote the construction of rural energy, primarily biomass energy, was accelerated.[32]

In the Scheme for Development of Agricultural Technology (2001–2010) issued by the State Council in April 2001, research and development work in relation to "production and effective utilization technologies for feed, farm and sideline products" and "non-pollution utilization techniques for crop straws and agricultural and forest wastes" was included in the "Ten Technological Initiatives" for the period of the Tenth Five-Year Plan.[33] In the Scheme of Sustainable Development of Science and Technology in 2001–2010 established by the Chinese Ministry of Science and Technology, the development of marsh gas technology and the acceleration of improvements in technology for the utilization of rural biomass energy are also noted as key areas for scientific and technical research.[34] In the Action Scheme for Sustainable Development at the Beginning of the 21st Century, the vigorous development of marsh gas and energy saving stoves and the need to improve rural energy structures are also listed as key areas for sustainable development in China at the beginning of the twenty-first-century.[35]

4.2 State and Local Authorities Formulate Normative Documents Concerning Management of Agricultural Renewable Energy

Although there are still no regulations or rules specifically concerned with the utilization and management of agricultural renewable energy in China, certain laws, regulations, and department rules formulated by the National People's Congress, State Council, local People's Congress, authorities under the State Council, and local governments contain related provisions concerning the rational utilization and management of agricultural renewable energy.

Related Regulations at the Level of State Legislation

In April 1999, the State Environmental Protection Administration of China and the Ministry of Agriculture formulated the Methods for the Prohibition of Straw Burning and Integrated Utilization, which sets out the scope of the definition of "straw," the competent administrative authorities responsible for the supervision of the implementation of bans on straw burning, and instructions for the integrated utilization of straw are clarified. Approaches for the integrated utilization of crop straw and the objective of a graded integrated utilization ratio are also set out. Finally, the powers of local governments, which are responsible for environmental protection and agriculture, are also prescribed with respect to biomass energy.[36] In May 2001, the State Environmental Protection Administration of China prescribed in Methods on Control of Pollution Caused

---

[32] Ministry of Agriculture, *China's Agenda 21 – Action Plan of Agriculture*, Agriculture Press (Beijing, 1991).

[33] State Council, Scheme of Development of Agricultural Technology (2001–2010), *see* http://apply.cpst.net.cn/law/state/1026807516-2.shtml.

[34] Ministry of Science and Technology, *Scheme of Sustainable Development of Science and Technology in 2001–2010*, *see* http://www.acca21.org.cn/kjgy.html.

[35] "Action Scheme of Sustainable Development in the Beginning of 21st Century," *China Environment News*, Edition 1, July 30, 2003.

[36] State Environmental Protection Administration, Ministry of Agriculture, *Methods on Prohibition of Straw Burning and Integrated Utilization*, April 16, 1999, Great Collections of China Laws and Regulations (State Collections).

by Animal Husbandry that integrated utilization issues should be considered during the construction of animal production farms. For example, issues such as the transformation of wastes into manure, marsh gas production, the manufacture of organic fertilizers, and renewable feed production should be considered.[37]

In November 1987, the Ministry of Forestry and Ministry of Agriculture, Animal Husbandry and Fisheries issued the Joint Notice on Strengthening Management of Bamboo Forest and Preventing Over Felling and Digging, which clearly demanded the implementation of quotas for tree felling and a system of felling certificates. This was to address problems of overfelling and digging of Mao Bamboo and bamboo shoots in Southern provinces.[38] In the Report on the Vigorous Development of Straw Resources to Develop Herbivorous Livestock in Rural Areas by the Ministry of Agriculture, forwarded to provinces, municipalities, and autonomous regions by the General Office of the State Council in May 1992, it was provided that "understanding the significance of developing straw resources should be further enhanced." Also "feasible policies and methods should be formulated or completed, centred on straw development," while also suggesting that governments at all levels include animal husbandry with straws in their policy schedules.[39] In January 1999, the Notification on Further Support of Development of Sustainable Renewable Energy and Related Issues, jointly issued by the State Development Planning Commission and the Ministry of Science and Technology, clearly prescribed that the state will offer financial discounts by way of support for construction projects of a certain scale that generate electricity from renewable energies, including biomass energy.[40]

In addition, the Law of Agriculture of the People's Republic of China prescribes the integrated utilization of straws and other wastes, treatment and integrated utilization of animal excrement and other wastes, and the development and utilization of rural renewable energy.[41] The Energy-Saving Act of the People's Republic of China stipulates the obligations that governments at all levels have in relation to capital arrangements for the development of renewable energy, and the development and construction of rural renewable energy.[42] The Law of Soil and Water Conservation of the People's Republic of China regulates any action which damages surface vegetation, such as the uprooting of turf and digging of tree stumps on steep slopes and in dry regions.[43] The Air Pollution

---

[37] State Environmental Protection Administration of China, Methods on Control of Pollution Caused by Animal Husbandry, May 8, 2001, Great Collections of China Laws and Regulations (State Collections).

[38] Ministry of Forestry, Ministry of Agriculture, Animal Husbandry and Fisheries, Joint Notice on Strengthening Management of Bamboo Forest and Preventing Over Felling and Digging, November 24, 1987, Great Collections of China Laws and Regulations (State Collections).

[39] Ministry of Agriculture, Report on Vigorous Development of Straw Resources to Develop Herbivorous Livestock in Rural Areas, May 29, 1992, Great Collections of China Laws and Regulations (State Collections).

[40] State Development Planning Commission, Notification on Further Support Development of Sustainable Renewable Energy and Related Issues, January 12, 1999, Great Collections of China Laws and Regulations (State Collections).

[41] Standing Committee of the National People's Congress, Law of Agriculture of People's Republic of China, December 28, 2002, Arts. 65 and 57, Great Collections of China Laws and Regulations (State Collections).

[42] Standing Committee of the National People's Congress, Energy Saving Act of People's Republic of China, November 1, 1997, Arts. 11 and 38, Great Collections of China Laws and Regulations (State Collections).

[43] Standing Committee of the National People's Congress, Law of Soil and Water Conservation of People's Republic of China, June 29, 1991, Art. 13, Great Collections of China Laws and Regulations (State Collections).

Control Law of the People's Republic of China clearly defines areas in which the burning of straws and fallen leaves in the open air is forbidden.[44] The Forest Law of the People's Republic of China prescribes in detail the types of timberland where firewood chopping is forbidden as well as sanctions for violations of this law.[45]

Related Regulations at the Level of Local Legislation

Local legislation concerning the integrated utilization and management of agricultural renewable energy deals primarily with the following four areas: the management of rural energy; farmland conservation; protection of the agricultural ecological environment; and straw burning.

At present, seven provinces (autonomous regions) have formulated and enforced regulations or approaches for the management of rural energy and the management of rural energy construction. These provinces are Hubei, Shandong, Hunan, Anhui, Gansu, Heilongjiang, and Guangxi. In the approaches formulated, rural energy is clearly defined to include biomass energy, such as marsh gas, straw, and firewood. These approaches also stipulate that local governments at all levels should: first, integrate rural energy construction into their local economies and the national economy and social development plans; second, bring the cost of rural energy construction into their fiscal budgets; third, establish programs for the development and utilization of rural energy; and fourth, develop and promote technology for the integrated utilization of marsh gas, biological gasification and solidification, and the utilization of woodfuel forests. Regulations in Hubei Province also provide that new rural energy technology cannot be demonstrated and promoted until it is assessed according to the Law on Dissemination of Agricultural Technology of People's Republic of China and passes this assessment.[46] Regulations in Anhui Province provide that in the case of rural areas that are appropriate for the development of family methane facilities, local governments should include the construction of these facilities in their construction plans.[47] Regulations in Hunan Province stipulate that in areas with abundant straw resources, the competent authorities responsible for rural energy should improve instruction in relation to the integrated development and utilization of straw, and demonstrate and promote applied gasification and solidification technology according to identified plans.[48] Regulations in Helongjiang Province provide that competent authorities responsible for rural energy at all levels should strengthen management of integrated utilization of straws.[49] Shandong Province also provides regulations concerning affixing

---

[44] Standing Committee of the National People's Congress, Air Pollution Control Law of People's Republic of China, April 29, 2000, Art. 41, Great Collections of China Laws and Regulations (State Collections).

[45] Standing Committee of the National People's Congress, Forest Law of People's Republic of China, April 29, 1998, Arts. 23 and 44, Great Collections of China Laws and Regulations (State Collections).

[46] People's Government of Hubei Province, Methods of Rural Energy of Hubei Province, December 16, 1998, Art. 9, Great Collections of China Laws and Regulations (Local Collections).

[47] People's Government of Anhui Province, Regulations on Construction and Management of Rural Energy of Anhui Province, August 15, 1998, Art. 14, Great Collections of China Laws and Regulations (Local Collections).

[48] People's Government of Hunan Province, Methods on Rural Energy Construction of Hunan Province, June 7, 2001, Art. 13, *see* law.chinalawinfo.com/newlaw2002/SLC/SLC.asp?Db=lar&Gid=16799908.

[49] People's Government of Heilongjiang Province, Provisions on Rural Energy of Heilongjiang Province, November 1, 1997, Art. 11, Great Collections of China Laws and Regulations (Local Collections).

responsibility for the violation of laws by staff of competent authorities responsible for rural energy construction.[50]

To date, seven provinces (Heilongjiang, Shandong, Hunan, Hebei, Gansu, Hubei, and Henan Provinces) have established regulations in relation to farmland conservation and basic farmland protection concerning straw utilization. All these relevant regulations contain common substantive content concerning the management of agricultural renewable energy, particularly in relation to changing straw into manure directly, or in the form of animal excrement. Under the methods proposed in Hebei Province, governments at all levels should "grant awards to and encourage farmland users to return straw directly to farmlands or in the form of excrement," and "impose fines and affix the leader's responsibility for the burning of straw randomly and the waste of organic fertiliser sources, depending on the circumstances."[51]

Currently, there are approximately twenty provinces (municipalities and autonomous regions) all over China which have established local regulations concerning the protection of agricultural ecological environments. These regulations do not specifically refer to the integrated utilization of renewable energy. Their objectives are: "to protect and to improve agricultural environments, to prevent pollution and damage to agricultural environments, to promote sustainable development of agricultural production and to guarantee quality of products";[52] and "to protect and to improve agricultural ecological environments, to prevent pollution to agricultural ecological environments, to comprehensively develop and rationally utilize agricultural resources and to promote sustainable development of agriculture."[53] It is only the regulations formulated in Fujian, Jiangsu, Shandong, Jilin, Hubei, Hunan, Hebei, Anhui, and Tianjin (nine provinces and municipalities) which contain related articles on the integrated utilization of agricultural renewable energy. They state that "people's governments at all levels should promote the technology of integrated utilization of agricultural resources and agricultural wastes, and develop and utilize new rural energy."[54] Furthermore, the Conservation Regulations on Agricultural Environment of Hubei Province provide that the integrated utilization of agricultural wastes be made the subject of preferential policies such as tax reduction and remissions as well as low-interest loans, through related State legislative provisions.[55] In order to assist the implementation of Methods of Straw Burning and Integrated Utilization, Jinan and Chengdu established

---

[50] People's Government of Shandong Province, Administrative Provisions on Rural Energy Construction of Shandong Province, April 14, 1997, Art. 33, Great Collections of China Laws and Regulations (Local Collections).

[51] People's Government of Hebei Province, Methods for Soil Conservation of Farmland of Hebei Province, January 30, 1988, Arts. 13 and 16, Great Collections of China Laws and Regulations (Local Collections).

[52] NPC Standing Committee of Inner Mongolia Autonomous Region, Conservation Regulations on Agricultural Environment of Inner Mongolia Autonomous Region, January 12, 1995, Art. 1, Great Collections of China Laws and Regulations (Local Collections).

[53] NPC Standing Committee of Fujian Province, Conservation Regulations on Agricultural Ecological Environment of Fujian Province, July 26, 2002, Art. 1, Great Collections of China Laws and Regulations (Local Collections).

[54] NPC Standing Committee of Shandong Province, Conservation Regulations on Agricultural Environment of Shandong Province, April 21, 1994, Art. 14, Great Collections of China Laws and Regulations (Local Collections).

[55] NPC Standing Committee of Hubei Province, Conservation Regulations on Agricultural Environment of Hubei Province, February 25, 1993, Art. 16, Great Collections of China Laws and Regulations (Local Collections).

special supporting regulatory methods. Chengdu provides that governments at city and county levels should increase the input of funds needed for straw burning and integrated utilization. Science and technology authorities, as well as institutions concerned with agriculture and agricultural machinery, should be engaged in the research and promotion of new technology for the integrated utilization of straw, to solve the problem of atmospheric pollution caused by straw burning.[56] Jinan also provides that governments at county, village, and town levels must strengthen instructions for the burning of straw, each sign responsibility letters, and should conduct strict assessments. Moreover, governments at all levels should encourage the research and development of new technology concerning the integrated utilization of straw, vigorously promote achievements in relation to such integrated utilization, such as the transformation of straw into manure through mechanical processes, straw gasification, and the development of industrial raw materials. Governments should also offer support in terms of policy and the input of funds. Agricultural authorities are responsible for issuing instructions and enforcing rules in relation to the integrated utilization of straw.[57] The general offices of the governments of Jiangsu Province and Sinkiang Autonomous Region have also issued the government notification on Methods on Straw Burning and Integrated Utilization, issued jointly by the State Environmental Protection Administration of China and the Ministry of Agriculture.

4.3 Chinese Governments Have Made Significant Progress in the Development and Utilization of Agricultural Renewable Energy

Since the beginning of the 1990s, Chinese governments at all levels have continuously devoted significant manpower, material resources, and financial resources to the research, application, promotion, and popularization of technology for developing and utilizing agricultural renewable energy. After ten years of such government efforts, more rural areas in China have changed their traditional lifestyle and energy structures, while the quality of ecological environments in such regions has also gradually improved.

First, in terms of the development and integrated utilization of agricultural renewable energy and its engineering construction, according to the data provided in Statistical Information of China Agriculture (2001), in 2001, the total amount of capital invested in China for rural energy construction was 703,000,000 yuan, of which 523,000,000 yuan was directly funded by the government through its annual budget and construction loans totalled 180,000,000 yuan. By the end of 2001, in total there were 9,567,900 marsh gas ponds for rural families constructed all over China, with a total output of marsh gas of 2,982,000,000 m^3. Also 1359 large- or medium-scale marsh gas projects had commenced operations, with a total cellar capacity of approximately 639,200 m^3. Waste treatment capability measured approximately 34,039,000 tonnes and the annual output of marsh gas was approximately 169,000,000 m^3, and the capability existed to supply such gas to approximately 163,600 families. Furthermore, 1171 of the marsh gas projects that were initiated were for the treatment of agricultural

[56] People's Government of Chengdu, Methods on Prohibition of Straw Burning of Chengdu, February 27, 2001, Art. 9, Great Collections of China Laws and Regulations (Local Collections).
[57] People's Government of Jinan, Notification on Prohibition of Straw Burning, September 29, 1999, Arts. 3 and 5, Great Collections of China Laws and Regulations (Local Collections).

wastes, with a total cellar capacity of approximately 319,400 m^3, waste treatment capability of approximately 14,006,000 tonnes, annual output of marsh gas at approximately 35,511,000 tonnes and gas supply capability for approximately 53,800 families. Also seeds soaked with marsh liquid covered 73,100 ha; pigs fed with marsh liquid totalled 10,030,000 herds; fish fed with marsh liquid covered 53,400 ha; mushrooms planted with marsh residues totalled 24,300 tonnes; and crops stocked through marsh gas totalled 73,100 tonnes. Altogether, 189,000,000 firewood stoves were promoted at provincial levels and 20,077,900 firewood kangs were constructed. The annual gross of marsh gas produced all over China equalled approximately 3,200,000 tonnes of standard coal produced during the same period of time.[58]

Second, in terms of the prevention of agricultural pollution and control of agricultural ecological environments, China's construction of agricultural renewable energy projects also plays a significant role and has made a favorable contribution. In connection with the role of rural renewable energy construction, in 2000, the annual output of marsh gas was 2,712,000,000 m^3. This means that 52,500,000 tonnes of alternative energy like firewood and straws were saved, the amount of carbon dioxide discharged into the atmosphere was reduced by 75,520,000 tonnes, of which 4,885,700 tonnes was due to the use of marsh gas, while a further 50,617,000 tonnes resulted from alternative energy saving.[59] Furthermore, thanks to local enforcement of the Methods on Straw Burning and Integrated Utilization and Methods on Prevention of Pollution Caused by Animal Husbandry, as well as improvement in the integrated utilization of agricultural wastes like straws and animal excrement, environmental degradation has gradually been controlled. This includes reductions in atmospheric pollution, aquatic environment pollution, damage to vegetation, and soil erosion caused by the random felling of trees.

5 LIMITATIONS OF CURRENT CHINESE LEGISLATION IN RELATION TO AGRICULTURAL RENEWABLE ENERGY

Despite all the initiatives mentioned in Section 3, this author believes that the following limitations still exist with respect to China's legal framework for managing agricultural renewable energy.

5.1 Relevant Legislative Systems for the Management of Agricultural Renewable Energy at State Levels Are Still Incomplete

The incompleteness of the state legislative system is demonstrated by:

1. a lack of legislation concerning the management of agricultural renewable energy. Not only is there no specific legislation on this issue, there is even a lack of relevant provisions in related legislation. In terms of state legislation, only certain laws, such as the Law of Agriculture and Law of Energy Saving, are concerned with the integrated utilization and management of agricultural renewable energy. There are

[58] Ministry of Agriculture of People's Republic of China, "Statistical Information of China's Agriculture (2001)," *Rural Energy*, China Agriculture Press, (Beijing, 2002).
[59] Wang Gehua, "Contributions of Constructions of Rural Renewable Energy Made to Deduction of CO$_2$ Discharge and Actions" (2002) 1 *Energy of Jiangxi* 1–3.

also only two departmental statements formulated by the State Administration of Environmental Protection and the Ministry of Agriculture that touch on the issue of agricultural renewable energy substances from the perspective of rural environment protection. It is obvious, therefore, that provisions concerning the management of agricultural renewable energy, in related legislation, do not provide full legislative authority for actions in this area; and

2. the unbalanced approach of current State legislation is reflected in legislation concerning energy management more generally. Although the annual resource output of agricultural renewable energy in China totals more than one-third of the annual output of fossil fuel energy, certain laws normalize the exploitation and trade of fossil fuel energies, such as coal, petroleum, and natural gas. Such laws also provide for taxation and the management and maintenance of resources and equipment to different extents. In terms of legislation concerning energy management, there is still no authority to enact any specific legislation concerning agricultural renewable energy from the perspective of resource management.

5.2 No Effective Legislative Guarantee Is Provided for the Enforcement of Related State Policies, Programs, Schemes, or Plans

State schemes for the development of the national economy, the protection of ecological environments, renewable energy development, as well as related plans and programs, have been put forward. For example, the Ninth Five-Year Scheme of Energy Saving and Integrated Utilization put forward preferential polices such as "taxation adjustment, financial subsidies and discounted government loans."[60] The Tenth Five-Year Scheme on Energy Saving and Integrated Utilization of Resources put forward policies such as the "transfer of tax and tax burdens" and "public financial support."[61] The Tenth Five-Year Scheme on State Environmental Protection put forward the objectives that the integrated utilization rate of straws all over China reach eighty percent, and seventy percent of animal excrement be turned into resources.[62] The Development Scheme of Projects of Changing Straws to Manure in Form of Animal Excrement (1996–2000) required that the "Ministry of Agriculture and all governments at the provincial level should set up a long- and mid-term scheme and an annual implementation plan for projects for changing straw to manure in the form of animal excrement."[63] However, the related strategies and policies established in the development scheme, plan, and program of government have not been translated into legislation and so their objectives cannot be guaranteed by relevant legal systems and legal measures.

5.3 Central Legislation Is Lacking and Cannot Actively and Effectively Inform Local Legislation

In comparison with local legislation, central legislation is obviously lagging behind in relation to the management of agricultural renewable energy. Although there is still no

---

[60] *Supra* note 26. [61] *Supra* note 28.
[62] *Supra* note 30.
[63] Ministry of Agriculture, Development Scheme of Projects of Changing Straws to Manure in Form of Animal Excrement (1996–2000), *see* http://scmysp.net/zcfg/qgfg/zh/qgzhfg027.htm.

specific legislation for agricultural renewable energy in current local law, local legislation has begun to be enacted. This is before central legislation has been enacted. Furthermore, although almost all provincial people's congresses and governments all over China have established detailed local supporting rules and regulations in accordance with the Law of Energy Saving of the People's Republic of China, most local regulations and rules have not combined development of agricultural renewable energy with energy saving. Some have not even included agricultural renewable energy or biomass energy within the administrative scope of supporting regulations or rules. While there is no central government legislation to support local legislation, it is difficult for local legislation to have any impact in establishing administrative principles and an administrative system.

5.4 Related Provisions in Current Laws and Regulations Lack Sufficient Constraining and Compelling Force

As most of the provisions in current laws and regulations are merely provisions to encourage the development of alternative energies, no related legal obligations and legal responsibilities are provided for managers and users of renewable energy. There is also no legal framework for integrating energy development and environmental protection. Moreover, there is no clear relationship between authorities' legal rights and responsibilities. It is quite obvious that existing legal provisions are insufficient in their operation, constraining power, and compelling power. As a result, the implementation of related state policies is not prescribed in laws nor guaranteed by laws. Some departmental statements were simply established as restrictive measures aimed at administrative officials who violate the public interest and public environment. Such statements stipulated the means of punishment and legal responsibility for these people, while no detailed provisions were provided in relation to the rational utilization and protection of agricultural renewable energy. For example, in Methods on Straw Burning and Integrated Utilization and Methods on Control of Pollution Caused by Animal Husbandry, it is not clear which are the competent administrative authorities to perform governmental duties, legal responsibilities, and obligations in relation to the treatment of straws and animal excrement.

5.5 Management of Agricultural Renewable Energy Has Not Attracted the Common Concern or Recognition of Lawmakers

There is still no specific legislation in relation to the management of agricultural renewable energy, and most local legislation for the protection and management of agricultural renewable energy does not cover the integrated utilization of renewable energy. There is also no discussion on the need for agricultural renewable energy legislation in the mass media or in academic discourse. The management of integrated utilization of agricultural renewable energy has not yet attracted the concern or recognition of most lawmakers and legal researchers. If the integrated utilization of agricultural energy resources can be identified and developed, then the protection of rural ecological environments can be achieved. Yet in order to realize this objective, legislation is needed to effectively and fairly normalize the utilization of such substances and related management behavior.

5.6 Local Comprehensive Legislation on Agricultural Resources Does Not Provide for Agricultural Renewable Energy as an Object for Management

Although Liaoning, Jilin, Zhejiang, and Hubei Provinces have enacted local legislation relating to agricultural resources and their management, such enactments only refer to soil, water, organisms, and climate from the perspective of agricultural production. They do not provide for agricultural wastes generated in the course of agricultural production that can be utilized comprehensively as elements within the category of agricultural resources. For example, in Provisions on Comprehensive Management and Protection of Agricultural Resources of Liaoning Province, agricultural resources are defined as "agricultural natural resources that can be utilized in crop cultivation, forestry, animal husbandry and fishery, such as soil, water, organisms and climate."[64] In the General Administrative Regulations on Agricultural Resources of Jilin Province, agricultural resources are defined as "natural resources that can be utilized in crop cultivation, forestry, animal husbandry, fishery, and specialty industries, such as soil, grassland, water, organisms, and climate."[65] In Administrative Regulations on Agricultural Natural Resources of Zhejiang Province, agricultural natural resources are defined as "natural resources that are related to productive activities of crop cultivation, forestry, animal husbandry, and fishery, such as soil, water, forest, and organism."[66] In the General Administrative Regulations on Agricultural Natural Resources of Hubei Province, agricultural natural resources are defined as "natural resources that are related to productive activities of crop cultivation, forestry, animal husbandry, and fishery, such as soil, water, organism, and climate."[67] As local enactments have not included agricultural renewable energy within the definition of agricultural resources, even though these local regulations are enforced, they do not provide a mechanism for the management of agricultural renewable energy.

6 THE GOVERNMENT'S RESPONSIBILITIES AND OBLIGATIONS IN RELATION TO THE MANAGEMENT OF CHINA'S AGRICULTURAL RENEWABLE ENERGIES

This chapter has discussed the concept of agricultural renewable energy in China, the problems with its utilization, the current status of policies and legislation, and the incompleteness of legislation. The author now suggests that it is necessary to place particular emphasis on the legal responsibilities and legal obligations of governments at all levels in relation to the management of agricultural renewable energy.

Of the state or local regulations and rules related to agricultural renewable energy that are enforced, many are concerned mainly with the environmental pollution caused

---

[64] NPC Standing Committee of Liaoning Province, Provisions on Comprehensive Management and Protection of Agricultural Resources of Liaoning Province, December 3, 1997, Art. 2, Great Collections of China Laws and Regulations (Local Collections).

[65] NPC Standing Committee of Jilin Province, General Regulations on Agricultural Resources of Jilin Province, December 19, 1997, Art. 2, Great Collections of China Laws and Regulations (Local Collections).

[66] NPC Standing Committee of Zhejiang Province, Regulations on Agricultural Natural Resources of Zhejiang Province, November 1, 1999, Art. 2, Great Collections of China Laws and Regulations (Local Collections).

[67] NPC Standing Committee of Hubei Province, General Regulations on Agricultural Natural Resources of Hubei Province, July 28, 2000, Art. 2, Great Collections of China Laws and Regulations (Local Collections).

by such substances. These regulations and rules mostly provide normative rules for pollution control and investigation to determine responsibility for such pollution.

Undoubtedly, behavior that leads to environmental pollution falls within the usual administrative functions of governments and relevant parties are duty bound to obey state laws, statutes, and regulations, and to submit to supervision and management by competent administrative authorities of the government. However, the limitation of current laws and regulations is that they exclusively, or almost exclusively, focus on environmental pollution, instead of emphasizing or paying attention to the treatment and rational utilization of agricultural renewable energy substances.

Strictly speaking, the rational utilization of resources and protection and management of ecological environments are both the functions and obligations of the government. Government involvement and action is critical for achieving the objectives of the rational utilization of resources, the protection of ecological environments, and sustainable development. These governmental responsibilities should inform the behavior of resource developers and users, environment users and destroyers. Government should also take into account the following:

1. The government is duty bound to provide technology for the rational utilization and proper treatment of agricultural wastes, and to adopt related policies and measures to support the use of such technologies;
2. The government is duty bound to offer related preferential policies and encouragement for the development and promotion of technology for the integrated utilization of agricultural renewable energy substances, irrespective of whether such development or promotion is productive or nonproductive;
3. The government is duty bound to establish related plans and programs for the rational utilization of agricultural renewable energy, as well as technical development and promotion, within its jurisdiction, so as to guarantee the development of relevant undertakings;
4. The government is duty bound to offer related financial support for the development and promotion of technology for the integrated utilization of agricultural renewable energy, and incorporate such support in the annual fiscal budget of the government;
5. The government is duty bound to offer policy encouragement in the form of investment, taxation, and loans to those enterprises or individuals who invest in the development, application, and promotion of technology for the integrated utilization of agricultural renewable energy, and also provide related preferential policies for the benefit of such persons;
6. The government is duty bound to assume responsibility for energy wastes and environmental pollution caused as a governmental nonfeasance, specifically as a result of its lack of encouragement and support for the development of technology for the rational utilization and proper treatment of agricultural wastes, and for its failure to provide and promote the technology in a timely manner.

Therefore, this author suggests that in legislation related to the management of agricultural renewable energy, the responsibilities and obligations of governments at all levels should be noted with emphasis and specifically prescribed.

PART THREE

INTERNATIONAL ENERGY LAW

11 International Law and Global Sustainable Energy Production and Consumption

Adrian J. Bradbrook* and Ralph D. Wahnschafft**

1 INTRODUCTION

Over the past fifty years, the intergovernmental consultation process under the umbrella and the framework of the United Nations, its General Assembly, and its various subsidiary organs and commissions has produced a large number of international conventions and protocols under which nations have committed themselves to agreed principles of international law and global standards. While conventions and protocols form the core of binding international law, the world community has always recognized the value of achieving consensus in the formulation of nonbinding principles and universal policy guidelines through which policy issues of international concern can be addressed.[1]

Growing recognition of the need to achieve an ecologically more sustainable socioeconomic development has clearly marked the international development debate throughout the past decade.[2] In the same context, the need to urgently address energy–environment related issues and to work toward a sustainable energy future for all humankind has been widely recognized.[3] In spite of the increased global concerns for greater environmental protection and greater integration of environmental concerns into energy sector and economic decision making, and in spite of a considerable potential for international consensus on global policy guidelines in this field, no universal "code of conduct," "guideline," "action plan," or other form of "soft law" has yet been established.[4]

---

[1] The use of such principles and guidelines has its origin in 1948 in the Universal Declaration of Human Rights (UNGA Res 217A UN Doc A/810), probably the best known and most frequently cited soft law document.

[2] The importance of sustainable development was brought to international prominence in 1987 by the report of the World Commission on Environment and Development (the Brundtland Commission), created by the UN General Assembly in 1983: *see Our Common Future*, OUP, 1987.

[3] For example, in November 2000 the UN ESCAP organized in Bali, Indonesia, the Asia-Pacific NGO Symposium on Regional Perspectives and Initiatives for Achieving a "Sustainable Energy Future for All." The authors of this chapter were invited participants.

[4] For a discussion of the role of "soft law," *see* C. Chinkin, "The Challenge of Soft Law: Development and Change in International Law" (1989) 38 *Int & Comp LQ* 850; P. Dupuy, "Soft Law and the International Law of the Environment" (1991) 12 *Michigan J. Int. L.* 215.

* Bonython Professor of Law, School of Law, University of Adelaide, Australia.

** Economic Affairs Officer at the Energy Resources Section of the United Nations Economic and Social Commission for Asia and the Pacific (UNESCAP), based in Bangkok, Thailand.

This chapter seeks to remedy this omission and propose draft guidelines on sustainable energy production and consumption applicable to both developed and developing countries.

2 THE TERMS OF THE PROPOSED STATEMENT OF PRINCIPLES

The possible terms of a Statement of Principles, as drafted by the authors, are set out in full in the Annex to this chapter. Readers should refer to this text when considering the discussion of the terms in this section of the article.

While the majority of the terms of the proposed Statement of Principles contain novel ideas developed by the authors, some of the articles have been influenced by other soft law documents, in particular Agenda 21[5] and the Nonbinding Authoritative Statement of Principles for a Global Consensus on the Management, Conservation, and Sustainable Development of all Types of Forests.[6] The adoption of ideas from analogous documents, where appropriate, is considered sensible from a political standpoint in light of the anticipated difficulty in achieving the necessary international consensus to secure the adoption of the proposed Statement of Principles by the majority of nations. Where a particular clause or framework has been successfully negotiated in other parallel contexts, it would seem more likely to be regarded by the international community as acceptable in this context in comparison with other possible solutions.

A number of the minor provisions of the proposed Statement of Principles are self-explanatory and require no comment. The discussion in the remainder of this chapter will explain the meaning and significance of the important provisions.

2.1 Preamble

There is no consistency as to the length of preambles in modern international legal instruments. The goal should be to ensure that the context and background of the issue to be addressed by the document is adequately explained.

The proposed preamble seeks to make the following points:

- There should be universal access by the world population to clean and affordable energy resources. This is considered important in light of the fact that approximately two billion people in the world today (approximately one-third of the entire world population) is without access to electricity.[7] In areas without electricity supplies, people are obliged to rely on burning wood and animal manure for their energy requirements, which is unsustainable and causes severe health problems due to indoor air pollution.[8]
- Energy is a key component in the drive toward sustainable development.

---

[5] A/Conf 151/26. *See* N. A. Robinson (ed.), *Agenda 21: Earth's Action Plan*, Oceana Press, Dobbs Ferry, NY, 1993.

[6] (1992) 31 ILM 881.

[7] United Nations Development Programme, United Nations Department of Economic and Social Affairs and World Energy Council, *World Energy Assessment: Energy and the Challenge of Sustainability*, United Nations, New York, 2000, at 44.

[8] *Id.*, at 68.

- The needs of future generations must be taken into account in determining energy policy. This is consistent with the newly emerging principles of international environmental law.[9]
- The current heavy reliance on fossil fuels for energy production is unsustainable in the long term.
- The principle of common but differentiated responsibility[10] dictates that different energy solutions will be required in respect of developed and developing countries. As the current unsustainable energy production and consumption patterns were created initially by the developed countries, it is appropriate that the lead in introducing reforms and changes leading to sustainable energy patterns should be introduced and financed by the developed countries. This is consistent with other modern international environmental law instruments, where developed countries have taken primary responsibility for change.[11]

2.2 Objectives

Articles 1–3 contain a wide range of objectives of the Statement of Principles. The major features of these are as follows:

- Sustainability in the energy context is not inconsistent with the right of each state to promote economic development. However, it is the responsibility of each state to ensure that such development is not inconsistent with environmental objectives and reduces possible adverse impacts on human health to an absolute minimum.
- Energy security is a valid concern when considering sustainable energy policies.[12] This dictates a need for the international community to promote energy efficiency and to shift from fossil fuels to other energy resources. The past heavy reliance on oil and gas has caused international instability and tension and has led to armed conflict. For example, the current international dispute involving the People's Republic of China, Viet Nam, and the Philippines over sovereignty in the Spratly Islands in the South China Sea appears to concern the ownership of the suspected energy reserves in the seas surrounding the islands and to have little (if any) relevance to the sovereignty of the islands themselves.[13]

---

[9] *See generally* E. Brown Weiss, *In Fairness to Future Generations: International Law, Common Patrimony and Intergenerational Equity*, Oceana Press, Dobbs Ferry, NY, 1988; E. Brown Weiss, "Our Rights and Obligations to Future Generations for the Environment" (1990) 84 *American J. Int L*. 198; L. Gündling, "Our Responsibility to Future Generations" (1990) 84 *American J Int L* 207. This principle was first recognized in Principle 2 of the Stockholm Declaration on the Human Environment (1972) 11 ILM 1416. It is also referred to in Principle 3 of the Rio Declaration on Environment and Development ((1992) 31 ILM 874), Article 4 of the UNESCO Convention for the Protection of the World Cultural and Natural Heritage ((1972) 11 ILM 1358) and in a number of UN General Assembly Resolutions (for example, Protection of Global Climate for Present and Future Generations of Mankind, G. A. Res 43/53 Dec. 6, 1988, UN Doc A/Res/43/53 Jan. 27, 1989.

[10] Proclaimed in Principle 7 of the Rio Declaration on Environment and Development (1992) 31 ILM 874.

[11] *See e.g.*, the United Nations Framework Convention on Climate Change (1992) 31 ILM 849 and its associated Kyoto Protocol (1998) 37 ILM 22.

[12] On the importance of national energy security, particularly for developed countries, *see, for example*, R. Belgrave, C. K. Ebinger, and H. Okino (eds.), *Energy Security to 2000*, 1987; G. C. Georgiou, "US Energy Security and Policy Options for the 1990s" (1993) 21 *Energy Policy* 831; C. L. Orman, "The National Energy Strategy – An Illusive Quest for Energy Security" (1992) 13 *Energy L.J.* 251.

[13] See D. Ong, "The Spratlys Dispute Over Marine Resources: Time for a New Approach?" (1994) 12 *Oil and Gas Law and Taxation Rev.* 352; D. Ong, "Joint Development of the Spratly Islands' Marine Resources:

- The development of appropriate national energy laws and regulations, as well as energy policies, is an important element in the promotion of sustainable energy production and consumption. The exact form that such measures might take is considered in more detail below.[14]
- The need for additional financial assistance to developing countries to adopt sustainable energy policies together with technology transfer. This factor has been reiterated in all major environmental conventions in recent years.[15]
- The need to reduce wastage of fossil fuels based on past energy production and consumption practices. While still plentiful, coal, oil, and gas reserves are finite and will eventually be exhausted. Reduction in wastage will allow additional time for the world to develop adequate alternative renewable energy resources.
- The promotion of energy efficiency and renewable energy resources represent the best sustainable path for the world to take.
- When assessing the economic viability of alternative energy paths, consideration must be given to external environmental costs. The present system of energy accounting largely ignores such issues and makes traditional fossil fuel based energy policies appear to be artifically cheap. For example, when comparing the economics of road and rail transport for the transportation of goods, no allowance is traditionally made for costs such as road damage caused by heavy vehicles, damage to health caused by poor air quality in cities as a result of vehicle exhaust, or public hospital costs resulting from vehicle accidents. Similar comparisons can be made in the context of the costs of alternative forms of electricity generation.[16]

2.3 Common Principles

The two proposed common principles articles attempt to deal with the difficult balance between respecting each state's sovereignty with the need to control transboundary environmental damage. In *Trail Smelter*[17] an Arbitration Tribunal awarded damages to the United States in respect of air pollution damage caused by a Canadian smelter and required Canada to take appropriate control measures to ensure the cessation of the harm. The Tribunal stated that no state has the right to use or permit the use of its territory in such a manner as to cause injury by fumes in or to the territory of another.[18] Article 4 seeks to incorporate this decision within the energy context and to expand the principle so as to include all forms of environmental damage resulting from energy production and consumption. It is consistent in its wording with Principle 21 of

---

Legal Problems and Prospects for Solutions" (1993) 11 *Oil and Gas Law and Taxation Rev* 158; G. M. Valero, "Spratly Archipelago Dispute: Is the Question of Sovereignty Still Relevant?" (1994) 18 *Marine Policy* 314; L. G. Cordner, "The Spratly Islands and the Law of the Sea" (1994) 25 *Ocean Development and International Law* 61.

[14] *See* notes 48–49 *infra*, and accompanying text.

[15] *See, e.g.*, Articles 11–12 of the United Nations Framework Convention on Climate Change ((1992) 31 ILM 849); Article 11 of the Kyoto Protocol to the Framework Convention on Climate Change ((1998) 37 ILM 22); Article 10–10A of the Montreal Protocol on Substances that Deplete the Ozone Layer ((1987) 26 ILM 1541).

[16] *See* the seminal work by Pace University Center for Environmental Legal Studies, *Environmental Costs of Electricity*, Oceana Publications Inc., New York, 1990.

[17] (1939) 33 AJIL 182 and (1941) 35 AJIL 684; 1931–1941 3 UN RIAA 1905.

[18] (1941) 35 AJIL 684 at 716.

the 1972 Stockholm Declaration on the Human Environment[19] and Principle 2 of the Rio Declaration on Environment and Development,[20] which are regarded as reflecting customary international law.[21] Article 5 goes somewhat further by seeking to ensure that all state energy policies are consistent with sustainable development. This is outside the scope of Principle 21, but would be within the newly emerging customary right to a decent environment.[22]

In light of the difficulties caused to the development of international environmental law by sovereignty, it may be questioned whether it is a sensible idea to refer to sovereignty at all in the Statement of Principles. The argument could be made that the right of sovereignty is backward looking and inconsistent with the aim and purpose of the Statement of Principles. There appear to be three answers to this possible objection. First, to be effective the Statement of Principles will need to be adopted by the maximum possible number of states. The references to sovereignty in Articles 4 and 5 may reassure reluctant and hesitating states, which fear a loss of sovereignty, to become signatories. Second, there seems little advantage in trying to disguise the current state of environmental law by omitting references to sovereignty. Third, the inclusion of references to sovereignty would reduce the likelihood of arguments arising that the Statement of Principles is inconsistent with sovereignty and reduce the credibility of such arguments.

2.4 Efficiency in Energy Supply Systems

The need to improve the energy efficiency of energy supply systems and to reduce the use of fossil fuels in energy production is a key issue in achieving energy sustainability. Traditional coal-fired power plants are notoriously inefficient and as a consequence are major sources of transboundary air pollution. One major problem is acid rain.[23] The problem varies in gravity around the world, depending on geography and climatic conditions, and the sulphur content of the coal consumed. The problem has become of acute concern in the eastern part of North America, where Canadian forests have suffered as a consequence of airborne sulphur from power stations in the Midwest of the United States that burn high sulphur content locally produced coal. East Asia also suffers

---

[19] Principle 21 reads:

> States have, in accordance with the Charter of the United Nations and the principles of international law, the sovereign right to exploit their own resources pursuant to their own environmental policies, and the responsibility to ensure that activities within their jurisdiction do not cause damage to the environment of other States or of areas beyond the limits of national jurisdiction.

[20] This provision repeats the terms of Principle 21 of the Stockholm Declaration, except that the phrase "and developmental" is added after the phrase "pursuant to their own environmental."

[21] See, e.g., L. Sohn, "The Stockholm Declaration on the Human Environment" (1973) 14 *Harvard Int L. J.* 423.

[22] See H. Hohmann, *Precautionary Legal Duties and Principles of Modern International Environmental Law*, Graham & Trotman, London, 1994, 191–203.

[23] For a general discussion of the problem of acid rain, see C. C. Park, *Acid Rain: Rhetoric and Reality*, Methuen, London, 1987; H. Dowlatabadi and W. Harrington, "Policies for and Mitigation of Acid Rain; A Critique of Evaluation Techniques" (1989) 17 *Energy Policy* 116; D. P. Adams and W. P. Page, *Acid Deposition. Environmental, Economic and Policy Issues*, Plenum Press, New York, 1985. For a discussion of the legal problems associated with acid rain, see, e.g., J. L. Regens and R W Rycroft, "Options for Financing Acid Rain Controls" (1986) 26 *Natural Resources J.* 519.

from the use of high sulphur coal in China.[24] Perhaps the greatest problem is global warming. By far the greatest problem in the global warming issue is the increasing release of carbon into the atmosphere, the bulk of which results from coal-fired power stations, although the use of oil and gas also makes a significant contribution.[25] Approximately two-thirds of the global warming problem is caused by energy use and production.[26] Other problems attributable in part to energy supply systems include local air pollution in cities and ozone depletion.

While coal is the major pollutant among traditional energy supply systems, lesser but still significant problems caused by oil- and gas-fired plants exist. The other pollutant is nuclear energy. While this does not produce the problems referred to above, and in particular causes no atmospheric carbon emissions, the accidental release of radiation resulting from an accident at a nuclear power plant can cause catastrophic transboundary environmental harm, as evidenced in 1986 at Chernobyl.

The Statement of Principles seeks to reduce these sources of transboundary environmental harm by a variety of different strategems. Foremost amongst these is the use of a variety of different forms of renewable energy technologies as alternative supply-side options. Many of the options contained in Article 6 are self-explanatory. The list seeks to be as broad as possible to take account of the differing availability of the various resources in different countries and regions of the world. For example, solar energy is best suited to equatorial and subequatorial regions, while wind energy tends to predominate in high latitudes. Wind energy would include not only traditional land-based wind farms, but also newly emerging offshore wind turbines.[27] A variety of different solar energy technologies exist, and all are supported by Article 6. These include direct heat applications, photovoltaic conversion, and solar thermal power stations.[28] Small-scale hydropower schemes, which are based on run-of-the-river technology requiring no dams, is encouraged, but not the traditional large-scale applications. Although hydropower is clean and nonpolluting, large-scale applications have resulted in massive social and environmental disruption as a result of the physical displacement of native peoples and the drowning of fertile and productive land.

Article 7, which supports and promotes the use of energy efficiency, is another important key toward achieving a sustainable energy future. This is designed to emphasize the importance of energy efficiency in maximizing energy efficiency in energy production, and not only in energy consumption, where it has received most emphasis

---

[24] A. J. Bradbrook, "Energy Use and Atmospheric Protection" (1996) 3 *Australasian J. Natural Resources L. and Policy* 25, at 28–29.

[25] *Id.*, at 30.

[26] The exact figure may vary from country to country depending on its energy mix. *See, e.g., Green Paper on Sustainable Energy Policy for Australia*, AGPS, Canberra, 1996, at 20; R. J. Fowler, "International Policy Responses to the Greenhouse Effect and their Implications for Energy Policy in Australia," in D. J. Swaine (ed.), *Greenhouse and Energy*, 1990, at 462; D. A. Lashof and D. Tirpak, *Policy Options for Stabilising Global Climate*, U.S. Environmental Protection Agency, Washington, DC, 1990.

[27] *See* K. C. Tong, "Technical and Economic Aspects of a Floating Offshore Wind Farm" (1998) 74 *J. Wind Engineering and Industrial Aerodynamics* 399; A. J. Bradbrook and A. S. Wawryk, "The Legal Regime Governing the Establishment of Offshore Wind Turbines in Australia" (2001) 18 *Environmental and Planning Law Journal* 30.

[28] For a discussion of the different solar technologies, *see* World Energy Council, *New Renewable Energy Resources*, Kogan Page, London, 1994; A. J. Bradbrook, *Solar Energy and the Law*, Law Book Co., Sydney, 1984, Ch. 1; S. F. Kraemer, *Solar Law*, Shepards Inc., Colorado Springs, 1978, Ch. 3.

in the past. The draft article refers to the need to achieve the full benefit of energy efficiency throughout the energy cycle. "Energy cycle" should be understood to mean the entire energy chain, including activities related to prospecting for, exploration, production, conversion, storage, transport, distribution, and consumption of the various forms of energy, and the treatment and disposal of wastes, as well as the decommissioning, cessation, or closure of these activities, minimizing harmful environmental impacts.[29]

A particularly pervasive form of energy waste is transmission losses arising from electricity transmission cables. Depending on the distances that electricity is required to be transmitted, losses of up to ten percent are not uncommon. While some transmission losses are inevitable, technology has advanced to the extent that they can be substantially reduced. While this matter would be included within the general wording of Article 7, it was thought appropriate in light of the importance currently attached by the world community to extending electricity grid systems into remote areas in developing countries[30] to highlight the need for energy conservation in this respect by the inclusion of a special provision, Article 8.

Articles 9 and 10 refer to the vexed and controversial issues of the privatization of the energy supply industries and the future use and expansion of nuclear energy. The majority of the developed countries have either undertaken or are in the process of undertaking structural reforms promoting privatization of the electricity and natural gas industries.[31] Such reforms are justified by the increased efficiencies that private participation has promised. While privatization can produce useful economic savings in the production of energy supplies, the danger exists that the public interest will be sacrificed in the name of increasing corporate profits. The public interests that need protecting are many and varied, including, for example, the need to ensure the preservation of a minimum level of supplies to needy people. The public interest also embraces the advancement of energy efficiency and renewable energy supplies. Unfettered, the drive toward profit maximization may well lead private electricity companies to abandon the use of renewable energy technologies and increase the use of traditional, fossil fuel technologies on the ground of cost competitiveness. Similarly, as corporate profits will only be generated by the sale of energy, energy conservation and efficiency runs counter to the private interests of companies. The answer is to ensure that provisions are included in national electricity and gas legislation requiring privatized companies to ensure a minimum use of renewable energy for electricity generation and to adopt specified measures in support of energy efficiency.[32] As such legislation could take a variety of possible forms, it would be inappropriate for the Statement of Principles to specify the exact form that it should take. It would be sufficient for the Statement merely to

---

[29] This definition is taken from Article 19(3)(a) of the Energy Charter Treaty ((1995) 34 ILM 360) and article 2(4) of its related Protocol on Energy Efficiency and Related Environmental Aspects ((1995) 34 ILM 446).

[30] World Energy Assessment, *supra* note 7, at 381.

[31] *See, e.g.*, A. R. Lucas, "Impact of Privatisation and Deregulation of Energy Industries on Canadian Environmental Law and Policy" (1996) *14 J. Energy and Natural Resources L.* 68; G. Kühne, "Incremental Regulatory Reform and Antitrust Law in the Energy Sector" (1996) 14 *J. Energy and Natural Resources L.* 76; U. Hammer, "Reorganisation of the Norwegian Electricity Market" (1996) 14 *J. Energy and Natural Resources L.* 95.

[32] *See, e.g.*, Electricity Act 1989 (UK), §§ 32–33.

require appropriate measures to be taken in this regard. The wording of the proposed Article 9 has been drafted accordingly.

In light of current polarized opinions as to the future of nuclear energy, it would be impossible to achieve world consensus for the inclusion of a clause in the Statement of Principles recommending either the expansion of the industry or its eventual abolition. While nuclear energy is being enthusiatically promoted in some countries (France, Belgium, and Japan), it is being phased out in others (Germany, Sweden, and Switzerland). Opinions differ fundamentally as to whether the risk of future accidental large-scale releases of radiation is real, whether there is yet a satisfactory solution to the disposal of nuclear wastes, and whether the use of nuclear energy for peaceful purposes can be separated from its possible military application. While past incidents culminating in 1987 in Chernobyl have placed a brake on the expansion of nuclear energy in some countries, the passage of time since that accident and the emergence of global warming as a major international environmental issue have led to a reconsideration in other countries. The latter issue is potentially very significant as the nuclear energy cycle avoids atmospheric carbon emissions.[33] The wording of Article 10 of the Statement of Principles is designed to achieve a compromise between the two factions by not prohibiting the future use and expansion of nuclear energy, but making such use and expansion conditional on a satisfactory resolution of the problems of nuclear waste disposal and the accidental release of radiation.

2.5 Efficiency in Energy Consumption

It is in the field of energy consumption that energy efficiency can make its most effective contribution in the short to medium term. Energy efficiency measures can be adopted in all sectors of the economy, including industry, transportation, domestic appliances, and buildings. This is recognized by the wording of Article 11, which encourages appropriate state action in respect of each of these sectors. Articles 12–17 seek to expand on the type of measures considered appropriate.

Articles 12 and 13 refer to energy efficiency measures to curb industrial energy consumption. Article 12 does not impose actual measures on states, but rather leaves it to their discretion to determine the appropriateness of possible alternative measures. A wide body of literature exists on the various alternative measures.[34] Article 13 seeks to supplement such legislative responses by the use of regular energy and environmental auditing of resource use in industry and by the use of trained energy managers.[35]

Article 14 refers to energy efficiency in home and office appliances and promotes the use of energy efficiency standards and energy labeling programs.[36] Such standards

---

[33] Nuclear energy is not entirely free of carbon emissions as significant carbon emissions result from the construction of nuclear plant.

[34] *See, e.g.,* A. Bradbrook, "Energy Conservation Legislation for Industry" (1992) 10 *J. Energy and Natural Resources L.* 145.

[35] *Id.,* at 153–155.

[36] *See* A. J. Bradbrook, "The Development of Energy Efficiency Laws for Domestic Appliances" (1990) 12 *Adelaide L. Rev.* 306; W. H. Lawrence and J. H. Minan, "The Use and Implementation of Solar Energy Equipment Standards" (1982) 3 *Solar Law Reporter* 781; California Energy Commission, *California's Appliance Efficiency Standards: An Historical Review, Analysis and Recommendations,* Report at 400-83-020, 1983.

and programs already exist in many industrialized countries.[37] The problem caused by electricity consumption in the standby use of electricity for office and home equipment has increased to such an extent in recent years that it is thought necessary to make special mention of the need for remedial measures.

The need to improve the fuel efficiency of motor vehicles is referred to in Article 15.[38] This issue is particularly significant in light of the fact that little fuel switching to renewable energy resources has occurred in this sector,[39] and that the sector is still overwhelmingly reliant on oil. The article promotes the use of fuel efficiency standards, labeling for fuel efficiency, and the mandatory inclusion of fuel efficiency information in model-specific vehicle advertising.

Energy efficiency in the building sector is addressed in Articles 16 and 17.[40] The Statement of Principles favors the adoption of a combination of measures for all categories of buildings, the most important being minimum insulation standards, energy rating schemes, building energy audits, and training schemes for professional personnel.

A major difficulty is in securing agreement on the most appropriate measuring system for energy consumption. Without such a system, no comparative records could be kept. Energy intensity is used by the various articles in the Statement of Principles as the appropriate measure. This can be defined as the level of energy needed per unit of output. While energy intensity has never been employed in the past in any international agreement, it is commonly employed by energy specialists as an accurate measure of testing comparative energy efficiency levels.[41] The essence of energy intensity is that any given manufactured item requires a certain amount of energy to produce. The country that produces the given item using the smallest level of energy will have the lowest energy intensity (and vice versa). The aim is to record the lowest measure of energy intensity possible.

Energy intensity is not the only possible measuring system for energy consumption. If energy intensity is considered to be too complex, it would be possible to adopt a system

---

[37] *See, e.g.,* United States: Energy Policy and Conservation Act 1975, Pub. L. 94-163, 89 Stat. 871; Australia: Electricity (Energy Labeling of Electrical Appliances) Regulation 1995, made pursuant to Electricity Act 1945 (New South Wales), § 37(2); Electricity (Electrical Articles) Regulation 1994, made pursuant to the Electricity Act 1994 (Queensland), § 266; Electrical Products Regulations 1990, made pursuant to the Electrical Products Act 1988 (South Australia), §8.

[38] *See* Office of Technology Assessment, *Improving Automobile Fuel Economy: New Standards, New Approaches,* US Government Printing Office, Report OTA-E-504, 1991; A. J. Bradbrook, "Alternative Legal Measures to Improve the Fuel Efficiency of Motor Vehicles," in Economic and Social Commission for Asia and the Pacific, *Energy Efficiency: Compendium of Energy Conservation Legislation in Countries of the Asia and Pacific Region,* United Nations, New York, 1999, at 105ff; A. J. Bradbrook and A. S. Wawryk, "Legislative Implementation of Financial Mechanisms to Improve Motor Vehicle Fuel Efficiency" (1998) 22 *Melbourne U. L. Rev* 537.

[39] In some countries, ethanol and methanol have acquired a significant market share. The most spectacular success is Brazil, where 70% of all motor vehicles now rely on ethanol rather than gasoline. For a discussion of the situation in Brazil, *see* J. Goldemberg, *Energy for a Sustainable World,* Wiley Eastern Ltd., New Delhi, 1988, at 239ff; A. de Oliveira, "Reassessing the Brazilian Alcohol Programme" (1991) 19 *Energy Policy* 47. *See generally,* A. J. Bradbrook and A. S. Wawryk, "Energy, Sustainable Development and Motor Fuels: Legal Barriers to the Use of Ethanol" (1999) 16 *Environmental and Planning L. J.* 196.

[40] *See* A. J. Bradbrook, *Energy Conservation Legislation for Building Design and Construction,* Canadian Institute of Resources Law, Calgary, 1992; G. P. Thompson, *Building to Save Energy: Legal and Regulatory Approaches,* Ballinger Publishing Co., Cambridge, MA, 1980.

[41] For a general discussion of energy intensity, *see* H. Khatib, "Energy Intensity: A New Look" (1995) 23 *Energy Policy* 727; W. H. Golove and L. J. Schipper, "Restraining Carbon Emissions: Measuring Energy Use and Efficiency in the USA" (1997) 25 *Energy Policy* 803.

of percentage reduction of either total energy consumption or fossil fuel consumption. The use of either of these alternatives would involve only minor changes to the wording of the Statement of Principles.

2.6 Energy Pricing

The pricing of energy is crucial in shaping the world's energy future. The past and continued predominant use of fossil fuels for both energy production and consumption in all sectors of the economy is a reflection of the fact that fossil fuels have been priced more cheaply than possible alternatives. In addition, the relative affordability of traditional petroleum supplies has fueled the exponential use of petroleum for private motor vehicles since the end of the Second World War.

Under existing pricing policies it is unrealistic to expect widespread adoption worldwide of sustainable energy futures. A reshaping of energy pricing policies is a vital precursor to increasing the use of energy efficiency measures and renewable energy technologies and to preserving the existing stocks of fossil fuels for future generations.

The Statement of Principles contains three measures on energy pricing in Articles 18 and 19. First, environmental costs and benefits should be incorporated into energy pricing mechanisms. The traditional failure to do so in the past has resulted in the price of fossil fuels being kept artificially low. The adoption of environmental effects into fossil fuel prices would have a dramatic effect. It would mean, for example, that the cost of road freight would have to be increased to take account, inter alia, of increased damage to the highways caused by trucks, the increased health costs posed by vehicle exhaust emissions, and the increased hospital costs resulting from road accidents. Such increased prices might well result in the transfer of most road freight to rail, a much more efficient and environmentally friendly alternative. It would also mean that energy utilities using coal as the principle source of fuel for electricity generation would have to adjust their prices upward to take account of the environmental problems caused by coal combustion, including global warming, acid rain, the health and safety effects of coal mining, and local air pollution degradation.[42]

Second, Article 19 recommends the gradual adjustment of energy prices upward in order to enhance sustainable energy production and consumption. This is particularly important in the major developed countries, which are collectively responsible for the majority of the world's fossil fuel consumption. Some European nations have already taken the first steps in this regard. An illustration of this is Germany, which has introduced an ecological tax on petroleum whereby the price is increased by annual increments of approximately 3 euro cents over the rate of inflation over a period of years.

Third, Article 19 calls for existing price subsidies in favor of conventional energy technologies to be phased out. Such subsidies exist in nearly all developed countries, although their details and operation differ. They are not designed to deter the development of energy efficiency and renewable energy technologies, but incidentally have this effect. One useful illustration is the adverse effect that cheap, off-peak electricity tariffs have had on the market for solar hot water systems. The introduction of such

---

[42] *See* Pace University Center for Environmental Legal Studies, *Environmental Costs of Electricity*, Oceana Publications Inc., New York, 1990.

preferential tariffs were designed with the laudable goal of promoting energy efficiency in electricity generation and to avoid the need for electricity utilities to construct new electricity generating stations for peak supply periods, but have had the effect of pricing solar energy for water heating out of the market. Solar energy systems have a high initial capital cost that is gradually recouped by savings made in electricity supply charges. With cheap, off-peak tariffs for water heating, the time taken for purchasers of solar systems to recoup their initial capital outlay (the "pay-back period") has increased to such an extent that the systems are no longer economically justifiable in many countries.

2.7 Mitigation of Environmental Impacts

Although the environmental impacts of energy production are referred to in the Statement of Principles in other contexts, the issue is regarded as sufficiently important to justify separate treatment in the document. The relevant Articles are 20, 21, and 22.

Article 20 draws the link between forest preservation and energy policies. The provision reflects the increased importance attached to forest management and preservation since the Rio Conference on Environment and Development in 1992 and the adoption in that year of the Statement of Forestry Principles.[43] Much forest damage in the past has resulted from energy production, particularly from coal-fired power plants. The proposed article requires all pollutants from energy production which are capable of harming forest ecosystems to be strictly controlled by all levels of government.

Article 21 makes the general statement that governments must ensure that the possible adverse environmental consequences must always be taken prior to adopting any policies, programs, and plans in support of energy production by the use of fossil fuels. This is followed by a proposed practical means of implementing this requirement contained in Article 22. This article focuses on environmental impact assessment (EIA) as a tool for controlling pollution from fossil fuel fired power plants. The majority of developed nations have already adopted EIA procedures for all significant land developments, although the effectiveness of their procedures and their applicability in the energy context varies from state to state depending on the terms of the national legislation. EIA is generally regarded by environmental lawyers as one of the major methods of preventing and controlling actual and potential environmentally harmful developments. The Statement of Principles proposes that all activities involving the use of energy by the use of nonrenewable energy resources that are likely to have an adverse effect on the environment be evaluated before approval. Such evaluation must be effective and transparent.

2.8 Consumer Information and Environmental Education

Sustainable energy development involves the introduction of a wide range of consumer products incorporating renewable energy and energy efficiency technologies. Consumer education and consumer confidence is essential to the widespread introduction of these new consumer products.[44]

---

[43] *See supra* note 7 and accompanying text.

[44] *See* J. H. Minan and W. H. Lawrence, "Product Standards and Solar Energy," in J. H. Minan and W. H. Lawrence (eds.), *Legal Aspects of Solar Energy*, Lexington Books, Lexington, MA, 1981, at 153ff;

This has been highlighted in the past by both the United Nations and international consumer organizations. In 1999, the United Nations General Assembly amended its Guidelines for Consumer Protection so as to include sustainable consumption, based on a recommendation of the Third Session of the Commission for Sustainable Development.[45] The new Guidelines state that the promotion of sustainable consumption is one of the principle objectives of consumer protection (cl. I(h)), and that the promotion of sustainable consumption should be one of the features of a strong consumer protection policy which all governments are urged to develop and maintain (cl. II.3(g)). Energy is specifically included as an area of consumer concern. This same theme was adopted by the Asia-Pacific NGO Forum on Effective Consumer Information for Sustainable Energy Use, held in May 1999 in Seoul, Republic of Korea, and organized jointly by the United Nations Economic and Social Commission for Asia and the Pacific (ESCAP) and the Citizens' Alliance for Consumer Protection of Korea. This Forum consisted of representatives of the leading consumer organizations of the majority of countries of the Asia-Pacific region. The Forum published a document entitled "Conclusions and Recommendations for Future Action by Consumer Organizations to Promote Sustainable Development and Sustainable Energy Use."[46] Recommendation 6 states: "A comprehensive system of legislation designed to protect consumer interests is essential. Consumers investing in renewable energy devices and energy efficiency equipment deserve particular protection from misleading information."

The Statement of Principles builds on this theme in Articles 22–24. Article 22 states that greater public awareness and understanding of the environmental impacts of energy production and consumption is an essential prerequisite to more environmentally conscious consumption patterns. Article 23 supports the development of consumer information programs as to energy consumption, including product energy labeling for comparative energy efficiency and independent product testing. Education is seen as the key element in Article 24, both for the purposes of influencing consumer choice and indirectly for influencing electricity producers and product manufacturers. The article states that education is required as to sustainable energy consumption, and that emphasis should be given to targeting children as future consumers.

2.9 Policies and Strategies for Implementation

The Statement of Principles recognizes in Article 25 that the achievement of a sustainable energy future will depend on a combination of policy initiatives rather than one large measure. The article adopts the conventional wisdom that the combination of measures

---

W. H. Lawrence and J. H. Minan, "The Role of Warranties and Product Standards in Solar Energy Development" (1981) 34 *Vanderbilt L. Rev.* 537; A. J. Bradbrook, "Eco-Labeling: Lessons from the Energy Sector" (1996) 18 *Adelaide L. Rev.* 35.

[45] The original ECOSOC Guidelines for Consumer Protection were drafted in 1985 and adopted by General Assembly Resolution 39/248 of April 9, 1985. The Commission on Sustainable Development recommendations are contained in document E/1992/31, Par. 45, § E. The revised Guidelines for Consumer Protection were adopted in ECOSOC Resolution 1999/7 of July 26, 1999.

[46] *See* A. J. Bradbrook, "The Development of a Regulatory Framework on Consumer Protection and Consumer Information for Sustainable Energy Use" (2000) 5 *Asia Pacific Journal of Environmental Law* 239.

must consist of three separate types of measures: regulations, financial stimulatory measures, and educational reforms.[47] Regulations, sometimes referred to disparagingly by economists as "command and control measures," ensure that minimum levels of reforms are achieved. This type of reform includes such measures as energy efficiency standards for appliances, maximum fuel consumption laws for motor vehicles, and the compulsory purchase by electricity supply companies of specified minimum levels of supply from renewable energy sources. Such laws typically penalize nonperformance by fines. The weakness of such measures is that they only ensure compliance by companies with the minimum standards specified in the legislation and give no incentives to companies to exceed these standards. This is the role of financial stimulatory measures. Such measures may consist of investment allowances, income tax or company tax deductions for investment costs, and special grants or tax concessions for expenditure on research and investment. The combination of regulations and stimulatory measures has been referred to as the "carrot and stick" approach to reform, with regulations (the stick) being supplemented by financial incentives (the carrot).[48] This would appear to be the ideal combination.

Educational measures promoting the importance of sustainable energy development are often overlooked, but are fundamental for building the public understanding and support for the type of reforms that will be necessary to take us away from the fossil fuel era into a future built on renewable energy technologies. The measures required will be at all levels, ranging from energy education at school to new professional courses offered at tertiary institutions and to general educational courses for the general public at continuing education centers. An important element in the educational process is the provision of information on energy consumption. Hence some reforms that have already been made (for example, the provision of energy consumption labels on motor vehicles and domestic appliances) relate primarily to the educational goal and show that progress has already been made. There is a link between regulation and education, as sometimes the purpose of a mandatory law is not to punish individuals for breaching the law but rather to educate them as to the correct course of action. The real purpose of the labeling legislation is not to punish companies for breaching the law but rather to ensure that the public is educated and persuaded to change its behavior. Outside the energy sector there are many examples of this, such as laws requiring the mandatory wearing of seat belts in cars and crash helmets for motor cycles, and laws requiring a health warning to be displayed on tobacco products.[49]

Articles 26–32 support the general policy enunciated in Article 25 in a variety of different ways with a number of specific proposals. Article 27 makes the important point that action will be required by all levels of government to address the sustainable energy question. While some reforms will be the responsibility of national governments (for example, taxation reforms and fiscal incentives to manufacturers), others may devolve on local or state governments. An illustration of the latter would be legislation designed

---

[47] On this issue, *see* A. J. Bradbrook, "Energy Law as an Academic Discipline" (1996) 14 *J. Energy and Natural Resources L.* 190, at 214–15.

[48] *Id.*, at 215.

[49] *See, e.g.*, Canada: Tobacco Products Control Act, Stats Can 1988, c. 20; New Zealand: Smoke-Free Environments Act 1990 (NZ); Hong Kong, China: Smoking (Public Health) Ordinance 1982.

to protect solar access to solar collector panels.[50] The division of legislative responsibility will depend on the constitution of each country.

Articles 30 and 32 are particularly significant for the future of sustainable energy development. Article 30 states that scientific and technological research in relation to sustainable energy production and consumption should be strengthened. This recognizes that there has been a very significant shortage of research funds available in the majority of countries in recent years to conduct research into sustainable energy technologies. This is presumably because governments have failed to recognize the importance of this area of research for future development. In addition to the increased provision of direct research grants in this area by governments to industries and universities, the article could best be satisfied by the introduction of significant tax incentives for private investment in sustainable energy research and development. The cost to consolidated revenue would be minimal in comparison with the boost that such a measure would give to sustainable energy technologies.

Article 32 seeks to prohibit developed countries from exporting old, polluting technologies in to developing countries. This form of dumping already occurs in many parts of the world. One illustration is the sale by Japan to many countries of the Asia-Pacific region of motor vehicles over a certain age that are no longer allowed to be registered in Japan under national legislation. Dumping of outmoded energy consuming equipment merely shifts the source of pollution from the exporting to the importing nation and fails to address the need for energy efficiency on a worldwide basis. Such a measure also condemns developing countries to suffer major health and other environmental problems caused by the use of polluting technologies.

The key to the introduction of reforms in favor of sustainable energy technologies is the availability of government revenue. Article 29 seeks to address this issue by providing for the creation of specific national funds for this purpose created from revenues produced from direct or indirect forms of energy consumption taxation. While such an energy consumption tax would doubtless prove unpopular in the short term, there are many examples of the use of taxes or levies to fund environmentally worthwhile national or local projects.[51]

2.10 International Cooperation

The proposed articles on international cooperation, Articles 33–41, contain a variety of measures designed to ensure that all states, particularly developing countries, participate in and derive benefit from the drive toward the introduction of sustainable energy technologies. Without such participation, the wealth gap between developed and developing countries will only get worse as the world comes to rely increasingly on energy efficiency measures and renewable energy sources.

Many of the proposed measures are self-evident and require no commentary. Perhaps the most important provisions are Articles 39, 40, and 41. Consistent with other

---

[50] For a discussion of solar access legislation, *see* A. J. Bradbrook, *Solar Energy and the Law*, Law Book Co., Sydney, 1984; M. M. Eisenstadt, "Access to Solar Energy: The Problem and its Current Status" (1982) 22 *Natural Resources J* 21; J. W. Gergacz, "Legal Aspects of Solar Energy: Statutory Approaches for Access to Sunlight" (1982) 10 *Boston College Environmental Affairs L. Rev.* 1.

[51] In Australia, for example, *see* Water Management Act 2000 (NSW) and Emergency Services Funding Act 1998 (SA).

modern international environmental law agreements, Article 39 seeks from developed countries the provision of new and additional financial resources to be made available to developing countries. The specified purpose of Article 39 is to enable developing countries to introduce sustainable energy production and consumption policies. This is linked to Article 41, which asks developed countries to provide access to and transfer of environmentally sound technologies and corresponding know-how on favorable terms, including on concessional and favorable terms. In light of the existing wealth imbalance between developed and developing countries and the problem of external indebtedness of the majority of developing countries, it is quite unrealistic to expect developing countries to be able to finance unaided the development and implementation of sustainable energy technologies or to develop the necessary know-how and scientific and technical expertise.

Article 40 is noteworthy in that it makes the link between energy and climate change. As noted above, energy production and consumption is the major source of atmospheric carbon emissions and the leading cause of global warming.[52] If the three flexibility mechanisms prescribed in the Kyoto Protocol to the United Nations Framework Convention on Climate Change (the clean development mechanism, joint implementation, and emissions trading) are to play an effective role in reducing carbon emissions, it will be vital that such mechanisms include new sustainable energy projects.

3 CONCLUSION

A sustainable energy future has long been recognized as one of the essential elements in the drive toward sustainable development. Specific mention in international documents as to the importance of energy for sustainable development go back at least as far as the Brundtland Report in 1987. While progress in developing internationally agreed sustainable energy policies since then has been slow, the recently concluded World Summit on Sustainable Development Plan of Implementation gives new hope to the development of international law in this area in the future. In contrast to Agenda 21, where the relevant part of the report, Chapter 9, makes scant reference to energy, the new Plan of Implementation sees energy as an integral part of world poverty eradication and the changing of unsustainable consumption and production patterns.

As the first major international soft law instrument to recognize and address energy production and consumption as part of sustainable development, the Plan of Implementation is inevitably vague and general in relation to the concrete actions proposed. The authors believe that the next stage forward will be the development of a nonbinding statement of energy principles. This should form the basis of a further international conference and negotiations. The adoption of such a statement was eventually accepted at the 1992 UNCED conference as the most appropriate policy in respect of forest management, an area of similar difficulty in achieving consensus. The proposed statement of energy principles expounded in this article is designed as the basis for negotiation of a future international agreement. While many may regard a statement of energy principles as too weak to be effective and would consequently prefer the negotiation of a new Convention on Energy or a new Energy Protocol to the United Nations Framework

---

[52] *See* World Energy Assessment, *supra* note 7, at 86–95.

Convention on Climate Change, it is submitted that such a binding treaty would as a practical matter be impossible to achieve in the short to medium term. This would need to be left to a third stage of international law development.

ANNEX
NON-LEGALLY BINDING STATEMENT OF PRINCIPLES FOR A GLOBAL CONSENSUS ON SUSTAINABLE ENERGY PRODUCTION AND CONSUMPTION

PREAMBLE

(a) Access to clean and affordable energy is a precondition for all social and economic development. These Guidelines endeavor to lay out a universally acceptable framework for national policies and international cooperation in pursuit of the sustainable development objectives laid out in Agenda 21. Adherence to these guidelines is expected to facilitate the achievement of "a sustainable energy future for all."

(b) Energy resources should be sustainably managed to meet the social, economic, and ecological needs of present and future generations. The currently prevailing patterns of energy production and consumption are predominantly based on finite fossil fuel reserves and are therefore not sustainable in a longer term perspective. Growing environmental concerns also call for a stringent review of energy policies.

(c) Unsustainable patterns of energy production and consumption threaten to harm the global environment. Industrialized countries should take the lead in achieving sustainable energy production and consumption patterns; developing countries should seek to achieve sustainable energy production and consumption patterns in their development process, having due regard to the principle of common but differentiated responsibilities. The special situation and needs of developing countries in this regard should be fully taken into account.

(d) States should strive to promote an international economic climate conducive to the continued and environmentally sound development of sustainable energy production and consumption in all countries.

OBJECTIVES

1. The guiding objective of these principles is to allow for economic development to occur in all states with the minimum possible adverse impact to human health and the environment and to preserve the existing reserves of fossil fuels for the benefit of future generations.

2. The objectives of this Statement of Principles are as follows:

    (a) To act as a framework for a world energy strategy aimed at concerted international, national, and regional programs for harmonious and sustainable economic and social development;

    (b) To encourage states to cooperate and, as appropriate, assist each other in developing and implementing policies, laws, and regulations designed to promote sustainable energy production and consumption;

    (c) To promote energy efficiency policies consistent with sustainable development;

(d) To create framework conditions that induce energy producers and consumers to use energy as economically, efficiently, and environmentally soundly as possible, particularly through the organization of energy efficient markets and a fuller reflection of environmental costs and benefits;

(e) To advance the sustainable energy policies agreed to in Chapter 9 of Agenda 21, relating to the protection of the atmosphere;

(f) To encourage and facilitate programs for fuel switching from high carbon to low carbon sources of energy and for the substitution of fossil fuels by environmentally benign sustainable energy technologies;

(g) To ensure financial and technological assistance for developing countries to adopt sustainable energy production and consumption policies; and

(h) To preserve dwindling global reserves of fossil fuels from further unnecessary waste due to past unsustainable patterns of energy production and consumption.

3. Energy conservation and energy efficiency are important features of energy security, and their promotion can enhance the prospects of economic development and world peace.

COMMON PRINCIPLES

4. States have, in accordance with the Charter of the United Nations and the principles of international law, the sovereign right to exploit their own energy resources pursuant to their own environmental policies, but have the responsibility to ensure that activities within their jurisdiction or control do not cause damage to the environment of other states or of areas beyond the limits of national jurisdiction.

5. States have the sovereign and inalienable right to utilize, manage, and develop their existing energy resources in accordance with their development needs and level of socioeconomic development, but subject to policies consistent with sustainable development.

EFFICIENCY IN ENERGY SUPPLY SYSTEMS

6. States should promote the greater use of renewable sources of energy and energy efficiency as far as possible throughout all sectors of the economy. Renewable sources of energy include, among others, the following: (a) biomass fuel (including crop residues, wood mill wastes, forest residues, municipal solid wastes, and ethanol); (b) solar energy (in all its applications); (c) wind energy; (d) geothermal energy; (e) tidal and wave energy; (f) salt gradient energy; (g) ocean thermal energy conversion; and (h) small-scale hydropower (of capacity of ten megawatts or less).

7. States should strive to achieve the full benefit of energy efficiency throughout the energy cycle. To this end they should, to the best of their competence, formulate and implement energy efficiency policies and cooperative or coordinated actions based on cost-effectiveness and economic efficiency, taking due account of environmental aspects.

8. In the maintenance and development of supply-side energy systems, conversion and transmission losses need to be minimized to the extent technically possibly and economically feasible.

9. The facilitation or increase of private sector participation can be an important option for the development of the energy supply infrastructures, in particular in developing countries. Where this occurs, legislative measures must be taken to ensure that the use of energy efficiency measures and renewable energy technologies is enhanced.

10. The future use and expansion of nuclear energy should only proceed if the problems of the disposal of nuclear wastes and the environmental risks associated with the accidental release of radiation are adequately addressed.

EFFICIENCY IN ENERGY CONSUMPTION

11. States should formulate, implement, publish, and regularly update national programs containing measures to reduce energy intensity. These programs concern all sectors of the economy, including, inter alia, industry, transportation and commercial, institutional, and residential buildings.

12. In most industrialized and new industrializing countries industry accounts for the largest share of final energy end use. At national level appropriate measures should be considered with a view to raising the energy efficiency of industrial production, in particular in those sectors and industrial establishments that are characterized by energy intensities significantly above world average.

13. Measures to promote periodic, regular energy and environmental auditing of resource use in industry are useful for enhancing productivity. However, adequate training of designated energy managers is a further important factor in advancing energy conservation programs in industry.

14. In consultation with manufacturers and consumer organizations, states should seek to promote higher levels of energy efficiency in electrical home and office appliances. The introduction of minimum energy efficiency standards and energy labeling programs for enhanced consumer information can be cost-effective tools for energy efficiency promotion. Measures aimed at reducing electricity leakage and standby losses will be significant for the long term development trend in energy use.

15. Increasing the fuel efficiency of automobiles is another effective policy measure for reducing harmful atmospheric emissions. The introduction of fuel efficiency standards and fuel efficiency labeling, and the mandatory inclusion of fuel efficiency information in model-specific vehicle advertising are among the policy options through which vehicle fuel efficiency can be improved.

16. In many of the developed and the rapidly developing economies, commercial and institutional buildings account for a growing share in energy consumption, in particular electricity consumption. Building codes and standards requiring improved building insulation can be effective tools to reduce energy consumption. The introduction of preconstruction permits, building energy audits, and training of professional personnel are among the most effective optional measures for energy efficiency promotion. In addition, the promotion of bio-climatic building designs and maximum use of daylighting have also proven effective measures in both developed and developing countries.

17. Mandatory building codes or energy rating schemes for residential buildings have shown to be an important energy saving measure, in particular in countries with cold climates. In developing countries such schemes are less relevant and less applicable.

ENERGY PRICING

18. The incorporation of environmental costs and benefits into market forces and mechanisms, in order to achieve sustainable energy production and consumption, should be encouraged.

19. States should seek to enhance sustainable energy production and consumption by adjusting energy prices upward to reflect the real cost of energy supply and to enable energy efficiency projects to compete financially on a level playing field with other technologies. Existing subsidies in favor of conventional energy technologies distort the market and discourage energy efficiency initiatives. Such subsidies should be phased out.

MITIGATION OF ENVIRONMENTAL IMPACTS

20. Pollutants from energy production and consumption, particularly airborne pollutants, including those responsible for acidic deposition, that are harmful to the health of forest ecosystems at the local, national, regional, and global levels should be strictly controlled.

21. States should take appropriate measures to ensure that before they adopt policies, programs and plans relating to energy production by the use of nonrenewable energy resources that are likely to have a significant adverse effect on the environment, the environmental consequences of such actions are duly taken into account.

22.(a) States should establish or strengthen national environmental impact assessment procedures to ensure that all activities involving the production of energy by the use of nonrenewable energy resources that are likely to have a significant adverse effect on the environment are evaluated before approval.

(b) States should designate appropriate national authorities to ensure that environmental impact assessments are effective and conducted under procedures accessible to concerned states, international organizations, persons, and nongovernmental organizations.

(c) States should conduct periodic reviews both to determine whether activities approved by them are carried out in compliance with the conditions set out in the approval and to evaluate the effectiveness of the proposed mitigation measures.

CONSUMER INFORMATION AND ENVIRONMENTAL EDUCATION

23. Greater public awareness and understanding of the environmental impacts of energy production and consumption is an essential precondition to achieving more environmentally conscious patterns of consumption.

24. Consumers should be entitled to full information on visible and invisible product qualities, including comparative energy efficiency. Independent product testing, publication of comparative market surveys, and other measures such as energy or environmental labeling are important elements in consumer information programs.

25. The task of supporting and expanding consumer education and awareness programs in the field of sustainable energy consumption, especially targeting children as

future consumers, is of vital importance. States should recognize that education is the key to influencing electricity producers and consumers to adopt sustainable energy policies.

POLICIES AND STRATEGIES FOR IMPLEMENTATION

26. Sustainable energy production and consumption can most effectively be promoted by a combination of policy initiatives and financing. State initiatives may take the form of regulation, financial stimulation, or educational measures.

27. States should strive to implement national energy management and energy conservation laws. Such laws should provide basic mandates for institutional development or for national advisory services, improved energy efficiency in power generation and transmission, minimum energy efficiency standards for motor vehicles, industrial equipment, domestic appliances, and buildings, and improved market transparency resulting from energy labels or other measures designed to enhance public or investor awareness for the benefit of energy efficiency investments.

28. Recognizing that the responsibility for sustainable energy production and consumption is in many states allocated among federal/national, state/provincial, and local levels of government, each state, in accordance with its constitution and/or national legislation, should pursue these principles at the appropriate level of government.

29. States should promote and provide opportunities for the participation of all interested parties, including local communities and indigenous people, women, industries, labor, and nongovernmental organizations, in the development, implementation, and planning of national sustainable energy policies.

30. States should establish, consolidate, or expand national energy efficiency promotion or energy conservation funds, based on domestic revenues from direct or indirect forms of energy consumption taxation used for the purpose of providing financial incentives for energy efficiency investments.

31. Scientific and technological research in relation to sustainable energy production and consumption should be strengthened.

32. Institutional capabilities in education, training, science, technology, economics, law, architecture, and social aspects of energy production and consumption are essential to the development of sustainable energy production and consumption policies and should be strengthened.

33. States should control the importation of old, polluting energy technologies into developing countries.

INTERNATIONAL COOPERATION

34. The implementation of national policies and programs aimed at sustainable energy production and consumption, particularly in developing countries, should be supported by international financial and technical cooperation, including through the private sector, where appropriate.

35. International institutional arrangements, building on those organizations and mechanisms already in existence, as appropriate, should facilitate international cooperation in the field of sustainable energy production and consumption.

36. International exchange of information on research into sustainable energy production and consumption should be enhanced and broadened, as appropriate, making full use of education and training institutions, including those in the private sector.

37. States should promote international awareness and information exchange on their relevant energy efficiency and renewable energy programs and standards and on the implementation of those programs and standards.

38. New and additional financial resources should be provided to developing countries to enable them to introduce sustainable energy production and consumption policies. The efforts of developing countries to implement policies consistent with sustainable energy production and consumption should be supported by the international community, taking into account the importance of redressing external indebtedness. In this respect, special attention should also be given to countries undergoing the process of transition to market economies.

39. States should endeavor to support the development of sustainable energy production and consumption in developing countries by the use of the flexibility mechanisms (the clean development mechanism, joint implementation, and emissions trading) prescribed in the Kyoto Protocol to the United Nations Framework Convention on Climate Change.

40. In order to enable, in particular, developing countries to adopt sustainable energy production and consumption policies, the access to and transfer of environmentally sound technologies and corresponding know-how on favorable terms, including on concessional and preferential terms, as mutually agreed, in accordance with the relevant provisions of Agenda 21, should be promoted, facilitated, and financed, as appropriate.

12 Policy Options

Kui-Nang (Peter) Mak and Friedrich Soltau*

1 INTRODUCTION

Unsustainable patterns of energy use are harming the local and global environment. Global climate change is already making itself felt, from the thinning of the Arctic ice cap to the retreat of glaciers across the world, as well as in the emerging link between climate change and the increase in extreme weather events. At the same time access to safe and effective energy remains largely out of reach in many developing countries. Some two billion people, one-third of the world's population, rely almost completely on traditional energy sources, and are unable to take advantage of modern forms of energy, such as electricity, that are taken for granted in the developed world.[1] For instance, in most of sub-Saharan Africa the electrification rate is as low as ten percent, falling even further in rural areas.

Energy consumption in developing countries, although growing rapidly, remains low in absolute terms (*see* Table 12.1). Access to modern energy for the poor will not be achieved without massive additional investment, which so far seems unforthcoming.[2] Although the developing country share of energy consumption is low, it is set to grow dramatically – according to some calculations, from thirty percent in 2000 to forty-three percent in 2030 – with long-term consequences for sustainable development. Two important points can be made about the link between energy production and use and sustainable development. The first is the importance of adequate energy services for satisfying basic human needs, improving social welfare, and achieving economic development. The second is that the production and use of energy should not endanger the quality of life of current and future generations.[3] Crucial choices need to be made to ensure that the increased energy consumption minimizes local, regional, and global environmental risks. In this context, energy for sustainable development is energy that is produced and used in a manner that will support human development in the long run, in all its social, economic, and environmental dimensions.[4] It is a concept that is

---

[1] World Energy Assessment, UNDP, UNDESA, WEC (2000), at 3.
[2] Randall Spalding-Fecher, Harald Winkler, and Stanford Mwakasonda, "Energy and the World Summit on Sustainable Development: What Next," *Energy Policy* (Winter 2003).
[3] World Energy Assessment, *supra* note 1, at 31.   [4] *Id.*, at 3.

* The authors are, respectively, Chief, Energy and Transport Branch, and Associate Sustainable Development Officer, Energy and Transport Branch, United Nations Department of Economic and Social Affairs, New York. This chapter is written in the authors' personal capacity and does not reflect the views of the United Nations.

Table 12.1 Detailed commercial primary energy use by region

Region	Million tonnes of oil equivalent (Mtoe)		2002 as share of world total (percentage)	Percentage growth 1990–2002
	1990	2002		
North America	2,315.8	2,715.4	28.86	17.4
South & Central America	321.1	448.2	4.75	39.6
Middle East	257.6	403.1	4.29	56.5
Africa	222.9	291	3.08	30.6
Europe and Eurasia	3,205	2,829.5	30.07	−11.7
Asia Pacific	1,28.4	2,717.8	28.90	48.6
World Total	**8,150.8**	**9,405**	**100.0**	**15.4**
EU 15	1324.2	1468.9	15.62	9.84
OECD	4589.5	5346.1	56.8	14.13
Former Soviet Union	1424.4	946.1	10.06	−33.6

Source: Adapted from BP, 2003

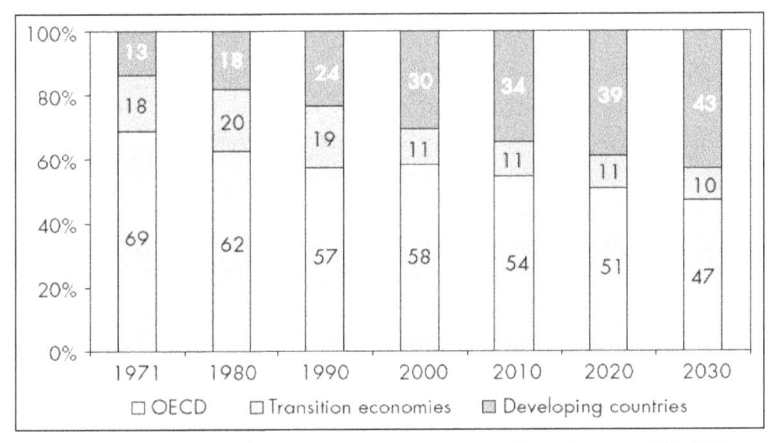

Figure 12.1 Commercial primary energy use 1971–2030. *Source:* IEA, 2002

being actively developed and serves as a framework for work on energy issues, including in the field of law.

This chapter focuses on law and energy for sustainable development. It is not written from a purely legal perspective, rather it is a survey of developments in the field of energy, sustainable development, and law, from a vantage point of policy development within the United Nations. In this chapter our central contention is that law – and energy law in particular – needs to be harnessed, reinterpreted, and adapted to advance sustainable development. The purpose of such an endeavor is to integrate social and environmental concerns into energy laws, so that energy laws can complement environmental protection laws and anticipate environmental considerations. Precisely how that should be done lies, at least partly, within the domain of the legal specialists gathered under the umbrella of the IUCN Academy of Environmental Law. We will only seek to outline some areas where this revaluation and reinterpretation has already begun, or might fruitfully be pursued. In doing so, we also attempt to sketch some features of energy law for sustainable development, and examine how law can contribute to the achievement of sustainable development, particularly in the field of energy. We also outline some of the contributions that the United Nations has made in this process.

In Section 2 we briefly analyze the concept of sustainable development, before proceeding to trace the genesis of energy for sustainable development.

2 SUSTAINABLE DEVELOPMENT

The era of globalization has brought into stark relief the inequalities of global society. Globalization can be usefully defined as "the intensification of worldwide social relations which link distant localities in such a way that local happenings are shaped by events occurring many miles away and vice versa."[5] Sustainable development is linked to globalization in a number of ways. For instance, the climate change caused by greenhouse gas emissions poses a global threat; the production and consumption patterns of persons in Europe and America impact on the livelihood of Pacific islanders. At the same time, the existence of the mass media, information and communication technology, and air travel facilitates the efforts of small island developing states (SIDS) to coordinate their participation in the international climate change negotiations. The response to climate change, from the science to the political action, demands action at the global level. In the era of globalization, law also faces new challenges and demands.

The 1987 report of the World Commission on Environment and Development, more popularly known as the Brundtland Report, defined sustainable development as development that "meets the needs of the present without compromising the ability of future generations to meet their own needs."[6] Sustainable development has been criticized for essentially becoming an empty buzzword that cannot be employed to inform public policy.[7] It is also commonly pointed out that differences arise depending on whether "sustainability" or "development" is emphasized. Thus, at the Rio Conference, the environmental aspect of sustainable development was emphasized. Most recently, at the World Summit on Sustainable Development (WSSD) a shift was detectable to an approach that stressed the economic and social pillars of sustainable development. This shift, reflecting the influence of the developing countries, has caused some to believe that this constitutes a conflation that will hamper progress with regard to the environmental aspects.

As with so many contested concepts, the debate over definitions can quickly become sterile, satisfying few but those engaged in it. Thus it is reassuring that in parallel with the quest for analytic rigor, the concept is being translated and specified for practical application in a range of fields, including energy. A good example is in the field of sustainability indicators, where the United Nations[8] and other organizations are active.[9]

---

[5] Anthony Giddens, *The Consequence of Modernity* (1990), at 64.
[6] Our Common Future, at 8.
[7] Daniel Esty, "A Term's Limit," *Foreign Policy*, Sept.–Oct. 2001.
[8] United Nations Department of Economic and Social Affairs, *Indicators of Sustainable Development: Framework and Methodology* (2001), at 44; accessible at: http://www.un.org/esa/sustdev/csd/csd9_indi_bp3.pdf.
[9] The International Institute for Sustainable Development (IISD) maintains a compendium of indicator initiatives: http://iisd1.iisd.ca/measure/principles/; indicators for the Millennium Development Goals, accessible at: http://www.oecd.org/dataoecd/30/28/2754929.pdf; and the World Bank indicators on environment: http://lnweb18.worldbank.org/ESSD/envext.nsf/44ByDocName/EnvironmentalEconomicsandIndicators.

The United Nations and other energy institutions have developed sustainable energy indicators as part of the overall sustainable development indicator work to enable more complete and comprehensive analyses of energy policies at the national level within the context of sustainable development. The sustainable energy indicators are currently being applied in a number of developing countries with a view to providing relevant information for energy policy decisions. An interagency group, comprising a range of energy and statistical organizations within and outside the United Nations, is writing a methodological guide for the indicators. This kind of work provides a yardstick, admittedly crude at times, to assess public policy and to identify unsustainable policies and practices. It also generates data that can be fed into decision making, which can help to make environmental debates turn on data and analysis rather than rhetoric.[10] Lawyers and legal scholars should not remain aloof to methodologies that can provide tangible information about the effects, and possible shortcomings, of legal rules that they formulate, implement, and study.

Section 3 outlines how the link between energy and sustainable development has been articulated in the United Nations' intergovernmental process.

3 ENERGY FOR SUSTAINABLE DEVELOPMENT

Energy underpins and drives the productive capacities of global society. It is woven into the fabric of society. Questions of energy extraction, production, and use touch the very basic facts of economic life. Attempts to shift the patterns of energy use have profound political and welfare implications. Small wonder then that it has been very difficult to achieve agreement on this issue. This section will examine the idea of energy for sustainable development, drawing on the deliberations at the Ninth Session of the Commission on Sustainable Development (CSD-9) and the World Summit on Sustainable Development (WSSD).

3.1 Background

Energy was a controversial topic at the historic United Nations Conference on the Environment and Development (UNCED) in Rio in 1992, and was not addressed explicitly in Agenda 21, the major outcome of that conference. Although no chapter was dedicated to energy, energy issues were addressed indirectly in relation to other subjects, such as human settlements, protection of the atmosphere, and agriculture and rural development. The failure to address energy as a distinct topic was the result of its political sensitivity. In 1997, the General Assembly, at its Nineteenth Special Session, held to review Agenda 21, decided that the Commission on Sustainable Development should consider energy at its Ninth Session.

The United Nations Framework Convention on Climate Change was adopted at UNCED. With the aim to stabilize atmospheric concentrations of greenhouse gases (GHGs) at safe levels, the Convention lead to debate on energy, because of the role that the production, and consumption of energy plays in climate change. The Kyoto Protocol, containing the binding targets absent from the Convention, was adopted in

---

[10] Daniel Esty, "Toward Data-Driven Environmentalism: The Environmental Sustainability Index" (2001) 31 *Environmental Law Reporter* 10603.

1997. It calls for industrialized countries, as a whole, to reduce GHG emissions by a total of five percent from 1990 levels between 2008 and 2012. The decision by the United States not to ratify the Protocol dealt it a severe blow, but the other parties rallied in November 2001 and agreed to the so-called Marrakesh Accords, which settled key details for the implementation of the Protocol.[11] At the time of writing this chapter, the coming into force of the Protocol hinges on ratification by the Russian Federation.

The discussions around the Convention and the Protocol have fueled a healthy debate on the science of climate change, as well as the costs and feasibility of climate change mitigation measures. The successive reports of the Intergovernmental Panel on Climate Change (IPCC) have established the scientific consensus that GHG emissions from human activity are responsible for some of the observed warming that has taken place.[12] Meeting climate change commitments, beginning with the first Kyoto commitments, will necessitate a transition to a less carbon intensive economy in industrialized nations. That is one aspect of the challenge of energy and sustainable development; the other is the need to bring access to energy to populations in the developing world, in a way that does not compound climate change. This second part of the sustainability agenda, given that its advocates are the developing countries, with less of a voice in the international system, has received less attention.

The United Nations was closely involved in one effort to highlight and explore, in as comprehensive and objective a fashion as possible, the linkages between energy and sustainable development. The World Energy Assessment, a joint project of the United Nations Department of Economic and Social Affairs (UNDESA), the United Nations Development Programme (UNDP), and the World Energy Council (WEC), was intended as a guide to decision makers, containing an analysis of energy's relationship to sustainable development and a set of policy recommendations.

Institutionally, no single body in the United Nations system has overall responsibility, or even a primary coordinating role, for energy; various agencies and programs deal with different aspects of energy. Despite efforts at coordination, a unified system-wide response to the challenge of energy and sustainable development has not yet materialized.[13] Important players are also found outside the United Nations system, such as the International Energy Agency (IEA), which serves as the think-tank of the OECD countries, or Organización Latinoamericana de Energía (OLADE), at the regional level in Latin America, and the Organization of Petroleum Exporting Countries (OPEC).[14] The WSSD disappointed those who thought that it would be the occasion for an overhaul of global environmental governance, with the existing institutions in effect being tasked with implementation, and the creation of new bodies not on the horizon. As demonstrated by the debate around a world environment organization, the establishment of a single body on energy faces an uphill battle.

---

[11] See UN Doc. FCCC/CP/2001/13/Add.1–4.   [12] See IPCC, Third Assessment Report (2001).

[13] Jayarao Gururaja "Energy for Sustainable Development: Review of National and International Energy Policies" (2003) 27 *Natural Resources Forum* 58.

[14] For a survey of international organizations in the field of energy law and the role they play in the development of energy law and policy, *see* Thomas W. Wälde, "The Role of Selected International Agencies in the Formation of International Energy Law and Policy Towards Sustainable Development," in Adrian J. Bradbrook and Richard L. Ottinger (eds.), *Energy Law and Sustainable Development*, IUCN Environmental Law and Policy Paper no. 47 (2003).

On the institutional side, various regions have adopted initiatives that have a bearing on energy and sustainable development. One prominent example is the New Partnership for Africa's Development (NEPAD), which has as one of its aims to secure sustainable development for Africa. It is a fact that the North–South divide underlies different understandings of sustainable development. Rather than strive for an illusive degree of theoretical coherence, progress is being made on the ground, including in the articulation of regional norms. Work is also being done in relation to other bodies such as APEC and ASEAN. The United Nations plays a role through the work of its regional commissions.[15]

3.2 CSD-9: Energy for Sustainable Development

Through the intergovernmental process the United Nations has sought to bring energy – the driver for development – into the wider debate on sustainable development. A major milestone in this effort was the Ninth Session of the United Nations Commission on Sustainable Development (CSD), which marked the first time that energy issues were considered in their totality in the context of sustainable development within the United Nations system. The Commission was established after the Rio Summit with the mandate to enhance international cooperation and rationalize the intergovernmental decision making capacity for the integration of environment and development issues, and to examine the progress of the implementation of Agenda 21 at the national, regional, and international levels.[16] It is a functional Commission of the Economic and Social Council (ECOSOC), to which it reports. The Commission consist of fifty-three elected governments, serving three-year terms. In the first years of its existence it organized its work program in accordance with the chapters of Agenda 21.

In preparation for Ninth Session, known informally as CSD-9, the United Nations prepared a range of background documents on energy, atmosphere, and transportation, which included possible actions and recommendations. At the same time, the Ad Hoc Open-Ended Intergovernmental Group of Experts on Energy and Sustainable Development considered and made recommendations on all key issues relating to energy for sustainable development, including energy sources, a range of energy policies and approaches, market issues, transfer of environmentally sound and economically viable energy technologies, as well as addressing financial resources and capacity building for developing countries.

Energy was one of the three sectoral themes considered at CSD-9 and was dealt with in considerable detail. The other sectoral themes were atmosphere and transportation, with information for decision making and participation and international cooperation for an enabling environment falling under the heading of cross cutting issues. The Commission's decision on energy begins by affirming that "[e]nergy is central to achieving the goals of sustainable development."[17] The Commission explicitly cast the challenge in terms of the approximately two billion people who have no, or inadequate, energy

---

[15] The Economic Commission for Africa (ECA), the Economic and Social Commission for West Asia (ESCWA), the Economic Commission for Europe (ECE), the Economic and Social Commission for Asia and the Pacific (ESCAP), and the Economic Commission for Latin America and the Caribbean (ECLAC).

[16] G.A. Resolution A/RES/47/191.

[17] Commission on Sustainable Development, Report of the Ninth Session, U.N. doc. E/2001/29, Decision 9/1 at para. 1, accessible at: http://www.un.org/esa/sustdev/csd/ecn172001-19e.htm.

services while at the same time recognizing that current patterns of energy production, distribution, and utilization are unsustainable. The Commission also notes clearly that foremost in developing country priorities is the eradication of poverty. It is recognized that energy for sustainable development will be achieved by providing cost-effective access to a mix of energy resources. The basic approach advocated is to give "a greater share of the energy mix to renewable energies, improving energy efficiency and greater reliance on advanced energy technologies, including fossil fuel technologies."[18] The decision on energy is notable for the list of "key issues" it identified, based on work of the Ad Hoc Open-Ended Intergovernmental Group of Experts on Energy and Sustainable Development. This exercise identified challenges and recommendations for seven energy issues – accessibility, energy efficiency, renewable energy, advanced fossil fuel technologies, nuclear energy technologies, rural energy, and energy and transport.

The work of the Commission marked the first such detailed consideration of energy issues at the intergovernmental level and established a baseline of consensus. This remains true even in the absence of numerical targets and new means of implementation. The negotiations demonstrated that the nexus of energy, environment, and development is a knotty one, and the process frustrated many, especially those lacking familiarity with the limits of the intergovernmental process. However, it is true to say that the importance of the conclusions reached at CSD-9 was revealed at the WSSD, where they formed the starting point for the negotiations and served as a basis for the decisions on energy. In part this reflected the fact that the CSD-9 negotiations had foreshadowed the same splits between the North and the South that were displayed at the WSSD.

Looking to the future, the Commission decided at its Eleventh Session in 2003 that its multi-year program of work would be organized on the basis of seven two-year cycles, with each cycle focusing on selected thematic clusters, as well as cross-cutting issues. The two-year cycle will consist of a review session and a policy session, with the idea being to make the work of the Commission more focused and consistent. Energy for sustainable development, atmosphere/air pollution, industrial development, and climate change comprise the thematic cluster for the 2006–2007 cycle. The next cycle, spanning 2004–2005, will consider the thematic cluster of water, sanitation, and human settlements. Although energy is thus not specifically on the agenda of the Commission for the next two years, it is of relevance to the topic of human settlements. The United Nations will be engaged in carrying out the Johannesburg Plan of Implementation (JPOI), adopted at the WSSD, and report to the CSD on the progress made.

3.3 World Summit on Sustainable Development

The Plan of Implementation of the WSSD did not please all critics.[19] It did not benefit from the adoption of important multilateral environmental agreements – on climate change, desertification, and biodiversity – as had been the case at the Rio Summit. For better or for worse, the divisions among the participating countries meant that the focus was less on the articulation of new obligations, and more on implementation, including

---

[18] *Id.*, para. 4.
[19] Geoffrey Lean and James Plamer, "Earth Summit: After Days of Intense Negotiations, Leaders Settle on a Blueprint to Keep the Planet Alive," *The Independent*, Sept. 3, 2002, at 3; Kenneth R. Weiss, "World Summit Reaches Pact to Sustain Planet," *Los Angeles Times*, Sept. 3, 2002, at 1; Naomi Klein, "The Summit That Couldn't Save Itself," *The Guardian*, Sept. 4, 2002.

in the form of partnerships. As is well known, no agreement was reached on a target for renewable energy, despite a relatively modest proposal from the European Union (EU) and a more ambitious one put forward by Brazil. However, it was decided to halve the estimated 2.4 billion people living without basic sanitation (linked to the Millennium Development Goal to halve the number of people without access to safe drinking water), to restore fish stocks by 2015, and to significantly cut the rate at which rare species are becoming extinct. The Summit also endorsed the NEPAD goal of ensuring access to energy for at least thirty-five percent of Africa's population within twenty years.

Energy was undoubtedly one of the most crucial issues at the Summit. The importance of energy for sustainable development was affirmed in the course of the discussions on energy and through the reference and borrowing of the conclusions of CSD-9.[20] Among other things, there was also agreement that action should be taken to increase the use of renewable energy, ensure more efficient use of energy, and promote greater reliance on advanced and cleaner fossil fuel technologies. Although the lack of agreement on a target for renewables was viewed by many as a setback, the Summit agreed that countries should "with a sense of urgency substantially increase the global share of renewable energy sources." Renewable energy, energy efficiency, and cleaner fossil fuel technologies are referred to several times in relation to their development, dissemination, and the diversification of the energy supply.[21] Specific mention is made of the establishment of domestic programs for energy efficiency. It is also recommended that the policies of international financial institutions and other agencies support developing countries, as well as economies in transition, "in their own efforts to establish policy and regulatory frameworks which create a level playing field between the following: renewable energy, energy efficiency, advanced energy technologies, including advanced and cleaner fossil fuel technologies, and centralized, distributed and decentralized energy systems."[22] The Plan of Implementation also mentions policies to promote energy systems compatible with sustainable development, through the use of improved market signals and by removing market distortions, including restructuring taxation and phasing out harmful subsidies, bearing in mind "the specific needs and conditions of developing countries" and minimizing the adverse impacts on their development.[23] Reference is also made to the phasing out of subsidies in the energy area where they inhibit sustainable development, again with due regard to the situation of developing countries, and governments are also encouraged to improve the functioning of national energy markets so that they support sustainable development but "taking into account that such policies should be decided by each country."[24] These references to policy and legal frameworks should be of particular relevance and interest to lawyers.

The Plan of Implementation also reaffirmed the goal of the UNFCCC to stabilize greenhouse gas concentrations at a level that will prevent dangerous anthropogenic interference with the climate system, "within a time frame sufficient to allow ecosystems to adapt naturally to climate change, to ensure that food production is not threatened and to enable economic development to proceed in a sustainable manner."[25] States that have not signed the Kyoto Protocol are urged to do so by states that have. Earth

---

[20] Report of the World Summit on Sustainable Development, UN Doc. A/CONF.199/20, Annex (Plan of Implementation), para. 20.

[21] *Id.*, para. 20 (c), (d), (e), (i), and (k).   [22] *Id.*, para. 20 (j).

[23] *Id.*, para. 20 (p).   [24] *Id.*, para. 20 (q) and (r).

[25] *Id.*, para. 38.

observation, cooperation to reduce air pollution, including transboundary air pollution, as well as support for the Montreal Protocol regime are also covered.

Section 4 of this chapter briefly analyzes linkage between sustainable development and law, followed by a survey of key areas at the intersection of law, energy, and sustainable development.

4 SUSTAINABLE DEVELOPMENT AND LAW

The linkage between law and sustainable development can be examined on two broad levels. First, it may be considered at the level of broad principles and general rules of international law. There is considerable evidence of emerging principles of law that can be located under the international law of sustainable development. Some of those principles can then also be applied to advocate for change and to present new analyses of global problems, including the field of energy. At a second level, one may engage with law and sustainable development in the quest to see whether specific law and legal provisions, usually at the domestic level, promote sustainable development.[26] This can be understood as a "sustainability audit" to determine whether the laws, as they are applied and interpreted, hinder or advance sustainable development.

Chapter 38 of Agenda 21 calls upon governments to commit themselves to the "further development of international law on sustainable development, giving special attention to the delicate balance between environmental and developmental concerns." Developments since the Rio Summit have lead to the emerging consensus that sustainable development is an objective of the international community, as well as a concept with increasing normative force in international law.[27] More recently, in the spirit of implementation, the WSSD Plan of Implementation, in paragraph 163, also underlines that each country has the primary responsibility for its own sustainable development, and that countries should promote "sustainable development at the national level by, *inter alia*, enacting and enforcing clear and effective laws that support sustainable development." At past sessions the Commission on Sustainable Development has considered the role of law in sustainable development; most recently, the JPOI stipulates that the CSD shall follow significant legal developments in the field of sustainable development. This will form part of the Commission's more focused program of work.

The principle of interrelationship and integration can be identified as one of the underpinnings of sustainable development.[28] At its best, the concept of sustainable development is able to act as a unifying factor, bringing together disparate areas of law. It does not mandate particular legal solutions, but it encourages integration of

---

[26] This approach is advocated by William Futrell, President of the Environmental Law Institute, in his 2003 Garrison Lecture, delivered at Pace Law School on March 31, 2003.

[27] International Law Association, Legal Aspects of Sustainable Development, Fifth and Final Report, 2002, at 5. The report collects some of the international agreements that refer to sustainable development, including the United Nations Framework Convention on Climate Change, the Convention on Biological Diversity, and the Anti-Desertification Convention, as well as the preamble to the Agreement on the Establishment of the World Trade Organization.

[28] This point is made from a legal perspective in the Report of the Expert Group Meeting on Identification of Principles of International Law for Sustainable Development, para. 11. Report of a meeting held at Geneva, Switzerland, Sept. 26–28, 1995, and prepared for the Fourth Session of the Commission on Sustainable Development, accessible at: http://www.un.org/documents/ecosoc/cn17/1996/background/ecn171996-bp3.htm.

thinking and approaches. Different disciplines and even different jurisdictions will arrive at slightly – or perhaps even widely – divergent solutions and proposals. Sustainable development will be advanced when an effort is first made to achieve compatibility between competing legal rules.[29]

Section 5 briefly explores how energy, law, and sustainable development are linked in a number of specific areas.

5 LAW, ENERGY, AND SUSTAINABLE DEVELOPMENT: A FOCUS ON KEY AREAS

This section examines the intersection between law, energy and sustainable development in four areas: trade and investment, access to energy, energy efficiency, and responses to climate change.

Until quite recently one could not have spoken of an international energy law. Today there is a body of law largely centered around the fossil fuel industry, particularly hydrocarbon extraction dealing with oil concessions, contracts, and so forth. This is a well-developed and specialized area of law. To it may be added regional agreements on energy trade and development, such as the Energy Charter Treaty. And as briefly explored below, the international law of trade and investment is also becoming of increasing relevance to an understanding of energy at the international and national level. This body of law is primarily aimed at regulating legal relationships to permit the efficient and profitable exploitation of energy resources. It exists somewhat uncomfortably with laws that proscribe marine pollution or require environmental impact assessments.

Broadly speaking, the question of energy and sustainability can be looked at from the supply and demand (consumption) sides; policy measures and laws can be adopted to regulate either. On the supply side, one can ask what national regulatory measures can be adopted, or have an impact, on the provision of energy that is produced in a sustainable manner. How can the efficiency gains flowing from power sector reform also be harnessed to benefit the environment and, in developing countries, address the question of access to energy? Investments in energy infrastructure are as a rule long term in nature, with a lifespan of twenty to thirty years. The required investment to bring energy to those without access is massive.[30] The transition to a less fossil fuel intensive energy future will require the revamping of regulatory frameworks, so that the cleaner technologies can be more rapidly adopted. In this regard, attention has been drawn to lowering subsidies to the fossil fuel industry. The practice of export credit and investment insurance agencies, whose financing is largely devoted to fossil fuel projects, has also been the subject of criticism.[31] At the same time, experience shows that, at least in the early stages, renewable energy sources require some sort of support, frequently in the form of subsidies.

5.1 Trade and Investment

Among the emerging issues in connection with energy and sustainable development is trade. It is predicted that the trade in energy is set to increase dramatically.[32] Most

---

[29] *Id.*, para. 13. [30] Spalding-Fecher et al., *supra* note 2.
[31] *Id.*
[32] *World Energy Outlook*, International Energy Agency (2002).

of this trade will be of fossil petroleum and associated fossil fuels. However there will also be greater trade in natural gas. Such developments have implications for energy security, in particular as fossil fuel reserves will continue to be concentrated in the Middle East.

The further growth in pipelines, especially transboundary projects, has implications for energy law, both in the more technical aspects, as well as on the social and environmental fronts. The potential problems and the difficulty in balancing the various interests is illustrated by projects such as the Camisea gas field and pipeline project in Peru,[33] the Chad-Cameroon pipeline,[34] as well as the continuing debate in the United States concerning the proposed exploitation of the Arctic National Wildlife Refuge (ANWR). From the more technical side, the proliferation of the transboundary pipelines brings into play the need for agreements between the countries concerning passage rights, as well as security and guarantees for investors. Such norms have been developed in the context of the Energy Charter Treaty and its Optional Protocol. It is likely that the standards for investor protection developed under Bilateral Investment Treaties (BITs) and the North American Free Trade Agreement (NAFTA) will inform the conclusion of agreements relating to pipeline construction and operation. On the environmental and social side, it is clear that securing funding, especially from sources such as the World Bank, the regional development banks, and export credit agencies increasingly requires impact assessment and environmental mitigation measures. Even where active steps are taken to improve the environmental and social performance of a project, the results can still be mixed. Extractive industries will face the pressure to improve the sustainability of their operations, from local populations that face resettlement and the potential destruction of livelihoods, as well as NGOs that utilize the courts in developed countries to influence the corporations involved, for instance through suits brought under the Alien Torts Claims Act in the United States.[35]

Developments are also taking place at the regional level. For instance, a proposal under the New Partnership for Africa's Development (NEPAD) would see the adoption of an Energy Protocol, to establish an environment conducive to investment and to harmonize laws and standards, to further regional integration and energy trade. Africa has abundant energy resources, but these are unevenly distributed and not exploited for the benefit of all countries. Thus it makes sense to tap and transmit the rich hydropower resources of Central Africa. Similar circumstances are present in other regions of the world. Large-scale hydropower developments pose significant challenges, but without them in the mix it will be difficult to provide the required electricity. In all regions where the potential for electricity trading is only beginning to be exploited, there is a need for the creation of legal and institutional frameworks. Trade in electricity will likely assume importance if the goals of providing greater access are to be realized in a sustainable manner. The development of policies and laws to govern interconnections between country grids for the purpose of trading will be important, in tandem with overcoming other technical barriers.

---

[33] Juan Ferrero, "Gas Project in Peru Gets Crucial Loan," *New York Times*, September 11, 2003, at W1.
[34] Elizabeth Becker, "World Bank Inaugurates Oil Pipeline In Africa," *New York Times*, Oct. 3, 2003, at W1.
[35] 28 U.S.C. § 1350.

The broader alignment between the international trade regime and sustainable development also deserves further examination. The relationship between the WTO and its rules and the various multilateral environmental agreements (MEAs) is somewhat obscure. At the Summit language was proposed that would have tilted the balance in favor of the WTO rules.[36] In the end, a delicate balance was maintained: the Plan of Implementation refers to the "mutual supportiveness between the multilateral trading system and the multilateral environmental agreements, consistent with sustainable development goals, in support of the work programme agreed through the WTO, while recognizing the importance of maintaining the integrity of both sets of instruments."[37]

A great deal of work is being done in the area of trade and sustainable development. A body of law is being developed under NAFTA and in decisions of the ICSID (International Centre for the Settlement of Investment Disputes) tribunals under Bilateral Investment Treaties (BITs). The latter have proliferated, growing to around 2,000. Arbitral decisions under these instruments are putting national laws under the spotlight in the context of claims by investors, and a new body of international law is developing, which should also be ripe for analysis from a sustainability angle.

Energy is moving into the trade arena in the form of the General Agreement on Trade in Services (GATS), which is currently under negotiation. The GATS negotiations on energy services are the first attempt to address aspects of energy policies with a view to bringing them within the disciplines of the multilateral system.[38] Two issues raised in the negotiations are access for upstream services – the activities related to the fossil fuel services sector – and transmission and transit issues.[39] Given that cross-border trade is dependent on networks, the lifting of trade barriers alone is not sufficient, because proactive measures need to be taken to open up networks to imported energy.[40] Regulatory frameworks and regulators are required to ensure access.

The GATS negotiations also raise a number of other broad questions, some particular to the WTO, such as the condition for the accession of OPEC members, and others bearing on what the liberalized trade in energy services means for social and environmental concerns in the host countries. How will a liberalized electricity market promote access for the poor?

However, a narrower set of questions arises in relation to energy and trade. For instance, do trade rules permit a country to discriminate, when engaged in transboundary trade, against power generated from nuclear power or "dirty" fossil fuels and in favor of green sources? In the context of climate change mitigation, can imports from countries that are not undertaking mitigation measures be subjected to a "climate levy," so that domestic industries are not disadvantaged? Article 3(5) of the UNFCCC states

---

[36] Geoffrey Lean and James Palmer, "After Days of Intense Negotiations, Leaders Settle on a Blueprint to Keep the Planet Alive," *The Independent*, Sept. 3, 2002, at 3.

[37] Report of the World Summit on Sustainable Development, *supra* note 20, para. 98.

[38] Murray Gibb, "Energy Services, Energy Policies and the Doha Agenda," in *Energy and Environmental Services: Negotiating Objectives and Development Priorities*, UNCTAD, 2003, at 14.

[39] *Id.*, at 6–10.

[40] Thomas W. Wälde and Andreas J. Gunst, "International Energy Trade and Access to Energy Networks," in *Energy and Environmental Services: Negotiating Objectives and Development Priorities*, UNCTAD, 2003, at 118.

that "[m]easures undertaken to combat climate change should not constitute a means of arbitrary or unjustifiable discrimination or a disguised restriction on international trade." The principle is similarly restated in Article 2(3) of the Kyoto Protocol.[41] The relationship between the WTO and climate change regimes has not been sufficiently explored.[42] Measures under the Kyoto Protocol, such as energy efficiency standards, energy taxes, subsidies, the use of specific environmentally sound technologies, eco-labels, and government procurement policies all have potential trade implications.[43] In addition, the manner in which governments allocate emission allowances will affect the international competitiveness of their industrial sectors.

It has been suggested that one way to avoid the potential for conflict between the climate regime and the WTO rules is to actively pursue multilaterally agreed, WTO-consistent measures. Since aspects of the applicable trade rules[44] do indeed provide that regulations adopted pursuant to international standards enjoy a presumption of consistency with rules, measures instituted pursuant to recommendations or mandates of the UNFCCC and the Protocol would be found more acceptable than unilateral measures.[45] Achieving the sustainable use of energy will require closer cooperation to ensure that the compliance with the Protocol can be achieved without infringing on the core trade rules. Those rules may need to be amended, or at the very least reinterpreted, to ensure effective, least cost climate change mitigation. Since the full-scale amendment of the rules is cumbersome and risks opening up unrelated issues, the adoption of "understandings" on the interpretation of the trade rules in relation to climate change mitigation could be considered. At the very least, both the Kyoto process and the WTO may need to devote more attention to these questions, so that climate change mitigation is not treated as an environmental issue, but rather as the cross-sectoral question that is reaching deep not only into national economies, but also with implications for the international trading system.

5.2 Access to Energy

This section will briefly highlight the challenges of broadening access to sustainable energy, focusing on some of the legal and policy challenges. At the heart of any sustainable energy strategy lie policies to widen access to reliable and affordable modern energy supplies and reduce the negative health impacts related to energy use.[46] In Africa firewood and charcoal make up some 67 per cent of primary energy use, and the use of such fuels is associated with indoor air pollution from toxic substances such as carbon

---

[41] The Article states that: "The Parties included in Annex 1 shall strive to implement policies and measures under this Article in such a way as to minimize adverse effects, including the adverse effects of climate change, the effects on international trade, and social, environmental and economic impacts on other Parties, especially developing country parties and in particular those identified in Article 4, paragraphs 8 and 9, of the Convention, taking into account Article 3 of the Convention."

[42] Lucas Assunção and Zhong Xiang Zhang, *Domestic Climate Change Policies and the WTO*, 2002, UNCTAD, at 2, accessible at: http://r0.unctad.org/ghg/sitecurrent/download_c/publications.html.

[43] Murray Gibb, *supra* note 38, at 17.

[44] For instance, Article 2.5 of the Technical Barriers on Trade (TBT) Agreement states that a regulation is presumed not to contain any unnecessary obstacles to international trade if it is established in accordance with "relevant international standards."

[45] Assunção and Zhang, *supra* note 42, at 15.   [46] World Energy Assessment, *supra* note 1, at 417.

monoxide and particulates.[47] Focus on access to safe energy was affirmed at CSD-9 and at the WSSD, with its emphasis on poverty alleviation.

Energy sector reform will have a significant impact on the provision of access. Taking Africa, the lack of suitable transmission infrastructure and weak local demand are the two key factors holding back optimal utilization of Africa's diverse energy resources. The changes in the donor priorities, from development planning to structural adjustment and reforming governance, has had a major impact on the electricity sector, with the multilateral institutions moving away from grants and "soft loans" for project finance, preferring to leave this to the private sector.[48] In Africa the power sector faces problems such as small size, limited exploitation of opportunities for interconnections, poor management performance, inability to mobilize the funds needed for expansion, weak maintenance capacity, inappropriate tariff rates, and inadequate revenue collection mechanisms. Among the prescriptions for utilities to improve performance and remain solvent are: setting tariffs based on real cost, pursuing revenue collection, and minimizing wastage and loss in the delivery of energy services.[49]

The move to a private sector model has also seen a shift to emphasize "cost recovery" of services. However, given the low levels of consumption the private sector may frequently be unable to make a financial return on investment.[50] The challenges are brought into stark relief when it is considered that extending grid-based electricity supplies can cost seven times as much as in urban areas, and even where rural densities are high, the cost is likely to be fifty percent higher than in urban areas.[51] Faced with the high cost of grid extension, other energy sources such as solar and Liquefied Petroleum Gas (LPG) are advocated. Affordability remains a problem – South Africa's oft-cited off-grid solar voltaic electrification program requires the government to subsidize the capital cost of the equipment, and to break even the consumers would have to be charged 30 times the residential electricity tariff.[52] The same problems with affordability have been experienced elsewhere in Africa, leading to the call for a more diversified renewable energy policy, one that emphasizes solutions that catalyze income generation.[53] Accordingly, priority should be given to highlighting the real and tangible economic benefits – such as job and income generation – that a renewable energy program can deliver, while focusing policies on the implementation of projects that have proven track records and that maximize the use of local resources, expertise, and available finance. Lack of expertise, poor maintenance of equipment, and problems with obtaining credit

[47] Ogunlade Davidson and Youba Sokona, A New Sustainable Energy Path for African Development: Think Bigger Act Faster, Energy and Research Development Centre, Cape Town, and Environmental Action in the Third World, Dakar, 2002, at 28.

[48] Randall Spalding-Fecher, Harald Winkler, and Stanford Mwakasonda, "Energy and the World Summit on Sustainable Development: What Next," Energy Policy (Winter 2003).

[49] Xolani Mkhwanazi, Power Sector Development in Africa, background paper prepared for the Workshop for African Energy Experts on Operationalizing the NEPAD Energy Initiative, Dakar, June 2003, available at: http://www.un.org/esa/sustdev/sdissues/energy/op/ nepadmkhwanazi.pdf.

[50] Davidson and Sokona, supra note 47, at 29.

[51] World Bank, Rural Energy and Development: Improving Energy Supplies for Two Billion People, Washington, D.C., 1996.

[52] Spalding-Fecher, et al., supra note 2.

[53] Stephen Karekezi and Waeni Kithyoma, "Renewable Energy Strategies for Rural Africa: Is a PV-Led Renewable Energy Strategy the Right Approach for Providing Modern Energy to the Rural Poor of Sub-Saharan Africa?" (2002) 30 Energy Policy 1071.

are all problems that have been identified in relation to energy access in rural areas. Access to commercial energy is most effective when combined with other development activities to improve water supply, agriculture, and transport.[54]

The restructuring and reform of the power sector has implications for the objective of increasing access. It is true that the old model of vertically integrated state monopolies, or private monopolies, has failed in developing countries to bring about access to electricity. The public sector agencies or companies are not in a position today to roll out access, lacking in many cases the managerial and technical skills, and are often mired in debt. Of course, counter-examples exist – Eskom, the South African utility is still state-owned and was only recently incorporated, and has managed to bring electricity into the homes of some two million people. (It is also the fifth largest electric utility in the world, with extensive technical and financial capacity, so that it is not a good marker for comparison.) Furthermore, universal access in industrialized countries was undertaken almost entirely by public utilities. Nonetheless, in the present circumstances, the question remains how to meld the demands and need for market reform with the agenda of energy for sustainable development. In many ways the reform of the power sector is in fact a "reregulation" as public utilities, acting under administrative oversight and subject to government policy, are replaced by private corporations, often with a separation of generation, transmission, and distribution functions. It is now recognized that the operation of the market in such circumstances requires a well-designed and functioning regulatory structure. That legal structure needs to be cast in such a manner that public benefits, such as access and environmental protection, are promoted.

Since it is recognized that the market cannot deliver services where it is not an economic proposition – such as in rural areas – governments will need to intervene carefully, with policy and legal instruments that promote rural access. Where the infrastructure exists, steps could be taken to guarantee a basic "lifeline," as the evidence is clear that in many cases full cost recovery of a basic service such as electricity is simply not viable. The benefits of access – as measured in the effects on human health (respiratory illnesses and fires) and the environment (deforestation avoided) – warrant the extension of access at affordable rates. While the relevant human rights instruments do not contain a right of access to energy, the argument for access could be framed in the wider context of socioeconomic rights. Interpreting the right to housing in the South African Constitution, the Constitutional Court recognized that the realization of this right may require the provision of other services. The Court stated that:[55]

> The state's obligation to provide access to adequate housing depends on context, and may differ from province to province, from city to city, from rural to urban areas and from person to person. Some may need access to land and no more; some may need access to land and building materials; some may need access to finance; some may need access to services such as water, sewage, electricity and roads.

The challenge is thus for lawyers to be active participants in the discussion on access and to focus attention on how this goal – as well as environmental protection – is being addressed in the restructuring and reform of the energy sector.

[54] World Energy Assessment, *supra* note 1, at 421.
[55] *Government of the Republic of South Africa and Others v. Grootboom and Others*, (11) BCLR 1169, para. 37. Judgment available at: http://www.concourt.gov.za/files/grootboom1/grootboom1.pdf.

5.3 Energy Efficiency

More efficient energy use is a key option for achieving sustainable development.[56] Energy efficiency is achieved when energy intensity – the amount of energy required per unit of output – is reduced in a specific product, process, or area of production and consumption. Many jurisdictions enacted energy conservation laws and standards following the oil price shocks of the mid-1970s and early 1980s, which frequently made provision for the stockpiling of strategic reserves, market intervention, and emergency price regulation. Energy efficiency promotion legislation covers areas such as standards and energy use in industries, transportation, electrical appliance standards, including labeling and consumer awareness, as well as energy codes for buildings. In addition, laws on land use and zoning also have an indirect impact on energy use.

At the international level the Energy Charter Treaty, which relates largely to international energy trade and investment, does contain a provision on energy efficiency, but it is phrased in nonbinding terms and its environmental objective are subordinated to economic considerations.[57] The Protocol on Energy Efficiency and Related Matters is legally binding and contains quite comprehensive provisions, but a closer analysis reveals that the Protocol does not impose enforceable obligations on parties to take specific measures.[58] The Kyoto Protocol lists "enhancement of energy efficiency" as one of the policies and measures available to Annex I parties to achieve their emission reduction commitments under the Protocol.[59] Energy efficiency projects – covering both the supply and the demand side – have also been included in the list of small-scale Clean Development Mechanism (CDM) projects, for which simplified baseline and monitoring procedures have been approved under the Kyoto machinery. For instance, a project resulting in the adoption of energy efficient equipment, such as lamps or motors, would be eligible for carbon credits based on emissions avoided.[60]

Energy efficiency improvements face a variety of barriers, including the observed expectation of a higher rate of return investments in energy efficiency, as opposed to investments in supply.[61] This may in part be due to lack of information, which makes efficiency improvements seem less tangible than investment in new capacity. In developing countries serious problems include the lack of awareness of potential benefits, the pervasiveness of inappropriate energy pricing and cross-subsidies, the lack of trained staff, and the desire to minimize initial costs, often the result of lack of capital or high financing costs.[62] Below-cost energy pricing and cross-subsidization are not consistent with market policies, but alternative regulatory options will need to be found

---

[56] World Energy Assessment, *supra* note 1, at 175.

[57] Adrian Bradbrook, "Regulatory Framework for Promotion of Energy Conservation and Energy Efficiency in Australia," in *Compendium of Energy Conservation Legislation in Countries of the Asia and Pacific Region*, ESCAP, 1998, at 30–1. The Compendium is available at: http://www.unescap.org/esd/energy/publications/compend/cec.htm.

[58] Adrian Bradbrook, *Id.*, at 31–3. *See also*, Adrian Bradbrook, "Energy Efficiency and the Energy Charter Treaty" (1997) 14 *Environmental and Planning Law Journal* 327.

[59] Article 2(a)(i).

[60] For small-scale CDM projects, aggregate energy savings from the project may not exceed the equivalent of 15GWh per year. *See* "Indicative simplified baseline and monitoring methodologies for selected small-scale CDM project activity categories," Appendix B of the Simplified Modalities and Procedures for Small-scale CDM project activities, document FCCC/CP/2002/7/Add.3. The simplified methodologies and baselines are available at: http://cdm.unfccc. int/pac/howto/SmallScalePA/ssclistmeth.pdf.

[61] World Energy Assessment, *supra* note 1, at 201.   [62] *Id.*, at 202–3.

to ensure that objectives such as affordable access for the poor can be achieved, even as industry and other large consumers are weaned off underpriced energy.

The barriers facing energy efficiency investments in developing countries are considerable. The need exists to update or establish legislation and institutions, while recognizing that very good results can be achieved using different models, corresponding to the political and economic specificities of a country.[63]

5.4 Responses to Climate Change

The debate on climate change has been dominated by the economic analysis of the costs of mitigation and adaptation. This section will briefly examine the nexus between law, energy, and sustainable development.

The accumulation of greenhouse gases, which remain in the atmosphere upward of 100 years exerting their heat-trapping effects, is an unintended consequence of human development, more particularly the carbon fuels – coal and oil – that have powered it. Climate change poses a challenge for scientists, philosophers, economists, lawyers, and politicians. It is the classic over-the-horizon problem – policy steps need to be taken today, with largely no return in the near term, even as scientists are still engaged in putting the precise outlines to the threat. By the time scientists have full information and the effects of climate change become a political issue, it will be too late to reverse or even halt it. It truly puts to the test the principles of fairness and intergenerational equity that underpin sustainable development.

The scientific consensus concerning climate change is contained in the reports of the Intergovernmental Panel on Climate Change (IPCC). According to the IPCC, the global average surface temperature has increased by 0.6–0.2 C since the late nineteenth century; the ten warmest years since 1860 have occurred since 1987, with 1998 the warmest on record and 2002 in second place.[64] The latest reports of the IPPC date from 2001, with three thematic working groups addressing: the scientific basis for climate change; the impacts, adaptation, and vulnerability; and mitigation. In its report on the science of climate change the IPCC concluded that: "In the light of new evidence and taking into account the remaining uncertainties, most of the observed warming over the past 50 years is likely to have been due to the increase in greenhouse gas concentrations."[65]

Scientists were able to draw this conclusion based on essentially the following evidence: the observed increase in the concentration of GHGs in the atmosphere stemming from human activity (fossil fuel combustions); painstaking analysis of meteorological records that revealed a rise in global mean surface temperature; and computer models that support the conclusion that the increase in temperature is the result of

---

[63] For an examination of labeling standards in the Philippines and Thailand, *see* Kristina Egan, "Energy Efficiency Standards for Electrical Appliances: Regulatory and Voluntary Approaches in the Philippines and Thailand," in *Compendium of Energy Conservation Legislation in Countries of the Asia and Pacific Region*, ESCAP, 1998, at 123. The *Compendium* is available at: http://www.unescap.org/esd/energy/publications/compend/cec.htm.

[64] World Meteorological Organization, *WMO Statement on the Status of the Global Climate in 2002* (2002) press release WMO-No. 684, available at: http://www.wmo.ch/index-en.html. In mid-2003, well in advance of its yearly statement on the global climate, the World Meteorological Organization issued an unusual press release noting an increase in severe weather events in 2003, with a possible link to climate change. *See* press release WMO-No. 695, pf July 2, 2003, accessible on the WMO's Web site.

[65] *IPCC Climate Change 2001: The Scientific Basis*, J. Houghton et al., eds., 2001, at 60.

human activity, not natural phenomena such as sunspots or the natural variability of the climate system. The emerging evidence indicates that, rather than being a gradual, linear process, changes to the climate may occur rapidly, the result of so-called "positive feedbacks."[66]

The UN Framework Convention on Climate Change (UNFCCC) and its Kyoto Protocol are the only multilateral treaties that have indirect, but quite far-reaching implications for energy consumption patterns. This is particularly true of the Kyoto Protocol, whose genesis was painful and whose coming into force has been protracted and filled with pitfalls. Contrast this with the Montreal Convention, widely hailed as the most successful multilateral environmental agreement (MEA), which, agreed and ratified in short order, demonstrates how the international community can respond to a global environmental threat. Indications are that after thirty years of ozone depletion the protective layer has begun to regenerate.[67] Why has this effort succeeded, while the multilateral measures to mitigate GHGs have had such a difficult birth? Space does not permit a full analysis, but it is clear that the ubiquity of energy militates against an easy solution. The substances causing ozone depletion – primarily chlorofluorocarbons (CFCs) – are used in a limited number of applications (refrigeration) and products. Substitutes were available. Not so with fossil fuels, whose combustion releases carbon dioxide (CO_2), the main GHG. Furthermore, countries have associated energy security closely with sovereignty.

Climate change mitigation means initiating fundamental changes in the production and consumption patterns of society. Quite aside from this, past and future emissions – even based on the most optimistic scenarios – mean that the world is already committed to climate change. Increasing attention is thus being paid to the question of adaptation. In this context, studies show that some of the most adverse effects of climate change will be manifested in developing countries, where populations are most vulnerable and have the least capacity to easily adapt to climate change.[68]

Under the UNFCCC parties have pledged to stabilize "greenhouse gas concentrations in the atmosphere at a level that would prevent dangerous anthropogenic interference with the climate system."[69] However, the Convention confines itself to general goals and does not contain binding targets for GHG and reductions. The industrial nations (Annex 1 countries) agreed to take the lead in modifying the trend in long-term anthropogenic emissions with the aim of reducing GHG emissions to 1990 levels by 2000.[70] The Conference of the Parties (COP) to the Convention was established as the key negotiating mechanism, paving the way for the adoption of the Kyoto Protocol in 1997 and the subsequent efforts to put in place the mechanisms for its operation. The appearance that the climate change agreements are devoid of legal obligations for non-Annex 1 (developing country) parties needs to be avoided. Article 10 of the Kyoto Protocol, in essence reiterating commitments contained in Article 4 of the UNFCCC, requires all parties to formulate a program to improve the gathering of emissions data, formulate and implement a program containing measures to mitigate climate change,

---

[66] *Stabilisation and Commitment to Future Climate Change: Scientific Results from the Hadley Centre,* Hadley Centre, October 2002, at 6–7, available at: http://www.metoffice.com/research/hadleycentre/pubs/brochures/B2002/global.pdf.

[67] Peter N. Spotts, "After 30 Years, Ozone is Recovering," *Christian Science Monitor,* Aug. 1, 2003.

[68] IPCC Third Assessment Report, Synthesis Report (2001).

[69] Article 2.   [70] Article 4(2) (a) and (b).

and to facilitate adaptation, as well as cooperate on scientific and technical research. The formulation of a program to improve the quality of emission data is to be undertaken to "the extent possible" and where it is "cost-effective." Thus the capacity constraints of non-Annex 1 parties are clearly borne in mind. In addition, mention is also made of the transfer of, and access to, environmentally sound technologies and know-how, as well as the strengthening of capacity for participation in international research and scientific observation.[71]

The turning point of the Kyoto process, at Marrakesh (COP-7), saw the adoption of the key provisions required for the operation of the market-based mechanisms for GHG reductions.[72] A sophisticated and well-developed architecture has been pieced together to ensure the environmental integrity of the agreement and promote compliance with its provisions. For instance, strict eligibility criteria apply to Annex I parties engaged in emissions trading with other such parties, and provision is made for a "commitment period reserve," a minimum of credits that such a party must hold at any one time.[73] Detailed enforcement procedures, encompassing review, evaluation, and sanctioning for noncompliance have been set out.[74] Parties have taken important steps to lay the groundwork to meet their commitments – the EU has outlined its emissions trading system, and member states will shortly be allocating emission entitlements. Important institutions such as the Executive Board of the Clean Development Mechanism are operating. Once the Russian Federation ratifies it, the Protocol will be in force.

Vigilance is required at the national level in Annex I countries to ensure that emissions trading and joint implementation (JI) retain their environmental integrity. Transparency and openness will be critical for monitoring and evaluation. For developing countries, the CDM holds much promise, but capacity building efforts will be required for them to capitalize on this source of investment, and to ensure that CDM projects are not simply concentrated in a small group of countries. In this respect the United Nations is preparing to play a role. At the same time, host countries will need to create the legal framework for investment, including the articulation of sustainable development criteria for CDM projects.

6 CONCLUSION

The fragmentation of legal standards and competing priorities – trade versus environmental protection – would seem to call out for some form of unifying principle. Yet the very forces of globalization that propel change will likely frustrate any effort at harmonization. To knit bodies of law together through reference to universal principles may simply not be feasible. However, some alignment and accommodation is crucial, because if we are to achieve sustainable development then laws on trade or energy policies, for instance, cannot operate compartmentalized from environmental laws or policies to promote access to energy for the poor. We have argued that an alignment of laws and policies in the area of energy is possible, with the aim of advancing the cause of sustainable development. To this end, environmental lawyers and practitioners should

---

[71] Article 10(c) and (d).   [72] UN Doc. FCCC/CP/2001/13/Add.1–4.
[73] Annex, decision 18/CP.7, UN Doc. FCCC/CP/2001/13/Add.2.
[74] Annex, decision 24/CP.7, UN Doc. FCCC/CP/2001/13/Add.3.

no longer regard their branch of law as separate and distinct from issues of social and economic development.

Looking to the future, for its part the United Nations will continue to promote energy for sustainable development through its normative, analytical, and technical assistance activities. In relation to energy, the normative function in support of the CSD will assume particular importance in 2006–2007, when the Commission considers energy for sustainable development, atmosphere/air pollution, industrial development, and climate change. Bearing in mind that the WSSD mandated the CSD to follow significant legal developments in the field of sustainable development, it can be expected that the nexus between law and energy will feature more prominently in future. In this context, one area of interest is the elaboration, in accordance with each country's needs, of appropriate national legal frameworks, an area where legislatures and other decision makers play a key role. The United Nations will continue to facilitate the exchange of information and experiences on national laws, as well as promote capacity building initiatives upon request. The United Nations will also endeavor to provide a forum for further discussion of international cooperation in promoting enhanced frameworks for the development of energy in a sustainable manner.

13 Financing Energy for Sustainable Development

Jayarao Gururaja*

1 INTERNATIONAL DIALOGUE ON ENERGY FOR SUSTAINABLE DEVELOPMENT

Financing energy for sustainable development is a crucial element of the challenges posed by the implementation of Agenda 21.[1] Although it was considered crucial for development, energy for sustainable development was not explicitly addressed at the Rio Conference.[2] However, energy, in relation to the environment and development, has been specifically treated in Agenda 21, in chapters 9 ("Atmosphere"), 14 ("Agriculture and Rural Development"), and 7 ("Human Settlements").

International dialogue in relation to energy and the challenge of sustainability is relatively recent and in fact, energy, in its entirety, was discussed for the first time at an intergovernmental level during the Ninth Session of the UN Commission on Sustainable Development (CSD-9).[3] One significant feature of this dialogue was that it involved consultation with, and input from, relevant stakeholders: it was a more inclusive process than ever before. Following CSD-9, energy figured prominently at the World Summit on Sustainable Development (WSSD).[4]

The outcomes of CSD-9 and the WSSD Johannesburg Plan of Implementation[5] (Johannesburg Plan) on energy for sustainable development have focused attention on certain key energy issues as well as options and strategies to address them. The inputs provided by different stakeholders – academia, business and industry, nongovernmental organisations (NGOs), and other members of civil society – as well as several analytical studies and reports, notably the World Energy Assessment (WEA), as well as reports by the World Energy Council and the International Energy Agency (IEA) have proved valuable and indeed, helped to shape these outcomes. There is thus broad consensus as to the actions that need to be taken at various levels – national, regional, and global – in order to move from current unsustainable patterns of production and use of energy to those that are sustainable. However, since no new institutional arrangements or funding mechanisms at an international level emerged from the WSSD, the implementation of

---

[1] Available at http://www.un.org/esa/sustdev/documents/agenda21/english/agenda21oc.htm.
[2] *See* http://www.un.org/esa/sustdev/documents/UNCED_Docs.htm.
[3] *See* http://www.un.org/esa/sustdev/csd/CSD9.htm.
[4] *See* http://www.johannesburgsummit.org/html/documents/documents.html.
[5] Available at http://www.un.org/esa/sustdev/documents/WSSD_POI_PD/English/POIToc.htm.

* Senior Interregional Adviser, Energy and Transport Branch, Division for Sustainable Development, Department of Economic and Social Affairs, United Nations, New York.

tasks that energy for sustainable development calls for, as reflected in the Johannesburg Plan, is a major challenge facing the international community.

Mobilization of financial resources to tackle energy for sustainable development is of vital importance if the goals and objectives of sustainable development are to be achieved. Thus, the challenges of financing energy for sustainable development are a part of a broader set of challenges confronting national and international players in translating the agreements reached at CSD-9 and the Johannesburg Plan into concrete actions.

To place this issue in perspective, Section 2 of this chapter discusses some of the policy underpinnings of energy for sustainable development as they impact on financing issues. Section 3 discusses the challenges relating to the financing of renewable energy development.

2 POLICY UNDERPINNINGS OF ENERGY FOR SUSTAINABLE DEVELOPMENT

2.1 Goals and Challenges of Implementation

Viewed against the backdrop of the challenges facing developing countries in achieving the goals of sustainable development, the three most critical energy-linked threats to sustainability are accessibility, social equity, and environmental impacts. Emerging from the deliberations of CSD-9 and WSSD forums in relation to energy strategies is the understanding that, in order to address the challenge of sustainability, the three broad areas in which policy initiatives and practical actions are essential in all countries are:

- Improvements in the efficiency of the energy system to the maximum extent possible;
- Progressive increases in the contribution of renewable sources of energy to the energy mix within nations and internationally; and
- Progressing to the next generation of advanced fossil fuel technologies.

Financing issues and challenges in each of these three broad areas of action depend on the specific circumstances in individual countries. Investments in conventional energy systems will continue to follow financing modalities that are currently in vogue; however, sustainable energy policies will increasingly influence the direction of these investments. As the role of the private sector in mobilizing investments for the energy sector increases, the challenge for developing countries is to establish appropriate legal, regulatory, and policy frameworks and build institutional capacity to deal with investment issues in an expeditious and transparent manner.

According to the World Energy Council and WEA studies, expected global economic growth over the next twenty to thirty years has the capacity to generate the necessary resources for energy investments estimated at US$500–900 per year, depending on the particular energy options chosen for sustainable development. It is in the area of renewable energy that new and innovative financing mechanisms are needed in order to achieve the goal of increasing the contribution of renewable energy to the total energy mix. While targets and timetables for this renewable energy contribution were not agreed upon at WSSD, there is considerable interest among many industrialized and developing countries in aiming for a ten to twelve percent target (for the contribution of renewable energy to the total energy mix) by 2015. However, achieving this target level presents immense financing challenges.

While focusing attention on the three aspects of energy development mentioned above would constitute a basic approach to sustainable energy, the overarching challenge of securing affordable access to energy services for two billion people remains as one of the most compelling of a full range of steps that will have to be taken, in order to achieve sustainability.

Currently, policy makers in developing countries face the daunting task of putting in place policies that simultaneously address economic growth, social justice, and environmental protection with only limited domestic resources being made available to them. In a somewhat circular fashion, the mobilization of external financial resources depends to a large extent on the policy environment and governance structures that are already in place at a national level.

2.2 Financial Implications of the Millennium Development Goals: Ensuring Access to Energy Services

To achieve the poverty reduction goals set out in the UN Millennium Development Declaration[6] (known as the Millennium Development Goals (MDGs)), one billion people (that is, half of the two billion people estimated to be living on less than US$1 a day) would need to have access to modern energy services, as this is an important precondition for the eradication of poverty. Assuming an average figure of five persons per household, this goal can be translated into the provision of:

- First, a basic level of energy service that can meet, at least, basic requirements for home lighting, fans, radio, television, efficient appliances for cooking and fuel needs; and
- Second, further services that could facilitate people's engagement in income generation activities,

to 200 million households in the period between 2004 and 2015.

To gain some understanding of the magnitude of this challenge, let us look at an estimate of the costs involved in reaching the first MDG goal of access to basic energy services. This estimate is based on the provision of a minimum of 100 watts (W) of electrical capacity per household, plus the cost of providing access to liquid and/or gaseous fuels and efficient appliances for cooking, with the further proviso that in a number of low income countries the use of biomass based fuels and improved stoves may continue for practical reasons. Assuming that forty percent of the 200 million households cited above are to be covered by decentralized systems and the remaining sixty percent by grid extensions, the total cumulative investment for meeting the above-mentioned goal by 2015 has been estimated to be in the range of US$200–400 billion or US$20–40 billion per year, including the estimated cost of LPG diffusion at US$2.5–4 billion per year. While different sets of assumptions could obviously be made in relation to the share of centralized and decentralized systems and the like, the fact remains that significant financial resources need to be mobilized to address problems of access to basic energy services. Various factors influence the actual cost within the broad ranges cited, including

---

[6] United Nations General Assembly, 55th Session, A/55/L.2, Sept. 18, 2000.

the choice of technology, location, and infrastructure. The operational challenge that remains however is how to mobilize the needed resources on such a vast scale.

The challenge for the international community is to assist developing countries through efforts aimed at building capacity, facilitating the transfer of technologies, and the mobilization of financial resources to achieve sustainable development goals, taking into account the specificities and circumstances of individual countries.

Many developing countries are facing, on the one hand, growing and competing local demand for public finance and, on the other, declining financial resources from international agencies to state energy entities and public sector electricity utilities. Therefore, the challenge for these developing countries is increasingly how to attract the private sector in order to mobilize needed investments for sustainable energy development. Private sector investment can come from local savings mobilized through efficient financial institutions as well as through international finance from global markets. Creating favorable conditions for private sector investment in sustainable energy through appropriately tailored policy instruments is one of the key steps necessary for mobilizing such financial resources.

In most developing countries there are always competing requirements for investment in infrastructure development. Private sector capital for investment in sustainable energy will materialize only when investment opportunities are perceived as yielding sufficiently high risk-adjusted net returns on the relevant investments. The risk-reward ratio will largely determine the priority that investors will attach to sustainable energy projects and the speed with which such projects materialize. It is estimated that fifty to sixty percent of the Memoranda of Understanding (MOUs) for energy projects (mostly conventional energy projects) signed in developing countries since 1990 have either failed to secure financing or the relevant energy projects have subsequently failed to materialize. Inadequate policy support, cumbersome bureaucratic procedures, high risks, and low return situations have been some of the reasons for this situation. While most economies in transition, and some larger developing countries particularly in Asia and Latin America, are, by and large, able to service the requirements of international investors and repatriable returns, the situation in many less developed countries, particularly in Africa, of poorly managed state-owned energy entities, faltering pricing policies, inadequate financial and institutional frameworks, and a lack of adequate legal and regulatory mechanisms, makes it very difficult to attract private sector financing for energy investments.

3 FINANCING RENEWABLE ENERGY DEVELOPMENT

It is not possible to deal comprehensively in this chapter with all issues relating to financing energy for sustainable development. Consequently, this section will be confined to some of the challenges and opportunities evident in financing renewable energy projects.

3.1 Financing Renewable Energy Projects: Challenges and Options

Policy instruments have been, and continue to be, designed to accelerate the implementation of sustainable energy systems in many countries. These policy instruments and legislative measures all tend to encourage an increase in the share of renewable energy in the overall power supply mix.

In the United States, the Public Utility Regulatory Policies Act[7] (PURPA) promoted the installation of biomass fueled power generation in the 1980s, as well as the development of wind power and, to a lesser extent, solar thermal power generation. Policies targeted toward increasing the share of renewable energy in the power supply mix include the Renewables Non-Fossil Fuel Obligation[8] (NFFO) in the United Kingdom and the Renewable Portfolio Standard[9] (RPS) in the United States and several other countries. The German Act on Granting Priority to Renewable Energy Sources[10] (EEG) came into force on April 1, 2000 and is also aimed at increasing the share of renewable energy-based electricity generation in the total power supply mix. Further, India, China, and Argentina have also developed policies, including incentives as well as institutional arrangements, to promote investment in renewable energy development. For instance, India has established a separate ministry and a dedicated financial institution for renewable energy investment in order to spearhead a wide ranging renewable energy development program.

In a number of developing countries however, the policy environment and adequate institutional arrangements, including legal and regulatory structures for sustainable energy investments, are not yet properly established.

This section will now discuss first, some of the barriers to investment in renewable energy projects and second, potential means for overcoming these barriers.

3.2 The Nature of Renewable Energy Projects

Renewable energy projects differ from conventional energy projects in terms of:

- Scale;
- Capacity;
- Energy resource characteristics;
- Point of sale for output;
- Technological diversity;
- Level of maturity of technology; and
- Commercial status.

3.3 Barriers to Financing Renewable Energy Projects

Set out below are the main barriers to financing renewable energy projects.

public perceptions of renewable energy projects
- Renewable energy projects are generally perceived as being more expensive than conventional energy projects;
- Renewable energy projects often attract inaccurate perceptions of the risks attaching to the project. Proven and reliable information on renewable energy systems is not readily available or easily accessible to potential investors and financial institutions or commercial banks. Renewable energy systems are usually incorrectly perceived as something promoted by "environmental radicals." The reality of the commercial

---

[7]   16 U.S.C. §§ 2601 et seq.
[8]   Available at http://www.british-energy.com/environment/factfiles/nonffobligation.html.
[9]   Available at http://www.ucsusa.org/clean_energy/renewable_energy/page.cfm?pageID=109; *see also* http://www.awea. org/policy/rpsbrief.html.
[10] "Gesetz für den Vorrang Erneuerbarer Energien," *Federal Law Gazette* I, at 305.

success of such projects has not seeped into mainstream consciousness. It is perhaps fair to say that while renewable energy systems are reliable, the information about them is not; and

- Generally, inadequate data and infrastructure hampers project development processes for renewable energy projects.

specific financial requirements for, and cost structures of, renewable energy projects

- Renewable energy projects have a high capital to operations and maintenance cost ratio, which is more than twenty, as compared to approximately five to ten for conventional energy systems. This still acts as an impediment to project financing even though renewable energy projects can have a lower NPV of all costs when compared to conventional energy systems;
- Renewable energy projects also have a high project development to investment cost ratio;
- Renewable energy projects have small total investment requirements. Most commercial banks, utilities, and independent power producers (IPPs) are not interested in pursuing small investments for the simple reason that the time and costs involved in undertaking "due diligence" on renewable energy projects are high, as are the perceived risks. Accordingly, such large investors are not attracted;
- Renewable energy projects require longer-term debt financing. Due to high initial capital costs, the renewable energy project developer must usually seek longer-term debt financing arrangements to minimize the annual debt service burden on the project. Put simply, higher capital costs require longer-term loans and make renewable energy projects less attractive;
- Renewable energy projects provide a weak basis for nonrecourse project financing. Small, independent, and newly established entrepreneurs or project developers (ESCOs) often lack the institutional track records and financial inputs (equity) necessary to secure nonrecourse project financing. Financial institutions, due to the limited marketability of renewable energy assets as opposed to conventional energy systems, do not readily accept valuations of renewable energy project assets;
- Higher financial costs attach to renewable energy services. Compared to conventional energy systems, which often enjoy built-in or hidden subsidies that provide them with a financial edge, renewable energy systems are not given any cost advantages on the basis of their environmental benefits, but instead, are burdened with taxes and duties if imported. The net result is that renewable energy systems face higher financial costs when compared to conventional energy systems. In practice, it appears that the benefits of renewable energy systems are taxed, while the damage caused by conventional systems is subsidized; and
- Project developers of renewable energy systems are usually financially weak. Smaller entities with weaker financial positions are not able to leverage financial resources and as a result are unable to attract equity investors or secure debt financing.

decentralized nature of renewable energy projects

- Dispersed and small-scale renewable energy projects result in higher and more complex legal, regulatory, and engineering transaction costs and further, do not benefit from the economies of scale which are common to large conventional energy projects; and

- Offering guarantees as to the project's cash flow is a key element for project financing. Renewable energy projects are generally decentralized and as such, lack enforceable guarantees for purchases of project output. This in turn makes it extremely difficult to guarantee the project's cash flow. Without these guarantees it is difficult to secure the necessary financing. The old adage – "banks don't take risks, borrowers do" – is perhaps apt in this context.

3.4 Strategies for Addressing Barriers to Financing

The financing choices available to project developers depend on the type of renewable energy system which is at issue and its scale. Financing strategies that are currently employed, and those still being developed, for small-, medium-, and large-scale renewable energy systems are discussed below.

3.4.1 Small-Scale or Nongrid Systems

Small-scale or nongrid systems mainly involve solar PV home systems or wind battery chargers which are sold or leased directly to the end user. Such systems face the barrier of high up-front costs. Set out below are potential financing strategies for such projects, some of which are still evolving.

finance leasing programs. The end user leases the unit rather than purchasing it outright. Aggregation of such programs into a larger project becomes feasible and projects are then more easily appraised and managed. Also, the leasing company can take advantage of tax and depreciation benefits. The main disadvantage of such a program is that leasing involves additional costs which results in higher financing costs for the end user.

finance service providers. "Micro utilities" sell services and it is the service provider, rather than the hardware seller, who relieves the end user of operational and maintenance responsibility. Financing can be aggregated at the level of service provision rather than at the level of the end user. Periodic payments are made by the end user as in the case of conventional energy

mortgage financing. This approach essentially allows homeowners to incorporate the cost of installing renewable energy systems into the overall cost of their homes through mortgage financing. Aggregation is possible; however, the disadvantage of this approach is that it excludes low-income end users and those end users who are not homeowners.

3.4.2 Medium-Scale or Isolated Grid Systems

Isolated grid systems, such as small hydropower schemes, biomass gasifiers and cogeneration systems, wind/diesel/solar hybrids, and other energy systems within the range of 100kW to 10MW, are all included in this category. Clients include state utilities, rural electric cooperatives, and private sector companies. Financing strategies for isolated grid systems are still evolving. Such energy systems pose significant financing challenges as risk factors are high and isolated grid systems are also difficult to develop and implement.

3.4.3 Large-Scale or Grid-Connected Systems

Financing strategies for large projects depends on the individual characteristics of the particular project and specific local circumstances. The sizeable investments required for such projects are usually mobilized with the involvement of the private sector, international financial institutions, host country establishments including nonfinancial banking institutions (for example, the Indian Renewable Development Agency Ltd.) and commercial banks. Long-term power purchase agreements, tax incentives, risk management instruments and astute financial engineering are all preconditions for investment in such projects.

3.5 Evolving Sources of Project Finance

Set out below are potential sources of equity financing:

- Project developers;
- Venture capitalists;
- Equity fund investors;
- Equipment suppliers;
- Regional development banks; and
- Institutional and individual investors.

International and national commercial banks are the main sources of debt financing. However, other sources include multilateral development banks (MDBs) and international finance corporations, debt/equity investment funds, equipment suppliers, and private investors.

Sources of grant financing include:

- Global environmental facilities (UNDP/World Bank/UNEP);
- International and bilateral agencies;
- Foundations; and
- National and local agencies.

3.6 Types of Support Available for Renewable Energy Project Development

3.7 Innovative Financing Mechanisms

Given the challenges posed in relation to the financing of renewable energy projects, new and innovative financing mechanisms are of crucial importance in promoting renewable energy. Currently, several different financing mechanisms are being adopted while others are being explored. These include:

- Renewable energy leasing companies;
- Renewable energy vendor credits;
- Targeted project credits;
- Direct consumer credits;
- The acceptance of equipment as collateral by suppliers;
- Support for project preparation and development;
- Global environmental facilities;
- Jointly implemented activities;

Table 13.1 Multilateral development agency support for sustainable energy projects

Type of service	World bank	IFC[a]	MIGA[b]	RDBs[c]	UNDP[d]
Feasibility studies and assistance for project development	X	X		X	X
Equity investment		X		X	
Debt financing	X	X		X	
Investment co-financing	X	X		X	
Loan guarantees			X		
Lease guarantees			X		
Political risk insurance			X		
Technical assistance and training					X

[a] International Finance Corporation
[b] Multilateral Investment Guarantee Agency
[c] Regional development banks
[d] United Nations Development Programme

Table 13.2 Private sector investor support for sustainable energy projects

Type of service	Commercial banks	Venture capitalists	Institutional investors	Individual investors	Equipment suppliers
Equity investments		X	X	X	X
Debt investments	X		X	X	
Debt-equity swaps	X				
Project financing	X				
Equipment financing	X				X

- Clean development mechanisms;
- The Solar Development Group;
- The PV Market Transformation Initiative;
- Prototype carbon funds; and
- The Shell Foundation's sustainable energy program.

4 CONCLUSION

While various kinds of government incentives and subsidies have, until now, driven renewable energy development, in the long term the challenge lies in operating financing schemes in a commercial environment that is still driven by incentives but devoid of unnecessary subsidies.

14 The Clean Development Mechanism and UNFCCC/Kyoto Protocol Developments

Maria Socorro Z. Manguiat*

1 INTRODUCTION

Of the three flexible mechanisms created under the Kyoto Protocol to the United Nations Framework Convention on Climate Change (UNFCCC),[1] the Clean Development Mechanism (CDM) has generated the most interest. This is due to at least two reasons: (a) the eligibility of nonAnnex I Parties (mostly developing country parties) to participate in CDM project activities as host countries;[2] and (b) the fact that it is the only mechanism for which credits can be earned prior to the beginning of the first commitment period (2008 to 2012).[3]

For many people, the CDM connotes a potential source of funding for projects in the energy and forestry sectors. While this is true, the statement needs to be qualified in many ways. Project developers should realize that many conditions attach to a CDM project activity, which could affect the expected revenues to be derived from the project.

2 THE CDM: A FEW BASIC CONCEPTS

The CDM has two purposes: For non-Annex I Parties, the CDM is meant to assist in achieving sustainable development and in contributing to the ultimate objective of the Convention, i.e., stabilization of greenhouse gas concentrations in the atmosphere at a level that would prevent dangerous anthropogenic interference with the climate system.[4] On the other hand, the CDM aims to assist Annex I Parties (developed country Parties) in achieving compliance with their quantified emission limitation and reduction commitments (QELRCs), set out in Article 3 of the Kyoto Protocol, in relation to its Annex B.

---

[1] Hereinafter referred to as the "Kyoto Protocol."   [2] Art. 12.3(a), Kyoto Protocol.

[3] Par. 13, decision 17/CP.7, Modalities and procedures for a clean development mechanism as defined in Article 12 of the Kyoto Protocol, FCCC/CP/2001/13/Add.1 (hereinafter referred to as "decision 17/CP.7) and par. 1(c), decision -/CP.9, Guidance to the Executive Board of the Clean development mechanism (Advance unedited version available at http://www.unfccc.int). Based on these two decisions, a CDM project activity starting anytime from January 1, 2000 until before December 31, 2005 and registered before December 31, 2005 can use a crediting period that begins at the start of the project activity, even if this is before the date of project activity's registration.

[4] Art. 2, United Nations Framework Convention on Climate Change. Hereinafter referred to as "UNFCCC."

* Legal Officer, IUCN Environmental Centre, Bonn, Germany.

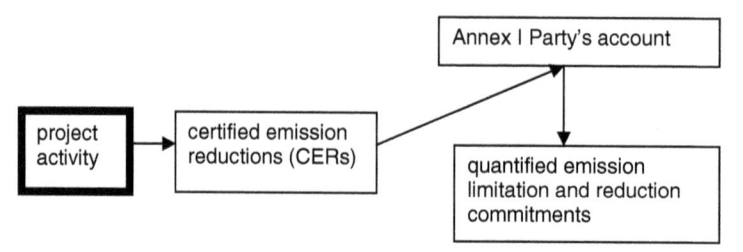

Figure 14.1 The basic concept of a CDM project activity.

The way in which the second objective can be achieved, as illustrated in a simple[5] way, is this: A project activity is located in a nonAnnex I country (known as the "host country"). At some point, this project activity will start to earn emission reduction credits, known as certified emission reductions (CERs), which can then be transferred to an Annex I Party's account. Assuming these CERs remain valid throughout the commitment period,[6] they will then count toward the Annex I Party's QELRC. Figure 14.1 illustrates the basic concept of the CDM project activity.

3 ENERGY FOR SUSTAINABLE DEVELOPMENT WITHIN THE CDM

With regard to the second objective of the CDM, it is the host country Party's prerogative to determine whether a CDM project activity assists in sustainable development.[7] Regardless of the variety of criteria to be used by host countries in determining compatibility with its sustainable development goals, decisions of the Conference of the Parties (COP) to the UNFCCC indicate a preference for certain types of energy projects. In particular, decision 17/CP.7 recognizes that Annex I Parties "are to refrain" from using CERs generated from nuclear facilities to meet their QELRCs.[8] Moreover, CDM project activities "should lead to the transfer of environmentally safe and sound technology and know-how."[9] In addition, the list of small-scale CDM-eligible energy project activities, i.e., those subject to simplified modalities and procedures,[10] and presumably, lower transaction costs,[11] concentrates on renewable energy project activities and energy efficiency improvement project activities, to wit:

a. Renewable energy project activities with a maximum output capacity equivalent of up to 15 megawatts (or an appropriate equivalent);

---

[5] And even oversimplified way, for the purposes of clarifying some concepts.

[6] There is an elaborate set of rules governing CERs, found in decision 17/CP.7 and decision 19/CP.7, Modalities for the accounting of assigned amounts under Article 7, paragraph 4, of the Kyoto Protocol, FCCC/CP/2001/13/Add.2.

[7] 4th prefatory clause, decision 17/CP.7.   [8] 5th prefatory clause, decision 17/CP.7.

[9] 8th prefatory clause, decision 17/CP.7.

[10] See Annex II (Simplified modalities and procedures for small-scale clean development mechanism project activities) to decision 21/CP.8, Guidance to the Executive Board of the clean development mechanism, FCCC/CP/2002/7/Add.3 (hereinafter referred to as "decision 21/CP.8").

[11] Both through the simplification of modalities and procedures, and the actual lowering of fees, such as the share of proceeds to cover administrative expenses of the CDM and registration fees. Par. 21, Annex II (Simplified modalities and procedures for small-scale clean development project activities) to decision 21/CP.8.

b. Energy efficiency improvement project activities that reduce energy consumption, on the supply and/or demand side, by up to the equivalent of 15 gigawatt/hours per year; and

c. Other project activities that both reduce anthropogenic emissions by sources and directly emit less than 15 kilotonnes of carbon dioxide equivalent annually.[12]

It is also worth highlighting the additionality requirement for CDM project activities, i.e., it is not enough to simply implement an energy project: the project participants must demonstrate that the reduction in emissions is additional to any that would have occurred in the absence of the certified project activity.[13] In establishing the baseline[14] over and above which emission reductions will be considered additional, project participants shall take into account "relevant national and/or sectoral policies and circumstances, such as sectoral reform initiatives, local fuel availability, power sector expansion plans, and the economic situation in the project sector."[15] Arguably then, a host country party with a progressive renewable energy policy may find that its proposed CDM energy project activities will not meet the test of additionality, since the project would have been implemented anyway, even in the absence of the CDM. It has thus been argued that the CDM may, in some cases, act as a disincentive to the institution of certain energy policies.

4 THE CDM PROJECT CYCLE[16]

An essential part of understanding the costs and benefits associated with a CDM project activity is reviewing the project cycle. Before a CDM project activity is officially registered as such, a project design document (PDD)[17] must be prepared, and the project must undergo validation, a process of independent evaluation of the project activity by

---

[12] Par. 6 (c), decision 17/CP.7. These categories are mutually exclusive. In a project activity with more than one component that will benefit from simplified modalities and procedures, each component shall meet the threshold criterion of each applicable type. Par. 7, Annex II (Simplified modalities and procedures for small-scale clean development project activities) to decision 21/CP.8. The Executive Board agreed to draw up an indicative list of eligible project activities/sectors, as proposed in Annex II of the annotated agenda of its third meeting. *See* http://cdm.unfccc.int/EB/Meetings/003/eb03annan2.pdf. The list will evolve and be further elaborated over time as new project activities are proposed and registered. Par. 2, Annex II, Simplified modalities and procedures for small-scale clean development project activities, to decision 21/CP.8.

[13] Art. 12.5, Kyoto Protocol.

[14] The baseline for a CDM project activity is "the scenario that reasonably represents the anthropogenic emissions by sources of greenhouse gases that would occur in the absence of the proposed project activity. Par. 44, Annex (Modalities and procedures for a clean development mechanism) to decision 17/CP.7.

[15] Par. 48, Annex (Modalities and procedures for a clean development mechanism) to decision 17/CP.7.

[16] This description is largely taken from decision 17/CP.7, Modalities and procedures for a clean development mechanism as defined under Article 12 of the Kyoto Protocol, the Draft COP/MOP decision attached thereto, and the accompanying annex and appendices, all found in FCCC/CP/2001/13/Add.2. A slightly different set of modalities and procedures for afforestation and reforestation project activities under the CDM have been developed, and adopted at the recently concluded ninth session of the Conference of the Parties to the UNFCCC. *See* the advanced unedited version of decision -/CP.9, Modalities and procedures for afforestation and reforestation project activities under the clean development mechanism in the first commitment period of the Kyoto Protocol found in http://www.unfccc.int.

[17] The information required in a project design document is outlined in Appendix B to the Annex (Modalities and procedures for a clean development mechanism) to decision 17/CP.7.

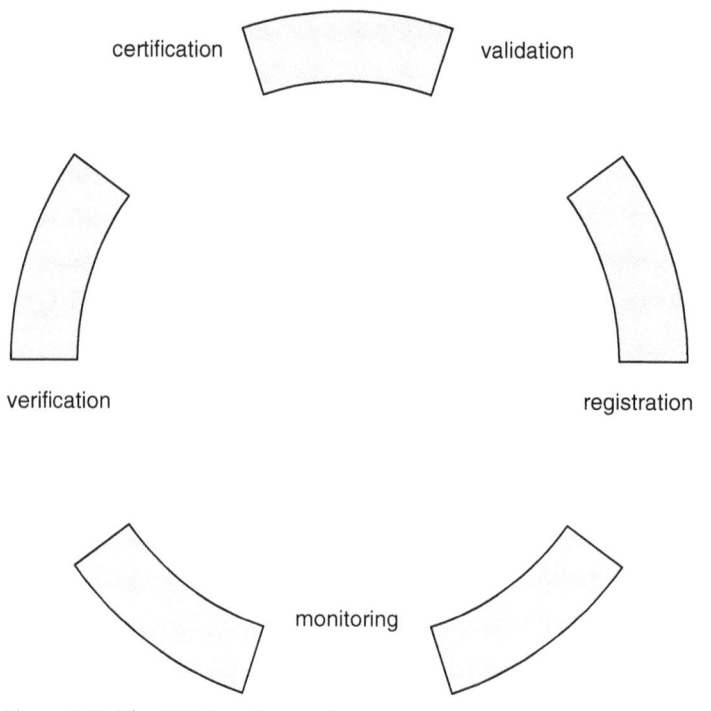

Figure 14.2 The CDM project cycle.

a designated operational entity (DOE).[18] Upon formal request of the DOE, the project activity is then registered.[19] Throughout the project lifetime, periodic monitoring must be conducted in accordance with Part H of the modalities and procedures for afforestation and reforestation projects under the CDM and the monitoring plan submitted with the PDD.

For the CERs to be issued, the project activity must undergo verification.[20] Based on the verification report, the DOE will certify in writing that, during the specified time

---

[18] Par. 35, Annex (Modalities and procedures for a clean development mechanism) to decision 17.CP.7. Validation is to be made on the basis of decision 17/CP.7, the Annex to the decision, relevant decisions of the Conference of the Parties serving as the Meeting of the Parties to the Kyoto Protocol, on the basis of the project design document.

[19] Registration is the formal process of acceptance by the Executive Board of a validated project activity. Par. 36, Annex (Modalities and procedures for a clean development mechanism) to decision 17/CP.7. The registration fee ranges from US$5,000 for a project producing a reduction of up to 15,000 average tonnes of CO_2 equivalent per year over the crediting period to a maximum of $30,000 for a project producing a reduction exceeding 200,000 average tonnes of CO_2 per year over the crediting period. Par. 70(b), Report of the Executive Board of the clean development mechanism to the Conference of the Parties (2002–2003), FCCC/CP/2003/2, Sept. 22, 2003. The registration becomes final eight weeks after the date of receipt by the Executive Board of the request for registration, unless a Party involved in the project activity or at least three members of the Board request a review of the proposed CDM project activity. Par. 41, Annex (Modalities and procedures for a clean development mechanism) to decision 17/CP.7. Annex II (Procedures for review as referred to in paragraph 41 of the clean development mechanism modalities and procedures) to decision -/CP.9, Guidance to the Executive Board of the clean development mechanism, sets out the review procedures in greater detail. An advance unedited copy of the decision is available at http://www.unfccc.int.

[20] The periodic independent review and ex post determination by the designated operational entity of the monitored reductions in anthropogenic emissions by sources of greenhouse gases that have occurred as a result of a registered CDM project activity during the verification period. Par. 61, Annex (Modalities and procedures for a clean development mechanism) to decision 17/CP.7.

period, the project activity achieved the verified amount of reductions in anthropogenic emissions by sources of greenhouse gases that would not have occurred in the absence of the CDM project activity.[21] This certification report will constitute a request to the Executive Board for the issuance of CERs equal to the verified amount of reductions of anthropogenic emissions by sources of greenhouse gases.[22]

Figure 14.2 shows, in a nutshell, the CDM project cycle.

5 GETTING THE CERs

The financing of an energy project through the CDM comes from funds that an investor is willing to pay for the CERs to be obtained from the project activity. The number of CERs actually received by project participants from a project activity is not, however, necessarily equivalent to the certified emission reductions for the activity, and may often be less. First, the DOE has to account for baseline reductions and leakage in computing the CERs.[23] Furthermore, two levies are to be imposed on CERs arising from a project activity: a two percent charge to cover adaptation costs of the developing country Parties that are particularly vulnerable to the adverse of effect of climate change,[24] and another charge to cover the administrative expenses.[25] The project implementer may also decide not to have the full amount of CERs issued at the point of verification and certification as part of the project risk management plan.

On the matter of when the funds actually flow into a project activity, unless there is an agreement between the project participants for an up-front payment for the expected CER yield of a project activity upon its commencement, it appears more likely that funding will be received after the actual issuance of CERs, or as close to this date as possible. Since the crediting period will be either a maximum of seven years, which may be renewed at most two times, or a maximum of ten years with no option of renewal,[26] the waiting period for payment may be substantial. An agreement for an up-front payment would, in all likelihood, be made only if the project implementer agrees to a discounted rate for the CERs.

---

[21] Par. 63, Annex (Modalities and procedures for a clean development mechanism) to decision 17/CP.7.

[22] Par. 64, Annex (Modalities and procedures for a clean development mechanism) to decision 17/CP.7.

[23] A CER is equal to one metric tonne of carbon dioxide equivalent. The number of CERs to be issued for a project activity is derived by subtracting the measured emissions by sources from baseline emissions, and adjusting for leakage. Par. 59, Annex, Modalities and procedures for a clean development mechanism, to decision 17/CP.7. "Leakage" is defined as "the net change of anthropogenic emissions by sources of greenhouse gases which occurs outside the project boundary, and which is measurable and attributable to the CDM project activity." Par. 51, Annex (Modalities and procedures for a clean development mechanism) to decision 17/CP.7.

[24] Par. 15, decision 17/CP.7. Note, however, that if the project is located in a least developed country Party, as the term is defined under the UNFCCC, the project will not be subject to this two per cent (2%) levy.

[25] The Executive Board has been tasked to determine this fee. Par. 16, decision 17/CP.7. In its latest report to the COP, the Executive Board concluded that "a determination of what share of proceeds shall go towards meeting the administrative costs of the CDM should only be undertaken once more reliable information is available on, inter alia, the value/price of a CER and the likely volume of CERs issued annually." The Executive Board did not, therefore, make a recommendation on the rate of this charge, but expects to be in a position to do so in 2004. Par. 48, Annual report of the Executive Board of the clean development mechanism to the Conference of the Parties (2002–2003), FCCC/CP/2003/2, 22 September 2003.

[26] Par. 49, Annex (Modalities and procedures for a clean development mechanism) to decision 17/CP.7.

6 COSTS AND BENEFITS: DO THEY BALANCE OUT?

As the brief illustration of the CDM project cycle demonstrates, transaction costs may constitute a considerable portion of the project costs. In addition, there are the costs associated with project preparation, setup, operation, and decommissioning. Dedicating the resources to an energy project may also result in opportunity costs. Finally, early entrants into the market may have to directly or indirectly bear most of the institutional costs associated with the CDM, such as the costs associated with setting up a designated national authority[27] and the costs of evaluating and, if necessary, realigning the policies and laws relating to, or impacting on, CDM project activities.

7 SOME PARTING QUESTIONS

Will proceeds from CERs arising out of a CDM project activity be sufficient to cover these costs, and to provide a sufficient rate of return to project participants? This does not appear to be the case in all instances. Will other sources of funding outside of the CDM be available? If so, these other sources of funding should be examined. It is worth noting at this point that decision 17/CP.7 clearly states that "public funding for clean development projects from Parties in Annex I is not to result in the diversion of official development assistance (ODA) and is to be separate from and not counted towards the financial obligations of the Parties included in Annex I."[28] Thus, unless an exception to ODA financing is made in the case of some project activities,[29] ODA cannot be counted on to provide this additional financing.

There is the additional challenge of promoting equitable geographic distribution of CDM project activities at regional and subregional levels.[30] As the distribution of these project activities is clearly to be influenced by market forces, how can measures be undertaken to ensure a more equitable geographic distributing, without undue interference to market forces? These are among the questions that need to be answered as more experience is gained in the development of CDM project activities.

---

[27] Parties wishing to participate in the CDM need to identify a designated national authority or DNA, which, inter alia, will provide written approval of voluntary participation by each Party involved in the CDM project activity, and, in the case of the host country Party, confirms that the project activity assists in achieving sustainable development. Pars. 29 and 40(a), Annex, Modalities and procedures for a clean development mechanism, to decision 17/CP.7. *See* also par. 1(f), decision 21/CP.8 and par. 1(f) of decision -/CP.9, Guidance to the Executive Board of the clean development mechanism.

[28] 7th prefatory clause, decision 17/CP.7. Thus, the PDD for a CDM project activity is required to include information on source of public funding from Annex I Parties, with an affirmation that such funding does not result in diversion of official development assistance and is separate from and not counted towards the financial obligations of the Annex I Party. Par. 2(f), Appendix B, decision 17/CP.7.

[29] This suggestion has been informally made in the case of small-scale afforestation and reforestation project activities under the CDM, in an effort to facilitate their implementation.

[30] *See* the 6th prefatory clause, decision 17/CP.7. Thus, the COP/MOP shall, among other things, review the regional and subregional distribution of CDM project activities with a view to identifying systematic or systemic barriers to their equitable distribution and take appropriate decisions based, inter alia, on a report of the Executive Board. Pars. 4(c) and 5(h), Annex (Modalities and procedures for a clean development mechanism) to decision 17/CP.7.

15 The Report of the World Commission on Dams: Some Implications for Energy Law

Achim Steiner* and Lawrence J. M. Haas**

1 INTRODUCTION

Among the international commissions reporting so far this millennium on water and energy development issues, the World Commission on Dams (WCD) through its report, "Dams and Development: A New Framework for Decision Making," has issued perhaps the clearest and most comprehensive call to action for the legal fraternity and law making constituencies in this field. The WCD report refers to itself as a milestone in the evolution of dams as a development option. Observers have characterized the multistakeholder processes that gave birth to the Commission, and around which it deliberated and produced its recommendations, as a watershed in global governance – one that also serves as a model for other resource development fields.

As agreed from the outset, the Commission dissolved itself when it submitted its final report to the international community in London in November 2000. Through its findings and recommendations the Commission explicitly called for the inclusion of a number of key principles in the growing body of national legislation, laws and, regulatory frameworks for water and energy development, and for these to be reflected in international approaches. It felt the framework and principles that it offered would not only go a long way to respond to the controversy over large dams, as one option for water management and energy supply, but would markedly improve decision making processes and outcomes. Moreover, such steps would help to lower the risks faced by all stakeholders, and ultimately improve access to financing for initiatives that emerged from consultation and negotiation processes.

The Commission's work applies not only to new initiatives, but also to new ways of managing the world's existing 45,000 large dams and their associated service delivery infrastructure. Here the Commission emphasized the scope to address "remaining problems," to use the Chinese vernacular, that have led to many of today's controversies over large dams; and perhaps most important, to realize opportunities for high return investments to optimize the social, environmental, and economic performance of existing infrastructure.

This chapter draws directly from the WCD report and knowledge base and analysis of the responses to it. Here energy law is viewed in its broadest sense. That is, the

With valuable contributions from John Scanlon and Maria Socorro Manguiat of the Environmental Law Centre in Bonn, Germany.

* Director General, IUCN.
** Formerly Team Leader in the Secretariat of the World Commission on Dams (WCD).

body of policies, legislation, and legal and regulatory frameworks that circumscribe water and energy development, as well as more specific legal instruments and tools such as contracts and agreements. Strategic and project level decision making processes also provide different entry points to apply laws that influence or enable new decision processes and outcomes.

The Commission proposed five core values and a "rights-and-risks" approach, with supporting strategic priorities and guidelines to better integrate these perspectives in decision making on water and energy development. The rights-and-risks approach is particularly helpful as an integrating mechanism for project level decision making. It enables effective negotiation initially on the decision whether to proceed with a particular project, and if approved, to support further negotiation at key decision points through the project life cycle, particularly where rights may be significantly transformed or affected. It offers a way to include all legitimate stakeholders in negotiating development choices and agreements, including voluntary and involuntary risk takers and marginalized voices, and goes to the core of many issues in the dams controversy.

At the other end of the spectrum, strategic decisions define the rules that promote sustainable use of water and energy resources, and how these rules are applied. This includes questions critical in the dams debate such as what options are actually on the table to achieve sustainable development, and how they get there, how options are subsequently considered and weighed, and whether a "level playing field" exists for options, or in fact, whether policy or regulatory measures to correct for nonmarket factors are to be invoked. In this respect, an important theme in the WCD Report was to engage stakeholders in comprehensive options assessment processes at a strategic level, before embarking on project level approval processes.

2 THE GENESIS OF THE WCD, THE PROCESS, AND ITS OUTCOME

The debate on large dams is at the intersection of many debates over the impacts of globalization, human rights, equity, and sustainable development. The proposal for an independent commission on large dams was born as a response to this controversy, in a multistakeholder process involving representatives of civil society, the private sector, and governmental, nongovernmental, and multilateral organizations. There was a powerful convergence of interest from all sides in the debate to move beyond stalemate, which not only delayed or threatened investment in large dams, but also was affecting alternative investments to meet priority needs. The World Bank and IUCN – The World Conservation Union – brokered this agreement in a meeting in Gland, Switzerland, in 1997. Based on that outcome, the WCD began work in 1998 under the chairmanship of Professor Kader Asmal, then South Africa's Minister of Water Affairs and Forestry and later the Minister of Education.

The Commission's two mandated tasks were:

- to review the development effectiveness of large dams and assess alternatives for water resources and energy development; and
- to develop internationally acceptable criteria, guidelines, and standards, where appropriate, for the planning, design, appraisal, construction, operation, monitoring, and decommissioning of dams.

On the first agenda, the Commission's unanimous agreement was that dams have made an important and significant contribution to human development, and the benefits derived from them have been considerable. In too many cases an unacceptable and often unnecessary price has been paid to secure those benefits. More specifically:

- lack of equity in the distribution of benefits has called into question the value of many dams in meeting water and energy development needs when compared with the alternatives;
- by bringing to the table all those whose rights are involved and who bear the risks associated with different options for water and energy resources development, the conditions for a positive resolution of competing interests and conflicts are created; and
- negotiating outcomes will greatly improve the development effectiveness of water and energy projects by eliminating unfavorable projects at an early stage, and by offering as a choice, only those options that key stakeholders agree represent the best ones to meet the needs in question.

The five core values the Commission applied to inform its understanding of the issues were equity, efficiency, participatory decision making, sustainability, and accountability. It proposed a generic framework for decision making based on recognizing the rights and assessing the risks of all interested parties. This framework was elaborated in seven strategic priorities for gaining public acceptance, comprehensively assessing options, addressing existing dams, sustaining rivers and livelihoods, recognizing entitlements and securing benefits, ensuring compliance, and sharing rivers across boundaries, supported by practical criteria and guidelines.

The Commission felt this framework could be applied in all governance settings. It would require more work up front for dialogue processes, and to put in place the enabling mechanisms for negotiation, but would ultimately serve to reduce risks, reduce overall cost and time, and deliver more equitable outcomes. It would help to integrate social, environmental, economic, and technical dimensions in decision making, add value to recent thinking on development, and add flesh to participatory planning principles advocated in the past decade, particularly starting with the Bruntland Commission on Sustainable Development (1987).

Moreover, by documenting the sources of controversy, and pointing to an alternative framework that avoided sources of controversy, the Commission offered no verdict, but an understanding and analysis of "what was broken and needs to be fixed or adapted." It did not prescribe a development model or outcome, but proposed a framework for effective and transparent decision making. And it did not prejudge whether a dam should be built, but instead offered criteria to enable societies to identify preferred options themselves. Most important, it did not preempt whole societies from making an informed choice which is their sovereign and human right, but offered a principled way forward to address the issues, and how the international community may support that endeavor.[1]

---

[1] The WCD report and its knowledge base consisting of all the regional consultations, submissions, thematic papers, cases studies, presentations, and constituency reactions to the interim and final report are available at http://www.dams.org and the on the Web site of the UNEP sponsored follow-up initiative discussed later in Section 5.2 at http://www.unep-dams.org.

3 THE CHANGING CONTEXT THE WCD ADDRESSED

The changing development context and trends in water and energy resource provided the rationale for the Commission's call to action. But certainly, the WCD's own work was not without precedent or peers. It worked on common ground with a number of other integrating global initiatives to address the challenges in water, energy, environment, and sustainable development for the new millennium. These included processes around the World Water Forum (WWF) and Global Water Partnership (GWP), the UNEP-WEC World Energy Assessment Report (WEA-2000), and the Intergovernmental Panel on Climate Change (IPCC) supporting the United Nations Framework Convention for Climate Change (UNFCCC). Though the WCD had a more specific mandate, the same influences that are shaping governance and development thinking today informed each process.

3.1 The Changing Governance and Development Context

A number of overall trends in governance have significantly altered the context for decision making on large dams and alternatives over the past twenty-five years. In fact, part of the Commission's challenge was to offer ways to better translate these changes to new decision making processes on dams. The first is the dramatic number of transitions from authoritarian to democratic rule. The democratizing trend has in turn been deeply interconnected with the spread of human rights norms and the proliferation and strengthening of civil society organizations, both domestically within countries and internationally. A further trend involves the globalization of development issues, and in particular, the increased prominence of market-oriented economic models and institutional processes for environmental protection and conservation.

Within this, there is a detectable shift in the way public interest is defined from one that placed a premium on strict technical or economic interests, to one that places much more weight on the rights and interests of people and communities affected by development activities, with a focus on equity in the spread of costs and benefits from development, including the concept of intergenerational equity in dealing with resource use. This applies to consumptive uses of water, as well as finite energy resources. It fundamentally shifts the basic perspective on management of resources from a technical and economic optimization exercise to an emphasis on human development and sustainability, and puts management of resources to optimize social needs and welfare as a foremost criteria.

At the same time roles and responsibilities among the public and private sectors and civil society are changing. This is not to say that the role of governments has become less important; simply that its role is changing in character in most governance settings. The role of civil society organizations has, by contrast, expanded and their legitimacy in representing and defending interests, in participating in decision making on development, and in monitoring compliance is increasing, although not unchallenged. The private sector has also considerably expanded its role, undertaking service provision and other functions that were once – and not long ago – the exclusive remit of government.

The recent emphasis on good governance is shifting to insistence on transparent and participatory decision making, which requires that the range of stakeholders not only be consulted but be empowered to negotiate in processes making key decisions affecting them. Within this, the concepts of legitimacy and accountability are becoming pillars of the new order, and decisions that have not been taken in a context that guarantees their legitimacy are increasingly being challenged. Legitimacy is being evaluated on the grounds of transparency, openness, and participation. And stakeholders are developing ways to hold decision makers and developers accountable for the fulfillment of their undertakings.

There is also a growing body of international instruments relating to human rights, as well as institutions to oversee their further development and application. While little of this may be binding and enforceable, there is a growing sense that development activities will be increasingly open to question and challenge if they infringe on these rights in a substantial and systematic way. International instruments will also continue to inform the development of national laws, and mechanisms for oversight of human rights are growing steadily stronger and more influential, both at national and international levels. These strengthen the arguments in favor of greater transparency, participation in decision making, and accountability for compliance.

Similarly, the notion of the right to development is beginning to develop a normative framework for specifying responsibilities in applying the human rights approach to development. In future, it is unlikely that approaches based on a narrow assessment of costs and benefits of specific actions will be tolerated if they do not adequately take into account the real impact of those actions on the rights and welfare of all those affected.

3.2 Sustainable Management of Fresh Water Resources

Global trends in water demand and supply reinforced what follows from analysis governance and development trends – that is, in spite of difficulties, negotiated outcomes offer the only practical way forward and basis for improved development outcomes.

The WCD knowledge base shows the dramatic impact of water withdrawals from the world's lakes, rivers, and ground aquifers, and how the growing water stresses impact on interdependent human and natural systems. By 2025, there will be approximately 6.5 times as many people as today, or 3.5 billion people, living in water stressed countries. At present two billion people lack adequate, safe drinking water supply and sanitation. The unfolding scenario for water use in many parts of the world is one of increasing concern about access, equity, and the response to growing needs. This will increasingly affect relations:

- within and between nations;
- between rural and urban populations;
- between upstream and downstream interests;
- between agricultural, industrial, and domestic sectors; and
- between human needs and the requirements of a healthy environment and functional ecosystems.

Moreover, the evidence is compelling that climate change will bring additional pressure to the world's hydrological systems, watersheds, river basins, and wetlands, increasing the uncertainty and scale of the challenge.

In face of this evidence, the Commission's view was that real strategic decisions are not about dams as such, but about wider options for water, energy, and sustainable development. The challenge was not to mobilize so as to compete successfully, but to cooperate in reconciling competing needs and adapt successfully to changing circumstances. It is to find ways of sharing water resources equitably and sustainably; ways that meet the needs of all people, as well as those of the environment and economic development. The Commission recognized that these needs are all intertwined.

3.3 Sustainable Development of Energy (Electricity) Systems

Fortunately, the global energy resource outlook is not as acute as that for fresh water, particularly for electricity generation. The WEA-2000 suggested that while individual countries have different energy resource endowments, there is no shortage of renewable energy or conventional fossil resources, or conversion options at all scales, to meet future electrical needs well into this century. The immediate concerns relate more to closing the equity gap, where close to one-third of humanity live with no access to electricity services, and to expand electrical services in developing countries to support growth and modernization, leaving aside the question of how those services are provided. A second pressing issue, related to sustainability, is how to address the causal linkage between present patterns of energy resource conversion and use and climate change, given that power generation directly accounts for up to thirty percent of human-generated GHG emissions, mostly from coal plants.

The WCD knowledge base showed that the power sector in virtually all countries is undergoing structural change, more rapidly so than the water sector. The motivations vary. But apart from allowing new forms of ownership and financing, the regulatory reforms facilitate market entry of renewable and more efficient conventional technologies, formation of decentralized or distributed electrical systems, and introduction of consumer-oriented energy services. Where enabling conditions are present in rural areas (e.g., political will and financial capacity), advances include the adoption of new decentralized, stand-alone systems such as solar units that "leapfrog" conventional approaches to service provision. At the other end of the spectrum, the regulatory reform processes in the power sector coupled with political changes are redefining energy security, less in national terms, and more in regional terms. This evidence is in the dramatic increase in the number of agreements for interconnection of regional power grids, regional power pool arrangements, and gas and oil pipelines crossing national boundaries to supporting power generation in neighboring countries.

Especially in Europe, the concern over global warming of conventional thermal generation has translated into a new impetus for regulation to promote renewable and nonconventional power generation options, and systems where the consumer can choose the generation source at some cost premium. EU governments have established "minimum resource portfolios" with tariff, tax, and other subsidy equalization or leveling measures to achieve new targets for renewable generation in the supply mix. For instance, they now require a minimum ten percent of total electrical generation from renewable energy sources by 2010. It is anticipated that such targets would be increased as climate change mitigation and adaptation strategies are finalized. This trend is not restricted to developed economies. China and India are moving toward setting renewable energy generation targets, though how the hydropower option is treated in the renewable equation varies from country to country and is a source of ongoing debate at international levels.

It is also clear that many aspects of the regulatory reforms remain controversial, especially the ownership issues and tariff-related equity impacts. Certainly without adequate institutional safeguards such transparent regulation and credible rules, divestiture or the opening up of power markets to private investors may contribute to market failure by increasing rent seeking and introducing new opportunities for corruption, the recent concerns about power trading in California notwithstanding.

3.4 Applying the Rights-and-Risks Framework To Seek Negotiated Outcomes

Few disagree that large dams fundamentally alter rivers and transform resources, frequently reallocating benefits and entitlements from local riparian users to new groups of beneficiaries at the regional or national level. In the Commission's view, issues of equity, governance, justice, and power to decide entitlements were at the heart of the dams debate, and negotiated approaches best served to reconcile the competing needs and entitlements. The Commission felt that a rights-and-risks approach provided an effective framework to determine who has a legitimate place in consultation on overall water and energy policy, what issues need to be on the agenda, and what legitimate groups need to be at the negotiation table on specific projects.

The rights-and-risks approach empowers decision making processes based on the pursuit of negotiated outcomes, conducted in an open and transparent manner, and inclusive of all legitimate actors involved in the issue. While this will present greater demands at early stages, it leads to greater clarity and legitimacy for subsequent steps in project level decision making and implementation and reduces the risks faced by all stakeholders. It shifts the basic perspective on management of resources to place more emphasis on human development dimensions.

The Commission did not have to look far to identify principles on rights. They are the same principles that emerged from the global debates on human rights, development, and sustainability. The emergence of a globally accepted framework of norms rests on the adoption of the Universal Declaration of Human Rights and later resolutions including the Declaration on the Right to Development adopted by the UN General Assembly in 1986, and the Rio Principles agreed upon in 1992.

In practice these have to be translated to the context. For upstream and downstream riverine communities affected by dams, there are a "bundle of rights" that potentially may come into play. These range from customary and traditional rights of ownership, tenancy, resources access, and livelihood benefit that may be uncodified, to other more formal rights encoded in legislation. Rights may also belong to the individual, household, or family, a traditional user or neighborhood group, or to a community or public body, or other defined social entity, such as indigenous people. At the other end of the spectrum are the rights of those who may be recipients, or the main beneficiaries from a resource transformation occurring elsewhere, including their right of access to water and energy services essential to their right to develop, welfare, and livelihood.

The second element in the rights-and-risk approach, the assessment of risk (including rights at risk), adds an important dimension to understanding to what extent an intervention may impact on people's rights in a significant or systematic way. Traditional practice has been to restrict the definition of risk to that of the larger national economy in terms of avoided cost, or nationally defined water or energy security, or to the corporate investor or developer, in terms of loan repayment and expected returns on equity. In contrast, the WCD's Global Review showed that risks faced by a far larger group of stakeholders in dam projects were not addressed. Often these groups had risks imposed on them *involuntarily* and managed by others, including risks that directly affect their livelihoods, quality of life, and culture. Typically, these involuntary risk bearers have little or no say in overall water and energy policy, in the choice of specific projects to meet their needs, or in subsequent project design and implementation, thus denying them a stake in the decision making process commensurate with their exposure to risk.

In the Commission's view, *voluntary* risk takers have the capacity to define the level and type of risk they wish to take and explicitly to define its boundaries. Involuntary risk bearers must engage with risk takers in a transparent process to negotiate equitable outcomes, in ways appropriate to the governance context. What the Commission proposed was that governments have a responsibility to establish the enabling framework for good faith negotiations to take place. To be effective, this framework would include procedures for more effective mediation and adjudication, either through political or judiciary means, in the case of intractable disputes. Governments nonetheless retained ultimate responsibility for all processes, decisions, and their sovereignty.

3.5 Using the Planning and Project Cycle

What the Commission identified was five generic decision points in the strategic planning and project cycle where an appropriate group of stakeholders should be involved, such as identified with the rights-and-risks approach.

The decision points at the strategic level were:

1. needs assessment – validating the needs for water and energy services; and
2. selecting alternatives – identifying the preferred development plan consisting of a mix of complementary options from among the full range of development options.

And where a dam emerges from this process, three further critical decision points are:

3. project preparation – verifying that agreements among stakeholders are in place before tendering construction contracts;
4. project implementation – confirming compliance with agreements before commissioning; and
5. project operation – adapting to changing contexts.

The five stages and associated decision points need to be interpreted within the overall planning and regulatory contexts of individual countries such as for government and privately licensed projects. And to some extent strategic and project level planning activities are interactive. The steps also illustrate points of entry to apply different legal instruments and tools, and how comprehensive options assessment can be lifted out of project level debates to strategic decision making levels.

4 SOME OF THE LEGAL IMPLICATIONS ARISING FROM THE WCD REPORT

4.1 Strategic Priorities

The Commission suggested, and in fact urged, governments to review their national policies, regulations, and institutional frameworks in light of the WCD report, using multistakeholder processes. And while different states are at different stages in developing legal and regulatory systems and institutional capacity, much of the work in translating new policy to legal and regulatory instruments would be accomplished with local legal knowledge, capacity, and expertise. There are areas where it may also be advantageous for national legal entities to draw on international law centers and networks, such as the IUCN Environmental Law Center in Bonn and the IUCN Commission on Environmental Law, a network of over 820 lawyers in more than 130 countries.

Following are three of the Commission's seven strategic priorities and possible implications for policy and legal provisions. A discussion of possible entry points for legal measures to act on the remaining four strategic priorities is provided in Section 4.2.

Strategic Priority 5: Recognizing Entitlements and Sharing Benefits
Key Message: Joint negotiations with adversely affected people result in mutually agreed and legally enforceable mitigation and development provisions. These provisions recognize entitlements that improve livelihoods and quality of life, and affected people are beneficiaries of the project. Successful mitigation, resettlement, and development are fundamental commitments and responsibilities of the state and the developer. They bear the onus to satisfy all affected people that moving from their current context and resources will improve their livelihoods. Accountability of responsible parties to agreed mitigation, resettlement, and development provisions is ensured through legal means, such as contracts, and through accessible legal recourse at national and international level.

Effective implementation of this strategic priority depends on applying these policy principles:

- Recognition of rights and assessment of risks is the basis for identification and inclusion of adversely affected stakeholders in joint negotiations on mitigation, resettlement, and development related decision making.
- Impact assessment includes all people in the reservoir, upstream, downstream, and catchment areas whose properties, livelihoods, and nonmaterial resources are affected. It also includes those affected by dam related infrastructure such as canals, transmission lines, and resettlement developments.
- All recognized adversely affected people negotiate mutually agreed, formal, and legally enforceable mitigation, resettlement, and development entitlements.
- Adversely affected people are recognized as first among the beneficiaries of the project. Mutually agreed and legally protected benefit sharing mechanisms are negotiated to ensure implementation.

Among the possible arrangements national policy makers and the legal fraternity may use to improve the recognition of entitlements and sharing of benefits, depending on whether these provisions are currently embodied in existing laws and statutes, include steps to:

- consolidate and clarify ambiguous laws and regulations on traditional, customary, and formal entitlements and rights to be considered in negotiations;
- introduce formal requirements for negotiation on projects, and clarifying procedures and mechanisms to determine effective stakeholder involvement;
- clarify roles, authorities, and responsibilities of governments, licensing agencies, regulators, and developers (public or private) in such negotiations;
- introduce support mechanisms for the poorest and most vulnerable stakeholders, such as funded access to independent legal advice;
- clarify policies and procedures for either political resolution, or arbitration and legal recourse for dispute settlement; and
- develop models for contracts and agreements among stakeholders such as for benefit sharing, new entitlements, and for resettlement and compensation agreements.

The rights-and-risks framework offers a useful starting point for a number of these tasks. The WCD knowledge base showed there are surprisingly few mechanisms for benefit sharing in widespread use today, despite the fact that models exist for different governance settings, especially for hydropower projects that generate a revenue stream. The WCD knowledge base also shows many instances of benefit sharing for projects with limited revenue streams such as irrigation and flood control projects. These are typically livelihood entitlement approaches that arise from negotiation, and that go well beyond one time cash compensation for lost and property assets. These include new entitlements to replace those entitlements lost, provide access to services generated by the dam to its host community, and ongoing financing of local enterprise development to enhance long-term welfare and livelihoods.

Strategic Priority 6: Ensuring Compliance

Key Message: Ensuring public trust and confidence requires that governments, developers, regulators, and operators meet all commitments made for the planning, implementation, and operation of dams. Compliance with applicable regulations, criteria, guidelines, and project specific negotiated agreements is secured at all critical stages in project planning and implementation. A set of mutually reinforcing incentives and mechanisms is required for social, environmental, and technical measures. These should involve an appropriate mix of regulatory and nonregulatory measures, incorporating incentives and sanctions. Regulatory and compliance frameworks use incentives and sanctions to ensure effectiveness where flexibility is needed to accommodate changing circumstances.

Effective implementation of this strategic priority depends on applying these policy principles:

- A clear, consistent, and common set of criteria and guidelines to ensure compliance is adopted by sponsoring, contracting, and financing institutions and compliance is subject to independent and transparent review.
- A compliance plan is prepared for each project prior to commencement, spelling out how compliance will be achieved with relevant criteria and guidelines, and

specifying binding arrangements for project specific technical, economic, social, and environmental commitments.

- Costs for establishing compliance mechanisms and related institutional capacity, and their effective application, are built into the project budget.
- Corrupt practices are avoided through enforcement of legislation, voluntary integrity pacts, debarment, and other instruments.
- Incentives that reward project proponents for abiding by criteria and guidelines are developed.

Governments and other stakeholders need to be satisfied that once agreements are reached, all parties can monitor and ensure compliance with obligations throughout the life of a project. Indeed the Commission felt that past conflicts over dams arose all too frequently from the failure to fulfill voluntary and other commitments that were made to observe statutory regulations and abide by internal guidelines. Compliance mechanisms largely exist for construction, engineering, and equipment performance aspects of dams. The concern here is to extend compliance provisions to cover environmental and social performance, reflecting agreements reached in this regard. This is consistent with a shift toward optimizing the performance of infrastructure away from strict technical and economic criteria to enhance human development returns.

Among the possible measures to ensure effective compliance, that should be in place to improve compliance when a decision is taken to proceed with a new dam, or to significantly alter an existing dam include steps to:

- introduce requirements for compliance plans in regulations and licenses for new projects that complement existing requirements such as for resettlement and environmental mitigation and management plans, and when relicensing existing facilities;
- clarify roles, authorities, and responsibilities of governments, licensing agencies, regulators, and developers (public or private) and affected stakeholders in developing compliance plans, monitoring, and compliance, and to provide accessible means to address and remedy noncompliance;
- define incentives and sanction measures (rewards and penalties) to include in project agreements and subagreements among stakeholders, appropriate to different circumstances; and
- provide model compliance plans and monitoring indicators for stakeholders to be consulted on, or agree to as appropriate.

Legally based sanctions for noncompliance would apply to projects, private concessions, and licenses to quasi-public entities. The WCD report suggested that environmental performance bonds supported by financial guarantees are a possible mechanism, where there is some experience in mining and the construction industries. Bonuses and other incentive mechanisms have also been used for different purposes. Different instruments may be required for public entities building and operating dams, or where a government ministry or agency is responsible separately for resettlement, environmental mitigation, and compensation components of a project. Forming an independent panel for compliance review is one measure that may be implemented quickly for these circumstances. Trust funds that hold and manage funds set aside for a particular purpose (such as resettlement or environmental measures) with transparent disbursement is another possible measure. Other longer-term steps being advocated are standards and certification approaches, working with recognized international standards groups such as the International Standards Organization (ISO), of which many governments are members.

Strategic Priority 7: Sharing Rivers for Peace, Development, and Security

Key message: Storage and diversion of water on transboundary rivers has been a source of considerable tension between countries and within countries. Dams are specific interventions for diverting water that require constructive cooperation. The use and management of resources increasingly become the subject of agreement between states that promote mutual self-interest for regional cooperation and peaceful collaboration. There is a shift in focus to sharing rivers and water and the benefits deriving from them. States are innovative in defining the extent of issues that form the scope of negotiations and do not restrict themselves to seeking allocation of a finite resource.

Effective implementation of this strategic priority depends on applying these policy principles:

- National water policies make specific provision for basin agreements in shared river basins. Agreements are negotiated on the basis of good faith among riparian states. They are based on principles of equitable and reasonable utilization, no significant harm, prior information, and the Commission's strategic priorities.
- Riparian states go beyond looking at water as a finite commodity to be divided, and embrace an approach that equitably allocates not the water, but the benefits that can be derived from it. Where appropriate, negotiations include benefits outside the river basin and other sectors of mutual interest.
- Dams on shared rivers are not built in cases where riparian states raise an objection that is upheld by an independent panel. Intractable disputes between countries are resolved through various means of dispute resolution including, in the last instance, the International Court of Justice.
- For the development of projects on rivers shared between political units within countries, the necessary legislative provision is made at national and subnational levels to embody the Commission's strategic priorities of "gaining public acceptance," "recognizing entitlements," and "sustaining rivers and livelihoods."
- Where a government agency plans or facilitates the construction of a dam on a shared river in contravention of the principle of good faith negotiations between riparians, external financing bodies withdraw their support for projects and programs promoted by that agency.

The need to pursue negotiated outcomes is perhaps most visibly demonstrated in the case of states sharing rivers. There are 216 international river basins worldwide, most do not have agreements covering water allocation, certainly there are few agreements covering shared, beneficial use of ground water aquifers.

As shown in the WCD knowledge base, the negotiation of agreements between riparian states has proceeded on a case-by-case basis without an overarching globally binding legal instrument. With the intensifying scarcity of water, pressures will grow for mechanisms to resolve disputes between riparian states. Broad international consensus has been reached on some overarching principles, such as embodied in the 1966 Helsinki Rules on Use of Water in International Rivers, as well as more recent agreements, such as the Petersburg Declaration, which saw water as a catalyst for cooperation, the Dublin Water Principles (1992), and the Ministerial Declaration and Bonn Recommendations for Action from the International Conference on Freshwater (2001). But in the absence of effective international agreements, other measures need to be invoked.

An approach the WCD offered was for riparian states to constructively widen the considerations for negotiated outcomes on sharing rivers to a broader framework of cooperation. This would shift the primary focus from one of negotiation about how to allocate finite water quantities, to negotiation of sharing benefits that derive from the use of water in a wider development context, inclusive of other synergies such as in wider terms of trade. This approach may help avoid water disputes from becoming polarized and entrenching negotiating positions. Other avenues include support for integrated basin management, including river basin organizations and regulatory bodies and enforcement agencies. Many countries internally, and international financing agencies almost without exception, now embrace the principle of integrated river basin management (such as the EU Directive 2000/60/EC establishing a framework for Community action in the field of water policy). Legal and regulatory reforms within countries, such as arrangements to share resources among provinces or states within countries, build toward and help improve the enabling environment for eventual international agreements. This also offers an integrating framework and entry point for many cross cutting laws including those concerned with water allocation and conservation, water quality, and ecosystem restoration and protection.

4.2 Some Implications for Legal Mechanisms and Tools for the Remaining Four Strategic Priorities

The following highlights issues where policy and legal mechanisms may need to be introduced, or strengthened, to better achieve the underlying aims of the four remaining strategic priorities of the WCD, namely: gaining public acceptance, comprehensively assessing options, addressing existing dams, and sustaining rivers and livelihoods. The Commission recognized that the approach and timeframe to revise policies and put supporting tools in place is country and context specific.

Gaining Public Acceptance

Laws that provide better more open access to information is one central and comparatively easy measure to gain public acceptance and confidence. This is not only for stakeholders directly involved in project related negotiation, but also for the wider stakeholder constituencies. Enabling laws are also needed to ensure that information such as environment impact assessment reports on new project proposals and monitoring reports on the performance of existing projects are more accessible and understandable to the public. Although regional in scope, the adoption of the Aarhus Convention is of global significance in setting a regional framework for gaining more open access to information.

Comprehensive Options Assessment

A feature that the Commission proposed that was new or not widespread practice was an assessment of all of the options of interest to stakeholders, and to move options assessment processes "upstream" to strategic planning level. In some cases, assessments and limited debates on options are now carried out within, or prompted by project approval processes for specific dams. Revisions to planning and regulatory systems to accommodate this may not be difficult, but may be gradual. Beyond this step, laws and regulations will need regular assessment and possible revision to ensure a level playing field for all options. This will take into account, for example, direct and hidden subsidies, or at a minimum, to make these explicit in decision making processes. This also provides scope to identify laws and regulatory provisions to accelerate the adoption of options, or more sustainable practices where appropriate. Such measures not only apply to supply options, but also to demand measures to encourage longer-term structural efficiency in water or electricity demand.

Addressing Existing Dams

What the Commission called for that was new, or not widespread practice, was to ensure that improvements in existing dams are part of comprehensive options assessment (i.e., improving social, environment, technical, and economic performance), and secondly, to involve stakeholders in adaptive management of existing dams, particularly where changes in the operation would significantly affect upstream or downstream communities and ecosystem services. It also recommended a review of policies and legislation to addresses unresolved claims and disputes that were unforeseen or unintended outcomes of existing dams. An important step in this direction is to ensure that all dams have licenses that stipulate roles, responsibilities, and entitlements of all stakeholders in how the dam is managed and operated.

Sustaining Rivers and Livelihoods

Many countries have developed new policies and laws relatively recently to address a range of environment protection and restoration concerns related to rivers, watersheds, wetlands, and aquatic ecosystems that directly and indirectly concern dams. At present, 177 countries have accepted, approved, or acceded to the Biodiversity Convention and 122 to the Ramsar Convention on Wetlands. The WCD report calls for the better integration of these measures in dam related decision making, and in options assessments processes to ensure the full range of options for sustainable management of water resources are debated. What the Commission called for that was new, or not in widespread practice, was the consideration of policies on intact rivers and environmental flows, where there are numerous models and precedents to draw upon.

5 RESPONSES AND FOLLOW-UP TO THE WCD REPORT

While reaction to the WCD report when it was issued in November 2000 was largely positive, there was no unanimous endorsement of all its aspects by all constituencies. In some instances there were different responses even from international and national committees of the same organizations. Some – notably, on both sides of the debate – felt the weight of some findings unbalanced against their respective positions, or that recommendations could have gone further, or went too far. Yet the overwhelming consensus was that, despite their remaining differences in perspectives, the Report provided a solid reference point for all parties to move forward, both individually and collectively.

5.1 Initial Responses after the WCD Report Was Launched in November 2000

As an immediate response, a number of governments, NGOs, civil society representatives, development agencies, professional associations, and engineering companies engaged in the WCD process issued statements indicating that the philosophy of the report and its specific recommendations would be reflected in their policies and practices.

NGOs and civil society groups collectively called for full and complete adoption of the WCD report by all governments as a starting point, but especially by the multilateral financing agencies, bilateral agencies and Export Credit Agencies (ECAs). A coalition of a number of people's movements and NGOs also called for a moratorium on dams until a time bounded program to implementing the report's major recommendations was agreed on. Many industry groups and professional associations welcomed the report unconditionally. Other key groups, such as the International Commission on Irrigation and Drainage (ICID), International Commission on Large Dams (ICOLD), and International Hydropower Association (IHA), while noting basic agreement on the strategic priorities and principles, indicated concerns about what they felt was a negative tone of the review of past performance of dams. They also felt the report's criteria and guidelines, while based on best practices, could make it too difficult to construct any new dams, and thus could be interpreted as antidam, or even antidevelopment. The World Bank and Asian Development Bank immediately welcomed the report, but the World Bank also said that the critical test for it would be whether its country members represented by the major borrowers accepted the Commission's recommendations.

Reactions after the WCD held a series of regional launches to present the report to governments and constituencies in the debate indicated substantive agreement emerging across the spectrum of interests on some of the following points:

- that the linkage between water, dams, and wider development challenges was correctly identified in the report, and that an increasing number of countries are facing an urgent need to proceed with investments;
- that countries should review their national policies, legislation, and large projects in the context of the WCD report;
- that multilateral and bilateral financing agencies should review their policies in the context of the WCD report;
- that core values and strategic priorities the Commission offered were appropriate for these reviews;
- that a fair and realistic assessment of all options is needed early in the planning process;
- that sector and river basin studies are needed to get a broadly acceptable portfolio of projects;
- that there should be a greater focus on refurbishment and optimizing technical, economic, and environmental performance of existing dams and other assets;
- that guarantees for the social and environmental mitigation work are needed and compliance plans are needed that clearly specify responsibilities; and
- on the need to continue the dialogue among the constituencies so as not to miss the window of opportunity presented by the WCD process and its momentum.

A number of developing countries responded to the report at the regional launches in different capitals, or in a direct response to the WCD Chair, or through the outreach work of the World Bank and Asian Development Bank (ADB) canvassing their members' reactions. Some, but certainly not all, agreed with many aspects of the report, especially the core values, strategic priorities, and policy principles. Many expressed strong concerns about the practicality of the detailed guidelines, amidst concerns that the WCD report, if adopted in total by international financing agencies, would lead to greater conditionality. Moreover, because they had not directly authored or negotiated key aspects of the report, many developing government representatives wanted time to consider its implications more fully, using multistakeholder processes in some cases.

The majority view of members of the WCD Forum at its final meeting in February 2001 was that an information clearinghouse function was needed to support the national dialogues spawned by the report, and build on the unprecedented interest in the report, while negotiations proceed at the international level on the next steps.

5.2 Two Years after the Release of the Final WCD Report

In response to the WCD Forum request, the United Nations Environment Programme (UNEP) agreed to host the Dams and Development Project (DDP). Building on the dialogue of the WCD and the WCD's core values and strategic priorities, the aim of this two-year program is to promote a dialogue on improving decision making, planning, and management of dams and their alternatives based on the WCD core values and strategic priorities. For this, the UNEP has constituted a fourteen-member Steering Committee, a support Secretariat, and a Dams and Development Forum of ninety representatives from different constituencies, fifty of whom were formerly WCD Forum members. UNEP also sees the DDP and the broad representation of the Steering Committee as a model for more substantive national processes to follow in digesting and taking action on the report. The first Forum meeting was held in Nairobi in June 2002.

A number of organizations actively participating in the DDP will channel further responses to the WCD report and how it may be applied in different countries and at international levels through the DDP platform for dialogue. Some countries and organizations have already taken steps to assess how to integrate the WCD report in their own activities, or have launched complementary initiatives to achieve this. A sampling of these is noted as follows. This is not comprehensive, but rather indicates the nature of the follow-up.

Activities at the National Level

Separate from the WCD launch meetings in different capitals, over twenty-two national governments have arranged or have participated in activities ranging from multistakeholder seminars and workshops to national forums to gather responses to the report and decide further practical steps. A few countries have moved ahead with more substantive, multistakeholder reviews of their policies and programs, and many more are likely using the report as a reference in ongoing programs. For instance, the South African government is using the WCD Report to scrutinize their national policies and procedures on dams with open stakeholder processes. The government of Pakistan has initiated a one-year process with donor support to consult with stakeholders in all provinces and territories, and have a national debate to help generate recommendations for policy reforms by the government through enhancing understanding of the WCD report, combined with national issues.

Most OECD countries members indicate that they have already implemented, or will take steps to implement WCD recommendations in their development assistance programs, and reflect them in the export credit agency policies. They have indicated they will continue to take similar positions as board members of multilateral agencies and would explore further mechanisms to harmonize policies among bilateral programs on these matters. For example, the U.S. Senate Committee on Appropriations in its report in 2001 urged the World Bank to continue to engage with the full range of interested parties in the implementation of the WCD's report, and to integrate these guidelines to the fullest extent practicable into the Bank's relevant operational policies and directives, including those relating to resettlement, environmental assessment, and water and energy policies.

Multilateral Development Banks

After its initial internal review and canvassing of borrowing country reactions, the World Bank launched it own initiative under a Dams Planning and Management Action Plan. The stated aim of the initiative is to improve the quality of its operations by building on the core values and strategic priorities of the WCD report. This includes a series of initiatives to identify best practice, such as on stakeholder involvement, benefit sharing, and comprehensive options assessment. The World Bank is also participating on the DDP steering committee. Similarly, the Asian Development Bank, after sponsoring regional dialogue among its members on the report, including a workshop with delegations from fifteen member countries, including China, India, Pakistan, Nepal, Indonesia, Thailand, The Philippines, and Malaysia, indicates that that it will determine the extent to which the report's recommendations may necessitate changes in its existing procedures. Agencies including the African Development Bank, Inter American Development Bank, and European Bank for Reconstruction and Development indicated similar intentions to apply the WCD principles in their lending policies.

International Development Organizations and Conventions

UNEP is hosting the DDP and will be a primary vehicle to bring the WCD report directly into intergovernmental discussion forums. IUCN – The World Conservation Union – apart from resolutions to respond to the recommendations of the WCD report passed at the World Conservation Congress and subsequent resolutions of the IUCN Council, is participating on the DDP Steering Committee and has established a program of work to respond to the WCD report. Other international development organizations working with the WCD report include the OECD-DAC Environmental Development Committee and the OECD Export Credit Agency Working Party, who indicate they will incorporate reviews made of the WCD recommendations in their efforts to harmonize guidelines and ECA activities. The members of the Convention on Biological Diversity and the Ramsar Convention on Wetlands are similarly conducting assessments on how the report can be integrated in the Conventions' activities.

Private Sector and Professional Associations

Private sector groups, including equipment manufactures and consulting firms, are represented on the DDP Forum and DDP Steering Committee. The Hydro Equipment Association (HEA) has been formed to represent the hydro equipment industry in the follow-up dialogue and actions with other stakeholders resulting from the WCD

Report. IHA has subsequently joined the Steering Group of the DDP. While ICOLD and ICID remain cautious about engaging directly in the DDP process, subsequent to the WCD report ICOLD has established an ad-hoc Committee on dams to "Implement the ICOLD Position Paper on Dams and Environment" and extend it to Governance of Dam Projects, including ethical points of view. ICID has formed a new task force for "Promoting Appropriate Decision Making Procedures for New Dams, Particularly for Irrigation, Drainage and Flood Management."

Civil Society and NGO Community

NGOs and advocacy groups have been actively disseminating the WCD report to their constituencies and have brought the report into national policy dialogue processes and project specific consultations in different countries. For example, the international Rivers Network has published a Citizens' Guide to the WCD. Key civil society and NGO groups are actively involved in the DDP follow-up process, participating on the DDU Forum and Steering Committee, and specifically have been monitoring the responses of the key donor agencies, the development banks, and companies to the report. They have, for instance, increased pressure on the World Bank and OECD country ECAs for the adoption of the report. Other NGO groups have been helping to sponsor national or regional dialogue on the WCD report inviting governments and all constituencies.

6 FROM POLICY TO PRACTICE

The WCD report is certainly not the last word on large dams, or on how the issues raised in the dams debate should be tackled. It derives its significance from the rapidly changing context into which the Commission's recommendations are offered, at a time when sustainable water resources management concerns are rapidly moving to the top of the global development agenda, as is most evident from the United Nations Millennium Declaration and the outcomes from the World Summit on Sustainable Development, the Johannesburg Political Declaration and Plan of Implementation. The WCD's own legitimacy in offering a way forward was that it engaged the entire spectrum of participants in the dams debate, and at all levels, in an open process. It offered itself as model for what can be achieved at the national level. Certainly after two years of intense study, dialogue, and reflection, the Commission felt its rationale and framework offered scope for progress on this issue that no single perspective on its own may offer. In its "Call to Action" the Commission declared that the WCD report itself was not a blueprint. It encouraged all parties to use it as "a starting point for discussions, debates, internal reviews, and reassessment of existing procedures." As the Commission hoped, stakeholders have moved on with the dams debate, largely informed by, and in large measure with constant reference to the Commission's work. The acknowledged task now is to move from policy to practice. And in this respect the legal fraternity in countries and working at the international level will have a significant role to play.

16 International Issues for Energy for Sustainable Development: IUCN Perspectives

John Scanlon*

1 IUCN – THE WORLD CONSERVATION UNION: A UNIQUE GLOBAL PARTNERSHIP

The perspectives of IUCN – The World Conservation Union on energy for sustainable development relate directly to what the institution is and stands for.

IUCN is a unique global partnership established in 1948 in Fontainebleau, France.[1] It is a membership based organization, which today has close to 1,000 members, including states, government agencies, and nongovernment members.[2]

There are several components of IUCN, all of which play complementary roles. The highest organ of IUCN is the World Conservation Congress, which is where all IUCN members meet and set IUCN's "general policy," and approve the program and financial plan for the Union. At the Congress the membership also elects its office holders, including the President, members of Council, and Commission Chairs.[3] The other components of IUCN are the Council, National and Regional Committees of Members, Commissions,[4] and the Secretariat.[5]

IUCN was granted United Nations Observer status in 2000, and is the only conservation organization in the world to enjoy such status. IUCN is also recognized as an intergovernmental organization with most convention secretariats it works with and the UNEP Governing Council.

IUCN's vision is: "a just world that values and conserves nature" and its mission[6] is to: "***influence, encourage and assist*** *societies throughout the world to conserve the*

---

[1] Statues were adopted in 1948, which have since been amended, most recently at the World Conservation Congress in Montreal 1996.

[2] For more information visit www.iucn.org.

[3] The World Conservation Congress takes place every three to four years.

[4] There are currently six Commissions, including the Commission on Environmental Law.

[5] With its Headquarters being based in Gland, Switzerland. There are 42 regional and country offices, including the IUCN Environmental Law Centre, Bonn, which is regarded as an "out-posted" office of Headquarters.

[6] The IUCN Mission repeats its Statutory Objectives. *See* Article 2.

* Head, IUCN Environmental Law Programme, Director, IUCN Environmental Law Centre, Bonn, Germany. Views expressed by the author in this chapter do not necessarily represent the views of IUCN or its members. With thanks to Jeffrey McNeely, IUCN Chief Scientist: *see* J. McNeely, "Energy and Biodiversity: Understanding Complex Relationships," in Adrian J. Bradbrook and Richard L. Ottinger (eds.), *Energy Law and Sustainable Development*, IUCN, Gland, Switzerland and Cambridge, UK, 2003, 31.

integrity and diversity of nature and to ensure that any use of natural resources is equitable and ecologically sustainable" [emphasis added]. It can be readily seen from our vision and mission that IUCN is all about People; Nature; Equity; Sustainability.

All of the various components of IUCN are required to act in conformity with its Statutory Objectives,[7] and reference to the manner in which the Statutes anticipate the Objectives being attained provides a good insight into what IUCN is all about.

The Statutes provide[8] that the IUCN Objectives are to be attained, among other things, by:

- Building alliances for conservation;
- Strengthening institutional capacity;
- Promoting enhanced cooperation;
- Encouraging research;
- Providing a forum for discussion;
- Developing expert networks; and
- Influencing national and international legal and administrative instruments.

This is exactly what we see happening at the First Colloquium for the IUCN Academy, which will be discussed in Section 5.

2 RECENT INTERNATIONAL AGREEMENTS AND PROCESSES

There have been numerous recent events and processes going on that are of major interest to the global community and to IUCN. Perhaps the most important of these are the Millennium Development Declaration[9] and the World Summit on Sustainable Development outcomes. Other chapters address each of these in detail, hence this chapter only seeks to highlight their importance.

2.1 Millennium Development Declaration

The Declaration sets out a number of key objectives (often called "goals") identified by states as being of special significance. The objectives seek to promote development and the elimination of poverty, while at the same time protecting our common environment.

2.2 World Summit on Sustainable Development (WSSD)

The Johannesburg Plan of Implementation addressed the importance of improved access to energy services for sustainable development and linked this directly to the millennium development goals and the eradication of poverty. Two brief extracts from Paragraph 8 warrant direct reference:

> ... to work together at all levels to improve access to reliable and affordable energy services for sustainable development sufficient to facilitate the achievement of the millennium development goals ... including actions to ... Improve access to reliable,

---

[7] *See* Article 1.   [8] *See* Article 3.
[9] Resolution Adopted by the UN General Assembly September 18, 2000.

affordable, economically viable, *socially acceptable and environmentally sound* energy services and resources ... [emphasis added]

The importance of energy policies and regulatory frameworks to create the right conditions for socially acceptable and environmentally sound energy services and resources was also highlighted in the Plan.[10]

3 MAJOR CHALLENGE FROM IUCN'S PERSPECTIVE

Looked at in the context of the Millennium Development Declaration and the WSSD outcomes, the major challenge from an IUCN perspective can be quite simply stated as: "How do we collectively achieve these goals and targets in an equitable and sustainable manner that serves to conserve the integrity and diversity of nature?"

The challenge also gives rise to a number of key questions regarding what needs to be addressed in meeting the challenge.

4 KEY QUESTIONS FROM IUCN'S PERSPECTIVE

We all need and use energy – and there are many different sources including hydroelectricity, nuclear energy, biomass energy, fossil fuel energy, wind energy, solar energy, and other forms, all of which have been addressed by others.

One thing is clear – each source of energy has its own direct or indirect environmental and social impacts. It is essential that we properly assess the environmental and social impacts of *all* energy development projects to ensure we are making sound and informed choices.

The key questions from an IUCN perspective can be seen as:

Question 1: What is the relationship between human uses of energy and the conservation of biodiversity – with a particular focus on the impacts on biodiversity of climate change driven by the use of fossil fuels to generate energy?

Question 2: What are the practical challenges we face to provide everyone with adequate and affordable access to energy, while conserving biodiversity?

Question 3: What does "socially acceptable and environmentally sound energy services and resources" actually mean in practice?

Question 4: How can we best use international and national law and policy to respond to the challenges ahead?

Question 5: How can we build the necessary capacity to respond to these challenges?

IUCN does not purport to have all of the answers. But it does seek to raise the key questions, to stimulate critical thinking, and to forge the necessary alliances, expert networks, and partnerships to find the answers. This is well reflected in its response to the challenge and the key questions.

---

[10] *See e.g.*, Paragraph 8(e), for example.

5 IUCN'S RESPONSE TO THE CHALLENGE
AND KEY QUESTIONS

It is one thing to set out a challenge and to articulate the key questions, but quite another to take action to achieve real "on ground" change. IUCN is already well advanced in striving to do this, and its efforts can be directly related back to its Statutory Objectives. For example, in the context of law, policy and governance issues it has been active in:

- *Building alliances for conservation.*
  This includes the creation of the IUCN Environmental Law Programme (ELP),[11] its 900 Commission on Environmental Law members in 130 countries, its numerous partners, including a network of thirteen "centres of excellence" in eleven countries and the twenty-five IUCN Members active in environmental law. Coupled with the IUCN Environmental Law Centre, and regional and country offices, this collectively represents an extraordinary alliance for conservation.

- *Strengthening institutional capacity.*
  IUCN ELP benefits from being part of a broader multidisciplinary knowledge based institution. Professor Alexandre Kiss highlighted the importance of this association when he said, "From the beginning of the existence of international environmental law there was the understanding that environmental problems need an interdisciplinary approach. Law needed the findings of other branches of science, including economy and sociology." IUCN links science with law and policy through its network of Commissions and interdisciplinary approach. The capacity of IUCN members, partners, and recognized "centers" is built through collaborative endeavors, such as this Colloquium.

- *Promoting enhanced cooperation.*
  Many examples can be provided, but by way of example, IUCN and The World Bank sponsored the creation of the World Commission on Dams, an independent Commission that addressed the "dams debate." Whether all of the ultimate findings were universally supported or not, the Commission provided a platform for enhanced cooperation among those of competing views regarding large dams and the satisfaction of energy needs more generally. The Commission's report[12] highlighted the importance of policy and regulatory frameworks, and effective compliance and enforcement.

- *Encouraging research.*
  This goes to the very heart of the conceptual approach of the IUCN ELP since its inception in the 1960s, with the "conceptual development" of the law and the "generation of knowledge" being two of the four pillars of its work. IUCN CEL has sought to further the opportunity for research, and attract additional funds to support it, through the IUCN Academy. IUCN ELP has also encouraged the publication of research and academic endeavor through its Environmental Policy and Law series, including through the recent publication of "Energy Law and Sustainable Development,"[13] edited by Professors Adrian Bradbrook and Richard Ottinger.

---

[11] For more information, visit http://www.iucn.org/themes/law.
[12] *Dams and Development: A New Framework for Decision Making*, 2000. *See* Chapter 15.
[13] Paper No. 47 in the series and available free of charge from http://www.iucn.org/themes/law.

- *Providing a forum for discussion.*
  No better example can be given than the creation of the IUCN Academy and the decision to hold this Colloquium on the issue of the Law of Energy for Sustainable Development. However, reference can also be made to the collaborative efforts with FAO and UNEP in working with African and Asian delegations participating in the conferences of the parties to the Framework Convention on Climate Change (FCCC).
- *Developing expert networks.*
  Through the Commission on Environmental Law (CEL), IUCN has created the CEL Specialist Group on Climate and Energy, an expert network of the world's leading energy and climate law specialists, and now the IUCN Academy, a network of the world's leading academic institutions teaching and carrying out research on environmental law.
- *Influencing national and international legal and administrative instruments.*
  IUCN ELP and other programs are taking steps to facilitate linking the Convention on Biological Diversity, the UNFCCC, the Kyoto Protocol Clean Development Mechanism, and the Commission on Sustainable Development deliberations. It is also taking steps to provide technical assistance to developing countries to enable them to successfully participate in the current policy debate, such as its collaborative endeavors with FAO and UNEP to facilitate two regional meetings to assist the Asian and African groups in preparing for the ninth session of the Conference of the Parties to the UNFCCC.

6 NEXT STEPS

IUCN will continue to mobilize its members, commissions, and partners to forge, and support, alliances, expert networks, and partnerships to ensure that the global community – from global to local – is best able to:

- understand the relationship between energy development, the conservation of biodiversity, and sustainable development;
- put into place sustainable and equitable energy laws and policies; and
- effectively implement what is put into place.

IUCN looks forward to working with all its partners, and the IUCN Academy in achieving these goals.

17 Enhanced Implementation and Enforcement of International Environmental Laws by the Judiciary

Alfred Rest*

1 INTRODUCTION

At present, an environmental crisis looms large, for which two major interrelated causes can be identified: continuing environmental degradation and a lack of respect for the law,[1] together with a changed approach to ethical and moral values. Recent monitoring and data collection systems evidence increasing, and somewhat frightening, threats and damage to the environment. These are sometimes of a transboundary/transnational nature and have deleterious global and national effects.[2]

2 INTERNATIONAL EFFORTS TO FORMULATE AND IMPLEMENT SUSTAINABLE DEVELOPMENT POLICIES

Although endeavors, on national and international levels, to prevent environmental risks and infringements have intensified since the Rio Conference,[3] the goals of environmental protection have not yet been adequately achieved. This has been confirmed in the UN Millennium Development Declaration[4] of September 2000 (Millennium Declaration) and again by the Johannesburg Declaration on Sustainable Development[5] in September 2002 (Johannesburg Declaration). In particular, paragraph 13 of the Johannesburg Declaration provides: "The global environment continues to suffer. Loss of biodiversity

---

[1] *See* P. L. Stein, "Judges Active in Promoting Environmental Law Capacity Building" (2003) 33 *Environmental Policy and Law* 2.

[2] *See* A. Rest, "Rechtsschutz von Nichtregierungsorganisationen vor einem internationalen Umweltgerichtshof: Die neue Rolle des Permanent Court of Arbitration," in *CIPRA-Jahreskonferenz* 2002 "Die Rolle von Nichtregierungsorganisationen in Berggebieten" Schaan, 2003 at 21. *See also* http://www.cipra.org/d/publikationen/ grosse_schriften/2002_Rest_Gerichtshof.pdf.

[3] *See* Rio Declaration on the Environment and Development, UN General Assembly, A/CONF.151/26 (Vol. I), August 12, 1992.

[4] UN General Assembly, 55th Session, A/55/L.2, Sept. 18, 2000, see also (2000) 30 *Environmental Policy and Law* 263.

[5] (Sept. 4, 2002), available at http://www.un.org/esa/sustdev/documents/WSSD_POI_PD/English/POI_PD.htm.

* Dr. Jur., Academic Director at the Institute of Public International Law and Comparative Public Law, University of Cologne, Germany. Consultant of UN, ECE, EU, OECD, Council of Europe, IUCN, PCA, and the German Federal Ministry for Environment, Nature Protection and Security of Nuclear Installations. This contribution is an enlarged version of A. Rest, "Enhanced Implementation of International Environmental Treaties by Judiciary – Access to Justice in International Environmental Law for Individuals and NGOs: Efficacious Enforcement by the Permanent Court of Arbitration" (2004) 1 *Macquarie Journal of International and Comparative Environmental Law* 1–28.

continues, fish stocks continue to be depleted, desertification claims more and more fertile land, the adverse effects of climate change are already evident, natural disasters are more frequent and more devastating and developing countries more vulnerable, and air, water and marine pollution continue to rob millions of a decent life."[6]

As a blueprint for change, the Millennium Declaration stressed the urgent need to implement and respect principles of equity and social justice; of tolerance; and the eradication of poverty. Also a new ethic of conservation and stewardship of our common environment with a greater respect for nature is needed, in order to guarantee peace and security on our planet. Emphasising the opportunities generated through globalization, the Millennium Declaration states that: "at present [globalization's] benefits are very unevenly shared, while its costs are unevenly distributed."[7] In order to translate these shared values into action, the Millennium Declaration postulates the development of instruments to promote more efficient capacity building, good governance and democracy, and the promotion of the protection of human rights, inter alia, by peaceful dispute resolution in conformity with the principles of justice and international law.[8]

The World Summit on Sustainable Development[9] (WSSD), which can be characterized as a "summit for implementation, accountability and of partnership,"[10] addressed and emphasized these goals. It further undertook to accelerate the improved and more effective implementation of Agenda 21[11] and to implement further political commitments as set out in the Johannesburg Plan of Implementation[12] (Johannesburg Plan). Regrettably however, the WSSD and the Johannesburg Plan did not directly address the issue of access to courts, in particular, questions of standing and jurisdiction – and only addressed the position of nongovernmental actors in a very general way (in the context of building partnerships with governments).[13]

3 THE ROLE OF THE LAW: FUNDAMENTAL LEGAL DOCTRINES AND LEGAL INSTITUTIONS

The development of international sustainable development policies presents a unique challenge and opportunity, inter alia, for national and international lawyers to promote and support the implementation of such policies. Such implementation requires the development of innovative legal instruments, such as progressive environmental laws and international agreements, as well as ensuring their implementation and execution. Unfortunately however, a significant deficiency in the application of legal norms still remains as judicial control and enforcement of such laws through independent institutions is indispensable.

---

[6] UN General Assembly, A/Conf.199/L.6 Rev. 2 and Corr. 1 adopted on Sept. 4, 2002; the text is also published in (2002) 35 *Environmental Policy and Law* 234.

[7] *See* para. 5.   [8] *See* para. 4.

[9] *See* http://www.johannesburgsummit.org/html/documents/documents.html.

[10] K. Töpfer, UNEP Executive Director, Speech at the WSSD Opening Plenary Meeting of 26 Aug. 2002, cited in M. A. Buenker, "Setting a Path for Improved Implementation of Agenda 21" (2002) 32 *Environmental Policy and Law* 190–2.

[11] *See* http://www.un.org/esa/sustdev/documents/agenda21/english/ agenda21oc.htm.

[12] UN General Assembly, A/CONF.199/20, Report of the World Summit on Sustainable Development, Johannesburg, South Africa, 26 Aug.–4 Sept. 2002. The Plan of Implementation is annexed to this report. *See* http://www.un.org/esa/sustdev/documents/WSSD_POI_PD/ English/POIToc.htm.

[13] *See* paras. 163 and 168 of the Plan of Implementation.

According to the theory of separation of powers, it is a hallmark of systems governed by the rule of law that at least one independent judicial institution is empowered to guarantee the implementation, due application, and impartial execution of the law, including in relation to the actions of the legislature and executive. Without such a doctrine, the existence and effective operation of any legal system is endangered.

3.1 International Policies Governing the Development of Legal Institutions

This author, who for more than three decades has recommended that more attention be paid to legal issues and the role of the judiciary[14] in the context of sustainable development, welcomes the Johannesburg Principles on the Role of Law and Sustainable Development adopted at the Global Judges Symposium in August 2002.[15] In the author's view, the judges remembered well the concept of a community of states and the duty of states and all parts of society to respect, uphold, strengthen, and enforce the rule of law. The author also considers that the judges were right to affirm that "an independent judiciary and judicial process is vital for the implementation, development and enforcement of environmental law, and that members of the judiciary, as well as those contributing to the judicial process at the national, regional and global levels, are crucial partners for promoting compliance with, and the implementation and enforcement of, international and national environmental law."[16] The judges stressed that the "judiciary has a key role to play in integrating human values [as] set out in the [Millennium Declaration]"[17] Through the four key principles[18] adopted at the Global Judges Symposium and the precise, concerted, and sustained program of work set out at that Symposium – involving data exchange, information, environmental law education, and access to justice – the judges have proposed fundamental environmental law capacity building instruments to promote the implementation of Montevideo Programme III,[19] and to effect sustainable development in the future. It is noteworthy that Montevideo Programme III, through its twenty objectives[20] and highly detailed prescribed actions, laid a strong general foundation for the further development of environmental law and for making such laws more effective.

---

[14] A. Rest, "International Protection of the Environment and Liability," *The Legal Responsibility of State and Individuals in Cases of Transfrontier Pollution*, (Berlin, 1978); A. Rest, *The More Favourable Law Principle in Transfrontier Environmental Law: A Means of Strengthening the Protection of the Individual?*, (Berlin, 1980); A. Rest, "The Role of the Permanent Court of Arbitration as an International Court of the Environment," in A.Vlavianos-Arvanitis (ed.), *Biopolitics International Organisation, Bio-Syllabus for European Environmental Education* (Athens, 2002) at 538; A. Rest, "Der Ständige Schiedshof als Internationaler Umweltgerichtshof. Die neuen Verfahrensregeln zur schiedsgerichtlichen Streitbeilegung von Ressourcen-Nutzungs- und Umweltkonflikten" (2002) 10 *Umwelt Wirtschafts Forum* 92.

[15] *See* (2002) 32 *Environmental Policy and Law* 236.

[16] *See* paras. of the Johannesburg Principles on the Role of Law and Sustainable Development.

[17] *Id.*

[18] *See* (2002) 32 *Environmental Policy and Law* 237 at paras. 1–4.

[19] Draft program for the development and periodic review of environmental law for the first decade of the twenty-first century, UNEP/ENV LAW/4/4, *see* (2000) 30 *Environmental Policy and Law* 309.

[20] *Id.* These objectives include: 1. Implementation, compliance, and enforcement of environmental law; 2. Capacity building; 3. Prevention and mitigation of environmental damage; 4. Avoidance and settlement of international environmental disputes; 5. Strengthening and development of international environmental law; 6. Harmonization and coordination; 7. Public participation and access to information; 8. Information and technology; 9. Innovative approaches to environmental law.

The UNEP Governing Council, in its Decision 22/17 on Governance and Law adopted on February 7, 2003[21] (Decision 22/17), recalling, inter alia, the six regional judges' symposia on environmental law convened by the UNEP Programme during the period 1996–2001, noted with appreciation the Global Judges Symposium. Decision 22/17 calls on the Executive Director to support, within Montevideo Programme III, the improvement of judicial capacity-building commitments. Decision 22/17 further stresses that it is necessary to improve "the capacity of those involved in the process of promoting, implementing, developing and enforcing environmental law at the national and local levels, such as judges, prosecutors, legislators and other relevant stakeholders, to carry out their functions on a well informed basis with the necessary skills, information and material, with a view to mobilizing the full potential of the judiciaries around the world for the implementation and enforcement of environmental law and promoting access to justice for the settlement of environmental disputes, public participation in environmental decision-making, the protection and advancement of environmental rights and public access to relevant information."[22]

This statement reflects Principle 10 of the Rio Declaration[23] and the objectives, which have been implemented in the meantime, by the Aarhus Convention.[24] It must be stressed that such approach is restricted to the national law level and may fail in solving transnational environmental law disputes as will be demonstrated later. The section of Decision 22/17 on "Enhancing the Application of Principle 10 of the Rio Declaration" merits some special attention as it provides that: the Governing Council requests the Executive Director "to assess the possibility of promoting, at the national and *international levels*, the application of Principle 10 . . . and determine, inter alia, if there is value in initiating an intergovernmental process for the preparation of guidelines on the application of Principle 10."[25]

The actual content and meaning of this statement remains somewhat ambiguous, however. Could, for instance, such potential guidelines enable concerned citizens and victims of transnational environmental damage to bring an action against state organs, even against foreign polluting states and grant such persons legal access to international courts, such as the International Court of Justice? Such assumptions would certainly be unconventional, as they run directly counter to principles of state sovereignty and, traditionally, states are most unwilling to relinquish such sovereign rights. States currently appear to prefer to decide complex problems of legal access at the level of private actors, that is, on the level of domestic or comparative national law. This tendency is manifest first, in the promotion of instruments reflecting civil liability concepts[26] and second, the lack of progress in formulating obligations which are binding upon states

---

[21] Decisions adopted by the UNEP Governing Council at its 22d Session/Global Ministerial Environment Forum, February 2003 at 48, available at www.nyo.unep.org/pdfs/gc2217.pdf.

[22] *Id.*, at para. 2.

[23] For the text, *see* (1992) 22 *Environmental Policy and Law* 268.

[24] Convention on Access to Information, Public Participation in Decision-Making and Access to Justice in Environmental Matters (Aarhus Convention), June 25, 1998, available at http://www.unece.org/env/pp/documents/cep43e.pdf, also published in W. Burhenne, *International Environmental Law: Multilateral Treaties*, under No. 998:48.

[25] *See* Decision 22/17 under II, B, para. 3 at 51, *supra* note 21.

[26] *See* for instance, Objective 3 of Montevideo Programme III, *supra* note 19.

as evidenced by the work of the International Law Commission[27] (ILC). It remains to be seen whether this "private actors" approach can meet sufficiently current and future environmental challenges. Nevertheless, enhancing access to national courts according to the law on conflicts and international procedural law is a step in the right direction.

The UNEP Governing Council has also requested the Executive Director to submit a progress report on the implementation of Decision 22/17 at its 23d Session.[28] It is important to clarify at the outset that it is not only those individuals, whose legal interests are directly or potentially affected, who must be granted standing to bring actions for violations of international environmental law. Rather, standing should be granted to all individuals. All civil society organizations, such as environmental interest groups and NGOs that represent common societal and environmental interests should also be granted standing. Note, Montevideo Programme III stressed that new ways of "advancing the effective involvement of non-state-actors in promoting international environmental law and its enforcement at the domestic level" needed to be developed.[29] Regrettably, this has not yet been explicitly recognized at an international level.

This chapter examines the exercise of national jurisdiction in Germany and other European Member States, to consider whether the current domestic approach, relying on the rulings and jurisdictional powers of national judiciaries, is sufficient or whether this approach needs to be changed, expanded, and amended by new instruments which vest international jurisdiction in national courts and international tribunals.

3.2 The Current Approach: Limitations on the Efficacy of Domestic Court Proceedings in the Context of Transnational Environmental Disputes

The Exercise of Domestic Jurisdiction in Germany and Other European States

There is no doubt, that in states that possess advanced legal systems and with established doctrines of jurisdiction, as well as developed mechanisms for the exercise of jurisdiction, judicial control plays a major role in the implementation and execution of environmental law. In Germany, according to long standing doctrines of jurisdiction, potentially injured legal persons and individuals can rely on the lawful execution of national environmental law by bringing actions in competent German courts. Under the German system, judicial decisions can also, indirectly, bring about legislative developments, through constructive criticism by judges of ambiguities in existing regulations. Insofar as such litigation relates only to a national dispute and the application of national environmental law, the German legal system, including the judiciary, provides effective legal protection.

However, when transboundary or transnational effects and the objectives of international environmental law are at issue, domestic jurisdiction may be deficient or even

---

[27] A. Rest, "Ecological Damage in Public International Law: International Environmental Liability in the Drafts of the UN International Law Commission and the UN/ECE Task Force," (1992) 22 *Environmental Policy and Law* 31.

[28] *See* Decision 22/17 under II, A, para. 5 and B, para. 5 at 50 et seq., *supra* note 21.

[29] *See* Action I,1,1 of Montevideo Programme III, *supra* note 19.

fail. This can be seen in German case law, such as the cases of *Chernobyl*,[30] *Sandoz*,[31] and the nuclear power plant at *Lingen*.[32] All these decisions reflect the general proposition that in cases of transboundary or transnational pollution, the injured individual victims have no prospect of success and only limited opportunities to bring actions in national courts against a foreign polluter and specifically, against a foreign polluter state or its organs.[33] Cases like the *Dutch-French Litigation Concerning the Salinisation of the River Rhine*[34] and the judgments of Austrian and Swiss courts in the *Chernobyl* cases or cases concerning the nuclear power plants of *Mochovce, Temelin* (Slovakia), and *Cattenom* (France), as well as the Slovenian hydropower plant at *Soboth*, demonstrate that the same proposition is true for almost all European States.[35]

The American Society of International Law's Interest Group's project on "International Environmental Law in Domestic Courts" in 1997,[36] examined the work and decisions of national judiciaries in Australia, Canada, Holland, Germany, India, Japan, and the United States and reiterated the view that international environmental law aspects were not sufficiently considered in depth and were not implemented by national courts, with the exception of the Dutch courts. A further notable exception, where a domestic court considered the protection of the global commons and the implementation of principles of intergenerational equity and responsibility, is the decision of the Supreme Court of the Philippines in the *Oposa Case* of 1993.[37] The plaintiffs, all minors, duly represented by their parents, successfully brought a court action to halt the continuing deforestation of domestic tropical rainforests on the basis that these forests constituted an indispensable natural resource for the life of present and future generations. This case remains an exception, however.

At a symposium held by UNEP and the South Asia Cooperation Environment Programme (SACEP) from July 4–6, 1997 at Colombo, Sri Lanka on "The Role of the

---

[30] A. Rest, "Tschernobyl und die internationale Haftung: Völkerrechtliche Aspekte," *Versicherungsrecht* (1986) at 609; A. Rest, "Tschernobyl und die internationale Haftung: International-privatrechtliche Aspekte und Ansprüche" (1986) *Versicherungsrecht* 833.

[31] A. Rest, "The Sandoz Conflagration and Pollution of the Rhine: Liability Issues" (1987) 30 *German Yearbook of International Law* 160.

[32] A. Rest, "International Environmental Law in German Courts" (1997) 27 *Environmental Policy and Law* 409.

[33] A. Rest, "The Need for an International Court for the Environment: Underdeveloped Legal Protection of the Individual in Transnational Litigation," in G. Cordini and A. Postiglione (eds.), *Towards the World Governance of the Environment, IV*, International Conference Venice (Pavia, June 2–5, 1996) at 591.

[34] A. Rest, "Internationaler Umweltschutz vor Verwaltungs-, Zivil- und Strafgerichten. Der niederländisch – französische Rheinverschmutzungsprozeß" (1985) 35 *Österreichische Zeitschrift für öffentliches Recht und Völkerrecht* 225.

[35] *See* A. Rest, "The Need for an International Court for the Environment?" (1994) 24 *Environmental Policy and Law* 173; for further cases *see* M. R. Albus, "Zur Notwendigkeit eines Internationalen Umweltgerichtshofs - zugleich eine Analyse der Staatenpraxis zum Internationalen Umwelthaftungsrecht und der Rechtsschutzmöglichkeiten bei grenzüberschreitenden Umweltbeeinträchtigungen," *Kölner Schriften zu Recht und Staat*, Peter Lang Publishing Co. (Frankfurt/Main, 2000).

[36] Workshop of the ASIL Interest Group for Environmental Law, April 9, 1997, Washington D.C. The preliminary report of national jurisdiction in the various countries is partially published in (1998) 7(1) *Review of European Community International Environmental Law* (RECIEL) 63, *see also* M. Anderson and P. Galizzi (eds.), *International Environmental Law in National Courts*, The British Institute of International and Comparative Law (London, 2002).

[37] *Re Minors Oposa v. Secretary of the Department of Environment and Natural Resources(DENR)*, July 30, 1993, ILM 33 (1994) 173; A. Rest, "The *Oposa* Decision: Implementing the Principles of Intergenerational Equity and Responsibility" (1994) 24 *Environmental Policy and Law* 314.

Judiciary in Promoting the Rule of Law in the Area of Sustainable Development,"[38] it was recommended and emphasized, that national judiciaries have a responsibility to mold emerging environmental law principles, such as the "polluter-pays" principle, the precautionary principle, the principle of continuous mandamus and *erga omnes* obligations, with a view to giving these principles a sense of coherence and direction.[39] The conference further emphasized problems relating to the identification of an "aggrieved person" and of *locus standi* in the context of transnational disputes. The published Compendium of Summaries of Judicial Decisions in Environment Related Cases[40] also evidences a current deficiency in national jurisdiction mechanisms in relation to the application of international environmental law.

For the purpose of actions brought before German courts, as in most other jurisdictions, distinctions need to be made between civil, public, and criminal law cases. When it comes to litigation before the civil courts of the polluted state, both claims for compensation and actions to halt environmentally harmful and hazardous activities meet with failure.[41] Moreover, meager attention is paid to the question of protecting the global commons.[42] There are a number of reasons for this, including:

- individuals usually refrain from bringing legal actions because of the potentially high costs of litigation and the problem of litigating in a foreign language;
- immunity from jurisdiction may hinder the competence of courts of the polluted state as well as courts of the polluter state;
- pursuant to the rules of the law of conflicts or of the *ordre public*, the application of domestic substantive law can be excluded; and
- immunity from enforcement can defeat the actual enforcement of a foreign decision.

As regards lawsuits brought before the administrative courts of the polluter state, *ius standi* can be highly problematic. In particular, the application of domestic substantive law, dominated by the principle of territoriality, can be refused if it does not protect foreign legal interests. Before its domestic courts, the polluter state can argue that the court's decision cannot be enforced abroad by reason of immunity from enforcement. By reason of the doctrine of state sovereignty, courts of the polluted state have no competence to examine questions of foreign public law.

With regard to environmental protection through criminal courts, the German Supreme Criminal Court has emphasized, in a case concerning the transboundary movement of hazardous waste from Germany to Poland, that the German criminal

[38] L. Kurukulasuriya, "The Role of the Judiciary in Promoting Sustainable Development" (1998) 28 *Environmental Policy and Law* 27.

[39] *Id.*, at 28.

[40] SACEP/UNEP/NORAD, *Compendium of Summaries of Judicial Decisions in Environment Related Cases, with special Reference to Countries in South Asia*, Publication Series on Environmental Law and Policy No. 3 (1997).

[41] For numerous decisions on this issue *see* A. Rest, "International Environmental Law in German Courts" (1997) 27 *Environmental Policy and Law* 412; for details of litigation in the 1950s and 60s *see* A. Rest, *The More Favourable Law Principle in Transfrontier Environmental Law: A Means of Strengthening the Protection of the Individual?* (Berlin, 1980) at 69.

[42] For a discussion on the global commons, common heritage, common concerns and interests, and *erga omnes* obligations, *see* A. Rest, "Ecological Damage in Public International Law" (1992) 22 *Environmental Policy and Law* 31.

law does not protect the interests of foreign injured individuals and will only apply on German territory.[43]

Accordingly, domestic court proceedings are still generally ineffective in the context of transnational environmental disputes as domestic courts lack the requisite legal authority. Moreover, lengthy litigation sometimes lasting longer than a decade – as in the *Dutch-French Litigation Concerning the Salinisation of the River Rhine* and the case concerning the nuclear power plant at *Lingen* – also undermines the value of domestic courts as a means of legally protecting environmental rights. The protection of the global commons remains outside the scope of domestic jurisdiction and courts generally refuse, or are very reluctant to guarantee such legal interests, through legal interpretation grounded in principles of public international law.

Environmental Law Education for Domestic Judiciaries

It is possible that the task of interpreting public international environmental law demands too much from local judges who are perhaps not so experienced in this area of law. For this reason, the proposal put forward at the Global Judges Symposium to strengthen international environmental law education[44] is welcome.[45]

It is worth noting that the Supreme Court of India recently called for the establishment of special national environmental courts composed of judges highly qualified in environmental law and technical experts and scientists who are also highly proficient and experienced in environmental matters.[46] The Permanent Court of Arbitration has already implemented a similar proposal through its adoption of Optional Rules for the Arbitration of Disputes Relating to Natural Resources and/or the Environment.[47]

Summary

In countries such as Germany, with advanced legal systems and highly developed doctrines of jurisdiction, there remains a deficiency in the ability of courts to adequately apply international environmental law and protect individual and communal rights granted by international environmental law. It is not surprising then, that in countries that have not yet established legal systems, the inability to implement principles and rules of international environmental law is even greater. In order to support the development of such an international legal order and to further enable principles of international environmental law to be brought within the jurisdiction of domestic courts, instruments and institutions at the level of public international law need to be established first.

---

[43] For details on this case and other criminal law cases, *see* A. Rest, "International Environmental Law in German Courts" (1997) 27 *Environmental Policy and Law* 419.

[44] *See* para (d) in (2002) 32 *Environmental Policy and Law* 237.

[45] A. Rest, "From Environmental Education to 'Education for Sustainable Development': The Shift of a Paradigm" (2002) 32 *Environmental Policy and Law* 79; *see also* A. Vlavianos-Arvanitis (ed.), *Biopolitics International Organisation, Bio-Syllabus for European Environmental Education* (Athens, 2002).

[46] *A. P. Pollution Control Board II v. Prof. M. V.Nayudu*, Judgment of Dec. 1, 2000, 2000 SOL Case No. 673 under Nos. 65 et seq.

[47] Approved June 19, 2001 by the Administrative Council of the Permanent Court of Arbitration, available at http://www.pca-cpa.org/PDF/ENRrules.pdf.

Insofar as the idea of establishing an international environmental court – postulated since 1988[48] by the International Court of the Environment Foundation (ICEF), Rome – remains open for further consideration, such a court could be the proper institution for monitoring the application of rules of international environmental law as agreed in environmental treaties. Further, such a court could also provide guidance to national courts as to the application of international environmental law within the parameters of national law.

It is highly desirable that actions before such an international court be able to be brought by NGOs, environmental interest groups, enterprises, and individuals as well as by states and international organizations, and further, that national courts be able to refer matters concerning conflicts between international and national environmental law to such a court, to be decided by a procedure of preliminary decision or by interpretation. The decisions of an international environmental court could certainly have a significant impact and abiding influence on the further development of national environmental laws.

4 THE NEED FOR INTERNATIONAL JUDICIAL INSTITUTIONS AND JUDICIARIES

Although there is not the slightest doubt about the indispensability of domestic judiciaries for the effective enforcement of environmental law, cases with transnational effects cannot always be adequately resolved. In order to provide for the appropriate resolution of transnational environmental disputes, it is necessary for national legal systems to be flanked by an international judicial institution and judiciary. This is indispensable for the following reasons:[49]

- the behavior of states must fall within judicial control, as states themselves may commit or tolerate environmental destruction;[50]
- only an independent judicial institution can scrutinize the implementation and enforcement of international treaty law and international law obligations if states, at an earlier stage, have failed to achieve compliance through "political nonconfrontational" mechanisms or agreements; and
- the necessary protection of the global commons and the development of *erga omnes* obligations[51] as well as of human rights jurisprudence concerning the right to a safe and healthy environment[52] can be best ensured and promoted by an international judiciary.

---

[48] A. Rest, "Zur Notwendigkeit eines Internationalen Umweltgerichtshofes," in G. Hafner, G. Loibl, A. Rest, L. Sucharipa-Behrmann, and K. Zemanek (eds.), *Liber Amicorum* in honor of Prof. I. Seidl-Hohenveldern, Kluwer Law International (The Hague, 1998) at 575, 577.

[49] For further reasons *see* A. Rest, "An International Court for the Environment: The Role of the Permanent Court of Arbitration," in PCA (ed.), *International Alternative Dispute Resolution: Past, Present and Future*, Centennial Papers (The Hague, 2000) at 53, 57.

[50] For example, forest burning in Indonesia was tolerated by the government although existing law prohibited such activities. For details of this case and further examples *see* A Rest, *supra* note 48, at 575, 579.

[51] For discussion of the global commons and *erga omnes* obligations, *see* A. Rest, "Ecological Damage in Public International Law" (1992) 22 *Environmental Policy and Law* 31.

[52] Considering the problem of the incorporation of such a right in the EU Charter on Basic Rights, *see* Conseil Européen Du Droit de L'Environnement (CEDE) (ed.), *Le Droit À L'Environnement, Un Droit*

Another significant current problem concerns the initiation of an international dispute settlement procedure if, not only state interests, but the interests of individuals or nongovernmental environmental associations, are at issue. States are, not infrequently and usually for political reasons, very reluctant (or simply refuse outright) to support their injured nationals and to bring proceedings against another polluter state, for instance in the *Chernobyl Case*. State interests, in particular economic priorities, can conflict with the interests of its citizens and the environment.[53] Therefore individuals, enterprises, and NGOs should also be granted direct access to international judicial institutions. This proposition has been supported by two Resolutions of the Institut de Droit International.[54] In order to adequately and properly control state activities, as well as those of private players, the engagement of NGOs, environmental interest groups and individuals as legal guardians in relation to the protection of environmental rights should be upheld. Such nonstate players have already demonstrated the will to act in such a capacity. Recollect, for instance, Greenpeace's protests against the introduction of toxic substances into rivers and the North Sea, against nuclear tests on the Mururoa Atoll, its campaign against the disposal of the oil platform "Brent Spar," and also the numerous activities of the IUCN in connection with nature protection and biodiversity.

While an international judicial institution competent to decide transnational environmental disputes remains indispensable, it is not an automatic solution to problems concerning the implementation of international environmental law. Even such a tribunal or a court cannot itself engender, or replace, the will of states to effectively implement their obligations under international environmental agreements. This is largely because the competence of such an international judicial institution is also dependent on the will of the states, as reflected in the agreement or legal instrument establishing the relevant judicial institution and establishing its competence under public international law. Nevertheless, once established and with sufficiently wide jurisdictional powers, the decisions of an international institution, supported by the ability to impose relevant sanctions, may press states to properly fulfill their obligations under international environmental law.

The importance of peaceful settlement of environmental disputes is emphasized in Principle 26 of the Rio Declaration, in Agenda 21 and in Montevideo Programme III.[55] Paragraph 39.10 of Agenda 21[56] emphasizes, inter alia, the importance of the judicial settlement of such disputes. It calls on states "to further study mechanisms for effective implementation of international agreements, such as modalities for dispute avoidance

---

Fundamental Dans L'Union Européenne (Funchal, 2001); for a comprehensive survey, *see* A. Kiss and D. Shelton, *International Environmental Law* (New York, 1991) at 21.

[53] On several occasions this was noted by A. Postiglione, *The Global Village without Regulations: Ethical, Economical, Social and Legal Motivations for an International Court for the Environment*, ICEF (Florence, 1992) at 24; A. Rest, "The Indispensability of an International Environmental Court" (1998) RECIEL at 63–4.

[54] Institut de Droit International, Session de Strasbourg, *Resolution on Environment*, adopted on September 3, 1997, Annuaire IDI, 76(II) (1998) at 476; *see also* Articles 11, 26–28, *Resolution on Responsibility and Liability under International Law for Environmental Damage*, adopted on September 4, 1997, Annuaire IDI, 76(II) (1998) at 476.

[55] *See* para. 4, b, V.

[56] *See* N. A. Robinson (ed.), *Agenda 21: Earth's Action Plan*, IUCN Environmental Policy & Law Paper No. 27 (1993) at 626.

and settlement." It also identifies a full range of methods available to states for such dispute resolution, such as prior consultation, fact finding, commissions of inquiry, conciliation, mediation, noncompliance procedures, arbitration, and judicial settlement of disputes. Paragraph 4 of Montevideo Programme III, which seeks to concretize the relevant aims of Agenda 21, particularly emphasizes the need "to consider innovative approaches to dispute avoidance."[57]

There appears to be a general consensus among states that preventive instruments calling for dispute avoidance should be favored. In this regard political, nonconfrontational mechanisms such as compliance procedures,[58] as well as conferences of the parties (COPs), should be considered.[59] It should be noted that no compliance mechanism[60] is included in the Convention on Biodiversity[61] although Article 23 does provide for a COP mechanism. In the event that agreement cannot be reached by further negotiation or through the COP mechanism, Article 27(3) provides for an agreed compulsory settlement of disputes either by arbitration, or by submission of the dispute to the International Court of Justice. Accordingly, the Convention on Biodiversity also recognizes the indispensability of judicial mechanisms if all other modalities for dispute avoidance are unsuccessful.[62] Laudable though this approach is, it must be stressed that these nonjudicial instruments operate only as between state organs. NGOs or private third parties are not involved and also cannot participate in the noncompliance procedure. This is true for the vast majority of international treaties and agreements. A unique exception is the new compliance procedure mechanism set out in the Convention for the Protection of the Alps and its Protocols, adopted in November 2002.[63] This enables NGOs, under certain conditions of confidentiality, to participate in mechanisms concerning the implementation and enforcement of the Convention. Such an innovative approach reflects the idea of participation as described in the UN Secretary General's Report Implementing Agenda 21.[64] This report emphasizes that "participation generates shared values, mutually reinforced commitments, joint ownership and partnership, which are crucial to achieving sustainable development . . . The increase in major group participation has been a key area of success in the post-*Rio* period."[65] Also of note is the report's criticism in relation to the participation of nonstate actors at national and international levels: such "participation is often based on temporary and ad hoc

---

[57] *See* para. 4 (a), i–V.
[58] For details concerning compliance procedures in various international environmental treaties see P. Széll, "Compliance Regimes for Multilateral Environmental Agreements – A Progress Report" (1997) 27 *Environmental Policy and* Law 304; W. Lang, "Compliance-Control in International Environmental Law: Institutional Necessities" (1996) 56 *Zeitschrift für Ausländisches Öffentliches Recht und Völkerrecht* (*ZaöRV*) 685; P. H. Sand, "Institution Building to Assist Compliance with International Environmental Law: Perspectives" (1996) 56 *ZaöRV* at 774, 786–8, 793.
[59] Art. 6, Convention for the Protection of the Ozone Layer, ILM (1987) at 1516, has incorporated the COP mechanism as well. Together with the amending Montreal Protocol on Substances that deplete the Ozone Layer, ILM (1987) at 1541, this mechanism is combined with the noncompliance procedure rule in Art. 8.
[60] *See* Széll, *supra* note 58, at 305.
[61] (June 5, 1992), available at http://www.biodiv.org/doc/legal/cbd-en.pdf.
[62] A. Rest, "Enhanced Implementation of the Biological Diversity Convention by Judicial Control" (1999) 29 *Environmental Policy and Law* at 32, 41.
[63] *Supra* note 2. *See also* T. Enderlin, "A Different Compliance Mechanism" (2003) 33 *Environmental Policy and Law* 155.
[64] UN Doc. E/CN.17/202/PC.2/Advanced Unedited Text.
[65] *Id.*, at 37.

rather than permanent and reliable mechanisms and procedures. A strengthened sense of ownership of the decisions taken among participating stakeholders would help in implementing many decisions relating to sustainable development."[66]

It can be seen, therefore, that there is a clear need for the establishment of an international judicial institution competent to decide matters of international environmental law and an international judiciary. Accordingly, the next question is whether existing international courts or tribunals are capable of resolving transnational environmental disputes or whether a new, separate international court for the environment is needed.

5 EXISTING INTERNATIONAL JUDICIAL INSTITUTIONS

5.1 International Court of Justice

Even though the International Court of Justice (ICJ), in 1993, established an ad hoc chamber for environmental matters, the ICJ is not the proper forum for the resolution of transational environmental disputes as states alone have direct access to the ICJ. This is a regrettable limitation as otherwise, due to the very purpose and functions of the ICJ, it could be the proper institution to control the implementation of environmental treaty obligations, as demonstrated in the *Gabcikovo-Nagymaros Project Case*.[67] The ICJ could develop its environmental jurisdiction further and improve international environmental law, to concentrate on the immediate problem of protecting the global commons by applying the concept of *erga omnes* obligations.

Sooner or later, due to the current efforts of the state community to strengthen and enhance the legal position of NGOs, nonstate actors will also be granted standing to address the ICJ. Such a step requires states to cede a certain measure of their sovereignty[68] and expose themselves to potential legal proceedings. While necessary, such reform of the ICJ Statute[69] and of the UN Charter appears unrealistic at this time.[70]

5.2 International Tribunal for the Law of the Sea

For the purposes of protecting marine environments, under Article 20 of the Statute of the International Tribunal for the Law of the Sea,[71] the state parties to the Convention on the Law on the Sea[72] can submit disputes concerning the interpretation and implementation of relevant regulations to the International Tribunal for the Law of

---

[66] *Id.*, at 38, §170.

[67] *Case Concerning the Gabcikovo-Nagymaros Project between Hungary and Slovakia,* Judgment of September 25, 1997, ICJ Reports No. 92; for further details *see* A. Rest, *supra* note 49, at 581.

[68] What is necessary is a new understanding of sovereignty which can meet the environmental challenges of our world in transition. *See* S. Bhatt, "Ecology and International Law" (1982) *Indian Journal of International Law* at 422.

[69] *See* www.icj-cij.org/icjwww/ibasicdocuments/Basetext/istatute.htm.

[70] F. Orrego Vicuña and C. Pinto, in PCA (eds.), *The Peaceful Settlement of Disputes: Prospects for the Twenty-First Century,* Report prepared for the 1999 Centennial Commemoration of the First Peace Conference, The Hague at paras. 173 et seq.

[71] Annex VI (21) ILM 1982 at 1345, *see* www.itlos.org/ documents_publications/documents/statute_en.pdf.

[72] (21) ILM 1982, at 1261, available at http://www.un.org/Depts/los/convention_agreements/texts/unclos/closindx.htm.

the Sea (ITLOS), established in Hamburg in October 1996.[73] Pursuant to Article 20(2), ITLOS is also open to entities other than states in cases provided for in Part XI of the Convention on the Law of the Sea.

Part XI concerns the competence of the special Sea-Bed Disputes Chamber with regard to sea-bed activities. The Chamber can hear cases brought by, or against, the International Sea-Bed Authority, parties (including nonstate parties) to a contract, as well as prospective contractors.[74] The same provision further extends the jurisdiction *ratione personae* of ITLOS in "any case submitted pursuant to any other agreement conferring jurisdiction on the Tribunal which is accepted by all the parties to that case."[75] According to Article 187(c) in connection with Article 153, private natural persons may bring disputes before the Chamber but only with the consent of states. In general, it must be emphasized that Articles 20 et seq. of the ITLOS Statute only provide for limited jurisdiction for ITLOS in the context of disputes concerning marine environments. Furthermore, the term "entities"[76] still needs to be more precisely defined for the purpose of establishing and understanding the scope of ITLOS' jurisdiction in the future. Finally, it is doubtful whether the ITLOS Statute and the Convention on the Law of the Sea actually provide for comprehensive protection of the marine environment, as evidenced, inter alia, by Article 135, which provides that these instruments and ITLOS' decisions "shall not affect the legal status of the waters super-adjacent to the Area [within ITLOS' jurisdiction] or that of the air space above those waters."

ITLOS has handed down some very significant judgments, however. While the *M/V Saiga*[77] and *Camouco*[78] cases concern the arrest of ships and, therefore, are not specifically related to environmental matters, the *Southern Bluefin Tuna Case*[79] concerned the protection of marine mammals. In this case, ITLOS imposed provisional measures against Japan for the catches. Marine pollution was the subject of the *MOX Plant Dispute.*[80] In this case, Ireland requested the imposition of provisional measures against the UK to stop the activities of the plant. The dispute stemmed from the UK's authorization for the opening of a new MOX facility in Sellafield. The facility was designed to reprocess spent nuclear fuel into a new fuel that combined reprocessed plutonium with uranium, and is known as mixed oxide fuel (MOX). The Irish government pointed out that the plant would contribute to the pollution of the Irish Sea and emphasized the potential risks involved in the transportation of radioactive material to and from the plant. By its order of December 3, 2001,[81] by way of provisional measures, ITLOS ordered cooperation between the two governments in exchanging information concerning risks

---

[73] R. Wolfrum, "Der Internationale Seegerichtshof in Hamburg" (1996) *Vereinte Nationen* 205; T. Treves, "The Law of the Sea Tribunal: Its Status and Scope of Jurisdiction after November 16, 1994" (1995) 55 *ZaöRV* 421.

[74] T. Treves, *id.*, at 428.

[75] Cf. Art. 20, second sentence and also Art. 21 (21) ILM 1982, p. 1348.

[76] For the definition of "entities" *see* Arts. 1(2) and 305(1)(b), (c), (d), (e), and (f) of the Convention on the Law of the Sea.

[77] For the judgments and order of provisional measures in *Saint Vincent and the Grenadines v. Guinea* in 1997, 1998, and 1999, *see* ILM 37 (1998) 362; ILM 38 (1999) 1323.

[78] For the judgment of February 7, 2000 in *Panama v. France, see* Press Release, ITLOS, Press 35, available at http://www.un.org/Depts/los/Press/ITLOS/ITLOS-35.htm.

[79] For the details of the order of August 27, 1999, *see* list of cases Nos. 3 and 4 available at http://www.un.org/Depts/los/ITLOS/Order-tuna34.htm.

[80] For a survey, *see* (2002) 32 *Environmental Policy and Law* at 25.

[81] Available at http://www.itlos.org.

or possible effects arising from the operations of the MOX plant and the development of means of addressing these issues.

It should be noted that on June 18, 2001, the Irish government initiated a second international arbitration process, this time through the Permanent Court of Arbitration (PCA). This arbitration concerns access to information under Article 9 of the OSPAR Convention for the Protection of the Marine Environment of the North-East Atlantic[82] in relation to the authorization of the MOX Plant. By Final Award of July 2, 2003 the claim of Ireland was dismissed.[83]

As neither NGOs nor individuals are able to access ITLOS independently and generally for the purpose of resolving environmental disputes, this Tribunal does not offer a complete solution to the problem of future protection of international marine environments. Nor does it offer a complete solution to the problem of resolving transnational environmental disputes. However, ITLOS unquestionably plays a very significant and progressive role in international environmental law.

5.3 The Court of First Instance and the Court of Justice of the European Communities

In Europe, NGOs, enterprises, and individuals have access to the Court of First Instance, which was established in 1988, and the Court of Justice of the European Communities (ECJ) (also a court of appeal) in matters concerning the interpretation of primary and secondary European environmental laws, or concerning the proper implementation and application of EU Regulations and Directives. However, claims brought by legal and physical persons are admitted only if their rights are potentially injured directly and individually. This proposition was confirmed in a judgment of the ECJ of April 2, 1998 where Greenpeace International and concerned residents tried, in vain, to bring a claim against a subvention granted by the European Commission for the establishment of two electric power installations in *Gran Canaria* and *Tenerife*.[84] The claim of three French nationals, residents of Tahiti, in relation to the testing of atomic bombs on Mururoa Atoll were also rejected as well.[85]

In general, the courts can be proud of their extensive case load in environmental matters,[86] but given the restricted regional field of application for European law, the jurisdiction of these courts does not extend as far as is desirable for global environmental protection. Nevertheless, the courts' importance for the further development of regional environmental law and general environmental principles remains unquestioned.[87]

---

[82] Available at http://www.ospar.org/eng/html/convention/welcome.html.

[83] For the details, *see* ILM 42 (2003), 1118–86.

[84] *Re C-321/95 P*, E.C.R. (1998) Part I at 1651 and 1702; B. W. Wegener, "Keine Klagebefugnis für Greenpeace und 18 andere" (1998) *Zeitschrift für Umweltrecht* (*ZUR*) 131.

[85] *See* E.C.R (1995) Part II at 3051.

[86] For further ECJ decisions, *see* E. Hey, "The European Community's Courts and International Environmental Agreements" (1998) *RECIEL* 4; L. Krämer, "Die Rechtsprechung des Gerichtshofs der Europäischen Gemeinschaften zum Umweltrecht 1992–1994" (1995) *Europäische Grundrechte Zeitschrift* (*EuGRZ*) 45; D. Stamatakos, "International and European Environmental Legislation," in A. Vlavianos-Arvanitis (ed.), *Biopolitics International Organisation, Bio-Syllabus for European Environmental Education* (Athens, 2002) 484.

[87] For judgments in the *Gran Canaria, Tenerife* and *Mururoa Atoll* cases, *see* A. Rest, "Friedliche Streitbeilegung internationaler Umweltkonflikte durch den Ständigen Schiedshof: Seine zukünftige Rolle als internationaler Umweltgerichtshof," in Dörr, Fink, Hillgruber, Kempen, and Murswiek (eds.), *Die*

5.4 European Court of Human Rights

The jurisdiction of the European Court of Human Rights[88] (ECHR) offers new ways of improving environmental protection through an expanded concept of human rights and by linking these bodies of law which, traditionally, have been treated separately. In its groundbreaking *López-Ostra* decision in 1994,[89] the ECHR opened the door for the protection of human rights against almost all sources of environmental pollution, as opposed to only noise emissions and radiation, as had been the case in the 1970s and 80s.[90] This laudable progressive decision provides for more comprehensive environmental protection through the protection of individual rights and stimulates discussion concerning the existence of a human right to a safe and healthy environment.[91]

The factual background of the *López-Ostra* case was relatively simple. In 1988, Gregoria López-Ostra, living with her family close to Lorca (in Murcia, Spain), suffered as a result of emissions from a waste treatment plant, built on municipal property just twelve meters from her home and subsidized by the government. Foul smells and gas fumes, which caused health problems, were emitted from the installation which operated without a required permit. The López-Ostra family lived there until February 1992. Even though the local council ordered the cessation of some plant activities in September 1988, the family continued to suffer health problems and noted some deterioration in the surrounding environment and quality of life. Doctors confirmed that López Ostra's daughter suffered from nausea, vomiting, allergic reactions, bronchitis, and anorexia because of her residence in a highly polluted area. Authorities for the Murcia region also reported health risks from the plant following many complaints from residents. López-Ostra urged local government authorities to find a solution to the problem of emissions from the waste treatment plant. When these efforts by Lopez-Ostra failed, she filed complaints with the Administrative Division of the Murcia Audiencia Territorial, the Supreme Court, and the Constitutional Court. These complaints were based on violations of fundamental rights under the Spanish Constitution. Each of these courts rejected her complaints or found them inadmissible, notwithstanding official reports concerning the health dangers arising from the operations of the waste treatment plant. Two of López-Ostra's sisters-in-law, living in the same building, also brought administrative and criminal complaints. Although the courts in these proceedings ordered the closure of the plant, the orders were suspended due to appeals. In February 1993, the family bought a new house and moved.

In May 1990, López Ostra brought her claim before the ECHR complaining that local authorities' inaction violated her rights under the European Convention for the

---

Macht des Geistes: In honour of H.Schiedermair, C. F. Müller Publishing Co. (Heidelberg, 2001) at 937, 956.

[88] A. Rest, "Improved Environmental Protection Through an Expanded Concept of Human Rights?" (1997) 27 *Environmental Policy and Law* 213; A. Rest, "Europäischer Menschenrechtsschutz als Katalysator für ein verbessertes Umweltrecht" (1997) *Natur und Recht* (*NuR*) 209.

[89] *López-Ostra v Spain*, ECHR Series A, Vol. 303/C; A. Rest, "Improved Environmental Protection," *supra* note 88, at 215.

[90] For judgments concerning noise pollution and the airports Gatwick (*Arondelle v. UK*) and Heathrow (*Baggs, Powell and Rayner v UK*) and other cases, *see* A. Rest, "Improved Environmental Protection," *supra* note 88, at 213, 215.

[91] A. Kiss and D. Shelton, *Manual of European Environmental Law* (New York, 1993) at 42.

Protection of Human Rights and Fundamental Freedoms.[92] Lopez-Ostra's claims were based on Article 8 of this Convention ("Right to respect for private and family life") and Article 3 ("Prohibition of torture and inhuman and degrading treatment") and she claimed compensation on this basis. She asserted that the Spanish government failed to protect her privacy rights by maintaining a passive attitude toward the disturbances caused by the waste treatment plant. She further contended that emissions from the plant caused severe distress and constituted degrading treatment. The European Commission, which found a violation of Article 8 but rejected the Article 3 claim, referred the case to the ECHR.

The ECHR handed down its unanimous judgment on December 9, 1994, holding that the pollution from the waste treatment plant and the inaction of the Spanish government violated Article 8. The Court held that states have both a *positive* duty to take measures to secure rights under Article 8 as well as a *negative* duty to refrain from taking actions, or failing to take actions, which would interfere with the enjoyment of rights under Article 8. The ECHR stated that here "the State did not succeed in striking a fair balance between the interest of the town's economic well-being – that of having a waste treatment plant – and the applicant's effective enjoyment of her right to respect for her home and her family life." The judges rejected the claim based on Article 3. The ECHR further observed that the applicant undeniably "sustained non-pecuniary damage. In addition to the nuisance caused by gas fumes, noise and smells from the plant, she felt distress and anxiety as she saw the situation persisting and her daughter's health deteriorating." Therefore, the Spanish government was held liable for four million pesetas in damages and more than one million pesetas for costs and expenses.

Overall, the judgment in the *Lopez-Ostra* case demonstrates jurisprudential flexibility and judicial willingness to view environmental infringements as human rights harms. It has also enhanced the legal protection of victims of environmental harms, enabling them to bring claims in relation to almost all sources of pollution under Article 8. However, it should be borne in mind that the disadvantage of relying solely on Article 8 is that paragraph 2 provides for the lawful restriction of such individual rights on the basis of security, safety, morality, or economics. Thus, it is desirable to consider whether the environmental rights of individuals could be strengthened in the future by bringing such claims under Article 2, on the basis that the right to life of individuals encompasses the concept of a right to a safe and healthy environment. Alternatively, such claims could potentially be brought under Article 3, as an element of the right to physical integrity and health. Neither Article 2 nor 3 contain limiting provisions comparable to Article 8(2). Accordingly, rights conferred under Articles 2 and 3 are not subject to the same broad exceptions. A further positive development is the ECHR's promotion of the concept of state liability, which has been considered and debated by the ILC for over thirty years and the scope of which still remains unresolved.

Regrettably, however, in its judgment in the *Mühleberg Case* of 1997,[93] the ECHR did not pursue or extend its progressive approach to the interpretation of human and

---

[92] Available at http://www.echr.coe.int/Convention/webConvenENG.pdf.
[93] The judgment of August 26, 1997 in the case of *Balmer-Schafroth and Others v. Switzerland* is published in (1997) 43 *European Court of Human Rights: Reports of Judgements and Decisions* at 1347; for a critical review, *see* A. Kley, "Gerichtliche Kontrolle von Atombewilligungen" (1999) 26 *EuGRZ* 177.

environmental rights under the European Convention for the Protection of Human Rights and Fundamental Freedoms. In the *Mühleberg Case*, the applicants – living within a radius of four or five kilometers from the nuclear power station – appealed against the extension of the nuclear installation's operating license for an indefinite period and maintained that the power plant did not meet current safety standards. The applicants argued that the risks that they were exposed to of an accident occurring were greater than usual and, therefore, that their civil rights had been adversely affected. The applicants also stressed their lack of access to competent Swiss courts in order to appeal the decision of the Swiss Federal Council (the executive, administrative authority) to extend the installation's operating license. Accordingly, the applicants claimed that the Swiss government had violated Articles 6 and 13 of the European Convention for the Protection of Human Rights and Fundamental Freedoms. By a majority of twelve votes to eight, the ECHR rejected the applicants' claims.

The ECHR held that the applicants "did not establish a direct link between the operating conditions of the power station which were contested by them and their right to protection of their physical integrity, as they failed to show that the operation of the Mühleberg power station exposed them personally to a danger that was not only serious but also specific and, above all, imminent."[94] The repercussions for the Swiss population of any accident or harm caused by the operation of the installation were hypothetical only. However, in the dissenting opinion of seven judges, on the question of proof of a link between the operation of the installation and a relevant harm and also of a potential danger, it was emphasized that the majority "appear[ed] to have ignored the whole trend of international institutions and public international law towards protecting persons and heritage, as evident in European Union and Council of Europe instruments on the environment, the Rio agreements, UNESCO instruments, the development of the precautionary principle and the principle of conservation of common heritage."[95] The dissenting judges also highlighted the importance of the Convention on Civil Liability for Damage Resulting from Activities Dangerous to the Environment [96] stressing that the special hazards are posed in relation to certain installations, which need to be protected against through new international law measures, and through the availability and imposition of effective remedies for such harms. Such statements are laudable and encourage the view that, in the future, courts will take into account such new jurisprudential trends in international environmental law and pursue the progressive approach to fundamental rights taken by the *López-Ostra* judiciary.

Unfortunately, in general, judicial decisions concerning nuclear energy appear to develop their own set of rules due to political considerations and the political importance of nuclear energy. It was not surprising therefore, that in its judgment of April 6, 2000 concerning the Swiss nuclear power plant *Beznau II*[97] – in nearly identical circumstances to the *Mühleberg Case* – the ECHR again rejected claims brought by local residents in relation to the operating license granted to the Beznau plant. The ECHR stressed that the applicants had failed to prove that they were being personally and directly exposed to an imminent nuclear risk.

---

[94] *Balmer-Schafroth and Others v. Switzerland, id.*, at 1359 para. 40.
[95] For the dissenting opinion of Judge Pettiti, joined by Judges Gölcüklü, Walsh, Russo, Valticos, Lopes-Rocha, and Jambrek and of Judge Foighel, see *id.*, at 1361, 1363, 1367.
[96] (June 21, 1993), ILM 32 (1993) 1228, available at http://www.conventions.coe.int/treaty/en/Treaties/Word/150.doc.
[97] Judgment in the *Case of Athanassoglou and Others v. Switzerland*, April 6, 2000, Application No. 27644/95.

More recently, the ECHR considered a case concerning the right to a safe environment under Article 2 (and Article 1 of Protocol No. 1) of the European Convention for the Protection of Human Rights and Fundamental Freedoms. In the *Oneryildiz v Turkey* case,[98] the applicant and members of his family lived in an illegally built house in the vicinity of a rubbish tip in Umraniye (Istanbul). Members of the applicant's family died and their house was destroyed as the result of a methane explosion from the rubbish tip. In its judgment of June 18, 2002, the ECHR held that the death of the applicant's family members and the ineffectiveness of the Turkish judicial mechanism in the prevailing circumstances violated Article 2 and Article 1 of Protocol No.1. However, this judgment is not final as the case has been referred to the Grand Chamber under Articles 43 and 44 of the European Convention for the Protection of Human Rights and Fundamental Freedoms.[99]

Despite the progress in environmental and human rights jurisprudence achieved by the ECHR, the primary problem of direct access to the ECHR still remains. An individual is only allowed to bring a claim before the ECHR after having exhausted local remedies, that is, after having pursued claims in competent institutions of his or her home state. Such time consuming and complex procedural requirements considerably limit the protection of environmental human rights.

5.5 International Criminal Court

A conceivable future approach could involve the International Criminal Court (ICC), which was established on July 17, 1998 by the United Nations Diplomatic Conference of Rome.[100] According to Article 5 of the Rome Statute of the International Criminal Court,[101] the ICC has jurisdiction for the most serious crimes that are of concern to the international community as a whole. These crimes are the crime of genocide, crimes against humanity, war crimes, and the crime of aggression. The inclusion of an autonomous, explicit category of "crimes against the environment" within the subject matter jurisdiction of the ICC, as previously suggested in Article 19(d) of the ILC's Draft Articles on State Responsibility,[102] regrettably failed to gain support in the deliberations leading up to the adoption of the Rome Statute of the International Criminal Court.

In the course of the work of the Preparatory Committee on the Establishment of an ICC, a large majority of states wanted to limit the jurisdiction of the ICC to the core crimes mentioned and refused to include so-called "treaty crimes."[103] Instead, it was decided to include environmental aspects in a modified form under the heading of

---

[98] Judgment in the case of *Oneryildiz v. Turkey*, June 18, 2002, Application No. 00048939/99.

[99] For this and various other environment related cases, *see* A. Mularoni, "The Right to a Safe Environment in the Case Law of the European Court of Human Rights," manuscript published in *Symposium on Environmental Law for Judges*, (Rome, May 9–10, 2003).

[100] Edited by UN Diplomatic Conference, Rome, Press Release L/ROM/22, July 17, 1998.

[101] C. Rosbaud and O. Triffterer (eds.), *Rome Statute of the International Criminal Court*, Nomos Publishing Co. (Baden-Baden, 2000), *see also* www.un.org/law/icc/statute/romefra.htm.

[102] Art. 19(d) provides: "the serious breach of an international obligation of essential importance for the safeguarding and preservation of the human environment, such as those prohibiting massive pollution of the atmosphere or of the seas" is an international crime. *See Yearbook of the International Law Commission* (YILC) *1980*, Vol. II Part Two at 30, 32.

[103] O. Triffterer (ed.), "Article by Article: Annotation to Article 5" in *Commentary on the Rome Statute of the International Criminal Court*, Observers' Notes, Nomos Publishing Co. (Baden-Baden, 1999) at 98.

either a crime against humanity or a war crime. Article 8(2)(b)(iv) of the Rome Statute of the International Criminal Court includes within the definition of a war crime: "intentionally launching an attack in the knowledge that such attack will cause incidental loss of life or injury to civilians or damage to civilian objects or widespread, long-term and severe damage to the natural environment which would be clearly excessive in relation to the concrete and direct overall military advantage anticipated."[104] Although this Article does not provide for the comprehensive protection of the environment, in general this approach is a preliminary step in the right direction. The issue of extending the ICC's jurisdiction to include prosecution of environmental crimes may be raised again in the near future, if environmental crimes cannot be stopped and instead, steadily increase and also if, at a propitious moment, Article 19(d) becomes binding treaty law.

Although criminal law approaches are based on "individual responsibility," this concept could also easily be extended to encompass the responsibilities of state organs. The ICC's competence, in general, should not be regarded as contrary, or substantially different, to the competence and purview of the other courts and international tribunals discussed in this chapter, simply because the ICC is specifically concerned with criminal law and criminal responsibility. On the contrary, in combination with other international judicial institutions and acting as a complement to these institutions, the ICC could provide an effective means of combating international environmental pollution. However, this aim will only be realized if NGOs and individuals are able to bring claims before the ICC.

5.6 Summary

Currently, the existing, international judicial institutions cannot fully resolve the problems posed by transnational environmental disputes and cannot provide optimum solutions for the protection of the environment and injured individuals. Accordingly, their role, while important and desirable, is a complementary one.

It may be that proposals for a new International Environmental Court, mentioned in Section 4, with mandatory jurisdiction over transnational environmental disputes will be accepted. If not, the author is of the view that the Permanent Court of Arbitration in The Hague (PCA) is the most appropriate international judicial institution for the resolution of such disputes.

6 THE PERMANENT COURT OF ARBITRATION: THE PROPER FORUM FOR THE RESOLUTION OF TRANSNATIONAL ENVIRONMENTAL DISPUTES

In the absence of a special international environmental court with mandatory jurisdiction, the Permanent Court of Arbitration (PCA) could be the appropriate forum for the settlement of environmental disputes.[105] This idea was born at the First Conference of

---

[104] For discussion of the problem of concretizing "war crimes" under Art. 8(2), *see* C. Kress, "War Crimes Committed in Non-International Armed Conflict and the Emerging System of International Criminal Justice" (2000) 103 *Israel Yearbook on Human Rights* 103 at 134.

[105] In support of this idea, *see* C. P. R. Romano, *The Peaceful Settlement of International Environmental Disputes: A Pragmatic Approach*, Kluwer Law International (The Hague, 2000) at 125; T. T. van den Hout, "Resolving Environmental Disputes: From Negotiation to Adjudication," *Biopolitics, The Bio-Environment*, Vol. VIII (Racing to Save the Environment) (Athens, 2001); A. Rest, "An International

the Members of the Court in September 1993.[106] The author introduced the idea at the ICEF-Venice Conference 1994,[107] where it found strong support, inter alia, from the Secretary General of the International Bureau of the PCA.[108] In the meantime, numerous resolutions have stressed the potential for the PCA to act as a competent institution for the settlement of environmental disputes, such as the Resolutions of the George Washington University and the American Bar Association, Washington, April 1999; of ICEF, Rome, October 2000;[109] and of the Biopolitics International Organization, Athens, 2001.[110] The Second Conference of the Members of the PCA, by its Resolution of May 1999, also called upon the Secretary General and the International Bureau of the PCA "to expand the Court's role . . . including the area of environmental disputes, taking into account the entire range of international dispute resolution mechanisms administered by the Court."[111]

6.1 General Principles and Rules Governing Dispute Resolution at the PCA

There are good reasons supporting the view that the PCA is the appropriate institution for the resolution of transnational environmental disputes. First, this institution, with its roots in The Hague Peace Conferences of 1899 and 1907 and in particular the Conventions for the Pacific Settlement of International Disputes,[112] is well recognized and accepted by numerous member states of the UN. Second, it is a highly flexible and unique institution, because it offers facilities for four of the dispute settlement methods listed in Article 33 of the Charter of the United Nations:[113] inquiry, mediation, conciliation, and arbitration.

The PCA established Optional Conciliation Rules[114] in 1996, enabling the parties, including states, international organizations, NGOs, companies, and private associations to use conciliation mechanisms. These Rules are based on the UNCITRAL Conciliation

---

Court for the Environment: The Role of the Permanent Court of Arbitration" (1999) 4 *Asia Pacific Journal of Environmental Law* 107.

[106] PCA and Stichting T. M. C. Asser Instituut (eds.), *First Conference of the Members of the Court*, September 10–11, 1993 (The Hague, 1993); I. Diaconu, *Background paper* at 94, 96; Prince B. Ajibola, *Background papers* at 98, 99.

[107] A. Rest, "The Need for an International Court for the Environment. Underdeveloped Legal Protection for the Individual in Transnational Litigation," in *a cura di* A. Postiglione, *Towards the World Governing of the Environment, IV*, International Conference June 2–5, 1994 (Venice, Pavia, 1996) at 178.

[108] P. J. H. Jonkman, "Resolution of International Environmental Disputes: A Potential Role for the Permanent Court of Arbitration," *supra* note 108, at 435.

[109] The Resolutions are published in A. Postiglione, *Giustizia e Ambiente Globale: Necessità di una Corte Internazionale* (Milano, 2001) at 170, 175.

[110] Vlavianos-Arvanitis (ed.), *supra* note 14, at 533.

[111] PCA Members' Resolution of 17 May 1999, in PCA (ed.), *International Alternative Dispute Resolution: Past, Present and Future, Centennial Papers* (The Hague, 2000) at 237; *see* in particular para. 9 of the Resolution at 238.

[112] Available at http://www.lawschool.cornell.edu/library/pca/1899english.htm and www.lawschool.cornell.edu/library/pca/1907english.htm.

[113] Available at http://www.un.org/aboutun/charter/.

[114] PCA, Optional Conciliation Rules of July 1, 1996. All Optional Rules concerning Conciliation and Arbitration are published by the Secretary General and International Bureau of the PCA, Peace Palace, The Hague, in Basic Documents, Conventions, Rules, Model Clauses and Guidelines, (1998), available at http://www.pca-cpa.org/ENGLISH/BD/conciliationenglish.htm.

Rules[115] and enable conciliation to be linked with possible arbitration. Significantly, the PCA has further established Optional Rules for the Conciliation of Disputes Relating to Natural Resources and/or the Environment.[116]

In 1992, the PCA adopted Optional Rules for Arbitrating Disputes between Two States,[117] and, in 1993, Optional Rules for Disputes between Two Parties of Which Only One Is a State.[118] The PCA has also adopted Optional Rules for the Arbitration of Disputes Relating to Natural Resources and/or the Environment.[119] Consequently, disputes between a nonstate actor and a state can be submitted to the PCA. In May 1996, the PCA extended its Optional Rules to include Rules for Arbitration involving International Organisations and States[120] as well as between International Organisations and Private Parties.[121] By widening its jurisdiction to encompass all parties of the community of states, including organizations and all members of society, the PCA's jurisdiction extends well beyond the competence of the ICJ.

Third, the extra financing that would be required to establish a new international court for the environment is a further argument in support of utilizing the PCA with its existing administrative and logistical infrastructure. Under the PCA system, the costs of arbitration proceedings are borne by the parties. Moreover, the PCA Financial Assistance Fund for the Settlement of International Disputes of 1995[122] grants financial support to those states that require financial help in order to meet the costs involved in dispute resolution proceedings. In the future, this funding model should be extended to include nonstate actors.

Fourth, the flexibility of the PCA with regard to the place of arbitration should also be noted. For transnational environmental disputes in particular, the place of arbitration can be extremely important in terms of providing evidence of the harm that has occurred. It is possible that this can be decided by agreement between the parties. Where there is no agreement, arbitration takes place at The Hague, the seat of the PCA.

Fifth, it is highly advantageous that the PCA is very experienced in matters of trade law, investment law, and socioeconomic matters, such that this body of interdisciplinary knowledge can be applied in the context of environmental law issues. Taking into account the interdependence of all these fields is indispensable in our rapidly globalizing world.

While for all these reasons the PCA is the most appropriate international institution for the settlement of environmental disputes, it is important to remember that it is only through the agreement of the parties, or by compromise, that the competence of the PCA can be established. If the parties are states or only one of the parties is a state, this substantial impediment must be overcome. Ultimately, the submission of a dispute to the PCA depends on the political preparedness of a state. Very significant progress could be made in this regard if states, in future environmental treaties, were to include

---

[115] The Rules of the United Nations Commission on International Trade Law of December 1976 are published in A. Bülow, K. H. Böckstiegel, R. Geimer, and R. A. Schütze, *Der Internationale Rechtverkehr in Zivil-und Handelssachen*, Vol. II Loose-leaf-collection (1997), No. 753.

[116] Available at http://www.pca-cpa.org/PDF/envconciliation.pdf.

[117] Optional Rules of October 20, 1992, *supra* note 114, at 41.

[118] Optional Rules of July 6, 1993, *supra* note 114, at 69.

[119] *See* http://www.pca-cpa.org/ENGLISH/EDR/ENRrules.htm.

[120] Optional Rules of July 1, 1996, *supra* note 114, at 97.

[121] *Id.*, at 125.

[122] PCA Financial Assistance Fund for Settlement on International Disputes: Terms of Reference and Guidelines as approved by the Administrative Council on December 11, 1995, *supra* note 114, at 233.

a special dispute settlement clause that automatically established the competence of the PCA, as seen for instance in the Bonn Convention on the Conservation of Migratory Species of Wild Animals of 1979[123] and as foreshadowed in the IUCN Draft International Covenant on Environment and Development of 1995.[124] In 1998, the PCA developed guidelines for negotiating and drafting such dispute settlement clauses.[125]

Nevertheless, what is encouraging is the increasing number of arbitral decisions of the PCA in the last decade. For the first time the Optional Rules for Disputes between Two Parties of Which Only One Is a State were applied in a dispute between Technosystem SpA (Italy) and Taraba State and Nigeria, resulting in an award on November 25, 1996.[126]

6.2 The PCA Optional Rules for the Arbitration of Disputes Relating to Natural Resources and/or the Environment

Through the recent Optional Rules for Arbitration of Disputes Relating to Natural Resources and/or the Environment of June 19, 2001[127] – unanimously adopted by ninety-four member states – the PCA has offered yet another approach for the peaceful settlement of international environmental disputes. In a unique manner, these Rules, which seek to address the principal lacunae in environmental dispute resolution, meet most of the relevant requirements of the Montevideo Programme III and ensure first, that nonstate actors have access to an international judicial institution, and second, legal protection and effective control through the implementation and enforcement of international environmental treaty obligations and international environmental law in general. These Rules, which have been drafted by a special PCA Working Group on Environmental and Natural Resources Law,[128] are structured in four main sections: Introductory Rules (Section I, Arts. 1–4); the Composition of the Arbitral Tribunal (Section II, Arts. 5–14); the Arbitral Proceedings (Section III, Arts. 15–30); and the Award (Section IV, Arts. 31–41). The Rules are also supplemented with an Explanatory Memorandum.

The Rules contain the following significant innovations:

1. As the Introduction emphasizes, the Rules will be available for the use of all parties who have agreed to apply them. That means states, intergovernmental organizations, NGOs, and private entities, including, inter alia, corporations, companies, environmental interest groups, and individuals, can have recourse to the forum offered.

---

[123] Art. XIII of the Bonn Convention of June 23, 1979, ILM 19 (1980) 15, at 26.

[124] Art. 62(2) of the Draft International Covenant on Environment and Development of the World Conservation Union in cooperation with the International Council of Environmental Law, *Environmental Policy and Law Paper* No. 31, Gland, 1995; the second edition and updated text has been published in *IUCN Environmental Policy and Law Paper* No. 31, Rev. (2000).

[125] Prepared by P. Sands and R. MacKenzie, *Guidelines for Negotiating and Drafting Dispute Settlement Clauses for International Environmental Agreements*, International Bureau of PCA (The Hague, January 1998).

[126] PCA, 96th Annual Report, No. 21 at 9; for further decisions, *see* P. Hamilton, H. C. Requena, L. van Scheltinga, and B. Shifman (eds.), *The Permanent Court of Arbitration: International Arbitration and Dispute Resolution, Summaries of Awards, Settlement Agreements and Reports* (The Hague, 1999).

[127] Published by the Secretary General and the International Bureau of the PCA (The Hague, 2001), available at www.pca-cpa.org.

[128] For details of the history of the Rules, *see* A. Rest, "The Effective Role of the Permanent Court of Arbitration as International Court for the Environment," in A. Postiglione (ed.), *Giurisdizione e Controllo per L'Effettività del Diritto Umano all'Ambiente, Giornata Ambiente, 2000* (Naples, 2001) at 87, 103.

The Rules thus permit greater flexibility in the number and nature of parties than currently exists elsewhere.

2. In order to rapidly provide both scientific and juridical resources to the parties seeking resolution of a dispute, the Rules provide for the optional use of:

    a) a panel of environmental scientists nominated by the member states and the Secretary General respectively who can provide expert scientific assistance to the parties and the arbitral tribunal;[129] and

    b) a panel of arbitrators with experience and expertise in environmental and natural resources law nominated by the member states and the Secretary General respectively.[130]

3. Where arbitrations deal with highly technical questions, provision is made for the submission to the tribunal of a document agreed by the parties summarizing and providing background information on any scientific or technical issues which they wish to raise in their memorials or at oral hearings.[131]

4. The tribunal is empowered, unless in their *compromis* the parties chose otherwise, to order any interim measures necessary to prevent serious harm to natural resources and the environment.[132]

5. As time may be of the essence in environmental disputes, the Rules provide for arbitration in a shorter period of time than under the previous Optional Rules or the UNCITRAL Rules. The tribunal itself can be constituted rapidly as, if the parties cannot agree on arbitrators, the Secretary General is able to appoint them, rather than simply designating an appointing authority, as is the case under the UNCITRAL Rules.

6. Measures to protect the confidentiality of information provided by the parties are specifically set out in Article 15(4)–(6). While these powers were previously deemed to be inherently vested in the tribunal, the specific description in the Rules of an optional mechanism for resolving confidentiality issues is intended to save the time required for the tribunal and/or the parties to design a system to ensure accountability for confidentiality.

The Rules contain a number of innovative mechanisms that will contribute to enhanced judicial control in relation to the application of international environmental law and strengthen the legal position of NGOs as well as of the individual victims of harmful environmental activities. The Secretary General has further announced an intention to explain the aim and content of the various Articles in these Rules in a comprehensive Commentary in the near future.[133]

6.3 Environmental Protection Cases at the PCA

Two cases concerning environmental protection were recently brought before the PCA.[134] On June 18, 2001, Ireland initiated arbitration proceedings against the United

---

[129] *See* Art. 27, para. 5.   [130] Art. 8, para. 3.

[131] Art. 24, para. 4.   [132] Art. 26, paras. 1–3.

[133] For a convincing review of the Rules, *see* D. Ratliff, "The PCA Optional Rules for Arbitration of Disputes Relating to Natural Resources and/or the Environment" (2002) 14 *Leiden Journal of International Law* 887.

[134] Available at http://www.pca-cpa.org/English/RPC.

Kingdom pursuant to Article 32 of the OSPAR Convention for the Protection of the Marine Environment of the North-East Atlantic.[135] The case concerns access to information under Article 9 of the Convention in relation to the authorization of the MOX plant located at the Sellafield nuclear facility in the UK. By Final Award of July 2, 2003 Ireland's claim was dismissed. By majority decision the PCA found "that Ireland's claim for information does not fall within Article 9(2) of the OSPAR Convention."[136]

In the second case, which began in summer 2001, The Netherlands brought a claim against France to compel the application of the Convention on the Protection of the Rhine against Pollution by Chlorides of December 3, 1976,[137] and the Additional Protocol of September 25, 1991, and further, to compel France's compliance with the provisions of this Convention. The arbitration procedure was initiated on the basis of the Optional Rules for Arbitrating Disputes between Two States of 1992. Aspects concerning relevant compensation are also at issue in the dispute.

In general, it is clear that the PCA plays a significant role in international environmental dispute resolution and its practice in this area of law has grown immensely.

6.4 The PCA Optional Rules for Conciliation of Disputes Relating to Natural Resources and/or the Environment

A further progressive instrument for the peaceful and nonconfrontational settlement of environmental disputes is the PCA's Optional Rules for the Conciliation of Disputes Relating to Natural Resources and/or the Environment, which were adopted by ninety-six member states on April 16, 2002.[138] Primarily based on the PCA's Optional Conciliation Rules of 1996 and the UNCITRAL Conciliation Rules, these Optional Rules reflect the particular characteristics of disputes that concern natural resources, conservation, or environmental protection. Moreover, these Rules emphasize maximum flexibility and party autonomy. For example, the Rules may be used for dispute resolution between two or more state parties to a bi- or multilateral agreement relating to access to, and utilization of, natural resources in a dispute concerning the interpretation or application of such an agreement.

It is particularly important – as stressed in the Introduction – that the Rules and the services of the Secretary General and the International Bureau of the PCA are also "available for use by private parties, other entities existing under national or international law, international organisations and states."[139] This statement clarifies that nonstate actors, in addition to states, can initiate conciliation procedures if their legal interests are affected.

In keeping with the general preventive aims of conciliation, such procedures should be used prior to arbitration and, to the extent that it is possible, should replace arbitral proceedings. Article 15 of the Rules provides: "The parties undertake not to initiate,

---

[135] For the text of the Convention, *see* W. Burhenne *International Environmental Law, Multilateial Treaties* under No. 992:71.

[136] For the details, *see* ILM 42 (2003) 1118–86, in particular at 1152.

[137] Available at http://www.oup.co.uk/pdf/bt/cassese/cases/part3/ch17/1304.pdf.

[138] The Rules are published by the Secretary General and the International Bureau of the PCA (The Hague, 2002), available at www.pca-cpa.org.

[139] Introduction, under (i).

during the conciliation proceedings, any arbitral or judicial proceedings in respect of a dispute that is the subject of the conciliation proceedings, except that a party may initiate arbitral or judicial proceedings where, in its opinion, such proceedings are necessary for preserving and/or the interim protection of its rights." According to Article 1(1) of the Rules, "conciliation" is defined as "a process whereby parties request a third person, or a panel of persons, to assist them in their attempt to reach an amicable settlement of their dispute relating to natural resources and/or the environment." It should be emphasized that the "characterisation of the dispute as relating to the environment or natural resources is not necessary for application of these Rules, where all Parties have agreed to settle a specific dispute under these Rules."[140]

The appointment of the conciliator – which could be one, three, or five persons[141] – is by the free choice of the parties. If a party has not appointed its conciliator, or the parties have not agreed on the conciliator within sixty days, the Secretary General of the PCA can make such an appointment within thirty days.[142] The parties are free to choose conciliators from the PCA Panel of Arbitrators constituted under the PCA Optional Rules for Arbitration of Disputes Relating to Natural Resources and/or the Environment or members of the PCA. The parties are also free to choose expert witnesses from the PCA Panel of Scientific and Technical Experts constituted under the Optional Rules for Arbitration of Disputes Relating to Natural Resources and/or the Environment.[143] However, in general, the choice of conciliators or experts is not limited to PCA panels.[144]

Under Article 7(1), the role of the conciliator consists of assisting the parties in an independent and impartial manner in their attempt to reach an amicable resolution of the dispute. At any stage of the conciliation proceedings, the conciliator can make proposals and may communicate with all the parties together or with each of them separately.[145] When it appears to the conciliator that elements of a settlement exist that would be acceptable to the parties, the conciliator formulates the terms of a possible settlement and submits them to the parties for their observations.[146] If the parties reach agreement, they draw up and sign a written settlement agreement which is binding on all parties to the dispute and ends the dispute.[147] Of special interest in relation to the implementation of settlement agreements is the establishment of an Implementation Committee that can monitor the implementation of such agreements and guarantees the enforcement of settlement agreements.[148] Finally, it should be emphasized that conciliation procedures are confidential, unless the parties agree otherwise or disclosure is required by a court or tribunal of competent jurisdiction.[149]

These Rules offer an innovative, effective mechanism for the resolution of disputes concerning the use of natural resources and the environment in an amicable manner, before initiating arbitral dispute settlement procedures. Such preventive, non-confrontational procedures realize the aims of "political compliance procedures" as set out in other international legal instruments and extend this concept to include nonstate

---

[140] Art. 1, para. 1, sentence 2.

[142] Art. 4, para. 1, subparas. (d) and (e).

[144] Introduction (v).

[146] Art. 12.

[148] Art. 12, para. 4(c).

[141] Art. 4, para. 1, subparas. (a)–(c).

[143] Introduction, under (iii) and (iv).

[145] Art. 7, para. 5 and Art. 8, para. 1.

[147] Art. 12, paras. 2 and 3.

[149] Art. 13.

actors, as such actors can initiate conciliation processes and ensure the direct protection of their rights.

7 CONCLUSION

Through the Johannesburg Principles on the Role of Law and Sustainable Development, the Global Judges Symposium – which built on the work of six previous regional judges' symposia convened by UNEP and various partners – laudably stressed the indispensability of the judiciary for the effective implementation of environmental law at national and international levels, and for the promotion of sustainable development. For too long, the role of the judiciary – which also constitutes a branch of government – has received meager attention and has not been concretized in environmental policy making.[150] Now, through the Global Judges Symposium, judges have provided a highly necessary policy approach, recalling and highlighting the importance of the rule of law and of the judiciary. In postulating the enhancement of national jurisdiction and stressing the urgent need to strengthen the capacity of judges, prosecutors, and legislators, the judges have properly identified existing areas of concern in the context of international environmental law.

As evidenced in numerous legal studies by academics and practicing lawyers concerning national jurisdiction and environmental law in various regions of the world, and particularly in the context of the German and European court systems, national judicial mechanisms are still highly ineffective where transnational environmental harms are concerned. Therefore, it is necessary to focus on the limits on the jurisdiction of national courts. As a first step to resolving the problems currently faced in the resolution of transnational environmental disputes, the jurisdiction of judicial mechanisms called upon to resolve such disputes must be extended beyond national boundaries. Accordingly, alongside national courts and tribunals, international judicial control is indispensable for the proper protection of the environment on a regional and global level, as well as for the protection of the global commons and the human rights of those individuals that are threatened or injured in cases of transnational pollution. International judicial control is also strongly needed to control the activities of states, to remind them of their collective responsibility for the protection of environment and to guarantee the implementation and application of international environmental agreements, and of international environmental law in general.

Courts such as the ICJ, ITLOS, the Courts of the European Community, the ECHR, and ICC cannot offer optimal solutions for the resolution of international environmental problems at this time. These institutions either do not have comprehensive jurisdiction to protect the environment sufficiently or cannot guarantee the rights of NGOs or individuals, as such nonstate actors lack standing. Nevertheless, these international institutions remain critical for the progressive development of international environmental law. Moreover, they could certainly play an important complementary role to support the work of the PCA.

---

[150] A. M. Hindman, "Global Judges Symposium. A Step Forward in the Judiciary's Role in Sustainable Development" (2002) 32 *Environmental Policy and Law* 240.

In the absence of an international environmental court, the PCA is the most appropriate forum for the resolution of transnational environmental disputes. Through its Optional Rules for Arbitration of Disputes Relating to Natural Resources and/or the Environment the PCA offers new innovative instruments for the effective application of national and international environmental law. The Optional Rules for the Conciliation of Disputes Relating to Natural Resources and/or the Environment contain new preventive mechanisms allowing for the amicable and nonconfrontational resolution of such disputes. Both sets of Optional Rules provide a new approach for dispute avoidance and dispute settlement and have translated numerous policy statements into practical regulations, as proposed in Montevideo Programme III and the Millennium Declaration. In enabling private parties and other nonstate actors[151] to initiate conciliation and arbitration processes and to participate in these procedures, the Rules are unique. In this way, the Rules take into account the increasing importance of NGOs, environmental interest groups, and individuals in the field of environmental protection and emphasize the "vital role that NGOs play in the shaping and implementation of participatory democracy."[152]

Transnational environmental problems can only be effectively solved through cooperative efforts at national and international levels. States need the cooperation and support of private institutions. Equally, these private elements must be more extensively incorporated within current interstate mechanisms, especially international environmental treaties, in order to give such nonstate actors a real chance to make effective contributions in decision making, as well as in implementing international environmental law. To meet the challenges of our modern, globalized world, states must cooperate with nonstate actors, albeit within certain limitations imposed by principles of state sovereignty.

Taken together, the PCA Optional Rules can play a model role for the enhancement of the standing of nonstate actors and for the development of an international environmental judiciary in general. This aim could also be realized and supported by the inclusion or amendment of dispute settlement clauses in existing environmental agreements and the inclusion of such clauses in future treaties. The PCA Guidelines for Negotiating and Drafting Dispute Settlement Clauses for International Environmental Agreements of 1998[153] offer welcome assistance in this regard. While the PCA currently provides an appropriate forum for the resolution of environmental conflicts, the open question of whether we need a new international court for the environment with mandatory jurisdiction over such matters still needs further consideration.[154]

---

[151] In relation to the need for nonstate actors to be granted access to international judicial mechanisms, *see* T. T. van den Hout, "Towards an International Court of the Environment," *Biopolitics International Organisation, Bio-Syllabus for European Environmental Education* (Athens, 2002) at 551.

[152] *See* Agenda 21, Chapter 27.   [153] *Supra* note 125.

[154] For the numerous recommendations and resolutions demanding the establishment of such a court, *see*: The Global Demand for an International Court of the Environment, International Report 1998 of the International Court of the Environment Foundation (ICEF) (Rome, 1998); *see also* A.Vlavianos-Arvanitis, International Court of the Environment, in: *Biopolitics International Organisation, Bio-Syllabus for European Environmental Education* (Athens, 2002) 532; for a general discussion, *see* E. Rehbinder and D. Loperena, "Legal Protection of Environmental Rights: The Role and Experience of

Taken as a whole, however, the recent activities of judges recalling and asserting first, the importance of the rule of law and second, the indispensability of judicial mechanisms for environmental protection at national and international levels are valuable contributions toward more effectively realizing the aim of sustainable development in the future.

the International Court of Environmental Arbitration and Conciliation" (2001) 31 *Environmental Policy and Law* 282, 285. The authors demonstrate the jurisdiction of a court registered as a civil association under Mexican Law.

PART FOUR

COMPARATIVE ENERGY LAW

18 UNDP: China's Energy Portfolio

Rusong Li*

1 UNDP'S APPROACH TO ENERGY

The United Nations Development Program (UNDP) is the UN's global development network, advocating for change and connecting developing countries to the knowledge, experience, and resources that will enable people in developing nations to build better lives for themselves. UNDP is active in 166 countries, working with these countries to provide their own solutions to the international and national development challenges they face. As these countries develop local capacity to address such challenges, they draw on the people of UNDP and its wide range of partners.

UNDP's efforts in energy for sustainable development support the UN Millennium Development Declaration's[1] (Millennium Declaration) goal (millennium development goal (MDG)) of reducing the proportion of people living in poverty by 2015 by half. None of the agreed upon MDGs can be achieved without significant improvements in energy services in the developing world. UNDP's experience with integrated development solutions gives it a unique perspective for addressing the multiple social, economic, and environmental aspects of sustainable energy approaches. As the development coordinator within the UN system, UNDP works to identify strategic entry points for enhancing policy frameworks through developing local capacity, assisting with grants, and providing technical support for pilot projects.

UNDP supports sustainable energy activities through global, regional, and national level projects and programs. UNDP's Thematic Trust Fund on Energy for Sustainable Development (Thematic Trust Fund), launched in the fall of 2001, defines UNDP's corporate energy priorities. It also serves as a vehicle for mobilizing additional resources to support national activities.

The four priority areas in the context of sustainable energy development for UNDP are:

- Strengthening national policy frameworks to support energy for poverty reduction and sustainable development;
- Promoting rural energy services to support growth and equity;

[1] UN General Assembly, 55th Session, A/55/L.2, Sept. 18, 2000.

* The author wishes to acknowledge and thank Susan Mcdade, Manager, Sustainable Energy Programme, BDP, UNDP and Maria Suokko, Cluster Head for Energy and Environment, UNDP China for their valuable comments and guidance.

- Promoting clean energy technologies for sustainable development; and
- Increasing access to investment financing for sustainable energy.[2]

At a global level, UNDP undertakes advocacy and analysis on energy trends and linkages between energy and development goals, and also promotes dialogue on energy and development issues within the international community.

At a regional level, UNDP's five Regional Cooperation Frameworks are helping countries access and share knowledge and best practices in relation to sustainable energy, drawing on established institutions and programs in their regions.

At the country level, UNDP funds activities in developing countries and countries with economies in transition, both through its Thematic Trust Fund and in its role as an implementing agency of the Global Environment Facility (GEF). The GEF provides grants to developing countries to address certain global environmental issues, including climate change. The Thematic Trust Fund complements the GEF by funding activities that are not eligible for GEF support, but are essential for addressing local sustainable development needs. UNDP-GEF primarily focuses on developing capacity within governments and civil society to respond to the challenges of global climate change, focusing on removing barriers affecting energy efficiency and renewable energy technologies and also promoting low-emission technologies and sustainable transport.

In addition to UNDP's core resources and government cost sharing, the primary sources of funding for UNDP's work are the Montreal Protocol[3] and the GEF. UNDP's ongoing Environment and Energy projects have an overall budget of approximately US$200 million.[4]

2 UNDP CHINA'S ENERGY PORTFOLIO

Providing support to the Chinese government in furtherance of its obligations as a party to multilateral environmental agreements, the promotion of environmental governance and holistic support for biodiversity conservation are some of the focus areas of UNDP China's work in the field of the environment and sustainable energy. The promotion of sustainable energy for sustainable development and poverty alleviation play a central role in UNDP's work.

As part of the UNDP China Country Office, the Environment and Energy Cluster seeks to make a critical contribution to reducing poverty in China by supporting initiatives to achieve growth with environmental sustainability. Supporting the Chinese government in its efforts to integrate environmental and energy related objectives into macroeconomic and sector policies, and also capacity building to negotiate and implement global environmental commitments, are focus areas in UNDP China's work. As the "scorekeeper" and "campaign manager" for the MDGs, UNDP China has drawn from its experience in integrated development solutions to assist China in advancing its sustainable development by addressing these development challenges in a holistic way.

The promotion of sustainable energy for sustainable development and poverty alleviation plays a central role in UNDP China's work. UNDP China has a sizeable energy

[2] UNDP, *Energy Brochure.*
[3] Montreal Protocol on Substances that Deplete the Ozone Layer (1987) 26 ILM 1541.
[4] UNDP, *China Brochure.*

portfolio, including energy efficiency, renewable energy and clean energy technologies. UNDP has also taken a lead role in developing a program for End Use Energy Efficiency. This umbrella program aims to foster a strategic approach to developing, implementing, and enforcing a comprehensive and effective energy conservation policy and regulatory system.

Generally, the Chinese government has been paying close attention to energy conservation efforts and the decoupling of energy consumption and economic growth has been realized in China in recent years. UNDP China has been contributing to this process through several UNDP-GEF supported projects such as the Green Lights, the Refrigerator, Township and Village Enterprises (TVEs) projects. One of the lessons learned from these projects is that energy conservation efforts only touch on the huge barriers that exist to improve energy efficiency. Without interministerial coordination, the enforcement of regulations and some transformation of the market, such improvements are extremely difficult to achieve.

Based on those experiences, the Chinese government set more ambitious targets for further energy conservation and energy efficiency improvement for major energy intensive sectors (industry, building, and transportation) in the Tenth Five-Year Plan period (2000–2005). The Chinese Government came to UNDP with a proposal for UNDP support of a flagship project to set up and implement this roadmap for improvements in energy efficiency. The program's aim is to foster a strategic approach to developing and implementing a comprehensive and effective energy conservation policy and regulatory system, and to removing institutional, technical, financial, and informational barriers to the widespread application of energy efficiency improvements in major energy intensive sectors. "Supporting China's Strategy for Sustainable Energy Development" has enhanced China's national capacity to formulate long-term energy development strategies. Several energy standards and labeling schemes for products and services have been developed through UNDP funded projects.

UNDP also provides technical assistance and expertise through pilot projects and ensures that the findings of UNDP-supported initiatives feed into policy formulation and institutional development for sustainable environment and energy services. For example, in March 2000, the Jilin Provincial Government and UNDP China, in partnership with the UN Foundation, launched a program for modernized biomass utilization to provide improved rural energy services based on agricultural residues. This biomass project in Jilin province is the first one to demonstrate the feasibility of combined heat and power (CHP) generation by using agricultural residues. Through dissemination of the results of this project at a national level, the project will promote the replication of such technologies in other parts of China.

Demonstration sites have been established by provincial authorities to generate gas from corn residues, which can then be used for heating and cooking purposes. The gas is also used to generate electricity for local use and for sale to the electricity grid as a means of making the project financially viable. By supporting the construction of a CHP generation site with technical assistance and capacity development, UNDP is helping to introduce a new approach to rural energy in China. The objective of the project is to provide cleaner, more energy efficient rural energy services to support local sustainable development. Modern biomass-based power can promote rural industrialization and generate well-paying jobs in rural areas. This project is also helping local people and industries reduce their reliance on coal, improving the living conditions of rural Chinese, especially women and children, who currently face indoor air pollution associated with open burning of agricultural residues.

Finally, UNDP has also assisted the Chinese government to introduce market-based instruments for energy conservation. Several GEF-UNDP projects have used market-based approaches to create both "supply push" and "demand pull" to increase the adoption of energy efficient products, services and practices.

19 Implementing the Kyoto Protocol beyond the WSSD at Johannesburg – The Japanese Perspective

Akio Morishima*

1 INTRODUCTION

After the adoption of the Marrakesh Accords,[1] global climate change negotiations went into the implementation stage of the Kyoto Protocol. Annex B Parties to the Kyoto Protocol expedited their processes toward achieving the quantified GHGs (Greenhouse Gases) targets inscribed in Annex B so that they could ratify the Protocol by 2002, the tenth anniversary of the adoption of the United Nations Framework Convention on Climate Change (UNFCCC). Japan, as one of the Annex B parties, prepared a domestic policy to combat global warming and ratified the Protocol on June 4, 2002, with a view to contributing to the implementation of the Protocol in time for the World Summit for Sustainable Development (WSSD).

This chapter discusses the essence of the decisions of the Kyoto Protocol, and the development of Japanese domestic policy to achieve the targets set out in the Protocol.

2 THE KYOTO PROTOCOL

Some of the key elements set out in the Kyoto Protocol are: (1) the quantified GHG reduction targets; (2) introduction of flexible mechanisms; and (3) considerations on land use, land use change, and the forest sector. In this section, each of these will be discussed in some detail.

2.1 The Quantified Reduction Targets of GHGs

The Kyoto Protocol set out in its Annex B the differentiated reduction targets of GHG emissions from Annex I parties,[2] with a view to reducing their total emissions in average by five percent relative to the 1990 levels, during the commitment period from year 2008 to 2012. This was great progress in the efforts toward realizing the Convention's spirit of "common but differentiated responsibilities." According to Annex B, Japan is committed to reducing its GHG emissions by a six percent average per year from the 1990 level for the period from 2008 to 2012.

---

[1] The Marrakesh Accords are a set of 24 decisions adopted by the Conference of the Parties to the United Nations Framework Convention on Climate Change during its seventh session (COP7) held in Marrakesh, Morocco. The Accords may be found in documents FCCC/CP/2001/Add. 1 to 3.

[2] Under the UNFCCC. They are sometimes referred to as the "developed country parties."

* Professor and Chair, Board of Directors, Institute of Global Environmental Strategies (IGES) Japan.

2.2 Flexible Mechanisms

The Protocol introduced three innovative and epochal mechanisms in the implementation phase of the protocol. These are:

(a) the Clean Development Mechanism (CDM);
(b) Joint Implementation (JI); and
(c) Emissions Trading (ET).

These three mechanisms, known as the "Kyoto Mechanisms," were designed to reduce the costs of curbing emissions of the parties by providing them with alternatives for meeting their targets.

The Clean Development Mechanism (CDM)

Under the CDM defined in Article 12, an Annex I party can receive the certified emission reductions (CERs) when it finances a project that will reduce the net emissions of nonAnnex I parties. This mechanism has the potential to meet the needs of both industrialized and developing countries. The CERs generated by the project will be counted as reductions of the Annex I party and help them meet the target at a lower cost. At the same time, the nonAnnex I party will be able to obtain capital for technology transfer that will help them achieve sustainable development and, eventually, contribute to the process of global warming mitigation.

Joint Implementation

Joint Implementation, the idea of which is defined in Article 6, enables an Annex I party to receive the emission reduction units (ERUs) when it finances a project that reduces the net emissions of another Annex I party. ERUs generated by the project will be counted as the reduction of the Annex I party that conducts the project, but to avoid double counting, the necessary subtraction will be made from the reduction credits of the host party. This mechanism is most likely to take place in the economies in transition (EITs) where the cost of reduction is lower than the other Annex I parties. This mechanism has been tested as Activities Implemented Jointly (AIJ)[3] to accumulate more experiences both for investing and hosting Parties.

Emissions Trading (ET)

Through emissions trading (defined in Article 17), Annex I parties will be able to acquire the assigned amount units (AAUs) from other Annex I parties that find the reduction relatively easy. An Annex I party that would like to exchange their AAUs and other units (CERs, ERUs, etc.) will record their transfers and acquisition of these units through national registries.

2.3 Land Use, Land Use Change, and Forestry (LULUCF)

Under the Protocol, parties can take into account net changes in carbon stocks (calculated as emissions minus removals) through carbon sinks and other activities in the LULUCF sector (e.g., afforestation, reforestation, and deforestation) in their efforts to

---

[3] http://unfccc.int/program/coop/aij/aij_back.html.

Table 19.1 GHG Emissions for Japan in 1988		
Electricity Generation	7 %	Increase – 5.7 %
Industries	45 %	Increase – 3.2 %
Business/Households	23 %	Increase – 12.6 %
Transportation	25 %	Increase – 21.1 %

meet the reduction targets. The amount of GHGs removed from the atmosphere in the LULUCF sector is called "removal units" (RMUs) and can be used by Annex I parties at a lower cost, although there are still uncertainties in the method of calculating emissions and removals of GHGs in the sector. According to the Bonn Agreement, which sets out the maximum amount for the use of sinks, Japan was allowed to use sinks up to thirteen megatons (Mt),[4] which accounted for around 3.9 percent of the total emissions in 1990.

3 GHG EMISSIONS IN JAPAN

As shown in Table 19.1, CO_2 comprised nearly 90 percent of the total GHG emissions in Japan in 1998, of which the power generation and other industrial sectors accounted for one-half of the total emissions. The other half is composed of emissions from the business/household sector and the transportation sector, which accounted for a quarter of the total emissions respectively.

As for the rate of increase in GHG emissions in 1998 compared with emissions in 1990, only the industrial sector showed a decrease of 3.2 percent, while the power generation sector, the business and household sectors and the transportation sector all experienced increases of 5.7 percent, 12.6 percent, and 21.1 percent respectively.

The rate of increase in total GHG emissions in 1998 was 8 percent as compared to 1990 and, in order to achieve the target of 6 percent reduction, Japan needs to implement measures to reduce its GHG emissions by some 14 percent. It will not be easy for Japan to meet the quantified reduction target for the first commitment period from 2008 to 2012. Naturally, there were serious discussions in the process of deliberation at the Diet on whether to ratify the Kyoto Protocol or not, even though the Protocol itself was adopted in Kyoto.

4 MEASURES TO COMBAT CLIMATE CHANGE ISSUES IN JAPAN

In this section, an outline of the measures and laws developed in Japan since COP3 will be discussed.

Just after the Kyoto Conference (COP3), the Cabinet organized the Global Warming Prevention Headquarters (GWPH) to deliberate on ways to reduce CO_2 and other GHG emissions generated from various sectors in Japan. In June 1998, GWPH publicized the Guidelines on Measures to Prevent Global Warming, which was essentially a wish list of all possible measures to be taken, submitted by the ministries concerned. Some 300 measures were listed, without any indication of their priorities.

---

[4] *See* "Review of the Implementation of Commitments and of other Provisions of the Convention," FCCC/CP/2001/L.7, p. 11, para. 6(c).

Table 19.2 Japan's Response to the Kyoto Protocol

Dec. 1997	Global Warming Prevention Headquarters (GWPH) was established in the Cabinet (Cabinet Decision)
1997	Law Concerning Special Measures for the Promotion of New Energy Use
June 1998	Guideline of Measures to Prevent Global Warming (GWPH)
1998	Amended Law Concerning Efficient Use of Energies (Energy Saving Law)
Oct. 1998	Law Concerning the Promotion of Measures to Cope with Global Warning
Apr. 1999	Basic Principles Concerning Measures to Cope with Global Warming (Cabinet Decision)
Jan. 2002	Central Council's Report on Domestic Measures towards the Ratification of the Kyoto Protocol (GWPH)
Feb. 2002	Principles towards the Ratification of the Kyoto Protocol (Cabinet Decision)
Mar. 2002	The Amended Guidelines on Measures to Prevent Global Warming (GWPH)
Apr. 2002	Amended Law Concerning the Promotion of Measures to Cope with Global Warming

After the submission of the Guidelines, the Central Environment Council deliberated on a rather comprehensive law, entitled "Law Concerning the Promotion of Measures to Cope with Global Warming,"[5] to prescribe the role of the central government, local governments, industries, and citizens in combating global warming.

Following this law, the Cabinet decided on the basic principles concerning global warming.[6] Apart from the laws and decisions directly related to global warming, the Basic Law for Establishing the Recycling-based Society[7] was enacted in June 2000 at the request of the Central Environment Council. The main issue to be addressed by this law is the management of waste disposal, one of the most serious problems in both urban and rural areas throughout the country. This new law sets out the principles to reduce waste through the "three Rs – Reduce, Reuse and Recycle." Based on this law, several laws concerning recycling were enacted to promote the recycling of used cars, electrical appliances, etc.

Responding to the rising awareness of global warming issues, the Ministry of International Trade and Industry (MITI), which has the jurisdiction of energy issues, also took various actions. Just before COP3, MITI introduced the Law Concerning Special Measures for the Promotion of New Energy Use,[8] a special law concerning the promotion of innovative technology for renewable energy. After COP3, in accordance with the target set forth in the Kyoto Protocol, MITI also revised the Amended Law Concerning the Efficient Use of Energies,[9] which was originally promulgated just after the oil shortage in 1978. At that time, due to the lack of petroleum, the government tried to persuade or force industries to reduce their consumption of fuel and to change the energy sources

---

[5] Chikyuondanka Taisaku Suishin Ho, 1998, No. 107.
[6] Chikyuondanka Taisaku Suishin Taiko decided by GWPH in 1998.
[7] Junkangata Shakai Keisei Suishin Kihon Ho, 2000, No. 110.
[8] Shinenerugi Riyo tou no Sokushin ni Kansuru Tokubetsu Sochi Ho, 1997, No. 37.
[9] Enerugi no Shiyo no Gorika ni Kansuru Horitsu, amended in 1998, No. 96.

from petroleum to natural gas and nuclear power. In 1998, this law was amended with a view to promoting energy efficiency in order to tackle global warming. To attain this objective, the new idea of "Top Runner Method" was introduced to require the private sector to produce products, including cars, electrical appliances, and housing materials, using the best available technologies.

The energy issue is closely linked to global warming issues. However, in Japan, while environmental issues are under the jurisdiction of the Ministry of the Environment (MoE), energy related issues are controlled by the Ministry of Economy, Trade and Industry (METI, formerly, MITI). This has made the deliberation process time consuming and caused much inefficiency in decision making.

By 2000, Japan had made certain progress in preparing for the measures to achieve its reduction target set out in the Protocol with the initiatives of MoE and METI, and was anticipating the decisions to be made at COP6 in The Hague where the Protocol's rulebook, the operational details to implement the Protocol, was to be discussed and decided. Since the rulebook would affect the ways of commitments of the Parties, the discussion was heated and decisions were postponed to the COP7 in Marrakech, October/November 2001. After Marrakech, most of the parties, including Japan, started the process of ratification of the Protocol, aiming for the time of the World Summit for Sustainable Development in Johannesburg in August/September 2002.

In Japan, the Central Environment Council submitted a report to the Prime Minister in January 2002 on the implementation of the Kyoto Protocol by national and local governments as well as those by private sector. The GWPH, responding to the report of the Central Environment Council, also published a report on the prerequisites for the ratification of the Protocol. Still there was much opposition from various sectors against the ratification, particularly from heavy industries which discharged a large amount of CO_2.

In March 2002, GWPH revised the Guideline of Measures to Prevent Global Warming, which was followed by the Amended Law Concerning the Promotion of Measures to Cope with Global Warming[10] submitted by the Ministry of the Environment, based on the Central Environment Council's report. At that point, the Japanese government was still unsure if consensus could be established among domestic actors to ratify the Protocol, despite the huge efforts made. The ratification was realized in June 2002, after intensive discussions at the Diet.

5 CONCLUSION

This chapter has given an overview of the process of preparation for the ratification of the Kyoto Protocol as well as the possible measures to combat global warming in Japan. It will now discuss the effectiveness of different policy instruments for tackling climate change issues. Traditionally, the command and control approach has been widely used to achieve policy goals. Economic incentives are also used as policy instruments. In the climate change policy, some other new approaches have been introduced.

Many people say that the command and control approach may not be appropriate in order to achieve the GHG reduction target because of the nature of the climate change issues. It is necessary to promote innovative energy saving technology by urging industries to improve their energy efficiency standard. However, the innovation of

---

[10] Chikyuondanka Taisaku Suishin Ho, amended in 2002, No. 61.

Table 19.3 Policy Measures to Meet the Kyoto Protocol

Command and Control	Top Runner Method (Cars, Electrical Appliances, Housing) 3R (Reduce, Reuse, Recycle)
Planning:	Energy Saving Plan
Economic Incentives:	Environmental Tax, Subsidies
Voluntary Commitment	ISO 14001
Labeling and Reporting:	Eco-Label, Environmental Report
Capacity Building:	Environmental Education
International Cooperation:	CDM

technologies cannot be realized only through voluntary efforts of the industry. As described in Section 4, the Top Runner Method was introduced in the Amended Law Concerning the Efficient Use of Energies, with a view to raising the energy efficiency standards of products such as automobiles, electrical appliances, and housing materials. The principle of "three Rs" prescribed in the recycling law also had some effect in promoting the production of products in resource saving way. This shows that the command and control approach is still effective as a basis to promote and facilitate advanced technology in the manufacturing sector, which accounts for large CO_2 emissions.

In addition to the conventional "command and control" method, planning is also useful. The Amended Law Concerning the Efficient Use of Energies[7] requires industry to draft an energy saving plan for the factories. Based on the plan, both the central and local governments may provide advice or even financing to promote energy efficiency in the production process.

With regard to the economic incentives, the Japanese government could not reach a consensus on the introduction of the environmental tax. Intensive discussions on this issue are still continuing. The industry sector is unwilling to accept the environmental tax or carbon tax, expressing concerns on possible adverse effects on the economy, which has been sluggish and does not show any upward momentum in the past years. Considering the current recession, many companies claim that they cannot shift the tax to consumers by raising the price of products, which means that the industry would incur the whole burden introduced by the environmental tax. Before the ratification of the Protocol, the Central Environment Council as well as other governmental organizations had serious discussions on this issue but the introduction of the tax was not accepted by the public.

On the other hand, subsidies are still a favored mechanism. The cases of subsidies for purchasing hybrid cars and solar panels are typical examples.

Despite strong opposition from industry, the environmental tax is considered as one of the indispensable measures to achieve the reduction target set out in the Protocol, which is clearly seen in various examples from the countries of Europe. In the Amended Law Concerning the Promotion of Measures to Cope with Global Warming,[10] the phased approach is taken from 2002 to 2004 to make the best use of the existing legal system for the realization of sustainable society. Toward the end of 2004, the Central Environment Council will review and check the emission status to see if emissions are still increasing. If the decrease is not sufficient, another step will be taken from 2005 to 2007, keeping in mind the possibility of introduction of the environmental tax.

With regard to voluntary commitment, which is favored by industry, various approaches are taken by various companies. Most large companies in Japan as well as the Ministry of the Environment acquired the certification of ISO-14001. The number of Japanese entities with this certification is the largest in the world. Eco-labeling and environmental reporting are also popular in Japan, which enables consumers and other stakeholders to evaluate the attitude of the company to reduce the impact of its products and activities on the environment.

Japan also places considerable importance on international cooperation in tackling global warming issues, especially in the policy area. At Johannesburg during WSSD, Prime Minister Koizumi made a statement that Japan will contribute more than 4.5 million Japanese yen[11] for the initiation of capacity building programs internationally, and that international cooperation is one of the important pillars in combating global warming, in the operation of the Kyoto Protocol.

After long discussions, Japan succeeded in preparing laws and measures to cope with global warming issues and was able to ratify the Kyoto Protocol. However, whether Japan will be able to achieve the six percent emission reduction target wholly depends on how effectively these measures will be implemented in the future. Considering the uncertainty of many elements in the issues relating to climate change and the lack of appropriate technology to tackle global warming, evaluation and monitoring are also very important for the better operation of the system, which is to be established in the course of the implementation of measures. To establish a good system of implementation, there is a need to work toward improvement of policy measures based on such evaluation.

[11] Approximately US$82,500 at the exchange rate prevailing on November 11, 2002.

20 Strategy, Policy, and Law Promoting Renewable Energy Resources in China

Wang Xi,* Mao Runlin,** and Maggie Dong***

1 INTRODUCTION

Based on an analysis of both current energy structures and strategies for developing renewable energy resources, this chapter makes a number of suggestions for an appropriate legislative and systems framework for further development of the sector.

Energy resources are essential for social and economic development, as well as for the everyday life of a human being. They are part of the physical basis for human survival and constitute a critical pillar for the development of modern industry. The whole process of human civilization has been witness to the development and usage of energy resources. Per capita measures of energy resources, energy efficiency, and the environmental impacts of energy production and usage are some of the important indicators for assessing a country's level of modernization. Nowadays, the overdevelopment and consequent overuse of energy resources is one of the primary causes of many types of environmental problems. Maintaining a balance between the development and use of energy resources while simultaneously protecting the environment and ecological systems is a global problem. The establishment of a sustainable energy system, crucial for sustainable development, has been identified as a top priority for many countries. Sustainable development refers to development that meets "the needs of present generations without compromising the ability of future generations to meet their own needs." As such, it requires the utilization of natural resources in a sustainable way. Law plays an important role in establishing such a sustainable energy system.

2 THE CONCEPT OF RENEWABLE ENERGY

Renewable energy resources may be defined as "new and renewable energy resources developed by new technology and new material, different from conventional fossil fuel resources as they can be developed continuously, obtained endlessly, can be renewed and supplied after use, produce little or no pollution, and have no harm to the

* Professor, Director, Environmental and Resources Law Institute (ERLI); Associate Dean, School of Law, Shanghai Jiao Tong University, Shanghai, China; Member, Commission on Environmental Law, IUCN – The World Conservation Union;

** LLM (Environmental Law) Candidate, School of Law, Wuhan University, China.

*** Ph.D. (Environmental Law) Candidate, School of Law, Shanghai Jiao Tong University, China.

environment."[1] Renewable energies can be classified into the following types of energy: solar; wind; biomass; geothermal; and marine.

Notwithstanding this clear definition, certain differences between countries are evident in the detail of such definitions. For instance, many countries, including China, define hydraulic power as a conventional energy source, rather than a renewable source. The State Planning Commission of China classified small-scale hydroelectric stations, with a capacity lower than 25,000 kW, as a source of renewable energy in its Tenth Five-Year Plan on Renewable Energy Development. China defines all other hydroelectric stations as conventional energy resources. Note however, that China's Agenda 21[2] explicitly includes hydroelectric energy within the definition of renewable energy resources. It provides that "renewable energies, including water energy, biomass energy, solar energy, wind energy, geothermal energy and marine energy, which can be supplied and renewed after use and produce little or no pollution, will be the base of the energy structure in future."[3] Countries such as Denmark, Italy, and the UK do not consider hydraulic power as a renewable energy resource. However, the United States and Canada do define hydraulic power as a source of renewable energy.

3 ENERGY RESOURCES: THE STATUS QUO IN CHINA

3.1 Exhaustible (Nonrenewable) Energy Resources: The Status Quo

Exhaustible, or nonrenewable energy, resources include fossil fuels like coal, oil, and natural gas. China is rich in a diverse range of energy resources including vast reserves of conventional energy resources. Coal is the major conventional energy resource in China with reserves totaling 5,059.2 billion tonnes, of which 2,600 billion tonnes are located more than 1000 meters underground.[4] Up to the end of 2000, discovered coal reserves reached 1,007.7 billion tones, making China the world's third largest known source of coal.[5] Total oil reserves are estimated at 100 billion tonnes, of which 16 billion tonnes have already been discovered, making China the world's sixth largest discovered source of oil.[6] China has natural gas reserves of 38,140 billion stere, of which 2,060 billion stere have been discovered, making this the sixteenth largest discovered natural gas reserve in the world.[7] China also has vast uranium reserves.

Coal is the major pillar in China's current energy structure. China is the largest coal producing and coal consuming country in the world and one of only a few countries that have coal as their sole primary domestic energy resource. In 1993, coal output totaled 11,497,000 tonnes, a share of 72.8 percent of China's total energy consumption.[8] Coal provided seventy-five percent of overall industrial fuel and power and 80 percent of residential energy.[9] Such heavy consumption of coal has caused serious air pollution

---

[1] *See* Yan Changle (ed.), *Report on Energy Development of China*, Economic Management Press (Beijing, 1994) at 207.

[2] China's Agenda 21, Chapter 13.   [3] *Id.*

[4] Editorial Committee of Chinese Report on Energy Development, *Chinese Report on Energy Development*, Chinese Computation Press (2001) at 35.

[5] *Id.*   [6] *Id.*

[7] *Id.*, at 39.

[8] *Encyclopedia of Energy*, Chinese Encyclopedia Publishing House (Beijing, 1997) at 7.

[9] *Id.*

in Chinese cities. For example, in 1993, pollution levels of 179,500 tonnes of sulphur dioxide (ninety percent from coal consumption) and 141,600 tonnes of soot (seventy percent from coal consumption) were recorded.[10] Moreover, as the geographical distribution of coal resources can barely meet productivity requirements, "north-to-south" and "west-to-east" coal divisions have developed.

It is most likely that increasing demand for energy services in China in the following decades will be met mainly through coal fired power generation. Accordingly, much greater pressure will be placed on both the environment and transportation services as a result of the increasing production and usage of coal.

3.2 Renewable Energy Resources: The Status Quo

The future of renewable energy is optimistic since, unlike fossil fuel energy, renewable energy sources can be continually developed. China's hydroelectric power capacity totals 378 million kW, of which only eleven percent has been developed. Biomass energy in the form of crop stalks, firewood, and organic garbage of all kinds, has a capacity which is equal to 260 million tonnes of standard coal. Other types of renewable energy available in China include: more than 0.6 million joules per sq cm per year of solar energy; 1.6 billion kWs of wind power capacity; geothermal reserves equivalent to 462.6 billion tonnes of standard coal, of which only 0.001 percent has been used. Marine energy resources are also abundant, for example, more than 20 million kW of the tidal energy is available for productive use.[11]

There has been considerable development in the renewable energy sector in China over the past twenty years and it has become an indispensable part of China's current energy system. Renewable energy resources, primarily biomass energy that has not yet been commoditized, provide energy that is equivalent to that produced by more than 300 million tonnes of standard coal. They have played an important role in promoting China's national economy and meeting the demand for energy services in rural areas.

The development and operation of small hydroelectric power schemes has been a great success. More than 60,000 such schemes had been implemented by the end of 1993, providing electricity for ninety-seven percent of townships, ninety-two percent of villages, and eighty-seven percent of rural families across China.[12] As an effective source of energy in rural areas, small hydroelectric power schemes have made a significant contribution to electrification in rural areas. To date, primary electrification has been achieved in 109 rural counties and a further 200 counties have embarked on electrification processes.[13]

Significant progress has also been made in the establishment of plantation forests for firewood. During the thirteen years following the implementation of the "Sixth Five-Year Plan,"[14] plantation forests expanded in extent from 4.72 million hectares to 5.4 million hectares.[15] The development of plantation forests has played an important

---

[10] *Id.*
[11] China New Energy Net, Outline for New and Renewable Energy Development in China (1996–2010), available at www.newenergy.org.cn.
[12] *Id.*   [13] *Id.*
[14] The Sixth Five-Year Plan for Economic and Social Development of China (1981–1985).
[15] *Supra* note 11.

role in providing energy to local communities and in protecting natural forests, vegetation, and the environment.

Significant progress has also been made in biomass technologies. Approximately fifty percent of Chinese farmers are using the efficient coal saving stove, which can reduce fuel consumption by approximately thirty-three to fifty percent.[16] The use of biogas to meet the basic energy needs of families has reached a stage of stable development. China's 5.25 million biogas ponds produce more than 1.2 billion stere of gas per year. Large and medium biogas programs have developed rapidly. There are more than 600 such programs, each with a capacity of over 100 stere and 84,000 families can now enjoy centralized gas supply.[17] The integrated application of biogas with bio-agriculture has led to increasing levels of sustainable development in rural areas in recent years. In order to improve biomass technology and increase its efficiency, research and development of new technologies, such as technologies that transform garbage into gas and liquefied fuel, have been initiated and relevant demonstration projects have been established.

The application of solar energy technology has entered a new stage. Chinese technologies for solar water heaters, solar stoves, passive greenhouses, and solar dryers have become mature and are used all over China. According to incomplete 1993 statistics, China's achievements in relation to the development of solar technologies were already significant: For instance, at that time, 2.3 million sqm of solar water heaters had been installed, 1.8 million sqm of passive greenhouses were installed, 342,000 hectares of solar greenhouses for crops were installed, and 140,000 solar stoves and 132,000 solar dryers were in use. These developments have continued. The application of solar technologies has an obvious effect on energy conservation. For instance, Chinese solar water heaters can save approximately 100–150kg per sqm of standard coal annually. Passive solar greenhouses can save approximately 20–40kg per sqm of standard coal per year during their operation and each solar dryer can save approximately 500–700kg of firewood per year.[18]

China accelerated the development of photovoltaic technology in 1982. The seven production lines for solar batteries introduced, from the United States and Canada during 1983 to 1987, increased the production capacity of photovoltaic cells from 200 kW per year in 1984 to 4.5 MW in 1988. Solar batteries, with sales of 1.1 mW per year, have been used mainly in communication systems and remote areas that do not have access to conventional electricity services. Solar batteries have played, and will continue to play, an important role in the supply of electricity as there are still twenty-eight counties, thousands of villages, and islands that lack conventional electricity services. Of the nine counties in Tibet that have no hydroelectric power or electricity, two have established solar power plants with capacities of 10 kW and 20 kW respectively, while similar plants in the remaining seven counties are under construction. In relation to research concerning solar batteries, monocrystalline silicon batteries increased energy efficiency by up to twelve to thirteen percent, polycrystalline silicon batteries increased efficiency by up to nine to ten percent, and other kinds of batteries increased efficiency by up to five to six percent.[19]

---

[16] *Id.*

[18] *Id.*

[17] *Id.*

[19] *Id.*

Wind energy continues to develop. The total capacity of wind power generators in China has reached 26,000 kW. Mini-wind power generators, each with a capacity of 50–200 W, have been developed and become operational since the 1980s. The number of these mini-generators totals more than 120,000. They help to solve the energy problems of fishermen and herders in rural and coastal areas that have no electricity network like the areas of Neimeng, Xinjiang, and Qinghai. Small and medium-sized wind power generators, each with a capacity of 1–20 kW have commenced their first stage of production while medium to large generators, each with a capacity of 50–200 kW are still being researched. Commercial demonstrations of large-scale local wind-powered generators have just begun. There are fourteen medium- to large-sized wind farms currently under construction. China has also successfully developed wind powered water pumps. National surveys concerning the performance of technologies like wind power have improved. These include the synthesized usage of wind energy, foreign technology as well as experimentation in, and the operation of, wind-powered electricity fields.[20]

Development of other renewable energies has also been successful. Current usage of geothermal resources is the equivalent of four million tonnes of standard coal. The Yangbajing geothermal power station in Tibet, which is the largest such power station in China, has a capacity of 25,000 kW and provides ninety-seven million kW of electricity per year, which amounts to fifty percent of the capacity of the electricity network in Lhasa. As to the development and usage of marine energy, current tide-driven power stations have a total capacity of 5,930 kW, providing 10.21 million kW of electricity per year, while experimentation continues in relation to wave-driven power stations.[21]

Notwithstanding the rapid development of renewable energies in China, renewable energy technologies are still in the initial stages of their development and the level of development of such technologies has fallen below levels in developed countries. The underdevelopment of technology is linked to the fact that China is a developing country. The relatively high costs of such technologies, the lack of an inspiring policy framework, and the existence of only small-scale markets for such technologies all operate as significant obstacles to the sustainable development of renewable energy technologies.

3.3 Problems with the Current Energy Structure

For historical reasons, the Chinese government's overall energy strategy is deeply influenced by the abundant availability of coal. Coal fired power generation accounts for approximately seventy-five percent of all energy consumption in China.[22] Development and consumption of natural gases and renewable energies, by comparison, is still very low, given the projected growth in total energy consumption across China. Clearly, the current energy structure, with its overdependence on coal, is in need of reform. A lack of efficiency in the use of fossil fuels, such as coal, results in the rapid exhaustion of such resources and constitutes an unsustainable form of energy consumption. The current unsustainable energy structure in China makes it very likely that coal resources will be quickly exhausted. China has an extremely large population and, when measured on a per capita basis in comparison with other countries, China does not have significant

---

[20] *Id.* [21] *Id.*
[22] The Energy Consumption in China, available at http://www.chinaenvironment.com.

energy resources. Accordingly, if China is to achieve a level of development and prosperity comparable to that in developed nations, energy efficiency levels in China need to be higher than in developed countries. Energy efficiency in China reached 34.3 percent in 1995. In the early 1980s, energy efficiency levels in China equaled levels in OECD countries.[23]

Further, the geographical distribution of energy resources in China is uneven. On a per capita basis, China's major mineral reserves, excluding coal, and its oil reserves, are approximately half of the global average.[24] Approximately 60.8 percent of discovered coal reserves are located in the north of China and seventy percent of hydroelectric power production is located in southwest China, a considerable distance away from points of consumption.[25] In South China, the eight provinces and one city, which have more developed economies, more centralized industries, and where approximately thirty-seven percent of the Chinese population lives, have only a very small share of China's energy resources.[26]

Moreover, the current energy structure in China, which focuses on coal, is a significant contributor to air pollution problems. The total amount of soot released in 1997 reached 18.73 million tonnes, of which seventy percent was emitted from coal-fired power stations. According to monitors in eighty-seven cities in China, the TSP (Total Suspending Particulars) reaches 32–741 micrograms per stere per day every year and averages 291 micrograms per stere nationally, which is higher than the second class of national air quality standards (the second class of the standards is set at the level of 200 microgram per stere).[27] Moreover, in some Chinese cities, the TSP is three to seven times higher than the recommended standard of the World Health Organization (WHO).[28] Soot pollution is so serious in some cities that these cities are invisible in satellite photographs.[29]

The national total of sulphur dioxide emissions in 1997 reached 23.46 million tonnes, making China the world's leading emitter of sulphur dioxide. The concentration of sulphur dioxide in Chinese cities is two to eight times higher than the recommended standard of the WHO. Moreover, acid rain levels caused by sulphur dioxide emissions have increased and acid rain now affects approximately forty percent of China.[30]

Carbon dioxide emissions caused by energy consumption account for approximately eighty percent of total greenhouse gas emissions in China and this figure is set to increase as overall energy consumption increases in China. According to calculations by the International Energy Agency (IEA), global emissions of carbon dioxide in 1995 totalled 22 billion tones, while in China that year they were 3 billion tonnes, accounting for 13.6 percent of the global figure. China was second only to the United States, which contributed 5.229 billion tonnes and accounted for 23.7 percent of global emissions.[31]

It is clear that the current Chinese energy structure, which relies heavily on coal, will worsen regional environmental pollution in China, put more pressure on the global

---

[23] Project team of Macroeconomists of the State Planning Commission, "Research Report on Nuclear Driven Electricity's Status in the Chinese Energy Structure," *Macroeconomic Studies*, Issue 7 (1999).

[24] *Supra* note 11, at 8.   [25] *Id.*

[26] China New Energy Net, Energy Consumption in China, available at http://www.chinaevironment.com.

[27] *Supra* note 23, at 41.

[28] The WHO standard for Annual Maximum Concentration of SO_2 is 60 microgram per stere.

[29] *Supra* note 23, at 41–5.   [30] *Id.*

[31] *Id.*

environment, increase China's international environmental responsibilities, and generate new problems in relation to economic development and foreign trade.

China's particular circumstances and energy needs make it imperative for China, as a developing country, to rapidly reform its energy sector and to develop new energy resources. This would be consistent with international trends.

4 THE IMPORTANCE OF DEVELOPING RENEWABLE ENERGIES

Today, the conflict between energy production and protection of the environment is intensifying, which compels all countries to search for means of resolving this conflict. Developing renewable energy resources is one important solution. The renewable energy sector is currently enjoying rapid development demonstrating its potential to be the dominant source of energy in the twenty-first century. Renewable energy resources create little or no environmental pollution. They currently provide much needed supplementary energy and will constitute the basis of future energy sectors. The development of renewable energy resources is highly significant in the context of implementing sustainable development strategies and relieving global environmental pressures.

The development of renewable energy resources can enhance the energy sector and promote sustainable development. Sustainable development is one of China's basic national policies and should be grounded in the rational exploitation of natural resources, including energy resources. Accordingly, China must develop its energy framework in a way that results in a greater contribution of clean energies to China's overall energy consumption, thereby enabling sustainable economic and social development in China. Zero or low emission technologies are the basis for sustainable energy systems in the future. For this reason, the development of high quality renewable energies that are compatible with local conditions is of great importance for the harmonious development of Chinese society, China's economy, and the environment.

As a developing country, China places significant emphasis on environmental protection and has decided not to follow the historically disastrous road of "polluting first, improving later." The Chinese government has made environmental protection a basic national policy. The Chinese Premier Li Peng signed the UN Framework Convention on Climate Change[32] (UNFCCC) on China's behalf at the Rio Conference.[33] In 1994, the Chinese government published China's Agenda 21, which proposed a specific scheme for the sustainable development of China's society, economy, and environment in the twenty-first century. The development of renewable energy resources is one important part of China's Agenda 21.

5 CHINESE STRATEGY FOR DEVELOPING RENEWABLE ENERGIES

5.1 Strategic Objectives for the Development of Renewable Energies

The Chinese government has paid close attention to the development of renewable energy resources since 1992. Shortly after the Rio Conference, the State Council issued a document entitled "Ten Countermeasures on the Environment and Development,"

---

[32] (May 9, 1992), available at http://www.unfccc.int/resource/docs/convkp/conveng.pdf.
[33] Available at http://www.un.org/geninfo/bp/enviro.html.

which explicitly calls for the development and promotion of clean energies, such as solar, wind, geothermal, tidal, and biomass. The Energy Conservation Law of PRC (1998)[34] clearly provides that the "development of renewable energy is encouraged."[35] Moreover, the Outline for Developing New and Renewable Energy in 1996–2010,[36] issued by the State Planning Commission, State Science Commission, and State Economic Commission further provides that both the development of renewable energy technologies and the process of industrializaton need to be speeded up. China has designed long-term and short-term development objectives for new and renewable energy resources in China's Agenda 21 and the Tenth Five-Year Plan. Targets have also been set for social and economic development by 2010.

Long-Term Objectives

China's Agenda 21 provides that the overall objective is: "to establish and implement a policy and legal framework that is suitable for a market economy; to develop and promote advanced and environmentally harmless technology for the production and consumption of energy; to improve energy efficiency; to use resources rationally; to reduce environmental pollution; to achieve sustainable development of the energy industry and to meet the development requirements of society and the economy by enhancing integrated planning and administration of the energy sector."[37] China's Agenda 21 also requires: the development of renewable energy resources as a priority of China's energy strategy; increased investment in the energy sector; participation by local government and energy users through appropriate financial encouragement and market measures; a reduction in electricity production costs; and an increased share of renewable energy resources in the energy mix."[38]

Short-Term Objectives

The energy objective of the Tenth Five-Year Plan is to achieve significant progress in the adjustment of the energy structure away from conventional energy resources toward renewable energies; to further improve energy efficiency; to establish a competitive energy sector, equipment production, construction and operation; and to achieve progress in the development of energy services in the middle and west of China on condition that total energy capacity and consumption meet the requirements of national economic and social development goals.[39]

To promote the development of renewable energy resources, China developed the Tenth Five-Year Plan for Industrial Development of New and Renewable Energy. The plan provides that "with the market as a guide, enterprises should provide technical support to: cultivate and regulate energy markets; standardize products; localize technology; and promote new and renewable energy industries."[40] The Plan's specific

---

[34] The Law of the People's Republic of China on Energy Conservation (1998).

[35] *Id.*, Art. 4.

[36] China New Energy Net, Outline for New and Renewable Energy Development in China (1996–2010), available at http://www.newenergy.org.cn.

[37] Agenda 21, § 13.3.   [38] *Id.*

[39] Song Chaoyi, Official in Basic Industry Department of State Development and Planning Commission, "A Brief Introduction to the Tenth Five-Year Plan for Energy," Workshop for New Technology for Energy Conservation and New Energy of China and Germany 2001, China New Energy Net, available at http://www.crein.org.cn.

[40] Tenth Five-Year Plan for New and Renewable Energy Industry, National Economy, Trade and Resources, 2001, Issue 1020, Art. 3(1).

targets include the development of new and renewable energies (excluding small-scale hydraulic power and traditional usage of biomass energy) to the level where they are equivalent to 13 million tonnes of standard coal per year by 2005. This in turn will reduce greenhouse gases equivalent to approximately 10 million tonnes of carbon and 600,000 tonnes of sulphur dioxide and dusts. It would also provide electricity services to 1.3 million families (noting that, approximately five to six million people live in rural areas and that such services would create employment opportunities for approximately 200,000 people). The Plan also provides that by 2005, the annual production capability of solar water heaters is to reach 11 million sqm, and the total amount is to reach 64 million sqm; the annual production capacity of photovoltaic cells is to reach 15 gigawatts and a photovoltaic industry is to be established; the capacity of wind power generators is to reach 1.2 million kW and essentially meet domestic demand; total geothermal heating area is to reach 200 million sqm; and a supply capacity of 2 billion cubic meters of biogas must be established.[41] The "Long Term Target for Energy Development in 2010" contains similar provisions to the Tenth Five-Year Plan.

The development of renewable energy resources will continue to implement the so-called "Chengfeng Plan" (Wind Riding Plan), which requires the acceleration of development in localized wind powered equipment; the acceleration of the "Bright Project," which aims to provide electricity to people in areas which currently lack them; and the improvement of integrated energy infrastructure in rural areas. In general, the objective is to implement policies first, which favor the development of renewable energy resources; second, regulate competition in the market; third, promote the localized use of renewable energy resources; fourth, increase the share of renewable energies in the overall energy system; improve the energy structure in China and contribute to environmental protection.[42]

6 LEGISLATION AND THE ENERGY SYSTEM

The development and use of renewable energies has a short history in China given the government's historical commitment to fossil fuel technologies. Renewable energies were not deployed or used in rural areas until the 1970s. Despite the significant progress which has been achieved in the past twenty to thirty years, there is still no specific legislation, as opposed to policies, governing renewable energies. The Chinese government began to implement national legislation governing the development of energy resources in rural areas in the 1980s. Certain administrative documents have been adopted since then, such as the The Outline for New and Renewable Energy Development in China (1996–2010).[43] Those administrative normative documents have established a basic framework for the development of renewable energy resources. They provide valuable experience in developing regulatory frameworks for renewable energies in the future.

---

[41] *Id.*, Art. 3(2).
[42] Speech of Mr. Song Caoyi, Offical of Infrastructure Development Department, State Commission on Development and Planning, delivered at the Sino German Energy Conservation and New Energy Technology Symposium, available at http://www.crein.org.cn.
[43] *Supra* note 11.

6.1 Governmental Institutional Arrangements

All departments of the State Council have their own specific responsibilities in connection with the overall development of energy resources in rural areas. The State Development and Reform Commission (together with its predecessor, the State Planning Committee) is responsible for planning, design, and correspondence between departments. The former Energy Ministry (now part of the State Development and Planning Commission) is responsible for energy production and industrial management. The Ministry of Water Resources is responsible for the development of small-scale hydraulic power schemes. The Forest Administration is responsible for the development of plantation forests for firewood. The Ministry of Agriculture is responsible for the development of noncommercial energy resources, such as firewood and biogas pools. Finally, local governments at all levels also have relevant responsibilities.

6.2 Planning and Design for Renewable Energy Development

Energy development in rural areas has been incorporated into plans for national economic and social development at all governmental levels. Relevant industrial and regional plans for the development and promotion of renewable energy resources have been made and implemented, such as plans for promoting firewood saving stoves, biogas stoves, biomass energy, hydraulic power, solar energy, wind energy, geothermal energy, and marine energy.

6.3 Financing of Renewable Energy Development

The development and implementation of renewable energy projects in rural areas is encouraged in China. Special loans for rural energy development, with interest rates set by the State Economic and Trade Commission, are available for all renewable energy resources development projects in rural areas. These loans, introduced in 1987, have supported more than 500 renewable energy projects and have greatly promoted the industrialization and commercialization of renewable energy.[44]

China's national investment policy gives priority to self-financing projects by collectives or individuals, while providing for supplementary government funding. On both national and local levels, rural energy resources development is earmarked in government budgets every year. As of 1990, government financing totaled 33 million yuan. In 1991, the Chinese national government added another 5 million yuan per year to this investment.[45] The State also provides special funds for research projects in relation to renewable energy resources.

Finally, the Chinese government also provides tax reductions and exemptions for renewable energy resources projects, such as biogas pool projects.

6.4 Renewable Energy Technologies and Infrastructure

The Chinese government supervises the development of renewable energies and renewable energy infrastructure through establishing technology standards for energy

---

[44] China Energy Net, The Existing Incentive Policies, available at http://www.newenergy.org.cn.
[45] Xiao Qiangang and Xiao Guoxing, *Energy Law*, Law Press (1996) at 215.

resources projects. For instance, the National Standard for Checking the Quality of Water Pressure Driven Biogas Pools in Rural Areas[46] has been applied to monitor the construction of energy projects in rural areas.

The government is responsible for promoting and demonstrating renewable energy technologies particularly in relation to the development of small-scale hydraulic power schemes and plantation forests. Governments at all levels actively promote the development of wind energy, solar energy, geothermal energy, marine energy, and biomass energy crops.

7 THE NEED FOR LEGISLATIVE REFORM

7.1 The Need for a Legal Framework Governing the Development of Renewable Energies

The law provides the basis for administering China's energy resources. Accordingly, serious consideration must be given to the need for, and feasibility of, legislation governing the development of energy resources in China. Generally speaking, legislative imperatives include: the need for an integrated system; consideration of the impact of foreign or international law; political frameworks; as well as public sentiment.[47] Finally the overall need for economic, social, and cultural development must be considered. All of the above reasons combine to make specific energy legislation in China a necessity.

The Need for Specific Legislation Regulating the Administration of Renewable Energy Resources

The development and use of renewable energy in China relies largely on the Chinese government, which is principal decision maker for all relevant activities. First, the government is the designer of the energy sector. The government holds powers of resource distribution, regulatory powers, and overall authority in relation to energy projects. The government also controls the scope and significance of development activities. However, current processes of governmental decision making are technically and democratically deficient and need to be improved. In the area of renewable energy resources, some local governments have not realized fully the strategic significance of such resources and have not prioritized their development as part of the government's agenda.

A legislative framework that regulates the administration of energy resources and energy projects is the preferred solution. Legislation specifically governing renewable energy resources can regulate the process of governmental decision making to make it more democratic, technically sound, and rational.

Second, the government is the primary investor in the development of renewable energy resources. It provides direct investment, the provision of loans with low interest rates, and preferential tax treatment. However, current levels of government investment in renewable resources are clearly not sufficient. For instance, Chinese government

---

[46] National Standard for Checking the Quality of Water Pressed Biogas Pool in Rural Areas (GB/T4751–2002).

[47] Ye Junrong, *Environmental Policy and Law*, China University of Political Science and Law Press (2003) at 99–102.

investment in this regard is less than that of India. Low government financial support results in poor infrastructure, slow development, low levels of industrialization and low levels of commercialization of renewable energy technologies. In order to change this situation, traditional models of government administration must be reformed. This is necessary in order to: provide for incentives based regulation through a legal framework; to ensure open financing channels for such development and the realization of government investment; to accelerate the market entry of renewable energy technologies and products; to improve the competitiveness of renewable energy technologies; to establish market share for these technologies; and, finally, to achieve favorable cycles of development.

Third, although the government is responsible for the overall supervision of the development of renewable energy resources, there is no single department providing an integrated approach to the development of renewable energy resources in China. Relevant functions are distributed between various government departments, such as the State Development and Reform Commission, the State Economic and Trade Commission (now part of the Ministry of Commerce), the Ministry of Agriculture, the Ministry of Water Resources, and the Forestry Administration. The lack of uniform administration has resulted in significant overlaps and duplication in the development of the energy sector and has also weakened overall control of such development by the government at a macro level. This has led to weakness and inefficiency in the administration of the energy sector. Not much can be done to change this outcome unless China establishes a department responsible for the overall and uniform management of renewable energy resources. An integrated administrative system should define the responsibility and authority of each relevant institution. Legislation providing participatory processes for interested parties, such as enterprises and the general public, will also have to be developed.

It is clear, then, that renewable energy legislation is needed to overcome current problems with government decision making, the lack of investment in the energy sector, and administrative confusion.

The Need for a Legislative Framework to Promote Investment in, and the Development of, Renewable Energy Technologies

As a developing country, China faces twin pressures of increasing economic growth and ensuring environmental protection. Changing current methods of energy production and consumption in China, and developing renewable, clean energy resources is the only way for China to achieve continuous economic growth without destroying its environment. As the technical and infrastructure risks associated with renewable energy development are considerable, high levels of investment are required. Currently, mechanisms for entry into the renewable energy technology market have not been developed and projected returns for such investments are low. So private investors demonstrate little enthusiasm for participation and investment in the development of renewable energy resources in China.

At the same time, in many other countries laws and regulations are being drafted and implemented to promote investment in this area. The market share of renewable energy products has grown. It is obvious that many countries have agreed upon, and increased their efforts to, encourage and promote investment in, and development and innovation of, renewable energy resources.

Legal reform seems to be the best option for promoting the development of renewable energy resources. Guided by the law, financial investment vehicles and institutions can encourage the direction of capital and labor to areas of technical innovation, like renewable energy resources. The law can provide measures to regulate markets for renewable energy resources and so create a more favorable legal environment for investment in renewable energy technologies.

Legislation Is an Efficient Way of Restricting the Use of Fossil Fuels in China's Energy Sector

The essential deficiency in China's energy sector is its current overreliance on fossil fuels, such as coal. Together with a lack of efficiency in the utilization of energy and the rapid depletion of exhaustible resources, the current energy sector has a significantly detrimental impact on the environment. In order to overcome these problems, an adjustment away from conventional energy resources toward renewable energies is required. Restrictions on the use of fossil fuels can be achieved through various legal mechanisms.

Legislation Is Required for the Pursuit of Sustainable Development

Sustainable development policies can assist countries to resolve the conflicts between energy needs, environmental problems, and economic underdevelopment. China has already identified sustainable development as its future development strategy. Renewable energy resources are perfectly aligned with the concept of sustainable development, making them the inevitable choice for sustainable energy systems.

Unfortunately, at present, China's policies on energy resources and environmental protection are not properly integrated. Legislation governing renewable energy resources could play an important role in solving these problems, Such legislation can improve the current legal framework governing the energy sector while complementing the existing legal framework for environment protection. In this way, specific legislation governing renewable energy resources will almost inevitably facilitate the attainment of sustainable development.

7.2 The Feasibility of Implementing a Specific Legislative Framework

Karl Marx said that law reflects social and economic relationships. Roscoe Pound believed that the value of law is realized in its balancing of various, possibly competing, societal interests. Whether legislation is valuable or not depends not only on whether it reflects all relevant interests, but also on whether its implementation can integrate and balance the conflicts between them. Accordingly, legislation must be reasonable, feasible, and practicable in order to ensure that the relevant legislative objectives can be incorporated within the existing legal system and realized in practice.

Existing Regulations and Policies Provide a Strong Basis for the Proposed Legislative Framework

While no well-developed legislation in relation to renewable energies currently exists, the Chinese government has gained valuable experience in the administration of renewable energy resources development. The government promulgated a number of administrative regulations such as the Outline for New and Renewable Energy Development in

China (1996–2010)[48] and relevant technical regulations such as the National Standard for Checking Water Pressure Biogas Pools in Rural Areas.[49] The government has also proposed guidelines for the development of renewable energy resources which "adjust measures for local conditions, provide for measures which are complementary as between different sources of energy, provide for integrated usage and place emphasis on efficiency" and "focus on both energy resources development and energy conservation."[50] The Chinese government adopted special systems governing public investment in energy resources development, preferential tax treatment, and the provision of low interest loans in order to encourage the development of renewable energy resources. In reality, most of these policies and regulations have proven to be appropriate and practicable. Accordingly, they can be translated into binding law through legislative enactment of their provisions.

International Best Practice Is a Useful Guide

Legislative history in recent decades in China demonstrates that reviewing international best practice can be an effective means of improving Chinese legislation. Compared with the short history of administration and legislation in relation to renewable energy resources in China, some countries have had a long history of government involvement in this area and demonstrate remarkable achievements. This can act as a valuable guide for China.

The German government, for example, has enacted the Renewable Energy Sources Act 2000 (RESA) to facilitate the sustainable development of energy supply.[51] RESA deals with the purchase of, and the compensation to be paid for, electricity generated exclusively from various renewable energy sources by utility companies that operate grids for public power supply (grid operators).[52] The different compensation rates[53] to be paid to the generators of different types of renewable energy, specified in RESA, have been determined by means of scientific studies.[54] The purpose of this pricing regime is to bring renewable energy sources closer to conventional energy sources in terms of their competitiveness. The compensation rates will decline over time and remain in effect for a limited period of time. The fact that the rates will be reviewed every two years guarantees that they will be updated continuously and at short intervals to reflect market and cost trends.[55] The costs associated with connecting the electricity derived from renewable energy sources to the technically and economically most suitable grid connecting point is borne by the renewable energy generators.[56] Transmission grid operators are required to record any differences in the amount of energy purchased and compensation payments and to equalize such differences amongst themselves.[57]

Japan adopted the Law of New Energy in 1997.[58] Denmark, The Netherlands, and the UK have also achieved similar progress in relation to implementing legislation for

---

[48] *Supra* note 11.
[49] *Supra* note 46.
[50] *Dictionary of Agriculture*, Agriculture Press, Beijing (2003) at 1176.
[51] *Renewable Energy Sources Act 2000* § 1.
[52] *Id.*, § 2
[53] *Id.*, §§ 5–9.
[54] *Id., see* Explanatory Memorandum.
[55] *Id.*
[56] *Id.*, § 10(1).
[57] *Id.*, § 11(1).
[58] Guangzhou Industrial Information Net, "Inspiration from Foreign Policy on Renewable Energy," available at http://www.gzii.gove.cn.

renewable energy resources.[59] Legislative developments in all these countries demonstrate that renewable energy legislation is needed to underpin governmental financial support, market mechanisms, government regulation, and institutional arrangements.

Such international experience is meaningful for China and should be absorbed and used as a valuable reference for the development of similar Chinese legislation. The following elements of foreign legislation which are particularly useful in the context of China are:

- the inclusion of the development of renewable energy resources in long-term development planning;
- the examination of the status and capacity of enterprises and individuals devoting themselves to renewable energy;
- the encouragement of participation by foreign investors;
- the improvement of development and research on renewable energy; and
- the promotion of the combination of new technology and traditional industry.

It is of particular significance for the design of renewable energy systems that proven international experience is properly reflected in Chinese legislation. In this way, Chinese legislation in this area may reflect legislation in leading countries.

Adjustment of China's Development and Energy Strategy Provides a Good Opportunity for Legislation

The strategy of sustainable development was confirmed by the Chinese government in the 1990s. Significant adjustments in the details of China's development strategy have taken place since then. Most importantly, the Chinese strategy for energy development has been adjusted along with the national development strategy. For example, China's Agenda 21 and the Tenth Five-Year Plan for New Energy require improvements in China's energy sector, increases in energy efficiency and the market share of renewable energies, and also the achievement of sustainable development in the energy industry. The adjustment of the national energy development strategy provides a good opportunity for the implementation of legislation governing renewable energy resources. Such legislation will close the current gap in this area and help to satisfy the demands of sustainable development.

8 RECOMMENDATIONS REGARDING THE LEGAL FRAMEWORK FOR PROMOTING RENEWABLE ENERGY RESOURCES

Having established the need for, and feasibility of, the implementation of such legislation, the specific formulation of a Law on Renewable Energy Resources still requires consideration. On its own, such a law will do little to realize the overall objective of the sustainable development of energy resources in China. Additional regulations, rules, and systems will be necessary to establish a complete legal framework governing renewable energy resources. In this sense, the establishment and improvement of the relevant legal system is as important as the recognition of the significance of such a law. This section suggests that the relevant legal framework should focus on the following issues.

---

[59] *Id.*

8.1 Adopting a Law on Promoting Renewable Energy Resources

The establishment of a Law on Promoting Renewable Energy Resources is a precondition for an effective legal framework in the area of renewable energy resources. Administrative documents alone, as currently exist, cannot adequately promote the development of renewable energy resources in China. They tend to be temporal and fragmentary in nature, causing administrative chaos in the management of renewable energy resources. The new Law on Promoting Renewable Energy Resources will serve as the backbone of a comprehensive legal framework for the development of renewable energy resources. All administrative regulations and rules should be compatible with this law. This law should enjoy a leading and guiding status in the Chinese energy sector.

8.2 Adopting Implementing Administrative Regulations and Rules

First, relevant ministries and departments of the State Council, as well as local governments, will need to adopt administrative regulations and rules for implementing the Law on Renewable Energy Resources. Second, relevant technical standards in relation to renewable energy resources must be adopted in law as compulsory standards. Third, all engineering projects for renewable energy resources will need to be regulated under the Law on Promoting Renewable Energy Resources. In this way, the Law on Promoting Renewable Energy Resources will help to bring about a uniform legal environment for the management of renewable energy resources and provide a healthy and orderly investment environment for the development of renewable energy resources.

8.3 Relevant Laws and Regulations Should Be Amended According to the Law on Promoting Renewable Energy Resources

Ministries and local governments have already adopted some regulations on the basis of the authority vested in them under existing laws. These existing regulations will need to be reviewed and amended according to the provisions of the Law on Promoting Renewable Energy Resources. Such laws and regulations that may require amendment include intellectual property and tax laws. Intellectual property laws, especially patent laws, should enhance the protection of technical innovations in renewable energy technologies to encourage their development and promotion. Tax laws should provide for favorable tax treatment in order to stimulate the enthusiasm and creativity of enterprises and individuals in the context of the renewable energy industry. Also, existing technical standards for renewable energy resources will need to be amended so that they are consistent with the Law on Promoting Renewable Energy Resources.

9 DESIGN OF THE LAW ON PROMOTING RENEWABLE ENERGY RESOURCES

This chapter has suggested the adoption of a Law on Promoting Renewable Energy Resources. It now sets out the purpose of, and the principles for, guiding the development of renewable energy resources, as well as the essential regulatory framework. It is hoped that this proposal will be helpful for the legislative activities of the National People's Congress.

9.1 Purpose of the Law

Identifying the purpose of relevant legislation is the first step. The stated purpose of legislation can specify the social relationships that are to be adjusted by the law, the interests to be balanced, the values or objectives to be achieved, and the status such legislation is intended to enjoy in the legal system. The purpose of law is not only to guide legislative activities but also to provide a norm for the future implementation of, and compliance with, relevant legislation.

The purpose of the Law on Promoting Renewable Energy Resources should be defined as "the regulation of government administration with respect to investment and innovation in, as well as the development and use of, renewable energy resources, the promotion of the renewable energy industry, the sustainable utilization of energy resources, and environmental protection." The proposed law is designed to improve government regulation of the energy sector. The Law on Promoting Renewable Energy Resources should define the responsibilities of each government department and clarify and coordinate various administrative responsibilities related to the development of renewable energy resources. The Law on Promoting Renewable Energy Resources should strictly regulate and harmonize the relationship between government and nongovernment entities. Finally, the law should provide rules for regulating all aspects of the development and use of renewable energy resources. In this way, the Law on Promoting Renewable Energy Resources will serve as a framework law for the systematic development of the entire body of law governing renewable energy resources in China. The ultimate goal of the Law on Promoting Renewable Energy Resources is to achieve the sustainable utilization of energy resources and environmental protection.

9.2 Guiding Principles Recognized by the Law for the Development of Renewable Energy Resources

Guiding principles recognized in legislation reflect the nature and guiding concepts of the legislation. The principles recognized in a law govern the regulatory systems and institutional arrangements stipulated in the law and guide the implementation of, and compliance with, the relevant law. In this sense, the design of the Law on Promoting Renewable Energy Resources should incorporate principles that will influence the whole process of development of renewable energy resources in China.

Principle of Government Dominance

Experience in China, and in other countries, demonstrates that governments generally adopt a dominant role in the development of renewable energy resources. Governments are the major financial investors in the development of renewable energy resources. They also tend to be the major buyers and consumers of renewable energy products, as well as being the central planners for the development of renewable energy resources. Governments are also responsible for the regulation of the renewable energy industry and markets. Because of this, they are well placed to be powerful promoters of renewable energy resources. Therefore, the Law on Promoting Renewable Energy Resources must recognize the central role of governments in the development of renewable energy resources. However, governments cannot dominate this area to the exclusion of other participants, but rather should limit their role to those functions best carried out by government entities. Governments must also allow the private sector and energy markets to function to support renewable energy resources.

The government should, first, carry out its planning function by designing a technically sound and rational path for the development of renewable energy resources. Second, the government should foster the development of a market that is favorable to the growth of the renewable energy industry. The market should allow investors to gain reasonable financial profits from their investments in renewable energies and also allow consumers access to safe, stable, and cheap renewable energy. The Law on Promoting Renewable Energy Resources should specify these central governmental functions to ensure the implementation of the principle of overarching governmental involvement in this area.

Principle of Economic Incentives

Following China's transition from a centrally planned economy to an emerging market economy, many Chinese laws have been amended to change traditional, compulsory government regulations into incentive based market mechanisms. Modes of government administration have also changed from a purely "command and control" model to a combination of "command and control" and economic incentive mechanisms. The Law on Promoting Renewable Energy Resources should also apply these principles to realize its objectives.

The government should focus on cultivating renewable energy markets and guiding and indirectly adjusting the development and involvement of market participants by using the economic information implicit in the market. China is currently seeing a lack of participants in renewable energy markets and a lack of enthusiasm to enter such markets. Accordingly, the government should stimulate the enthusiasm and creativity of existing and new participants through the provision of relevant economic incentives, such as: direct financial support; price allowances; tax reductions or exemptions; low interest loans and loan security. It should also ensure that market participants are able to access market information on a timely basis and realize reasonable profits. The Law on Promoting Renewable Energy Resources should encourage the application of such economic incentives. Renewable energies will hold an increasing share in China's future energy structure. Therefore, economic incentives, such as those discussed in this section, should be adopted as a relevant legislative mechanism.

Principle of Encouraging Innovation

The renewable energy industry is a new one that requires creative thinking, new technology, investment, and a new mode of development. First, the development of renewable energy products relies on technical innovation. The protection of new technologies and the provision of capital support for research and development through the implementation of appropriate laws is critical to the achievement of rapid progress in renewable energy technologies. Second, creative thinking is needed in relation to investment and financing methods, project development, and the marketing of renewable energy products. Accordingly, the Law on Promoting Renewable Energy Resources should encourage innovation in renewable energy technologies and in marketing the development of renewable energy resources.

9.3 Major Systems Arrangements

A good regulatory and administrative system, designed in accordance with the stated legislative purpose and principles of the Law on Promoting Renewable Energy Resources, is fundamental for the development of renewable energy resources. This section now considers the main legal arrangements that should be provided for in the Law on Promoting Renewable Energy Resources.

System of Investment in the Development of Technologies

Investment in renewable energy technologies is different from conventional investments that are capital based operations aimed only at the achievement of continuous profits. Investment in renewable energies requires consideration of social costs or externalities. Therefore, such investment requires special arrangements and protection under law, including provisions on the composition of investments and the scope and manner of capital investments. Investment composition can usually be divided into government investment and private investment. Government investment is currently the main financial source for the development of renewable energy resources. It can be divided into direct government funding for the provision of renewable energy services (through budget allocations and subsidies) and funding for the development of renewable energy technologies. Direct government funding for renewable energies is based on annual government budgets, whereas funding for the development of renewable energy technologies is usually based on an agreement between the government and relevant researchers.

System of Governmental Financial Support

Governmental financial support is a basic financial means for the promotion of the renewable energy industry. However, the current level of financial support for the renewable energy industry is clearly inadequate. Until now, the development of renewable energy infrastructure has not been included within usual government budget allocations loans in a similar manner to conventional energy projects. It is estimated that the total investment required for the development of renewable energy resources is approximately 89 billion yuan, that is, 5 billion yuan per year.[60] The rapid development of the renewable energy industry in other countries is the result of governmental financial support in accordance with existing legislation. Few members of the OECD provided government support for basic research in relation to renewable energy resources, such as photovoltaic cells, prior to 1973. However, most OECD countries greatly increased government financing for the development of renewable energies after that time. Between 1977 and 1985, government financing for renewable energies reached US$7 billion. In 1993, this amount was US$716 million, that is, 7.5 percent of total government financing for the energy industry, excluding nuclear power. Of this amount, the United

---

[60] Lu Ming, Problem and Solutions about Sustainable Usage of Renewable Energy in 21st Century (2002) 3 *Journal of Qufu Normal College.*

States contributed US$226 million, Japan provided US$188 million, and Germany provided US$1.13 million. Research and development in relation to renewable energies continued to develop following the Rio Conference. The U.S. government greatly increased its budget allocations for energy conservation and clean energy projects. By 1994, U.S. government funding for renewable energies increased to US$347 million. The EU also increased its total capital investment in research and development in relation to renewable energies to 580 million ECU during the four years from 1994 to 1998.[61]

Governmental financial support can be provided in the following ways.

- **Government subsidies**
  Financial subsidies are an important means for the development of renewable energy resources in all countries. Such subsidies can usually be divided into those provided by central or national governments and subsidies provided by local governments. The central governmental subsidy includes: subsidies to institutions; research and development subsidies; subsidies to encourage investment; and subsidies for the development of specific projects. Local government subsidies play important, even decisive, roles in the development of renewable energy technologies. Such subsidies can be used to support research institutions that are responsible for the administration, promotion, and demonstration of renewable energy technologies and to support activities for the promotion and popularization of renewable energy technologies.[62]

- **Tax**
  Tax is the most popular method of providing relevant economic incentives in the world. Generally, such incentives comprise two different tax policies. One is favorable tax policy, such as: preferential tariff treatment; preferential tax treatment for fixed assets; and preferential tax treatment in relation to value added taxes and income tax (for both enterprises and individuals). Preferential tax treatment does not require large amounts of government investment, although it does reduce certain governmental revenue. As the market for renewable energies in China is relatively small, such preferential tax treatment will have little impact on the overall tax balance of the country as a whole. Accordingly, tax reductions or exemptions are relatively easily provided. And, as experience has shown, if such policies are abolished some renewable energy technologies and industries barely survive. For example, sales of solar water heaters fell from 1,746,000 in 1980 to 1,026,000 in 1990 and the number of manufacturers fell by 200 after the preferential tax policies were abolished in the United States. Moreover, the LUZ, a world famous manufacturer of solar driven generators, is currently facing the threat of bankruptcy.[63]

  The second type of taxation policy is compulsory tax policies, such as levies for urban garbage and waste water from chicken farms and stock farms. Successful experiences in other countries suggest that such a properly constructed, high, and intensive taxation policy can force enterprises to adopt advanced technologies and to improve their levels of technical expertise. In this sense, such a policy is also a necessary incentive.

---

[61] *Id.*   [62] *Supra* note 44.

[63] China New Energy Net Comparison and Analysis of Energy Policy of China and United States, available at http://www.newenergy.org.cn.

- **Low interest loans**

  Governments can provide certain amounts of capital to developers of renewable energy resources in the form of low interest loans. These loans are a kind of government investment in the renewable energy industry. Low interest loans have specific target projects, objectives, amount restrictions, conditions, and a specific scale. They can be implemented by financial organizations consigned by the government or by an authorized government agency. In 1996, the Chinese government decided to promote and apply energy technology in rural areas on the basis of a loan of 120–130 million yuan from the Industrial and Commercial Bank and the Agricultural Bank. The Central Government paid fifty percent of the commercial loan interest by way of a subsidy to those enterprises that received such loans. Furthermore, the State Economic and Trade Commission (now part of the Commerce Ministry) provided loans for alternative technology development. Such loans can also be used for the development of renewable energy resources.[64]

- **Preferential prices**

  Favorable price policies are an effective means of promoting the development of renewable energy resources. Many countries allow renewable energy products to be preferentially priced in order to maintain a competitive market position. For example, the Public Utility Regulatory Policies Act of the United States[65] provides that an electric power company must buy electricity produced through thermo-electricity combinations or from renewable energy resources on the basis of preferential prices.[66] In China, the former Ministry of Electricity Power had implemented some favorable price policies in relation to wind powered electricity generation. However, there are some differences in the effectiveness of the national policies of these two countries. The United States' favorable pricing policy covers all relevant renewable energy technologies, while the Chinese policy is limited to wind power. Also, the U.S. regulation is a federal law, whereas the Chinese policy consists of plans permitted by Ministries.

- **Credit guarantees**

  Governments can provide credit guarantees to banks for developers of renewable energy resources. Such credit guarantees help developers to obtain loans from banks for the purpose of developing renewable energy technologies. For example, the U.S. Department of Energy provided US$500 million in credit guarantees for loans for the development of geothermal energy and US$240 million in credit guarantees for loans in relation to ethanol fuel in 1978.[67]

Planning for the Development of Renewable Energy Resources

For the healthy development of renewable energy resources, governments at all levels should plan such development comprehensively and adopt technically sound strategies. Such plans and strategies should provide the scope, degree, timetable, and specific programs for the development of renewable energy resources. The development of the renewable energy industry should follow the guidance of such plans. Planning is a popular mechanism under the current administration of renewable energy development

---

[64] *Supra* note 60.
[65] Public Utility Regulatory Policies Act of 1978, 92 Stat. 3117, 16 U.S.C. § 2601 et seq.
[66] *Id.*   [67] *Supra* note 45, at 213.

in China. One problem, however, is that current plans are not firm. They are instead frequently changed at random or even abandoned by governments altogether. The Law on Promoting Renewable Energy Resources should specify the subject, content, measure, and planning process for relevant plans so as to ensure that the process is transparent and the resulting plans are technically sound and reasonable. Moreover, the law should guarantee that government plans in relation to the development of renewable energies will be respected and implemented.

9.4 Institutional Arrangements

There is no single government department in China responsible for the overall development of renewable energy resources. Rather, relevant responsibilities are undertaken by the State Development and Reform Commission, the Ministry of Commerce, the Ministry of Water Resources, the Forestry Administration, and the Ministry of Agriculture. The administration of renewable energy development is undermined by this multi-institutional arrangement, which causes problems of scattered financial aid, duplication, isolation of information, and conflicts in regulatory powers.

It is suggested that the Central Government should designate a specific department or ministry to be responsible for the development of renewable energy resources in China under the proposed Law on Promoting Renewable Energy Resources. This department or ministry should be responsible for the uniform management of all kinds of renewable energy resources. Various other ministries that currently have responsibilities in this area should transfer their functions to this department or ministry and cooperate with it in implementing the Law on Promoting Renewable Energy Resources. Local governments should reform their relevant institutional arrangements in keeping with the arrangements provided for by the Central Government.

10 CONCLUSION

China adopted a strategy of sustainable development in 1992. The current coal based energy structure in China is a major challenge to the transition from traditional economic growth and consumption to sustainable development. Developing renewable energy resources is one way of helping China to realize this transition. China has already adopted a strategy for the development of renewable energy resources and a number of laws have been adopted that contain provisions relevant to the development of renewable energy resources. However, a law specifically designed for the promotion of renewable energy resources is needed. Based on relevant provisions of existing laws and administrative regulations, it is feasible to construct a comprehensive legal framework for promoting renewable energy resources in China. The proposed Law on Promoting Renewable Energy Resources can serve as a backbone for this legal framework and should be adopted now.

21 Energy Development and Utilization in Africa

Ibibia Worika*

1 BACKGROUND

In Africa, as in many parts of the developing world, the lack of clean and reasonably priced energy is a significant impediment to sustainable development and a principal contributor to a host of environmental and social problems, particularly health problems.[1] While approximately forty percent of the world's peoples lack modern energy services, in Africa the number exceeds eighty percent. In fact, the vast majority of African peoples rely on wood, dung, and other biomass fuels for cooking and heating and use such fuels in polluting and inefficient ways. Moreover, these energy sources are equally under threat from overuse, creating additional environmental challenges. In percentage terms, it is estimated that at least eight out of every ten Africans have no access to electricity. Table 21.1 provides comparative data on access to electricity services for some African populations. Approximately fourteen percent of the world's population lives in Africa, and as Africa's population is growing far more rapidly than rural access to electricity services, the emerging energy crisis is perhaps only better left to the imagination.

There is, however, abundant energy resource wealth in Africa, most particularly petroleum[2] as a source of commercial energy. However, energy resources are unevenly distributed: two-thirds are located in North Africa, in Algeria, Libya, and Egypt; the remaining one-third in sub-Saharan Africa, with a near monopoly held by Nigeria and Angola.[3] Aside from the fact that petroleum is exhaustible, the extraction, transportation and use of petroleum, and more particularly crude oil, has a detrimental impact on peoples and their environment on global, regional, and local levels, thus raising questions in relation to its long-term sustainability.[4]

---

[1] Facts and Figures, available at http://www.uneptie.org/energy/REED-Media-kit/docs/energy-facts.pdf.
[2] In its most comprehensive sense, "petroleum" comprises all hydrocarbons occurring in the earth. In its narrower, more commercial sense, it is usually restricted to the liquid deposits known as crude oil, the gaseous ones being known as natural gas and the solid ones as bitumen or asphalt. *See* Elsevier, *The Petroleum Handbook*, 6th Edition, Shell International Petroleum Company (The Netherlands, 1983) at 1.
[3] I. L. Worika, *Environmental Law & Policy of Petroleum Development: Strategies and Mechanisms for Sustainable Management in Africa*, Anpez Centre for Environment & Development (Port Harcourt, 2002) at 2.
[4] Energy production and consumption directly and indirectly affects local and regional environments. Such effects include, but are not limited to, air pollution through the release of particulates and toxic gases formed during the consumption of fossil fuels; acidification of ecosystems from acid deposition

* Senior lecturer, Faculty of Law, Rivers State University of Science & Technology, Senior counsel, OPEC.

Table 21.1 Access to electricity services in Africa

S/No.	Country	% of population with access to electricity
1.	Sierra Leone	4%
2.	Uganda	5%
3.	Malawi	5%
4.	Kenya	25%
5.	Zimbabwe	25%
6.	Ghana	30%
7.	Senegal	30%
8.	Cote d'Ivoire	35%
9.	Gabon	40%
10.	Nigeria	40%
11.	South Africa	45%

Source: Karl G. Jechouteck, World Bank, "Energy for Sustainable Development," Kumasi, Ghana, March 24–April 2, 2000 and A. Olugbenga M, "Elysian Energy for a Sustainable Nigeria." *See* www.worldenergy.org/wec-geis/publications/default/tech-papers/17th-congress_2_3_03.asp.

Yet energy production, transmission, and consumption lie at the very core of modern industrial societies. If Africa is to be transformed from a predominantly rural to an industrial economy, it must adopt sustainable energy policies almost as a matter of necessity.[5] The preponderance of existing literature places a disproportionate level of emphasis on the economic and social aspects of sustainable energy for Africa, while legal aspects have been largely neglected. Accordingly, this chapter attempts to fill an existing gap in the literature of sustainable energy for Africa by evaluating the comparative law on sustainable energy in Africa.

The main focus of this chapter is sub-Saharan West Africa, using Nigeria and Ghana as case studies.[6] This does not preclude references to other African countries as necessary, particularly where this would shed further light on the subject matter of discussion. Nevertheless, traditional constraints in research of this nature are unavoidable.[7]

This chapter contains five sections. First, an introductory background. Section 2 considers the concepts, issues, and trends in energy development and utilization in Africa.

---

and mine drainage; contamination of marine and inland waters due to oil spills; habitat destruction through mining and drilling operations and dam constructions; application and release of herbicides to maintain transmission and pipeline rights-of-way; noise pollution from power plants and internal combustion engines; deforestation from unsustainable harvesting of woodfuels. *See* UNEP – Energy & Environment, available at http://www.uneptie.org/energy/env/index.htm.

[5] For more information on the links between energy, poverty, and economic growth, *see* D. Lallement, "Delivering Sustainable Energy Services for Poverty Reduction and Economic Growth," available at http://www.worldbank.org/html/fpd/esmap/pdfs/wec_dl.pdf.

[6] The reasons for this are varied. Sub-Saharan West Africa is geographically homogenous. The choice of countries within Sub-Saharan Africa is predicated on the need to be much more accurate in data collection, research, and analysis; and to have a mix between predominantly oil exporting Nigeria and essentially agrarian Ghana. Also, the fact that these are English speaking countries reduces the linguistic hurdles in interpreting relevant texts and materials. But, more importantly, the need to be much more detailed rather than providing brief generalizations in analysis has been the overriding factor.

[7] In contrast to Nigeria, getting good quality primary data and source materials from Ghana was problematic. In the circumstances, Internet resources were helpful and were heavily relied upon.

Section 3 covers the current energy regulatory framework in Africa with particular references to Nigeria and Ghana in West Africa, covering policy, legislation, and institutional mechanisms for sustainable energy. Section 4 provides an assessment of existing regulatory frameworks, covering policy, legislation, and regulatory institutions for both Ghana and Nigeria. Section 5 summarizes the major findings of this chapter with recommendations for a pan-Africa sustainable energy regulatory framework.

2 CONCEPTS, ISSUES, AND TRENDS IN ENERGY DEVELOPMENT AND UTILIZATION IN AFRICA

2.1 Energy

Energy, in its broadest sense, is "the capacity of objects or systems to do work."[8] The concept emerged during the mid-nineteenth century, when it was realized that moving bodies could be made to move against resisting forces, thus doing work. There are various forms of energy: chemical, thermal (heat), electrical, nuclear, wind, and solar being the most common.

2.2 Energy Resources

The term "energy resources" simply refers to natural sources of useful energy. For more than a century, the world's primary sources of energy have been fossil fuels.[9] Hydroelectricity and nuclear energy together contribute some nine percent to present world annual energy consumption, and biofuels, in the form of firewood or other combustible plant or animal materials, are thought to provide approximately ten percent of the global total. Across Africa, exploration for, exploitation of, and use of, fossil fuels only began in the twentieth century; with the exception of South Africa, fossil fuel discovery and use did not begin until about the 1950s.

The Second World War reinforced the importance of petroleum energy.[10] Even after the war, the need to rebuild Europe, reduce dependence on Middle East oil, as well as ensure security of supply, all combined in varying degrees to drive increased production of oil and gas in Africa. Although disproportionately distributed, the relative cheapness and convenience of oil made it the preferred commercial energy for domestic, mechanical, and industrial heating.

However, the finite nature of fossil fuel energy resources has raised questions about the long-term sustainability of such resources. The intricate interplay of demand and supply coupled with technological innovations has, thus far, enabled energy supply to keep pace with increased demand. However, concerns have also been raised in relation to the environmental impact of burning fossil fuels. Accordingly, serious consideration is being given to alternatives to fossil fuels.

---

[8] *Oxford World Encyclopedia*, Oxford University Press, (Oxford, UK, 1998) at 472.

[9] Fossil fuels are carbon based fuels, such as coal, crude oil, and natural gas. All fossil fuels, whether solid, liquid, or gaseous, are the result of organic material being covered by successive layers of sediments over the course of millions of years. *Id.*, at 529.

[10] D. Yergin, *The Prize: An Epic Quest for Oil, Money and Power*, Simon & Schuster Ltd. (London, 1991). *See* also UNEP, *Global Environmental Outlook*, Earthscan Publications Ltd. (London, 2000) at 113.

2.3 Sustainable Energy

The term "sustainable energy" must therefore be considered within this context. Flowing from the definition of sustainable development,[11] "sustainable energy" is energy that is capable of meeting the needs of present generations without compromising the ability of future generations to meet their own energy needs. Within this context, the concept of sustainable energy encompasses the principles of intergenerational equity, sustainable use, equitable use or intragenerational equity, and integration.[12] Adopting this broad view, the World Energy Assessment (WEA) defines sustainable energy as "energy, which is produced and used in ways that support human development over the long term, in all its social and economic and environmental dimensions."[13]

2.4 Commercial Energy Consumption

Admittedly, Africa's share of world commercial energy consumption is relatively small (approximately three percent of total). However, commercial energy consumption is growing throughout Africa. Growth in energy demand in Africa averaged 2.7 percent annually from 1980 through 1997 and grew slightly between 1990 through 1997, averaging 3.1 percent per annum. Currently, energy demand in Africa is growing at approximately four percent per year.[14] All African countries consume at least some petroleum, regardless of the availability of domestic supplies. Fewer than fifty percent of African countries have any domestic refining capacity and many of the countries that do have very small facilities.

Oil, as a relatively easily transportable and usable (fungible) fuel, is consumed throughout Africa. Coal and gas, on the other hand, are not as fungible as oil. Their use, therefore, depends heavily on the availability of either domestic or closely located foreign resources and the extent to which these resources, armed with the necessary transportation infrastructure, have been developed.

Almost exclusively, countries with gas reserves and production facilities consume natural gas. Algeria, Egypt, Libya, and Tunisia (all in North Africa), plus Nigeria (in West Africa), account for ninety-four percent of total African natural gas consumption. The near absence of natural gas consumption in most other African countries is largely the result of a lack of pipeline infrastructure. This, in turn, is the result of several factors,

[11] The Brundtland Report defines "sustainable development" as "development that meets the present without compromising the ability of future generations to meet their own needs." *See* World Commission on Environment and Development, *Our Common Future*, Oxford University Press (Oxford, UK, 1987) at 43.

[12] E. B. Weiss, *In Fairness to Future Generations: International Law, Common Patrimony and Intergenerational Equity*, Transnational/United Nations University (New York, 1989); E. B. Weiss, "Our Rights and Obligations to Future Generations" (1990) *American Journal of International Law* 198. *See also* P. Ariansen, "Beyond Parfit's Paradox" in E. Aguis et al., *Future Generations and International Law*, Earthscan Publications Ltd. (London, 1998) at 13–17.

[13] IUCN Commission on Environmental Law and its Climate and Energy Working Group, "Brainstorming Session in the World Energy Assessment and Sustainable Energy Outreach," March 12, 2003, at 1.

[14] U.S. Department of Energy/Energy Information Administration (USDOE/EIA), Energy in Africa – Africa in a World Context, available at http://www.eia.doe.gov/emeu/cabs/africa.html, at 3.

including cost, terrain, and politics. South Africa is the only country in Africa with large natural gas reserves that also consumes significant amounts of coal.[15]

However, there is still widespread use of noncommercial or "traditional" energy in Africa. There are several reasons for this.[16] First, Africa's enormous commercial energy resources are largely underdeveloped. Second, Africa has poorly developed commercial energy infrastructure, including pipelines and electricity grids, to deliver commercial energy to customers. Third, widespread and severe poverty means that Africa's peoples cannot afford to pay for conventional energy resources and must instead rely on biomass and other like fuels. Fourth, many countries in Africa are landlocked, which makes the importing of commercial energy resources even more difficult and expensive.[17]

Within Africa, certain regions consume more traditional fuel than others. North Africa, for instance, consumes very little biomass, mainly as a result of the lack of wood in this arid environment. Central and East Africa, on the other hand, consume large amounts of biomass. Generally speaking, the consumption of traditional fuels is highly labor intensive, inefficient, polluting, and destructive of the environment, as it leads to deforestation and desertification.[18]

2.5 Commercial Energy Production

Since the 1970s, commercial energy production in Africa has nearly doubled and is expected to increase another 68% by 2020. African commercial energy production grew from 14.8 quads in 1970 to 26.5 quads in 1997 and is forecast to reach 45.5 quads in 2020. Natural gas production grew the most, by 3.9 quads, followed closely by growth in oil and coal (3.8 and 3.6 quads respectively), hydroelectricity (0.4 quads), and nuclear power (0.1 quads).[19] However, as a share of world total commercial energy production, Africa's production levels have remained constant at approximately 7% and this is expected to continue through to 2020.[20]

Oil accounted for over 86% of African commercial energy production in 1970, with coal a distant second at 11%, hydroelectricity at 2%, and natural gas at 0.5%. As of 1997, oil had declined to 6%, while coal had increased to 19%, natural gas to 15%, hydroelectricity to 2.3% and nuclear power to 0.5%.[21]

As stated earlier, commercial energy production is distributed unevenly throughout the continent. Approximately 99% of Africa's coal output, for instance, is in Southern Africa (mainly South Africa). Natural gas production, on the other hand, is overwhelmingly concentrated in North Africa (mainly Algeria and Egypt), as is crude oil production (Algeria, Egypt, and Libya). Crude oil production facilities are also located in West Africa (Angola and Nigeria). While East Africa produces almost no coal, gas, or

---

[15] It is to be noted that there are other countries with smaller but significant oil and gas reserves. These are Cameroon, Sudan, and Tunisia. Mozambique and Namibia (and to a lesser extent, Tanzania) have significant natural gas reserves but no oil.

[16] Africa is the world's largest consumer of biomass energy calculated as a percentage of overall energy consumption. Wood, including charcoal, is the most common and the most environmentally detrimental biomass energy source. Firewood accounts for approximately 65% of biomass use and charcoal accounts for approximately 3%. *See* http://www.eia.doe.gov/emeu/cabs/chapter7.html at 1.

[17] *Supra* note 14.

[18] USDOE/EIA. *See* http://www.eia.doe.gov/emeu/cabs/chapter3.html at 1.

[19] *Supra* note 15, at 4.   [20] *Id.*

[21] *Id.*

oil, it has the largest concentration of geothermal energy on the continent, which could be tapped for sustainability purposes.[22]

2.6 Carbon Emissions

Africa's carbon emissions from fossil fuel consumption (excluding natural gas flaring) are growing rapidly, albeit from a very small initial basis. Carbon emissions in Africa roughly tripled from 72 million metric tons (Mmt) in 1970 to 202 Mmt in 1997 and are projected to reach 325 Mmt by 2020. Africa's share of world carbon emissions has increased slightly from 2% in 1970 to approximately 3% in 1997 and is expected to remain constant at this level through to 2020.[23] As of 1997, emitting the same amount of carbon as Germany or India alone, the entire African continent had the lowest level of carbon emissions due to fossil fuel consumption of any continent in the world.[24]

In some ways, this has fueled the skepticism of African governments and peoples in relation to global climate change concerns,[25] on the basis that Africa is a very negligible contributor to the problem. Taking this approach, efforts to tackle this problem are deemed to be largely the responsibility of the industrialized north, including perhaps India or China as they have very large populations and are rapidly developing economies in the Asian subregion. Further, attempts to put a stop to Africa's conventional energy production and consumption patterns, in the interest of the global environment, are considered to be diversionary and aimed at stifling and frustrating Africa's desire for rapid economic growth. Considering that most of Africa's commercial energy resources are underdeveloped, it is difficult, if not impossible, to realistically dissuade African peoples from continuing to exploit domestic energy resources on the basis that it is not in the interests of the global environment to do so: even more so, while Africa's economies remain underdeveloped and African peoples continue to be mired in abject poverty.[26] The imperative for Africa generally, therefore, is to develop conventional energy resources in a sustainable manner for the benefit of present and future generations, while exploring renewable substitutes in the short, medium, and long term.

Cynicism aside, there are compelling reasons for global climate change to be taken seriously in an African context. First, sub-Saharan Africa is home to the world's second largest rain forest, in West Africa. It is, accordingly, one of the world's carbon sinks.[27] There are, therefore, persuasive reasons for the world to be interested in the implications of global climate change for Africa. Second, although Africa contributes only a negligible

---

[22] *Id. See also Eastern Africa Geothermal Market Acceleration Conference – Market Assessment Report* (2003), available at http://www.bcse.org/adobefiles/geothermalconferenceoverview.pdf at 1–138.

[23] As of 1997, oil's share of total carbon emissions stood at 44%, coal was 42%, and natural gas, 14%. By 2020, oil's share is expected to increase to 52%, natural gas to 15%, while coal is expected to fall slightly to 33%. See *supra* note 14, at 5.

[24] *Id.*

[25] The argument that environmentalism is an orchestrated master plan by some interest groups in the North to stifle developing countries' desire for rapid economic growth is sometimes attributed to the former Malaysian Prime Minister. *See* T. Walde, "Environmental Laws Towards Mining in Developing Countries" (1992) 10(4) *Journal of Energy and Natural Resources Law* 340.

[26] *See for instance* "Development and the Environment: Dirt Poor," *The Economist*, March 21, 1998, at 1.

[27] Carbon sinks capture carbon dioxide from the atmosphere.

percentage of the world's total carbon emissions, the net contributions of individual countries within Africa, relative to other countries, are quite high.[28]

2.7 Electric Power

In the late 1990s, electric generating capacity in Africa totaled nearly 94 gigawatts, approximately three percent of the global total. Most of Africa's generation capacity (76%) is thermal. This is particularly the case in North Africa (88%) and Southern Africa (81%). In North Africa, thermal capacity is mainly a mix of oil and natural gas. In Southern Africa, it is also a mix, of mainly coal and oil.[29]

Hydroelectric capacity accounts for about 22% of total electric generating capacity in Africa. Hydroelectricity represents the primary source of electricity in East and Central Africa, and nearly half of West Africa. Reliance on hydropower is 80% or greater in Cameroon, the Democratic Republic of the Congo, Ghana, Mozambique, Rwanda, Uganda, and Zambia. Further, hydropower reliance is greater than 70% in several other African countries.

Nuclear power accounts for only 2% of total African electric generating capacity and nuclear generation facilities are located in South Africa.

Geothermal generating plants constitute approximately 0.1% of total electric generating capacity in Africa. Ethiopia, and Kenya account for all of this capacity.

Access to a central power grid is a major challenge for Africa. Outside of Southern Africa and, to a lesser extent, North Africa, electrification rates are very low. As a result, per capita electricity consumption is very low in Central, East, and West Africa. In those regions, biomass is largely substituted for electricity from a power grid.

3 REGULATORY FRAMEWORK FOR SUSTAINABLE ENERGY IN AFRICA

This section will examine first, sustainable energy policies; second, energy legislation; and third, institutional mechanisms for sustainable energy in Africa, with particular reference to Nigeria and Ghana.

3.1 Pan-Africa Policy Instruments

Shortly after independence, various African countries took predictable strides toward economic self-sufficiency. Economic cooperation and development became national priorities, as evidenced by the adoption of the African Declaration on Cooperation, Development and Economic Independence[30] (Development Declaration). While the Development Declaration does not strictly constitute Africa's policy on sustainable energy, it contains references to "natural resources," which encompass both energy

---

[28] Although steps are being taken currently to drastically reduce flaring of gas in Nigeria, for instance, as of 1991 the flaring of natural gas as a percentage of gross gas production was as high as 76%. In Libya, it was 21%, while in the United States it was only 0.6%, and 0% in Holland. *See* Escravos Staff Appraisal Report, *Defining an Environmental Strategy for the Niger Delta*, WACD (Nigeria, 1995) at 59.

[29] *Supra* note 18, at 2.

[30] OAU Document CM/ST. 12 (XXI) of May 12, 1973, reproduced in 12 I.L.M. 996 (1973). The tenth Ordinary Session of the Assembly of Heads of States and Governments of the OAU Meeting in Adis Ababa, Ethiopia adopted this Declaration on May 28, 1973.

resources and the environment. Broadly, the Development Declaration could be understood to set out general guidelines in relation to energy resources development and environmental protection. Article 8 of the Development Declaration enjoins member states, among other things, to:

> Undertake a systematic survey of all Africa's resources, with a view to their rational utilisation and joint exploitation where appropriate, in order to accelerate the continent's development.

Further, Article 43 requires member states to:

> Ensure that the problems of environmental protection are seen within the contexts of economic and social development of the African countries, whose developmental policies should accordingly pay greater attention to the questions of natural resources conservation and management, the improvement of physical and human conditions in urban and rural areas, the eradication of endemic diseases, which have been extensively eliminated in many parts of the world.

Article 33 of the Lome IV Agreement[31] acknowledges that:

> In the framework of this Convention, the protection and the enhancement of the environment and natural resources, the halting of the deterioration of land and forest, the restoration of ecological balances, the preservation of natural resources and their exploitation are basic objectives that the ACP States concerned shall strive to achieve with a view to bringing an immediate improvement in the living conditions of their populations and to safeguarding those of future generations.

Moreover, the Treaty Establishing the African Economic Community[32] (AEC), adopted under the auspices of the Organization of African Unity (OAU), seeks to achieve its social and economic objectives by, inter alia, requiring the progressive harmonization and coordination of member states' environmental policies.[33]

3.2 National Sustainable Energy Policies

3.2.1 Nigeria

The Nigerian National Policy on the Environment[34] (NPE) provides that the goal of this policy is the achievement of sustainable development in Nigeria and, in particular, to:

(a) Secure a quality of environment adequate for good health and well being; and
(b) Conserve and use the *environment and natural resources* for the benefit of present and future generations. [emphasis added]

---

[31] (December 15, 1989), EU Official Journal L 229, 17/08/1991, p. 003–0280, Document No. 291A0817(01), available at www.acpsec.org/gb/lome/lomeiv_e.htm.
[32] (June 3, 1991), available at www.africa-union.org/Official_documents/Treaties_%20Conventions_%20 Protocols/AEC_Treaty_1991.pdf.
[33] Art. 58 of the AEC Treaty specifically provides that: "Member States undertake to promote a healthy environment. To this end, they shall adopt national, regional and continental policies, strategies and programmes and establish appropriate institutions for the protection and enhancement of the environment."
[34] FEPA Revised Edition (1999).

The strategies for implementation, as set out in the NPE comprise detailed provisions in relation to biological diversity,[35] natural resource conservation,[36] water resources,[37] mining and mineral resources,[38] energy,[39] and oil and gas.[40] Article 4.13 of the NPE, concerning energy, provides, among other things, that:

> In energy production and use, therefore, attention should be focused on the following:
> * Energy source;
> * Mode of procuring the energy fuel on sustainable basis;
> * Mode of power generation;
> * Energy transmission and use; and
> * Conservation.[41]

Strategies identified in the NPE to achieve these objectives include:

(a) implementation of detailed Environmental Impact Assessments (EIAs) for all planned energy projects, backed by detailed baseline ecological data against which subsequent environmental changes and/or impacts can be measured;

(b) developing a rational National Energy Utilization Master Plan[42] (Master Plan) that balances the need for conservation with the utilization of premium energy resources for premium socioeconomic needs;

(c) encouraging the use of energy forms that are environmentally safe and sustainable, particularly solar energy;

(d) establishment of stringent safety standards in all national energy production processes while promoting safe and pollution free operations in energy production and use;

(e) prescribing and enforcing stringent standards for the disposal of radioactive and toxic wastes from energy production processes and controlling the level of human exposure to nuclear radiation at mines, power plants, and reactors through periodic audit checks of ambient radiation levels at such environments;

(f) monitoring and controlling the levels of particulates, toxic chemicals and noxious gaseous effluents of energy production and use such as CO, CO_2, NOX, SO_2, and nonmethane hydrocarbons;

(g) monitoring the ambient temperatures and other physical and chemical properties of cooling effluents of energy plants to prevent or reduce their severe impacts on human health and the aquatic plants and animals;

(h) ensuring that site selection for energy construction projects emphasizes the right-of-way of transmission lines, in such a way as to ensure minimal loss or disturbance of habitats, vegetation, wetlands, wildlands, and human habitation;

(i) adoption of a multi sectoral approach to the monitoring and control of environmental problems associated with energy production and use;

(j) licensing and periodic inspection and monitoring of all energy waste disposal sites;

[35] *Id.*, Art. 4.4 of the NPE.   [36] *Id.*, Art. 4.5.
[37] *Id.*, Art. 4.8.   [38] *Id.*, Art. 4.11.
[39] *Id.*, Art. 4.13.   [40] *Id.*, Art. 14.
[41] *Supra* note 41, at 19.
[42] Note there is no such policy as the National Energy Utilization Master Plan.

(k) encouraging research and development programs that promote environmentally sound utilization of the abundant coal resources as a domestic energy source through the reduction of the ash and noxious chemicals content;

(l) establishment of standards for the control of fuel additives especially with respect to trace metals such as Pb and Zn compounds;

(m) promotion and encouragement of research for the development and use of various locally available energy sources especially nonconventional resources such as geothermal, solar, wind, and bitumen or tar sands;

(n) preparation of guidelines for energy production and use in consonance with the environmental implications of the National Energy Policy[43] (NEP);

(o) ensuring a mandatory environmental audit of all major existing energy projects; and

(p) ensuring capacity building to enhance sustainable use and monitoring of energy resources.

The first Draft Policy Statement for the Electric Power Sector (DPSEP) was issued in April 2000, followed by an in-depth expert study under the auspices of the National Council on Privatization (NCP). In July 2000, the NCP issued an Electric Power Policy Statement for Nigeria, a document that became the subject of public debate at a workshop organized by the Bureau of Public Enterprises (BPE) in August 2000. The DPSEP then underwent further reviews by the Electric Power Sector Reform Implementation Committee (EPIC). Currently, the final product is the National Draft Policy for Electric Power.[44] The Draft Policy reiterates the federal government's determination to modernize, expand, and reform the electricity supply industry in Nigeria. Implementation strategies will involve the unbundling of the National Electricity Power Authority (NEPA), the reform of power generation and sales/marketing processes, licensing of private electricity generation and distribution firms, and the establishment of the National Electricity Regulation Commission (NERC) as an independent regulatory agency to monitor the operations of the electric power sector.

3.2.2 Ghana

In Ghana, the evolution of national energy policies can be traced to the enactment of the Provisional National Defense Council Law 62 in 1983 (PNDC), which provided the statutory foundations for the establishment and operations of a board known as the National Energy Board (NEB). Among other things, NEB was responsible for formulating recommendations on energy policy and submitting the same to the PNDC.[45] The current policy document guiding the development of the energy sector in Ghana is the Energy Sector Development Program (ESDP). According to

---

[43] There is no National Energy Policy in Nigeria. A national daily, *The Guardian*, reported that the Nigerian President ordered a reform of the oil and gas sectors at a National Oil and Gas Policy Stakeholders' Workshop held at the Nicon Hilton, Abuja. *See The Guardian*, Friday, September 19, 2003, at 1.

[44] Dated December 2000 (Draft Policy).

[45] I. Edjekumhene et al., *Implementation of Renewable Energy Technologies – Opportunities and Barriers: Ghana Country Study*, UNEP Collaborating Centre on Energy and Environment (Denmark, 2001) at 22.

Part II of the ESDP, Ghana's energy sector policies are informed by the following principles:

(a) The need to plan for the sustained provision and security of energy supplies;
(b) The need to increase the reach of energy resources to all sections of the country to facilitate their socioeconomic improvements, especially the majority rural people;
(c) The need to overcome the constraints in existing energy resources via measures to resuscitate dilapidated infrastructure and institutional weaknesses in the energy operating entities;
(d) The need to consolidate the gains achieved since the inception of the Economic Recovery Program (ERP); and
(e) The need to enhance private sector investment in the development of the energy sector.[46]

Within this overarching framework for meeting Ghana's energy requirements for sustained growth and development, the energy sector's specific goals are:

(a) to restore improved productivity and efficiency in the procurement, transformation, distribution, and use of all energy resources;
(b) to reduce the country's vulnerability to short-term disruptions in the energy resources and supply bases;
(c) to consolidate and further accelerate the development and use of the country's indigenous energy sources, particularly woodfuels, hydropower, petroleum, and solar energy; and
(d) to secure the future power supply through thermal complementation of the hydrobased electricity generation.[47]

The Ministry of Mines and Energy (MME) has designed action programs and projects for the energy sector over the short, medium and long term. The programs and projects currently being implemented by the MME fall under the following broad categories:

(a) The Renewable Energy Development Programme (REDP);
(b) The National Liquefied Petroleum Gas (LPG) Promotion Programme;
(c) The Power (Electricity) subsector;
(d) The Petroleum subsector; and
(e) The Energy Efficiency & Conservation Program.

The broad short-term objectives for the future development of renewable energy resources in Ghana, under the REDP, are:

(a) Improvements in efficiency of production, conversion, and use of woodfuel;
(b) Demonstrations and evaluations of renewable energy technologies (RETs) with the potential to meet the needs of the prioritized socioeconomic well being of the people;
(c) Provision of support for research, development, and the demonstration of RETs with the greatest potential to increase and diversify the country's future energy supply base;
(d) Promotion of the development of renewable energy industries that have strong indigenization prospects over the short and medium term; and

---

[46] *Supra* note 56, at 25.   [47] *Id.* at 26.

(e) Development of relevant information bases on the stock and status of renewable energy resources, RETs, and end use patterns for the purpose of establishing a planning framework for the rational use of the country's renewable energy resources.[48]

The broad medium term objectives of the REDP are:

(a) To demonstrate and evaluate renewable energy technologies with the potential to meet the needs of the prioritized socioeconomic well-being of the people;
(b) To provide support for research, development, and demonstration of RETs with the greatest potential to increase and diversify the country's future energy supply base; and
(c) To develop the relevant information base on the stock and status of renewable energy resources, suitable technologies, and end use patterns for the purposes of establishing a planning framework for the rational use of the country's renewable energy resources.[49]

These medium-term objectives have been designed to improve the production and use of wood energy resources; to expand the productivity and use of existing bioenergy resources, such as the production of charcoal briquettes from logging and wood processing residues; and to encourage the substitution of other energy sources, such as LPG and electricity, for cooking. The REDP will also examine incentives necessary to encourage private sector investment in woodlots and implement appropriately tailored policies. To complement these measures, policy guidelines for the environmentally friendly production of charcoal and fuelwood at district and community levels should be developed.

The REDP covers a number of specific projects that can be grouped under two broad headings: biomass and solar energy. The MME is implementing a number of biomass projects, including pilot projects to tackle the issue of woodfuel supply and attendant environmental problems. The aim of such projects is to determine the most technologically and cost-effective solutions for optimizing the use of existing resources, resuscitating degraded areas, and increasing Ghana's sustainable bio-energy resource base. The strategy adopted for the achievement of these objectives in the biomass sub-sector seeks to:

(a) Conserve forest resources through improved methods of charcoal and firewood production;
(b) Decrease consumption of firewood and charcoal by using more efficient cooking devices;[50]
(c) Expand the productivity and use of existing bio-energy resources such as production of charcoal briquettes from logging and wood processing residues;
(d) Examine the use of animal and human wastes to provide biogas for cooking, lighting, and electricity generation;[51]

---

[48] *Supra* note 56, at 27.   [49] *Id.* at 28.

[50] Among the measures is the development and introduction of improved woodfuel cookstoves. The chief outcome of this measure is a locally designed stove called the "Ahibenso improved coalpot," which saves between 35–40% of charcoal as compared to the traditional coal pot.

[51] In pursuing this, a community based biogas project has been established at Appolonia, a village near Tema. This project aims to determine the socio-economic conditions necessary to ensure the success of

(e) Plan for future security of biomass supply through the implementation of sustained program of forest regeneration and afforestation, especially in areas where intense charcoal production activities have destroyed the land and created environmental and ecological problems;[52] and

(f) Substitute LPG and other fuels such as electricity for firewood and charcoal.

The implementation strategy for all renewable energy projects is to be driven by demand, within the following parameters: sustainability; payment for service and cost recovery; the full involvement of potential consumers; environmental considerations; and the basic needs of the community or individual consumers. Further, as most RETs are still in their infancy, the MME proposes to subsidize interested investors in this sector in order to encourage the accelerated penetration of RETs in the market.[53]

The MME has instituted a National Solar Energy Program (NASEP) to assess, demonstrate, and evaluate the technical, economic, and social viability of appropriate solar energy technologies. NASEP is also concerned with solar applications that are able to facilitate the realization of the major goals of the ERP, especially the development of rural areas. The solar energy action programs being implemented are focused around a strategy whose principal objectives are:

(a) To evaluate the technical and economic viability of proven solar technologies capable of meeting prioritized socioeconomic and developmental needs of the country; and

(b) To promote the development of solar energy industries that have strong indigenization prospects over the short- to medium-term future.[54]

Further, the MME has developed the Power Sector Development Program (PSDP), a strategy and action plan aimed at achieving the following objectives:

(a) Rehabilitation and expansion of deteriorated infrastructure, with restoration of effective maintenance of generating plants, transmission and distribution equipment, extension of distribution and subtransmission systems;

(b) Extension of reach of electricity to all parts of the country, especially to the rural areas, under a National Electrification Scheme (NES) by the year 2020;

(c) Assuring future supply of power by developing new hydro resources as well as complementing the predominantly hydropower generation capacity with other energy sources such as thermal generation;

(d) Reducing electricity wastage through energy conservation and demand side management programs; and

(e) Instituting structural reforms in the electricity industry in order to enhance efficiency and competition.[55]

---

the technology. This information will be used to promote and popularize the technology in other areas of the country.

[52] The MME is currently collaborating with the Ministry of Lands and Natural Resources, the Forestry Commission, Ghana Timber Association, as well as the District Assemblies in the major charcoal producing areas to enforce measures that require charcoal producers to cultivate sustainable woodlots to support their activities.

[53] *Supra* note 56, at 28–29.   [54] *Supra* note 56, at 29.

[55] *Supra* note 56, at 30. Note, that in order to achieve the stated objectives, a number of programs have been implemented, including the extension of transmission and distribution systems, increasing the capacity of power generation systems, and legal and institutional reforms to strengthen the sector's operational efficiency and improve competitiveness.

3.3 National Sustainable Energy Legislation

3.3.1 Nigeria

hydrocarbons. Nigeria's estimated proven oil reserves stand at between 24–31.5 billion barrels.[56] A larger part of the reserves are found along the Niger Delta coast of Nigeria, although newer reserves have also been discovered in deeper waters offshore. Nigeria's crude oil gravities range from 21° API to 45° API.[57] The main export blends are Bonny light (37° API) and Forecadoes (31° API). Nigeria produces approximately 2.01 million barrels of oil per day (b/d).[58] In recent times, however, despite the potential of Nigeria's reserves to produce even more oil, it has been difficult to sustain this level of production because of social unrest in the Niger Delta of Nigeria,[59] where approximately 60% of Nigeria's crude oil production takes place.

A plethora of energy laws on the licensing, operations, and fiscal regimes of energy investments across Africa exist throughout the continent. An examination of Nigerian legislation in this regard should begin with the current Constitution of the Federal Republic of Nigeria (1999),[60] in which its Exclusive Legislative List (ELL), more particularly Items 39 and 41 of Schedule II, make provision for mines and minerals, including oil fields, oil mining, geological surveys, and natural gas and nuclear energy. Accordingly, exclusive legislative competence in relation to hydrocarbon operations in Nigeria is vested in the federal government (National Assembly), as opposed to its constituent units (states or local governments of the federation).[61]

In furtherance of the powers already vested in the federal government, several enactments have been promulgated in the oil and gas sectors: the Petroleum Act 1969[62] (Petroleum Act), Mineral Oils (Safety) Regulations of 1962, Petroleum Regulations of 1967, the Petroleum (Drilling and Production) Regulations of 1969, Petroleum Refining Regulations of 1974, Crude Oil (Transportation and Shipment) Regulations of 1984 all regulate oil and gas operations in Nigeria.[63] The oil and gas sectors have been, and continue to be, the backbone of Nigeria's economy, contributing close to 90% of the nation's foreign exchange earnings and approximately 25% of gross domestic product (GDP).

The general purpose of the Petroleum Act is to provide for exploration for petroleum in territorial waters and the continental shelf of Nigeria and also, to vest ownership

---

[56] EIA Country Analysis Briefs, available at http://www.eia.doe.gov/emeu/cabs/nigeria.html.

[57] 65% of Nigeria's crude oil production is light (35 API) and sweet with very low sulphur content.

[58] For more information on the major Nigerian oil production joint ventures, *see* EIA, Nigeria, April 2003, available at http://www.eia.doe.gov/emeu/cabs/ngia.iv.html. For more information on Nigerian licensing Round Blocks and Awards, *see* http://www.eia.doe.gov/emeu/cabs/ngia_blocks.html.

[59] The unrest is as a result of what the indigenes of the Niger Delta perceive as both government and oil companies' neglect of the "goose that lays the golden egg," a situation that is further compounded by frequent oil spills and inadequate oil spill contingency measures.

[60] *See* http://www.nigeria-law.org/ConstitutionOfTheFederalRepublicOfNigeria.htm.

[61] In addition to the foregoing, section 44(3) of the Nigerian Constitution provides: "Notwithstanding the foregoing provisions of this section, the entire property in and control of all minerals, mineral oils and natural gas in, under or upon any land in Nigeria or in, under, or upon the territorial waters and the Exclusive Economic Zone of Nigeria shall vest in the Government of the Federation and shall be managed in such a manner as may be prescribed by the National Assembly."

[62] Cap. 350, L.F.N. 1990.

[63] All these various regulations were consolidated under the Petroleum Act Chapter Cap. 350, L.F.N. 1990. Note the Mineral Oils (Safety) Regulations 1962 have been replaced with the Mineral Oils (Safety) Regulations) 1997.

of such petroleum resources, and all onshore and offshore revenue from petroleum resources derivable from these areas, in the federal government. Matters that are ancillary to these activities also fall within the scope of the federal government's authority.[64] Although such petroleum resources are the property of the state, individuals or investors can obtain various licenses for the purposes of exploration, prospecting, and mining.[65] There are, however, restrictions on those persons or companies who may qualify for a license or lease under the Petroleum Act.[66]

Although the Petroleum Act defines "petroleum" to include oil and gas, successive Nigerian governments, conscious of the enormous oil revenues capable of being derived simply through exploring and exploiting crude oil deposits, have, over the years, emphasized oil to the detriment of gas, with the result that as of 1991, well over 75% of Nigeria's associated and nonassociated gas was flared. Notwithstanding this, gas has always combined with oil in contributing toward both Nigeria's foreign exchange earnings and GDP. Nigeria is essentially a "gas province" and has the world's ninth largest natural gas reserves, at approximately 124 trillion cubic feet (Tcf). However, consumption of gas in Nigeria is limited as approximately 75% of the gas produced in conjunction with crude oil is flared. There are also huge proven, but undeveloped, offshore reserves of nonassociated gas in Nigeria. Like oil, ownership and control of natural gas resources and revenues is vested exclusively in the federal government of Nigeria.

Attempts to reinject natural gas or to utilize it were only begun in the late 1970s with the promulgation of the Associated Gas Reinjection Act of 1979[67] (Associated Gas Reinjection Act). The Associated Gas Reinjection Act was enacted to compel all companies producing oil and gas in Nigeria to submit preliminary programs for gas reinjection and detailed plans for the implementation of gas reinjection or utilization.[68] Moreover, the Act fixes a time limit within which gas flaring must cease as well as providing for penalties for violations of its provisions.[69] Difficulties experienced in meeting the deadline set under the Associated Gas Reinjection Act led to the promulgation of the Associated Gas (Continuous Flaring of Gas) Regulations of 1984 (Associated Gas Regulations). Under these Regulations and section 3(2) of the Associated Gas Reinjection Act, the Minister could issue a certificate allowing the continued flaring of gas in a particular field or fields,[70] exempting the relevant entity from complying with section 3(1) of the

---

[64] In Nigeria, ownership of petroleum is vested in the state by section 1(1) of the Petroleum Act, which provides that "the entire ownership and control of all petroleum in, under or upon any lands to which this section applies shall be vested in the State." *See also* § 44(3) of the Nigerian Constitution.

[65] Under the Petroleum Act, three types of licenses may be granted: Oil Exploration Licences, Oil Prospecting Licences, and Oil Mining Leases. *See* § 2(1) of the Petroleum Act.

[66] Under section 2(2) of the Petroleum Act, licenses can only be granted to a citizen of Nigeria or a company incorporated under the Companies and Allied Matters Act, or other corresponding law in Nigeria.

[67] Cap. 26, L.F.N. 1990.

[68] Section 1 of the Associated Gas Reinjection Act requires submission to the Minister of a preliminary program for: (a) schemes for the viable utilization of all associated gas produced from a field or group of fields; (b) project or projects to reinject all gas produced in association with oil but utilized in an individual project.

[69] Section 3(1) provides that gas flaring is to cease after January 1, 1984.

[70] Regulation 1 of the Associated Gas Regulations. However, permits are subject to the following conditions: (a) more than 75% of the produced gas is effectively utilized or conserved; (b) the produced gas contains more than 15% impurities, which render the gas unsuitable for industrial purposes; (c) where an ongoing

Associated Gas Reinjection Act. Practical realities also led the federal government to impose fines in certain cases for the flaring of associated gas.[71] Note, further measures being adopted to utilize natural gas can be seen in the government's liquefied natural gas (LNG) project at Bonny.[72]

coal. Nigeria also has vast reserves of coal.[73] The Nigerian Coal Corporation Act[74] is the principal enactment regulating the exploitation of coal deposits. Coal mining falls within the exclusive preserve of the Nigerian Coal Mining Corporation (NCMC) by virtue of section 4 of the Nigerian Mining Corporation Act,[75] which sets out the functions of the NCMC, including working and winning the coal in coal mines transferred to the NCMC under the Act and also working and winning coal in other deposits made available to the NCMC under license.

The eventual discovery of oil coupled with the potential of foreign exchange earnings from oil exports meant that coal was largely deprioritized by successive Nigerian governments. In any event, as one of the most polluting fossil fuels, coal was unlikely to be a prominent sustainable energy resource in Nigeria.

electricity including hydropower. Nigeria has approximately 5,900 megawatts (MW) of installed electric capacity, through three hydro-based stations and five thermal stations. The two main sources of electricity generation in Nigeria are fossil fuels and hydropower. The former accounts for approximately 64% of electricity production, while the latter contributes 36%. Also, despite the inadequacy of electricity supply in Nigeria, electricity is exported to neighboring countries such as Chad and Niger at an estimated rate of 19 million KWh annually, while Nigeria itself consumes only approximately 14.768 billion KWh annually.[76] Generally, Nigeria's electricity subsector operates below capacity, as evidenced by the decline in electricity generation from power plants and frequent power outages.

Both federal and state governments in Nigeria have legislative competence in relation to electricity and electric power[77] as it is a matter on the Concurrent Legislative List (CLL) of the Constitution. Section 13 of schedule 2 vests legislative competence in

---

utilization program is interrupted by equipment failure, which is not too frequent and the period of any one interruption is not more than three months; (d) where the ratio of the volume of gas produced per day to the distance of the field from the nearest gas line or possible utilization point is less than 50,000 SCF/KM, provided that the gas to oil ratio of the field is less than 3500 SCF/bbl and that it is not technically advisable to reinject the gas in that field; and (e) where the Minister, in appropriate cases as deemed fit, orders the production of oil from a field that does not satisfy any of the conditions specified in these Regulations.

[71] The President announced in January 2003 that the official date to end natural gas flaring has been reset for 2004.

[72] For more information on the purchase agreement signed with the Nigerian LNG Company, *see* www.eia.doe.gov/emeu/cabs/ngia_lng.html.

[73] At Enugu, the capital of the Enugu State of Nigeria.

[74] Cap. 299, L.F.N. 1990.   [75] Cap. 317, L.F.N. 1990.

[76] Note, this is based on 2000 estimates.

[77] A plethora of legislation and subsidiary instruments govern the electricity subsector in Nigeria. It is not possible to undertake a detailed examination of all relevant laws. Accordingly, only a few of the most significant laws and regulations will be examined in this section.

relation to electric power in the federal government (National Assembly).[78] Section 14 of Schedule 2 of Part 1 also vests the power to make laws for the state with respect to:

(a) electricity and the establishment in that state of electric power stations;
(b) the generation, transmission, and distribution of electricity to areas not covered by a national grid system within that state: and
(c) the establishment within that state of any authority for the promotion and management of electric power stations established by the state, in a House of Assembly of any of the states of the Federation.[79]

The Electricity Act[80] (Electricity Act) is essentially "an Act to provide for the regulation and control of electricity installations, and of the generation, supply and use of electricity energy."[81] Every undertaking operating in this subsector must comply with the Electricity Act. Section 2 provides as follows:

> This Act and the regulation made thereunder shall apply in respect of any undertaking for the manufacturing, distribution or supply of electricity established by the Government of a state or any of its agencies to the same extent as the Act and regulations apply in respect of any such undertaking established by any other person or authority.

The Electricity (Amendment) Act of 1998[82] (Electricity Amendment Act) amends the Electricity Act, providing that:

(a) Licenses under the Electricity Act may be granted to any person other than NEPA, a State Government or any of its agencies; and
(b) A holder of such license has the same rights and obligations as the entities mentioned above, i.e., NEPA, a state government or its agency.

The National Electric Power Authority Act[83] (NEPA Act) established a central operating agency, NEPA, which is statutorily empowered to develop and maintain an efficient, coordinated, and economical system of electricity supply for all parts of the Federation

---

[78] It provides that:

> the National Assembly may make laws for the Federation or any part thereof with respect to: (a) electricity and the establishment of electric power stations; (b) the generation and transmission of electricity in or to any part of the Federation and from one State to another State; (c) the regulation of the right of any person or authority to dam up or otherwise interfere with the flow of water from sources in any part of the Federation; (d) the participation of the Federation in any arrangement with another country for the generation, transmission and distribution of electricity for any area partly within and partly outside the Federation; (e) the promotion and establishment of a national grid system; and (f) the regulation of the right of any person or authority to use, work or operate any plant, apparatus, equipment or work designed for the supply or use of electrical energy.

[79] Section 15 of the Second Schedule then goes on to clearly define the meanings of "distribution," "management," "power station," and "transmission" as used in the context. In examining sections 13 and 14 of the Second Schedule, one cannot but come to the inescapable conclusion that the powers of the states are still limited to specifics of legislating for electricity as well as the establishment of state electric power stations to generate, transmit, and distribute same in areas outside of the national grid system (e.g, some remote communities in local government areas) as well as the establishment of state institutions for the purpose of managerial control.

[80] Cap. 106, L.F.N. 1990.
[81] Electricity Act, Preamble.
[82] Act No. 28 of 1998.
[83] Cap. 256, L.F.N. 1990.

and any matters ancillary to the provision of this service.[84] To date, NEPA has not met performance expectations as a result of exorbitant investment in excess generating capacity and meager expenditure on distribution facilities and maintenance. This has led the BPE to put NEPA up for privatization and to shop around for independent power producers to generate and sell electricity to NEPA.

The NEPA (Amendment) Act[85] (NEPA Amendment Act) essentially demonopolizes NEPA by repealing provisions in the NEPA Act that inhibited competition in electricity generation or otherwise reserved participation in the market for electricity generation to government agencies. The NEPA Amendment Act further provides that licenses under the NEPA Act may be granted to persons or entities other than NEPA, a state government, or any of its agencies.[86]

The Customs, Excise Tariff (Consolidation) (CETEC) (Amendment) Act[87] (CETEC Amendment Act) further amends the CETEC Act No. 4 of 1995 (as previously amended by the CETEC (Amendment) Act No. 13 of 1996). Under the provisions of the CETEC Amendment Act, machinery, equipment, and spare parts imported for use in gas-fired power generation and other like operations, are exempt from import duties.[88]

Following the trend of liberalization in the power sector through the Finance (Miscellaneous Taxation Provisions) Act,[89] the Petroleum Profits Tax Act[90] (PPTA) was amended to grant significant tax relief to companies that utilize gas for power generation.[91] The Utilities Charges Commission Act[92] (UCC Act) establishes the Utilities Charges Commission (UCC) to, among other things, evaluate trends in tariffs charged by public utilities and to determine permissible increases in these tariffs.[93]

In addition to principal enactments, there are further regulations affecting the electricity power sector. The Electricity (Private Licences) Regulations of 1965 is one of several anachronistic regulations that give NEPA overriding powers over the electricity sector: despite subsequent enactments demonopolizing NEPA and liberalizing electric power markets, these anachronistic regulations have not been repealed.[94] The Electricity

---

[84] Section 1 of the NEPA Act establishes the Corporation and vests it with its powers. Section 2 establishes the Board of Directors (BOD) of NEPA and its composition. The combined effects of sections 7 and 8 are to vest NEPA with certain functions specified thereunder.

[85] Act No. 29 of 1998.

[86] *See* § 4 of the NEPA (Amendment) Act 1998. A bill is currently being proposed as the Electricity Power Sector Reform Act. When the bill is finally passed into law, it shall see to the formation of initial successor and private companies and the transfer of assets and liabilities of the National Electric Power Authority. The new law should hopefully open up the electricity space by deregulating the subsector thereby making electricity much more easily affordable and accessible to all Nigerians.

[87] Act No.16 of 1997.   [88] CETEC Amendment Act, § 2.

[89] Act No. 18 of 1998.   [90] Cap. 354, L.F.N. 1990.

[91] Section 4 of the Finance (Miscellaneous Taxation Provision) Act No. 18 of 1998 introduces a new s. 28G into the PPTA, which grants: (a) initial tax holidays for 3 years, renewable for another 2 years to companies utilizing gas for power generation. The holiday period starts to run on the day the company commences production; (b) tax free dividends during the tax holiday, where the investment in foreign exchange was not less than 30% of the equity capital of the company; and (c) accelerated capital allowance: 90% annual allowance with 10% retention for investment in plant and machinery; and 15% additional investment allowance that will not reduce the value of the asset.

[92] Act No. 104 of 1992.   [93] *See* UCC Act, § 1–6.

[94] Upon application for private license, NEPA is empowered to determine if it can either undertake the functions for which the license is sought, or otherwise object to the issuance of such license (*see* Regulation 5(1)). In addition, NEPA may at any time give a 90-day notice to a licensee requiring the licensee to cease operations, except in emergency situations, if it feels that it can provide the service being undertaken by the licensee (*see* Regulation 10(1)).

(Annual Returns) Regulations of 1974 require returns to be filed twice a year, providing details of any electricity generation plants that have been sold and the proprietor's personal details.[95]

The Water Resources Act[96] establishes a legal framework for the development of water resources in Nigeria. The Act places ultimate responsibility for the proper development of Nigeria's water resources on the Ministry of Water Resources and Rural Development. The Act vests ultimate rights to the use and control of Nigeria's water resources in the state.[97] However this does not preclude the ability of individuals to take and use water for domestic[98] or industrial purposes, including the generation of hydropower.[99] Even so, a license is required for any person to undertake hydraulic work on the waterways or underground.[100] The mode of application for such a license is set out in section 10 of the Act, which requires applications for the grant of a license to be made to the Secretary in the prescribed form and manner and further, that such applications contain all required information and attach any required documents.[101]

nuclear energy. Nigeria neither produces nor utilizes nuclear energy. Nevertheless, as far back as the mid-1970s, the then Federal Military Government promulgated the Nigeria Atomic Energy Commission Act No. 46 of 1976[102] (NAEC Act). By its preamble, this Act established the Nigeria Atomic Energy Commission (NAEC), responsible for the development of atomic energy and all matters relating to the peaceful use of atomic energy.

The Nuclear Safety and Radiation Protection Act of 1995 establishes the Nigerian Nuclear Regulatory Authority, responsible for controlling and regulating the use of radioactive substances, material, and equipment emitting and generating ionizing radiation. Further, this Act prohibits the acquisition and use of such substances and

[95] Regulations 1 and 2. The Electricity Installation Regulations (EIR) 1996 regulate electrical installations on private and public premises in order to prevent electrical hazards and accidents from such installations. The Electricity Supply Regulations (ESR) 1996 among other things regulate the following: (a) the application process for obtaining a license to supply electricity; (b) stipulates the conditions precedent to issuance of such a license by the Minister; (c) stipulates the manner in which electricity is to be supplied to the consumers; (d) prescribes safety measures to be applied by the licensee for the protection of life and property; and (e) prescribes the penalties for contravention of the Regulations.

[96] Decree No. 101 of 1993.

[97] Section 1(1) provides: "The right to the use and control of all surface and groundwater and of all water in any water course affecting more than one state as described in the schedule to this Decree together with the bed and banks thereof, are by virtue of the Decree and without further assurance vested in the [g]overnment of the federation."

[98] See Water Resources Act, § 2.

[99] Section 3 of the Act states as follows: "Any person or any public authority may acquire a right to use or take water from any water-course or any ground water described in the schedule to this Decree for any purpose in accordance with the provisions of the Decree and any regulation made pursuant thereto."

[100] Water Resources Act, § 9(1).

[101] The Secretary referred to here is the Secretary charged with the responsibility for matters relating to water resources. The federal government with the Japanese government's technical assistance through the Japanese International Cooperation Agency (JICA) prepared a National Water Resources Master Plan. The project started in 1992 and was concluded in 1995. In addition, there is also a Register of Dams in the country, which was completed in 1995. This was necessitated by the dangers of dam breaks as evidenced by the failure of the Barauda Dam in 1988 and the attendant destruction of lives, property, and downstream ecology. The program was geared toward the verification and distribution of the vital statistics of dams. There is also an ongoing rehabilitation works to restore the dams to safety.

[102] Cap. 295, L.F.N. 1990.

equipment on any premises, vehicle, ship, or aircraft except as prescribed in the Act. It also prohibits the disposal of radioactive waste without permission and provides for penalties to be imposed for infringement of its provisions.

biofuels. Biofuels, in the form of wood, charcoal, and biomass, constitute at least 70% of energy consumed across Nigeria. Overall demand for wood fuels, for instance, is expected to increase by approximately 350% by 2030 and urban consumption, in particular, is expected to grow by 250% within the same period.[103] Regulation to halt the destruction of forest resources can be traced back to the Nigerian Constitution which, in section 20, provides that:

> It is an obligation of the state to protect and improve the environment and safeguard the water, air and land, **forest** and wild life of Nigeria.
> [emphasis added]

Moreover, Article 24 of the African Charter on Human and Peoples' Rights (Ratification and Enforcement) Act[104] provides: "[a]ll people shall have the right to a general satisfactory environment favourable to their development."

The requirement of environmental impact assessment in respect of any project embarked upon by any private or public authority with likely environmental impact under the Environmental Impact Assessment Act No. 86 of 1992 all combine to reduce the trend towards massive deforestation in Nigeria.

At a more local level, there are also state forestry laws in Nigeria. The forestry law of Delta State of Nigeria, for instance, defines "forest" to include forest reserves, protected forests, and communal forestry areas.[105] This law prohibits acts capable of dwindling the state's forests and grants the state governor the right to take and declare communal forests to be "forest reserves" or "protected forests" for the purposes of this law, under agreement with local communities. Pursuant to powers granted under section 28 of the forestry law, the state governor promulgated Forestry Regulations that were incorporated in the forestry law as subsidiary legislation to guide and regulate the exploitation and conservation of forest products and timber resources. However, these state laws have not led to a reduction in the spate of deforestation in Southern Nigeria caused by the overwhelming use of fuel wood. The situation is even worse in Northern Nigeria, which is naturally prone to desertification.

renewable energies. Renewable energy sources, such as solar power, wind power, geothermal energy, and wave power, that could, in principle, meet almost all of Nigeria's energy needs are not given any specific regulatory prominence. Such renewable

---

[103] Deregulation of the downstream oil industry with incremental removal of petroleum subsidy without a commensurate increment in the wages of Nigerians will continue to escalate the demand for wood fuels as cheaper alternatives, which in turn may lead to further deforestation.

[104] Cap. 10, L.F.N. 1990.

[105] The law seems to be a comprehensive piece of legislation designed for the preservation and control of forests and its resources. The law is divided into 5 parts with subsidiary legislation attached to it. Part 1, which is the preliminary part, deals with the interpretational aspect of the law. Part 2 deals with provisions relating to forest reserves and protected forests. Part 3 deals with general provisions. Part 4 deals with the protection and management of forests, while part 5 deals with savings provisions. The subsidiary legislation deals essentially with forestry regulations.

energy resources could not only ease current pressures on fossil fuel reserves, they are also cheaper and cleaner to use, causing little environmental pollution. None of these renewable energies alone could solve the problem of finding a substitute for crude oil products as an energy source for Nigeria and beyond: the relevant issue from a sustainability perspective therefore, is developing the most appropriate over-all framework for coordinating various RETs and policies for various renewable energy resources.

The Energy Commission of Nigeria Act[106] establishes the Energy Commission of Nigeria, responsible for coordinating and maintaining general supervision over the systematic development of the various energy resources of Nigeria, including new and renewable energy resources.[107]

Nigeria, by virtue of its location in the tropics, is richly endowed with solar energy resources, receiving daily solar irradiation of between four and six kWh/m^2 and corresponding annual sunshine duration of 1800–3000 hours. As no specific studies have been done on Nigeria's wind energy potential, it is difficult to draw any conclusions in relation to wind power. Nevertheless, with worldwide improvements in instrumentation and measuring capacity, it is reasonably safe to conclude that with increasing governmental and scientific interest in wind power, it would not be impossible to find areas along the Nigerian coast with wind speeds adequate for power generation. To date, Nigeria does not have any wind farms.

3.3.2 Ghana

hydrocarbons. Ghana is not a resource rich country, however it does have modest hydrocarbon resources. The major deposits are in the Tano, Saltpond, Accra/Keta, Voltaian, and Cape Three Points Basins.[108] Natural gas reserves are modest and they are primarily located in the Tano Fields. Studies show that Ghana's estimated natural gas reserves are sufficient to power a 250MW power plant for ten years.[109]

Petroleum operations (upstream) are generally regulated under the Petroleum (Exploration and Production) Law of 1984, which sets out administrative rules governing licensing, the operations of, and decommissioning of, oil and gas installations, including secondary recovery and prevention of waste in oil and gas operations.

The downstream section of the hydrocarbon industry in Ghana is now governed by the Energy Commission Act of 1997[110] (Energy Commission Act). Among other things, this Act establishes the Energy Commission,[111] which is responsible for the regulation, management, development, and utilization of energy resources;[112] the granting of licenses for the transmission;[113] wholesale supply, distribution, and sale of electricity

---

[106] Cap. 109, L.F.N. 1990.   [107] *See* Energy Commission Act, § 1 (2).

[108] The Saltpond Oil Fields, which were operated by AGRI-PETCO in the 1980s, are to be reproduced by exploiting the remaining reserves. The production is expected to average about 1,000 bbl/day. The conservatively estimated recoverable reserves are 1.2 million barrels of oil. The project agreements are presently undergoing statutory governmental approvals. *See* A. Kan Dapaah, Minister for Energy, Ghana, "Expanding Ghana's Energy Resources," *4th Annual Conference on Oil and Gas in the Gulf of Guinea* at 8.

[109] Based on discussions with private investors, the necessary government approvals are being sought for the exploitation of the Tano Field for firing a 125MW barge mounted power plant.

[110] Act 541 of 1997.   [111] Section 1 of the Energy Commission Act, § 1.

[112] *Id.*, § 2(1).   [113] *Id.*, § 2(e).

and natural gas;[114] refining, storage, bulk distribution, marketing, and sale of petroleum products;[115] and related matters.[116]

Even with effective electric power generation, the development of transmission and distribution operations could pose formidable challenges which, if not addressed carefully within an enabling regulatory framework, could jeopardize all efforts to make electricity more easily available and affordable. It is within this context that the Energy Commission Act should be considered. Some of the functions and objects of the Energy Commission are:

(a) to receive and assess applications and grant licences under the Energy Commission Act for the transmission, wholesale supply, distribution and sale of electricity and natural gas;

(b) to establish and enforce, in consultation with PURC, standards of performance for public utilities engaged in the transmission, wholesale supply, distribution and sale of electricity and natural gas; and

(c) to promote and ensure uniform rules of practice for the transmission, wholesale supply, distribution and sale of electricity and natural gas.[117]

Part II of the Energy Commission Act governs licensing, providing in section 11 that no person or entity may engage in any business or any commercial activity for the transmission, wholesale supply, distribution or sale of natural gas unless licensed to do so under the Energy Commission Act. Under section 12, licenses may only be granted to citizens of Ghana, body corporates registered under the Companies Code of 1963, or partnerships registered under the Incorporated Private Partnerships Act of 1962.

The licensing process under the Energy Commission Act has been streamlined as the Energy Commission must, upon receiving an application supported by relevant documents and payment of the prescribed fee, acknowledge receipt of the application within ten working days and inform the applicant in writing of the Commission's decision within sixty days after this ten-day period.[118] Further, by its terms the Energy Commission Act makes it almost obligatory for the Energy Commission to grant licenses where applications have been made in accordance with law.[119]

Part III of the Energy Commission Act governs the transmission, wholesale supply, and distribution of electricity and natural gas. Sections 23(1) and (2) essentially provide that the Energy Commission shall determine the national interconnected transmission system for the delivery of electricity and natural gas throughout Ghana, upon application by public utilities for licenses to provide such services. Such licenses are called

---

[114] *Id.*, § 2(e), (f). [115] *Id.*, §§ 2(h).

[116] Other provisions under Part 1 of this enactment include general directions of the Minister relating to public interest functions of the Commission; composition of the Commission, tenure of office of members of the Commission; allowance to members; meetings of the Commission; disclosure of interest of members of the Commission; as well as committees of the Commission.

[117] *Supra* note 111, §§ 2(e), (f), (g). [118] *Id.*, § 13(2).

[119] *Id.* Section 14 provides that: "Subject to this Act, an application under section 13 shall be granted by the Commission unless there are compelling reasons founded on technical data, national security, public safety or other reasonable justification which shall be communicated to the applicant." Other provisions of this Act include conditions of license; nontransferability of license; duration and renewal of license; power to modify license; suspension or cancellation of license; complaint to Minister; settlement of disputes by arbitration; gazette publication of licenses; interconnection transmission systems and transmission license; conditions for transmission license; wholesale supply license for electricity; as well as license for the distribution and sale of electricity.

"transmission licenses." Section 23(4) prohibits the granting of more than one transmission license at any particular time in the country, effectively creating a monopoly over the transmission of electricity or natural gas. The public utility granted any such transmission license is to be known as the Electricity Transmission Utility or the Gas Transmission Utility.[120]

A transmission license for either natural gas or electricity is subject to certain conditions as the Energy Commission shall determine and shall include the following conditions:

(a) for the safe, reliable, economic dispatch and operation of the national interconnected systems for the transmission of electricity and natural gas without discrimination to any wholesale supplier of electricity or natural gas licenses under the ECA; and
(b) that tariffs to be charged by the licensee for its services shall be subject to the approval of the Public Utilities Regulatory Commission (PURC).[121]

The Energy Commission may, on application by a public utility in the required form, grant the public utility a wholesale supply license to operate facilities and installations for the wholesale supply of electricity or natural gas.[122] A wholesale supply license for electricity or natural gas authorizes the licensee to produce electricity or natural gas for supply to distribution companies and bulk customers.[123] Such a license will only be granted if the Energy Commission is satisfied that it will promote the safe, reliable, and economic operation of the interconnected transmission systems in Ghana.[124] A wholesale supply license may be granted subject to certain specified conditions and must include:

(a) the location of the wholesale supply facilities or stations;
(b) the duration of the license; and
(c) a condition that charges for its services to distribution companies shall be subject to the approval of PURC.[125]

The Energy Commission may also, on application by a public utility, grant the public utility a license to distribute and sell electricity, or to distribute and sell natural gas, without discrimination in those areas or zones designated and specified in the license.[126] Moreover, there are additional provisions concerning standards for electricity and natural gas public utilities to be determined by the Energy Commission in cooperation with PURC; rules of practice to be set by the Energy Commission for electricity and natural gas public utilities licensed under the Energy Commission Act; and an Electricity and Natural Gas Technical Committee.

Under the Energy Commission Act, standards of performance for public utilities for the supply, distribution, and sale of electricity will govern voltage stability, maximum number of scheduled and unscheduled outages, the number and duration of load shedding periods, and metering. Such standards of performance will have the force of legislative instruments.[127]

---

[120] *Id.*, § 23(5).
[121] *Id.*, § 24(1).
[122] *Id.*, § 25(1).
[123] *Id.*, § 25(2).
[124] *Id.*, § 25(3).
[125] *Id.*, § 25(4).
[126] *Id.*, § 26(1).
[127] *Id.*, §§ 27(1), (2).

Where a licensee fails to meet any required standards of performance, in addition to any penalties provided for under the Energy Commission Act or any other enactment, licensees may also be required to pay compensation as determined by the Energy Commission to any person adversely affected as a result of the performance failure.[128] This requirement for payment of compensation will not limit rights to any other remedy at law which may be available to the complainant and further, does not prevent the Energy Commission from taking any other enforcement action or imposing any other penalties that it has a right to impose under law, in respect of the act or omission that constitutes the failure by the licensee.[129]

Part IV of the Energy Commission Act provides for special provisions in relation to petroleum products, which are particularly important in the context of rules for the conversion of crude oil into petroleum energy. The Energy Commission is empowered to grant licenses for the operation of refineries for the supply of petroleum products.[130] Such licenses entitle licensees to convert crude oil into petroleum products for sale without discrimination, to bulk customers of petroleum products and to those persons licensed under the Energy Commission Act to market petroleum products.[131] The Nigerian government is empowered to designate a network of strategic depots for petroleum products.[132] Further, there are provisions for operators of these strategic storage depots for petroleum products to be granted licenses to provide services for the storage and transshipment of petroleum products.[133] In addition to other conditions as specified, licenses for operators of strategic depots for petroleum products are subject to the following conditions:

(a) An obligation to provide services on request for the storage and transshipment of petroleum products to bulk customers and persons licensed under the Act on payment of the relevant charges without discrimination; and
(b) The approval of charges for its services by PURC.[134]

Finally, the Energy Commission may, on application, grant licenses to provide bulk transportation services for petroleum products, through pipelines, by barges, by rail tanker wagons, by road vehicle, or by any other means to be determined by the Energy Commission.[135] Licenses may also be granted that authorize relevant applicants to procure and sell petroleum products on certain terms.[136] Persons and corporate entities are prohibited from constructing or operating a petroleum products retail station, a petroleum products storage depot, a liquefied petroleum gas depot, or a petroleum depot without the prior written authorization of the Energy Commission.[137] Moreover, the Energy Commission is empowered to prescribe technical and operational practice

---

[128] *Id.*, § 27(3).
[129] *Id.*, § 27(4). It is to be noted that the Energy Commission Act supersedes the National Energy Board Law of 1983 (P.N.D.C.L. 62). Accordingly, the assets, rights, obligations, and liabilities of the National Energy Board were transferred to and vested in the new Commission. In addition, the following enactments were repealed by the Energy Commission Act: Excess Energy Consumption (Surcharges) Law of 1984 (P.N.D.C.L. 87); Electricity Corporation of Ghana Decree of 1967 (N.L.C.D. 125); Electricity Corporation of Ghana (Amendment) Law of 1987; and Electricity Corporation of Ghana (Amendment) Law of 1991.
[130] *Id.*, § 31(1).   [131] *Id.*, § 31(2).
[132] *Id.*, § 32.   [133] *Id.*, § 33.
[134] *Id.*, § 34(2).   [135] *Id.*, § 35(1).
[136] *Id.*, § 36.   [137] *Id.*, § 37.

rules governing licensees' refining, storage, bulk transportation, marketing, and sales operations in relation to petroleum products under the Energy Commission Act.[138]

electricity including hydropower. Following the 1983 drought, which substantially reduced water levels in the Volta Lake and resulted in the drastic curtailment of electricity production and supply to all regions in Ghana, the Ghanaian government was prompted to pursue programs for the expansion of the power generation base. This is to be achieved through the development of other, potentially more stable, hydro basins in Western Ghana, especially the Pra, Tano, and Ankobra Rivers, thereby reducing the nation's overreliance on the Volta basin. In addition to these hydro schemes, the government has completed financing arrangements for Volta River Authority (VRA) to install a 330 MW thermal power plant in the country. Ghana National Petroleum Company (GNPC) has also finalized financing arrangements for the installation of a 150 MW power plant utilizing natural gas from the Tano Gas Fields.[139]

Note, the VRA, established under the Volta River Act of 1961 is exempted from licensing requirements under the Energy Commission Act for the production and wholesale supply of electricity from the hydropower installations on the Volta River Basin.[140]

biofuels and renewable energy legislation. Biomass is the dominant source of energy in Ghana, as approximately 69% of national energy consumption is accounted for by biomass in either direct or processed form. Biomass is used in the domestic sector for cooking and other heat applications such as water heating. Woodfuel is the dominant biomass form used in Ghana. Most rural dwellers, representing 70% of Ghana's population, and a sizeable proportion of urban dwellers depend heavily on fuel wood and charcoal for all their domestic and other commercial activities that require heat.

PNDC Law 62 provided the regulatory background for the gradual evolution of national policies and legislation concerning RETs in Ghana, remaining in force as the primary enactment governing the implementation of renewable energy projects until 1996, when the ESDP was introduced.[141]

RETs are currently governed by the Energy Commission Act and the Public Utilities Regulatory Commission Act[142] (PURC Act). The Energy Commission is statutorily required to "recommend national policies for the development and utilization of indigenous energy resources."[143] The phrase "indigenous energy resources" obviously includes renewable energy resources that can be found in Ghana. This will include wind power, solar energy, hydropower, geothermal energy, and biomass.[144] The Energy Commission is also required to "secure a comprehensive data base for national decision

---

[138] *Id.*, § 38. The Energy Commission Act also repealed the following enactments: Petroleum Decree of 1973 (N.R.C.D. 187); Petroleum Decree of 1973 (Amendment) Act 1980 (Act 420); Petroleum Decree (Amendment) (No. 2) Act of 1980 (Act 427); and National Energy Board Law of 1983.

[139] This represents the plan for expanding the power generation base at the inception of the ESDP. The situation has, however, changed and plans are seriously under way to source funding for the development of Bui Hydro power. The VRA thermal generation has so far installed a 440 MW capacity plant at Aboade, near Takoradi.

[140] *Supra* note 111, § 30.

[141] The *ESDP* has been previously discussed in the Section 3.2.2.

[142] Act 538 of 1997.   [143] *Supra* note 111, § 2(a).

[144] *Id.*, § 57.

making on the extent of development and utilisation of energy resources available to the nation."[145]

Although most of the provisions of the Energy Commission Act are applicable only to electricity, natural gas, and petroleum products, Part V of the Act establishes an Energy Fund, which objectives include, inter alia, the "promotion of projects for the development and utilization of renewable energy resources, including solar energy,"[146] as well as "such other purposes as may be determined by the [Energy] Commission."[147]

As the Energy Commission is also empowered to "determine allocations to be made towards the objectives of the Fund"[148] and having regard to the objectives of the Energy Fund, including the "promotion of projects for the development and utilisation of renewable energy resources, including solar energy," more Energy Fund monies could be justifiably allocated for the development of RETs by the Energy Commission, realizing broader renewable energy aims under the Energy Commission Act.

3.4 Sustainable Energy Regulatory Institutions

3.4.1 Nigeria
hydrocarbons. The following regulatory institutions are relevant in the context of the oil and gas industry in Nigeria:

(a) the Federal Ministry of Petroleum Resources (FMPR);
(b) the Department of Petroleum Resources (DPR);
(c) the Nigerian National Petroleum Corporation (NNPC);
(d) the Federal Ministry of Environment (FME)/Federal Environmental Protection Agency (FEPA); and
(e) the Energy Commission of Nigeria (ECN).

FMPR is the executive arm of the Nigerian federal government responsible for overseeing the oil and gas industries. The Minister of Petroleum Resources (Minister) heads the FMPR. Under the Petroleum Act, the Minister is vested with broad supervisory powers, including licensing and regulatory powers.[149] The responsibilities assigned to the FMPR are:

(a) overall supervision of the Nigerian petroleum industry including the NNPC and its subsidiaries to ensure compliance with applicable statutes;
(b) issuing permits, licenses, leases, and granting authorizations and approvals as prescribed by statutes for a whole range of petroleum activities from seismic surveys to drilling, production, construction, and operation of processing plants, such as refineries, petrochemical and LNG plants, and for the marketing of petroleum products;
(c) policy responsibilities in relation to the granting of petroleum rights and the marketing of crude oil, natural gas, and their derivatives;

---

[145] *Id.*, § 2(d).
[146] *Id.*, 42(b).
[147] *Id.*, § 42(d).
[148] *Id.*, § 44 (1)(b).
[149] *See* Petroleum Act §§ 2–4. Section 8(a)–(h) provides for the powers and duties of the Minister as well as public officers under the Minister. Section 9 empowers the Minister to make regulations for the smooth operation of the petroleum industry. All the other Petroleum Regulations were made pursuant to the latter power.

(d) monitoring and control of environmental pollution associated with oil and gas operations and the administration and enforcement of environmental protection statutes and statutory provisions affecting such operations;

(e) fixing of allowable production levels and prices for crude oil, natural gas, petroleum products, and their derivatives;

(f) enforcement of oil and gas conservation laws and practices and monitoring petroleum activities to ensure proper conservation of oil and gas;

(g) giving such assistance to the petroleum industry as would enhance the industry in the overall interests of Nigeria; and

(h) duties relating to the following bodies –
   (a) Nigerian National Petroleum Corporation (NNPC);
   (b) Organization of Petroleum Exporting Countries (OPEC);
   (c) Petroleum Equalization Fund;
   (d) Petroleum Technology Development Fund;
   (e) Petroleum Training Institute, Effurum; and
   (f) African Petroleum Producers Association (APPA).[150]

Under the current democratic dispensation, the Nigerian President has not appointed a Minister. There is, however, a Special Adviser to the President on Petroleum, who acts in a de facto capacity as the Minister.

DPR began as an Inspectorate arm of the NNPC.[151] The NNPC was itself a merger between the then Ministry of Petroleum Resources and the Nigerian National Corporation (NNC) in 1977. By 1985, the Ministry of Petroleum and Energy was reestablished and in 1986 renamed the FMPR. What was previously known as the Petroleum Inspectorate arm of the NNPC was later transferred to the FMPR in 1988.[152] The DPR is the technical, supervisory, and enforcement arm of the FMPR[153] and its responsibilities include:

(a) ensuring that the activities of all the companies engaged in petroleum operations are conducted in accordance with all applicable laws and regulations in its capacity as the government agency for the enforcement of the Petroleum Act and the Oil Pipelines Act and regulations made thereunder;

(b) monitoring and controlling oil industry operations to ensure compliance with national goals and governing policies in relation to Nigeria's petroleum resources;

(c) enforcement of conservation measures and laws especially as to reservoir energy, production methods and practices and other oil field practices, rates of production and permissible quantities of production;

(d) issuing permits, licenses, leases, and giving authorizations and approvals as required under the enactments governing the whole range of oil and gas administration;

(e) keeping records of petroleum activities, data, production, and significant operational occurrences;

---

[150] "Assignment of Responsibilities," *Federal Government of Nigeria Official Gazette* No. 15, Volume 70, March 3, 1989.

[151] Nigerian National Petroleum Corporation Act, § 10(1), Cap. 320, L.F.N. 1990.

[152] However, Part II of Cap. 320 is yet to be amended or deleted in order to bring it into conformity with the transfer till date.

[153] M. M. Olisa, *Nigerian Petroleum Law and Practice* (2d ed.), Jonia Ventures Ltd. (Lagos, 1997) at 228.

(f) monitoring and control of environmental pollution associated with oil and gas operations;

(g) advising the Minister on parameters for fixing allowable production levels and prices for crude oil and petroleum products; and

(h) carrying out such duties as the Minister may from time to time delegate or direct.[154]

NNPC was formed through the merger of the then Nigerian National Oil Corporation (NNOC) and the then Ministry of Petroleum Resources in April 1977.[155] The NNPC had operational interests in, and was granted statutory powers in relation to, refining, petrochemicals, and products transportation as well as marketing. This was in addition to exploration and production activities carried out offshore and in the Niger Delta by the NNOC.[156] The Chairman of the Board of the NNPC is the Minister.[157]

Between 1978 and 1989, NNPC constructed refineries in Warri, Kaduna, and Port Harcourt and took over the 35,000 barrel Shell Refinery established in Port Harcourt in 1965. Further, the NNPC constructed several kilometers of pipelines, pump stations, and depots for the distribution of petroleum products throughout the country and also pioneered exploration activities in the Chad Basin. In 1982, product retail, which hitherto was firmly in the hands of major multinational oil companies, was deregulated to accommodate independent (indigenous) marketers. In 1990, with a view to improving the country's oil and gas reserve base, oil exploration, which has progressively moved further offshore from the Niger Delta, was further extended into frontier areas, including the deep offshore and the inland basins of Anambra, Benin, and Benue. Acreages were allocated to several multinational companies in these latter areas after they signed Production Sharing Contracts (PSCs) with NNPC.

FEPA has now been submerged within FME, created after the commencement of the new democratic dispensation. Although FEPA does not exist in fact, it does exist in law as its enabling statute (FEPA Act)[158] has not been repealed. Prohibitions in the FEPA Act on the discharge of hazardous substances (together with related offenses) and spillers' liability with concomitant general penalties are very relevant to hydrocarbon operations in both up- and downstream sectors.[159] Under section 4 of the FEPA Act, FEPA is responsible for the protection and development of the environment and environmental technology, including initiating policy in relation to environmental research and technology. FEPA is responsible for biodiversity conservation and developing the sustainable use of natural resources in cooperation with relevant international bodies as well as state and local government authorities. FEPA is also the institution responsible for implementing the Environmental Impact Assessment (EIA) Act[160] (EIA Act), which restricts the development of public or private projects without prior consideration of

---

[154] B. A. Osuno, "The Role of the Petroleum Inspectorate Division of the NNPC as the Guardian of the Nigerian Oil Industry," paper delivered at the National Workshop on Nigerian Petroleum Law, May 31, 1984.

[155] *See* the NNPC Act No. 33 of 1977, now Cap. 320, L.F.N. 1990. Its Preamble refers to it as "[a]n Act to dissolve the Nigerian National Oil Corporation and to establish the [NNPC] empowered to engage in all commercial activities relating to the Petroleum Industry and to enforce all regulatory measures relating to the general control of the Petroleum sector through its Petroleum Inspectorate Department."

[156] NNPC, "Introduction," *2003 Diary.*   [157] *Supra* note 151, § 1(3).

[158] FEPA was established by the FEPA Act, No. 131, L.F.N. 1990.

[159] It is currently undergoing review at the executive level before the amendment bill is sent to the National Assembly.

[160] Decree No. 86 of 1992.

the environmental impact of the project. The Schedule to the EIA Act sets out the mandatory study activities for EIAs. Paragraph 12 of the Schedule sets out provisions specifically concerning petroleum which is defined to include the construction of oil and gas separation, processing, handling, and storage facilities; the construction of oil refineries; and the construction of product depots for the storage of petrol, gas, or diesel (excluding service stations), located within three kilometers of any commercial, industrial, or residential areas and that have a combined storage capacity of 60,000 barrels or more.

electricity. In Nigeria, the following institutions are relevant in relation to electricity generation, transmission, and distribution:

(a) the Federal Ministry of Power and Steel (FMPS);
(b) the Federal Ministry of Water Resources (FMWR);
(c) the National Electric Power Authority (NEPA);
(d) the Federal Environment Protection Authority/Federal Minister of Environment (FEPA/FME);
(e) the Consumer Protection Council (CPC);
(f) the Utilities Charges Commission (UCC);
(g) the Energy Commission of Nigeria (ECN); and
(h) state/local government Electricity Boards.

FMPS is the executive arm of the Nigerian government responsible for overseeing the power and steel sectors of the Nigerian economy. FMWR is also an executive arm of the federal government, responsible for overseeing the water resources sector. Like all other ministries under the current democratic dispensation, two of the President's political appointees head both FMWR and FMPS respectively.[161] There are eight directorates under FMPS, the most important for sustainable energy purposes being the Electrical Inspectorate Services Division (EIS), which is responsible for:

(a) formulation of safety and other regulations binding on operators in the electric power sector;
(b) issuing licenses to operators in the power sector after approval of their application by the Minister;
(c) monitoring of compliance by operators with the various regulations affecting their operations;
(d) investigation of accidents; and
(e) monitoring and implementation of the rural electrification programs of the federal government.

The Department of Power under FMPS is responsible for:

(a) supervision and monitoring of NEPA's activities generally;
(b) formulation of such policies relating to the power sector as may enable the government to achieve its objective of supplying electricity to all parts of the country;

---

[161] The Minister for Water Resources and the Minister of State for Water Resources (junior Minister), which is also reflected in FMPS.

(c) initiation and implementation of development plans and policies for the power sector;

(d) monitoring and supervision of the construction of power stations and transmission lines nationwide;

(e) review and evaluation of the annual budget of NEPA before it is submitted to the Minister for approval;

(f) review and evaluation of NEPA's proposal for tariff increase before it is submitted to the UCC for approval; and

(g) regulatory oversight of the operation of independent power producers (IPPs).

NEPA was established by the NEPA Act,[162] as amended by the NEPA (Amendment) Act of 1998.[163] NEPA is the principal agency responsible for the development and maintenance of an efficient, coordinated, and economical system of electricity supply, power generation, transmission, and distribution throughout Nigeria. NEPA began as a monopoly service provider, but has gradually been unbundled with few privileges (deriving from its former position as a state-owned monopoly) remaining.[164] Nevertheless, NEPA is generally held to be underperforming.[165]

The Consumer Protection Council (CPC) was established by the Consumer Protection Council Act[166] and is responsible for overseeing issues of quality and costing in the provision of public services, including electricity. CPC safeguards the interests of consumers and is responsible for providing redress for consumer complaints in a timely manner through appropriate forms of dispute resolution. CPC also has power to enforce proceedings to ensure that a defaulting service provider complies with its directives.

The Utilities Charge Commission (UCC), established by the UCC Act,[167] is responsible, inter alia, for protecting consumer interests in relation to the setting of tariffs for utilities such as energy, water, and postal freight and to evaluate, on a continuing basis, trends in tariffs charged by such public utilities.

nuclear energy. The Nigerian Nuclear Regulatory Authority (NRA) is the institution responsible for the control and regulation of the use of radioactive substances, materials, and equipment emitting and generating ionizing radiation in Nigeria. NAEC is vested with the following powers:

(a) to prospect for and mine radioactive minerals;

(b) to construct and maintain nuclear installations for the purpose of generating electricity;

---

[162] Cap. 256, L.F.N. 1990.   [163] Act No. 29 of 1998.

[164] The Federal Ministry of Power and Steel would ordinarily not approve an application for power generation license in an area where NEPA is sufficiently operational. Besides, the Electricity (Private Licenses) Regulations give NEPA the exclusive prerogative of determining if it can undertake the functions for which a license is sought or if it has objections to the issuance of any such license. NEPA could also give a 90-day notice to quit to a licensee if it is of the view that it can provide the services being undertaken by the licensee.

[165] It can barely meet its overhead costs. It generates only a third of its installed capacity of 5,906 MW. Its transmission and distribution network is inadequate and frequently interrupted by vandals. As a result, it is only barely able to recover 35% of the cost of energy distributed. In fact, the agency is almost crippled by debt overhang.

[166] No. 66 of 1992.   [167] No. 104 of 1992.

(c) to produce, use, and dispose of atomic energy and carry out research into matters connected with the peaceful uses of atomic energy;

(d) to manufacture or otherwise produce, buy, or carry out research into matters connected with the peaceful uses of atomic energy;

(e) to make arrangements with universities and other institutions or persons in Nigeria for the conduct of research into matters connected with atomic energy or radioactive substances and to make grants to universities or other institutions or persons engaged in the production or use of atomic energy or radioactive substances or in research into matters connected with atomic energy or radioactive substances;

(f) to educate and train persons in matters connected with atomic energy and radioactive substances; and

(g) to advise the federal government on questions relating to atomic energy.

renewable energy. The Energy Commission of Nigeria (ECN), the agency responsible for the coordination and general supervision of the systematic development of Nigeria's energy resources, was established by the Energy Commission of Nigeria Act (ECN Act). Section 1(2) of the *Act* provides for the composition of ECN. The departments within ECN include Energy Planning and Analysis, which in turn includes Energy Efficiency Demand Management and Conservation; Rural Energy; and Alternative and New and Renewable Energy Sources.[168] ECN is charged with responsibility for the strategic planning and coordination of national energy policies, including consideration of all the ramifications of such policies; preparation, after consultation, where ECN considers appropriate, with government agencies whose functions relate to the field of energy development or supply; and the development of periodic master plans for the balanced and coordinated development of energy resources in Nigeria, including recommendations for the exploitation of new sources of energy as and when considered necessary. ECN is also responsible for formulating guidelines in relation to the optimal utilization of particular forms of energy for specific purposes.

3.4.2 Ghana

hydrocarbons. The major institutions responsible for overseeing the hydrocarbons industry in Ghana are the Ministry of Energy and the Ghana National Petroleum Corporation (GNPC). Overall responsibility for the control and direction of the hydrocarbons industry rests with the government through the Minister of Energy, a political appointee of the President, who heads the Ministry of Energy.[169] In addition to supervising the operations of state-owned petroleum and oil refineries, the Ministry of Energy oversees the two public utilities in the power sector, VRA and the Electricity Corporation of Ghana (ECG).[170] The Ministry of Energy also operates the nation's strategic reserve of petroleum products through the Bulk Oil Storage and Transportation Company (BOST).

---

[168] ECN Act, § 1(2)(b).

[169] This position under the military dispensation that used to be occupied by the Secretary of State for Fuel and Power.

[170] A. Kan Dapaah, "Expanding Ghana's Energy Resources," *4th Annual Conference on Oil and Gas in the Gulf of Guinea.*

GNPC is responsible for procurement, storage, and the bulk distribution of petroleum products to oil marketing companies.[171] The Petroleum (Exploration & Production) Law of 1984 empowers GNPC to operate on all open land in Ghana, alone or in association with foreign partners.

In late 1998, the Ministry of Energy established a seven-member Energy Commission, whose brief was to regulate and manage the utilization of energy resources in Ghana and also to coordinate energy policies. The Energy Commission was also responsible for the granting of licenses for the transmission, supply, and sale of natural gas.

Other important institutions in the hydrocarbon sector are the Tema Oil Refinery Company (TOR) with an operating capacity of 45,000 barrels per day, running on crude oil imported mostly from Nigeria and GNPC. In 1992, the Tema Lube Oil Company constructed a new oil blending plant designed to produce 25,000 tons of oil per year.

electricity. The Ministry of Energy is the principal institution responsible for establishing and implementing energy sector policy in Ghana, including overseeing the Volta River Authority (VRA) and the Electricity Corporation of Ghana (ECG). While ECG is responsible for the distribution of electricity supplied by VRA throughout Southern Ghana, VRA is responsible for the generation and transmission of electricity in Ghana and supplies electricity in bulk to ECG, Volta Aluminium Company (VALCO), an aluminum smelter at Tema, several mining operations, and other industrial concerns. Further, VRA also exports electricity to Communaute Electrique du Benin (CEB) in Togo and Benin. VRA also distributes power in Northern Ghana through its subsidiary, Northern Electricity Department (NED).

The primary regulatory institutions in the electricity subsector are the Public Utilities Regulatory Commission (PURC) and the Energy Commission. PURC is responsible for regulating and overseeing the provision of electrical and water utility services to consumers, including protecting the interests of both service providers and consumers, approving the rates charged by service providers, monitoring performance standards, and promoting competition among service providers.

The Energy Commission is responsible for regulating, developing, and managing the utilization of energy resources, such as electricity, natural gas, and petroleum products. The Energy Commission is also responsible for preparing indicative plans for the development of the energy sector; maintaining the licensing regime for public utilities for the transmission, wholesale supply, distribution, and sale of electricity and natural gas; and enforcing performance standards for public utilities.

renewable energy. A great deal of what has already been said about the Energy Commission applies in equal measure to the Commission's institutional responsibilities in relation to renewable energy policies, which include, among other things, the recommendation of national policies for the development and utilization of indigenous energy resources, as well as developing and providing a comprehensive database on the extent

[171] An Mbendi Profile: Ghana: Oil And Gas Industry – Overview, available at http://www.mbendi.co.za/indy/oil/af/gh/p0005.htm, at 1.

to which available energy resources have been developed and utilized in Ghana.[172] This database is to provide an information base for national decision making in connection with energy development projects and policies.

Important sections of the Energy Commission Act provide for the establishment of an Energy Fund.[173] Under the Energy Commission Act, monies generated through the Energy Fund are required to be used, among other things, for the promotion of projects for the development and utilization of renewable energy resources, including solar energy. The Energy Fund's revenue is derived principally through government levies on petroleum products, electricity, and natural gas, where a prescribed proportion of such levies is required to be paid into the Energy Fund.[174]

4 APPRAISAL AND RECOMMENDATIONS

4.1 Policy

The importance of a pan-Africa energy policy and domestic energy policies that are consistent with this cannot be overemphasized. Currently, regional and subregional conventions and protocols with very broad environmental provisions, requiring the rational utilization of environmental resources (including energy resources), belies the existence of a pan-Africa policy on sustainable energy.[175] Several plausible reasons can be offered to explain the current absence of a continental policy framework on sustainable energy in Africa. First, the uneven distribution of conventional energy resources that has resulted in uneven development within and between several African states. Second, revenues derived from the exploitation of energy resources are usually the exclusive preserve of the host governments and foreign investors. Third, environmental damage caused by the exploitation of energy resources is widely perceived to be localized. Fourth, it is only very recently that connections between energy and sustainable development have been emphasized globally. There is no doubt that current practices concerning the exploitation of energy resources and development are having increasingly detrimental impacts on human health and the environment, through global warming and atmospheric pollution. Furthermore, the widespread lack of access to affordable energy is perpetuating poverty and associated gender inequity.

In percentage terms, 40% of the world's people lack modern energy services. In Africa, this number exceeds 80%. Accordingly, securing affordable energy production, use, and availability is of the utmost importance. The regional and subregional agreements currently in place were never intended to govern sustainable energy needs. The provisions of these agreements are too general and broad to be of any real significance. A pan-Africa policy instrument that focuses attention on sustainable energy and

---

[172] *See* Section 3.3.2 of this chapter on Ghanaian renewable energy legislation.

[173] *Supra* note 111, § 41.

[174] The levy on petroleum products is one cedi per litre (¢1/litre), while that on electricity is ¢1.70/kWh.

[175] At the World Summit on Sustainable Development held in Johannesburg from August 26 to September 4, 2002, world leaders reaffirmed their commitment to securing a better future for all people in all countries, for all generations and identified five priority areas – water, energy, health, agriculture, and biodiversity (WEHAB). Despite the poignancy of these priority areas for Africa's sustainable development, there has not been any effort to harmonize development initiatives and goals within the context of a continental policy on Sustainable Development a year after the Johannesburg Summit.

environmental aspects of such energy projects could set guidelines, prescribe standards, and provide an overall framework for the sustainable management of Africa's vast energy resources, while using existing institutions at continental, subregional, and national levels for the effective implementation of policy goals.[176]

On a national level, Nigeria has no national energy policy. What it has is a National Policy on the Environment that articulates a national environmental policy on energy generally and more specifically in relation to oil and gas resources, but does not specifically provide for renewable energies. As with most such policy documents, it focuses on how to minimize the environmental, health, and safety risks posed by the development and use of energy resources. References in the National Policy on the Environment to a National Energy Policy and a National Energy Utilization Master Plan are essentially hollow, since no national policy or master plan exists.[177] In any event, the existence of a national environmental policy does not preclude the need for a national energy policy. A Nigerian National Energy Policy similar to the White Paper on the Energy Policy of the Republic of South Africa of December 1998[178] is urgently needed. Such a policy document should restate the Nigerian government's commitment to "the promotion of access to affordable and sustainable energy services for small businesses, disadvantaged households, small farms, schools, clinics, in our rural areas and a wide range of other community establishments."

Ghana is, perhaps, much more advanced in its articulation of a national energy policy. Ghana's Energy Sector Development Program (ESDP) could be said to be the equivalent of the White Paper on the Energy Policy of the Republic of South Africa, as it sets out the various factors that shape Ghana's energy sector policies, a framework for meeting its energy sector goals, and the programs currently being implemented by MME in all energy sectors, including renewable energy, power, petroleum as well as energy efficiency and conservation. What is particularly impressive about the ESDP is its identification of short-, medium-, and long-term objectives for future development of Ghana's renewable energy resources. What is urgently needed now in Ghana is the formulation of new energy laws or the amendment of existing energy laws with a view to consistency with, and complementary to, Ghana's policy goals in relation to sustainable energy.

More generally, other African states, and Nigeria in particular, should consider following Ghana's lead and the approach taken by Republic of South Africa in establishing national energy policies to ensure that national energy resources are sufficiently tapped and developed for the benefit of their respective nations and African peoples generally. In this way, energy production, transmission, and distribution can lead to a manifest improvement in the living standards of African citizens.

Such a national energy policy should first, identify the context, objectives, and priorities of a national sustainable energy policy in the short, medium, and long term;

---

[176] The African Union (AU) and various subregional bodies – Economic Community of West African States (ECOWAS), South African Development Cooperation (SADC), and East African Economic Community (EAEC) just to mention a few.

[177] Admittedly, there is the National Draft Policy on Electric Power of December 2000.

[178] The White Paper was developed by an active process of consultation, beginning with the publication of the Energy Policy Discussion Document in August 1995. This process was concluded in December 1998 when Cabinet approved this White Paper as government policy on Energy. The Introduction and the Appendix give more information on this consultation process.

second, identify and analyze demand and supply sectors as well as interrelated issues; and third, preserve an appropriate balance between energy demand and supply as well as a balance between the use of natural energy resources and environmental considerations.

In their respective national energy policies, African states must establish a clear distinction between their primary role in formulating policies and regulating the energy sector and their secondary role as facilitators in the supply of energy services. Moreover, such energy policies must go further to set out a framework for sustainable energy regulation which is stable, consistent, transparent, and nondiscriminatory, while at the same time strengthening institutional capacities to implement and enforce this regulatory regime. The rationale for such an energy policy is obvious. Governments all over the world are retreating from direct involvement in, and domination of, economic environments and instead, performing a more specialized role, that of an efficient regulator. This does not mean that the state does not operate in the market at all. Rather, a system of regulation developed and enforced by the state must necessarily be in place to ensure the proper and efficient functioning of markets, as well as to appropriately address broader social concerns such as consumer interests, environmental protection, and the need for sustainable energy.[179]

Generally speaking, laws should reflect policy concerns, as no legislation can or should be made in vacuum. The presence of a multiplicity of fragmentary energy laws in most African countries, which laws are not based on any particular overarching energy policy, may be one of the reasons why regulatory institutions are currently unable to effectively implement such laws and why sustainable energy development has continued to elude Africa.

4.2 Legislation

At a continental level, there is no multilateral investment treaty between African countries, similar to Europe's Energy Charter Treaty[180] (ECT) or the North American Free Trade Agreement[181] (NAFTA), with a focus on trade and energy investment in Africa. The reasons for the absence of such a treaty are varied. First, African countries are generally at similar levels of social and economic development and are basically capital importing developing countries.[182] Synergies for sustainable energy development and consumption are more easily established within an amalgam of capital exporting and capital importing countries all located within the same subregion.[183] Second, there is a

---

[179] C. Redgwell, "Privatisation and Environmental Regulation: Some General Observations" (1997) 15(1) *Journal of Energy & Natural Resources Law* 36.

[180] The ECT is an EU-driven international agreement that aims, amongst other things, to create a freer and more competitive energy market among its contracting parties through the establishment of negotiated discipline on the regulation of investment, transit, and trade in the energy sector. For more information, *see* T. Walde (ed.), *The Energy Charter Treaty: An East-West Gateway for Investment and Trade*, Kluwer Publishers (London, 1996).

[181] NAFTA is a U.S.-driven free trade agreement in North America with a special chapter devoted to energy products.

[182] The Republic of South Africa is possibly the only exception on the continent. South Africa is likely to play the role of a middle income capital exporting country.

[183] As between the more established capital exporting Western nations and the recently established capital importing Eastern European nations in transition, or between the superpower capital exporting United States and Mexico, a capital importing developing country within the North American subregion. *See* R. F. Housman & P. M. Orbuch, "Integrating Labor and Environmental Concerns into the North American

paucity of highly skilled indigenous human, institutional, and legal capacity in science and technology areas that are relevant for sustainable energy development in Africa. Accordingly, African countries are bound to look outward to Europe and America and also Asia (Japan and China) to source the much needed technical expertise to exploit its energy resources.[184]

However, together with technical assistance partnerships and the cooperation of sustainable energy companies from more economically advanced nations (MEANs), a cooperative approach by African countries to the development, distribution, transmission, and consumption of energy resources on the continent would, in the final analysis, provide far greater benefits to their respective national economies and peoples. Such cooperation and the resulting benefits can hardly be achieved in the absence of broadly consistent bilateral agreements or a multilateral sustainable energy charter treaty between participating African countries. The uneven distribution of energy resources across Africa; the gross underdevelopment of Africa's commercial energy resources; the landlocked position of many African countries and the consequent difficulty of importing commercial energy on an affordable basis; the widespread poverty in Africa; the poor development of commercial energy infrastructure; and the paucity of highly skilled technical expertise on the continent, all combine in varying degrees to make a cooperative approach toward the harnessing of resources for sustainable energy development in Africa the preferred option.

Some interesting findings arise out of a detailed comparative examination of current energy legislation in Nigeria and Ghana. First, such legislation reflects an understanding that an appropriate legal framework is a prerequisite for maximizing investment opportunities in the energy sector in both countries, as indeed in most countries in Africa and beyond. Table 21.2 sets out current energy legislation in Ghana and Nigeria. A plethora of administrative and private regulations for energy investments exist in both countries. Existing legislation in both Ghana and Nigeria is mostly rule oriented, requiring implementation processes that are basically coercive and provide for judicial remedies. This, in turn, requires an efficient and integrated judicial system. To be sure, both countries inherited a colonial system of judicial administration based, in part, on the English common law.[185] At common law, environmental protection in the context of energy investments is grounded largely in actions in nuisance, negligence, trespass or based on the rule in *Rylands* v. *Fletcher*, which covers liability for damage caused by the escape of noxious substances from land owned by the tortfeasor. However, both the applicability and usefulness of common law remedies are limited[186] first, by the common law's primary function to protect private personal and proprietary rights,

---

Free Trade Agreement: A Look Back and a Look Ahead" (1993) 8 *The American University Journal of International Law & Policy* 719.

[184] Within a globalized world these should not really be a problem. The fact is the absence of these key variables puts Africa at a serious disadvantage in negotiating with global capital exporting companies, institutions, or countries. In the absence of a Sustainable Energy Charter Treaty (SECT) in Africa, African countries are left to develop their respective national energy resources at their own pace and subject to their own rules. The prevailing competition for scarce international capital in a globalized environment imposes cutthroat competition for foreign investment, which consistently leaves Africa marginalized.

[185] The others are doctrines of equity, local legislation, and customary law.

[186] UNEP & UNDP, *Training in Environmental Law and Policy: The Case of Nigeria*, Report of the UNEP/UNDP Training Program in Environmental Law and Policy for Nigerian Lawyers conducted by UNEP, Nairobi, November 3–28, 1998 at 8.

Table 21.2 Summary of some major energy legislation in Ghana and Nigeria

ENERGY TYPES	ENERGY LEGISLATION IN GHANA	ENERGY LEGISLATION IN NIGERIA
Hydrocarbons	Petroleum (Exploration & Production) Law of 1984; Petroleum Regulations of 1959, L.N. 206; The Safety (Petroleum Rules), 1959, L.N. 207; and the Energy Commission Act, No. 541 of 1997.	Constitution of Nigeria 1999; Petroleum Act and Associated Regulations Cap. 350 L.F.N.; Associated Gas Reinjection Act, Cap. 26, L.F.N.; Deep Offshore & Inland Basin Production Sharing Contract Decree No. 9, 1999; Environmental Impact Assessment Act of 1992; Hydrocarbon Oil Refineries Act, Cap. 39, L.F.N.; Nigerian National Petroleum Corporation Act, Cap. 320, L.F.N.; Petroleum Profits Tax Act, Cap. 354, L.F.N.
Electricity including Hydropower	Volta River Act of 1961, Act 46; Public Utilities Regulatory Commission Act of 1997; Energy Commission Act of 1997, which has repealed the following enactments: 1 National Energy Board Law, 1983; 2 Excess Energy Consumption (Surcharges) Law, 1984; 3 Electricity Corporation of Ghana Decree, 1967; 4 Electricity Corporation of Ghana (Amendment) Law, 1987 and Electricity Corporation of Ghana (Amendment) Law of 1991.	Constitution of Nigeria 1999; National Electric Power Authority (NEPA) (Amendment) Act No. 29, 1998; Customs, Excise Tariff, Etc. (Consolidation) (CETEC) (Amendment) Act, No. 16, 1997; Finance (Miscellaneous Taxation Provision) Act, No. 18, 1998; Petroleum Profits Tax Act (PPTA), Cap. 354, L.F.N. 1999; Utilities Charges Commission Act, No. 104, 1992; Electricity (Amendment) Act of 1998 and a host of implementing Regulations.
Nuclear	N/A	Nigerian Atomic Energy Commission Act, No. 46, 1976; Nuclear Safety and Radiation Protection Act of 1995.
Renewable including Biofuels	Energy Commission Act of 1997 and the Public Utilities Regulatory Commission Act of 1997.	Constitution of Nigeria 1999; African Charter on Human and Peoples Rights (Ratification and Enforcement) Act, Cap. 10, L.F.N.; Nigerian Energy Commission Act, Cap. 109, L.F.N. 1990

Source: Compiled by Author; N/A: Not Available

whereas many environmental resources including energy are "public property," or "state property." Moreover, as the common law operates only where harm has been caused to an ascertainable individual or entity, rather than to the environment per se, its effectiveness is limited to the resolution of what may be termed "neighborhood" environmental problems. Second, intricacies resulting from technological developments also limit the applicability and usefulness of the common law: the principle of stare decisis, or judicial precedent means that the common law develops on a case-by-case basis. This process is ill suited to developing legal rules of environmental protection for sustainable energy. It is against this backdrop that a more specific investigation of current energy legislation in both Nigeria and Ghana has to be undertaken.

In Nigeria, mines, oil fields, oil mining, geological surveys, and like matters are all on the ELL and accordingly they fall within the exclusive legislative competence of the federal or central government. Overcentralization of regulatory authority over energy resources in Africa generally, and Nigeria in particular, has tended to result in the inequitable distribution of revenues derived from the exploitation of energy resources, usually in favor of those majority groups that control the federal or central government. Accordingly, rather than contributing toward poverty reduction in those areas where energy resources are mined, environmental degradation, despoliation, and deprivation, mostly in the Niger Delta of Nigeria, have largely been the results of energy resources exploration and exploitation.[187] And, in a somewhat circular manner, the resulting and incessant restiveness of youths and women in the Niger Delta is inimical to sustainable energy investment in the first place.

The Nigerian Petroleum Act of 1969 and associated regulations are outmoded. This observation is equally true of the Ghanian Petroleum Law of 1984. As part of the process of liberalizing oil and gas investments, sustainable energy legislation relating to oil and gas exploration and development should focus on minimizing environmental damage,[188] protecting health,[189] promoting safety,[190] and addressing broader social issues.[191]

In relation to downstream energy sectors, Ghana's regulatory framework is further advanced than Nigeria's.[192] Ghana's Energy Commission Act is currently the governing legislative framework, not just for petroleum products, but also for electricity and natural gas. By way of contrast, Nigeria's Hydrocarbons Oil Refineries Act and Petroleum Regulations for downstream sectors were promulgated in 1965 and 1967 respectively and are still operational in an era of economic liberalization. Although Nigeria's upstream sectors are the most important foreign exchange earners, refining and downstream sector operations actually impact on the citizenry directly. The availability, effective transmission, and distribution of petroleum products are driving forces behind any economy and impact on the prices of all other goods and services. Pervasive poverty in

---

[187] I. L. Worika, "Deprivation, Despoliation and Destitution: Whither Environment and Human Rights in Nigeria's Niger Delta?" (2000–2001) 8 *Nigerian Juridical Review* 85–125.

[188] Soil pollution, atmospheric pollution, pollution of the sea from land based and offshore sources, as well as oil and gas infrastructural damage to biodiversity.

[189] Some relevant provisions of the Public Health Laws of the former Regions in Nigeria such as the Public Health Law, Cap. 103, Laws of the Eastern Region, should be incorporated into modern sustainable energy laws. For example, Sections 7–10 of Cap. 103 on nuisance and its abatement as well as on the fouling of water could be part of health provisions of a sustainable energy law.

[190] It took thirty-four years for Nigeria to come up with the Mineral Oils (Safety) Regulations, which repealed the Mineral Oils (Safety) Regulations Law No. 45 of 1963.

[191] Government must clearly and adequately address employment and other social issues in the oil and gas industry to avoid unnecessary interference with petroleum operations by its workforce. While it would be difficult, if not impossible, to legislate the concept of corporate social responsibility into existence, the legislation could encourage or facilitate responsible corporate citizenship.

[192] A plausible reason for this could be that Ghana is a net importer of crude oil from Nigeria, which it refines to meet domestic needs. Accordingly, the problems of shipping, unshipping, loading, landing, and transportation/storage of petroleum products loom large.

Africa militates against total deregulation of these subsectors. Conversely, absent the political will to deregulate refining and downstream sectors in the hydrocarbons industry,
governments wittingly or unwittingly interfere with the energy market, distort prices,
sustain inefficient state-run enterprises, and generally misallocate scarce resources. Sustainable energy legislation for downstream sectors in the hydrocarbons industry must
seek to increase access to petroleum products at an affordable cost. What is needed in
Ghana is for the Energy Commission to prescribe technical and operational practice
rules for those persons licensed under the Energy Commission Act engaging in the
refining, storage, bulk transportation, marketing, and sale of petroleum products.

Electricity regulation in Nigeria, with the overall aims of liberalizing the power sector,
unbundling NEPA, and introducing new and independent players, is advancing at an
impressive pace.[193] It is commendable that electricity is on the CLL of the Constitution
of Nigeria, making it possible for both the federal government and its constituent
units (states) to legislate in relation to electric power. But, by limiting the power of
states to generate, transmit, and distribute electricity to only those areas not covered
by the national grid system within that state, the vast majority of those within the
national grid (including private investors in other economic sectors) are forced to
endure the recurring and painful experience of NEPA's epileptic power supply. This
issue must be addressed within the framework of constitutional amendments, otherwise
all subsequent amendments to both the NEPA Act and other electricity regulation may
later be declared unconstitutional.

The transmission, wholesale supply, distribution, and sale of electricity and natural gas in Ghana are regulated under the Energy Commission Act. This Act, which,
among other things, repeals the Electricity Corporation of Ghana Decree of 1967,[194]
the Electricity Corporation of Ghana (Amendment) Law of 1987,[195] and the Electricity
Corporation of Ghana (Amendment) Law of 1991, preserves the Electricity Corporation of Ghana (Electric Power) Regulations of 1988 (Electric Power Regulations). These
Regulations set out detailed rules for the safe regulation of electric power in Ghana. It
is also worth noting that the VRA is exempt from licensing requirements in relation to
the production and wholesale supply of electricity from the hydropower installations
on the Volta River Basin. But, through such exemptions, the VRA is left intact as yet
another regulatory institution in electricity markets, introducing an additional layer of
complexity in relation to coordination and cooperation in the context of energy policy
making and regulation.

As Ghana does not have significant petroleum resources, Ghanaian governments
have demonstrated an awareness of the need to harness Ghana's limited natural gas
resources to generate electric power. This is also a preferable alternative to hydroelectric power, which is afflicted now and then with low water levels during prolonged
dry seasons.[196] Like electricity, the Energy Commission Act regulates the transmission,
wholesale supply, and distribution of natural gas. While the Energy Commission Act
generally provides for a sound regulatory framework, sections 23(1) and (2) are highly
problematic. The combined effect of sections 23(1) and (2) of the Energy Commission

---

[193] USDOE/EIA, "Independent Power Projects in Nigeria: March 2003," available at http://www.eia.doe.
gov/emeu/cabs/nigeria-ipp.html.
[194] N.L.C.D. 125.   [195] P.N.D.C.L. 172.
[196] Dapaah, *supra* note 170.

Act is to create a monopoly over both electricity transmission and natural gas transmission, in sharp contrast to global trends toward the demonopolization of public utilities. Experience the world over, and particularly in Africa, demonstrates that monopolies are inefficient as a result of lack of competition. Accordingly, sections 23(1) and (2) should be repealed.

Nigeria's natural gas policies have significantly advanced from the time when these resources were wasting national assets. The underlying rationale has been first, the need to eliminate waste by turning gas that would have otherwise been flared into a source of valuable revenue; second, the community's need to eliminate gas flares that cause acid rain and devastate the environment; third, the government's resolve to diversify its mono-product economy and thus liberate the economy from the vagaries of an unstable international oil market. The Associated Gas Regulations, the Nigeria LNG (Fiscal Incentives, Guarantees and Assurances) Decree,[197] and the Oso Gas Condensate Project Decree[198] are all legislative expressions of the government's resolve to reinject or viably utilize natural gas in the interest of the national economy and its peoples.

The West African Gas Pipeline Project was one of the economic policies developed by the Economic Community of West African States (ECOWAS) for the development of a natural gas pipeline throughout West Africa. This project, which has been approved by core investors and the respective West African governments, will transport gas that would otherwise have been flared from Escravos in the Niger Delta through Lagos to Effasu in Ghana. Notwithstanding criticisms that the EIA for the project was not given adequate attention in feasibility studies, when viewed from a sustainable energy standpoint, the project's long-term benefits are immense.[199] Further, the development of this gas pipeline will provide an alternative energy source to wood fuels for urban residential and industrial use.[200]

The regulation of water resources for the purposes of hydropower services is overly centralized in Nigeria. This creates rigidity in the regulatory system and makes procedures for approving license applications unnecessarily bureaucratic, both of which are inimical to the development of small hydropower (SHP) schemes in the country.[201] Note, SHP schemes are those hydro installations rated at less than 10MW.[202] SHP schemes are a viable source of renewable energy and although various sites for such installations have been identified, none have been developed in Nigeria. By way of comparison, it is estimated that Ghana, potentially, has an additional 2,000MW of hydropower capacity. Approximately 1,205MW of this power is to be generated from proven large hydropower sources while the remainder will be sourced from SHP schemes. It is also estimated that there are approximately forty SHP sites in Ghana.

---

[197] No. 30 of 1990.   [198] No. 15 of 1990.

[199] USDOE/EIA, "West African Gas Pipeline (WAGP) Project," available at http://www.eia.doe.gov/emeu/cabs/wagp.html.

[200] *See* http://www.ase.org/ghanaef/advocacy.htm.

[201] Water from such sources as may be declared by the National Assembly to be sources affecting more than one state is within the Exclusive Legislative List, Part I, Second Schedule to the Constitution of Nigeria.

[202] Until recently, virtually all of Ghana's electricity was produced from two large dams on the Volta River at Alosombo and Kpong, which combined have a capacity of about 1.1 GW out of a total installed capacity of 1.5 GW. Despite its considerable resource base, no SHPs have been developed in the country. The absence of a policy framework for development of SHP has been found to be the major barrier to the development of this energy resource. *See* www.areed.org/country/ghana/overview.pdf.

Speculation that the Northeastern border of Nigeria was rich in radioactive materials led the then military administration into enacting the NAEC Act and the Nuclear Safety and Radiation Protection Act of 1995. Despite this legislation, Nigeria has, to date, been unable to harness and utilize nuclear energy for a number of reasons. First, the complexity of nuclear energy systems necessitates a very high degree of relevant scientific and technical expertise that is not available locally. Second, the severe environmental implications in case(s) of damage to, or leakage from, nuclear installations. Third, the likely detrimental effect of radioactive waste disposal on both humans and the environment. In any event, it is becoming increasingly clear that nuclear energy is unlikely to be considered a viable source of sustainable energy, even in more developed societies. Accordingly, it is unlikely that nuclear energy will play a significant role in meeting Nigeria's energy needs for the forseeable future.

There is no specific legislation regulating the use of biofuels in either Nigeria or Ghana. Existing legislation merely extrapolates from broadly applicable provisions in the African Charter on Human and Peoples' Rights, the Constitutions of Ghana and Nigeria and in the latter case, state forestry laws also. As biofuels, in the forms of wood, charcoal, and biomass, constitute at least 70% of energy consumed throughout Africa, more specific regulatory attention should be paid to biofuels.

The vast majority of existing legislation governing the energy sectors in both Ghana and Nigeria is skewed in favor of the hydrocarbon and electricity subsectors: both these subsectors are areas in which government and private investors believe they can quickly, clearly, and easily amortize their respective investments, while driving the respective countries toward rapid industrialization.[203] Notwithstanding this overarching trend, in practice the specific laws that apply to various energy subsectors, for instance the electricity subsector, have operated as major obstacles to the wider use of distributed resources for grid-power. In Kenya, Albert Muma's examination of the Electric Power Act of 1997 reveals a bureaucratic licensing system, a state dominated supply monopoly, and a weak regulatory framework leading to high tariffs. Further, the Kenyan law governing electricity generation and supply discourages small-scale energy generators from entering or expanding their operations in the market, fails to provide links with other licensing requirements (water permits/society registration) to allow for greater efficiency, fails to provide tax incentives and subsidies, and is implemented in an opaque and unfriendly manner.[204] In order to accommodate firm power purchase agreements that would enable cost recovery and profit making for independent power producers (IPPs) and other potential developers, all such laws need to be modernized and operate within a streamlined regulatory framework.

Other forms of renewable energy, such as wind and solar energy, are not granted any legislative prominence in Ghana or Nigeria and this situation is replicated in other

---

[203] Dr. Dominic Walubengo thinks electricity for all is wishful thinking. In canvassing increasing formal attention and funding for biomass use in Kenya, he opines that, "We shall not in the next 200 years provide electricity to all those who want it. We shall not be able to provide LPG to all those who want it. Therefore, we should pay attention to biomass energy and give it more prominence and more funding." See "Biomass Use in Kenya: Policy Considerations," available at http://www.policydialogekenya.energyprojects.net/links/Biomass_use_kenya.pdf.

[204] A. Muma, "Sustainable Energy and the Law in Kenya," available at www.policydialogue.energyprojects.net/links/A_Muma_Sustainable_Energy_Law.pdf; see also, S. N. Mutimba, "Fifth Policy Dialogue Meeting on Sustainable Energy in Kenya," available at http://www.policydialogue.kenya.energyprojects.net.

African countries.[205] The provisions concerning renewable energy in the Energy Commission Act and the ECN are merely palliative. There are no specific provisions governing necessary qualifications and the application processes for licenses; the grant of, as well as conditions on, licenses; or providing for incentives to harness any form of renewable energy. In fact, both statutes are silent on procedures for harnessing renewable energy or facilitating RETs. The absence of authoritative legal instruments establishing a framework for managing the various forms of renewable energy, regulating the rights and obligations of both host country and private investors, and imposing legally enforceable standards and obligations demonstrates the low prioritization of sustainable energy issues in most African countries. If indeed these forms of energy are to be harnessed and utilized in Africa, positive legislative measures for the promotion of renewable energy must be implemented.[206]

Ghana and Nigeria could follow Kenya's lead in the development of geothermal resources; such development in Kenya is guided by legislated environmental controls contained in the Geothermal Resources Act, the Water Act, the Wildlife Act and the Forest Act. The new Environmental Management and Coordination Act of 1999 (EMCA) was established to harmonize the aforesaid Acts and to supersede them in relation to environmental matters. Kenya's EMCA specifically covers acceptable methods of handling polluting agents arising from geothermal developments, such as liquid, gas, and thermal effluents; noise pollution; and toxic and hazardous waste. The EMCA also sets out the requirements for an EIA, to be concluded prior to any energy development activity.[207] Although the EMCA supersedes all previous legislation on matters relating to the environmental impact of geothermal development, the other Acts are still in force to the extent that they are not in conflict with the EMCA. Consequently, the EMCA provides a legislative framework for the sustainable use of natural resources in an environmentally friendly manner and also offers avenues for conflict resolution.[208]

The characteristic features of the energy industry (excluding noncommercial energy)[209] and the sometimes similar, occasionally entirely divergent, and frequently conflicting, objectives of the major players in the energy industry underscore the need for a dynamic and efficient regulatory system, if sustainability in energy exploration, development, transmission, distribution, and consumption is to be achieved in Africa. All

---

[205] The absence of renewable energy legislation in Ghana is much more surprising because unlike Nigeria, Ghana has a comprehensive policy on renewable energy.

[206] R. Munk Hanwen, "Legislative Measures for Promotion of Renewable Energy: Wind Energy Development in Denmark as a Case Study," in A. Bradbrook and R. Ottinger (eds.), *Energy Law and Sustainable Development*, IUCN Environmental Policy & Law Paper No. 47 at 115–137.

[207] K. Benjamin, *An Outline of Kenya's Environmental Laws and Regulations as applied to Geothermal Development*, Report on the Olkaria Geothermal Project, The Kenya Electricity Generating Company (KEGC) Ltd., Kenya (undated). Cited in *Eastern African Geothermal Market Acceleration Conference – Market Assessment Report* (2003) at 37.

[208] *Eastern African Geothermal Market Acceleration Conference – Market Assessment Report* (2003) at 38.

[209] One of the most important characteristics of the energy industry is that investment risks are very high and the venture capital is intensive, with very long gestation periods, indeed, sometimes over and above the onshore oil and gas industry operations. The reasons for this are varied depending in part on the energy type. For oil and gas resources, the challenging geological environment coupled with water depth make offshore oil and gas exploration and development particularly expensive. Investments that go into generating, transmitting, and distributing thermal, hydro, or gas powered electricity is equally expensive.

such regulatory systems require the performance of a number of policy making tasks: the goals of the energy regime must be established; those goals must then be translated into principles and rules which control behavior of the principal players; and there must be very clear and impartial procedures for explicating and enforcing these principles and rules, and for the adjudication of disputes arising from such implementation.[210] This is the basis from which Africa will begin to attract much needed investment for sustainable energy development projects.

4.3 Regulatory Institutions

A plethora of legal texts, legislation, and subsidiary instruments vest in certain government departments and special agencies (that are more or less independent of government) the responsibilities of licensing, operating (sometimes in various types of partnerships), supervising, implementing, and monitoring energy investments and also, the responsibility of enforcing compliance with the regulations and rules governing energy investments. This is the case in both Ghana and Nigeria, as it is in almost every other energy producing and consuming country in Africa and beyond, irrespective of the stage of economic development in the particular country, although the degree of government control, intervention, or involvement varies from one country to the other. Table 21.3 summarizes the major institutional arrangements for Ghana and Nigeria.

However, a multiplicity of public sector energy regulatory institutions is not synonymous with effective or coordinated regulation of the energy sector. It may actually imply that the energy sector is being heavily overregulated with little or no coordination between the various institutions.[211] This is the case in Africa, where there are very few integrated, efficient legal systems, with both juridical and administrative branches. Regulatory institutions in Africa are either overstaffed with semiskilled or unskilled workforces, or are understaffed with skilled personnel. In either case, the number of highly skilled and motivated personnel, able and willing to implement and enforce compliance with the energy regulatory regime, is entirely insufficient. This situation is further exacerbated by poor funding and a dearth of up-to-date equipment.

There is a clear need to direct existing resources to the development and training of indigenous personnel to effectively run the regulatory institutions and agencies in the energy sector, such that they can attain their goals in a highly professional manner. Further, the various regulatory institutions and agencies should enter into a Protocol Agreement for the effective monitoring and enforcement of environmental obligations in the energy sector, akin to the Protocol Agreement Between the Ministry of Environment and the Ministry of Energy, Mines and Petroleum Resources Concerning Inspection of Placer Operations in British Columbia, Canada in order to avoid jurisdictional overlap,[212] conflicts of authority, and mixed regulatory signals in the energy sector.

---

[210] A. Ogus, *Regulation: Legal Form and Economic Theory*, Oxford University Press (Oxford, 1994) at 99.

[211] A. Dias, "The Oil and Gas Industry in a Tangled Web of Environmental Regulation: Spider or Fly?" in Z. Gao (ed.), *Environmental Regulation of Oil and Gas*, Kluwer International Publishers (London, 1998) at 59–89.

[212] *See* Protocol Agreement Between the Ministry of Environment and the Ministry of Energy, Mines & Petroleum Resources Concerning the Inspection of Placer Operations, July 1988, available at http://www.env.gov.bc.ca/epd/cpr/protocol/pabtmoea.html at 1–4.

Table 21.3 Summary of Major Regulatory Institutions in the Energy Sector in Ghana and Nigeria

ENERGY TYPES	GHANA	NIGERIA
Hydrocarbons	Ministry of Mines & Energy (MME) Ghana National Petroleum Corporation (GNPC) Energy Commission (EC) Bulk Oil Storage and Transportation Company (BOST) Tema Oil Refinery Company (TOR) Ghana Oil Company (GOIL)	Federal Ministry of Petroleum Resources (FMPR) Department of Petroleum Resources Nigerian National Petroleum Corporation (NNPC) together with its subsidiaries Federal Ministry of Environment/ Federal Environmental Protection Agency (FEPA) Energy Commission of Nigeria (ECN)
Electricity including Hydropower	Ministry of Mines & Energy Volta River Authority (VRA) Northern Electricity Department (NED) Electricity Corporation of Ghana (ECG)	Federal Ministry of Power and Steel National Electric Power Authority (NEPA) Federal Environmental Protection Agency/Federal Ministry of Environment Consumer Protection Council (CPC) Utilities Charges Commission (UCC) Energy Commission of Nigeria (ECN) State and Local Government Electricity Boards
Renewable including Biofuels Nuclear	Energy Commission of Ghana N/A	Energy Commission of Nigeria Nigerian Atomic Energy Commission (NAEC) Nigerian Nuclear Regulatory Authority (NNRA)

Source: Compiled by author, N/A: Not available

The pervasive poverty in Africa, notwithstanding its wealth of natural resources, against the backdrop of mounting billions in external debt, means that African governments cannot afford to continue to take on significantly more than they can actually handle. Establishing a variety of energy related institutions and agencies and underfunding them without adequate regard being paid to principles of accountability, transparency, efficiency, and productivity is, needless to stress, wasteful of scarce public funds. Accordingly, if government institutions and agencies are to have a positive impact on energy investment in Africa, a complete overhaul of existing regulatory institutions will be required, in order to provide for a cleaner, more stable, more transparent, and more efficient regulatory framework for the energy sector. This will include internalizing the following principles: the principle of financial accountability;[213]

---

[213] This requires government agencies to satisfy certain standards of financial management by minimizing administrative costs and drastically reducing wastes. Financial accountability will invariably positively impact on productive efficiency.

the principle of procedural accountability;[214] and the principle of substantive accountability.[215]

Problems of accountability pose different challenges in a public institutional setting, as opposed to the private sector, for several reasons. First, there is no single, homogenous group of principals concerned with monitoring the performance of government agencies, but rather a diverse set of interest groups, for instance, bureaucrats, politicians, industrialists, trade unions, and ordinary citizens. Second, the performance of government institutions is, in any event, more difficult to monitor, as there are generally no conventional profit and loss accounts. Third, there is no market for the control of government agencies and the principals often cannot simply agree to dismiss ineffectual or corrupt officials.

In Africa, problems of accountability run even deeper.[216] Nevertheless, structural controls, which have been used in other countries to bring about greater transparency and efficiency in the activities of government regulatory institutions, could be adopted in Africa's local setting.[217] Africa has most of these structural controls in place already, but not in an absolute sense.[218] Note however, if integrity and principles are lacking in the individual personalities or character traits of persons in government, there are bound to be very wide distortions in the system.

5 EPILOGUE

Energy issues featured prominently in the discussions taking place at the WSSD, particularly the link between energy and sustainable development and further, the critical role energy plays in reducing poverty and improving environmental quality,[219] both

---

[214] The procedures adopted by government agencies must not only be fair, but must be manifestly seen to be fair and impartial. There must exist an appropriate framework for making rules and decisions that serve the public interest as opposed to some private or political interests.

[215] This seeks to ensure that rules and decisions of government agencies are themselves justifiable in terms of public interest goals of the regulatory system in question, whether they are economic, social, or environmental.

[216] Ethnicity and religion are inseparable in any discussions on accountability of regulatory authorities within a given national context. To dismiss a corrupt public officer of any particular ethnic stock may be viewed by the official's kin as a deliberate attempt to marginalize them and replace him or her with someone from another ethnic stock.

[217] These include the following: subjecting government regulatory institutions/agencies in the energy sector to periodic scrutiny by the legislature; subjecting government institutions/agencies to the scrutiny of the auditor general of the country; requiring government institutions/agencies to undertake an assessment of the costs to the energy industry on the one hand and the nation on the other, of complying with the rules, when making proposals for regulatory rules; by publishing all such findings as enumerated under the above bullet points; by subjecting government institutions/agencies' decisions to the due process, including the participating rights of interests groups; by subjecting government institutions/agencies to judicial control; and by granting unrestricted access to the press to publish matters of public interest relating to the performance of government institutions/agencies.

[218] For example, the impression is created that our legislature only scrutinizes executive departments and other government agencies in offshore oil and gas operations, when it has an axe to grind with the executive, which appoints the agencies' management. Similarly, the executive investigates the legislature only when it is either threatened with impeachment, or accused of other vices. But a consistent and regular scrutiny of government agencies based on the national interest (national energy policy) is often missing.

[219] UNEP, "World Summit Highlights Role of Energy in Sustainable Development," *Energy + Sustainable Development: A Newsletter of UCCEE and UNEP* (December 2002) at 1; *see also* http://www.uccee.org/ E+/December03.pdf.

of which are so much needed in Africa. True, no country in the world has ever succeeded in shaking loose from a subsistence economy without access to modern energy services. Undoubtedly, the peoples of Africa urgently need better access to the services which commercial energy provides and better management of traditional fuels, while simultaneously exploring other renewable energy alternatives.[220]

Promoting sustainable energy production and consumption patterns in Africa, a region that still grapples with satisfying the most basic human needs, is a daunting task for which there are no easy answers. Africa possesses enormous as well as diverse nonrenewable and renewable energy resources. But, these resources are underexploited for a variety of reasons, depending in part on the country and subregion that is the subject of analysis. Realizing that the challenges and opportunities that Africa's energy environment offers cannot be seized without a correlative paradigm shift toward a more specific and adequate legal and regulatory framework supported and implemented by effective institutional mechanisms, this chapter considered the comparative legal aspects of sustainable energy. In order to avoid the pitfall of bland generalizations, Nigeria and Ghana were considered as case studies in the West African subregion in order to shed some light on relevant regulatory frameworks for the energy sector in Africa, involving a detailed consideration of relevant policy, legislation, and regulatory institutions.

It is not, however, this chapter's intention to create the impression that the imperatives for sustainable energy are any less urgent in other African subregions than they are for the West African subregion and more particularly for Ghana and Nigeria, even though the East and Southern African subregions have made more considerable advances in the area of photovoltaic and geothermal power.[221] In the final analysis, African countries must address the regulatory and legal constraints that have militated against investment in the energy sector generally, while specifically promoting increased investment in nonbiomass renewable energy development. African legal systems must provide clear rules for all stakeholders in emerging energy markets; clearly define the responsibilities and obligations of new private energy companies; and strike a principled balance between protecting business and investor interests on the one hand, and the general public and consumers on the other. Furthermore, governments must provide tax incentives to financiers of energy efficient projects as well as importers and manufacturers of energy efficient and renewable energy equipment.

---

[220] The World Bank Group, "A Brighter Future? Energy in Africa's Development," available at www.worldbank.org/html/fpd/energy/subenergy/energyinafrica.htm.

[221] In Kenya, a series of rural electrification and other programs has resulted in the installation of more than 20,000 small-scale PV systems since 1986. These PV systems now play a prominent role in decentralized, sustainable electrification. For other projects in South Africa, Namibia, Zambia, and Zimbabwe, see www.eia.doe.gov/emeu/cabs/chapter7.html. For Kenya, Djibouti, Ethiopia, Eritrea, Uganda, Tanzania, and Zambia's geothermal potential and exploitation, see East African Geothermal Market Acceleration Conference – Market Assessment Report, 2003; see also K. K. Kariuki, "Enhancing Electrification in Kenya – The Role of New Renewable Technologies," available at http://www.policydialoguekenya.energyprojects. net/links/Enhancing_electrification_Kenya.pdf.

22 European Energy Law Initiatives

Bernhard Nagel*

1 INTRODUCTION

To evaluate European environmental policy initiatives in general and renewable energy initiatives in particular, it is necessary to take into account the links between energy policy, ecological tax policy, climate change policy, and strategies for sustainability in general. Looking at Europe, leading examples can be seen in each of these policy areas; moreover, significant variations can be seen between member states. For instance, Germany provides leading examples of energy and climate change policies, whereas in other fields such as ecological taxation, the Scandinavians and the Dutch took and still hold the leading position while Germany is catching up at best. It is doubtful whether Germany has a clear sustainability strategy in place. For the purposes of this chapter, "sustainability" means more than environmental policy; it also involves good education policies, intergenerational equity, and social cohesion. Again in this context, the sustainability strategies currently in place in Scandinavia are further advanced than German policies. Germany also is lagging behind in certain areas, particularly education policies.[1]

This chapter will concentrate on energy policy and draw certain cross connections to climate policy, a closely related policy area. It will cover legal as well as factual developments. Within the broad parameters of energy policy, this chapter will concentrate first, on the supply of electricity produced from renewable sources and second, on how such strategies can operate as a means for reducing greenhouse gas emissions in order to achieve the aims of the Kyoto Protocol.[2] Other related policy areas, such as the promotion of biofuels for transport and the promotion of cogeneration of heat and electric power will be covered very briefly only.

2 THE GERMAN RENEWABLE ENERGY SOURCES ACT OF 2000

2.1 Background Information

Germany historically has lagged behind most other EU member states in the promotion of energy produced from renewable sources. Two of the objectives of the previous Energy

---

[1] Nagel and Jaich, *Bildungsfinanzierung in Deutschland*, Endbericht an die Max Traeger Stiftung, Frankfurt/M, 2002; The PISA-Report (2002), noting Germany's weak performance in relation to education policy.
[2] Kyoto Protocol to the UN Framework Convention on Climate Change, December 11, 1997; *see* http://www.unfccc.int/resource/docs/convkp/kpeng.pdf.

* Professor of Law, University of Kassel, Germany.

Business Act of 1935[3] were to raise the consumption of energy and to preserve regional monopolies in the production of electricity. Following the reunification of Germany in October 1990, two laws changed this situation. The first was the Act on the Supply of Electricity from Renewable Energy Sources to the Public Grid (Electricity Supply Act) of December 7, 1990, as amended in 1998.[4] Klaus Toepfer was the Minister of the Environment at that time. The second was the Act on Granting Priority to Renewable Energy Sources (EEG), which came into force on April 1, 2000.[5] The EEG is still in force.

2.2 Purpose of the EEG

Intended as an environmental protection law, the purpose of the EEG is to increase the production of electricity from renewable energy sources (RES) as a share of total German energy consumption. To this end, the EEG imposes an obligation on grid operators to purchase all electricity generated from RES. The EEG then triggers a chain of purchase obligations that extend from the nearest grid operator to the electricity supplier as the final stage in the marketing process. The Act's general objectives are set out in Section 1:

> The purpose of this Act, in the interests of climate and environmental protection, is to facilitate the sustainable development of energy supply and to achieve a substantial increase in the contribution made by renewable energy sources to the power supply, in order to at least double the share of renewable energy sources in total energy consumption by the year 2010 in accordance with the objectives defined by the European Union and the Federal Republic of Germany.

The overall duty imposed in Section 1, to facilitate the improvement of environmental aspects of electricity generation, triggers a series of purchase and compensation obligations throughout the electricity supply chain, ultimately obliging electricity consumers to buy energy generated from renewable sources. In this way, eco-electricity is integrated into the electricity market.

2.3 The "Supply-In" Scheme: Obligations to Purchase and Pay Compensation under the EEG

To achieve its goals, the EEG relies on obligations to purchase and pay compensation (fixed prices) for eco-electricity.[6] In a "counter current process," the chain of purchase obligations triggers a corresponding chain of compensation obligations with different pricing regimes for the various renewable energies. The EEG essentially provides for a "supply-in" scheme with differentiation through fixed prices for each type of renewable energy.[7] All links in the supply chain are obliged to purchase the total amount of electricity supplied from renewable sources at fixed prices.

---

[3] Energiewirtschaftsgesetz, *see* http://www.energylaw.de/.
[4] "Stromeinspeisungsgesetz," *Federal Law Gazette* I, pp. 730, 734.
[5] "Gesetz für den Vorrang Erneuerbarer Energien," *Federal Law Gazette* I, p. 305.
[6] *See* Art. 3 of the EEG.   [7] *Id.*, Arts. 4–8.

Grid operators are required to pay compensation rates in advance in the form of varied, and for later investments degressive, fixed prices.[8] This means that the price is fixed for twenty years excluding the year of commissioning of the relevant installation,[9] but there is a degression every year. Accordingly, if an installation was built next year, the electricity producer who owned that installation would receive fixed prices that were approximately two percent lower than the prices received by an electricity producer who built an installation this year. The degressive reduction of the fixed prices will apply only to new electricity generation installations commissioned after 2002 and later. This is intended to safeguard investment, create investment incentives, and foster rapid development in order to avoid the degression in the fixed pricing regimes. These degressive fixed prices are then passed down through the supply chain to each successive purchaser. The ultimate payer is the consumer who receives a mix of "green" and "brown" (fossil fuel) electricity. These purchase obligations ultimately constitute an extended product responsibility for eco-electricity.

The EEG specifically avoids a simple overall quota system that would specify, to the various players in the electricity supply chain, the amount of eco-electricity to be produced as a percentage of total electricity. Further, the EEG does not fix a uniform price for eco-electricity, which would have the same effect. Instead, it opts for different prices to be paid to producers supplying electricity into the grid, based on the type of renewable energy source used. Prices are set according to the costs of producing electricity from the different renewable sources and these degressive fixed prices are intended to regulate the overall composition of electricity supplied from the different renewable sources. Accordingly, the consumer not only buys "mixed" electricity, but rather buys a combination of different types of eco-electricity.

The first purchaser in the supply chain obtains eco-electricity in the form which is first supplied to the grid, that is, if a hydropower installation supplies electricity into the grid followed by a wind power installation, the first purchaser will obtain electricity supplied first by the hydropower installation and then by the wind power installation depending on the purchaser's capacity requirements and overall demand throughout the grid. The price paid by this purchaser is calculated from the mean value of all prices for eco-electricity supplied in to the grid.

Under the former Electricity Supply Act, the costs of a percentage based pricing regime to promote renewable energies were borne by grid operators, who were obliged to purchase RES electricity. Under this Act, due to the location dependent amounts of eco-electricity generated, there were variations in the extent to which the burdens arising from the obligation to purchase eco-electricity were shared between grid operators and the producers and brokers supplying via these grids. In other words, the costs of supplying electricity generated from renewable sources into the power grid were distributed unequally.

This has changed under the EEG, as it opts instead for a nationwide equalization scheme. Under the EEG, electricity brokers must purchase a specific mix of eco-electricity, for which they pay an overall price calculated on the basis of the electrical capacity supplied from the various renewable sources. Under the EEG scheme, the advantage for those producers of electricity generated from renewable sources who also

---

[8] *Id.*   [9] *Id.*, Art. 9.

operate as brokers is that these two functions are now separate. Like other producers of eco-electricity, they receive appropriate compensation for the energy they generate from renewable sources, while as brokers, they pay the percentage purchase price for eco-electricity just as their competitors do.

In their capacity as brokers, producers of electricity generated from renewable sources who also act as brokers pay the same price as every other broker, irrespective of how much they are paid for supplying electricity into the grid (which depends on the particular renewable energy source at issue). The sum of all payments by brokers to the previous "link" in the purchase chain is equal to the sum of all compensation paid to producers supplying into the grid. The prices (compensation rates) paid to producers supplying into the grid vary, depending on the type of renewable energy source they use. In this way, the EEG aims to regulate the total amount of electricity produced from renewable sources with private investment and also ensures that, in terms of overall supply, the potential of the various sites, production methods, and installation sizes is utilized to the full.

The quantity/fixed price model established in the EEG can be called a "flow quota," because the precise amount of electricity supplied from the various renewable sources is not regulated by a direct quota, but is determined indirectly by the amount bought and the price paid to producers supplying electricity into the grid.

2.4 Increasing Competition in Electricity Markets

The EEG is not only an environmental protection law,[10] it also abolishes specific elements of the Electricity Supply Act that restrained competition. First, all producers generating electricity from the same renewable source are paid the same rates of compensation for supplying electricity to the grid, that is, the actual amount they receive depends on the capacity they supply in.[11]

Second, under the Electricity Supply Act, the operators of regional grids were not eligible for compensation. Unlike third party producers supplying electricity into the grid, grid operators who also supplied electricity had no guaranteed entitlement to compensation for generating their own eco-electricity and thus, had no incentive to produce eco-electricity themselves. The EEG improves the underlying conditions for achieving the environmental policy goals of increasing the share of eco-electricity in the total energy supply as it does not exclude anyone from the group of domestic energy producers entitled to compensation. Moreover, exporting brokers are treated in the same way as brokers operating abroad and the EEG precludes discrimination against grid operators.

The EEG therefore supports the European Community's efforts to secure nondiscriminatory grid access for electricity generated from renewable sources, in keeping with the Directive concerning common rules for the internal market in electricity.[12]

---

[10] Section 1 of the EEG. *Id.*, §1.   [11] *See Id.*, Arts. 4–8.
[12] Directive 2003/54/EC of June 26, 2003, O.J. L 176/37 of July 15, 2003; *see* http://europa.eu.int/eur-lex/pri/en/oj/dat/2003/l_176/l_17620030715en 00370055.pdf. This replaced Directive 96/92/EC of December 19, 1996, O. J. L 27, 30.01.1997, p. 0020–0029.

3 PRIORITIZING ELECTRICITY GENERATED FROM RENEWABLE SOURCES

Through the adoption of the EEG, the German government has reduced the disadvantages imposed for decades on the producers of electricity from renewable sources,
as compared to coal fired or nuclear power electricity generation installations.

3.1 Regulatory Protection of the Coal and Oil Industries

Ever since the adoption of the Energy Business Act of 1935, the signing of a cartel agreement between the coal and oil industries in December 1958 (initiated by the federal
government)[13] and the subsequent introduction of duties and a fuel oil tax, the market
position of hard coal has been supported by massive state subsidies. Initially, the government's intention was simply to defend the coal mining industry from the competitive
challenges posed by oil. Under government pressure, the oil industry signaled its willingness to exercise "voluntary self-restraint," that is, to adhere to the global amounts
permitted by the state.

Later, in 1965, 1966, and 1974, various Electricity-from-Coal Acts were adopted to
safeguard the future of the coal mining industry. In 1980, the Jahrhundertvertrag – a
long-term exclusive contract between coal producers and the electricity utilities – was
accompanied by a new Electricity-from-Coal Act that introduced a special levy (the
"coal penny" – "kohlepfennig"), ultimately amounting to 8.5 percent of the electricity
price paid by the consumer. In 1994,[14] the German Federal Constitutional Court finally
ruled that this special levy was unconstitutional and void.

3.2 Regulatory Protection of the Nuclear Energy Industry

Nuclear energy has also been heavily subsidized in Germany for decades. For example,
under the German Nuclear Energy Act of 1959[15] (NEA), Gundremmingen nuclear
power station was funded almost entirely by the state. The state also covered ninety
percent of any operational losses.[16] Direct state subsidies to the nuclear energy industry
still run into many billions of Euros. Further, indirect subsidies are also provided,
in the form of tax concessions. The funds set aside by the nuclear power companies
for subsequent decommissioning, and to fulfill their "safe disposal" guarantee, are tax
exempt. Today, the reserve funds for decommissioning alone amount to more than
€ 35 billion.[17]

This nuclear policy approach was changed in 2002. A compromise between owners
of nuclear generation facilities and the federal government signaled the end of nuclear
energy in Germany. There is no fixed date for the end of nuclear power generation, as

---

[13] *See* J. Schwalbach and A. Schwerk, "Stability of German cartels," Humboldt University–Berlin, available
at http://www.wiwi.hu-berlin.de/im/publikdl/98-2.pdf.

[14] Decisions of the Federal Constitutional Court (BVerf*GE*) 91, 186.

[15] The original citation for this Act is *Federal Gazette (Bundesgesetzblatt)*, 1959 I, p. 814 but note that there
have been several amendments to it.

[16] Radkau, "Die Entstehung der Atomwirtschaft in der Bundesrepublik Deutschland, technologische Al-
ternativen und historische Kontexte," (1980); Varchmin and Radkau, *Kraft, Energie und Arbeit*, Reinbek
(1981) at 170ff.

[17] Hermes, "Rückstellungen für die Entsorgung und Stillegung von Kernkraftwerken und EG-
Beihilferecht," ZNER, (1999) at 156 ff.

owners of nuclear generation facilities are allowed to set off quantities of currency in one plant against quantities of another, but importantly, the termination of the operations of all nuclear power generation plants is the definite goal under the revised NEA.[18]

4 LITIGATION OVER THE LAWFULNESS OF THE ELECTRICITY SUPPLY ACT AND THE EEG

4.1 Proceedings in the Kiel Regional Court in Relation to the Electricity Supply Act

From the outset, the fossil fuel based electricity generation industry used all legal and political means at its disposal to challenge the lawfulness of the Electricity Supply Act. Preussen-Elektra AG, which was part of the former Veba AG (today EON AG), sued its own group subsidiary, Schleswag AG, for reimbursement of compensation paid under the Electricity Supply Act. Without examining the corporate links between the plaintiff and defendant and the possibility of equalization of losses, the Landgericht (Regional Court) Kiel referred the question of the Electricity Supply Act's compatibility with European Community law to the European Court of Justice (ECJ) for a preliminary ruling.[19]

Germany had notified the Electricity Supply Act as state aid in 1990 for the purposes of Article 87 of the EC Treaty,[20] notwithstanding its legal opinion that this was unnecessary; however the amendments to the Electricity Supply Act in 1998 had not been notified.[21]

4.2 Legislative Processes in Relation to the EEG

While the case concerning the compatibility of the Electricity Supply Act with European Community law was still pending before the ECJ, the German Bundestag had before it a proposal to enact the EEG. There had been a substantial fall in electricity prices during 1999. In this context, the German Federal Government decided to draft the Bill on Granting Priority to Renewable Energy Sources (Draft EEG) to replace the Electricity Supply Act and halt the dramatic decline in the profitability of renewable energies. From the outset, the federal government aimed to avoid any conflicts between the proposed EEG and the state aid provisions of Article 87 of the EC Treaty. Therefore, the proposed legislative measures envisaged that the state would not contribute any financial or other resources or participate in the distribution of these resources to the beneficiary producers of electricity generated from renewable sources. Instead, under the EEG, there would be a system for the redistribution of financial resources within the electricity industry. The intention was to ensure that any producer of some electricity generated from renewable sources could benefit from the funding, even if they generated the bulk of their electricity from nuclear energy or coal or other non-renewable sources.

---

[18] *Federal Gazette*, 2002 I, p. 2674.
[19] LG Kiel ZIP (1999) at 757; Falk, *Die materielle Beurteilung des deutschen Stromeinspeisungsgesetzes nach europäischem Beihilferecht*, ZIP (1999) at 738.
[20] Consolidated Version of the Treaty Establishing the European Community, O.J. C 325/33, December 24, 2002, available at http://europa.eu.int/eur-lex/en/treaties/dat/EC_consol.pdf.
[21] Fouquet and Zenke, ZNER (1999) at 61–66.

Critically, if the ECJ had held that the 1990 Electricity Supply Act amended was incompatible with community state aid rules, the supply-in scheme provided for by the EEG would also be inadmissible.

4.3 The European Commission's Approach to State Aid Rules in the Context of the Electricity Supply Act and the Case before the ECJ

In a submission to the ECJ dated January 21, 1999, the European Commission stated that the Electricity Supply Act was incompatible with community state aid rules under Article 87 of the EC Treaty. The European Commission made it clear that it intended to move away from previous ECJ rulings and widen the definition of state aid. In its previous rulings,[22] the ECJ had consistently taken the view that only advantages granted directly or indirectly through state resources are to be regarded as state aid. In the case of the Electricity Supply Act, the European Commission wished to extend this definition to include "circumvention measures" that the Commission believed have the effect of state aid even though the financial burden does not fall directly or indirectly upon the State.

The European Commission's first argument was that at least some of the grid operators who were obliged to pay compensation under the Electricity Supply Act were largely publicly owned and, therefore, the "public purse" effectively paid an indirect state subsidy to producers of renewable energy. The general thrust of this argument was that the grid operators were companies in which the state held a 100 percent or majority stake. Theoretically, therefore, the Electricity Supply Act under which payment obligations lay with these grid operators could be deemed to be indirect state aid as defined in ECJ case law. In reality however, the state no longer held majority holdings in most major grid operators. The state's former majority voting rights, for example, in RWE, were abolished. And EnBW, the only company where the State had a (formal) majority holding, was taken over by Electricité de France, the French state owned company that generates electricity primarily from nuclear energy. The four main energy companies RWE, EON, Vattenfall/HEW, and EnBW/EdF currently operate in a similar manner to private market driven corporations. There are no apparent differences in their mode of operation attributable to state ownership. And it should also be borne in mind that the compensation costs incurred by these electricity companies are ongoing.

The European Commission's second argument was that, if the state passes a law under which private or public resources flow to beneficiary public companies, this constitutes state aid. The state itself need not sacrifice resources from the public purse. With this second argument the European Commission did not follow the ECJ's previous case law, where the ECJ had always held that state aid requires a financial sacrifice by the state.

Surprisingly, in response to the further question submitted by Kiel Regional Court, as to whether there had been a quantitative restriction on imports or a measure having an equivalent effect between member states pursuant to Article 28 of the EC Treaty (freedom of free movement of goods within the EU), the European Commission, in its

---

[22] ECJ, Joined Cases C-52-54/97, *Viscido / Ente Poste Italiane* (Rec. 1998), I-2629; the ECJ cites its earlier rulings in the cases of *Van Tiggele* (Rec. 1978), 25; *Sloman Neptun* (Rec. 1993), I-887; and *Kirsammer-Hack* (Rec. 1993), I-6185.

submission to the ECJ, answered in the negative. The European Commission argued that such a measure does not breach European Community law, provided that the amount of domestic electricity that has to be purchased is small and does not require measures corresponding with a community regulation.

4.4 The European Commission's Approach to State Aid Rules and the EEG

In response to an intervention by the European Commission's Directorate General IV (DG IV), the question of whether the EEG should be defined as notifiable state aid was debated on February 14, 2000 at a hearing of the German Bundestag's Committee on Economic Affairs. None of the legal experts invited by the governing parliamentary groups, or the opposition, supported the view held by the European Commission that the EEG constituted state aid. The participants in this hearing were aware that the German Federal Ministry of Economics had voiced doubts on this point. On the basis of these expert opinions, the German federal government did not notify the EEG to the European Commission, and the EEG was adopted soon afterwards by the Bundestag and the Bundesrat.

The EEG came into force on April 1, 2000. In a letter to the German federal government dated April 7, 2000, the European Commission DG IV threatened those companies, entitled to payments under the EEG, with the prospect of an obligation to repay all such monies in the event that the European Commission, or the ECJ, held that such payments constituted inadmissible state aid. At this time, the European Commission was already debating the Draft Directive on the promotion of electricity produced from renewable energy sources in the internal electricity market and had been doing so for some time. The Draft Directive was adopted by the European Commission on May 10, 2000.[23] This Directive aimed to fulfill the commitments to reduce greenhouse gas emissions entered into by the EU at the Kyoto Conference.[24] To this end, the Directive required action from the member states at a national level, but did not prescribe a specific community-wide approach. Moreover, the Draft Directive identified fixed price schemes as being particularly successful:

> Fixed price schemes, operating presently in several EU countries, and notably Germany and Spain, are characterised by a specific price being set for RES-E (electricity from renewable energy sources) that must be paid by electricity companies, usually distributors, to domestic producers of RES-E. In such schemes, in principle, there is no quota, or maximum limit for RES-E set in the Member States. This limit or quota is however set indirectly by the level at which the RES-E price is set.[25]

In this context, the actions of the European Commission in relation to the German laws on renewable energies – both the Electricity Supply Act and the EEG – appear highly inconsistent with this policy approach.

---

[23] COM (2000) 279 final; Rdok 9312/2000, Bundestag Printed Paper 383/2000, June 20, 2000; in the meantime, the Directive on the promotion of electricity produced from renewable energy sources in the internal electricity market of September 27, 2001, 2001/77, O.J. L 283/33 of October 27, 2001, was enacted.

[24] *See* unfccc.int.

[25] Draft directive, Explanatory Memorandum (Begründung) at 6.

4.5 The ECJ's Decision in Relation to State Aid Rules and the Electricity Supply Act

On March 13, 2001, the ECJ held that the Electricity Supply Act did not constitute an inadmissible form of state aid as the Act did not provide for or require any loss of financial means by the state.[26] The duty of a company under the Electricity Supply Act to buy electricity from relevant producers did not have any specific connection to the state budget. Further, this duty did not violate the rules of competition or the free movement of goods within the EU under Article 28 of the EC Treaty.

In response to the argument that grid operators were publicly owned and therefore, as producers of electricity generated from renewable sources received an indirect State subsidy under the Electricity Supply Act, the ECJ held as follows:

> This question should be understood as asking, essentially, whether legislation of a Member State which, first, requires private electricity supply undertakings to purchase electricity produced in their area of supply from renewable energy sources at minimum prices higher than the real economic value of that type of electricity, and, second, allocates the financial burden arising from that obligation amongst those electricity supply undertakings and upstream private electricity network operators, constitutes State aid within the meaning of Article 92(1) of the Treaty . . .[27]

> In connection [with Article 92 of the EC Treaty], the case-law of the [ECJ] shows that only advantages granted directly or indirectly through State resources are to be considered aid within the meaning of Article 92(1). The distinction made in that provision between "aid granted by a Member State and aid granted" through State resources does not signify that all advantages granted by a State, whether financed through State resources or not, constitute aid but is intended merely to bring within that definition both advantages which are granted directly by the State and those granted by a public or private body designated or established by the State (see Case 82/77 *Van Tiggele* [1978] ECR 25, paragraphs 24 and 25; *Sloman Neptun*, paragraph 19; Case C-189/91 *Kirsammer-Hack* [1993] ECR I-6185, paragraph 16; Joined Cases C-52/97, C-53/97 and C-54/97 *Viscido* [1998] ECR I-2629, paragraph 13; Case C-200/97 *Ecotrade* [1998] ECR I-7907, paragraph 35; Case C-295/97 *Piaggio* [1999] ECR I-3735, paragraph 35).[28]

> In this case, the obligation imposed on private electricity supply undertakings to purchase electricity produced from renewable energy sources at fixed minimum prices does not involve any direct or indirect transfer of State resources to undertakings which produce that type of electricity. Therefore, the allocation of the financial burden arising from that obligation for those private electricity supply undertakings as between them and other private undertakings cannot constitute a direct or indirect transfer of State resources either. In those circumstances, the fact that the purchase obligation is imposed by statute and confers an undeniable advantage on certain undertakings is not capable of conferring upon it the character of State aid within the meaning of Article 92(1) of the Treaty.[29]

---

[26] *PreussenElektra AG v. Schleswag AG*, Case C-379/98, March 13, 2001, available at http://europa.eu.int/jurisp/cgi-bin/form.pl?lang=en&Submit=Submit&docrequire=judgements&numaff=&datefs=2001-01-01&datefe=2002-01-01&nomusuel=&domaine=&mots=electricity+&resmax=100.

[27] *Id.*, para. 56. Note that Art. 92 is now Art. 87.   [28] *Id.*, para. 58.

[29] *Id.*, paras. 59–61.

In response to the second argument, that state aid rules extend to "circumvention measures" where the state passes a law to be financed by private undertakings, the ECJ, noting that the European Commission made this argument by drawing analogies with the ECJ's previous decision in relation to Articles 85 and 5 of the EC Treaty,[30] held as follows:

> In that respect, it is sufficient to point out that, unlike Article 85 of the Treaty, which concerns only the conduct of undertakings, Article 92 of the Treaty refers directly to measures emanating from the Member States. In those circumstances, Article 92 of the Treaty is in itself sufficient to prohibit the conduct by States referred to therein and Article 5 of the Treaty, the second paragraph of which provides that Member States are to abstain from any measure which could jeopardise the attainment of the objectives of the Treaty, cannot be used to extend the scope of Article 92 to conduct by States that does not fall within it.[31]

The decision of the ECJ can be summarized very briefly for the purposes of this chapter: the state as an institution must act as an intermediary between those who finance a particular measure and those who benefit from it. A financial sacrifice by the state must, therefore, be implicit in its role as an intermediary between the financiers and the beneficiaries in the context of any legislative measure. In this context, measures that are funded by public undertakings *can* constitute state aid but do not necessarily do so. Whether such measures constitute state aid will depend on the specific nature of the relevant legislative measures and the factual circumstances of the case.

4.6 The Aftermath of the ECJ's Decision

Even though the ECJ clearly held that both the Electricity Supply Act and the EEG were compatible with European Community law – rejecting both of the European Commission's arguments suggesting that these laws contravened state aid rules – the European Commission DG IV did not stop proceedings questioning the lawfulness of the EEG. It was only more than a year later, on May 22, 2002, that the European Commission finally recognized the EEG as being compatible with European Community law. This time lag was not at all helpful for enterprises investing, or seeking to invest, in renewable energies in Germany. In the interests of sound law and certainty in policy making, this author considers that the European Commission should have immediately followed the ECJ's decision of March 13, 2001 as well as adopting its reasoning in relation to the interpretation of state aid rules.

4.7 Summary

The EEG regulates grid operators' obligations to purchase and pay compensation for electricity generated from renewable sources via a fixed price mechanism. This means that, in essence, the EEG is a quantity based regulatory scheme, where fixed prices are simply the relevant cost unit. The purpose of this regulatory scheme is to increase the quantity of electricity produced from renewable sources.

---

[30] *Id.*, para. 63.   [31] *Id.*, paras. 64–65.

In order to achieve this aim, a fixed price is set by the state. This fixed price is funded proportionally by all electricity brokers and ultimately, electricity customers, via purchase obligations. The compensation rates for electricity suppliers to the grid are regulated through varied and degressive fixed prices and the purchase prices which are ultimately paid depend on the mix of electricity purchased. In this way, under the EEG the system is based on payments and services, but does not feature any taxes, other levies, equalization funds, or the like. The EEG also regulates who bears the costs of grid connections and upgrading.

Finally, the EEG establishes a system for the equalization of burdens among grid operators that does not involve the state. The state does not grant aid to specific companies. Every electricity producer can respond to relevant incentives (particularly, the degressive pricing regime) and switch to renewable energies. Nor does the state use its own resources to fund renewable energies. Rather, the state's overall purpose in establishing purchase obligations (that is, quantity based regulation) via a flow quota and setting a fixed price (price regulation) is to protect the environment and it merely promotes renewable energies indirectly to achieve this end.

5 DEVELOPMENT OF RENEWABLE ENERGIES UNDER THE EEG

5.1 Developments in Renewable Energy Technologies

Under the EEG, renewable energies in Germany have developed very successfully, particularly wind, photovoltaic, and geothermal energy. Biogas is not as far advanced as a specific law governing the development of this type of energy could not be passed before 2002. In general, it appears therefore, that the extended court proceedings concerning the lawfulness of the EEG and its predecessor, the Electricity Supply Act, did not significantly harm the development of renewable energies in Germany.

As of 2002, Germany had installed 12.001 MW in wind energy capacity. By way of comparison, Spain had installed 4.830 MW; Denmark, 2.880 MW; Italy, 785 MW; The Netherlands, 688 MW; the UK, 552 MW; Sweden, 328 MW; and all other EU member states together, 992 MW. Accordingly, Germany had installed more than fifty percent of total EU wind energy capacity.[32] This high share is due to the EEG, which provides for different payments depending on the site of the windmill. Seaside installations attract lower payments, whereas payments for inland installations are higher.

As of 2002, Germany had installed more than sixty percent of total photovoltaic capacity in the EU. Each year, total installation capacity in Germany grew by approximately forty percent. This extremely high share is also due to the EEG, which provides for fixed prices of 0.50 € per kWh for the first 350 MW installed.[33] For instance, the Shell Company, with a global market share of thirteen percent, installed 25 MW of photovoltaic capacity in Germany recently. In any event, more significant future developments are expected in connection with solar collectors, rather than photovoltaics. Solar collectors are expected to hold a world energy market share of more than twenty percent in 2050.[34]

---

[32] See Table 1, *WWF* Progress Report on the Implementation of the European Renewables Directive (Brussels, 2002) at 14.

[33] EREF, Missing Targets (Brussels, 2000) at 15.   [34] *See* Annex 1 to this chapter.

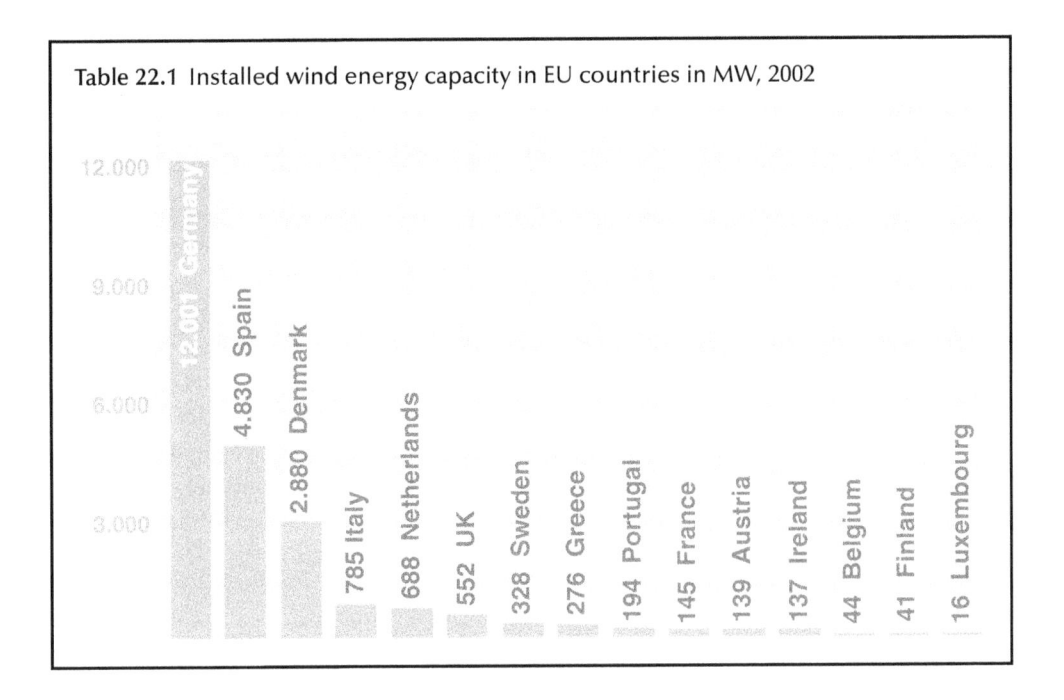

Table 22.1 Installed wind energy capacity in EU countries in MW, 2002

Germany, together with Japan, is also leading the way in thermal solar energy. Italy is the market leader in geothermal energy, while France is the European market leader in installed small hydropower capacity. The UK and Germany are joint market leaders in biogas.

5.2 Comparative Legislative Developments

Almost simultaneously with Germany, Spain introduced a law providing for supply-in tariffs for renewable energies. However, under the Spanish law, the premium has been set at a relatively low level and so the supply-in system has not been as successful as the EEG scheme in promoting the development of a specific energy technology. The same is true for Denmark as, under the Danish law, the supply-in premium was sufficient only for wind power and biogas; investment in all other renewable energy sources was effectively discouraged. Denmark also experienced legal difficulties with the European Commission and it took a significant amount of time for the Danish government to gain approval for a new regulatory scheme, introduced in Denmark post-2000.

6 EU REGULATORY DEVELOPMENTS IN RELATION TO RENEWABLE ENERGIES

6.1 The 1997 White Paper on Renewable Sources of Energy

In November 1997, the European Commission adopted a White Paper on renewable sources of energy,[35] which established a target of twelve percent for the contribution

---

[35] European Commission, Energy for the Future: renewable sources of energy – White Paper for a Community Strategy and Action Plan, COM (97) 599 final, November 26, 1997.

of renewable energies to the EU's gross inland energy consumption as of 2010. Furthermore, the European Commission was to report every two years on the progress achieved toward this goal. The first report of the European Commission was published in February 2001.

6.2 The 2000 Green Paper on Security of Energy Supply

As the EU depends on energy imports to satisfy approximately fifty percent of European demand for energy services and this dependence is projected to increase to approximately seventy percent as of 2030, the European Commission launched a Green Paper: Towards a European strategy for the security of energy supply in November 2000.[36] Renewables were considered one of the most attractive options for diversifying Europe's energy supplies. Since many of the renewable energy sources were relatively new on the market, the Commission urged a targeted legislative and commercial infrastructure to encourage market growth.

6.3 The RES-E Directive of 2001

The Directive on the promotion of electricity produced from renewable energy sources in the internal electricity market (RES-E Directive), released in draft form on May 10, 2000 by the European Commission, was finally adopted on September 27, 2001.[37] The RES-E Directive establishes national targets for all member states in relation to future consumption of electricity produced from renewable energy sources. The consumption of electricity produced from renewable energy sources, as opposed to electricity produced from nonrenewable sources, is projected to rise from fourteen percent in 1997 to 22.1 percent in 2010 if the targets under the RES-E Directive are met.

The RES-E Directive does not establish a harmonized community-wide support scheme for electricity produced from renewable energy sources. However, member states are required to ensure open access for electricity produced from renewable energy sources; issue guarantees of origin; and ensure that the calculations of the costs of connecting new producers of electricity produced from renewable energy sources, and of transmitting electricity produced from renewable energy sources, are transparent and nondiscriminatory.

As it is obliged under the RES-E Directive to monitor the progress made toward achieving these targets, the European Commission is obliged to propose a harmonized community-wide support scheme for electricity produced from renewable energy sources after four years if necessary. Note however, as the targets under the RES-E Directive are not obligatory, whether or not the fifteen member states will reach the projected targets is likely to be highly uncertain until 2010.

[36] Green Paper: Towards a European strategy for the security of energy supply, COM (2000) 769, available at http://europa.eu.int/comm/energy_transport/doc-principal/pubfinal_en.pdf. Note the European Commission's Final Report on this Green Paper, COM (2002) 321 final, is available at http://europa.eu.int/comm/energy_transport/livrevert/final/report_en.pdf.

[37] Directive 2001/77/EC, O.J. L 283/33, September 27, 2001, available at http://europa.eu.int/eur-lex/pri/en/oj/dat/2001/l_283/l_28320011027en00330040.pdf.

Table 22.2 Targets for 2010 and scenarios in UK, Germany, France, and Italy

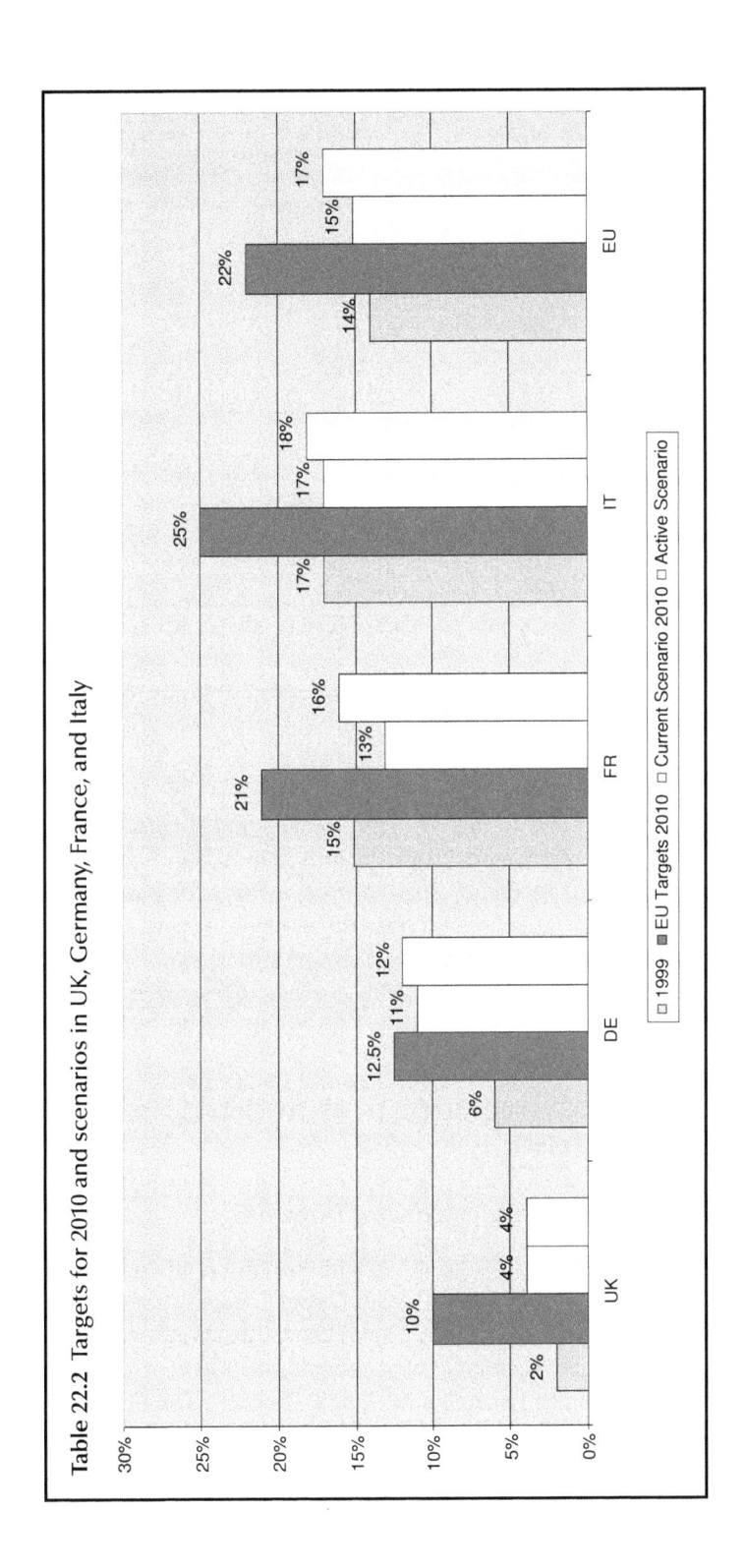

Table 22.3 Targets and Scenarios for All EU-Member States

	1999 %	EU Targets %	2010 Current scenario %	Active scenario %
AT	72%	78%	63%	63%
BE	1%	6%	1%	3%
DE	6%	12.5%	11%	12%
DK	13%	29%	23%	32%
ES	19%	29%	22%	28%
FI	26%	32%	31%	31%
FR	15%	21%	13%	16%
GR	10%	20%	12%	15%
I.E.	5%	13%	11%	15%
IT	17%	25%	17%	18%
LU	3%	6%	5%	5%
NL	2%	9%	6%	8.5%
PT	36%	39%	27%	38%
SE	50%	60%	57%	57%
UK	2%	10%	4%	4%
EU	14%	22%	15%	17%

Figures from WWF Progress Report and EREF (Brussels, 2002) at 9, based on PRETIR study 2002 (Ecofys, 3E, Fraunhofer).

6.4 Other EU Initiatives

There are further EU initiatives, such as the initiative supporting research and development through the Fifth Framework Program from 1998 to 2002[38] and the sixth Framework Program from 2002 to 2006.[39] Furthermore, in 2001 the European Commission adopted new community guidelines on state aid for environmental protection,[40] which provide for more transparent criteria for the circumstances in which the European Commission will hold state aid for renewable energies to be compatible with Article 87 of the EC Treaty.

7 EU REGULATORY DEVELOPMENTS IN RELATION TO GREENHOUSE GAS EMISSIONS TRADING

7.1 The Greenhouse Gas Emissions Trading Directive

The Directive establishing a scheme for greenhouse gas emission allowance trading within the community[41] (Greenhouse Gas Emissions Trading Directive) was adopted in July 2003 and published in October 2003. Under this Directive, member states are to adopt and implement laws, regulations, and administrative provisions necessary to comply with this Directive by December 31, 2003 at the latest. The aim of the Greenhouse

---

[38] *See* http://www.cordis.lu/fp5/about.htm.
[39] *See* http://europa.eu.int/comm/dgs/energy_transport/rtd/6/call_2/index_en.htm.
[40] O.J. C 37, February 3, 2001 at 3–15.
[41] Directive 2003/87/EC and amending Council directive 96/61/EC, O.J. L 275/32, October 13, 2003, available at http://europa.eu.int/eur-lex/pri/en/oj/dat/2003/l_275/l_27520031025en00320046.pdf.

Gas Emissions Trading Directive is an overall reduction of eight percent in greenhouse gas emissions in the EU from 1990 until 2012. The Directive covers emissions from large (more than 20 MW) stationary sources, including power and heat generators, oil refineries, ferrous metals, cement, lime, glass and ceramic materials, and pulp and paper.[42] The Greenhouse Gas Emissions Trading Directive provides for an entity based domestic cap and trade allowance scheme, starting on January 1, 2005. The first phase will run from 2005 to 2007, the second from 2008 to 2012.

The "bubble policy" and emissions trading will begin with carbon dioxide, as the most important of all greenhouse gas emissions, but will cover all greenhouse gases.[43]

Emissions trading will begin with a "grandfathering clause," that is, free allocation in the beginning. From 2005 to 2007, member states may auction up to five percent of their emissions and from 2008 to 2012, this figure will rise to up to ten percent. This is perhaps not very much, but it will hit the marginal plants, as the greenhouse gas cap per country will translate into a greenhouse gas cap per installation (firm). The amount of admissible emissions will be counted separately for every individual stationary source. In this way, "polluters" will have to pay more for their certificates than those who emit less carbon dioxide.

Each member state will have to draw up an ex-ante national allocation plan. Under Annex III of the Greenhouse Gas Emissions Trading Directive, member states will have to observe some common allocation criteria.

The Directive also provides for sanctions. For every tonne of emissions that is not covered by an allowance, a company will have to pay a penalty of €40 from 2005 to 2007 and €100 thereafter. Companies will also have to surrender a compensating amount of allowances in the subsequent year.

Finally, the Directive is very explicit in its provisions. It also provides for rules governing banking and borrowing, temporary exclusions, pooling, and force majeure.

8 EU REGULATORY SCHEMES: SUPPLY-IN REGULATIONS, QUOTAS OR BOTH?

8.1 Regulatory Schemes under the RES-E Directive and the Greenhouse Gas Emissions Trading Directive

Across Europe, there are currently two different regulatory schemes in operation, in relation to the promotion of "green" electricity under the RES-E Directive: supply-in schemes and quotas. Under the Greenhouse Gas Emissions Trading Directive however, there is only one regulatory scheme. The consequence of this latter Directive is that there is a de facto quota scheme in place, for polluting the atmosphere with greenhouse gas emissions resulting from the production of "brown" electricity from fossil fuels. Under the Greenhouse Gas Emissions Trading Directive, every company must buy certificates up to the amount of the polluting emissions it releases in connection with the production of such brown electricity. The effect of this regulatory scheme therefore, is that trading

---

[42] *See Id.*, Annex 1.
[43] The bubble policy and emissions trading will cover the following greenhouse gases: carbon dioxide (CO_2), methane (CH_4), nitrous oxide (N_2O), hydrofluorocarbons (HFG), perfluorocarbons (PFG), sulphur hexafluoride (SF_6).

on the basis of all such certificates is effectively a quota for brown electricity in the grid. This raises the question of whether these two regulatory approaches – supply-in schemes and quotas – are compatible with each other. Alternatively, whether an overall quota regime should be introduced within the EU.

8.2 Electricity Produced from Renewable Sources

In the context of electricity produced from renewable energy sources, supply-in regulations can be both advantageous and disadvantageous. If the price premium is too low, new technologies and new renewable sources of energy will not be developed. Alternatively, if it is too high, from a welfare economics point of view, this is inefficient and the state budget could be better spent for other purposes.

If a member state were to ask whether it will reach the target under the RES-E Directive there also is no clear answer. The price incentive may reach or overreach this goal, or may end up being above or below the target. As they are at different stages of development, each type of renewable energy must be treated differently, otherwise the supply-in scheme will only support those types of renewable energies which are closest to market prices. Accordingly, if the regulator sets prices at the correct level, the big advantage of supply-in schemes is that they provide more accurate incentives for research and development than quotas do. Moreover, if a guaranteed timeframe for the operation of the fixed prices is given, electricity producers have a secure base for planning investments in renewable energies. For instance, in Germany, with a high premium of 0.50 € per kWh for photovoltaic electricity and a price guarantee for twenty years – this industry can be supported more effectively and accurately than in other member states, where lower expected returns on investments advocate the development and installation of wind mills or hydropower plants, rather than photovoltaic solutions. Finally, supply-in regulations encourage new market entrants. Even consumers can take advantage of such regulations if they produce more electricity than they need.

As of 2003, the majority of EU member states had introduced supply-in tariffs. The UK and Ireland gave up their tendering schemes and moved to regulatory schemes imposing obligations and quotas. Sweden and Italy also adopted schemes imposing obligations with quotas. Belgium is divided, as Brussels has adopted a scheme involving supply-in tariffs, whereas Walloon and the Flemish regions have adopted quota systems.

8.3 Electricity Produced from Fossil Fuels

Emissions trading, in the context of brown electricity plants polluting the atmosphere with carbon dioxide and other greenhouse gases, covers existing plants and existing industries. It sets a cap on admissible emissions. Accordingly, the output of greenhouse gases can be predicted exactly provided that no accidents or force majeure events occur. Under the regulatory scheme provided for in the Greenhouse Gas Emissions Trading Directive, the externalities of existing industries are embedded in the price for brown electricity. This quota based solution is more efficient in relation to existing brown electricity production, provided that the speed at which certificates are reduced is not too fast or too slow. Such a scheme provides incentives for producers to move into

Table 22.4 RES Policy in EU Member States

Country	Major support instrument	Selection of additional instruments
Austria	TSO purchase obligation for RES-E with mandatory obligation to suppliers; fixed feed-in tariffs.	Rebates and feed-in tariffs for biomass (electricity and heat), solar thermal, PV, wind, and biogas.
Belgium	Feed-in tariffs (Brussels), renewables obligation and tradable green certificates (Walloon & Flemish region).	Rebates, investment-based tax exemptions.
Denmark	Feed-in tariffs for RES-E.	Tax relief for RES-E, e.g. from CO_2, tax, income tax. Compensation schemes; solar heat obligation in new buildings.
Finland	Tax relief, voluntary green pricing.	Rebates.
France	Feed-in tariff & purchase obligation (for wind energy, small hydro, PV, biomass and biogas, and electricity from CHP and wastes incineration).	Fiscal measures for PV, wind, solar thermal, wood burning heating devices (stoves, closed heaters, or boilers), heat pumps.
Germany	Feed-in tariffs for RES-E.	Soft loans, local rebates, green tariffs. Solar roofs program.
Greece	Feed-in tariffs for RES-E.	Subsidies and tax deduction.
Ireland	Tendering (AER program) with purchase obligation and feed-in tariff.	CO_2 tax, tax relief.
Italy	Renewables obligation.	Tax relief.
Luxembourg	Feed-in tariffs.	Compensation schemes.
The Netherlands	Feed-in system and purchase obligation proposed, combined with tax exemption and certificate system (Jan. 2003).	Feed-in tariffs, fiscal measures.
Portugal	Feed-in tariffs.	Rebate, compensation schemes.
Spain	Feed-in tariffs.	Compensation schemes, third party financing.
Sweden	Renewables obligation and certificate system as of Jan. 2003. Quota on new RES-E production from 6% in 2003 to 15% in 2010.	Feed-in tariffs for small generators, tax exemptions (largely to be phased out).
UK	Purchase obligation: 10% by 2010 and will continue (and increase) until 2027, tradable green certificates.	Pollution tax relief, green tariffs.

Source: Authors info based on ECOFYS 2003.
WWF Progress Report, (Brussels, 2002) at 7, 8.

markets for new energy technologies as it gradually raises the price of existing brown electricity production.

8.4 Summary

The conclusion to be drawn from such analyses is that both regulatory regimes, supply-in schemes for green electricity and quotas (through emissions trading) for brown electricity, are compatible. Both schemes still must resolve critical problems. First, the correct setting of the price for supply-in regulations for green electricity is crucial for the success of such regulatory schemes. Too low means too little or no investment at all, whereas too high means overinvestment and a waste of public resources. Second, the correct speed for the reduction of pollution certificates is crucial for the success of quota based regulations for brown electricity. Too fast means that companies are driven out of business and, at the same time, there is the specter of a scarcity of electricity. However, too slow means too much pollution and that the market share of green electricity cannot be expanded quickly enough from a welfare economics point of view and from an environmental protection policy standpoint.

9 OTHER RELATED ENERGY POLICY AREAS

9.1 Biofuels

The Biofuels Directive of May 2003[44] requires an increasing proportion of all fuels sold in member states to be biofuels. Whereas around 0.4% of the gasoline and diesel consumed in member states in 2000 were biofuels, Article 3 of the Biofuels Directive sets targets to increase this share to at least two percent by December 31, 2005 and 5.75% by December 31, 2010.

9.2 Cogeneration of Heat and Electric Power

The promotion of cogeneration of heat and electric power (CHP) is still not regulated by the EU. Following its initial proposal for a CHP Directive in July 2002[45] and amendments by the European Parliament on May 14, 2003, the European Commission further amended this proposal and submitted it for adoption in July 2003.[46] On January 26, 2004, the European Commission submitted a further Opinion to the European Parliament amending this proposal.[47] If the European Commission's cogeneration strategy

---

[44] Directive 2003/30/EC on the promotion of the use of biofuels or other renewable fuels for transport, May 8, 2003, O.J. L 123/42 of May 17, 2003; *see* http://europa.eu.int/eur-lex/pri/en/oj/dat/2003/l_123/l_12320030517en00420046.pdf.

[45] European Commission, Directive on the promotion of cogeneration based on a useful heat demand in the internal energy market, COM (2002) 415 final, July 22, 2002; *see* http://europa.eu.int/eur-lex/en/com/pdf/ 2002/com2002_0415en01.pdf.

[46] European Commission, Amended Proposal for a Directive on the promotion of cogeneration based on a useful heat demand in the internal energy market, COM (2003) 416 final, July 23, 2003; *see* http://europa.eu.int/eur-lex/en/com/pdf/2003/com2003_0416en01.pdf; *see also* Common Position (EC) No. 52/2003 of September 8, 2003, O. J. C 258/E, October 28, 2003 at 1.

[47] Opinion of the European Commission on the Directive on the promotion of cogeneration based on a useful heat demand in the internal energy market and amending Directive 92/42/EC, COM (2004) 49 final, January 26, 2004; *see* http://europa.eu.int/eur-lex/en/com/pdf/2004/com2004_0049en01.pdf.

is successful, the overall share of cogeneration in total EU electricity production, while only eleven percent in 1998, should increase to eighteen percent in 2010.[48]

The underlying reasons for the European Commission's pursuit of a cogeneration strategy are: first, cogeneration saves energy; second, it improves security of supply; and third, it is cost effective. As cogeneration installations are usually close to the points of consumption, less losses result on the electricity grid. Further, cogeneration has a positive competitive effect among producers and provides valuable opportunities for the creation of new businesses. Finally, cogeneration is well suited to isolated or ultra-peripheral areas.

It is important to note that the proposed Directive has not yet been adopted. A common position of the European Commission and Council was adopted on September 8, 2003.[49] The 18% target does not appear in this policy paper however. Moreover, it is uncertain whether the European Parliament will adopt this common position.

At a national level, Germany adopted the Combined Heat and Power Act in 2002.[50] This law is aimed at stabilizing the present share of cogeneration in Germany. Currently, cogeneration accounts for 14.2% of electricity produced in Germany, slightly above the EU average share (11%) but significantly lower than Sweden (85%), Finland (78.2%), Denmark (69.6%), Austria (71.7%), and The Netherlands (46.7%).[51]

10 CONCLUSION

The development of renewable energies and of policies governing the development of renewable energy sources has been very different across Europe. Germany, historically, lagged behind but has developed rapidly after the adoption of the Electricity Supply Act in 1990 and the EEG in 2000. The policy of the European Commission has not always been particularly helpful for the development of renewable energies or national laws and policies in this regard. There was a fierce court battle waged against both the Electricity Supply Act and the EEG. The European Commission maintained the assertion put forward by the plaintiff companies that the supply-in regulations under the two Acts constituted inadmissible state aid in violation of Article 87 of the EC Treaty. In 2001, the ECJ upheld the supply-in regulations. Subsequently, under the two Acts, there has been a rapid development of renewable energies in Germany, especially the wind and photovoltaic energy industries.

Under the RES-E Directive, the targets for member states to achieve the aims of the Kyoto Protocol[52] are indicative only. Under the Greenhouse Gas Emissions Trading Directive, an emissions trading scheme must be established in every member state, to commence in 2005.

For the promotion of green electricity, supply-in regulations are preferable as each type of renewable energy source can be treated differently. However, for the reduction of greenhouse gas emissions from brown electricity, emissions trading regimes with de

---

[48] O.J. C 291 E/182 v., 26 November 2002.   [49] COM (97) 514 (final).
[50] See http://www.energylaw.de/.
[51] Project Workshop "Green-X," Renewable Energy House, Brussels, September 23, 2003.
[52] Supra note 2.

facto quotas are preferable, as such schemes can set a cap on admissible emissions of greenhouse gases.

ANNEX 1 RENEWABLES, DEVELOPMENT, AND MARKETS

By Eva Maria Steiger

Types of Renewable Energy

This annex gives an overview of the most prominent types in the wide range of naturally occurring, replenishable energy sources, describing their function, focusing on their development states and giving future prospects of the various types in the member states of the European Union. The term renewable energy sources (RES) is defined in Article 2(a) of the renewables Directive as any "renewable non-fossil energy sources (wind, solar, geothermal, wave, tidal, hydropower, biomass, landfill gas, sewage treatment plant gas and biogases)." There are eighteen types of energy production classified as RES:

- Anaerobic digestion of agricultural wastes
- Biomass – Electricity (including CHP applications and co-utilization)
- Biomass – Heat (including domestic heat, district heating, and process heat for industry)
- Geothermal energy
- Hydrogen production from non-fossil fuels
- Landfill gas
- Large-scale hydropower
- Liquid biofuels (production)
- Municipal waste combustion
- Passive solar design of buildings and heat pumps
- Photo-chemical conversion
- Small-scale hydropower
- Solar PV
- Solar thermal (low temperature heating and cooling)
- Solar thermal electricity generation
- Tidal (including tidal streams)
- Wave
- Wind energy

Except for large-scale hydropower, which already operates at market conditions, all of these technologies, though growing and developing rapidly, are at a rather early stage of development. Due to a change in energy policy, which caused a switch away from fossil energy toward sustainable development and renewable energies, in recent years there have been several programs and stimulus to support the technologies across the EU and worldwide. As a result reliability has increased and costs have reduced. The EU has outlined in its 1997 White Paper and the directive outline as goals of the EU to foster the development of RES in the Union and to increase from 14% to 22% of gross electricity consumption by 2010. Still, except for large scale hydropower, energy from

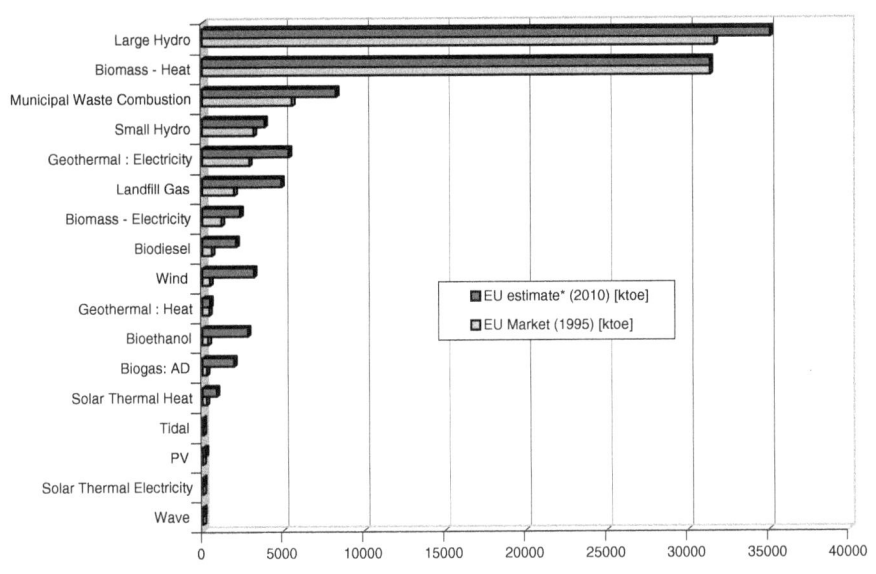

Figure 22.1 Current and prospective future deployment of RE technologies in the EU and Norway. *Source*: ATLAS Web site of the European Commission

clean sources is still considerably more costly than conventional fossil fuels in the short and medium run. However, it is widely recognized that increased deployment will help to bring down the costs of renewables, and such development largely depends on the extent of political commitment. There is no doubt, however, that in the long run the development of alternative energy sources is inevitable and that technical improvements will bring clean energy sources toward a cost level at which they can compete with the traditional sources.

The availability of renewable energy resources varies enormously between different countries and regions for reasons associated with their geographical features and climate. And not every kind of renewable energy is suited for the local conditions, as well as the conditions of the specific market. These conditions determine not only the technical possibilities, but also constitute the costs of the specific energy and its ability to compete with conventional alternatives. The graph in Figure 22.1 summarizes the share of the various types of clean energy in the EU in 1995 and its estimated share in 2010. In total in 1995 80,165 ktoe where produced with RES, and the EU strives to increase it to 102,799 ktoe by 2010.[53]

Technology Status

Due to support by the EU, national funding, and substantial cooperation between industry, research institutions, and academia, there had been development and maturing of some technologies and markets in the renewable sector. However, the stage of development differs significantly: Some technologies, e.g., large-scale hydropower and conventional domestic combustion of wood, are fully commercial, mature, and

[53] Numbers are taken from the ATLAS report and the website of the European Commission on New and Renewable Energies, http://europa.eu.int/comm/energy/res/index_en.htm.

approaching market saturation. Others, e.g., wind power, crystalline silicon PV power, and solar water heating, are becoming established in limited niche markets but have the potential to move into larger mass markets. A third category, which includes tidal and wave power and flash pyrolysis of biomass, are still essentially at the R&D stage.[54] Except for the first two, all types still require further research, optimization, and cost reduction in order to achieve competitiveness. We will shortly deal with each type of energy and state its technical specialities, current condition, and future prospects.

Wind Energy: Wind energy in Europe has matured rapidly over the last decade and the technology is now commercially available, particularly at medium (100–750kW) scale. The EU holds more than sixty-seven percent of newly installed capacities worldwide (vs. twenty-five percent in the United States), i.e., a supplementary installed power capacity of the order of 4,615 MW, with Germany being the uncontested leader with a total cumulated capacity of 8,750 MW, i.e., more than one-third of installed worldwide capacity. Nevertheless, Denmark's position is still a very enviable one, with a total capacity of 2,417 MW as of the end of this year. The EU estimates to have a capacity of 3,165 ktoe by 2010. Several aspects of the technology still need further development and cost reduction, including rotor technology and variable speed generators and drives, in particular the newly developed large-scale machines, of offshore applications, and of integration with electricity grids.

Solar PV: In 1995 photovoltaic accounted for only 4 ktoe of the energy supply, the EU estimated to accelerate the share to 151 ktoe. There has been considerable progress in PV technologies. Spain and Germany have invested in its development for several years. The German regulation, which guarantees 48 cents per kWh is accepted as a role model. Now Italy, France, and the UK have started considerable attempts to catch up.[55] As a result the use of photovoltaic technologies in isolated sites is now well established. The costs of PV modules and other system components have fallen substantially in the last five years and are expected to decline even further. Still, substantial future research in the field of thin film PV module technology is necessary to meet the estimated goals by 2010.

Solar Thermal (Heat and Electricity): Solar thermal technology operated at a scale of 224 ktoe p.a. in 1995 in the community. It is a well established technology for domestic water heating and swimming pool applications. Other applications are still being tested. Solar electricity is still at a very early stage (a production of 1 ktoe in 1995, the EU aims at an increase to 43 ktoe in 2010), although in California several prototypes have been operated during the last ten years. And researchers in the European Union have indicated that they are ready for large-scale demonstration within a hybrid system, in combination with conventional fossil fuel. Still, operating and maintenance costs are substantial and little experience on particular conditions in Europe has been gathered.

Biomass – Electricity and Electricity: Large-scale power (or combined heat and power) generation from biomass can be achieved by using a number of different fuels and technological approaches, and the spectrum of maturity for the conversion technologies is very wide. There is an established market for "conventional" industrial power or CHP generation using straightforward biomass combustion. The current size amounts to

---

[54] *See* ATLAS report on renewable energies, http://europa.eu.int/comm/energy_transport/atlas/home.html.
[55] *See* European Commission DG TREN, ALTENER II, Campaign for Take-off, Renewable Energy for Europe 2003 at 4–5.

1,170 ktoe and an increase is aimed at 2,322 ktoe in 2010. Still further research is needed especially in the field of gasification technologies (to increase efficiencies and reduce costs), for pyrolysis, fuel preparation, and energy crops.

The small-scale use of biomass (mainly wood) for domestic heating is widely used, but has low cost-effectiveness and creates considerable emissions. The EU aims at keeping quantities stable at about 31,399 ktoe, but shift to the large-scale industrial and district heating applications. Research on cost reduction and efficiency enhancement is still needed.

Municipal Waste Combustion: Municipal waste combustion technology is based upon conventional grate firing systems and operates in an established market. This is the most contested type of renewable energy, as it may create emissions due to insufficiently sorted waste. Therefore, further work is required to optimize the processing of wastes with respect to waste minimization and recycling. It currently operates at a scale of 5,590 ktoe and a moderate increase to 8,299 is expected by 2010.

Liquid Biofuels: The production of liquid biofuels (biodiesel and bioethanol) involves well-established industrial processes. It is currently used at a scale of 455 for biodiesel and 255 ktoe for bioethanol, and the use in 2010 is aimed at 3,165 and 1,924 ktoe. Nonetheless, further research is needed to reduce production costs.

Landfill Gas: The technology to produce electricity and heat from landfill gas is properly researched and developed. Also, there exists the necessary environmental legislation that requires the collection of the methane at landfill sites throughout the EU. Continuing growth (at a range from 1,944 to 4,902 ktoe in 2010) can therefore be expected in the production of energy from landfill gas in the short to medium term. Though legislation is also being introduced to limit the use of landfilling for waste disposal, in the longer term the market for landfill gas must be expected to decline again.

Anaerobic Digestion of Agricultural Wastes: Anaerobic digestion (AD) is widely used to treat sewage sludge at large-scale plants and the technology for this application is very well established. In contrast, the use of AD to treat agricultural wastes and the organic fractions of municipal solid wastes requires a smaller scale plant which is less well developed. Smaller scale AD plants do exist in the EU, but they are widely perceived to be too costly and to exhibit poor performance and reliability. Further RTD is therefore needed to build experience and confidence in the smaller scale plants, to enhance their gas yields, to reduce their costs and to promote new markets for the digested materials.

Geothermal Energy: Technologies for producing heat in the range from 50°C to 150°C from geothermal aquifers are well established and commercially available for use in district heating, fish farming, horticulture, and recreational uses. Since resources are limited, the EU aims only at a moderate increase, and future research will mainly focus on best practice. There is also considerable field experience with the exploitation of medium and high enthalpy geothermal resources (>150°C), which can be used for electricity production, but in this case further work to address problems associated with scaling and corrosion, and with reservoir management could lead to improved performance and cost-effectiveness.

Small Hydropower: Hydroelectric power generation is the most mature technology of all RES in the EU as well as worldwide. Italy and France remain the leaders in terms of installed power capacity, with respectively 2,229 MW and 2,018 MW. Spain has made the most outstanding efforts with an additional 570 MW installed between 1990 and

2000. However, improvements are possible to extend the range of the existing small hydro technologies, notably to develop new low head turbines, to use new construction materials, and to develop lower cost packaged systems for use in developing countries. The standardization of products and the development of load control equipment and head enhancement techniques such as inflatable weirs are also key areas for further technical development.

Wave: Wave technology is still at the development stage, and is not yet ready for commercial deployment. Designs for offshore devices are also still at an early stage of development. So far results look promising and the EU hopes to produce at a scale of 39 ktoe in 2010.

Tidal: Tidal barrage technology is a relatively mature technology, but the only existing full scale plant is the 240 MW barrage at La Rance in France, which has been operating successfully for over thirty years (since 1967). The EU plans no considerable increase in this technology. The main obstacles to more widespread use of this technology are the high capital costs and the environmental impacts created on the locality by the plant. Production of power from tidal streams is still at an early stage of research, and the prospects and estimated cost development of this technology are still unclear.

In conclusion, it can be said that considerable development takes place in the field of new and renewable energy, and, though the EU aims are ambitious, prospects are reasonable.

23 The Law of Energy for Sustainable Development in Britain

Andrew Warren*

The concept of a "balance of powers" is unknown in the British Constitution. The executive arm of government is entirely selected by the Prime Minister of the day from among those elected to the legislature. And the Prime Minister is in turn only elected by the members of the legislature. Thus, both Parliament and ministers are run via the same electoral mandate and, owing to the peculiar electoral system operating in the UK, will invariably be of the same, single party.

So, most legislation is conceived, prepared, and processed by the government of the day. As the influential House of Commons Environmental Audit Committee has somewhat acidly observed, energy efficiency is the exception to the rule. Practically every significant Act of Parliament over the past decade affecting the demand side of energy has emanated from initiatives undertaken by backbench Members of Parliament (MPs) – interestingly drawn from all three major parties.

In contrast, the one significant government sponsored measure – the Utilities Act 2000 – simply formalized a system of funding for household energy measures long required by the independent energy regulators.

The sole exception to this rule has been the use by the Chancellor of the Exchequer (finance minister) of his annual Finance Act to introduce fiscal measures designed to encourage energy saving investment (or not, as the case may be).

The classic taxation issue has long been that of the levels of Value Added Tax (VAT) imposed on energy conservation, as opposed to energy consumption. The level on the latter was introduced in 1994 at eight percent (making the UK the last European Union country to place this tax upon fuel). It was duly decreased to five percent by the incoming Labor government in 1997.

Previously their Treasury team had tried to amend the (final) Conservative budget to enable energy conservation measures to be taxed at the same level, rather than at the full 17.5 percent. In an impassioned speech, Dawn Primarolo, now Financial Secretary to the Treasury, described it as necessary in the name of "jobs, democracy and energy efficiency." The amendment was lost by just one vote. Once in government, it took a couple of budgets, but VAT levels were eventually equalized at five percent for some, but by no means all, energy saving measures.

A fairly eclectic list of artifacts qualify: cavity wall insulation, loft insulation (but not for self-installed purposes), heating controls (but not high efficiency boilers), microcogeneration (but not glazing), and so on. For all the measures excluded, there

* Director, Association for the Conservation of Energy, UK.

remains a fundamental distortion in the tax system that directly encourages excess consumption.

The other key Treasury measure has been the introduction of the Climate Change Levy in 2001. In common with all other northern European countries, the UK has an energy consumption tax. Unlike all others, it has placed it exclusively on the productive sector of the economy. In order to placate those who saw this as purely a "nice little earner" for the Treasury, for the first two years of the levy, there was a compensatory reduction in National Insurance (employment tax) levels, to simulate "revenue neutrality." That reduction has now been withdrawn.

Still in operation are the agreements negotiated with forty-six separate industrial sectors, whereby in exchange for an eighty percent reduction in levy rates, the sectors undertake to invest in energy saving measures (practically all of which would pay back within two years). That at any rate ensures some energy saving reductions, coupled as it is with a scheme to allow 100 percent capital allowance reductions in the first year of investments. Two years on, no figures are available on uptake.

So far as specific energy efficiency legislation is concerned, the Utilities Bill 2000 did formally codify requirements that energy regulators had been making since 1993 on residential gas and electricity suppliers, to allocate finances toward helping their customers save energy (the Energy Efficiency Commitment). It also allowed government to set the levels of these requirements, rather than regulators.

But the leading champions have been those backbench MPs. Each November, there is a tombola draw for MPs, enabling those who come high up on the list – effectively the top seven out of twenty – the possibility of acquiring enough parliamentary time to get a bill of their own choosing onto the statute book. The easy option is to adopt a bill prewritten by a government department, and that is what most do.

A few are prepared to prepare and present their own texts, and then negotiate with ministers, civil servants, other MPs, and external interest groups, to persuade them not to block their bill's progress. It is a tortuous and complex procedure, extraordinarily difficult to conclude satisfactorily. Since 1995, three MPs have successfully achieved this with energy saving measures – the Home Energy Conservation Act (Diana Maddock, Liberal Democrat), the Energy Efficiency Act 1996 (Alan Simpson, Labor), and in 2000 the Warm Homes and Energy Conservation Act (David Amess, Conservative).

The first two set duties for local authorities to prepare reports designed to improve the energy performance of all households in their areas by thirty percent over fifteen years. The most recent required government effectively to abolish fuel poverty by 2016.

In the interim years, each year one or more backbench MPs have chosen to promote a parliamentary bill designed to encourage energy efficiency – in offices, via mortgage surveys, via binding national intensity targets, and so on. All of these "ran out of Parliamentary time," usually at the very final stage.

This year another backbench MP, Labor's Brian White, has come sixth in the annual ballot. He is steering his Sustainable Energy Bill through Parliament at present. It seeks to embed into government policy all the aspirational targets, for cogeneration and renewables as well as residential energy efficiency, which decorate the Energy White Paper. If he succeeds, it will give great confidence to all the sustainable energy industries. If he fails, it will inevitably call into doubt the sincerity of government's official objectives.

In the meantime, we must look to Brussels for the most productive legislative support. The Energy Performance of Buildings Directive is but the latest in a line of directives that have a significant impact on the energy efficiency market.

This ensures that whenever a building changes occupancy, an energy survey is done. It requires all larger buildings, when upgraded, to meet contemporary energy efficiency standards. It also ensures that all larger commercial buildings, open to the public, overtly display their relative energy performance. It will also require a regular upgrading of the heat and power parts of the Building Regulations, itself a statutory instrument that greatly affects energy performance.

There has never yet been a government sponsored bill designed exclusively to improve energy efficiency. Perhaps that says it all about the relative priority given to the demand side.

HL BILL 92 53/2

Sustainable Energy Bill

Contents
1. Annual reports on progress towards sustainable energy aims
2. Energy efficiency of residential accommodation: Secretary of State
3. Energy efficiency of residential accommodation: National Assembly for Wales
4. Energy efficiency of residential accommodation: energy conservation authorities
5. CHP targets
6. Duty of Gas and Electricity Markets Authority to carry out impact assessments
7. Use of certain money held by Gas and Electricity Markets Authority
8. Financial provision
9. Citation, extent and commencement

A Bill to make provision about the development and promotion of a sustainable energy policy; to amend the Utilities Act 2000; and for connected purposes.

BE IT ENACTED by the Queen's most Excellent Majesty, by and with the advice and consent of the Lords Spiritual and Temporal, and Commons, in this present Parliament assembled, and by the authority of the same, as follows:–

1 Annual reports on progress towards sustainable energy aims

(1) The Secretary of State must in each calendar year, beginning with 2004, publish a report ("a sustainable energy report") on the progress made in the reporting period towards –
 (a) cutting the United Kingdom's carbon emissions;
 (b) maintaining the reliability of the United Kingdom's energy supplies;
 (c) promoting competitive energy markets in the United Kingdom; and
 (d) reducing the number of people living in fuel poverty in the United Kingdom.
(2) "The reporting period," for the purposes of subsection (1), means the year ending with 23 February in the calendar year in question.
(3) Accordingly, the report must be published in that calendar year within the period beginning with 24 February and ending with 31 December ("the publication period").
(4) A sustainable energy report may either be published as a single report or published in a number of parts during the publication period, and any such report or part may be contained in a document containing other material.

(5) A sustainable energy report must be based on such information as is available to the Secretary of State when the report is completed (except that if it is published in parts, each of those parts must be based on such information as is so available when that part is completed).

(6) For the purposes of this section a person is to be regarded as living in fuel poverty if he is a member of a household living on a lower income in a home which cannot be kept warm at a reasonable cost.

2 Energy efficiency of residential accommodation: Secretary of State

(1) The Secretary of State must within one week beginning with the coming into force of this section designate under this subsection at least one energy efficiency aim.

(2) For the purposes of this section an "energy efficiency aim" is an aim which –
    (a) is contained in a published document;
    (b) relates to the energy efficiency of residential accommodation in England; and
    (c) is compatible with Community obligations and any other international obligations of the United Kingdom.

(3) The Secretary of State may, at any time after designation under subsection (1), designate under this subsection a further energy efficiency aim or aims.

(4) Where an energy efficiency aim is for the time being designated under this section, the Secretary of State must take reasonable steps to achieve the aim.

(5) In deciding which steps to take for the purposes of subsection (4), the Secretary of State must consider steps relating to the heating, cooling, ventilation, lighting and insulation of residential accommodation.

(6) A designation under this section may be withdrawn, but not if its withdrawal would result in there being no energy efficiency aim designated under this section.

(7) If an energy efficiency aim designated under this section ceases to meet the condition in subsection (2)(c) it ceases to be designated under this section, but if this results in there being no energy efficiency aim so designated the Secretary of State must without delay designate a new energy efficiency aim.

(8) A designation of an aim under this section, or a withdrawal or cessation of such a designation, must be published in such way as the Secretary of State considers appropriate: a designation may be contained in the same published document as the aim itself.

(9) In this section "residential accommodation" has the meaning given by section 1 of the Home Energy Conservation Act 1995 (c. 10).

3 Energy efficiency of residential accommodation: National Assembly for Wales

(1) The National Assembly for Wales ("the Assembly") must within one week beginning with the coming into force of this section designate under this subsection at least one energy efficiency aim.

(2) For the purposes of this section an "energy efficiency aim" is an aim which –
    (a) is contained in a published document;
    (b) relates to the energy efficiency of residential accommodation in Wales; and
    (c) is compatible with Community obligations and any other international obligations of the United Kingdom.

(3) The Assembly may, at any time after designation under subsection (1), designate under this subsection a further energy efficiency aim or aims.

(4) Where an energy efficiency aim is for the time being designated under this section, the Assembly must (using the powers it has apart from this section) take reasonable steps to achieve the aim.

(5) In deciding which steps to take for the purposes of subsection (4), the Assembly must consider steps relating to the heating, cooling, ventilation, lighting and insulation of residential accommodation.

(6) A designation under this section may be withdrawn, but not if its withdrawal would result in there being no energy efficiency aim designated under this section.

(7) If an energy efficiency aim designated under this section ceases to meet the condition in subsection (2)(c) it ceases to be designated under this section, but if this results in there being no energy efficiency aim so designated the Assembly must without delay designate a new energy efficiency aim.

(8) A designation of an aim under this section, or a withdrawal or cessation of such a designation, must be published in such way as the Assembly considers appropriate: a designation may be contained in the same published document as the aim itself.

(9) In this section "residential accommodation" has the meaning given by section 1 of the Home Energy Conservation Act 1995 (c. 10).

4 Energy efficiency of residential accommodation: energy conservation authorities

(1) In this section an "energy efficiency direction" means a direction requiring each energy conservation authority to which it applies to take such energy conservation measures as that authority considers to be –
  (a) likely to result in achieving, by a date specified in the direction, an improvement so specified (which may be expressed as a percentage) in the energy efficiency of residential accommodation in that authority's area; and
  (b) practicable and cost-effective.

(2) For the purposes of this section, "the energy efficiency" of residential accommodation in an energy conservation authority's area has such meaning as may be specified in an order made by the Secretary of State.

(3) The Secretary of State may, after consulting the Local Government Association, give an energy efficiency direction which applies –
  (a) to one or more named energy conservation authorities in England;
  (b) to all energy conservation authorities in England; or
  (c) to a particular description of energy conservation authority in England.

(4) The National Assembly for Wales ("the Assembly") may, after consulting the Welsh Local Government Association, give an energy efficiency direction which applies –
  (a) to one or more named energy conservation authorities in Wales;
  (b) to all energy conservation authorities in Wales; or
  (c) to a particular description of energy conservation authority in Wales.

(5) With effect from the giving of an energy efficiency direction –
  (a) each energy conservation authority to which the direction applies must comply with the direction, using the powers it has apart from this section; and
  (b) the Home Energy Conservation Act 1995 (c. 10) ("HECA") shall cease to apply in relation to each such authority.

(6) In deciding which measures to take for the purposes of complying with an energy efficiency direction, an authority must give preference to measures which it considers would also contribute to –

  (a) achieving the objective mentioned in paragraph (d) of section 2(2) of the Warm Homes and Energy Conservation Act 2000 (c. 31) by the target date for the time being specified under that paragraph;

  (b) achieving any interim objectives for the time being specified under paragraph (c) of section 2(2) of that Act by the target date so specified.

(7) Different energy efficiency directions may be given in relation to different energy conservation authorities or different descriptions of such authority.

(8) The Secretary of State may after consulting the Local Government Association, and the Assembly may after consulting the Welsh Local Government Association, alter the date or the improvement (or both) for the time being specified in an energy efficiency direction given by the Secretary of State or (as the case may be) by the Assembly.

(9) An energy efficiency direction may be revoked, but only if each authority to which it applies either –

  (a) is subject to a new energy efficiency direction taking effect immediately on the revocation; or

  (b) no longer exists at the time of the revocation.

(10) The Secretary of State may give to energy conservation authorities in England, and the Assembly may give to energy conservation authorities in Wales, such guidance as he or it considers appropriate in relation to the exercise of an energy conservation authority's functions under this section.

(11) An energy conservation authority must have regard to any such guidance.

(12) The Secretary of State may by order –

  (a) amend this section so as to alter the body which must be consulted by him;

  (b) make transitional provision in relation to HECA's ceasing to apply in relation to an energy conservation authority in England.

(13) The Assembly may by order –

  (a) amend this section so as to alter the body which must be consulted by it;

  (b) make transitional provision in relation to HECA's ceasing to apply in relation to an energy conservation authority in Wales.

(14) Any power to make an order under this section is exercisable by statutory instrument which, in the case of an order made by the Secretary of State, shall be subject to annulment in pursuance of a resolution of either House of Parliament.

(15) In this section the following expressions have the meaning given by section 1 of HECA –

  "energy conservation authority";

  "residential accommodation";

  "area," in relation to an energy conservation authority;

  "energy conservation measures."

5 CHP targets

(1) Before the end of 2003, the Secretary of State must make a statement –

  (a) specifying one or more CHP targets; and

  (b) specifying the period that each CHP target is for.

(2) At any time after making the statement mentioned in subsection (1), the Secretary of State may make a further statement doing either or both of the following –
   (a) specifying as mentioned in that subsection;
   (b) revoking a CHP target contained in an earlier statement under this section.
(3) A CHP target is the percentage of the amount of electricity for government use in the period the target is for that the Secretary of State considers will be capable, at a reasonable cost to the government, of being supplied from CHP electricity.
(4) For the purposes of this section –
   "amount of electricity for government use in the period the target is for" means the amount of electricity that the Secretary of State estimates that the government will use in that period;
   "CHP electricity" means electricity that –
   (a) is generated by a generating station which is operated for the purposes of producing heat, or a cooling effect, in association with electricity; and
   (b) satisfies any other requirements specified in an order made by the Secretary of State.
(5) The Secretary of State may by order –
   (a) specify the departments and other bodies which (taken together) are to constitute "the government" for the purposes of this section;
   (b) provide for the exclusion from any estimation of the amount of electricity that the government will use in a period of –
      (i) the use of electricity for purposes specified in the order or in circumstances so specified;
      (ii) the use of electricity by any part of the government specified in the order.
(6) One of the periods specified under subsection (1)(b) must –
   (a) begin with 1 January 2010; and
   (b) end with 31 December 2010.
(7) The Secretary of State must lay any statement made under this section before Parliament.
(8) Any power to make an order under this section is exercisable by statutory instrument which shall be subject to annulment in pursuance of a resolution of either House of Parliament.
(9) No proceedings may be brought to enforce any CHP target contained in a statement made under this section or otherwise to review any act done, or any failure to act, in relation to any such CHP target.

6 Duty of Gas and Electricity Markets Authority to carry out impact assessments

After section 5 of the Utilities Act 2000 (c. 27) insert –

5A Duty of Authority to carry out impact assessment

(1) This section applies where –
   (a) the Authority is proposing to do anything for the purposes of, or in connection with, the carrying out of any function exercisable by it under or by virtue of Part 1 of the 1986 Act or Part 1 of the 1989 Act; and
   (b) it appears to it that the proposal is important;
but this section does not apply if it appears to the Authority that the urgency of the matter makes it impracticable or inappropriate for the Authority to comply with the requirements of this section.

(2) A proposal is important for the purposes of this section only if its implementation would be likely to do one or more of the following –
(a) involve a major change in the activities carried on by the Authority;
(b) have a significant impact on persons engaged in the shipping, transportation or supply of gas conveyed through pipes or in the generation, transmission, distribution or supply of electricity;
(c) have a significant impact on persons engaged in commercial activities connected with the shipping, transportation or supply of gas conveyed through pipes or with the generation, transmission, distribution or supply of electricity;
(d) have a significant impact on the general public in Great Britain or in a part of Great Britain; or
(e) have significant effects on the environment.
(3) Before implementing its proposal, the Authority must either –
(a) carry out and publish an assessment of the likely impact of implementing the proposal; or
(b) publish a statement setting out its reasons for thinking that it is unnecessary for it to carry out an assessment.
(4) An assessment carried out under this section must –
(a) include an assessment of the likely effects on the environment of implementing the proposal; and
(b) relate to such other matters as the Authority considers appropriate.
(5) In determining the matters to which an assessment under this section should relate, the Authority must have regard to such general guidance relating to the carrying out of impact assessments as it considers appropriate.
(6) An assessment carried out under this section may take such form as the Authority considers appropriate.
(7) Where the Authority publishes an assessment under this section –
(a) it must provide an opportunity of making representations to the Authority about its proposal to members of the public and other persons who, in the Authority's opinion, are likely to be affected to a significant extent by the proposal's implementation;
(b) the published assessment must be accompanied by a statement setting out how representations may be made; and
(c) the Authority must not implement its proposal unless the period for making representations about the proposal has expired and it has considered all the representations that were made in that period.
(8) Where the Authority is required (apart from this section) –
(a) to consult about a proposal to which this section applies, or
(b) to give a person an opportunity of making representations about it, the requirements of this section are in addition to, but may be performed contemporaneously with, the other requirements.
(9) Every report under section 5(1) must set out –
(a) a list of the assessments under this section carried out during the financial year to which the report relates; and
(b) a summary of the decisions taken during that year in relation to proposals to which assessments carried out in that year or previous financial years relate.

(10) The publication of anything under this section must be in such manner as the Authority considers appropriate for bringing it to the attention of the persons who, in the Authority's opinion, are likely to be affected if its proposal is implemented.

(11) References in sections 4AA, 4AB and 4A of the 1986 Act to functions of the Authority under Part 1 of that Act include references to any functions of the Authority under this section that are exercisable in relation to a proposal to do anything for the purposes of, or in connection with, the carrying out of any function of the Authority under Part 1 of the 1986 Act.

(12) References in sections 3A, 3B and 3C of the 1989 Act to functions of the Authority under Part 1 of that Act include references to any functions of the Authority under this section that are exercisable in relation to a proposal to do anything for the purposes of, or in connection with, the carrying out of any function of the Authority under Part 1 of the 1989 Act.

7 Use of certain money held by Gas and Electricity Markets Authority

(1) If the Secretary of State so directs, the person prescribed under section 33(1)(b) of the Electricity Act (collection of fossil fuel levy) must pay an amount into the Consolidated Fund out of money that has been paid under section 33(5A) of that Act.

(2) The total of the amounts directed to be paid under this section must not exceed £60,000,000.

(3) At any time which falls after the giving of a direction under this section, the Secretary of State is under a duty to spend the required amount for the purpose of promoting the use of energy from renewable sources.

(4) "The required amount," for the purposes of subsection (3), is an amount of money equal to the total of the amounts that at the time in question have been paid into the Consolidated Fund under subsection (1), less the total of any amounts that the Secretary of State has already spent under subsection (3).

(5) In subsection (3) "renewable sources" means sources of energy other than fossil fuel or nuclear fuel.

(6) In subsection (5) "fossil fuel" means coal, substances produced directly or indirectly from coal, lignite, natural gas, crude liquid petroleum, or petroleum products (and "natural gas" and "petroleum products" have the same meanings as in the Energy Act 1976 (c. 76)).

(7) The Secretary of State's duty under subsection (3) is without prejudice to any power or duty of his apart from this section to spend money for the purpose mentioned in that subsection.

(8) In this section –
   (a) "the Electricity Act" means the Electricity Act 1989 (c. 29); and
   (b) the references to section 33 of that Act are to that section as it has effect in England and Wales.

8 Financial provision

There shall be paid out of money provided by Parliament –

(a) any expenditure of the Secretary of State under this Act; and
(b) any increase attributable to this Act in the sums which under any other Act are payable out of money so provided.

9 Citation, extent and commencement

(1) This Act may be cited as the Sustainable Energy Act 2003.

(2) Except as provided in subsections (3) and (4), this Act extends to England and Wales, Scotland and Northern Ireland.

(3) Sections 2, 3, 4, 5 and 7 extend to England and Wales only.

(4) Section 6 extends to England and Wales and to Scotland.

(5) Sections 2, 4 (so far as it relates to England) and 5 shall come into force on such day as the Secretary of State may by order made by statutory instrument appoint.

(6) Sections 3 and 4 (so far as it relates to Wales) shall come into force on such day as the National Assembly for Wales may by order made by statutory instrument appoint.

(7) The other provisions of this Act shall come into force at the end of two months beginning with the day on which it is passed.

(8) An order under subsection (5) or (6) may appoint different days for different purposes.

PART FIVE

ELECTRICITY RESTRUCTURING

24 Some Environmental Lessons from Electricity Restructuring

Peter A. Bradford*

1 INTRODUCTION

Electricity restructuring is often analyzed in economic, legal, or technical terms. Its environmental implications are either not considered or are treated as secondary concerns.[1] The electricity industry's worldwide share of significant air pollutants is substantial, so any change in the industry's methods of operation will have environmental significance, even if unintended. Furthermore, in some countries reliance on nuclear power, or on the construction of large hydroelectric facilities, has significant impacts other than air emissions. The purpose of this chapter is to explore several lessons from recent experience with electricity restructuring in a way that gives a higher priority to these substantial environmental dimensions.

2 DEFINING ELECTRICITY RESTRUCTURING

It is important at the outset to establish what is meant by "electricity restructuring." The term has several different meanings, and considerable confusion can arise when a speaker has something different in mind than do the listeners. As used in the United States and other developed countries, electricity restructuring is likely to include at least some of the following concepts:

- the separation of formerly vertically integrated utilities into individual components of generation, transmission, and distribution;
- open access by all sellers of power over the monopoly transmission wires to the purchaser(s) of the power;
- an "independent" regulatory institution to set tariffs and issue licenses, normally with a goal of establishing tariffs that cover the full costs of producing and delivering electricity;
- competition among several different sellers of electricity generation;

---

[1] *See generally* papers by the Regulatory Assistance Project, Electric Industry Restructuring and the Environment (August 1999), available at www.raponline.org/Pubs/IssueLtr?Environment.pdf and Restructuring and the Environment (October 2000), available at www.raponline.org/Pubs/China/Detlmatt.pdf; *see also* Power Politics: Equity and Environment in Electricity Reform, Navroz Dubash et al., World Resources Institute (2003), available at http://pubs.wri.org/pubs_pdf.cfm?PubID=3159.

* Former Chairman, New York and Marine Utility Regulatory Commissions; Associate, U.S. Nuclear Regulatory Commission; Former Commissioner, Regulatory Assistance Project.

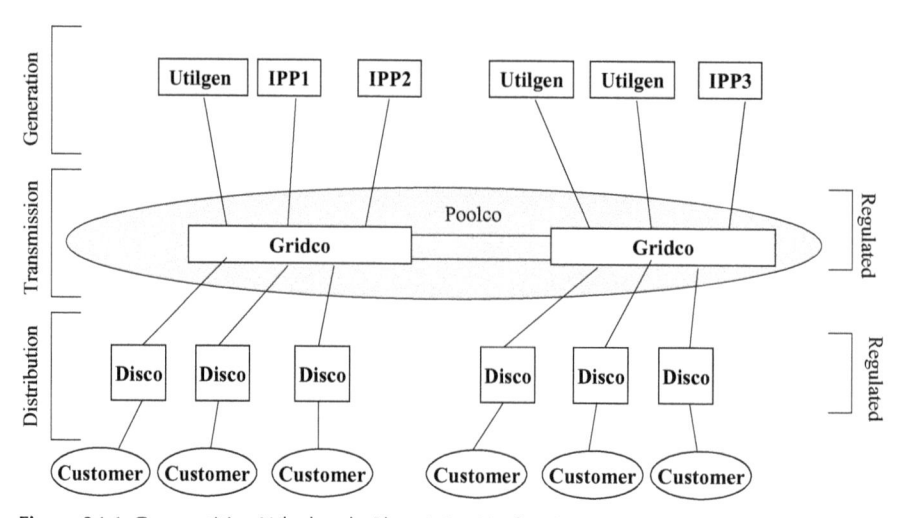

Figure 24.1 Competitive Wholesale Electricity Market Structure

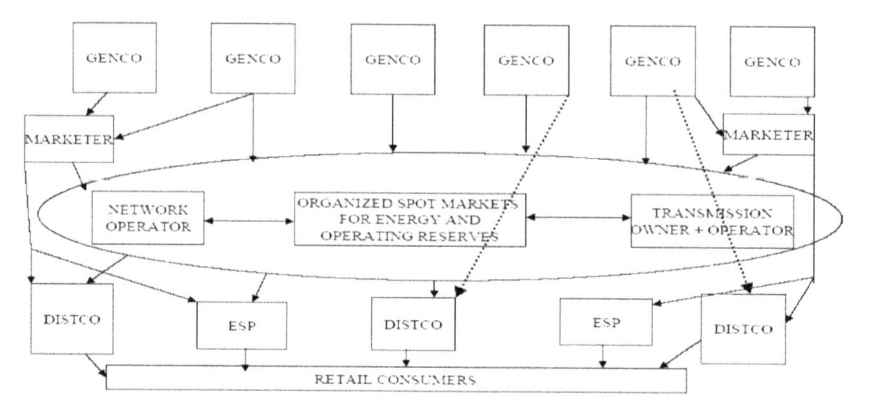

Figure 24.2 Comprehensive reform competitive wholesale + retail markets

- private ownership in the generation sector and perhaps transmission and distribution as well; and
- possible customer choice among different suppliers of electricity.

A simplified model of this type of restructuring, which includes competition among power suppliers but does not include customer choice, is shown in Figure 24.1. Note that regulation, which once applied to the entire vertically integrated utility structure, applies only to the "wires," i.e., transmission and distribution, while the generation segment has evolved into competition between Independent Power Producers (IPPs) and utility owned generators (Utilgen).

Figure 24.2[2] shows one potential evolution of the electricity industry when customer choice is introduced. This simplified model is intended to illustrate the appearance of

[2] Figure 2 is excerpted from "Electricity Sector Liberalization: Lessons Learned," a presentation by MIT Professor Paul Joskow, July 3, 2002, available at http://econ-www.mit.edu/faculty/download_pdf.php?id=545.

various new entities packaging services in a variety of ways, the quality and price of their offerings disciplined more by customer choice than by regulation, though a measure of regulation of the monopoly wires business remains necessary. Note in particular the ability of energy service providers (ESPs) to package together different arrays of generation and transmission services. These offerings may also include energy efficiency. A large customer may choose to act as its own energy service provider. Indeed, to date in the United States it is only the larger customers who have benefited significantly from the opportunity to choose among suppliers. The low profit margins in serving smaller customers, often compounded by rate caps imposed as part of restructuring legislation, have resulted in a paucity of competitors seeking to serve individual small customers. As a result, small customers have been bundled together into so-called "default" customer groups and auctioned off as "standard offer service," an approximation of franchise competition with frequent auctions. Restructuring in less developed countries may well involve quite different concepts. In particular, the ability of customers to choose among suppliers is unlikely to be of much importance. The electricity sector in less developed countries has almost invariably been government owned, and often badly mismanaged – to such an extent that it can neither provide adequate power to existing customers, nor attract capital nor extend service to customers not presently hooked up to the electricity system.[3]

In these countries, the restructuring process will necessarily put a greater emphasis on depoliticizing the electricity sector. In particular, the management of the electricity system and the process of setting the tariffs must become professional and free both of corruption and of calculations of political advantage. At the same time, national goals such as energy security and the extension of electricity services to people who do not presently have it, must be preserved. Restructuring may still include the components discussed earlier, but variations that offer customer choice to any but the largest industrial customers are not likely to be of much interest.

Finally, restructuring *never* – in any country – means "deregulation." Deregulation was a term applied to restructuring a few years ago in the United States in order to capitalize on the public hostility to the term regulation. However, even with regard to the introduction of competition into power supply (which comes the closest to eliminating the need for regulation) a substantial regulatory presence remains necessary to prevent market manipulation. With regard to other types of restructuring, regulation may be improved and redesigned, but it is never eliminated.

Among the potential benefits of restructuring is increased efficiency in the operations of the electricity sector, whether in advanced countries or in developing countries. Properly carried out, restructuring can provide substantial incentives to contain costs, to restore financial integrity, to reduce corruption, and to increase the level of potential investor confidence in the restructured electricity sector. With these improvements, countries can hope to see more reliable service extended to more people and also to see improvements in the technologies employed in all levels of the electricity power industry.

While the theory of restructuring seems straightforward and not difficult to implement, the actual experience has been far from successful. Combinations of

---

[3] According to the United Nations Development Program's World Energy Assessment, some 1.7 billion people (56 percent of the world's rural population) still lack access to electricity.

public backlash to tariff increases and to disconnection, worker resistance to job loss in the name of efficiency, bureaucratic resistance, and outright corruption have more often than not stymied restructuring efforts around the world. In advanced economies the record has been somewhat better, though even there combinations of price volatility and blackouts have shocked restructuring proponents and slowed the momentum.

3 EXPERIENCE WITH RESTRUCTURING

Here are some lessons on the restructuring of electricity sectors offered by experience:

1. Restructuring will not protect societal goals unless it is specifically designed to do so. Restructuring is designed to further economic efficiency, which is normally defined as prices that cover costs (whether embedded or marginal). As costs are driven down, restructuring leaves little room for objectives such as universal service, environmental improvement, national security, regional development, or even reliability – because all of these involve costs above the bare minimum that restructuring seeks to achieve.

   Put another way, effective restructuring must be designed to protect the societal values that are designed into the system that it will be replacing. Many of the world's electricity systems are indeed inefficient in classical economic terms, but some of this inefficiency comes from the ways that the electricity system has been woven into the welfare structure of the society.

   Excessive employment, energy subsidy programs that make little sense in energy terms,[4] limitations on disconnection for nonpayment may each be "inefficient" by developed country standards, both in terms of electricity pricing and in terms of a sensible welfare system. Nevertheless, these practices cannot just be eliminated. The reforms must include measures to preserve the legitimate social benefits that have been incorporated – however inefficiently – in the system being replaced.

2. Reconciliation of economic regulation and environmental goals must be part of the initial design and must be pursued aggressively. For reasons discussed in Section 1 of this chapter, the search for lower prices that accompanies all forms of restructuring will favor producers with lower costs, even if those lower costs are attained by avoiding pollution controls.[5] Only when the initial restructuring effort requires

---

[4] For example, the Republic of Georgia for many years offered electricity bill discounts of 50 or 100 percent to the following categories: invalids of World War II, invalids of wars for the territorial integrity of Georgia, families receiving pensions for those who died in World War II, people (or the families of people) who became invalids or died in the cleanup of the Chernobyl nuclear power plant accident, distinguished pensioners, employees of various ministries, victims of political repression, and persons employed in the practice of psychiatry. About 3000 customers received the Chernobyl subsidy, which is more than the total number of workers injured or killed at Chernobyl, most of whom did not come from Georgia.

[5] When the U.S. Federal Energy Regulatory Commission issued its initial restructuring order, it rejected requests from environmental intervenors that it consider the air emission impacts of its decision. Following intervention by the President's Council on Environmental Quality, it relented and announced that the impacts would be minimal and in any case not directly attributable to restructuring. Many of the impacts feared by the environmental intervenors have in fact occurred.

that energy and environmental planners work closely together and certify to the compatibility of their respective blueprints, can a country have reasonable assurance that its energy and its environmental goals will not constantly be undercutting each other.[6]

China, with its high growth rates, exceptional environmental problems, and its determination to avoid excessive dependence on imported oil, presents a particularly graphic example of a country that cannot leave the integration of its environmental and security concerns with its electricity restructuring to chance. If it does so, it may find itself in the security situation comparable to the United States, where every president since the 1960s has promised to avoid increased oil import dependence. However, oil imports have risen from about 2 million barrels per day (or sixteen percent of total consumption) to ten million barrels per day (or fifty-six percent of total consumption) during that time.

3. Successful restructuring requires careful attention to many forms of market power, all of which will be exploited wherever they are allowed to persist. Market power will not only stifle the potential price benefits of competition; it will also retard technological innovation and the development of markets that encompass the provision of energy efficiency.

Industries consisting of companies that have enjoyed a 100 percent monopoly market share granted by the government are especially hard to make competitive. The incumbents are not culturally predisposed to compete. New entrants face large capital requirements as well as essential facilities (such as transmission lines) and data bases that are under the control of their potential competitors.

These monopoly advantages and the potential for abuse will not recede on their own. Indeed, they will not recede at all unless government takes affirmative steps to shape the market structure by encouraging competitive entry.

The preconditions for competitive markets are well known. They include:

1 Several sellers, none with a market share large enough to set prices;
2 Ease of entry and of exit;
3 Access to essential facilities and related information on equal terms by all competitors; and
4 An effective regulator with a clear mandate to further competition.

However, competition policy is a separate and a crucial function that economic regulators, whose historic functions have been licensing, tariffs, and service quality, are often not well equipped to discharge.[7] In particular, competition policy in these formerly government created monopolies must rely on creating effective market

---

[6] For many years, New York had a particularly effective state energy planning process, conducted by the state Energy Office under the supervision of an energy planning board consisting of the Chair of the Energy Office, the chair of the state's utility regulatory agency, and the heads of the state's environmental department. The plan was updated every two years, and each of the agencies was required to give it deference in their ongoing decisionmaking. Ironically, the Energy Office was disbanded just as the state undertook to restructure its electric industry.

[7] At least the following types of anticompetitive behavior seem to have contributed to the 2000–01 California crisis, under the noses of federal and state regulators: manipulation of the transmission system, withholding of electric power generation in several ways, collusion among suppliers, and withholding of natural gas supplies.

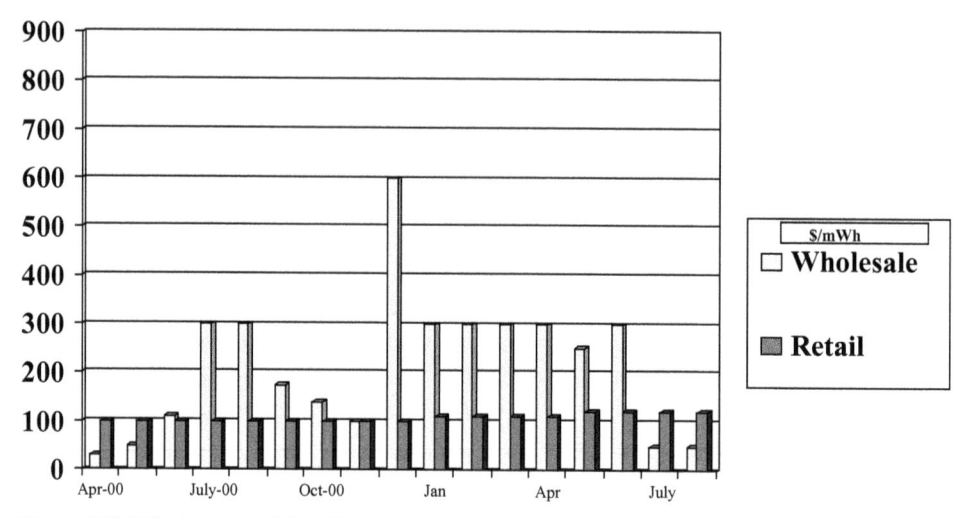

Figure 24.3 Wholesale and Retail Prices in California 2000–01

structures, not merely on policing of anticompetitive behavior,[8] and on doing so before reducing the protections afforded by traditional utility regulation. To achieve this result, regulators will need powers to require divestiture, to order structural separation of functions within corporations, to review and reject mergers, to monitor markets and take corrective actions, and to impose substantial penalties.

4. Energy efficiency, load management and power supply must be able to compete with each other in effective energy markets. A common failing in restructured electricity markets has been their failure to incorporate the willingness of customers to curtail usage at prices far below the cost of new generation. This is illustrated in Figure 24.3, a graph showing that power suppliers were buying power at prices several times what customers were paying for it. Because these are monthly averages, they understate the daily picture on the most costly days, when the utilities or the state were actually paying twenty or more times as much for electricity as the retail price being paid by customers. Because demand side management was not integrated into the market, customers who were willing to curtail usage at much lower prices than the cost of additional supply had no way to bid this willingness in ways that could make any difference.

In China in particular, with its combination of high load growth, environmental concern, and difficulty in attracting capital, study after study confirms that energy efficiency is an essential part of any strategy for minimizing the future costs of the Chinese electricity system. What remains to be seen is whether China will be more

---

[8]   Based on a century of experience, I would further emphasize that the Department [of Justice] is also highly skeptical of any relief that requires judges or regulators to take on the role of constantly policing the industry. Relief generally should eliminate the incentive or the opportunity to act anticompetitively rather than attempt to control conduct directly. We are institutionally skeptical about code-of-conduct remedies. The costs of enforcement are high and, in our experience, the regulatory agency often ends up playing catch-up, while the market forces move forward and the underlying competitive problems escape real detection and remediation.

J. Klein, U.S. Assistant Attorney General for Antitrust, "Making the Transition from Regulation to Competition," FERC Distinguished Speaker Series, January 21, 1998, at 12.

Table 24.1 The U.S. Nuclear Cost Problem

CASE	Real Levelized Cost ($$ Year 2002)[a]
	Cents/kWh
Nuclear (LWR)	6.7
Nuclear with spent fuel reprocessing	7.0
Pulverized Coal	4.2
CCGT (low gas prices, $3.77/MCF)	3.8
CCGT (moderate gas prices, $4.42/MCF)	4.1
CCGT (high gas prices, $6.72/MCF)	5.6

[a] Gas costs reflect real, levelized acquisition cost per thousand cubic feet (MCF) over the economic life of the project.

MIT Study, 8/03

successful than other countries have been in incorporating energy efficiency into its restructuring program.

5. Creation of an independent regulatory agency is necessary but not sufficient to assure that restructuring goes well. Regulation is a chain with several links. The legal framework must convey the necessary powers and duties, as well as providing for an adequate budget and separation from political and corporate influence. The enforcement regime must be sufficient to deter illegal or anticompetitive conduct in a context in which tens of millions of dollars can ride on each major decision. Furthermore, the top officials must be competent and dedicated, and training must be available to professional staff.

  The decisions of the regulatory agency will be the single largest determinant of the success of the restructuring program. There is no substitute for high quality in each of the aforementioned steps.

6. Improved transmission infrastructure and controls are essential to effective restructuring and to competition and cannot be neglected. One of the main impediments to effective competition and to reliable power supply is a transmission network incapable of moving power effectively among different regions. Transmission infrastructure tends to draw less attention than generation, but the reduction of transmission losses and the development of an adequate and flexible network are among the best guarantees of a flexible and reliable restructuring plan.

7. Without exception, countries that have allowed the market to decide what types of plants get built do not build new nuclear stations. Existing nuclear plants have generally responded effectively to the need to cut costs and to increase output. In the United States in particular, existing plants have increased their output by some thirty percent in the last fifteen years, but new units have not been able to compete with fossil fuels. Table 24.1 – which compares estimated costs of power from a new nuclear station to power from new gas and coal[9] – gives some indication why this is so: If world energy policies are in the future modified to reflect a significant value for fuels that do not emit greenhouse gases, then the economics of nuclear power may improve, though nuclear would still have to compete with energy

[9] Table 1 is derived from John Deutch and Ernest Moniz, "The Future of Nuclear Power: An Interdisciplinary MIT Study," Massachusetts Institute of Technology, 2003, at 7.

efficiency and with other non fossil fueled sources of electricity in such a scenario. Without policies that place a value on greenhouse gas avoidance, new nuclear units are very unlikely to be built under any restructuring that includes a real commitment to competitive power supply markets. This conclusion is even more emphatic for countries whose nuclear programs include a commitment to the reprocessing of used nuclear fuel, which adds to the expense both of nuclear waste disposal and of nuclear fuel procurement.

The foregoing list of seven lessons is by no means exhaustive. In particular, I have not addressed the important subjects of public participation and transparency in electricity sector reform. I have, however, sought to convey a sense of some of the major realities that should be observed if electricity sector restructuring is to avoid the disappointments, environmental and otherwise, that have too often followed in its footsteps in recent years.

25 The Implications of Electricity Restructuring for a Sustainable Energy Framework: What's Law Got to Do with It?

Rosemary Lyster*

1 INTRODUCTION

The restructuring of electricity markets is a worldwide phenomenon driven by broader programs of microeconomic reform. Since the 1970s, governments, driven by free market economics, have endorsed the introduction of competition in various sectors of the economy, including transport, telecommunications, water, gas, electricity, health services, and prisons. Extensive international research conducted by the author indicates that electricity restructuring has had indisputably serious environmental consequences. These include measurable increases in air pollution from sulphur dioxide and nitrous oxide emissions, and a marked escalation in greenhouse gas emissions. This chapter is concerned principally with the correlation between restructuring and increased greenhouse gas emissions, as well as the legal measures that should be enacted to counteract this phenomenon.

Given these well-documented environmental impacts, there is cause for concern about the future sustainability of the planet unless energy policies, which include electricity restructuring, actively counteract these impacts. Energy policy, which provides a framework for regulatory activity, cannot be developed in isolation. It must incorporate the principles contained in the international framework for ecologically sustainable development (ESD). The principles of ESD – intergenerational equity, the polluter pays principle, the precautionary principle, and conservation of biological diversity – are now well known. They were clearly articulated in the documents which emanated from the 1992 United Nations Conference on Environment and Development (the Rio Conference). These include the Rio Declaration[1] and Agenda 21.[2] In addition, imperatives for reducing greenhouse gas emissions were included in the United Nations Framework Convention on Climate Change[3] as well as the Kyoto Protocol.[4] At the 2002 World Summit on Sustainable Development (WSSD), the links between sustainable development and the supply of energy were reiterated in the Plan of Implementation.[5]

[1] (1992) 31 ILM 874.

[2] Available at http://www.un.org/esa/sustdev/documents/agenda21/english.

[3] (1992) 31 ILM 848.

[4] Kyoto Protocol to the United Nations Framework Convention on Climate Change (UNFCCC) (1997) 37 ILM 22, UN Doc. FCCC/CP/1997/L.7/Add.1.

[5] Available at http://www.johannesburgsummit.org/html/documents/summit_docs/2309_planfinal.htm.

* Senior Lecturer, Faculty of Law, University of Sydney, Australia; Consultant, PricewaterhouseCoopers Legal, Sydney. Rosemary Lyster would like to acknowledge the generous support of her research assistant, Alison Davidian, with the writing of this chapter.

Given what we know about the environmental consequences of electricity restructuring, it is argued that it is impossible to develop energy policy and subsequent energy law frameworks without reference to ESD. What is needed in Australia is a thorough overhaul of its policy on electricity restructuring so as to reflect the broader principles of ESD. Stationary energy sector policy has been, and still is, driven predominantly by National Competition Policy (NCP) without any attempt to integrate the process of restructuring and the principles of ESD. Environmental issues are being dealt with separately by way of voluntary programs, policies, and very little law. This is contrary even to the original intentions of NCP, which require that the principles of ecologically sustainable development be taken into account. Competition Policy, as it applies to the electricity industry, should be firmly integrated with the principles of ESD. A comprehensive array of legislative mechanisms should be enacted to deliver an ecologically sustainable electricity industry in Australia.

This chapter is divided into eight sections. In Section 2, principles of international environmental law are discussed to establish the basis for advocating a sustainable energy law framework for Australia. In Section 3, the international experience of the environmental impacts associated with electricity restructuring is canvassed, while Section 4 describes the Australian experience. Section 5 includes an initial assessment of whether or not Australia's policy for electricity restructuring is ecologically sustainable, while Section 6 discusses initiatives at the federal and state levels to reduce greenhouse gas emissions, especially in the electricity sector. Based on international experiences, Section 7 shows what more could, and should, be done to develop a truly sustainable energy law framework for Australia. Section 8 discusses the various reviews of energy policy and the electricity industry that are currently under way in Australia.

2 ECOLOGICALLY SUSTAINABLE ENERGY POLICY AT THE INTERNATIONAL LEVEL

The international law instruments developed at the 1992 Rio Conference leave one in no doubt about what governments should be doing to develop energy policies that are consistent with the goals of ESD. Agenda 21 stipulates that:

> [t]he need to control atmospheric emissions of greenhouse and other gases and substances will increasingly need to be based on efficiency in energy production, transmission, distribution and consumption, and on growing reliance on environmentally sound energy systems, particularly new and renewable sources of energy. All energy sources will need to be used in ways that respect the atmosphere, human health and the environment as a whole . . . the existing constraints to increasing the environmentally sound energy supplies required for pursuing the path towards sustainable development. . . . need to be removed.[6]

While Agenda 21 draws attention to the necessary links between climate change and energy, the United Nations Framework Convention on Climate Change and the Kyoto Protocol are the principal international law instruments for reducing greenhouse gas

---

[6] Agenda 21 Clauses 9.9, 9.10.

emissions. Article 3.1 of the UNFCC requires parties to:

> protect the climate system for the benefit of present and future generations of hu-mankind, on the basis of equity and in accordance with their common but dif-ferentiated responsibilities and respective capabilities. Accordingly, the developed country Parties should take the lead in combating climate change and the adverse effect thereof.

The Kyoto Protocol requires Australia, within the first commitment period 2008–12, to limit greenhouse gas emissions to 108 percent of 1990 levels.[7] The Protocol is expected to enter into force in 2004 when 55 Annex I countries representing at least fifty-five percent of total greenhouse gas emissions in 1990 ratify it.[8]

The Plan of Implementation, developed at the WSSD includes specific references to energy. Significantly, the Plan requires nations to integrate energy considerations, including energy efficiency, affordability, and accessibility into socioeconomic pro-grams.[9] They should also develop alternative energy technologies to secure a greater share of renewable energies in the energy mix.[10] The Plan also calls on governments to reduce market distortions to promote energy systems compatible with sustainable development. This could be done through the use of improved market signals, including restructuring taxation and phasing out harmful subsidies to reflect their environmental impacts.[11] Governments are also encouraged to improve the functioning of national energy markets in such a way that they support sustainable development, overcome market barriers, and improve accessibility.[12]

Importantly, the plenary session on energy at the WSSD[13] generated calls from a wide range of interest groups to move away from centralized high capital cost grid extensions and to focus on smaller renewable interventions and remote renewables projects. This recognizes that wider access to reliable, affordable, and socially acceptable energy ser-vices is a prerequisite for meeting the challenge of the Millenium Development Goals[14] of halving the proportion of people living on less than US\$1 a day by 2015. There were also calls for the removal of "perverse" subsidies,[15] the internalization of externalities, the reregulation of the energy market to take account of social and environmental ex-ternalities, and the setting of national and international renewable energy targets.[16]

---

[7] Kyoto Protocol Annex B; although this emissions reduction target represents a significant concession on the part of the international community to Australia, the federal government has indicated that it will not ratify the Protocol.

[8] *Supra* note 2, Art. 25.

[9] Plan of Implementation, Art. 19(b).

[10] *Id.*, Art. 19(c).

[11] *Id.*, Arts. 19(p), (q).

[12] *Id.*, Art. 19(r).

[13] The author attended the WSSD, including the plenary session on energy held on August 28, 2002.

[14] The Millennium Development Goals are an ambitious agenda for reducing poverty and improving lives that world leaders agreed on at the Millennium Summit in September 2000; *see* http://www.undp.org/mdg.

[15] Note that the Plan of Implementation does not include any targets for the removal of subsidies. This is in spite of the Draft Plan for Implementation recommending that countries "adopt, at the national level, policies leading to timetables for progressively phasing out energy subsidies which inhibit sustainable development. Developed countries should lead the way and, subject to a satisfactory review in 2007, they could be followed progressively by developing countries."

[16] Note that the Plan of Implementation does not include any renewable energy targets, in spite of the Draft Plan of Implementation requiring industrialized countries to increase the share of renewable energy sources of total primary energy supply by at least 2% of total energy supply by 2010 relative to 2000. During the plenary session on energy many stakeholders made representations calling for a global renewable energy target by 2010.

Interest groups also emphasized the importance of setting national energy efficiency targets and standards while structuring markets in a way that would give sustainable energy a chance.

The call for the internalization of the environmental externalities caused by electricity restructuring resonates with the Rio Declaration, which states quite clearly that "[n]ational authorities should endeavour to promote the internalization of environmental costs and the use of economic instruments, taking into account the approach that the polluter should, in principle, bear the cost of pollution, with due regard to the public interest and without distorting international trade and investment."[17]

2.1 The Key Messages for Energy Policy Development

What is quite clear is that since the 1992 Rio Conference, energy policy must be developed within the broader context of ESD and a carbon constrained economy. The international environmental law instruments, discussed in Section 2, contain a number of key messages for energy policy development. They are that: energy use should be ecologically sustainable; greenhouse gases should be reduced; renewable energy technologies should be promoted and adequately represented in the energy fuel mix; national energy efficiency programs should be pursued; market distortions and perverse subsidies, which impede a sustainable energy market, should be removed; national energy markets should function in a way that promotes sustainable development; and grid extensions are not necessarily the preferred method of increasing access to electricity.

Clearly, a sustainable energy policy and law framework for Australia cannot be developed solely within the context of liberalization, or, in accordance with National Competition Policy, as has occurred to date. More needs to be done to actively and deliberately integrate sustainable energy principles with the competition driven energy/electricity policy framework. However, as the international research, discussed in Section 6 of this chapter, indicates, unless this integration is *deliberately* pursued, there is little chance of the market delivering a sustainable energy future.

There is also no reason why, constitutionally, the federal government should not proceed to develop a sustainable energy law framework.[18] Given the international environmental law instruments governing energy and climate change, the federal government would be quite within its authority if it enacted effective national measures, consistently with the external affairs powers.[19]

3 RESTRUCTURING OF ELECTRICITY MARKETS AND ENVIRONMENTAL IMPACTS: THE INTERNATIONAL EXPERIENCE

The electricity industry has been viewed traditionally as a "natural monopoly," meaning that a single institution (usually the state) would undertake the tasks of generating,[20]

---

[17] Rio Declaration Principle 16.

[18] This may occur as a result of the energy policy review being undertaken as part of the Prime Minister's *Strategic leadership for Australia: Policy Directions in a Complex World (see* Section 7), but there is to date no indication of what the review will deliver.

[19] In fact the Commonwealth relied on this power to enact the Renewable Energy (Electricity) Act 1999 (Cth).

[20] "Generation" is the process used to create electricity.

transmitting,[21] and distributing[22] electricity. The notion is still widely held that transmission and probably distribution remain natural monopolies. However, support for the view that the electricity industry should operate as a vertically integrated monopoly is fading. In its place, several alternative models have emerged that would separate the operation, if not the ownership, of generating and transmission assets. The separation is intended to ensure equal and competitive access to the electricity grid for all electricity generators.[23]

Restructuring of the electricity industry has occurred in a number of overseas jurisdictions including the United States, many European Union (EU) countries (including the United Kingdom, Norway, Sweden, Finland, Denmark, and Germany), New Zealand, and many Asian jurisdictions. In developing countries, the restructuring of utilities is often a cornerstone of any lending policy. In addition to the restructuring that has taken place within individual EU jurisdictions, the EU has issued a directive that introduces some competition into the electricity markets in member countries.[24]

A striking aspect about the restructuring processes in these countries is the considerable amount of academic comment that they have engendered. There is a vast literature written from multidisciplinary perspectives,[25] about the serious environmental impacts

---

[21] "Transmission" is the process of transporting electricity at high voltages from where it is generated, often over long distances, to groups of electricity consumers.

[22] "Distribution" is the process or transforming electricity to lower voltages and transporting it over a shorter distance to individual consumers.

[23] *See* Dallas Burtraw, Karen Palmer, and Martin Heintzelman, *Electricity Restructuring: Consequences and Opportunities for the Environment* (Resources for the Future: 2000) p. 2–4.

[24] The Transmission of Electricity Through Transmission Grids (90/547/EEC).

[25] *See, e.g.,* Burtraw et al. *supra* note 23; Brad Jessup and David Mercer, "Energy Policy in Australia: A Comparison of Environmental Considerations in NSW and Victoria" (2001) 32 *Australian Geographer* 7; Rudy Perkins, "Energy Deregulation, Environmental Externalities and the Limitations of Price" (1998) 39 *Boston College Law Review* 993; Clive Hamilton and Richard Denniss, "Generation Emissions? The Impact of Microeconomic Reform on the Electricity Industry" (2001) 20 *Economic Papers* 15; Rich Ferguson, "Electric Industry Restructuring and Environmental Stewardship" (1999) (July) *The Electricity Journal* 21; Tim Woolf and Bruce Biewald, "Efficiency, Renewables and Gas: Restructuring as if Climate Mattered" (1998) January/February *The Electricity Journal* 64; Larry Parker and John Blodgett, "Electricity Restructuring: The Implications for Air Quality" (2001) CRS Report for Congress (http://cnie.org/NLF/CRSreports); John B. Gaffney, "What Blight Through Yonder Window Breaks?: A Survey of the Environmental Implications of Electricity Utility Deregulation in Connecticut" (2000) 32 *Connecticut Law Review* 1443; Michael Kantro, "What States Can Glean from the Environmental Consequences of Deregulating Electricity in California" (2000) 25 *William and Mary Environmental Law and Policy Review* 533; David Mallery, "Clean Energy and the Kyoto Protocol: Applying Environmental Controls to Grandfathered Power Facilities" (1999) 10 *Colorado Journal of International Law and Policy* 469; Karen Palmer, *Electricity Restructuring: Shortcut of Detour on the Road to Achieving Greenhouse Gas Reductions?* (Resources for the Future: 1999); *Air Polution Impacts of Increased Deregulation in the Electric Power Industry: An Initial Analysis* (Northeast States for Coordinated Air Use Management: 1998) (http://www.nescaum.org/archive.html); Karen Palmer, Dallas Burtraw, Ranjit Bharvirkar, Anthony Paul, *Restructuring and the Cost of Reducing Nox Emissions in Electricity Generation* (Resources for the Future: 2001); Jens Hauch, "The Danish Electricity Reform (2001) 29 *Energy Policy* 509; Edward A. Smeloff, "Utility Deregulation and Global Warming: The Coming Collision" (1998) 12 *Natural Resources and Environment* 280; Mark Diesendorf, "How Can a 'Competitive' Market for Electricity Be made Compatible with the Reduction of Greenhouse Gas Emissions" (1996) 17 *Ecological Economics* 33; Ann Berwick, "Environmental Implications of Energy Industry Restructuring" (1999) 33 *New England Law Review* 619; Robyn Hollander and Giorel Curran, "The Greening of the Grey: National Competition Policy and the Environment" (2001) 60 *Australian Journal of Public Administration* 42; Ann Brewster Weeks, "Advising Nature: Can we Get Clean Air from the Old Dirties?" (1999) 33 *New England Law Review* 707; Michael Evan Stern and Margaret Stern, "A Critical Overview of the Economic and Environmental

of electricity restructuring that leave one in no doubt that a wide range of measures is needed to counteract the dangers.

Who is it that is devoting so much time and research effort to uncover the impacts of restructuring? As the literature indicates, it is lawyers, policymakers, geographers, public administrators, economists, prestigious think tanks, industry groups, environmental nongovernment organizations, and many others. They are all concerned that when restructuring electricity markets, governments have focused mainly on price, without dealing seriously with the consequent rise in air pollution and greenhouse gas emissions. It seems that governments may have failed to realize that "[l]ow priced power may not be the same as low-cost power."[26] It has been suggested that the question for governments should not be "How can we obtain the cheapest power?" but "How can we obtain low-cost, reliable power in ways that advance our national environmental goals?"[27] It is quite clear that all too often governments fail to provide effectively for the twin objectives of low-priced power and ecologically sustainable development. It seems that if microeconomic reform and protection of the natural environment are both concerned with the efficient use of scarce resources, there should be no distinction between the two. However, a distinction has been drawn where microeconomic reform has been interpreted as competition policy with a focus on the minimization of costs.[28] As Hamilton and Denniss point out, "efficiency," whether allocative or dynamic, is never defined solely in terms of short-term cost minimization. This is not to say that cost minimization can never be allocatively efficient. However, this will only occur when markets are complete, information is perfect, and externalities are absent.[29]

According to commentators, price has repeatedly failed to signal the full costs of generating and using electricity, and a market, driven by price, may guide investment and consumption in directions that damage the environment, so increasing long-term costs. This is particularly so where consumers face the problem of information costs. It may take them a considerable amount of time to understand cost saving alternatives with respect to energy use, and with respect to sustainable energy choices. Consumers, who lack access to information about the market, are not likely to focus on environmental problems, like global warming, which may not manifest themselves for decades. The real cost of purchasing electricity is probably ignored in making current purchases in a competitive environment.[30] It probably goes without saying that the greatest risk associated with an electricity market focused on the cheap price of power, is that demand will increase therefore increasing generation and greenhouse gas emissions. Where demand increases, generators will also evaluate the relative costs of rehabilitating and using older, more polluting generating facilities compared with constructing new more sustainable capacity.[31]

The other principal concern of these commentators is that renewable energy technologies have difficulty competing in a restructured competitive environment, where

---

Consequences of the Deregulation of the U.S. Electric Power Industry" (1997) 4 *Environmental Lawyer* 79; R. Panasci, "New York State's Competitive Market for Electricity Generation: An Overview" (2001) *Albany Law Environmental Outlook* 25.

[26] Perkins, *Id.*, at 993.   [27] *Id.*, at 1031.
[28] See Hamilton and Denniss, *supra* note 25, at 15.   [29] *Id.*, at 16.
[30] See Perkins, *supra* note 25, at 1033–37; *see also* Kantro *supra* note 25, at 558.
[31] See Parker and Blodgett, *supra* note 25, at 6; *see also* Diesendorf, *supra* note 25, at 41.

fossil fuel generators enjoy many advantages and subsidies. For example, arrangements for the transmission of electricity do not allocate the full costs of transmission according to the location of generators and users. Cogenerators are disadvantaged when transmission losses, incurred as a result of long distance transmission, are averaged to the advantage of remote generators and consumers. This approach prevents the market from signaling that electricity generators should be located near their consumers, thereby reducing the cost of generation and reducing greenhouse gas emissions. Remote users also do not get the message that they should value more efficient use, or switch from grid supply to renewable remote area power supply systems.[32] This, it will be remembered, is one of the key concerns raised at the WSSD. Various other barriers of entry to the market for renewables exist, as will be described later.

Other types of impediments for market penetration of renewable energy technologies include the expenses associated with development in the early stages, institutional, political, and legislative barriers where the fossil fuel industry is favored, as well as planning regulations that do not cater for the installation of renewable technologies. Where these barriers exist, legislation may be needed if other measures and incentives do provide renewables with a level playing field.[33]

4 THE AUSTRALIAN EXPERIENCE OF ELECTRICITY RESTRUCTURING

In Australia, the energy market reform process has been consistent with a broader microeconomic reform process that has taken place under National Competition Policy (NCP). NCP has its origins in the decision in 1992 by the Council of Australian Governments (COAG)[34] to commission an Independent Commission of Inquiry into National Competition Policy chaired by Professor Fred Hilmer. Acting on the recommendations of the Hilmer Inquiry, COAG signed three agreements: the Competition Principles Agreement (CPA); the Conduct Code Agreement; and the Agreement to Implement the National Competition Policy and Related Reforms in 1995.

The reforms can be outlined as: the review and reform of all laws that restrict competition by the year 2000; the restructuring of public sector monopoly businesses covering the electricity, gas, water, and road transport industries; the introduction of competitive neutrality so that public businesses do not enjoy unfair advantages and to extend the operation of Part IV of Trade Practices Act 1974 to government business enterprises; to facilitate access to nationally significant infrastructure services to promote competition in related markets;[35] and the extension of price surveillance to government business enterprises which retain a market monopoly.[36]

The adverse environmental impacts of competition are supposed to be taken into account where the merits of reform are considered.[37] For example, Clause 1(3)(d)

---

[32] Hamilton and Denniss, *supra* note 25, at 22.

[33] See Annex I Expert Group on the United Nations Framework Convention on Climate Change, *Penetration of Renewable Energy in the Electricity Sector: Working Paper No. 15* (Organization for Economic Cooperation and Development: 1998) at 20.

[34] This Council comprises the Heads of the Federal government and the States and Territories.

[35] *See* Part IIIA of *Trade Practices Act*, which gives a firm right to require another firm to give it access to certain infrastructure it owns.

[36] "National Competition Policy – Some Facts" at 1; *see* http://www.ncc.gov.au.

[37] *See* Clause 1(3).

lists as relevant to this consideration "government legislation and policies relating to ecologically sustainable development"[38] while "the efficient allocation of resources" is made relevant by Clause 1(3)(g). Upon reviewing the restructuring of the electricity market and the introduction of competition into that market, these principles seem to have been forgotten.

Consistently with NCP, COAG decided to replace distinct state electricity markets with a national electricity market (the NEM). The basic principles of reform were that: generators should compete to supply electricity; there should be open access to the grid for new generation; and that customers should be able to choose their electricity supplier.[39] The states of New South Wales, Queensland, Victoria, the Australian Capital Territory, and South Australia now participate in the NEM. Tasmania's participation is imminent once the Basslink, linking Tasmania to Victoria, is completed. The rules of participation are outlined in the National Electricity Code which is administered by the National Electricity Code Administrator. The physical market is operated by the National Electricity Market Management Company (NEMMCO).[40]

Quiggan[41] explains that the restructuring of the Australian electricity industry has been conceived of as comprising processes which are essentially independent, but mutually supportive. They are: the establishment of the National Grid (via interconnectors) and the NEM; the corporatization of the government business enterprises involved in the electricity industry; the restructuring of the industry resulting in a separation between generation, transmission, distribution, and retail functions; the regulation of natural monopoly functions like transmission and distribution; and finally, the full privatization of the industry.

The restructuring process to date has seen the electricity industry broken into separate generation, transmission and distribution, and retail enterprises. Many integrated generators were reconstituted as a number of competing firms and distributors were given monopolies or franchises over discrete regions. Full privatization has only taken place in Victoria and South Australia.[42] However, full retail contestability (FRC)[43] in the electricity market has been introduced in New South Wales,[44] Victoria,[45]

---

[38] These would include the 1992 National Strategy on Ecologically Sustainable Development as well as the 1998 National Greenhouse Strategy.

[39] *See The Heat is On* (Senate Environment, Communications, Information Technology and the Arts References Committee: 2002) at 152.

[40] *See* The Allen Consulting Group, *Energy Market Reform and Greenhouse Gas Emission Reductions: A Report to the Department of Industry, Science and Resources* at 11.

[41] John Quiggan, "Market-Oriented Reform in the Australian Electricity Industry" (2001) 12 *The Economic & Labour Relations Review* 126 at 127.

[42] In other states, privatization of the electricity industry has been highly politicized with the Tasmania liberal government being defeated in 1998 in an election fought on the issue. In the 1999 election, the New South Wales Liberal opposition was defeated largely over the issue of privatization.

[43] FRC means giving customers a choice of supplier among competing vendors.

[44] This was introduced on January 1, 2000 under the Electricity Supply Amendment Act 2000 (NSW). The Electricity Supply (General) Regulation 2001 provides protections to small retail consumers of electricity. These include, among others, provisions relating to the discontinuance of electricity supply and the disconnection of customers from distribution systems, the establishment of customer consultative groups, setting out requirements for standard form customer contracts, the operation of the electricity ombudsman schemes, and social programs for energy.

[45] This commenced on January 13, 2002 under § 23 Electricity Industry Act 2000 (Vic).

and South Australia.[46] The Queensland government has decided not to introduce full retail contestability as it determined that the costs of FRC clearly outweighed the benefits.[47]

4.1 How the National Electricity Market Works

The National Electricity Market (NEM) was formally launched in December 1998. It was established to operate consistently with four principles: freedom of choice for consumers to trade with retailers and traders; open access to interstate interconnected transmission and distribution networks; no legislative or regulatory barriers discriminating against new participants in generation and retail supply; and no legislative or regulatory barriers discriminating against interstate and intrastate trade.[48]

The NEM is a wholesale electricity market, established under the National Electricity (South Australia) Act 1996, which operates across Queensland, New South Wales, Victoria, the Australian Capital Territory, and South Australia. Interregional trade between these jurisdictions is facilitated by interconnectors that transmit power between regions to meet energy demands that local generators cannot meet, or when the price of electricity in another region is sufficiently low that it displaces local supply. Tasmania will join the NEM when the construction of the Basslink between Victoria and Tasmania is complete.

The NEM was established by cooperative legislation being passed by all participating states to set up the NEM and to provide for access arrangements.[49] The operation of the NEM is regulated under the National Electricity Law[50] and the National Electricity Code.[51] Code participants include: generators,[52] market customers (electricity retailers and end-use customers),[53] network service providers who own, operate or control either a transmission (TNSPs) or distribution (DNSPs) system,[54] market network service

---

[46] This commenced on January 1, 2003 under Part 5A Electricity (General) Regulations 1997.

[47] *See* "Report on the Review of the Costs and Benefits of Full Retail Competition in the Queensland Electricity Industry" at http://www.energy.qld.gov.au/electricity/marketsnm.htm.

[48] See Ro Coroneos, "The Regulatory Framework of the NEM: its Impact on NSW Distributors and Opportunities for Further Reform" (1999) 7 *Australian Journal of Administrative Law* 5 at 7; *see also* Anne Rann, *Electricity Industry Restructuring – A Chronology* (Parliamentary Library Background Paper 21: 1997–8); and Quiggan, *supra* note 41.

[49] Electricity (National Scheme) Act 1997 (ACT), National Electricity (South Australia) Act 1996 (SA), Electricity – National Scheme (Queensland) Act 1997 (Qld), National Electricity (New South Wales) Act 1997 (NSW), National Electricity (Victoria) Act 1997.

[50] *See* the Schedule to National Electricity (South Australia) Act 1996 (SA).

[51] Agreed between all participating jurisdictions in accordance with § 6 of the National Electricity Law.

[52] National Electricity Code (NEC) para. 2.2.1(a); generators produce and sell electricity. There are four categories of generators: market generators whose entire output is sold on the NEM spot market; non-market generators that sell their entire supply directly to a local retailer or customer; schedules generators that have a capacity over 30 MW and whose output is regulated by NEMMCO's dispatch instructions; and nonscheduled generators that have a generating capacity of less than 30MW, but which are still required to register with NEMMCO.

[53] NEC para. 2.3.1(a); market customers comprise both electricity retailers and end-use customers. Retailers purchase wholesale electricity through the spot market, or from local generators who sell their entire output to them. The electricity is then sold to customers, increasingly within a contestable retail market. End-use customers purchase electricity directly from the spot market which they then consumer.

[54] NEC para. 2.5(a)(11); TNSPs control the high voltage transmission assets that carry electricity between generators and distributors, while DNSPs operate the low voltage substations and wires that transport

providers (MNSPs),[55] and special participants who may be appointed by NEMMCO to perform various functions like taking responsibility for operations during power system emergencies.[56]

The NEM is essentially a continuous time auction market[57] that allows generators and users of electricity to enter half hourly bids, indicating willingness to supply or demand electricity. Together, the bids form aggregate demand and supply schedules. Market clearing occurs every five minutes in recognition of the fact that available capacity and consumption can fluctuate. The dispatch price[58] is determined at the intersection of the aggregate demand and supply schedules. Generator bids that are equal to or less than the dispatch price are accepted as are user bids that are equal to or greater than the dispatch price. The spot price of electricity is determined when the dispatch prices are averaged over a half hour period, and this price is actually paid to generators by purchasers. Not all purchases occur in this way, however, as participants can enter into bilateral arrangements or trade electricity in a forward market. Based on the vagaries of supply and demand, the spot price for electricity can vary from $20MWh on one day to $10,000MWh on the next. However, $10,000 is the regulatory limit for the price of a MWh of electricity.[59]

The NEM is regulated in a number of different ways. Under the NEC, all market participants must be registered[60] with NEMMCO, which operates the spot market and is empowered to take action for the security of the grid. Civil penalties for breaches of the Code are imposed by the National Electricity Code Administrator (NECA).[61] The National Electricity Tribunal[62] is empowered to review the decisions of NECA and NEMMCO, to hear applications from NECA that Code participants have breached the Code,[63] and to review the civil penalties imposed by NECA for such breaches.[64] The Australian Competition and Consumer Commmission monitors competitive behavior in the NEM to ensure fair access to networks, under Part IV of Trade Practices Act 1974, and also authorizes the Code and changes to the Code. The Australian Securities and Investment Commission (ASIC) ensures that all energy trades are conducted consistently with the Corporations Law.

In addition, state legislation might apply to Code participants. For example, in New South Wales since generation, transmission, and distribution is corporatized, these functions are subject to the State Owned Enterprises Act 1983 (NSW), which requires adherence to community services obligations.

---

electricity from these substations to customers. Distributors hold a franchise over the regions in which their poles and wires are installed but must also be given access to customers outside their regions by using rival distribution networks; *see* Rann, *supra* note 48, at 3.

55 MNSPs are entrepreneurial interconnectors, with a minimum capacity of 30 MW, that offer their capacity to transport power into the market through a bidding process similar to that used by generators. Currently there is only one MNSP, called Directlink, which operates between New South Wales and Queensland. MNSPs are unregulated interconnectors whereas all other interconnectors are regulated, originally by state governments but increasingly by the ACCC. They receive a fixed rate of return that takes into account the value of their asset base and is reviewed every five years by the ACCC.

56 NEC para. 2.6(a).   57 *Id.*, para. 3.4.
58 *Id.*, para. 3.9.   59 *See* Quiggan, *supra* note 41, at 130.
60 National Electricity Law Part 3; NEC para 2.8.   61 National Electricity Law Part 4.
62 Established under Part 3 National Electricity (South Australia) Act 1996 (SA).
63 National Electricity Law § 12.   64 *Id.*, Part 5.

4.2 What Have Been the Environmental Impacts of the National Electricity Market?

The 2000 National Greenhouse Gas Inventory (NGI), released in August 2002, reported that Australia is currently eleven percent above its 1990 greenhouse gas emissions level. The NGI also shows that the stationary energy sector is responsible for 49.3 percent of Australia's greenhouse gas emissions. The net increase in the emissions from the stationary energy sector, particularly electricity generation, since 1990 is 26.6 percent. While the NGI figures seem encouraging, the CSIRO has recently warned that, according to its computer modeling, Australia threatens to overshoot its 1990 baseline level by between 170–230 percent by 2050. If the stationary energy sector is currently responsible for almost fifty percent of the net increase in emissions since 1990, and all indications point to escalating energy consumption, serious measures are needed to control emissions.

If one looks at the increase in emissions that has already occurred since the establishment of the NEM, it is clear that the market cannot continue to exist in an environmental policy vacuum driven principally by competition principles.

Hamilton and Denniss[65] argue convincingly that, although greenhouse gas emissions from the electricity sector have been increasing steadily since 1994, there was a 10.35 percent spike in emissions in 1998. This was the first year of the operation of the NEM. Their proposition has been supported by data released by the Australian Greenhouse Office.[66] Hamilton and Denniss point to the fact that the average prices charged to industrial and commercial users (which account for seventy percent of the market) fell by nearly twenty-two percent between 1991/2–1997/8.[67] The fall in price led in turn to a 6.3 percent increase in demand which exceeded the long-term average increase of around 2.5 percent. The authors ascribe the large fall in the price of electricity to attempts by Victoria's privatized brown coal generators to win market share at the expense of Victoria's gas generators and black coal generators in NSW. They show that in 1998, around 3,500 GWh was exported from Victoria into NSW, while only 600GWh flowed in the other direction (excluding flows from the Snowy Mountains Hydro-Electric Authority). This net energy transfer of 2,900 GWh northward is in sharp contrast with the pattern in preceding years, which saw nearly equal northward and southward energy transfers.

Hamilton and Denniss state that although the fall in the price of electricity to contestable customers is seen as the "jewel in the crown" of microeconomic reform in Australia, there is no doubt that this has been very damaging to the environment.[68] They conclude that:

> [a]s long as the impacts of economic activity on the environment are excluded from the definition of "economic efficiency" competition policy cannot guarantee improved welfare. Increased competition has the capacity to improve welfare in some situations, but only after significant market failures, particularly externalities, have been removed.[69]

---

[65] Hamilton and Denniss, *supra* note 25 at 18. *See also Greenhouse Gas Emissions and the Productivity Growth of Electricity Generators* (Productivity Commission: 2001) and *National Competition Policy: Some Impacts on Society and the Economy* (National Competition Council: 1999).

[66] *See* Analysis of Trends (Australian Greenhouse Office: 2000) at 18.

[67] Hamilton and Denniss, *supra* note 25, at 19.   [68] *Id.*, at 20.

[69] *Id.*, at 27.

5 DOES THIS MEAN THAT AUSTRALIA HAS DONE NOTHING TO COMBAT A RISE IN GREENHOUSE GAS EMISSIONS AND TO PROMOTE RENEWABLE TECHNOLOGY?

There have been various initiatives at both the federal and state government levels to combat the greenhouse gas emissions associated with the stationary energy sector. The question remains, however, whether or not these have been effective and what more needs to be done before Australia has a sustainable energy policy and law framework. The overall conclusion will be that to date the efforts to control greenhouse emissions, including the environmental externalities of the electricity restructuring process, are not sufficient. The largely voluntary measures resorted to by Australian governments have not delivered effective greenhouse emissions reductions. To be effective, mechanisms must be written into statute and be enforceable.

Section 5.1 assesses first federal and state government attempts to reduce greenhouse gas emissions, and then their initiatives to promote the commercialization of renewable energy technologies.

5.1 Responses to Greenhouse Gas Emissions

The Federal Government Response to Global Climate Change

The federal government has consistently refused to ratify the Kyoto Protocol unless the United States and developing countries ratify it. The government has claimed that without such ratification the Protocol will not be effective, and will damage Australia's economy. While it continues to insist that it will not ratify the Protocol, it will be difficult to construct an energy policy that is consistent with the principles of ESD. This is because the Protocol is regarded by the international community as an important instrument to begin combating one of the most significant barriers to ESD – global climate change.

To understand the federal government's stance on the Kyoto Protocol it is necessary to analyze the position which it adopted going into the Kyoto negotiations in December 1997. Prior to Kyoto, the federal government insisted that it wanted the outcome of the negotiations to be fair and achievable, defining a fair outcome as one where the costs of reducing greenhouse emissions would be shared equitably by all countries.[70]

In developing its pre-Kyoto position, the federal government relied on economic modeling undertaken by the Australian Bureau of Agricultural and Resource Economics (ABARE).[71] ABARE concluded that the cost to the Australian economy of reducing greenhouse emissions would be twenty-two times higher than the loss estimated by the average European country, and six times higher than America's. This meant that Australia would be expected to sacrifice jobs even though it only contributes one percent of the world's emissions compared with nineteen percent for the United States, and fourteen percent for the EU. For Australia to meet the proposed target it would have

---

[70] In the federal government's view, uniform international emissions targets, of reducing emissions to 5% below that of 1990, would not be fair while the EU allowed some countries to reduce their emissions by 30% while others would increase emissions by 40%. Furthermore, based on anticipated economic growth, Australia's emissions would probably increase by 40% compared with 1990 levels.

[71] ABARE is a public sector economic research agency located in Commonwealth Department of Primary Industry and Energy.

to sacrifice highly efficient coal mining, mineral processing[72] and agricultural production.[73] Australia also argued that the target would result in the displacement of emissions to neighbors.[74] As a result, Australia argued strongly for the principle of differentiation to be accepted and adopted when setting national emissions reduction targets as this would also encourage developing countries to participate in reduction programs.[75]

There has been a great deal of criticism of the government's position at Kyoto particularly since it relied entirely on ABARE modeling to reach the conclusions that it did. ABARE modeling did not consider the potential losses to Australia like the social, environmental, and economic costs of bushfires, floods, and tropical cyclones, natural disasters resulting in loss of crops and production and widespread property damage.[76] ABARE also did not account for benefits to the Australian economy of developing and selling renewable energy technologies like solar and wind, in which it has been recognized as a world leader.[77] In addition, the consultation process used by ABARE to draw its conclusions was found to be fundamentally flawed by a Commonwealth Ombudsman[78] investigation, instigated by the Australian Conservation Foundation.

Indeed, more recent studies refute ABARE's climate change modeling. The 2002 Warwick McKibbin Report concludes that the costs of participating in the Kyoto Protocol to Australia by 2010 is estimated to be 0.41 percent of GNP, or approximately $A3.4 billion. This loss rises over time to 0.58 percent of GNP in 2015 and 0.67 percent of GNP in 2020. However, where Australia does participate these costs are only 0.38 percent of GNP in 2015 and 0.30 percent in 2020.[79] Meanwhile, in 2003 the NSW Cabinet Office released the Report of the Kyoto Protocol Ratification Advisory Group: A Risk Assessment. The Advisory Group found that if Australia does ratify and meets its

---

[72] In particular, energy based commodities like the processing of aluminum which produces high emissions.

[73] Australia's food and fiber production results in high methane emissions from cattle and sheep (second highest per capita in the world).

[74] For example, if Australia were to be penalized for emissions produced in processing natural liquid gas for export to neighbors, neighbors would not get the benefit of a less polluting energy source.

[75] Note that ABARE forecast that by 2004 emissions from developing countries will exceed those from developed countries.

[76] Between 1989 and 1994 the federal government spent $280million on disaster relief.

[77] *See, e.g.*, The Allen Consulting Group, Sustainable Energy Jobs Report (2003) and the Sustainable Energy Jobs Report: Wind Manufacturing Case Study (2003). The reports conclude that in a competitive energy market, the states that establish a strong and dynamic sustainable energy sector will build a significant first mover advantage.

[78] Exercising powers under the Commonwealth Ombudsman Act 1977 (Cth). The ACF's principal complaint was that 45% of the costs of ABARE's modeling were borne by "sponsors" who had been offered a place on a "steering committee." With sponsors having to pay a $50,000 membership fee, participation was only affordable for industry groups. The Ombudsman found that: the constitution of the steering committee showed the close involvement of industry in modeling; the steering committee was not a proper one in accordance with the Australian Public Service because it had no proper terms of reference, should have ensured that all stakeholders were represented to give a balanced view, and that information should have been regularly disseminated to stakeholders; that it was highly unusual to charge a fee for participation in a steering committee; that greenhouse gas emissions are an important matter of public policy; that ABARE had made erroneous claims with regard to referees of the report; that ABARE had acted inappropriately; that ABARE must ensure that all sources of external funding be disclosed in research publications based on its climate change models; and that guidelines given to agencies to deal with external funds are not adequate; see Commonwealth Ombudsman, Report of the Investigation into ABARE's External Funding of Climate Change Modelling (February 1998), available at http://www.ombudsman.gov.au/publications_information/Special_Reports/abare.pdf.

[79] *See Modeling Results for the Kyoto Protocol*, Warwick McKibbin Report to the Australian Greenhouse Office, April 5, 2002.

targets using international emissions trading, the impacts are likely to be the following: GDP would be 0.11 percent ($875 million per year) lower than under a business as usual approach in the first commitment period. If Australia does not ratify and a domestic emission trading scheme is adopted, the impact is likely to be the following: GDP will be 0.26 percent ($2 billion) lower each year.

Responses from Civil Society in Australia to the Refusal to Ratify Kyoto

Civil society has been quite vociferous in its opposition to the federal government's stance on Kyoto. In February 2002, the Australia Institute, an independent think tank, produced a report that showed that the federal government has supported narrow industry interests by refusing to ratify.[80] The Institute notes that the Australian aluminum industry has been the most forceful opponent of policies to reduce greenhouse gas emissions, claiming that higher energy prices would damage its competitiveness and force it to move offshore. The industry consumes almost 15 percent of all electricity consumed in Australia, with emissions accounting for 5.9 percent of Australia's total emissions. In addition, the industry pays below market prices for electricity that represents a subsidy estimated to be between $210 million and 250 million.[81] The aluminum industry's claims about the costs of electricity in a carbon constrained economy have recently been refuted.[82]

Also, Environment Business Australia (EBA), the peak body for the environment and sustainability industry, has recently released a report entitled, "The Business Case for Ratification of the Kyoto Protocol."[83] EBA has identified three fundamental issues that need to be addressed: the need for comprehensive unbiased modeling that is not captured by a particular business sector and that analyzes the costs and benefits to Australia of not ratifying the Kyoto Protocol;[84] Australia's long-term competitiveness and economic growth; and the emerging environment and sustainability industry, like the renewable energy industry, that could become an important player in world markets.

All of the major environmental NGOs have rejected the Australian government's refusal to ratify. The Australian Conservation Foundation has accused the federal government of marooning Australia with "an old style smokestack economy." It pointed also to the fact that renewable energy, emissions trading, and energy efficiency

---

[80] *See* Hal Turton, *The Aluminium Smelting Industry: Structure, Market Power, Subsidies and Greenhouse Gas Emissions* (2002) at http://www.tai.org.au.

[81] Note that The Heat is On recommended greater transparency from large electricity consumers about the prices they pay for electricity if those prices are fixed outside the pool and especially where their low electricity prices are being subsidized by public monies; Recommendations 25–6; *supra* note 39.

[82] *See* an Origin Energy report, produced by McLennan Magasanik Associates, which refutes ABARE's claim that cutting greenhouse gas emissions could increase the cost of electricity by 50% by 2015. The report finds that a higher level of gas-fired generation coupled with increasing the Mandatory Renewable Energy Target to 10% under the Renewable Energy (Electricity) Act 2000 (Cth) would enable Australia to meet its Kyoto targets, without the rise in price predicted by ABARE. In fact, the report concludes that the impact on price would be minimal and would not impact on the cost competitiveness of Australian industries that are energy intensive.

[83] Environment Business Australia, The Business Case for Ratification of the Kyoto Protocol: Consultation Draft July 2, 2002.

[84] The EBA states that this modeling needs "to incorporate conflicting time scales, demographic pressure, perverse subsidies and the external costs of pollution, costs of mitigation or adaptation, new technologies and systems offering a low carbon future, and above all a framework that enable effective market to develop and operate"; *see id.*, at 5.

developments are being forced offshore.[85] Meanwhile, Greenpeace Australia Pacific released an opinion poll indicating that the majority of Australians reject the federal government's stance on Kyoto.[86] Of those polled[87] only seventeen percent of Australians agreed with the government while seventy-one percent believed it to be in Australia's interests to ratify. The poll also showed that sixty-two percent of respondents believed that ratifying would have a positive or no effect on the economy, with only twenty-two percent disagreeing.

The Australian Catholic Bishops have called on government to ratify the Kyoto Protocol.[88] Releasing their annual social justice statement, "A New Earth – The Environmental Challenge," the Bishops highlighted the fact that Australians are known to be the highest emitters of greenhouse gases in the world and that they owe a duty to their seven million Pacific Island neighbors to curb their excessive lifestyles. The Pacific Islanders survival is at risk from rising sea levels.

Finally, 250 of Australia's academic economists are signatories to a statement on climate change.[89] The 254 economists, including thirty-nine professors, have all urged the Prime Minister to ratify the Protocol citing the serious environmental,[90] economic, and social risks that Australia is likely to suffer as a result of global climate change. The economists claim that policy options are already available that would slow climate change without harming employment and living standards in Australia.

The Federal Government Adopts a "No-Regrets" Policy on Climate Change

Despite numerous calls to ratify the Kyoto Protocol, the federal government has not indicated any departure from its refusal to ratify and relies instead on a "no-regrets" policy. In terms of the policy, the government claims to have invested $1 billion in various voluntary greenhouse initiatives. One of the most significant of these initiatives was the establishment of the Australian Greenhouse Office (AGO), the world's first government agency dedicated to cutting greenhouse gas emissions. It was established in 1998 as a separate agency within the environment portfolio to provide a whole of government approach to greenhouse matters.

It also delivers the commonwealth government's $180 million climate change package, Safeguarding the Future: Australia's Response to Climate Change, and the $796 million greenhouse component of Measures for a Better Environment announced as part of Australia' s new tax system in 1999.

The Safeguarding the Future package includes a number of initiatives. The first is the development of the National Greenhouse Strategy.[91] In addition, the government has established a $180 million climate change package that includes the encouragement

---

[85] Australian Conservation Foundation, Australian-US "pollution" partnership Media Release, July 11, 2002.

[86] Greenpeace Australia Pacific Australians support Kyoto Media Release July 9, 2002.

[87] A telephone poll of 1,000 people was conducted across Australia between June 14–16, 2002 by Taylor Nelson Sofres.

[88] Media Release, Bishops' Committee for Justice, Development, Ecology and Peace, September 13, 2002.

[89] Australia Institute, Media Release, August 14, 2002.

[90] The economists, in expressing their concerns about climate change, referred to the Intergovernment Panel on Climate Change's, among others' assessment of the harm that Australia is likely to suffer.

[91] The Strategy has three principal objectives: to limit net greenhouse gas emissions to meet Australia's international commitment; to foster knowledge and understanding of greenhouse issues; and to lay the foundations for adaptation to climate change.

of renewable energy sources[92] and energy market reform. It also includes the reduction of emissions from motor vehicles,[93] national energy efficiency building codes,[94] and an investment in tree planting to absorb carbon.[95] The federal government has also set up the Greenhouse Challenge, which is a joint voluntary project between industry and the Commonwealth Government to reduce GHG emissions. As well, the government has committed $400 million to the Greenhouse Gas Abatement Program[96] to deliver cost effective abatement across all sectors of the economy. Finally, greenhouse measures are included in the revised tax system package, Measures for a Better Environment.[97]

The Senate Reviews the Federal Government's Response to Global Climate Change

There is no doubt that a significant amount of federal government funding has been spent on reducing Australia's greenhouse gases under the "no-regrets policy," and significant reductions in emissions have been achieved. However, on November 7, 2000, the Australian Senate Environment, Communications, Information Technology and the Arts References Committee tabled a Report[98] entitled The Heat is On: Australia's Greenhouse Future.[99] The report is critical of many aspects of the federal government's "no-regrets" policy, as well as some of the regulatory measures that have been attempted. The Committee made 104 recommendations, focusing on: the impacts of global warming; the Kyoto Protocol; Australia's greenhouse performance and strategy; the energy, transport and agricultural sectors, the Greenhouse Challenge; and emissions trading.

The following recommendations are worth noting: that the federal government take a leadership role in international negotiations on climate change to achieve ratification of the Protocol;[100] that the Council of Australian Governments (COAG) designate the

---

[92] *See* the Renewable Energy (Electricity) Act 2000 (Cth).

[93] The aim of this program is to impose new fuel efficiency standards to secure a 15% fuel efficiency improvement target by 2010 over business as usual. Note that the Fuel Quality Standards Act 2000 (Cth) has been passed by the federal government to enable it to make mandatory national quality standards for fuel supplied in Australia. In addition, a new labeling system for passenger vehicles sold in Australia has been introduced. The label is required under a new Australian Design Rule (ADR) 81/00 Fuel Consumption Labeling for Light Vehicles and must state the fuel consumption in liters per 100 km to enable consumers to make decisions based on fuel efficiency and environmental protection.

[94] In 2002, the federal and state and territory governments agreed to reduce Australia's greenhouse gas emissions by developing national energy efficiency standards for domestic and commercial buildings through better building design. As a result the ABCB has released RD/RIS 2002–1: Energy Efficiency Measures, BCA Volume 2 (Housing Provisions), Regulatory Proposal (Regulation Document) and Regulatory Assessment (Draft Regulatory Impact Statement), March 2002.

[95] This initiative aims to treble the Australian plantation estate by 2020: *see* The Heat is On, *supra* note 39, 115.

[96] The aims of the Program are: to fund initiatives that will result in sustained reductions in emissions during the first commitment period (2008–12); to be cost effective while having a least cost impact on the economy; be consistent with the principles of ecologically sustainable development; and generate the use of new technologies and provide opportunities particularly for rural and regional Australia; see The Heat is On, *supra* note 39, at 120.

[97] This package was announced in May 1999 as part of the introduction of the GST in Australia. It was negotiated with the Australian Democrats who allowed the GST legislation to pass in the Senate based on the additional greenhouse initiatives contained in the package.

[98] The References Committee conducted 13 public hearings as part of the inquiry and received 227 submissions, as well as holding a number or roundtables and site inspections.

[99] *Supra* 39; the Senate referred the global warming inquiry to the Committee on August 11, 1999.

[100] *Id.*, Recommendation 10.

reduction of greenhouse emissions as a goal of ongoing energy market reform;[101] that the Australian renewable energy industry capture five percent of the global market by 2015;[102] that the Greenhouse Challenge program be radically overhauled as it will otherwise severely constrain the government's capacity to achieve significant emission abatement;[103] that there be more substantial action in the transport sector across a broad range of government activity;[104] and that there is a need for a coordinated approach to emissions from the forestry, land management, and agriculture sectors.[105]

The federal government rejected a number of the key criticisms made by the Senate Committee. The essence of its response was simply to restate the programs and policies which it has implemented, in spite of the fact that many of these initiatives had been heavily criticized in the report.[106]

Recent Developments with the "No-Regrets" Policy

Since the Senate released The Heat is On, there have been further indications that all is not well with the no-regrets policy. The AGO was reviewed in 2002 and although it maintains its status as an executive agency, its powers have been subordinated to some extent to the Department of Foreign Affairs and Tourism. Also, the AGO is now required to report more formally to both the Minister for the Environment and Heritage and the Minister for Industry and Resources. This is to cure the perception that the AGO has displayed a bias toward environment rather than industry interests.[107] Given the fact that some industry interests have militated against the ratification of the Kyoto Protocol, this consultation requirement is likely to constrain the activities of the AGO, at least to some extent.

Meanwhile, the AGO's 2001/2002 Annual Report[108] shows that the federal government has underspent on climate change by $144 million. Much of the money that was not spent was allocated to the "Measures for a Better Environment Package," which was the package negotiated by the Democrats with the government, to secure Democrat support for the introduction of the GST. Another very successful scheme, the Photovoltaic Rebate Program, which offers a rebate to homeowners who install solar panels,

---

[101] *Id.*, Recommendations 30–32, 36, 37.
[102] *Id.*, Recommendations 41–44.
[103] *Id.*, Recommendations 84–95.
[104] *Id.*, Recommendations 45–65.
[105] *Id.*, Recommendations 66–83.
[106] Despite the AGO producing a 100-page AGO Government Response to The Heat is On, June 2001. See Senator Hill's Media Release where he reiterated the government's commitment to The National Greenhouse Strategy; National Greenhouse Gas Inventory; Measures for a Better Environment package; Safeguarding the Future package; Greenhouse Challenge; Energy Efficiency Best Practice program; various renewable and alternative energy initiatives; investigations into domestic greenhouse trading, credit for early action; and a greenhouse trigger in the Environment Protection and Biodiversity Conservation Act 1999 (Cth). Note that the greenhouse trigger has not yet been gazetted.
[107] Key recommendations include: revoking the AGO's status as an executive agency and incorporating in Environment Australia while retaining its distinct identity; allowing the AGO to continue to lead domestic greenhouse policy but requiring it to take a subordinate position to the Department of Foreign Affairs and Trade on international greenhouse issues; and that a whole-of-government approach be adopted to greenhouse policy, rather than favoring environmental interests; see Hon. Warwick L. Smith, Independent Review of the Australian Greenhouse Office (June 2002, released February 4, 2003), at iii.
[108] Australian Greenhouse Office Annual Report 2001 (Australian Greenhouse Office: 2002); see also Media Release, Shadow Minister for the Environment and Heritage, October 31, 2002. In particular, there has been a slower than expected uptake of monies allocated to the GGAP and the Remote Renewables Program.

was threatened with closure until the federal government agreed to refund it for two years. Can the slower than expected uptake of funding be attributed to the fact that to date the "no-regrets policy" is largely voluntary? Experience in New South Wales with greenhouse benchmarks for electricity retailers may provide a clue.

The New South Wales Government Takes a Firm Stand on the Electricity Industry and Greenhouse Gas Emissions

In 1995, the NSW government made it a condition of license for electricity retailers that they adopt greenhouse gas emission benchmarks. A 2001 review of compliance[109] with the license condition indicated that only two out of twenty-two retailers had complied with the condition. In January 2003, the NSW government introduced an enforceable greenhouse benchmark scheme (the Scheme) for electricity retailers and large users of electricity by enacting the Electricity Supply Amendment (Greenhouse Gas Emission Reduction) Act 2003 (NSW). The amending legislation inserted Part 8A into the Electricity Supply Act 1995 (NSW). In addition, the government has made the Electricity Supply (General) Amendment (Greenhouse Gas Abatement Certificate Scheme) Regulation 2003.

The Act requires participants to achieve a benchmark of 7.27 tonnes of carbon dioxide equivalent of greenhouse gas emission per head of state population by the calendar year 2007, which remains as a benchmark until the calendar year 2012.[110] This amounts to approximately twenty-five percent reduction in emissions compared with business as usual. It also makes a broad range of benchmark participants subject to the benchmark, including electricity retailers (as well as generators retailing electricity), large electricity users, and projects of state significance.[111] The Act establishes the NSW Independent Pricing and Regulatory Tribunal (IPART) as the regulatory body that will determine the liability of benchmark participants, and assess their compliance with the Scheme.[112] Benchmark participants are also required to lodge an annual greenhouse gas benchmark statement each year with IPART.[113]

The following activities[114] are recognized for the valid creation of a NSW Greenhouse Abatement Certificate (NGAC) equivalent to 1 tonne of CO_2eq abated: generation of electricity that results in reduced greenhouse gas emissions; reduction in electricity consumption; and carbon sequestration[115] that results in reduced greenhouse gas

---

[109] Independent Pricing and Regulatory Tribunal Electricity Distribution and Retail Licenses Compliance Report for 2000/01 – Report to the Minister for Energy at 4.

[110] Electricity Supply Amendment (Greenhouse Gas Emission Reduction) Act 2003 (NSW) § 97B.

[111] Id., § 97BB.   [112] Id., § 97H.

[113] Id., § 97CB.   [114] Id., § 97DA.

[115] Note that the New South Wales government has recognized a carbon sequestration right under the Carbon Rights Legislation Amendment Act 1998 (NSW). The Act defines carbon sequestration and a carbon sequestration right as follows: carbon sequestration by a tree of forest means the process by which the tree or forest absorbs carbon dioxide from the atmosphere, and a carbon sequestration right in relation to land means a right conferred on a person by agreement or otherwise to the legal, commercial, or other benefit (whether present or future) of carbon sequestration by any existing or future tree or forest on the land after 1990. The Act amends the Conveyancing Act 1919 (NSW) to recognize that rights associated with carbon sequestrated by trees and forests from the atmosphere may be a species of forestry right. This has been mirrored in other states by Forestry Act 1959 amended by Forestry and Land Title Amendment Act 2001(Qld), Forest Property Act 2000 (SA), and Forestry Rights Act 1996 (Vic).

emissions.[116] Large retail electricity users may elect to be directly liable under the Scheme and create Large User Abatement Certificates (LUACs) from reductions in greenhouse gas emissions associated with reduced consumption.[117]

Participants will be liable for a civil penalty of $10.50 per tonne of CO_2eq target shortfall for the relevant calendar year (the penalty may be CPI indexed under the regulations).[118] Criminal penalties may also be imposed for failure to comply with the operation of the Scheme, including the failure to cooperate with IPART.[119]

The Greenhouse Gas Benchmark Rules detail the methodology on how the Scheme will operate, for example, the calculations of the benchmark participants targets and possible shortfalls.

The Electricity Supply (General) Amendment (Greenhouse Gas Abatement Certificate Scheme) Regulation 2003 sets up the abatement certificate scheme, introduced into the licensing regime under Part 8A of the parent Act. The Regulation sets the criteria for the following aspects of the abatement certificate regime. In order to be eligible to create a certificate, the participant must be accredited by the Scheme Administrator.[120] Applications for the accreditation and the transfer of certificates must be made to the Scheme Administrator.[121] A register of accredited abatement certificate providers (ACPs) must be kept.[122] IPART or the Scheme Administrator may at any time conduct or require audits to be conducted of ACPs with respect to the creation of certificates, eligibility for accreditation and compliance with any condition of accreditation.[123]

The approach adopted by the New South Wales government to reduce emissions from the energy sector is in marked contrast to that of the federal government under the Generator Efficiency Standards program.[124] Under this scheme, generators using fossil fuels are *encouraged* to achieve best practice efficiencies in their power plants and so reduce greenhouse emissions. Standards apply to new electricity generation projects, significant refurbishments, and existing generation. Performance against the standards is determined on a plant by plant basis according to a methodology as set out in the Technical Guidelines for the measure.[125] The scheme is voluntary not mandatory and one wonders, given the lack of compliance with license conditions under the NSW scheme, whether it will be able to deliver significant greenhouse emissions reductions.

---

[116] The first forest dedicated to the reduction of greenhouse gases was planted on October 10, 2002. The forest is being established with the cooperation of Integral Energy, Planning NSW, and State Forests of NSW. The 5-hectare site will slowly be transformed with the planting of 5,000 native trees and shrubs. As the plants and shrubs grow they will soak in 50 tonnes of greenhouse gases each year during the forests' 40-year growth cycle. Each tonne can be converted into a carbon credit that could be traded and become of financial value to Integral Energy: see Media Release, NSW Minister for Forestry and Energy, October 10, 2002.

[117] *Supra* note 110, § 97EC(4).　　　　　　　　[118] *Id.*, §§ 97CA(2), (3).

[119] *Id.*, §§ 97CB(5), 97DD(5), 97EF(7).

[120] Electricity Supply (General) Amendment (Greenhouse Gas Abatement Certificate Scheme) Regulation 2003 Part 8B, Division 2.

[121] *Id.*, Division 3.　　　　　　　　[122] *Id.*, cl. 73LC.

[123] *Id.*, Division 8.

[124] The standards apply to any power generating plant that uses fossil fuels, whether on-grid, off-grid, or self-generating, that meets all of the following criteria: 30 MW electrical capacity or above; and 50 GWh per annum electrical output or more; and a capacity factor of 5% or more in each of the last three years: see http://www.greenhouse.gov.au/ges/qa.html#standards.

[125] These are available on the Australian Greenhouse Office Web site at http://www.greenhouse.gov.au/markets/ges/index.html.

5.2 Renewable Energy Initiatives at the Federal and State Levels

There have been a number of renewable energy initiatives at the federal and state government levels in Australia.

National Green Power Accreditation Program

The governments of South Australia, New South Wales, Victoria, Queensland, Western Australia, and the Australian Capital Territory signed on to the National Green Power Accreditation Program. The states all operate the accreditation program through a central program manager.[126] It is estimated that largely as a result of the Green Power program, about two percent of Australia's electricity is generated from renewable sources. Accredited Green Power products are those that: result in greenhouse gas emission reductions; have net environmental benefits; and are based primarily on a renewable energy source. Generation sources that could cause significant environmental or cultural damage, like major flooding hydro projects or biomass projects based on unsustainable native forestry, are not approved as Green Power.[127] Under the scheme, retailers must commit to the development of new renewable generation and source a minimum of eighty percent of their Green Power from new renewable sources developed since 1 January 1997. The accreditation program provides an assurance that any Green Power product with the "Government Approved" Green Power tick meets common standards and undergoes regular auditing to ensure the integrity of the product. The fact that the Green Power scheme does not have a legislative base has been identified as a possible shortcoming in the scheme.[128]

Renewable Energy (Electricity) Act 2000 (Cth)

Building on the relative success of the Green Power program the federal government has enacted the Renewable Energy (Electricity) Act 2000 (Cth).[129] The object of the Renewable Energy (Electricity) Act 2000 is to encourage an additional two percent generation of electricity from renewable sources by 2010. As a result of investment in hydroelectric schemes in Tasmania and New South Wales, ten percent of Australia's electricity supply was renewable before the introduction of the Act. Under the Act, accredited power stations will be given a 1997 eligible renewable power baseline. Power stations will create renewable energy certificates (RECs)[130] when they generate power

---

[126] The New South Wales Sustainable Energy Development Authority.

[127] *See*, by distinction, the renewable energy sources accredited under the Renewable Energy (Electricity) Act 2000 (Cth). These include the burning of biomass, which may constitute wood and wood waste harvested from native forests. See also The NSW government's decision to ban the burning of Australian native trees to generate electricity of 200kW under the Protection of the Environment Operations (General) Amendment (Burning of Bio-Material) Regulation 2003.

[128] Adrian Bradbrook, "Green Power Schemes: the Need for a Legislative Base" (2002) 22 *Melbourne University Law Review* 2.

[129] For a detailed discussion of this *Act*, *see* Adrian Bradbrook and Alexandra S. Wawryk, "Government Initiatives Promoting Renewable Energy for Electricity Generation in Australia" (2002) 25 *UNSW Law Journal* 124 at 146–153.

[130] Certificates must be created electronically containing a unique identification code, the electronic signature of the person who created the certificate, the date on which the electricity was generated, and the date on which the certificate was created. Certificates must be registered with the Regulator. Once registered the certificates can be transferred to any person subject to the Regulator being notified.

using renewable energy sources[131] that exceed the 1997 baseline.[132] Certificates can also be created by installations of solar hot water heaters that are installed after January 2001 and replace nonrenewable heaters.[133]

The legislation is directed primarily at "liable entities,"[134] that is, electricity retailers and wholesale purchasers of electricity. They are required to achieve individual renewable energy targets based on their projected market share of consumption, which can be projected three years in advance.[135] A liable entity must surrender RECs to the Renewable Energy Regulator in discharge of its renewable energy liabilities under the *Act*.[136] A liable entity will face a nontax deductible penalty of $40 MWh if it has not acquired sufficient RECs.[137] The regulation, made before March 31 of each year, will stipulate what the rate of liability is for a given year.[138] In the first year of the the operation of the *Act* 659,000 RECs were surrendered to the Regulator representing an oversupply of RECs for 2001 to a factor of 2.2.[139]

In early 2003, the Minister for the Environment and Heritage announced a review of the Act as required under the Act.[140] Early assessment of the legislation, however, indicates that the Act will not deliver the two percent increase in renewable energy. This is because energy consumption in Australia is likely to double by 2010. The legislation, as it currently stands will only deliver a 0.9 percent increase in renewable energy.[141] This is hardly impressive given the renewable energy targets set in other countries, as discussed in Section 6 of this chapter.

Establishment of Sustainable Energy Agencies at State Government Level

Most state governments have established sustainable energy agencies. The New South Wales government was the first to do so when it established the Sustainable Energy Development Authority under the Sustainable Energy Development Authority (SEDA) Act 1995 (NSW). The Western Australia government has established the Sustainable Energy Development Office (SEDO) to deliver the state's sustainable energy policy which focuses on nontransport related activities, while at the same time increasing jobs in related industries. Likewise, the Victoria government has also established a Sustainable Energy Authority to promote energy efficiency and support and facilitate the development and use of renewable energy.[142] In Queensland, the Office of Energy is responsible for the development of renewable energy policies and initiatives, and

---

[131] Eligible renewable energy sources are defined in Section 16 of the Act.

[132] *Id.*, § 18.   [133] *Id.*, §§ 18–30.

[134] *Id.*, § 35.

[135] *Id.*, §§ 36–43. Note that Green Power sales will not be able to be used by energy suppliers to meet their MRET obligations.

[136] *Id.*, § 41.

[137] *See* Renewable Energy (Electricity) (Charge) Act 2000 (Cth) § 6.

[138] For example, the renewable power percentage for the year commencing January 1, 2001 will be 0.24%. So if a party purchased 100,000MWh in 2001 it would have had to surrender 240 certificates to discharge its liability; *see* Renewable Energy (Electricity) Act 2000 (Cth) § 39.

[139] *See* http://www.orer.gov.au/pubs/bioenergy.pdf.

[140] The review must clarify various issues especially the extent to which the Act has contributed to reducing greenhouse gas emissions and encouraged the additional generation of electricity from renewable resources; *see* section 162 of the Act.

[141] *See* Origin Energy report, produced by McLennan Magasanik Associates, which shows that the legislation will only produce a 0.9% increase in renewable energy in 2010.

[142] *See* http://.sea.vic.gov/renewable/index.html.

provides advice on renewable energy issues. One of the key initiatives of the Queensland Energy Policy is the Gas Retail License Scheme which will require that at least thirteen percent of electricity sold by electricity retailers in Queensland must be generated from gas from January 1, 2005. This initiative will complement the Commonwealth's two percent Mandatory Renewable Energy Target.[143]

5.3 Assessment of Greenhouse Gas and Renewable Energy Initiatives in Australia

What is quite clear is that compared with legislative measures taken in overseas jurisdictions, there is very little law governing this area of environmental management. Other than the NSW greenhouse benchmarks scheme under the Electricity Supply Act 1995 (NSW) and the Renewable Energy (Electricity) Act 2000 (Cth), all other measures fall under the voluntary based "no-regrets-policy." The author believes that these voluntary type agreements are no match for enforceable legislative measures. In addition, there are too many barriers still confronting the developers of renewable energy technologies to allow them to effectively penetrate the National Electricity Market. While these economic, structural, and pricing barriers exist, it is unlikely that the market will deliver the commercialization of renewable energy technologies. As Crawford and Angel state, "To expect the market to deliver commercialisation of renewable unassisted energy is simply naïve."[144] These barriers are not necessarily unique to Australia.[145]

6 DESIGNING A SUSTAINABLE ENERGY LAW FRAMEWORK FOR AUSTRALIA: LEARNING FROM INTERNATIONAL EXPERIENCE WITH ELECTRICITY RESTRUCTURING

What the research shows is that the restructuring of the electricity industry will only be climate friendly by design. Although they may not have perfected the art, other countries undergoing electricity restructuring have attempted to achieve the twin goals of liberalization and environmental protection. The other crucial observation that must be made is that these twin goals have been written into law. The numerous provisions that appear in these countries' restructuring statutes suggest that policy makers are alive to the fact that price, on its own, will not deal effectively with externalities, or steer the purchasing of power to ecologically sustainable resources.[146] The negative externalities of restructuring must be internalized through regulation, not voluntary programs. This is in spite of the fact that the regulation of a restructured market is counterintuitive to the economic ideology that underpins the restructuring. However, to remain true to attempts to restructure the market, legal measures adopted to internalize the externalities should be congruent, as far as possible, with the restructured market. It is virtually impossible to avoid the calls made, both at the 2002 World Summit and in the literature, for the "reregulation" of the electricity market.

---

[143] *See* http://www.energy/qld.gov.au/sustainable/renewableenergy.htm.
[144] Sebastian Crawford and Jeff Angel, *Green or Black? Renewable Energy Policy in Australia* (Total Environment Centre: 2002) at 4.
[145] *See e.g.*, Annex I Expert Group, *supra* note 33.   [146] Perkins, *supra* note 25, at 1036.

6.1 The Need for Enforceable Legal Measures Rather Than Voluntary Programs

Despite the steps that have already been taken to reduce greenhouse gas emissions and to promote renewable energy technologies, Australian governments do not measure up to other jurisdictions with respect to the suite of enforceable legal measures that could be adopted to develop a sustainable energy framework. This is because the "no-regrets" policy is largely based on voluntary measures and government funding for various programs, and there is cause for skepticism that such measures will control the predicted escalation in greenhouse gas emissions. The author is in agreement with Mills, who states that "[w]here voluntary programs rely upon participating organizations to assess and monitor their own emissions reduction strategies, as is the case with Australia's Greenhouse Challenge, the integrity of the program may be undermined . . . The Greenhouse Challenge will encourage electricity utilities to reduce energy use in their own offices, but ignores the more important issue of the utilities' influence upon energy use throughout the nation." He goes on to say that "voluntary programs are not capable of ensuring the achievement of substantial emissions reductions" and are "best suited to limited application, as one component of an overall strategy for emissions reductions."[147]

Research into the international experience[148] shows that there is a raft of legally enforceable measures that Australia has not yet attempted, or if they have been attempted they are regional rather than national, or include ineffective targets. Effective legally enforceable measures are more likely in the long term to deliver the kinds of outcomes that Australia should be achieving. At a general level, Australia might follow the example of countries like the United States and Denmark.

United States

At a federal level, the U.S. Congress has consistently attempted to achieve the twin goals of restructuring and the development of renewable energy sources.[149] Each state has had a different experience with restructuring its own electricity industry. However, the policy at the federal level has been consistent. Restructuring began in 1978 when Congress passed the Public Utility Regulatory Act 1978 (PURPA).[150] PURPA amended the Federal Power Act[151] by allowing independent power producers, known as qualifying facilities, to generate electricity with a specific goal of developing alternative

---

[147] David Mills, "Reducing Greenhouse Gas Emission Through Electricity Industry Reform: A Market-Oriented Emissions Reduction Scheme" (2000) 12 *World Resources Review* 58 at 61–2.

[148] Wiser et al. *supra* note 116; Steven L. Clemmer, Alan Nogee, Michael C. Brower, Paul Jefferiss, *A Powerful Opportunity: Making Renewable Electricity the Standard* (Union of Concerned Scientists Publications, Cambridge: 1999); Jarmo Vehmas et al., "Environmental taxes on fuels and electricity – some experiences from the Nordic countries" (1999) 27 *Energy Policy* 343; Anwar Y. Al-Abdullah, "The Carbon-Tax Debate" (1999) 64 *Applied Energy* 3; Paul Ekins and Terry Barker, "Carbon Taxes and Carbon Emissions Trading" (2001) 15 *Journal of Economic Surveys* 325; Andrea Baranzini, Jose Goldemberg, und Stefan Speck, "A Future for Carbon Taxes" (2000) 32 *Ecological Economics* 395; Timothy J. Brennan, *Demand-side Management Programs Under Retail Electricity Competition* (Resources for the Future: 1998); Ryan Wise, Steven Pickle, and Charles Goldman, "Renewable energy policy and electricity restructuring: A California case study" (1998) 26 *Energy Policy* 465; Simone Espey, "Renewable Portfolio Standard: A Means for Trade with Electricity from Renewable Energy Sources" (2001) 29 *Energy Policy* 557.

[149] For a detailed discussion of the legal initiatives in the United States at 129–136.

[150] 16 U.S.C. §§ 2601 et seq.

[151] Inserting Section 3(17)(C) into the Federal Power Act.

electricity sources.[152] PURPA gave the Federal Energy Regulatory Commission (FERC) the power to require monopoly owners of transmission lines to allow qualifying facilities to use their transmission facilities.[153] In 1992, Congress passed the Energy Policy Act[154] to increase competition in the electricity industry but also to conserve energy and encourage efficiency,[155] to develop renewable energy resources,[156] and to address global warming.[157] The impact of this has been that qualifying facilities are no longer hampered by high costs of entry into the market as the industry is no longer regarded as a natural monopoly. In 1996, the FERC went further and promulgated Rule 888, which mandated the deregulation and restructuring of the electricity industry, in particular the separation of generation from transmission and distribution. Although the U.S. Environment Protection Agency publicly voiced its concern about the impacts of restructuring on the environment, it is clear that the U.S. Congress and the FERC have been concerned to promote restructuring while at the same time attempting to reduce global warming and other environmental impacts. As a result, the United States remains one of the world's leaders in renewables supply from wind, biomass, geothermal and solar.[158]

Denmark

In Denmark, the government has liberalized the market while at the same time ensuring that the market will not result in CO_2 emissions that are above Denmark's emissions reduction target under the Kyoto Protocol. A target has been set for CO_2 emissions from the electricity generation. These targets will be achieved using a system of tradeable emissions permits for electricity producers. In addition, twenty percent of Danish demand for electricity must be satisfied by the renewable energy market. Generators of renewable energy are awarded green certificates according to the amount of renewable energy produced and these must be purchased by distribution companies. In this way, producers of renewable energy are compensated through a market-based system to the extra costs associated with producing renewable electricity. Publicly guaranteed prices are paid based on the different renewable technology types.[159] Similar pricing arrangements apply in the German renewable energy market.[160]

The U.S. and Danish examples demonstrate the difference between energy frameworks that are based squarely on a price driven NCP, like Australia's, and those that attempt to integrate the goals of restructuring and ESD. It must be emphasized, therefore, that competition and ESD principles must be *deliberately* integrated into a sustainable energy policy.

---

[152] *Id.*, § 201; *see* Kantro *supra* note 25, at 537.

[153] PURPA § 203. The FERC may issue the order if it is in the public interest, would conserve significant amounts of energy, or would improve the reliability of the utility system.

[154] 42 U.S.C. § 13201. Note that the US Energy Policy Act 2002 has been through many iterations. To date (July 31, 2003) the Energy Policy Act of 2002 (Engrossed Amendment Agreed to by Senate) [H.R.4.EAS] has been passed by the Senate but not agreed to by the House of Representatives.

[155] *Id.*, Title I.   [156] *Id.*, Title XII.

[157] *Id.*, Title XVI; *see also* Kantro *supra* note 25, at 538.

[158] Wiser et al., *supra* note 116, at 469.   [159] Hauch *supra* note 25, at 509–10.

[160] *See* Stromeinspeisungsgesetz für Erneuerbare Energien 1991 (Act on Feeding into the Grid Electricity Generated from Renewable Energy Sources, referred to as Electricity Feed Law) and Gesetz für den Vorrang Erneuerbarer Energien (Erneuerbare-Energien-Gesetz) 2000 (the Renewable Energy Sources Act).

What the research also reveals is the way in which many jurisdictions adopt a "suite" of measures to counteract the greenhouse impacts of electricity restructuring. These include: energy and carbon taxes; emissions trading schemes; clean energy tax incentives; national market-oriented emissions reductions schemes; effective Renewable Portfolio Standards; systems benefits charges; demand-side management programs; energy efficiency standards; mandatory labeling of consumer bills; and feed laws. The strengths and weaknesses of each of these measures will be assessed in Section 6.2, including whether or not they are consistent with a restructured electricity industry.

6.2 Legal Measures to Counteract the Greenhouse Impacts of Electricity Restructuring

Energy and Carbon Taxes

It is generally agreed among economists that social welfare can be improved by imposing a tax on a good where the production or the consumption of the good results in negative externalities.[161] Many Scandinavian countries have used energy and carbon taxes to limit the negative externalities stemming from the use of fossil fuels. These have included taxes on the energy content of the energy source, carbon taxes based on the carbon content of the fuel, sulphur and nitrogen taxes on the sulphur dioxide and nitrous oxide content of the fuels, as well as an excise on electricity production and consumption. Estimations of the impact of these taxes indicate decreases in carbon dioxide of between three to fifteen percent.[162] Carbon taxes have not been used more widely, however, due to a fear that they might reduce national competitiveness through increasing costs to industry. Other policy and legal measures have been favored.[163]

Clean Energy Tax Incentives

The Maryland Clean Energy Incentive Act 2000 offers a set of tax incentives for energy efficiency and renewable energy products and services to Maryland residents and businesses. These include sales tax exemptions for purchases of a wide range of Energy Star® household appliances that meet specific energy efficiency guidelines. Excise tax reductions apply to electric and hybrid-electric vehicles, while income tax credits of fifteen percent of the installed cost of a solar or photovoltaic system apply. Credits are also awarded for using biomass fuel, such as cellulosic byproducts, wood trimmings, and chicken guano, to produce electricity. In an innovative measure, to promote purchases of Energy Star® appliances, the Maryland Energy Administration (MEA) works with the Comptroller's Office to inform retailers of the tax exemption through mailings and the Comptroller's monthly newsletter to retailers.

Energy incentives written into tax legislation is, in the author's view, a preferable mechanism for directing consumer behavior than schemes like the federal

[161] Ekins and Barker, *supra* note 148, at 328.

[162] See Vehmas et al., *supra* note 148, at 345, who indicate reductions of 3–4% in Norway, 4.7% in Denmark, 1.5% in the Netherlands, 15% in Sweden (including investment support for renewables), 4–5% in Finland. *See generally* Al-Abdullah, *supra* note 148; Ekins and Barker, *supra* note 148; and Baranzini et al., *supra* note 148.

[163] Vehmas, *supra* note 148, at 346; *see also* Annex I Expert Group, *supra* note 33.

government's Photovoltaic Rebate Program. There is a real danger that this scheme will close when funding runs out.[164]

National Market-Oriented Emissions Reductions Schemes for the Electricity Sector

A market-oriented emissions reductions scheme is precisely the type of scheme introduced by the Electricity Supply Amendment (Greenhouse Gas Emission Reduction) Act 2003 (NSW). The difficulty with this scheme is that is does not apply nationally. By distinction, the Danish government has introduced a national scheme under the Act 376 on CO_2 Quotas for Electricity Production, which came into force on July 15, 2000.[165] The scheme lays down a quota of 23 million tones of CO_2 in 2000 for electricity, which represent a radical reduction of twenty-four percent on 1994–98 levels. It is binding on producers of electricity, as opposed to retailers under the NSW scheme. Emissions allowances are allocated to existing electricity producers according to their historical emissions,[166] and are traded as the need arises.

Such a scheme is regarded as providing a theoretically optimum means of internalizing environmental costs in a competitive electricity market. The reason for this is that all liable parties, be they electricity retailers or generators, in the competitive market face the same requirement for reducing the greenhouse gas content of their energy supply. Competition is created when liable parties determine the most cost-effective means of reducing their greenhouse gas emissions. Such means will include advocating the most appropriate emissions reduction strategies to household and industrial users of electricity. Market-oriented emissions reductions schemes thus provide market-based drivers for the development of energy sources that are less greenhouse intensive. They also produce price signals that encourage an optimal mix of greenhouse sensitive energy services at the lowest cost to consumers.[167]

Participation in International or National Emissions Trading Schemes

Ratification of the Kyoto Protocol would allow Australia to meet its target through an international emissions trading scheme,[168] which would present Australia with a low cost abatement option.[169] However, the federal government is not pursuing this option. It has not ruled out, however, the possibility of establishing a domestic emissions trading scheme, and this may be an option that is pursued by the government as a result of various energy market reviews that are currently under way. Overseas experience shows that domestic and regional emissions trading schemes may be developed in advance of an international emissions scheme under the Kyoto Protocol. For example, the European Parliament voted in October 2002 to establish an ambitious new scheme for trading

---

[164] *See* Senate Hansard, February 11, 2003, p. 224.
[165] *See* http://www.ens.dk/sw1086.asp cited March 6, 2003; *see also* Sigurd Lauge Pedersen, "The Danish Emissions Trading System" (2000) 9 *RECIEL* 223; and Ekins and Barker, *supra* note 148.
[166] *See* Pedersen, *id.,* at 227.   [167] *See* Mills *supra* note 147, at 72.
[168] *See also* Jennifer Yelin-Kefer, "Warming up to an International Greenhouse Gas Market: Lessons from the US Acid Rain Experience" (2001) 20 *Stanford Environmental Law Journal* 221.
[169] GDP is likely to be 0.11% ($875m) per year lower than business as usual in the first commitment period but without ratifying GDP is likely to be 0.26% ($2b) lower; *see generally* Report of the Kyoto Protocol Ratification Advisory Group: A Risk Assessment (NSW Cabinet Office: 2003).

greenhouse gas emission rights throughout the EU. The scheme is mandatory but includes a proviso that member states should have limited rights to exempt individual installations as appropriate. For the period 2005–12, fifteen percent of the permits will be sold and the rest allocated for free under a grandfathering system. A cap will be placed on the number of permits issued to each member state. The Parliament has agreed that the EU will only recognize third countries' trading scheme if they are subject to the Protocol. Member states will not be allowed to use credits earned from projects that involve carbon sinks or nuclear energy sources.[170]

Effective Renewable Portfolio Standards

A Renewable Portfolio Standard (RPS) is the type of measure introduced by the Renewable Energy (Electricity) Act 2000 (Cth). As is clear from the Act, an RPS scheme typically requires retailers to purchase a proportion of their electricity from renewable energy sources. Renewable energy credits (RECs) are created which may then be traded between those retailers which have difficulty in meeting their legal obligations, and those which have the capacity to produce excess credits.[171] RPSs are a common measure for promoting the commercialization of renewable energy. The standard set in various countries is as follows: the Netherlands – 10% by 2020,[172] Denmark – 20% by 2010,[173] the United States – 10% by 2019,[174] and the United Kingdom – 10.4% by 2010.[175]

Despite the popularity of an RPS, the real question is whether or not an RPS scheme is consistent with a competitive electricity market. The reason that it is favored by regulators is that by creating a tradeable market in RECs it seems to require a minimal amount of government interference, and this is consistent with the economic theory underlying a restructured market. However, it is arguable that an RPS is not administratively simple. One has only to consider the role of the Renewable Energy Regulator under the Renewable Energy (Electricity) Act 2000 (Cth) to realize that the Regulator's task in verifying RECs, ensuring compliance with the scheme, and assessing penalties for breach of the Act is quite complex.[176]

Also, there is a legitimate debate about whether or not an RPS is competitively neutral when existing renewables are considered. Those utilities with an existing high level of renewables will be less severely impacted by an RPS than others.[177] In fact, suppliers with excess renewable energy credits may see rate reductions as they sell their excess

---

[170] *See* www.europarl.eu:int/press/index_publi_en.htm (cited March 11, 2003).

[171] *See generally* Woolf and Biewald, *supra* note 25; Palmer, *supra* note 25; Crawford and Angel, *supra* note 144; Wiser et al., *supra* note 116; Clemmer, et al., *supra* note 148; Mills, *supra* note 147; Annex I Expert Group, *supra* note 33; Wise, Pickle, and Goldman, *supra* note 149; Espey, *supra* note 148.

[172] Dutch Electricity Act 1998; *see also* Voogt et al., *supra* note 148 at 70–5.

[173] Energy 21; *see also* Hauch, *supra* note 25, at 510.

[174] Energy Policy Act 2002.

[175] The Renewables Obligation Order 2002 No. 914 made under the Utilities Act 2000 (UK); for a detailed discussion of the scheme *see also* Bradbrook and Wawryk, *supra* note 129 at 142–44.

[176] Renewable Energy (Electricity) Act 2000 (Cth) §§ 11–16, 41, 48–50, 52, 58–59, 69, 71–73, 102–105, 135–141; *see also* Wise et al., *supra* note 25, at 471.

[177] This has certainly been a concern in the Australian context where existing hydroelectricity generators were able to surrender the highest number of RECs in the first year of the operation of the Renewable Energy (Electricity) Act 2000 (Cth): *see* Bradbrook and Wawryk, *supra* note 129, at 150.

credits to other suppliers, whose rates increase. If competitive neutrality is a concern, it may be possible to limit the RPS to new renewable energy generation.[178]

Others note that the system gives renewable energy technologies an unfair market advantage in that customers and the market should select the types of electricity that are used, rather than being forced to select one source over another.[179]

Systems-Benefits Charge/Public Benefit Funds

A systems-benefits charge (SBC) is used to collect funds from customers to support various public benefit policies, including renewable energy programs. Under most SBC schemes, a volumetric fee is imposed on the use of electricity which is intended to be nonbypassable and competitively neutral.[180] The funds derived from SBCs are often used to support the development of higher cost emerging technologies, research and development, consumer education, green marketing, and manufacturing incentives. As such they are likely to play a critical role in supporting emerging technologies.[181] Bradbrook and Wawryk point to the California Public Utilities Code, as amended by the Assembly Bill 1890 of 1996[182] as a good example of a SBC. Under that Code large, privately owned utilities are required to collect revenue based on a rate of 0.37–0.45 percent per kW charged to customers. They report that US$540 million has been collected over four years to be spent on renewable energy technologies, and that the scheme has been extended to 2012.[183]

Demand-Side Management Programs

Demand-side management (DSM) refers to technologies, products, and programs that involve deliberately reducing buyer demand for electricity by substituting conservation on site for fuel use. DSM programs cover a variety of policies under which utilities have been directed to subsidize or otherwise encourage customers to install appliances that use less electricity to perform their functions. This will conserve fossil fuels, limit the environmental externalities caused by their use, and limit the need to build new power plants.[184]

In New South Wales, for example, the Independent Pricing and Regulatory Tribunal (IPART) has recently released its final report, Inquiry into the Role of Demand Management and Other Options in the Provision of Energy Services.[185] The key question posed by the Inquiry was whether demand management options that meet customers' energy needs at a lower cost, as well as with lower environmental impact, are being ignored in favor of a strategy to continue to build new generation facilities. IPART concludes that there are significant demand-management strategies that are cost effective but which are not being pursued. Importantly, IPART notes that the most significant barrier to DSM is that the full cost of energy is not reflected in the price.[186] One of

---

[178] Wise et al., *supra* note 25, at 472.

[179] *See* Bradbrook and Wawryk, *supra* note 129, at 133.

[180] *See* Wise et al., *supra* note 25, at 468.   [181] *See* Wiser et al., *supra* note 116.

[182] Cal. Stat. ch. 854 (1996).

[183] Bradbrook and Wawryk, *supra* note 129, at 136–7.

[184] *See* Timothy J. Brennan, *Demand-Side Management Programs Under Retail Electricity Competition* (Resources for the Future: 1998).

[185] *Inquiry into the Role of Demand Management and Other Options in the Provision of Energy Services* (Independent Pricing and Regulatory Tribunal: October 2002).

[186] *Id.,* at 31.

IPART's recommendations is the establishment of a Demand Management Fund,[187] funded at least partially by an SBC, described above.[188] The Fund would be used to facilitate sustainable generation and various energy efficiency programs. Similar initiatives have already been undertaken by at least twenty-one states in the United States as a fundamental part of the electricity restructuring process. All of the energy efficiency programs are provided for by statute.[189]

IPART also recommends the setting of energy efficiency benchmarks for government and commercial buildings,[190] as well as monitoring the impact of the design of the National Electricity Market and market rules on Demand Management initiatives.[191] These initiatives would both reduce consumption and greenhouse gas emissions,[192] as well as enhance the capacity and reliability of the electricity network.

It is the author's view that legally binding energy efficiency standards are an important mechanism for overcoming the market barriers that block cost-effective energy savings, including lack of awareness and uninformed consumers.[193] This view is reinforced by the fact that there have been recent initiatives in Australia to set national energy efficiency standards. These include the resolution by the Australian Building Codes Board, at its meeting on August 28–29, 2002, that energy efficiency measures for houses will be introduced in the BCA on January 1, 2003 under Amendment No. 12.[194] These standards will be enforced at a state level under environmental planning legislation. Also, the National Appliance and Equipment Energy Efficiency Committee (NAEEEC), consisting of representatives from commonwealth, state, territory, and New Zealand governments, has recently set Minimum Energy Performance Standards, requiring the labeling of household appliances.[195] The Standards must be implemented at the state level.[196] This brings Australia in line with other jurisdictions like the United States, where the National Appliance Energy Conservation Act of 1987 establishes standards for a dozen appliances.

Mandatory Labeling of Consumer Bills

There is strong support in the literature[197] for legally requiring retailers and wholesalers to disclose the fuel mix and the CO_2, NOX, and SO_2 emissions associated with electricity generation in a standard format on customer bills. As electricity markets

---

[187] *Id.*, at 40.   [188] *Id.*, Appendix 8 at 118.

[189] See, e.g., the District of Columbia which enacted the Retail Electric Competition and Consumer Protection Act of 1999 as well as establishing a SBC known as the Reliability Energy Trust Fund to protect low-income earners, promote energy efficiency and renewable energy technologies; for this and all other state initiatives *see* http://aceee.org/new/dc.pdf.

[190] IPART, *supra* note 145, at 50.   [191] *Id.*, at 98.

[192] IPART estimates that DM initiatives could reduce electricity consumption in NSW by 250MW (2%) and reduce emissions by $6000ktCO_{2-e}$ per annum (*id.*, at 29) and by 1,634MW and $3,462ktCO_{2-e}$ per annum, if renewables were fully operational; *id.*, at 30.

[193] *Id.*, at 22.   [194] *See* http://www.abcb.gov.au/content/whatsnew/.

[195] *See* http://www.greenhouse.gov.au/energyefficiency/appliances/naeeec/index.html. Note that there the addition of more appliances to this standard has been recommended under the National Appliance and Equipment Energy Efficiency Program; Work Plan and Project for 2002–2004 available at http://www.isr.gov.au/library/content_library/NAEEEP.pdf.

[196] In New South Wales, for example, they are implemented under the Electricity Safety Act 1945 (NSW) and the Electricity Safety (Equipment Efficiency) Regulation 1999.

[197] *See* Burtraw et al., *supra* note 23; Perkins, *supra* note 25, at 1037; Gaffney, *supra* note 25, at 1457; Kantro, *supra* note 25, at 43; Diesendorf, *supra* note 25, at 43; Crawford and Angel, *supra* note 144, at 7.

open to competition, retail consumers are increasingly gaining the ability to choose their electricity suppliers. It is crucial in a contestable market, that consumers have access to information about the price, source, and environmental characteristics of their electricity. As of August 2002, more than twenty states in the United States have environmental disclosure policies in place, which legally require electricity suppliers to provide information on fuel sources and, in some cases, emissions associated with electricity generation.[198]

Such a measure was proposed at the time that provisions of the Renewable Energy (Electricity) Act 2000 (Cth) were being debated. It was ultimately rejected by the federal government. The author believes that it is a mechanism which is consistent with the establishment of a contestable retail electricity market and that it should be written into legislation at the federal and state levels in Australia. Not only would it inform customers about the sources of energy, but it would also go toward counteracting one of the principal barriers to DSM – lack of consumer awareness.[199]

Feed Laws

Consistently with assessing various options for internalizing the externalities of a re-structured electricity industry, it is important to also consider whether Australia should adopt "feed laws." There have certainly been calls for the adoption of such laws to overcome barriers to grid access within the National Electricity Market.[200] These laws have been adopted in Germany, Denmark, and Spain whereby an electricity utility is obliged to let independent producers of renewable power "feed" their electricity into the grid against a guaranteed payment of a certain fee. In these three European countries, national legislation has been adopted to implement the scheme. Espey claims that "[i]t is owing exclusively to the national legislation of these three countries that the European Union witnessed the emergence of a wind turbine manufacturing industry which offers cutting-edge technology in the world market today."[201] Based on this experience, it may be wrong to assume that the introduction of minimum price systems hampers productivity. The feed laws have stimulated an efficient industry with considerable export opportunities, which has created jobs for over 20,000 people in Germany alone.[202]

The German feed laws operate under the Stromeinspeisungsgesetz für Erneuerbare Energien 1991 (Act on Feeding into the Grid Electricity Generated from Renewable Energy Sources, or Electricity Feed Law) as well as the Renewable Energy Sources Act (Erneuerbare-Energien-Gesetz) 2000 (RESA). The Electricity Feed Law regulated the purchase and price of electricity generated exclusively from hydropower, wind energy, solar energy, landfill gas, sewage gas, or biomass in the area of validity of this act by public electricity utilities.[203] Electric utilities were obliged to purchase the electricity generated from renewable energies in their supply

---

[198] For a full discussion of these measures, *see* http://www.eere.energy.gov/greenpower/disclosure.shtml.

[199] Note that the Victorian Minister for Environment and Water has announced that electricity retailers will be required to disclose to customers the amount of greenhouse gas that is being emitted as a result of their electricity consumption. The information will be detailed on the bill by way of a graph; Media Release, Australian Labor Party Victorian Branch, January 23, 2003.

[200] *See* Crawford and Angel, *supra* note 144, at 10.   [201] Espey, *supra* note 148, at 559.

[202] *Id.*

[203] Stromeinspeisungsgesetz für Erneuerbare Energien 1991 § 1.

area and to pay for the electricity fed into the system.[204] However, the compensation rates stipulated under the law were not sufficient to stimulate a large-scale market introduction of electricity generated from sources other than wind and hydro, especially photovoltaic cells and biomass. For this reason, the compensation rates have been modified in the RESA, which replaces the Electricity Feed Law, in order to promote large-scale generation of electricity from all kinds of renewable energy sources.[205] The Act also equalizes the costs for paying the rates among all transmission grid operators.

The purpose of the RESA is to facilitate a sustainable development of energy supply in the interest of managing global warming and protecting the environment. It is also to achieve a substantial increase in the percentage contribution made by renewable energy sources to power supply in order at least to double the share of renewable energy sources in total energy consumption by the year 2010.[206] The RESA deals with the purchase of, and the compensation to be paid for, electricity generated exclusively from various renewable energy sources by utility companies which operate grids for public power supply (grid operators).[207] The different compensation rates[208] to be paid to the generators of different types of renewable energy, specified in the RESA, have been determined by means of scientific studies.[209] The purpose of this pricing regime is to bring renewable energy sources closer to conventional energy sources in terms of their competitiveness. The compensation rates will decline over time and remain in effect for a limited period of time. The fact that the rates will be reviewed every two years guarantees that they will be updated continuously and at short intervals to reflect market and cost trends.[210] The costs associated with connecting the electricity derived from renewable energy sources to the technically and economically most suitable grid connecting point is borne by the renewable energy generators.[211] Transmission grid operators are obliged to record any differences in the amount of energy purchased and compensation payments and to equalise such differences amongst themselves.[212]

7 CURRENT AND FUTURE REVIEWS OF THE AUSTRALIAN ENERGY MARKET

Australia's entire energy market is currently under review. The Council of Australian Governments (COAG), which has overseen the establishment of the NEM, has recently undertaken a review of the market. It has released Towards a Truly National and Efficient

---

[204] *Id.*, § 2.

[205] Note that the German Bundestag and the German Federal Government have had to counter claims that the Renewable Energy Sources Act constitutes "state aid" granted by a member state or through state resources as defined in Article 87 of the Treaty Establishing the European Community.

[206] Renewable Energy Sources Act 2000 § 1.   [207] *Id.* § 2

[208] *Id.* §§ 5–9.   [209] See Explanatory Memorandum.

[210] *Id.*   [211] Renewable Energy Sources Act 2000 § 10(1).

[212] *Id.* § 11(1). How this works is that by March 31 of each year, the transmission grid operators must determine the amount of energy purchased in accordance with the Act and the percentage share which this amount represents, relative to the overall amount of energy delivered to final consumers either directly by the operator or indirectly via downstream grids. If transmission grid operators have purchased more energy than this average share, they are entitled to sell energy to, and receive compensation from, the other transmission grid operators, until these other grid operators have purchased a volume of energy which is equal to the average share mentioned above (§ 11(2)).

Energy Market. The report contains eight principle chapters: governance and regulatory arrangements; electricity market mechanism and structure; electricity transmission; electricity financial market development; demand-side participation and full retail contestability in electricity; increasing the wider penetration of gas; options to reduce greenhouse gas emissions; and rural and regional issues. It makes a number of significant recommendations. First, it recommends the introduction of a national economy-wide greenhouse gas emissions trading scheme[213] to replace the following: the mandatory renewable energy target under the Renewable Energy (Electricity) Act 2000 (Cth); the NSW greenhouse benchmarks scheme under the Electricity Supply Amendment (Greenhouse Gas Emission Reduction) Act 2003 (NSW); the Queensland 13% Gas Scheme; the Generator efficiency standards and the Greenhouse Gas Abatement Program – Stationary Energy projects.

The report also recommends the creation of a National Energy Regulator as a single independent regulator for all jurisdictions that would: replace the energy functions exercised by the ACCC, the state and territory regulators and the National Electricity Code Administrator; be responsible for the National Electricity Code, National Third Party Access Code Gas Pipelines, and other energy market codes; be responsible for the approval of code changes for gas and electricity; and have its decisions reviewable by the Australian Competition Tribunal. The Regulator would also introduce a mandatory code of practice governing arrangements between distribution companies and prospective embedded generators.[214]

In addition, in accordance with section 162 of the Renewable Energy Electricity Act 2000 (Cth), the Minister for Environment and Heritage has initiated an independent review of the operation of the Act. The Minister has now decided on the following terms of reference, amongst others: the extent to which the Act has contributed to reducing greenhouse gas emissions and encouraged the additional generation of electricity from renewable energy sources; the extent to which the objectives of the Act have been met and whether there is a need for any alternative approaches; the mix of technologies that has resulted from the implementation of the Act; whether or not the level of penalties under the Act is adequate; whether the renewable energy shortfall charge, payable when a retailer does not have enough renewable energy certificates to discharge its liability in a given year, should be linked to the Consumer Price Index; other environmental impacts that have resulted from the implementation of the Act, including the burning of forestry wood waste as biomass energy; the possibility of introducing a cap on the amount of energy that can be produced from sources that are greenhouse intensive – like biomass; and the level of the overall and interim targets.[215]

Finally, the Prime Minister has announced the development of a strategic long-term energy policy for Australia as part of his forward agenda for policy development in

---

[213] *See also Pathways and Policies* (Australian Greenhouse Office: 2002) relating to the approach to, and design of, such a scheme.

[214] *See also* Charles River Associates Asia Pacific Pty. Ltd. (CRA), *Distribution Network Barriers to Embedded Generation* 2002. CRA was engaged by the CoAG Energy Market Review Panel to consider certain allegations of impediments to embedded generation and to recommend means to overcome any associated barriers to entry in the National Electricity Market.

[215] Joint Media Release, Federal Minister for the Environment and Heritage, Dr. David Kemp and Minister for Industry, Tourism and Resources, The Hon. Ian Macfarlane, March 25, 2003

key strategic areas, known as Strategic Leadership for Australia: Policy Directions in a Complex World.[216]

8 CONCLUSION

It is too soon to analyze the extent to which reviews of the electricity market and strategic energy policy will result in a sustainable energy law framework for Australia. Such an analysis will be required at some time in the future. For present purposes, it is clear that currently Australia lacks a sustainable energy law framework. The key messages of ESD are being missed during the process of electricity restructuring. The increase in greenhouse gas emissions from the stationary energy sector in particular is not consistent with the principle of intergenational equity. If greenhouse emissions from this sector continue to grow, present and future generations will suffer the impact of global climate change. Australia is particularly vulnerable to this phenomenon.[217] It is also clear that the fossil fuel industry is not being made to pay for its emissions of air pollutants like sulphur dioxide and nitrous oxide. It is also being encouraged by NCP to continue to emit greenhouse gases. This is not consistent with the polluter pays principle.

In addition, there is surely a case to be made for Australian governments to apply the precautionary principle with respect to energy policy development. Where the exact parameters of the environmental consequences of restructuring are unknown, the international consensus is to adopt a precautionary approach. As applied to the electricity industry, a precautionary approach may mean that crude price mechanisms are inappropriate regulators where greenhouse gases are involved. As Perkins suggests, "[u]ntil the causal links of the global warming problem are more precisely understood, so that one tonne of CO_2 is known to cause about $X in harm, a precautionary approach argues against reliance on price alone as a guide to the optimal quantity of fossil-fueled electricity generations."[218] Similarly, reliance on the precautionary principle would place the burden on those advocating the introduction of increased competition to show that the expected benefits, arising from greater consumption, are greater than the expected losses due to more pollution. If this cannot be shown, then one would

---

[216] *See* http://www.dpmc.gov.au/leadership/strategicleadership2.cfm. The policy will be developed by a ministerial oversight committee, chaired by the Prime Minister, comprising the Deputy Prime Minister, the Treasurer, and the Ministers for the Environment and Heritage, and Industry, Tourism and Resources. The committee will be supported by a task force of senior officials chaired by the Department of the Prime Minister and Cabinet. The task force will draw on private sector advice as appropriate.

[217] *See* predicted impacts in Intergovernmental Panel on Climate Change, *Climate Change 2001: Impacts, Adaptation and Vulnerability* at 51–4. In July 2001, the CSIRO updated its regional climate projections and impacts for Australia in line with new findings by the Intergovernmental Panel on Climate Change showing expected changes in temperature, sea level, rainfall, evaporation, and moisture balance. Changes in climate will affect agriculture, forestry, natural systems, pests and weeds, water resources, and some coastal communities. Meanwhile, the World Wide Fund for Nature has urged the federal government to take immediate action to cut the nation's greenhouse gas emissions and to save the Great Barrier Reef from mass coral bleaching. A very large potential coral bleaching "hot spot" over large parts of the Reef has been discovered by the U.S. National Oceanic and Atmospheric Administration. The bleaching could threaten thousands of jobs in regional Queensland that depend on tourism associated with the Reef.

[218] Perkins, *supra* note 25, at 1044.

not be justified in assuming that society's welfare is enhanced by avoiding increased consumption.[219]

It will be most interesting to follow future energy policy and law developments to assess whether or not Australian governments have accepted the basic precepts for a sustainable energy law framework.

[219] Hamilton and Dennis, *supra* note 25, at 24.

26 Electricity Market Liberalization and Energy Sustainability

Barry Barton*

1 INTRODUCTION

Many countries have adopted a market approach to the reform of their electricity industries. Whether such changes help or hinder energy sustainability is debatable. Do they contribute to energy efficiency and conservation, and the uptake of renewable energy? This chapter examines the inherent characteristics of a market approach in comparison with a political or regulatory approach, for example in relation to energy pricing and investment. The role of subsidies is considered. It examines the legal design of energy market institutions and the manner in which the details of market design can affect energy sustainability, such as in demand-side management. It appraises policy instruments grafted onto a market strategy in order to improve energy sustainability. It concludes that, while the record is mixed, a market approach can make a contribution to energy sustainability.

2 ENERGY SUSTAINABILITY

Three elements can be identified in energy sustainability. Energy efficiency concerns the productivity we obtain from the primary energy we consume. Although in technical terms some energy is always wasted when it is converted from one form to another, or put to use, the amount can be reduced. Improvements in energy efficiency mean that the amount of economic output or satisfaction of human needs per unit of energy can be increased. Some countries, like Japan, have made dramatic improvements in the measure of gross domestic product obtained per unit of energy consumed. The second element, energy conservation, is the reduction of energy use, for example in eliminating unnecessary heating. The third element is renewable energy sources, replacing or avoiding dependence on fossil fuels.

Policies of energy sustainability have several justifications. There is the simple economic cost of investments in generation and capacity. At times supply has not been able to keep up with demand, and the need to avoid waste has been very evident. Energy security has been another reason to restrain demand and avoid dependence on fossil fuels, whether due to depletion of resources or due to political problems. In recent years more attention has turned to the environmental consequences of energy production and use. Air pollution has long been understood to be a significant adverse effect of

* Associate Professor of Law, University of Waikato, New Zealand.

the use of fossil fuels, especially coal, but it continues to be a severe problem in many regions. Other environmental consequences are pollution and thermal degradation of water, visual impact of generation and transmission facilities, and nuclear hazards. At a fundamental level, energy sustainability has a vital role in reducing the adverse effects of human activities on global climate. Energy use is the main source of anthropogenic carbon dioxide emissions, in the use of petroleum, natural gas, and coal. The reason why energy sustainability measures are so important is that there is no practical way to mitigate carbon dioxide emissions; they cannot be filtered out of the fumes or treated technically like other products of combustion. The amount of carbon dioxide emitted is tied firmly to the amount of fossil fuel energy used.

Energy sustainability faces barriers of various kinds. Its uptake is strongly affected by the availability and price of traditional fuels, which is in turn affected by the extent to which external environmental costs are externalized. Traditionally the price of oil, gas, and coal has not reflected pollution or climate change costs. Other barriers are the cost of capital investment and information. The special characteristics of renewable energy sources can also be a barrier; wind and solar, in particular, provide an intermittent supply of electricity that may or may not match demand. Renewables also have their own environmental burdens to carry. Biofuels can cause significant pollution; wind farms attract criticism for damaging amenity and affecting birdlife habitat; hydro dams affect rivers and lakes, and large ones affect whole regions. This chapter is particularly concerned with barriers of a legal and institutional kind.

Governments have a role in reducing these barriers. The Energy Charter Treaty is one international instrument that recognizes this role, and calls on ratifying parties, in nonbinding language, to improve energy efficiency and develop and use renewable energy sources.[1] An associated Protocol addresses energy efficiency specifically. Another protocol for energy efficiency and renewable energy, it can be argued, should be made under the United Nations Framework Convention on Climate Change, because of the role of energy use in the emission of climate change gases.[2]

3 CHARACTERISTICS OF THE TRADITIONAL ELECTRICITY INDUSTRY

It is convenient to start with the legal structures for the traditional electricity industry, where electricity and its delivery are assumed to be inevitably intertwined and provided by the one large monopoly organization. Large centralized organizations suit the generation technologies that have prevailed, at least up until the 1990s, because ever greater economies of scale could be obtained from large generation stations.[3] There are two main legal forms for the electricity industry under such circumstances. The first is as a government agency. Generation and transmission are in the hands of a department or ministry under the direct control of a politically accountable minister, or in the hands of a board or state owned enterprises substantially controlled by the minister. Distribution and sales may be part of that department or entity's work, but commonly they

---

[1] Energy Charter Treaty, Art 19. (1995) 34 ILM 360. Under it was made the Energy Charter Protocol on Energy Efficiency and Related Environmental Aspects 34 ILM 446, whereby the parties committed themselves to establish energy efficiency policies and appropriate regulatory frameworks.

[2] A. J. Bradbrook, "The Development of a Protocol on Energy Efficiency and Renewable Energy to the United Nations Framework Convention on Climate Change" (2001) 5 *NZJEL* 55.

[3] S. Hunt and G. Shuttleworth, *Competition and Choice in Electricity* (Chichester: John Wiley, 1996) p. 1.

are administered by local councils or boards on a nonprofit basis. The department has a legal monopoly and can (and often does) refuse to allow anyone else to build power stations. The local distribution and sales councils also have a legal monopoly. They have a corresponding duty to supply all paying customers. Prices are set by regulation and so are subject to direct political control. Price increases sometimes take place in the safer parts of the electoral cycle. Pricing often involves cross subsidy to reduce the electricity prices for home owners, who are after all voters. Investment decisions, in new power stations or new transmission lines, are government decisions. Staying ahead of demand is one of the main factors that a government will take into account, and it assumes that to be a necessity without comparing costs and benefits in any rigid way; it is a given that the government must provide electricity. But it is by no means the only purpose that governments pursue in electricity development projects. They see them as valuable means of job creation, which provide employment in construction and in coal mining, which contribute (in the case of hydro projects) to flood control and irrigation, and which act as vehicles for generalized regional development including roads and other infrastructure. This has been the dominant model in many parts of Europe, Canada, Australia, New Zealand, and developing countries.

Decisions about prices and investments are all made within the one integrated entity. Decisions about what fuel to purchase, what plant to run, and what capital works projects to invest in are taken in view of the well-being of the enterprise as a whole. There is no competition in any real sense between different sections of the enterprise. Accounting procedures are often different from in the private sector, focusing more on controlling the expenditure of taxpayers' money, and less on capital and the rate of return on capital. Political control also extends to decisions about fuel type and about renewables and energy efficiency. In some cases, however, political control is weak and the enterprise achieves high levels of autonomy. (Ontario Hydro from the 1920s to the 1990s is a leading example.) System operation and security is all dealt with as the enterprise's business.

The second main structure for a traditional electricity industry is privately owned companies subject to strict regulation. This pattern is found in Europe and is common in the United States. The companies are "investor owned utilities," in business to make a profit. However their profitability is subject to the oversight of a public utility board or like regulatory agency that has jurisdiction over prices and investment decisions. In exchange for the loss of control that this implies, each company obtains a franchise or legal monopoly for the supply of electricity in a particular territory, and the security of a reasonable income for the investors who hold its stocks and bonds. The public utility board regulates to control the prices that the monopoly company can charge, but to allow it to make a reasonable rate of return on its assets.[4] This requires an elaborate analysis of what investments can properly be included in the allowed asset base, before decisions on the rate of return and then the tariff for different classes of customer. Capital investment projects like new power stations require the board to grant a certificate of convenience and necessity. The legislation that gives the board its jurisdiction may direct the board to take energy efficiency into account as it performs its functions. Power companies operating under this kind of regulation are like government departments in many respects, for example, monopoly, integration, and close political direction. They are in

---

[4] *See* S. Breyer, *Regulation and its Reform* (Cambridge, Mass: Harvard Univ. Press, 1982).

a symbiotic relationship with their public utility boards in a regulatory compact. They share with government departments a predilection for capital works, because when prices and profits are controlled, the only way for the company to grow is by increasing the amount of the capital invested.

Whether investor owned or publicly owned, the traditional form of the industry has been the dominant paradigm for a century, and for good reason.[5] The vertically integrated organization allows the development of large-scale transmission systems, and enables the introduction of larger and larger generation stations to take advantage of the economies of scale that have prevailed at least until recently. The total monopoly of the vertically integrated entity makes it simple to maintain subsidies for social purposes or for the benefit of different fuel industries.

4 ENERGY SUSTAINABILITY CHARACTERISTICS OF A TRADITIONAL SYSTEM

What are the energy sustainability characteristics of these traditional forms of the electricity industry? First, they are designed to supply electricity in order to satisfy demand. Electricity is perceived as a public service, required for the nation's development and for the improvement of the lives of its factory workers, farmers, and householders. In the heyday of electrification in the 1920s and 1930s, electricity was the very essence of progress, and access to it was necessary for modern citizenship. Our dependence on electricity has only grown since; few of us in the developed world would know how to run our homes or offices, let alone our farms and factories, without a reliable supply. In many countries, demand has grown steadily and at a faster rate than the population.[6] The traditional model of the industry is therefore geared to supplying more electricity, come what may. It is all the more focused on supply when electricity prices are kept deliberately low, as they are in many developing countries for the purposes of modernization, economic growth, and social equity.[7] The consequences are that consumption is encouraged, although the consequences must fall on the state because the lower prices will discourage private investment in generation.

Second, in relation to investment decisions, there is a long record of governments forging ahead with energy schemes heedless of both environmental and economic risks. Hydroelectric development is especially prone to grandiose proposals. Kellow has documented examples in Canada, the United States, Australia, and New Zealand where governments have insisted on proceeding with projects without taking the environmental impact into account, and without considering closely the need for the electricity to be generated.[8] In New Zealand, the government in the late 1970s and early 1980s embraced the "Think Big" strategy of energy and natural resource development, putting both financial and environmental prudence to one side. The response, in the reforms later in the 1980s, brought together fiscal conservatives and environmentalists in an

---

[5] Hunt and Shuttleworth, *supra* note 3, at 31–38.
[6] Energy Information Administration, Per Capita (Person) Total Primary Energy Consumption, All Countries, 1980–2000, http://www.eia.doe.gov/pub/international/iealf/tablee1c.xls.
[7] F. P. Sioshansi, "Sobering Realities of Liberalizing Electricity Markets" International Association for Energy Economics (IAEE) Newsletter, Third Quarter 2002, p. 24.
[8] A. Kellow, *Transforming Power: The Politics of Electricity Planning* (Cambridge: Cambridge University Press, 1996).

unusual alliance.[9] The influence of government on investment decisions need not always be as bad as this; indeed, one would hope that at least occasionally it would be a positive influence. However, in a market system the government influence will generally need to be overt, through legal interventions.

Third, monopoly and integration favor large enterprises, large centralized power plants, and shut out new enterprises which may have new ideas and new technologies to contribute. Kellow draws out the point that traditional electricity departments are concerned above all with meeting demand, and therefore with development, expansion, and building new capacity. They tend to be dominated by an engineering ethos. Where circumstances change, for example, where demand drops because of economic recession, they find alternative rationales for their projects; Kellow called it "reverse adaptation."

5 SUBSIDIES IN THE TRADITIONAL SYSTEM

The last energy sustainability characteristic of traditional systems is that governments often maintain subsidies that work against sustainability. Some are general subsidies of production and consumption, in the form of reduced electricity prices, for purposes such as assisting agricultural irrigation, maintaining regional employment, or maintaining adequate supplies of energy to the poor.[10] Other subsidies or quotas help particular fuels, such as coal. A leading example was Germany's "kohlepfennig," a levy on the electricity industry to support the domestic coal industry. It was not removed until 1995, and even then it was replaced with direct state aid to the coal industry.[11] But subsidies distort price signals and fail to reflect the true economic costs of supply. They lead to inefficient levels of production. They exacerbate the negative externalities associated with energy supply in the form of environmental damage.

Other subsidies, however, have sought to inject energy efficiency measures into traditional electricity industries. Demand-side management, discussed in Section 11, is one. A leading example from the United States is the Public Utilities Regulatory Policies Act of 1978 (PURPA), which promoted cogeneration and small renewable power production.[12] It did so by requiring electric utilities to buy power production from such "qualifying facilities" at favorable prices, generally the avoided cost of new capacity. PURPA led to major advances in the construction of energy efficient electricity capacity. It also showed that it was possible for nonutility generators to connect to the grid and sell electricity and that economies of scale no longer dictated that generation be a monopoly. However, it led to excesses. No account was taken of the costs in relation to the benefits of purchasing from qualifying facilities. Regulators often overestimated avoided costs by a wide margin, especially at a time when oil prices were peaking. From 1984 new procedures lowered the avoided cost payments and put competitive pressure

---

[9] B. J. Barton, "From Public Service to Market Commodity: Electricity and Gas Law in New Zealand" (1998) 16 *JERL* 351.

[10] K. Schneider and M. Saunders, "Removing Energy Subsidies in Developing and Transition Economies" IAEE Newsletter, First Quarter 2001, p. 17.

[11] E. D. Cross, *Electricity Regulation in the European Union* (Chichester: Wiley, 1996) p. 132.

[12] T. J. Brennan et al., *A Shock to the System: Restructuring America's Electricity Industry* (Washington, DC: Resources for the Future, 1996) p. 28; Hunt and Shuttleworth, *supra*, note 3, at 4, 45.

on suppliers of new generation capacity. As a policy instrument PURPA was not viable, but it showed the way toward new possibilities in the way that the industry worked.

The legal regime for the traditional electricity industry makes it relatively easy to look after such social and economic objectives. A government department responsible for electricity can simply be directed by its minister to build this kind of power station and not that. It can be told to put more money into renewable energy or research and development. It can be told to alter its price tariff to encourage energy efficiency, to discourage high levels of use, or to assist low income customers. Investor owned utilities can be given similar directions through legislation or through orders of the public utility board. Either way, integrated monopoly utilities can simply pass the extra costs on to their customers, and (in the case of government departments) to the government in the form of lower or nonexistent return on investment. However, it is often difficult to tell the size of the subsidy.

6 CHARACTERISTICS OF A MARKET APPROACH

Many countries have taken a market approach to reform their electricity industries. While the pattern varies, the market approach involves the removal of monopoly rights to allow new companies to enter the field, and the removal of regulation of tariffs and capital spending, so that pricing and investment decisions are made in response to market supply and demand.[13] State owned enterprises are sometimes privatized. The industry is generally restructured by dividing integrated enterprises into smaller ones in order to improve competition, and to separate potentially competitive functions like generation from usually monopolistic ones like transmission and distribution. The underlying assumption is that the command-and-control relationships within a single firm can be replaced with contractual relationships between separate firms, and that the competition benefits outweigh the transaction costs.[14] A market approach became possible when new technology such as cogeneration and combined cycle gas technology reduced the economies of scale of large organizations. Improved information and communication technology also played a role in making markets possible, in managing complex system coordination, auctions to find spot prices every half-hour, and subsequent financial reconciliations.

An electricity industry that takes the form of a competitive market sees a number of generator companies offering electricity for sale in a wholesale market.[15] The electricity may be sold directly to large industrial users, or to retailers who then sell it on to individual businesses and households. For the transfer of energy from power stations to consumers, the generator and retailer companies enter into agreements with the owners of the high tension transmission system and the local distribution networks. The retailers will sometimes be the same companies who own the local distribution networks, or they may be the generator companies themselves, or third parties. In order

---

[13] Hunt and Shuttleworth, *supra* note 3.

[14] P. I. Joskow and R. Schmalensee, *Markets for Power: An Analysis of Electric Utility Deregulation* (Cambridge, Mass: MIT Press, 1983).

[15] For a discussion of different models, see Hunt and Shuttleworth, *supra* note 3. Also D. Sharma, "Australian Electricity Reform: A Regulatory Quagmire" IAEE Newsletter, Second Quarter 2002, p. 22; Barton, *supra* note 9; J. Surrey (ed.), *The British Electricity Experiment* (London: Earthscan, 1996); A. Pickering, "Contracting for Electricity Supply" (1998) AMPLA Ybk 245.

to facilitate these different sales and agreements, the industry establishes institutions for an electricity market and for system operation. The workings of the market allow supply and demand to be determined regularly, usually resulting in a spot price for every half-hour or hour during the day. Because spot prices will go up and down, companies may make hedge contracts and other financial arrangements in order to reduce the risks they face.

Motives for opening electricity supply to market forces have varied. Competition and choice are argued to result in greater efficiency, better use of existing plant, better investment decisions, lower energy prices, higher economic productivity, and increased domestic and international competitiveness.[16] Traditional price setting mechanisms are thought to insulate utilities from the consequences of their actions. Sometimes the incumbent utility has become inefficient and needs new incentives, but other incumbents want to be freed from constraints. Governments sometimes wanted to avoid further investment and investment risk themselves and get the private sector involved. Privatization policies have brought forward questions of markets and regulation where previously none had existed. Policies of small government, deregulation, and elimination of bureaucracy have played a part. The introduction of full competition will often be accompanied by scrutiny of subsidies that produce inefficiencies. Users have sought market choice – the freedom to choose from among competing suppliers. Alternative energy advocates have wanted to break the monopolies of traditional integrated utilities in order to have access to grids and customers.

The main benefit that is envisaged from market liberalization is the efficiency that market forces bring. Companies in competition are under pressure to keep their prices down and to offer a more attractive service to customers. On the other hand, prices will reflect the value of electricity and the inputs required to make it and bring it to the customer, that is, the fuel cost, the cost of required pollution abatement measures, the cost of capital to build power stations, the cost of transmission and of the distribution lines. Consumers in search of electricity will have to pay the market price in competition with other consumers; the price of electricity will reflect its scarcity. When electricity is more scarce, for example during a drought in a hydro dependent country, the price will rise. When prices are sufficiently high, companies will consider investing in further generation and transmission capacity. On the other hand, investing too early is penalized. There are a number of points of contrast, therefore, with the traditional system: the pressure of competition, price signals flowing through the system and reflecting scarcity and value, and the lack of government involvement in key industry decisions.

7 EXPERIENCE WITH MARKET SYSTEMS

The market approach is no longer a new idea, and we are gathering experience of how it works. Britain, Scandinavia, Germany, Australia, and New Zealand saw some of the earliest markets emerge.[17] North America has seen some liberalization but it

---

[16] Hunt and Shuttleworth, *supra*, note 3, at 11; Sharma, *supra* note 15.

[17] Generally, see R. J. Gilbert and E. P. Kahn (eds.), *International Comparison of Electricity Regulation* (Cambridge: Cambridge University Press, 1996); M. M. Roggenkamp, A. Rønne, C. Redgwell, and I. del Guayo, *Energy Law in Europe* (Oxford: Oxford University Press, 2001); Surrey, *supra* note 15; Barton, *supra* note 9; B. J. Barton, "Risk and Promise in Energy Market Liberalization: Consumer Choice in Buying Electricity" (1999) 64 *Applied Energy* 275–88.

is not evenly spread.[18] There is a new realization that it is not easy to restructure the electricity industry and throw it open to market forces.[19] Power markets are much more complex than many policy makers had realized. Electricity cannot be treated as merely another commodity; it is more fundamental to the economy than most things, it is still a public service in the eyes of many citizens, not a mere article in commerce, and it cannot be stored. Benefits such as higher operating efficiencies and lower retail prices do not automatically flow from the introduction of competition, and where they do occur they do not necessarily accrue to expected beneficiaries like small consumers. Newly liberalized markets do not automatically self-regulate. Competition is hard to produce, it takes a great deal of regulatory effort. Mere removal of legal monopolies and restructuring to break integrated companies up into pieces will not suffice. Markets, paradoxically, need constant and diligent monitoring and a powerful independent regulator. The role of regulators, and their workload, has usually increased following the introduction of competition in many jurisdictions. New Zealand is a clear example of the failure of competition to spark after restructuring.[20] Measures in 1998 and 2001 have reintroduced active management (although relying considerably on self-regulation) in order to foster the competition that the restructuring up to 1995 could not produce.

Along with this more mature understanding has come caution. The benefits of liberalization have flowed less freely than many had hoped. In California, liberalization was a fiasco, for a number of reasons; the deregulation of prices applied only to the wholesale level, so when wholesale prices climbed, retailers were stuck in the middle and went bankrupt.[21] Supply was already tight because there had been next to no building of generation or transmission for years, but customers were not exposed to the high prices that should have resulted. In spite of the scarcity of capacity, the power exchange bought energy only, not capacity. The legal and institutional regime for the market was too complicated; a dozen or more agencies had a hand in running it. A number of other U.S. states steered away from plans to open up markets, but Pennsylvania, New Jersey, and Maryland shine as examples of successful liberalization.

Britain's Pool was the pioneer of large deregulated electricity markets. Over the years since its inception in 1989 a number of difficulties emerged. It was centralized and its rule making procedures lacked flexibility. Its pricing mechanisms failed to reflect falling costs and increased wholesale competition. The New Electricity Trading Arrangements (NETA) replaced the Pool in March 2001.[22] The new system provides for a balancing and settlement mechanism to be operated by the National Grid Company to provide system security, but it plays a less central role than the Pool played. Only about two percent of the electricity produced now goes through the balancing mechanism, the rest that is in wholesale trade is sold in bilateral trades or through voluntary power exchanges. The NETA system is being extended to Scotland.[23] When NETA came into operation,

---

[18] M. Bailey and C. Eaton, "An Update on American Electricity Markets: Still Coming together at the Seams?" IAEE Newsletter, First Quarter 2002, p. 14.

[19] Sioshansi, *supra* note 7; Sharma, *supra* note 15.   [20] Barton, *supra* note 9.

[21] F. P. Sioshansi, "California's Electricity Crisis Continues" IAEE Newsletter, First Quarter 2001, p. 10.

[22] *See* http://www.ofgem.gov.uk/neta/index_neta.htm.

[23] It will be the British Electricity Trading and Transmission Arrangements (BETTA), an acronym deplorably calculated to release a spate of weak puns.

critics argued that it would be a major barrier to the deployment of renewables.[24] It put particularly heavy penalties on generators that need to buy electricity at the last minute for balancing purposes. Gas and coal-fired plants could run part loaded, under full capacity, and ramp up at the last minute to avoid penalties, but renewables could not do the same. Wind power is particularly vulnerable to a system which puts a premium on predictability. There is some evidence that part loading of thermal power stations has increased under NETA, and carbon emissions from the electricity sector have risen, but it is not easy to say how much is due to NETA and how much is due to the use of coal in place of gas, the price of which has risen substantially.[25] Wholesale prices have fallen by forty percent since 1998, although much of the fall is attributable to low fuel prices and over capacity rather than to the trading arrangements. Combined heat and power producers, however, have suffered from this fall in wholesale prices at the same time that gas prices have risen.

8 ENERGY SUSTAINABILITY CHARACTERISTICS OF A MARKET SYSTEM

Because the whole orientation of a market system is different from the traditional system, with its monopoly and emphasis on construction, it is capable of bringing considerable benefits in energy sustainability. The first benefit that we may identify is the accurate pricing of energy. Energy sustainability requires the accurate pricing of energy, free of subsidies and incentives to overconsume, so that consumption patterns are affected by the real costs of production. Users have to pay the true costs of energy resources. Competing companies will attempt to sell electricity at a lower price than the others, but they will not sell for less than what it costs them to produce it. Their investment decisions will be governed by these market prices. This can be very different from the pricing and investment policies of a government agency, which may have only a hazy idea of the costs of its inputs, and may be more concerned with the place of electricity projects and prices in general economic management. Under a market system, prices will rise if they have been set artificially low. That will not be congenial politically, but it may be necessary for energy efficiency and desirable levels of investment in alternative energy technologies. However, a market system may send pricing and investment signals that are relatively short-term in their outlook. Long-term investments, such as in research and development for alternative technologies, may be given less significance, especially where fuel is readily available.

A market system where price signals are transmitted without distortion puts more focus on the price of inputs. The price of different fuels cannot be hidden, and companies either reflect the price of fuels in their sales prices or go broke. In a more opaque system, such as an integrated government department, there may be routine cross subsidy between fuel types and very loose linkage of fuel costs with sales prices. There may not even be the information available about the cost-effectiveness of different fuels. A competitive company is more likely to have that information on hand and use it quickly to maximize its net returns.

---

[24] United Kingdom Parliament, House of Commons Environmental Audit Committee, Fifth Report of Session 2001–02, *A Sustainable Energy Strategy? Renewables and the PIU Review*, 22 July 2002, http://www.parliament.the-stationery-office.co.uk/pa/cm200102/cmselect/cmenvaud/ 582/ (UK Select Committee, 2002) para. 68.

[25] UK Select Committee, 2002, para. 79.

Inputs include environmental inputs: the environmental burdens that different kinds of generation impose on the environment – air pollution, climate change gases, water pollution, the adverse effects of gas production or coal mining, their transport, and waste disposal, whether fly ash or nuclear waste. In economic terms, these environmental burdens are called "externalities." All too frequently they are imposed on the public at large or on assets not within the market system, such as clean air, clean water, and the global climate. If there is no disincentive for imposing those negative externalities, whether by regulation or by some form of pricing, then they can be expected to continue. One of the benefits of a market system is that if imposed, those disincentives or prices will naturally flow back through the system to consumers, and affect their decisions about the use of energy. In contrast, in a traditional system, it will require a further decision to raise prices to reflect the environmental price being paid.

A further characteristic of a market system is that government has less influence in investment decisions. We noted above the problem of governments committing themselves to dramatic development programs, abetted by a construction ethos in the department or agency. Companies in a market system are not invulnerable to government influence, but they are working with their shareholders' money rather than taxpayers' money. The market imposes a financial discipline of its own. Where government does exercise influence in a market system, it will generally need to do so overtly, through legal regulation or direction.

Compared with an integrated one company industry, a market system is decentralized, made up of smaller companies that may differ in their strengths and philosophies. There is a greater opportunity for innovative technologies to be tried out and for new business models to be adopted. Companies in competitive markets are more likely to be dominated by an ethos of pursuing market share and increasing efficiency of production than an ethos of construction. On the other hand, they may be less likely to engage in long-term research and development.

9 SUBSIDIES IN A MARKET SYSTEM

The subsidies common in traditional systems were described in Section 5. They often produce poor results for energy sustainability, in increasing demand artificially, or favoring fuels such as coal. Subsidies are often removed or rearranged when a market system is approached, mainly because they can no longer be implemented by ministerial or regulatory directives to the monopoly power company. Where the subsidies have reduced the price of electricity to consumers, price rises will accompany the introduction of a market system – which makes restructuring politically unpopular in such cases. But with the reduction of energy consumption that can be expected will occur a reduction in pollution and greenhouse gas emissions, although the size of the reductions is open to debate.[26] The removal of different subsidies on different fuels can lead to fuel substitution, which is positive if it leads to cleaner fuels, although it can result in the old fuels being diverted to the export market.

---

[26] Schneider and Saunders, *supra* note 10, predict smaller reductions than International Energy Agency, *Looking at Energy Subsidies: Getting the Prices Right*, World Energy Outlook Insights Series (Paris: OECD, 1999).

10 DESIGNING ELECTRICITY MARKETS TO ENCOURAGE ENERGY SUSTAINABILITY: ELASTICITY OF DEMAND

In its early growth years the electricity industry was driven by the assumption that demand would only ever increase, and that it had to build more and more capacity to supply it. The assumption was based in experience, of course, in a new industry. When prices were set by regulation or by board order, they were fixed for months or years, and users of electricity had no incentive to reduce demand when supply was low. The price did not change no matter what the scarcity and no matter what their behavior. But the electricity sector is mature now. Where there is an electricity market, the real difference is the effect of price. Scarcity of supply, because of low generation capacity, constrained transmission, or low hydro lakes, means that prices will rise. The chief point is that if that price signal is passed on to users then they are likely to respond by cutting back their levels of consumption. If there is any elasticity of demand, then the quantity of electricity responds to a change in price. This has major implications for energy conservation. As Sioshansi puts it:[27]

> One of the enormously positive lessons of restructured markets is that there is a new recognition of the significance of *elasticity* of demand. There is now a much better understanding that customer demand can – and should – play a more active role in balancing supply and demand in real time. Markets provide the incentives – through market price volatility – to influence demand when and where it is cost-effective to do so.

Consumers can take steps to avoid using electricity in response to price signals, for example in peak periods, so promoting energy efficiency and reducing environmental impacts.

Price signals do not always contribute to energy efficiency so readily. Demand for electricity is often not as elastic as it is for other commodities; a bank or a hospital cannot stop using electricity because the price has risen. Households might switch to wood stoves for heating, but they are likely to keep buying it for their lighting and television no matter what the price. Another factor is the presence in the power bills of end users of fixed lines charges that do not reflect the scarcity of energy. The fixed lines charges are not paid to the generator but to the owners of the high tension transmission grid and local distribution network. For small consumers, that is often about half of the final power bill. It reduces the strength of the energy price signal, and reduces the cost of wasting power. It is worse if the allocation of costs between lines and energy is skewed to keep lines charges higher and energy charges lower. Small retail consumers will generally not be as responsive as larger industrial and commercial consumers. For reasons such as these, price elasticity of demand is thought to have decreased in recent years in American states that have restructured their retail markets.[28] The record of markets on elasticity is therefore not as clear as it should be. However, price elasticity seems to increase with consumer experience in participation in a market system.

---

[27] Sioshansi (2002), *supra*, note 7 [footnote omitted].
[28] Peak Load Management Alliance, *Demand Response: Principles for Regulatory Guidance* (Jupiter, Florida: 2002), http://www.peaklma.com.

11 DEMAND-SIDE PARTICIPATION

Demand-side participation is the conservation activity that consumers of electricity can carry out in order to avoid using electricity. At its simplest, it involves reducing load – turning things off – but it can have more sophisticated forms. Industrial and commercial users can engage in load shifting – rescheduling energy intensive processes to different days or different times of day. Water heating, space heating, air conditioning, and water pumping can be rescheduled in this way to reduce load in the heaviest use times of the day or week. Other industries have less flexibility; for example, an aluminum smelter, one of the largest individual consumers of electricity, runs continuously, and can only shut down a potline at great expense. Prolonged water shortage in a hydro system could justify such a decision. The demand side also participates where consumers turn to their backup power systems, for example, diesel generators, to reduce consumption from the grid. (Fortunately from an environmental point of view that is a less common response than reducing use.) In a household, demand-side participation may include the installation of energy efficient water heating and space heating, better insulation, and more efficient appliances. It may also appear in changes in the use of electricity through the day, putting off laundry until after the peak demand period has passed. It may also involve fuel switching, such as installing a wood stove for space heating. Demand-side participation yields environmental benefits in reducing emissions and the need for the construction of new power plants and transmission lines. It also yields benefits in system reliability (especially during emergency conditions), market efficiency, risk management (reducing exposure to price spikes), customer choice in managing their power use, mitigation of the market power of generator companies, and – of course – lower costs.[29]

The traditional legal framework for the electricity industry gave few incentives for demand-side participation except for the overall price, and that was often a poor reflection of the true cost of energy supply. Prices did not vary to reflect the increased scarcity of energy during peak periods. Prices were average cost prices, where new higher cost sources were averaged in with the lower cost sources, hiding the higher marginal cost of those sources and discouraging conservation. However, in the 1980s, American public utilities began to offer substantial demand-side management programs at the instance of their regulatory agencies, in order to encourage customers to reduce their electricity consumption.[30] The programs would reduce the need to build expensive and contentious new power stations, and were in fact a cheaper investment for the utility than those power stations. The programs offered free energy audits and subsidized purchase of energy efficient appliances. Larger users could be offered tariffs that allowed supply to be interrupted at peak periods. When demand-side management programs engaged in such peak load pricing, in an attempt to impose the full marginal cost of supplying electricity in a peak period, they contributed to the movement toward market liberalization.

At first blush, a competitive system should allow consumers to participate actively in the market, demand participating equally with supply, and should give consumers

---

[29] Id., para. 2.0.
[30] S. F. Bertschi, "Integrated Resource Planning and Demand-Side Management in Electric Utility Regulation: Public Utility Panacea or a Waste of Energy?" (1994) 43 *Emory L. J.* 815; Brennan, *supra*, note 12, at 122.

incentives to manage their demand. (Because neither supply nor demand is managed centrally, the older term "demand-side management" has given place to "demand-side participation" or "demand response.") The consumer participates by selling callable demand reductions to the power supplier or some other party. Large consumers can participate in wholesale markets on their own account, and small ones can participate indirectly because their retailer suppliers have an incentive to offer them tariffs that encourage demand response. However these theoretical possibilities have met with frustration in practice. In the United States, the Peak Load Management Association identifies the difficulties in retail markets as "lack of information, lack of incentives, lack of enabling technologies, lack of functional wholesale market, lack of customer choice."[31] Progress under the demand-side management programs of the 1980s has fallen back, because the programs were not readily reconcilable with an open-market system. In wholesale markets, jurisdictional fragmentation is a problem. So is the presence of price caps imposed by regulators to prevent pice spikes; the caps reduce the incentives on participants to protect themselves against them with demand response programs. Regulators seem to require particularly clear proof of the benefits of demand response programs. In England and Wales, even large users could only participate indirectly in the Power Pool. NETA, which replaced it, was intended to improve the situation, but it has not led to much growth in demand-side participation.[32] There is some progress in providing fast reserves and standing reserves as contracted balancing services to National Grid Company, the system operator. It has been argued that the complexity of the new arrangements is a deterrent.[33] In New Zealand even large consumers have difficulty with the price and complexity of monitoring wholesale market price information, and do not see the benefits of participation coming through to them.

Ways round these obstacles are emerging so that demand-side participation can occur in competitive markets. The Peak Load Management Alliance identifies a number of actions that regulators can take to stimulate greater use of economic demand response resources.[34] Markets can be designed to foster participation by customers of all types and sizes. Demand response participants should be on an equal footing with generator companies – rare in current market governance arrangements. Demand response has historically been an afterthought. Restrictions on consumer use of backup generation should be reexamined, and price caps should be phased out. In Australia the Independent Pricing and Regulatory Tribunal of New South Wales has made recommendations to pursue the same objective, finding again that a major obstacle is the traditional supply-oriented culture that pays little more than lip service to demand response.[35]

Alongside these regulatory solutions is the innovative possibility of voluntary techniques of demand response. Electricity retailers can engage with their customers as active trading partners without having to involve them in the wholesale market. "Customers

---

[31] Peak Load Management Alliance, *supra* note 28, para. 4.2.
[32] Office of Gas and Electricity Markets, *The Review of the First Year of NETA: A Review Document* (July 2002) (Ofgem 2002) p. 114.
[33] R. Lane, "The England and Wales Mid-Course Correction – Is it Working?" International Bar Association Section on Energy and Resources Law Conference, Edinburgh, April 2002.
[34] Peak Load Management Alliance, *supra* note 28, paras. 7.0–8.0.
[35] Independent Pricing and Regulatory Tribunal, *Inquiry into the Role of Demand Management and Other Options in the Provision of Energy Services: Final Report* (Sydney, NSW: The Tribunal, October 2002, Review Report No. Rev02-2), http://www.ipart.gov.nsw.au.

indicate their specific action plans based on market conditions. The economic benefits to the customer show up either in cash or as credits on their future electric bill. Interval metering and verification of electrical loads round out the balance of the process."[36] The retailer can use a Web site to post prices in the time windows for which it seeks demand reductions, and customers can state their offers in reply. This voluntary system can work whether or not electricity is subject to full market competition. It gives consumers an opportunity to learn how to modify their demand in interaction with constraints upon supply. Emergencies such as power shortages at different times in California and in New Zealand have stimulated voluntary measures. The challenge is to make them more common in ordinary circumstances. In this and more generally, we see that competitive electricity markets present significant problems for demand-side participation, but it is worth reminding ourselves how much the traditional electricity industry structure limited any such participation. As new problems emerge when markets are liberalized, so do new solutions.

12 REAL-TIME PRICING

Demand-side management in an open market for electricity raises the question of the point in time when prices are fixed. The usual way that electricity markets work to determine prices is after each trading period – half an hour in many countries, one hour in North America. This is "ex-post" pricing. It is usual because electricity markets working with an auction bidding system "discover" prices from the bids and indications made for each such trading period by buyers and sellers. From this supply and demand information, the spot price can be determined from the highest price of supply required to meet the demand. Market operators are at pains to deny that they decide the prices, let alone fix them. The consequence, however, is that they cannot discover the price until the period is over. This normal practice of ex-post pricing has implications for the demand side, that is, the decisions of electricity users, and in turn for energy efficiency and conservation. It prevents users from knowing the actual price they are paying in time to make load management decisions that would in turn affect price through reduced demand.

Ex-ante pricing is technically difficult to calculate. It requires the market to run the auction interactions right down to the last minute before the half-hour trading period begins. In contrast ex-post pricing takes what happened in the auction interactions and the period itself, and runs it through the market software to determine the price. Real-time pricing seems to be viable as an alternative to produce more accurate and timely information. The New Zealand Electricity Market has proposed a rule change to allow a trial of real-time pricing in late October 2002.[37] It will allow production of six five-minute ex-post indicator prices in each half-hour trading period directly after the completion of each five-minute period, and production of an indicative final price on completion of each half-hour period that is a time weighted average. If it is successful, it will allow users to know the actual price they are paying in time to make load management decisions that will in turn affect price.

---

[36] "Introducing the Demand Exchange," http://www.demx.com.
[37] Ofgem 2002, *supra* note 32, p. 4.

13 VOLATILITY OF THE MARKET

Prices go up and down in all open electricity markets; that is their whole point, after all. But the volatility of spot market prices can be higher in some markets than others, and that can affect alternative energy suppliers. Market rules have a significant effect on volatility. In England and Wales the Pool spot market was very volatile because the great majority of power was traded on long-term contracts. Volatility threatens all traders, and discourages use of the spot market. It is beyond the variability that ordinary hedging instruments can manage. It is particularly serious for small generators, because they have less ability to manage risk, and it is particularly serious for emerging wind generator companies. Because of the nature of wind energy, it cannot be guaranteed round the clock; if the wind is not blowing, then there will be no production. A wind company that has made supply commitments will have to make up its supply from the spot market, and in a volatile market they may have to pay exorbitant prices. If it cannot offer dependable supply, then it will have to sell at a discount. NETA in England and Wales have reduced volatility through the balancing mechanism; price volatility as reflected in balancing mechanism prices has declined from around £70/MWh at the start of NETA to £17 a year later.[38]

14 SMALL COMPANIES

Energy efficiency and alternative energy are often brought to the market by small operators. Market arrangements can vary in the expense they impose on participants, especially on small ones. Prudential requirements, for example, are required for purchasers, to ensure that the pool or market institution will be able to collect payment, often in the form of a letter of credit from a bank. But if too much is required, it can be especially burdensome for small retail companies. NETA in England and Wales has imposed new costs in new computer systems and trading desks, in credit cover and estimating demand. However, small generators, mainly renewables, are producing as much energy as they were before NETA.[39] This was good news because after the first two months of NETA they had reported a forty-four percent reduction in output. Prices being obtained by such generators are comparable with other generators, or higher where they attract government subsidies. A change to NETA balancing rules to reduce gate closure from three and a half hours to one hour gives market participants more time to balance their positions and reduce the risk of charges for being out of balance. This helps wind generators with their difficulty in predicting their output. Consolidation services are seen as desirable to improve the negotiating position of small generators and to reduce their costs. The lack of work on them has been criticized.[40]

15 GOVERNANCE AND REGULATION

The rules of an electricity market affect these matters of demand-side participation, real-time pricing, volatility, and the place of small companies. We need therefore to consider how the rules are made in electricity market institutions. Barker,

---

[38] NZEM update July 2002.
[39] Ofgem 2002, *supra* note 32, p. 5.
[40] UK Select Committee (2002), *supra* note 25, para. 73.

Tenenbaum, and Woolf[41] identify four categories of power exchange governance in use internationally:

(i) A Multiclass Stakeholder Board. A club or representative model in which different classes of participant (generators, buyers, marketers, etc.) are represented and given a fair voice.
(ii) A Nonstakeholder Board of Independent Directors. Members elect board members who have no financial interest in any of the market participants, but who are chosen for their professional experience to act independently. Hybrid boards have some such independent directors and some stakeholder representatives.
(iii) A Singleclass Board. All decisions are controlled by one class, e.g., generators or incumbent vertically integrated utilities.
(iv) A Single For Profit Corporation Not Affiliated with Market Participants.

Single class boards are likely to be dominated by generators, and even multiclass stakeholder boards are likely to suffer the same fate. Generators, left to their own devices, are unlikely to promote demand-side management unless there are incentives to do so. They are more likely to pursue extra sales and market share instead. Energy sustainability therefore depends in important measure on governance, and the extent to which generator-dominated market structures can be steered to promote demand-side management and real-time pricing in particular.

In New Zealand, the government insisted that the governance system change, not least for energy sustainability reasons.[42] The New Zealand Electricity Market had been governed under what started as a multiclass stakeholder model, to use Barker, Tenenbaum, and Woolf's parlance, but which became dominated by generators as independent retailers disappeared from the industry, making it more of a single class board. The government was concerned that the Market may have lost its focus on efficiency, on the functions of parties other than generators, and on social policy issues such as equity and sustainability. It required the industry to change to a nonstakeholder board of independent directors, and for the board to bring under its control the work of the Metering and Reconciliation Information Agreement and the Multilateral Agreement on Common Quality Standards as well as that of the NZEM. The new Electricity Governance Board (EGB) must adopt and implement Guiding Principles laid down by the government, including explicit requirements for energy efficiency and environmental objectives. Rules set by the EGB must be consistent with government policies on climate change and energy efficiency. The government has taken statutory powers by amendments to the Electricity Act 1992 to impose such a board, or to impose requirements on an industry board, but it has refrained from doing so, and instead it has allowed industry to reform its self-governing mechanisms to comply with the government's policy. The EGB is to include membership with expertise in energy efficiency and renewables, and its performance is to be monitored as to energy sustainability by the Parliamentary Commissioner for the Environment.

[41] J. Barker Jr., B. Tenenbaum, and F. Woolf, "Regulation of Power Pools and System Operators: An International Comparison" (1997) 18 *Energy L J* 261.
[42] Ministry of Economic Development, *Power Package: Government Decisions on Electricity Industry Reform* (Wellington: The Ministry, Oct. 3, 2000, http://www.med.govt.nz/ers/electric/package2000/index.html).

This pressure has caused the New Zealand Electricity Market to act on real-time pricing, even though it has had the matter under consideration from its inception. As well as the measures described above, the government required the EGB to ensure that its rules promote demand-side participation, facilitate demand-side bidding and set up a real-time market so that the demand side can see and respond to actual prices immediately they change.

NETA in the United Kingdom shows how policies of encouraging renewables can be adversely affected by ostensibly technical market affairs such as gate closure, the price of imbalance from predicted output, and the relative expense of participation in the market for small companies. On governance's positive side, NETA allows rule changes to be made to improve conditions, whereas the previous arrangements made rule changes very difficult to obtain, especially if the established generators were opposed. Regulatory arrangements have come under attack in the UK for failing to keep the regulator Ofgem and the Department of Trade and Industry to formal duties to promote sustainable development.[43]

16 POLICY INSTRUMENTS GRAFTED ON TO A MARKET SYSTEM: SUBSIDIES AND SOCIAL POLICY

A market system does not accommodate social objectives like sustainability as easily as the traditional system, where a minister or utility board can, as we have seen, simply direct the power monopoly to build this kind of power station or that, or to alter its price tariff one way or another, with the costs being passed on to consumers or government. The experience of environmental and advocacy groups has been that in a competitive market nobody will look after such social concerns.[44] Where there were mechanisms to look after them under the old system, market liberalization has tended to dismantle them as part of deregulation.

Should they be reintroduced? One widely held view is that they should not; the invisible hand of the market should be allowed to look after such matters, and that it is an error to intervene in markets. Certainly, market forces can deliver on some such social concerns in the energy sustainability area, as we have seen. But it does not follow that all necessary progress on energy sustainability can be delivered that way. Rather, we must use alternative measures if the market will not deliver. Legislation and regulatory activity is eminently justified to pursue social justice or environmental sustainability, and the free operation of market forces must be subordinate to those objectives.[45] Environmentally benign technologies require long-term investment and bankable contracts to cover their development. Left alone, liberalized energy markets do not readily support such long-term contracts, because they are oriented to shorter investment horizons. Some sustainability policy measures therefore represent compulsory long-term investments in new technologies.[46]

---

[43] UK Select Committee (2002), *supra* note 25, paras. 71, 82.

[44] Sioshansi (2002), *supra* note 7, p. 24–5.

[45] Generally on this theme, see C. Sunstein, *After the Rights Revolution: Reconceiving the Regulatory State* (Cambridge, Mass.: Harvard University Press, 1990); C. Sunstein, *Free Markets and Social Justice* (New York: Oxford University Press, 1997).

[46] UK Select Committee (2002), *supra* note 25, para. 76.

If indeed policy measures are to be introduced to promote sustainability, we cannot assume that the old mechanisms will work in the new competitive market. Legislative or regulatory mechanisms must be attuned to the facts of market competition, and must change market behavior, but must not introduce unwanted distortions and side effects into the working of the market. We need also to be aware of the importance of market design, market governance, and contractual arrangements as well as conventional regulation. On the positive side, where measures for sustainability are introduced into an electricity market system, their costs and benefits can be measured better than under a traditional system. This is because pricing under the traditional system is opaque and often masks the true costs and benefits of the nonmarket measure.

17 SMALL INTERVENTIONS IN A MARKET SYSTEM

New Zealand saw a number of small interventions or adjustments of a market system introduced in 2001 for energy sustainability purposes.[47] It was decided to require retailers to offer at least one tariff to domestic consumers with a fixed charge of no more than ten percent of the bill of the average domestic consumer (8,000 kWh a year). Renewable energy was given a boost by allowing distribution companies to employ it if they want to get back into electricity generation, from which they were banned by the Electricity Industry Reform Act 1998. Those companies were also given some latitude (up to two percent of a network's load or five MW, whichever is greater) to own generation if it is embedded or distributed generation connected to the local network rather than the national grid, thereby reducing transmission demand and line losses. Possible misuse of hydro resources also received attention. A mechanism ensures that hydro generation companies will have to provide more information about the amount of water they spill from hydroelectric storage dams without using it to generate electricity. This will disclose whether they are "gaming" the market and withholding hydro generation in order to lift market prices, but causing unnecessary hydro spill and increased consumption of natural gas.

Similar interventions or adjustments of a market system for energy sustainability purposes are administered in the United Kingdom, by the regulator, the Office of Gas and Electricity Markets (Ofgem). The first is the energy efficiency commitment which requires all major gas and electricity suppliers to improve the energy efficiency of customers' homes with better insulation, better plant, and equipment. Collectively it will entail expenditure of approximately £500 million over three years, with a view to saving 62TWh over the next three years. It is targeted particularly at disadvantaged customers. The second, the climate change levy exemption for renewables, exempts renewable electricity from the levy payable on sales of electricity to the business and public sectors. It therefore helps renewable producers to keep their prices competitive. The third element, the renewables obligation, is described in Section 18 in relation to green certificates. The

---

[47] Ministry of Economic Development (2000), supra note 42. Powers were taken by amendment of the Electricity Act 1992, but the policies are mostly being implemented by industry institutions in liaison with government. For background see Parliamentary Commissioner for the Environment, *Getting More for Less: A Review of Progress on Energy Efficiency and Renewable Energy Initiatives in New Zealand* (Wellington, 2000); D. Caygill, S. Wakefield, and S. Kelly, *Ministerial Inquiry into the Electricity Industry* (Wellington: 12 June 2000). Discussed by B. J. Barton, "Governance in the Electricity Industry" (2000) *NZLJ* 300; B. J. Barton, "Responsive Regulation in the Electricity Industry" (2000) *NZLJ* 347.

British government's target is for ten percent of electricity sales to come from renewables by 2010, subject to the costs being acceptable to the consumer, and for 10,000 MW combined heat and power (CHP) capacity by then.[48]

18 GREEN CERTIFICATES

Green certificates are receiving a great deal of attention in Europe as an alternative to old systems for subsidizing renewable energy.[49] The attention has been stimulated by a European Union Directive promoting electricity produced from renewable energy sources.[50] The Directive requires member states to set national indicative targets for the consumption of renewable electricity, and to establish a system of certification of renewable energy electricity. In a green certificate scheme, green certificates are issued to the generator of renewable environmentally friendly electricity (let us say green electricity) for every megawatt-hour of energy it produces. The demand for certificates can be structured in different ways. Certificates can be voluntary, so that holding them is a marketing advantage that allows an electricity retailer company to put itself forward as environmentally friendly. Firms buying from the retailer can in turn advertise that their inputs are environmentally friendly as to energy. In many schemes, however, certificates will be compulsory. Consumers must hold certificates to cover a quota or legislated percentage of their consumption in each accounting period. (Domestic consumers can be covered through their retailer.) This is envisaged in Denmark. In Italy, an alternative is envisaged, that a purchase obligation is imposed on the production side.[51] In the compulsory schemes, the quota or purchase obligation is necessarily imposed as a matter of public law.

The green certificates are tradeable, so that a market in them forms. Consumers of electricity (or others on whom a purchase obligation is imposed) purchase enough certificates to cover a percentage of their electricity consumption. There are two markets, one for the physical supply of electricity, and another for green certificates. Green certificates represent a splitting off of the benefits of ownership of renewable energy production from the physical supply of energy. They get around the fact that one cannot tell which part of a supply of electrical energy is from a green source and which is not. The renewable energy producer therefore adds the revenue from the sale of certificates to that from the sale of electricity, and can trade profitably when otherwise it could not. Green certificates therefore assist the uptake of renewables. The electricity market continues separately, and continues to impose market incentives and discipline on all participants, on purchasers, conventional producers, and renewable producers alike.

In the United Kingdom, green certificates take the form of "renewable obligation certificates." Statutory power has been taken for a scheme which began in April 2002 and obliges electricity sellers to obtain at least 3.0 percent of their electricity from

---

[48] Government Response to Ofgem's Reports "The New Electricity Trading Arrangements – Review of the First Three Months" and "Report to the DTI on the Review of the Initial Impact of NETA on Smaller Generators" of August 31, 2001 (London: Dept. of Trade and Industry, November 1, 2001).

[49] S. Grenaa Jensen, "Green Certificates and Emission Permits in the Context of a Liberalised Electricity Market," IAEE Newsletter, 1st quarter 2002, p. 24; B-O. Gram Mortensen, "Green Certificates in a Danish and EU Context," unpublished staff seminar, University of Waikato, Hamilton, New Zealand, 2002.

[50] Directive 2001/77/EC, September 27, 2001.

[51] Grenaa Jensen, *supra* note 49.

renewable generators in 2002–3, a figure which will rise to 10.4 percent in 2010–11.[52] Renewables generators apply to the regulator (the Office of Gas and Electricity Markets) for accreditation, and are issued one renewable obligation certificate per megawatt hour (MWh) generated. The certificates can be sold along with the electricity generated, or separately. Electricity sellers can meet their obligation to buy three percent renewable by buying certificates, or by paying a buy out price of £30/ MWh for the shortfall. Biomass is eligible, but not incineration of mixed waste, and the eligibility of large hydro and co-firing with fossil fuels is restricted.

In Denmark, legislation to establish green certificates (or Renewable Energy Certificates) has been enacted, but is not yet in force. It is uncertain whether changing government policy will see it come into force. However, there is strong interest from other countries in northern Europe, notably Sweden and the Netherlands. There are significant difficulties to be solved in introducing such a new system. Establishing a market for certificates will be no easier than establishing one for electricity. The size of the market could be a difficulty, if it is too small to sustain liquidity and active trading. Transaction costs will need to be contained. Stranded costs will need to be dealt with. Cross border trade will be complicated, even in the European Union, where one country may still be on an old subsidy system and the other on a new green certificate system. Scope and definitional questions need to be answered, for example, are new large-scale hydro dams included as green energy?

The emerging shape of the green certificate scheme indicates that its incentive system can be kept separate from the electricity market itself.[53] That may be the best arrangement for all such energy sustainability systems. In other cases the separation may involve clear arrangements for the proper pricing of inputs, so that externalities are captured, internalized, and properly reflected in the generator's costs. The price of thermal generation, for example, should reflect the price that society, or more properly the international community, considers should be paid for the effect of carbon dioxide on the global commons of the atmosphere. Carbon credits are likely to evolve into an international market that is separate from the electricity market.[54] In Denmark, the system of tradeable CO_2 emissions permits is expected to coexist not only with the electricity market but also with the green certificates market.[55] Arguably, at least, the price of hydro generation should include a figure for the value of the water, although putting a price on it is difficult. The same goes for geothermal generation, recognizing that in some cases a geothermal system is not infinitely renewable. The great contribution that an electricity market can make is to ensure that those costs are passed through promptly and accurately to consumers. A traditional system masks these costs.

---

[52] Renewables Obligation Order 2002 (2002 No. 914) made under the Electricity Act 1989 as amended by the Utilities Act 2000. The renewable obligation replaces the non-fossil fuel obligation which was introduced with the reforms of the UK electricity sector in 1988.

[53] They could be merged; the system operator or market rules could give priority in dispatch to verified issuers of green certificates, ensuring that they can run whenever they are able. But there seems to be greater risk of unpredictable market distortion.

[54] P. D. Cameron and D. Zillman (eds.), *Kyoto: From Principles to Practice* (The Hague: Kluwer Law International, 2001).

[55] Grenaa Jensen, *supra* note 49.

19 CONCLUSION

While the record is mixed, a market approach in electricity can make a contribution to energy sustainability. A market system's pressure for financial efficiency can often further energy efficiency and conservation. It prevents many of the perversities that seem to be inevitable in the traditional system, such as a tendency toward capital development, a resistance to new players and new technology, failure to connect costs with prices, and failure to signal explicitly the value of energy resources. The introduction of markets is generally accompanied by the removal of nonsustainable subsidies such as subsidies for the coal industry or for cheap electricity for farmers. However, market systems are not simple, and their design can include hurdles, preferences, and subsidies, whether intended or unintended. They call for careful scrutiny to ensure that they are really providing opportunities for the nonconventional technologies, for the renewables, for the small-sized enterprises, and for the new entrants.

PART SIX

FINANCING FOR
SUSTAINABLE ENERGY

27 Financing Clean Energy for Development

Alan S. Miller*

1 INTRODUCTION

Finance is a critical element in the range of strategies designed to make clean energy available for development. For this to occur, renewable energy technologies (RETs) must be available at competitive prices. Further, policy environments must allow clean energy to compete on fair terms recognizing, if possible, the societal and environmental benefits of clean energy. At a minimum, policies should avoid approving subsidies to more established, more pollution intensive alternatives. Human resources and institutions also have important roles to play in establishing effective private enterprises and distribution channels.

There are numerous sources of complexity in analyzing the availability of financing for clean energy investments. Because clean energy services tend to be relatively capital intensive, substituting capital for fuel, the cost and availability of capital is often a significant issue in economic comparisons with more conventional alternatives. Until fully proven over time, new technologies, including those for clean energy, also have a risk premium that adds to financing costs. Finally, in allocating capital, commercial enterprises often demand higher rates of return for energy investments than for investments that relate to their core business objectives.

As the energy sector is increasingly being privatized, the availability of financing has become an indicator of overall market maturity and investor confidence. At the same time, the limitations of overreliance on private financing for the provision of energy services have also become increasingly apparent, including the continued need for public subsidies to support poverty alleviation and the highly volatile character of much commercial investment. In the short to medium term, public support from national and bilateral sources will continue to be necessary to overcome these barriers. The resources available for such purposes will also have to increase if clean energy is to be provided in a manner consistent with meeting development goals.

2 THE AVAILABILITY OF FINANCING: ENERGY POLICY AND THE ORGANIZATION OF ENERGY SERVICES AND INSTITUTIONS

The availability of financing is, as with all aspects of the energy equation, a function of several variables, including government policies and regulations. While in global terms

---

* Global Environment Facility Coordinator and Team Leader, Climate Change, Environmental Finance Group, International Finance Corporation; previously Team Leader, Climate Change and Ozone, GEF. The views expressed are those of the author and are not endorsed by the IFC or GEF.

financial flows are largely a function of perceived risks and competition for investor dollars, markets for clean energy services in developing countries are constrained by the added barriers imposed in relation to new technologies in general. Small enterprises are often unable to borrow at reasonable rates. Low income consumers also have limited access to capital and often must pay very high rates of interest for short-term loans. This is a significant obstacle to the substitution of capital for fuel costs spread over time, as required for clean energy projects. To make clean energy available to the poor, microcredit must be extended much more widely, even when equivalent amounts are being spent on lower quality fuels.

The nonavailability of capital is often identified as a barrier to the development of markets for renewable energy systems which have high capital costs. In reality, financing is less often the major barrier to, or conversely the primary means of, promoting clean energy alternatives. In other words, if other necessary factors are in order, financing will generally be made available, leaving aside the case of low income populations which raise different challenges. For example, key barriers to the development of markets for wind energy systems typically relate to difficulties in establishing contracting arrangements with utility purchasers (themselves financially credible) for sufficient time periods at reasonable rates (tariffs). However, if the policy environment addresses these matters, technical performance is now sufficiently demonstrated such that in most regions financing could be secured from commercial sources on fair terms.

Less obviously, there is a financial bias in favor of large energy suppliers with access to capital and, frequently, the political influence to obtain a supportive policy environment. To attract financing on comparable terms, small-scale, dispersed technologies must be aggregated. The establishment of energy service companies (enterprises that identify and implement energy efficiency improvements in return for a share of the savings) are a partial response to the current need to find new institutions able to aggregate investments and reduce capital costs.

As regulated monopolies, utilities were becoming useful institutions for collecting resources for research and investments in energy efficiency in the 1980s. However, deregulation led to a rapid decline in such expenditures in the 1990s as utilities sought to minimize costs unrelated to their short-term profitability.[1]

3 THE SCALE AND SOURCE OF ENERGY FINANCE IN DEVELOPING COUNTRIES[2]

3.1 Capital Requirements

One of the most significant characteristics of a modern energy infrastructure is its capital intensity. Power plants, oil refineries, and transmission systems are among the most capital intensive projects in any economy. The cost of renewable energy systems is almost entirely made up of capital costs as, once operational, such systems have no fuel costs (with the exception of biomass systems) and minimal maintenance costs. Energy efficiency investments also typically require the payment of some modest,

---

[1] The same trend was responsible for a drop in expenditures on tree trimming and other measures necessary to maintain service during storms, leading to more frequent and longer outages.

[2] This section is updated from A. Miller, "Energy, Climate Change, and Sustainable Development," in M. Harris (ed.), *Energy Market Restructuring and the Environment*, U. Press (2002) at 247–70.

initially higher, capital cost in return for reduced operating (fuel) costs over time. The cost and availability of capital is, therefore, critical to making clean energy services available for development.

The terms and availability of financing are particularly important for developing countries that have limited credit and a wide range of investment needs. There are few estimates of capital requirements specifically for clean energy systems for developing countries, although such studies have been done at varying levels of detail for the United States and other industrialized countries.[3] These analyses recognize that demand and supply-side investments are fungible and, accordingly, require detailed modeling to allow for an assessment of the lowest cost societal options over time.

However, by any measure, it is evident that capital requirements for energy-related investments will be very large. In the recently published *World Energy Investment Outlook*, the International Energy Agency (IEA) estimates that between 2001 and 2030, total required investment in global energy infrastructure will be in the order of US$16 trillion, approximately half of which will be needed in developing countries.[4] This aggregate figure masks significant regional differences and even greater variations in needs between countries and regions, relative to GNP and capital availability. For instance, Russia's investment requirement is in the order of five percent of GNP, in Africa the requirement is approximately four percent, while within the much larger and more established economies of the OECD the burden is much less. Accordingly, the challenge is not so much the total investment amount, but rather, matching the investment climate and commercial realities with specific resources and those countries with unmet demand.

From a global perspective, these percentages are consistent with historic norms and while they are relatively large, are not infeasible. However, the context for raising these funds is changing. One difference is the sizeable increase in the share of energy-related capital requirements for developing countries which, according to a set of scenarios prepared jointly by two leading international sources of energy analysis,[5] is set to rise from around twenty-five to thirty percent in recent years to forty-two to forty-eight percent in 2020.

3.2 Bilateral Aid Flows

Since 1990, bilateral aid has been generally stagnant while private sources of investment have risen enormously, only to drop again in recent years (although remaining significantly above the levels of donor aid). Despite an agreed target at the Rio

---

[3] The Intergovernmental Panel on Climate Change (IPCC), an international consensus based review of climate change science and policy, summarizes a range of studies on the potential for low cost or cost saving reductions in greenhouse gas emissions in developing, as well as in industrialized, countries. *See* B. Metz, O. Davidson, R. Swart, and J. Pan, *Climate Change 2001: Mitigation*, Cambridge University Press (Cambridge, UK, 2001). These studies consistently show large technical possibilities for low cost reductions relative to business-as-usual projections, for example, negative costs to achieve an 80% reduction from the Brazilian baseline and a 36% reduction for India from the 2025 baseline. J. Hourcade and P. Shukla, "Global, Regional, and National Costs and Ancillary Benefits of Mitigation," *id.* at 511. *See also* various country studies published by the Pew Center on Climate Change, available at http://www.pewclimatecenter.org.

[4] IEA, *World Energy Investment Outlook*, OECD/IEA (Paris, 2003).

[5] The International Institute for Applied Systems Analysis (IIASA) and the World Energy Council.

Conference[6] to increase foreign aid to 0.7 percent of GNP, worldwide (nonmilitary) aid flows from industrialized to developing countries peaked at US$69 billion in 1991[7] but thereafter declined by approximately a third of this amount in real (inflation adjusted) terms.[8] In 1997, U.S. bilateral aid was only 0.08 percent of GNP, amounting to about US$7 billion compared with US$14 billion given by the largest donor, Japan.[9] More recently, U.S. aid has increased while aid from Japan has declined, restoring the position of the United States as the largest donor.

The availability of bilateral aid related to energy and the environment is difficult to distinguish from donor statistics, but one study suggests that total aid related to global environmental objectives – including biodiversity and other nonenergy objectives – is roughly twice the amount allocated to the Global Environment Facility (GEF).[10]

3.3 The Global Environment Facility

The Global Environment Facility (GEF) was initiated in 1991 as a pilot program in the World Bank with a budget of US$1 billion for three years and a mandate to provide finance to cover the added costs incurred by developing countries in achieving global environmental benefits.[11] The GEF serves as the financial mechanism for several environmental agreements, including the UN Framework Convention on Climate Change.[12] In 1994, the GEF was restructured by international agreement, with an independent thirty-two country Council for Governance, and a CEO and Secretariat for managerial oversight. Project development and implementation was to be managed through the World Bank, UN agencies, and four regional development banks. Since then, donors have pledged a total of approximately US$6.5 billion with an average of thirty-five to forty percent of these funds allocated for clean energy projects.[13] The role and outcome of GEF projects will be discussed in greater detail in Section 6.

3.4 Private Investment Flows

A key factor in any analysis of financing requirements for clean energy is the growing importance of private investment in developing countries. In contrast with aid flows, private investment has increased dramatically over the past decade. In 1990, private investment in developing countries constituted approximately half of the financial flows from North to South.[14] By 1998, private capital flows exceeded US$220 billion and

---

[6] *See* Rio Declaration on the Environment & Development, UN General Assembly, A/CONF.151/26 (Vol. I) (August 12, 1992).

[7] World Bank, *Assessing Aid: What Works, What Doesn't, and Why?* (1998) at 7. Note that the 1991 value of the dollar is expressed here in terms of its value in 1995 to account for changes in the value of the dollar.

[8] UN Development Program, *Human Development Report* (1999) at 30–31.

[9] *Supra* note 7, at 7.

[10] R. Clemencon, *Financing Protection of the Global Commons*, GEF (Washington, D.C., 2000). General information about GEF policies, procedures, and eligibility requirements is available at www.thegef.org.

[11] *See* A. Miller, "The Global Environmental Facility and the Search for Strategies to Finance Sustainable Development" (2000) *Vermont Law Review* 1229–44.

[12] (May 9, 1992), available at http://www.unfccc.int/resource/docs/convkp/conveng.pdf.

[13] Based on annual reports and information available at the GEF Web site, approximately US$1.4 billion has been committed to about 140 clean energy projects with a total value in excess of US$4.5 billion in more than 75 countries.

[14] *Supra* note 7, at 7–8.

constituted almost ninety percent of the funds entering developing countries.[15] Annual investment in the power sector in developing countries grew from around US$1 billion in 1990 to US$49 billion in 1997, before falling to approximately US$11 billion in 2001.[16] Over the same period, total private investment in infrastructure projects (including telecoms and water as well as power and gas) was an impressive US$754 billion.

Private investments, however, tend to be more volatile than aid and also tend to be focused on the most commercially promising environments. The rapid drop in private flows in recent years is generally attributed to several factors.[17] First, the fact that privatization transactions resulted in large but "one-off" investments, particularly in Brazil. Second, there was a decline in the investment environment as a result of fiscal problems in several large countries in Asia and South America. Third, recently declining equity markets in industrial countries and corporate governance problems affecting major energy companies and international investors have also resulted in reduced investment.

The flow of private investment dollars has also tended to be limited to a handful of countries.[18] More than eighty percent of such funds have been directed to approximately twenty countries and, within these countries, a relatively small percentage of the population often receives the vast majority of resulting financial benefits.[19] More than 100 countries receive less than US$100 million per year and their share has further declined in recent years.[20] The measure of financial flows can also be misleading as, with growth, more resources shift to mergers and acquisitions. Moreover, success in exports is no guarantee of either economic growth or an improved quality of life. For instance, countries in sub-Saharan Africa maintain a high export-to-GNP ratio due to an emphasis on the export of primary commodities, but nonetheless have low growth economies.

Nevertheless, the need to attract and retain private investment is fundamental. It is the only sustainable source of financing and the only source commensurate with investment needs where market conditions exist.

---

[15] H. French, *Vanishing Borders: Protecting the Planet in an Age of Globalization* (2000) at 6. Foreign investment in developing countries encompasses several very different types of financial transactions. The most important categories include the purchase of previously publicly owned assets like utilities; purchase of privately held companies or assets; new business ventures; loans to domestic enterprises; and the purchase of securities issued by local firms. *See* World Bank, *Entering the 21st Century*, World Development Report 1999/2000 (1999) at 6–7; S. Schmidheiny and B. Gentry, "Privately Financed Sustainable Development," in M. Chertow and D. Esty (eds.), *Thinking Ecologically* (1997) at 118–20. As much as 40% of global foreign direct investment goes to developing countries or countries with economies in transition, although this figure varies from year to year.

[16] World Bank, *Private Participation in Infrastructure: Trends in Developing Countries in 1990–2001*, World Bank (Washington, D.C., 2003). The report identifies four types of private participation in infrastructure projects: management and lease contracts; concessions; greenfield projects; and divestitures. *See also* estimates in R. Williams, "Addressing Challenges to Sustainable Development with Innovative Energy Technologies in a Competitive Electric Industry," (2001) v (2) *Energy for Sustainable Development*, 48–73.

[17] World Bank, *Private Participation in Infrastructure: Trends in Developing Countries in 1990–2001*, World Bank (Washington, D.C., 2003).

[18] UNDP, *Human Development Report* (1999) at 30–31; World Bank, *Global Development Finance* (1999) at 47–80.

[19] The inequity is less when investment is measured as a percentage of economic activity and in the last few years the distribution of investment dollars has increased with a greater tolerance of risk among investors, *supra* note 11, at 292.

[20] D. Mishra, A. Mody, and A. Murshid, "Private Capital Flows and Growth," (2001) 38(2) *Finance and Development* 2, available at http://www.imf.org/external/pubs/ft/fandd/2001/06/mishra.htm.

A recent World Bank survey found substantial investor interest in the power sector in developing countries despite past problems.[21] Four factors were perceived as being of greatest importance: first, tariff and collection policies that ensure adequate cash flow; second, the stability and enforceability of laws and contracts; third, administrative efficiency and processing time; and finally, minimal government interference. As the survey notes, "the results indicate a 'back to basics' approach in the international investor community." Moreover, the survey indicated that investors took for granted several underlying assumptions about the rule of law that too often proved invalid. Accordingly, the survey concluded that in order to reassure investors and attract or retain their interest, governments needed to focus attention on these four basic priorities.

4 THE ROLE OF THE WORLD BANK AND OTHER INTERNATIONAL FINANCIAL INSTITUTIONS

4.1 The World Bank

Prior to the early 1990s, the World Bank and other international financial institutions (IFIs) dedicated approximately twenty-five percent of their resources to the energy sector.[22] This percentage has declined to approximately ten percent in the case of the World Bank, from a figure of approximately US$3.7 billion in 1990 to approximately US$1.4 billion in 2001. This trend reflected several broader influences on the energy sector. One was the emphasis placed on the liberalization and privatization of infrastructure services as an alternative to traditional state owned monopolies, previously the focus of substantial support. This policy change to some extent mirrored the changes taking place in industrialized countries, where competition and regulatory reform had become powerful forces. An additional rationale for promoting such reforms in developing countries was that state owned enterprises in many developing countries were often poorly managed and financially weak or insolvent, as tariffs were kept below cost recovery in order to attract support from particular constituencies.

An example of the World Bank's efforts to achieve such policy reform was in Côte d'Ivoire, where in the mid-1990s the government agreed to transfer the management of electricity services to a private operator. The World Bank had applied considerable pressure through conditions attached to the release of an energy sector loan and also provided technical assistance as the basis for this change in management of the electricity utility. Similar World Bank–led reforms have been implemented in many other countries, particularly in Central America, parts of South America, and Eastern Europe.[23]

---

[21] R. Lamech and K. Saeed, "What International Investors Look For When Investing in Developing Countries, Results from a Survey of International Investors in the Power Sector," Energy and Mining Sector Board *Discussion Paper* No. 6 (May 2003).

[22] Energy Sector Management Assistance Program, "Economic Development, Climate Change, and Energy Security," Energy and Mining Sector Board, World Bank (2002).

[23] R. Dominguez, F. Manibog, and S. Wegner, "Power for Development: A Review of the World Bank Group's Experience with Private Participation in the Electricity Sector," World Bank Operations Evaluation Dept. (2003). The social consequences and governance issues created by these reforms proved challenging. The World Bank evaluation report found the portfolio of these projects "half-successful in pursuing the objectives of its reform agenda," *id.*, at 14. IFC projects, which tended to be in higher income countries, tended to be more successful. The challenges associated with the privatization of the power sector in Georgia is the subject of a recent documentary, "Power Trip," available at http://www.powertripthemovie.com.

In May 2001, the World Bank presented a revised strategy paper to its Executive Directors, the Energy Program for Poverty Reduction, Sustainability, and Selectivity. The paper emphasizes the linkages between energy and poverty reduction. In support of this strategy, the energy practice of the World Bank has set general quantitative targets for increasing access to, improving the finances of, and restructuring state owned energy utilities. Under these targets, by 2010:

- The percentage of households in developing countries with access to electricity must increase from sixty-five to seventy-five percent, the average carbon dioxide emission intensity of energy production must decline from 2.9 tons of oil equivalent (toe) to 2.75 toe and the average energy consumption per unit of GNP must decline from 0.27 toe per thousand dollars of output to 0.24 toe;
- The percentage of developing countries where the power industry is a burden on the government budget must decline from sixty-six to fifty percent;
- The percentage of developing countries where private ownership and financing are dominant in the energy sector must increase from twenty-five to forty percent and the percentage of countries where industrial consumers have a choice of supplier must increase from fifteen to forty percent; and
- The percentage of developing countries where utilities are regulated in a manner consistent with good economic principles must increase from thirty-five to fifty percent.

4.2 Other International Financial Institutions

The decline in public sector lending through the Bank was partially offset by an increase in private sector lending through the International Finance Corporation (IFC) and the Multilateral Investment Guarantee Agency (MIGA). In the 1990s, IFC approved fifty-seven projects with costs of US$14.4 billion compared with seven projects with costs of less than US$1 billion in the previous thirty years. IFC loans, like those of export credit agencies, are sometimes more important as an assurance to other investors that projects have an independent source of capital. This is particularly true with respect to oil and gas projects, which often have minimal economic risk but may be located in countries or regions that are politically unstable. The pending loan for a pipeline to export oil from the Caspian Sea is a recent example. The project is supported by BP but has been severely criticized by the World Wildlife Fund for Nature as a "potential ecological and social disaster." MIGA, which provides insurance against political risks, has seen a rapid rise in power sector related guarantees since it first provided such a guarantee in 1994. Approximately twenty percent of its liabilities are for seventy-two guarantees for thirty-nine electric power projects in twenty-five countries.

5 CONCESSIONAL FINANCING

With limited exceptions (primarily geothermal and small hydro projects), financing for clean energy in developing countries is still dependent on concessional financing. This is because efficient energy technologies and RETs are still rarely perceived as the "least cost, highest value" alternative even when they are marginally competitive, based on industrialized country experience. This may be due to a lack of practical experience, the absence of local financing, institutional biases (particularly among utilities), a lack of consumer awareness or the costs associated with introducing and servicing new products in countries that lack well-established infrastructure. The end result continues to be that some noncommercial financing is typically needed to facilitate clean energy lending in developing countries.

The World Bank renewable energy portfolio highlights the potential for using donor funds to leverage much greater investment.[24] As of mid-2001, the World Bank had twenty-six active investment projects for RETs with a total investment value of approximately US$4 billion. This amount reflected approximately US$1.4 billion in World Bank financing and US$123 million in GEF funds, the latter based on the most generous terms. The IFC had US$162 million in investments on its own account, plus US$68 million in syndicated loans and US$70 million in GEF funding, while MIGA had eleven contracts for small hydro and geothermal projects.

The largest source of funds for clean energy projects on concessional terms is the GEF. In the current four-year replenishment, donors have pledged a total of US$3 billion, of which approximately US$1.1 billion (that is, US$250 to US$300m/yr) is earmarked for climate change projects.[25] In a little more than a decade since its inception as a pilot program in the World Bank, the GEF has made financial commitments to a diverse range of clean energy projects, justifying such investments on the basis of their potential to reduce greenhouse gas emissions, in support of the aims of the UN Framework Convention on Climate Change.

The GEF approach to energy projects was originally outlined in an operational strategy and three operational programs.[26] These programs allowed for government subsidies in order to reduce the cost of RETs on the basis of first, commitments to avoid substantial greenhouse gas emissions and commitments to encourage commercial competitiveness with increases in scale (consistent with the level of GEF resources); and second, commitments to introduce measures to remove barriers to commercially competitive but underutilized efficient energy technologies and RETs. The former rationale has been applied to solar thermal power plants, biomass gasification, and grid connected photovoltaics; the latter has been used to justify low interest financing, appliance labeling and energy service companies as strategies to promote energy efficiency, as well as a range of demonstrations, financing for solar businesses, microcredit, utility reforms and other strategies for promoting solar home systems, wind energy, and to a lesser extent, biogas, solar water heating, and improved cookstoves.[27]

6 GEF FUNDING OF CLEAN ENERGY PROJECTS

6.1 Examples of GEF Funded Clean Energy Projects

Set out below are some examples of GEF funded clean energy projects in developing countries.

---

[24] ESMAP, "Economic Development," at 12.
[25] Proposed GEF financial commitments for the next four fiscal years are updated annually in the Corporate Business Plan, available at www.thegef.org.
[26] Both are available at the GEF Web site, http://www.thegef.org.
[27] Project documents and numerous evaluation reports are available at the GEF Web site www.thegef.org; see also E. Martinot, A. Chaurey, D. Lew, J. R. Moreira, and M. Wamukonya, "Renewable energy markets in developing countries" (2002) 27 *Annual Review of Energy and the Environment* 309–48.

Rural Electrification and Renewable Energy Development in Bangladesh

A World Bank project in Bangladesh, "Rural Electrification and Renewable Energy Development," offers an example of the integration of RETs and capacity building efforts. This project promotes solar energy in rural areas, implemented by rural electricity cooperatives, community based organizations, NGOs, microfinance institutions, and the private sector. The project supports:

a) increasing awareness of solar home systems (SHS) among consumers and providers;
b) building technical and management capacity to design, implement, and evaluate SHS programs;
c) providing technical and business development support to implementing institutions;
d) introducing standards and programs for testing and certification; and
e) financing grants to buy-down capital costs and increase affordability of SHS.

The project is expected to result in the installation of 65,000 solar systems, displacing fossil fuels and traditional biomass energy in rural areas. The project budget is US$38.6 million with US$8.2 million funded by GEF.

The Technology Transfer Network

The Technology Transfer Network (TTN) project, a UNEP project included in the May 2003 work program, aims to increase the quality and flow of environmentally sound private sector investments in developing countries and countries with economies in transition. The project's approach is based on strengthening and expanding a network of national agencies (the "TTN Local Desks") to seek out and facilitate environmentally beneficial private investments by providing access to information on technology and financing to business groups, potential investors and other interested parties. A central element of the project's approach is to link needs and opportunities at national and regional levels to the information and technical assistance available at the global level. The GEF contribution is US$2 million and builds on an earlier pilot project.

Biomass Power Generation Projects

In two projects focused on biomass power generation, the GEF has laid the groundwork for the commercialization of power production from bagasse and other agricultural resources in Brazil. In the course of the two projects, technology has been developed to harvest and use locally abundant sugar cane wastes in a more efficient and environmentally beneficial manner. A UNDP project, with US$8 million funded by GEF, established the technical and environmental feasibility of this technology in the Brazilian market and a US$40 million World Bank project is currently seeking to demonstrate the viability of this technology on a commercial scale, in partnership with local private interests.

Cogeneration of Electricity and Steam Using Sugarcane Bagasse and Trash in Cuba

The GEF/UNDP project, "Cogeneration of Electricity and Steam Using Sugarcane Bagasse and Trash" in Cuba, is attempting to provide a commercial demonstration of state-of-the-art biomass cogeneration technology and to satisfy the relevant preconditions for the utilization of a significant fraction of the biomass energy potential in Cuba, including creating necessary legal and financial instruments. In this case, a GEF grant of US$12.5 million will leverage additional investments of US$73.3 million. The first two activities support a demonstration of the technology, development of trash handling processes, and other activities necessary to be undertaken in adapting the technology to local resources and circumstances.

Household Energy in Mali
A World Bank project, "Household Energy" in Mali, was designed to:

(a) create an enabling regulatory and policy environment for project implementation; and
(b) provide technical assistance and training to charcoal makers, producers, and sellers of stoves, as well as urban consumers, to efficiently harvest and carbonize fuelwood in order to manage the natural forest in a sustainable manner and to effectively market and use improved kilns, biomass and kerosene stoves.

The project involved addressing the supply and demand for fuel wood and its efficient use; institution building in the energy sector; as well as information, education, and communication. As a result of the project, fuel wood is being marketed on a sustainable basis in 200 rural markets and stoves are produced by local blacksmiths. Energy sector institutions have also been improved as the project is being managed by central and local governments. A central unit responsible for the implementation of the Household Energy Strategy, with the objective of maintaining a continuing awareness campaign in cooperation with national energy authorities as well as with NGOs, is also responsible for some management of the project. NGOs as well as private sector operators play an important role in the project's ongoing management and GEF contributed US$2.5 million of the US$5 million project budget.

Energy and Environment Upgrading in Morocco
A medium-size (US$1 million) World Bank project in Morocco called "Energy and Environment Upgrading of the Industrial Park of Sidi Bernoussi Zenata, Casablanca," aims to promote improvements in energy efficiency through enhancing the capacity of the private sector, financial institutions, and local agencies to create sustainable and replicable business practices. The project supports information and awareness efforts; assistance to industrial clients on a cost sharing basis to identify eligible and effective projects; the development of contracts and legal arrangements; and performance monitoring. Moreover, the project includes the formulation, negotiation, and implementation of performance contracts.

These activities, together with a US$100,000 contingency loan, are expected to leverage private investments of nearly US$12 million. The project is implemented by a local industry association (IZDIHAR), which operates the industrial park, that will receive technical assistance in order to improve its operational efficiency, to increase social and environmental services for the park and to support energy and water saving initiatives.

Energy Projects in The Philippines
In The Philippines, two different GEF projects are linked to a large World Bank program in the energy sector. One focuses on improving the technical and management capacities

of a set of electricity cooperatives in order to improve the efficiency of power transmission and to reduce greenhouse gas emissions. The total cost of the project is US$62.5 million, with US$12.4 million coming from the GEF.

In the second project, a renewable energy component of the energy sector reform program is being introduced. This project, which focuses on rural electrification, has a total cost of US$43.4 million, with US$10 million being GEF financed. This project builds on previous capacity development efforts by other agencies, in this case ESMAP and local NGOs.

Transportation Projects

Since the adoption of its initial operational programs, the GEF added an additional program on transportation, encompassing both new technologies (for example, fuel cell buses) and modal shifts (for example, measures to promote the introduction and use of bus rapid transit and other less energy intensive forms of transportation).

Energy Projects in China

A large proportion of the GEF portfolio of clean energy projects is made up of projects located in China, consistent with China's status as the world's second largest source of greenhouse gas emissions and largest user of coal, and also, China's rapidly growing economy. The GEF has funded projects dealing with promoting renewable energy generally, and wind energy in particular; developing coalbed methane; improving the efficiency of coal boilers; enabling the conversion of coal boilers to gas; improving the efficiency of lighting, refrigerators, and buildings; and introducing fuel cell buses in Beijing.

6.2 The GEF's Funding Strategies

In its initial years, the GEF had more resources than eligible projects. As demand grew over time, the importance of using funds strategically increased. Further, pressure was placed on the GEF's resources due to political decisions to expand the GEF's role, including projects to address land degradation and persistent organic pollutants (POPs). With experience, it became apparent that some project concepts were more successful than others, adding to the need to refine the GEF's initial funding strategies. As a starting point, the GEF concluded that resources had to be used in a more more catalytic way, with greater emphasis on the sustainability and replication of results.

One way of doing this was to put more emphasis on leverage, for example, by using resources to achieve lasting policy reforms and domestic financial approaches with long-term effects. In May 2003, two projects were included that illustrate this approach. One will support utility policies in Mexico to expand the role of renewable energy, particularly wind energy systems, as a source of grid connected power. Similar to the "reverse auction" approach used in California, a financial mechanism developed under the project will use GEF funds to augment the base tariff, awarded to those project developers bidding the lowest total cost level required for their projects. A second project in Eastern Europe is designed to develop a sustainable financing mechanism for geothermal energy in the region.

The GEF has also refined its operational programs with the articulation of several strategic priorities based on learning from experience. In the renewable energy area, one focus is on the design of projects to include productive uses and income generating activities, such as water pumping. The list of the GEF's strategic priorities includes reform of the power sector (with respect to power purchase agreements, tariffs, and other impediments to clean energy) and promoting innovative sources of local finance. For new technologies, another goal is aggregating markets to reduce costs.

The GEF system has a significant commitment to learning from experience and includes a quasi-independent monitoring and evaluation unit and periodic reviews by independent experts. The resulting reports are publicly available, and typically include consultation with NGOs and affected community groups. An ongoing study relevant to financing is an M&E review of GEF's experience in engaging the private sector. Two interim reports have been released that highlight some of the mixed outcomes resulting from projects that were directly targeted to private sector engagement. For example, GEF funds were used as the basis for capital raising by several private funds targeted toward renewable energy enterprises in developing countries. The underlying rationale was that such funds could achieve near commercial returns and thus would serve as models for future financing. In reality, the profit levels projected proved to be overly optimistic and the funds are now being restructured. In contrast, those funds that included higher levels of local business support and worked more closely with locally based banks and financiers have been more successful.

7 TRADING OF CARBON OFFSETS

As a long-term source of resources, trading of carbon offsets pursuant to the Kyoto Protocol "clean energy mechanisms"[28] and related national programs may provide substantial funding for clean energy projects. The magnitude of resource flows from carbon offsets is dependent upon which countries commit to greenhouse gas reductions, national policies that are ultimately adopted, and eligibility requirements that are still to be defined. In the short term, the value of offsets has been low due to the absence of U.S. participation. Nevertheless, the likelihood is that this issue will remain and that as growth in greenhouse gas emissions will need to be curtailed, this will lead to an increase in the demand for carbon offsets.

Other chapters in this book address the topic of carbon offsets in more detail; I will simply make two observations about their potential role in promoting clean energy. First, the World Bank and other IFIs have become early leaders and innovators in helping to develop and demonstrate the concept. As relatively public and transparent investors, their actions (even when criticized) have established useful benchmarks for others to follow. Second, there may be significant opportunities for linking GEF and other donor aid to carbon offsets. The former may continue to assume much of the "up front" risk in establishing clean energy initiatives, while the latter can provide much needed sources of revenue for sustainability and replication.

Early experience under the World Bank Prototype Carbon Fund[29] has demonstrated some of the possible strengths and limitations of carbon funding. The most appealing projects have been those with low risk and high offsets per dollar, for example, landfill

---

[28] Kyoto Protocol to the UN Framework Convention on Climate Change, December 11, 1997, available at http://www.unfccc.int/resource/docs/convkp/kpeng.pdf.

[29] *See* http://www.prototypecarbonfund.org.

gas projects. Efficiency projects are possible but raise baseline issues, while small-scale solar projects are unlikely to be particularly attractive at low carbon prices (although the World Bank is working on a fund dedicated to community oriented projects as a kind of "green premium" for interested investors). The opportunity to mix carbon offset funds with other resources is also important in providing additional financial flexibility.

However, even if current optimistic predictions in relation to carbon revenues are realized, the need for clean energy financing is unlikely to be fully met. Carbon revenues will most likely be subject to the same limitations that shape private infrastructure investments generally, being concentrated in a subset of countries and tied to other investor biases and risk aversion.

8 GREENING THE FINANCIAL SECTOR

An entirely different approach in relation to the financial and investment community has been to promote "greening" from within. While still relatively new, this goal is being pursued from several different angles and has produced some interesting results.

One of the most exciting, recent developments is the formulation of the Equator Principles.[30] These include a commitment to abide by environmental and social policies based on those of the World Bank and IFC and were announced by a group of ten leading international banks in June 2003. With the subsequent addition of seven more banks, the initiative applies to more than seventy percent of privately financed project loans in developing countries. While operational details remain to be defined, including such key issues as scope for public disclosure and consultation, the approach directly addresses concerns in relation to the protection of the public interest. That is, rather than eventually be subject to external public interest regulation, such an approach preempts regulatory intervention by providing for the protection of the public interest through a (largely) self-designed policy measure.

Another development of potential importance for developing countries is the rise of socially responsible investment funds.[31] Such funds have grown rapidly globally and currently constitute a US$2.7 trillion industry with more than 760 retail funds and many institutional investors. However, such funds are primarily to be found in the US and Europe and have, thus far, had minimal application in developing countries. This may be subject to change, however, as the IFC and others work to create the requisite data and infrastructure to support investor interest.

One limitation of such initiatives is their definition of expectations for the evaluation of environmental and social consequences. For the most part, the focus of such initiatives has been on avoiding potential problems rather than advancing potentially greener, but initially risky, alternatives. Indeed, a major selling point for socially responsible investment has been evidence of higher returns. The head of ABP Investments, a Dutch public employees' investment fund that is the largest such fund in the world, recently noted that "there is a growing body of evidence that companies which

---

[30] Available at http://www.equator-principles.com.
[31] *See* IFC, "Towards Sustainable and Responsible Investment in Emerging Markets" (October, 2003). In addition to environmentally focused funds, the report describes the parallel influence of shareholder initiatives. While rarely successful, the attendant publicity can contribute to engaging a company in a more constructive dialogue producing changes in corporate behavior, *id.*, at 17–23.

manage environmental, social, and governance risks most effectively tend to deliver better risk-adjusted financial performance than their industry peers."[32]

The UNEP Financial Initiative (UNEP FI) attempts to take this approach further to engage financial institutions to promote linkages between environmental and financial performance. So far more than 275 such institutions are participating in a dialogue that includes not only the identification of environmental risk but also the development of financial products and services that promote environmental sustainability. In this context, the head of UNEP, Klaus Topfer, recently spoke to participating firms about the need for commitments to providing greater financial support for clean energy.

Another step toward using market forces for environmental purposes has been the advent of green products and services to capture consumer demand for products with superior environmental performance: shade grown coffee and sustainably harvested wood products are two examples. Clearly defined and credible criteria are key requirements and not always easily achieved. In the energy sector, an important recent example has been the advent of "green power": that is, electricity sold for a premium price because it derives from a defined renewable source (most often wind energy) or because the revenues collected will be used to acquire such resources. This concept has primary applicability among more affluent consumers in the industrialized countries, although there is some potential for the export of green power from developing countries, for example, wind energy from Mexico to the U.S. market and solar thermal power from North Africa to Europe.

---

[32] *Id.*, at 16. Advocates of this perspective frequently point to nuclear power, which was avoided by socially responsible investors well before performance problems led to declines in shareholder value.

28 Legal Aspects of International Project Finance for Sustainable Energy Development

Donggen Xu*

1 INTRODUCTION

The framework for international project finance for sustainable energy development provides for both conflicting and cooperative exchanges between parties to such contracts. Under the cooperative aspects of such contracts, host governments grant foreign investors exclusive licenses to develop and operate sustainable energy development projects. In order to ensure that the benefits of such projects are shared equitably, host governments supervise such energy projects. Limited financing options for sustainable energy projects increase the credit risk of project lenders. Specific clauses such as step-in clauses, substitution clauses, floating charges, negative pledge clauses as well as covenants clauses, are included in financing agreements for sustainable energy development. These are intended to eliminate and allocate the credit risk of project lenders.

2 INTERNATIONAL PROJECT FINANCE

International project finance is the primary global vehicle for financing cross-border investments. International project finance transactions are defined by the OECD as the "financing of a particular economic unit in which a lender is satisfied to consider the cash flows and earnings of that economic unit as the source of funds from which a loan will be repaid and the assets of the economic unit as collateral for the loan."[1] The OECD arrangement also specifies seven "essential criteria" to further define a project finance transaction:

1. Financing of export transactions with a legally and economically independent project company, for example, a special purpose company, in respect of "greenfield" investment projects generating their own revenues;
2. Appropriate sharing of risks between the partners in the project, for example, private or creditworthy public shareholders, exporters, creditors, off-takers, including adequate equity;

---

[1] OECD, "Project Finance: Understanding on the Application of Flexibility to the Terms and Conditions of the Arrangement on Guidelines for Officially Supported Export Credits in Respect of Project Finance Transactions, For a Trial Period," OECD Doc. TD/Consensus (98) 27 (July 30, 1998) at 5, see also http://www.oecd.org/ dataoecd/36/15/1887311.pdf.

[*] Professor of Law and Director, Institute of International Law, Shanghai Jiaotong University School of Law, and Vice-Chairman of the China Society of Private International Law. Graduate of Fribourg University Law School, Switzerland, 1992.

3. Sufficient cash flow for the project during the entire repayment period to cover operating costs and debt servicing for outside funds;
4. Priority deduction from project revenues of operating costs and debt servicing;
5. No sovereign repayment guarantee with regard to the project (not including government performance guarantees, such as off-take arrangements);
6. Asset based securities for the proceeds/assets of the project, for example, assignments, pledges, proceeds, or accounts; and
7. Limited or no recourse to sponsors of the private sector shareholders/sponsors of the project after completion.[2]

"Project finance" refers to the financing of large industrial and infrastructure projects.[3] Project finance was first used to fund power projects in the United States and the United Kingdom. Most project finance during the last two decades has taken place in developed countries.[4] Thereafter, its use has grown tremendously around the world. Between 1997–98, project finance transactions in developing countries accounted for an estimated US$184 billion, or a little more than half of all project finance transactions in the world.[5] The Asian financial crisis that began in 1997 significantly dampened any increase in the flow of investment dollars into developing countries.[6] Concerns have been voiced in relation to the detrimental effects of externalities in project finance transactions in developing countries.[7] Now, project finance is used widely in connection with sustainable energy development in developing countries, such as the exploitation of coal mines, crude oil, oil in the sea, and natural gas.[8]

2.1 Sustainable Energy Development Project Finance

Sustainable energy development project finance is a technique of nonrecourse financing that is not primarily dependent on the credit support of project sponsors, or the value of the physical assets involved, but depends instead on the expected performance of the project itself. The credit appraisal by the project lender is therefore based on the underlying cash flow from the revenue producing contracts of the project, independent of the project sponsor's credit in a traditional sense. If these cash flows prove inadequate for debt servicing, the project sponsor has no direct legal obligation to repay the project debt or to make interest payments.

Thus, host governments usually invite some foreign banks and private enterprise groups to join in these projects. This kind of financing is a cumbersome system and involves complex legal relationships involving the host government, project sponsors (usually foreign and/or domestic equity investors), the project company (a single purpose

---

[2] *Id.*, at 5–6.
[3] K. Miyamoto, "Measuring Local Legal Risk Premium in Project Finance Bonds," (2000) 40 *Virginia Journal of International Law* 1126.
[4] International Financial Corporation, "Project Finance in Developing Countries," (1999) 3 at 5, available at http://www.ifc.org/publications/pubs/loe/loe7/loe7.html.
[5] *Id.*
[6] W. M. Stelwagon, "Financing Private Energy Projects in the Third World," (1996) 37 *Cath. L.* 45.
[7] L. Lamkin Broome, "The Social Impact of Project Finance: A Comment on Bjerre," (2002) 12 *Duke Journal of Comparative & International Law* 444.
[8] D. Lamethe, "Le Financement de Projets et Leur Organisation Industrielle – L'exemple de la Construction et de l'exploitation de Centrales Electriques," in *Souverainete Etatique et Marches Internationaux a la Fin du 20eme Siecle – Melanges en l'honneur de Philippe Kahn* (2000) at 453.

company, partnership or other entity (created by the project sponsors to develop, own, and operate the project), the project lender, purchasing utilities, construction contractors, operations contractors, and fuel suppliers.

Host governments that participate in such projects are important legal actors in this kind of international financing. These governments play an important role in many aspects of the relevant transactions such as: choosing the project and sponsor; supervising the process; checking and granting approvals after completion of the project; and supervising the operation, management, and maintenance of the project. Further, the government grants licenses to the project sponsor through concession agreements, which allow the sponsor to invest in the exploitation and management of sustainable energy development in the designated time period and geographic area. In light of their need to pursue commercial interests and secure short-term returns, private capital is highly unlikely to invest in large-scale sustainable energy development projects without receiving certain guarantees from the host government. Accordingly, host governments usually assume certain obligations in the financing process to purchase some of the relevant project's products.

3 THE CONCEPT OF EQUITY AND ITS FUNCTION IN SUSTAINABLE ENERGY DEVELOPMENT PROJECT FINANCE

The concept of equity has a long history, with its rudimentary beginnings in the *Zhouyi*.[9] British judges also established the legal doctrine of equity, which has become an important part of the British legal system.[10] In legal practice, the concept of equity plays a positive role in overcoming the inflexibility and rigidity of laws, and recognizing the need for compromise and a harmonization of interests between two parties. The development of the legal doctrine of equity is one of the most splendid achievements in the historical development of the law. The views of distinguished American legal scholar, Justice Benjamin N. Cardozo, on balancing interests from the point of view of legal philosophy, have also made an important contribution.[11] Consequently, equity has become an important and instructive concept in harmonizing the interests of different parties.

Importantly, equity determines and reflects the balanced nature of rights and obligations in the construction of legal relationships in sustainable energy development project financing. In such transactions, there are core conflicts between the host government and corresponding project sponsor or lender, as the main participants in such legal relations. These parties may be regarded as both cooperative and conflicting legal actors. The host government represents public social interests, whereas the project sponsor or lender represents private interests. In these circumstances, the conflicting interests of the host government and the project sponsor or lender can become belligerent, if not properly managed and mediated. The law's function lies in reconciling conflicting interests in order to achieve a unification, harmony, and balance of interests. This requires private, individual interests to be subordinate to the overarching public interest, while simultaneously protecting individual interests to the extent that the

---

[9] *Zhouyi* is a Chinese philosophy book, written approximately 5000 years ago. *See* http://www.yxun.net/genduoneirong1/14.htm/.

[10] D. G. Cracknell, *English Legal System Textbook* (17th Edn.), HLT Publications (London, 1995) at 5–6.

[11] *Selected Writings of Benjamin Cardozo*, Fallon Law Book Co. (1947).

public interest is not harmed. The purpose and essence of the law in sustainable energy development project finance transactions is to realize a proper equilibrium between public and private interests.

With project finance contracts, equity dictates that host governments should supervise the project company to prevent it from increasing the price of relevant energy products and services via its exclusive licenses and privileged monopoly position. At the same time, the host government must ensure the regular and continuous operation of the project company to ensure that it can provide reliable energy products and services to the community.

The concept of equity also resolves conflicts between project lenders and the project company or sponsor. Project lenders provide financing to the project company. In light of limited recourse rights for project finance for sustainable energy development, the financing risks for project lenders are much higher than for common international business loans. To balance the interests of project lenders and the project company or sponsor, equity requires the design of a legal structure that applies other measures to convert the project lender's risks. Therefore, through intervention measures, substitution clauses, floating charges, and negative pledges, a balance can be maintained between the interests of project lenders and the project company. In the event of breach of contract, or a lack of good faith in the execution of contracts, project lenders can claim relevant relief, under contract, on the basis of the measures just mentioned.

In keeping with principles of equity, sustainable energy development project finance arrangements should reflect the conflicting and cooperative nature of the parties' interests. Through the use of complex contracts, agreements, and specific terms and conditions, the law can ensure that the rights, obligations, interests, and responsibilities of all parties are recognized in the project dealings.

4 IDENTIFYING THE LEGAL RISKS IN PROJECT FINANCE

An examination of the local legal risks, faced in relation to sustainable energy development project finance, may help to define the necessary elements of the operation of the "rule of law" in such a context. According to Jonathan Green, the fundamental difference between international and domestic project financing "is the importance of identifying and dealing with the local law aspects of the transaction."[12] Green notes further that "the importance and complexities of the domestic local issues pale in comparison to those faced when developing a project in another country where there is a totally different legal system."[13] Green also identifies a long list of various local legal issues pertaining to sustainable energy development project finance including: investment restrictions; concession agreements; the host country's regulatory scheme; the limitation on the creation and enforcement of security interests; and local bankruptcy laws.[14] However, in considering such lists of local legal issues, it is important to note the distinction between regulatory barriers or burdens, which may increase project costs, as opposed to the uncertainty arising from regulatory and legal risks, which increase the cost of capital.

---

[12] J. Green, "Managing Risks in International Power Projects," in Project Financing 669, 676, *PLI Commercial Law & Practice Course Handbook Series* No. A-672 (1993).

[13] *Id.*   [14] *Id.*, at 677.

Other practitioners have produced similar checklists of critical local legal issues. One such list provides a comprehensive set of factors including the choice of law, government guarantees, currency convertibility, changes in taxes and duties, import and export of equipment, national content requirements, force majeure, country risk, and the adequacy of the national regulatory framework (for instance, the nature of land title, foreclosure, international arbitration and adjudication conventions).[15]

James Otto developed a compendium of eighty-six questions to analyze a country's regulatory environment for foreign investment in mining operations.[16] Some of these questions are relatively straightforward, for example, "[I]s the exploration right transferable?"[17] Other questions are problematic in that they utilize vague criteria, for example, "[A]re all taxes reasonable and stable?"[18]

While it is difficult to identify precisely how to frame questions in relation to local legal systems, and the precise information that must be extracted about such systems, local legal risks must be identified and mitigated for the purposes of sustainable energy development project financing.

5 THE RIGHTS AND INTERESTS OF THE PROJECT SPONSOR OR PROJECT LENDERS IN SUSTAINABLE ENERGY DEVELOPMENT PROJECT FINANCE

The ultimate value of an investment in energy development in a particular country is highly dependent on the quality of that country's legal system. Countries that host infrastructure projects, particularly those countries with emerging economies, have varying levels of local regulation protecting investment. These laws and their enforcement mechanisms affect the likelihood of a project being successfully completed.[19]

The two main objectives of project lenders are to maintain a constant cash flow and the continuous operation of the project. To realize these goals, project lenders must use contractual documents to protect themselves against any potential threats. In other words, in the absence of market regulation, private contracts attempt to operate as a substitute but are more concerned with the interests of an individual consumer under a purchase contract than the interests of consumers, or the market as a whole.[20] Moreover, the host government always enjoys more favors due to its state power, manpower, and material resources in the country, while counterparties to such contracts, either foreign investors as the project sponsor or foreign project lenders, are always placed in a weaker position. Subject to these concerns, legal frameworks for sustainable energy development project financing can set more favorable guarantee mechanisms for the project sponsors or project lenders in accordance with principles of equity.

---

[15] J. B. O'Sullivan, "Power Sales Agreements and Project Financing," in Project Financing, 18, 100–101 *PLI Commercial Law & Practice Course Handbook Series* No. A-672 (1993) at 79.

[16] J. Otto, "Legal Risk Analysis for Mining Projects," Centre for Petroleum and Mineral Law and Policy (1994) at 9–12.

[17] *Id.*, at 10.   [18] *Id.*, at 11.

[19] Miyamoto, *supra* note 3.

[20] N. Nassar, "Project Finance, Public Utilities and Public Concerns: A Practitioner's Perspective," (2000) 23 *Fordham International Law Journal* 65.

5.1 The Host Government Grants to Project Sponsors an Exclusive License To Operate the Sustainable Energy Development Project by Concession Agreement

A "concession agreement" is a legal document executed between the project sponsor and the host government that grants the project sponsor the right to explore, develop, and operate the sustainable energy development project. It also establishes the principles that must be complied with during the development and operation of the project. Concession agreements are the premise for sustainable energy development project financing and, to a certain extent, determine the legal framework for project finance. Therefore, without such concession agreements, sustainable energy development projects would be unlikely to be developed and established.

Concession agreements also have great importance for project lenders, although lenders do not always take part in the execution of such agreements. As in some of the actual project financing arrangements, the project sponsor is most likely to assign certain rights under the concession agreement to project lenders as a form of security. The duration of the concession agreement and foreign exchange control of the principal and interest, under the project loan, both directly influence the interests of project lenders.

Host governments, project sponsors, and project lenders must reach an agreement in the concession agreement in relation to the following:

1. the grant of the concession right, the scope of the concession operation, and the duration and extension under special circumstances of the concession agreement;
2. issues arising during the process of developing and operating the sustainable energy development project, including, but not limited to, the standards for the design, construction, operation, and maintenance of the project, the quality standard of the project product, the connection of the project with existing facilities, the project duration, and obligations in the case of delay;
3. facilities from the host government, such as financial facilities, the availability of finance and security, guarantees of title and proceeds of land use rights and the means of providing such facilities;
4. financial aspects, including, but not limited to, the cost plan and the cost recapture proposal for the project and the exchange, transmission, and taxation of foreign exchange;
5. titles, including, but not limited to, whether the project company has ownership of the project facilities during the operating process, whether it has the right to set pledges or other securities over the project facilities, the procedure for, and security of, transferring title upon expiry of the concession agreement;
6. miscellaneous matters, including, but not limited to, insurance, the termination of the concession agreement, remedies in cases of default or violation, the settlement of disputes, the governing law, and force majeure.

The main characteristics of concession agreements are:

1. first, one party of the agreement should be the host government or other relevant authorities of the host country, while the other parties should be the relevant foreign investors;
2. second, there should be concessions for the development and construction of the sustainable energy development project from the host country; and

3. third, the host country should provide favorable treatment for, and commitment to, these foreign investors.

The balance of rights and obligations between the host government, the project sponsor, and project lenders is well reflected in the terms of such concession agreements. The host government has the right to censor, amend, and cancel the design proposal of the project sponsor; to supervise the project construction; to inspect, examine, and confirm the project during the completion process; to supervise the operations of the project; to enact relevant labor policy; and to take over the project. The host government also commits to provide the area for construction of the project, relevant resources, to realize the project's proceeds, and to offer temporary financial support. Meantime, the project company enjoys rights under charges, preferential tax treatment, priority of assignment, currency equivalency, and rights to apply for assistance and protection from the host country. The project company is also obliged to design and construct the project in accordance with the proposal as authorized by the host government, to charge prices under the relevant regulated standard, and to assure the integrity of the product when transferring ownership of the project.

5.2 The Host Government Grants the Project Sponsor and Project Lenders Security Interests under the Commitment Clause

The host government should provide foreign investors with guarantees in relation to political risks connected with project financing. "Political risks" refers to adverse influences on the construction and operation of the sustainable energy development project as a result of new policy or regulatory measures implemented by the host government, which were triggered by political causes or force majeure. Political risks include, but are not limited to, war, civil strife, nationalization and expropriation, the limitation on remittance of foreign exchange, the elevation of the tariff index, and controls on the supply of both labor resources and raw material.

Host government commitments to sustainable energy development projects are meant to guarantee the prosperity of the authorized projects and provide security for foreign investors. Commitment clauses reflect well the inclination of host governments to undertake the risks of the project and to grant special operating concessions to foreign investors. Subject to such commitment clauses, foreign investors have obtained operating rights for development projects which otherwise would only be held by host governments. Host governments are able to take over development projects smoothly, without the need for payments to foreign investors. Hence, such commitment clauses are the basis upon which foreign investors can seek legal remedies for any governmental breaches, provided that state immunity doctrines are slightly restricted in their operation. Certain devices in concession agreements represent a balance of rights and obligations such that host governments gain relevant rights based on their fulfillment of equivalent obligations. Accordingly, government commitments for sustainable energy development projects, as provided for in concession agreements, differ from the security provided by governments in relation to ordinary foreign investment projects.

Disputes between the developed and developing countries concerning the actual obligations of governments under commitment clauses are evident. Scholars in developed countries generally consider that the government's obligations are as follows: to provide guarantees for revenue, for noncompetition, guarantees of recision in cases of force majeure, warranties for environment protection, financial assurance, guarantees of special compensation, and warranties for the settlement of disputes.[21] From the perspective of developing countries, government guarantees for project financing should be divided into two categories: first, commercial guarantees, such as the return rate for investment; and second, political commitments to the project sponsor. This author believes that host governments have no obligation to provide commercial guarantees for the reasons which follow.

First, host governments should not commit to a particular rate of return for the project company, as this shifts debt obligations to host governments and reduces operating costs. The Notice on the Approval of the Concession Project to Foreign Investors,[22] issued jointly by the Central Planning and Developing Committee, the Electric Power Committee, and the Transportation Committee in China, provides:

> ... the project company should bear the risks in finance, construction, operation and maintenance, the government may not provide a guaranteed rate of return investment.

However, a floating rate of return could fully reflect the utility of relevant infrastructure, the availability and economic value of the project, the dynamic influence of existing economic factors during the development process, and the mobilization of investors during the construction, development, and operation of the project. In practice, the project to develop the highway from Guangdong to Shenzhen successfully adopted such a floating rate of return.[23]

Second, the Security Law of the PRC and the Regulation Regarding Guarantees Granted by Internal Institutions to Foreign Project Lenders issued by the Central Bank in China, provide that the Chinese government and state authorities may not provide security for commercial businesses in the context of international project finance for development projects. Such guarantees to any third parties are forbidden. Consequently, it is necessary to carefully consider means of resolving regulatory conflicts between the floating rate of return system and the current legislative framework in China.

Government policy commitments to the project sponsor cover issues such as preferential tax treatment, the risks in foreign exchange, the supply of raw material, and the expropriation of land. Such commitments are essential to ensure the workability of sustainable energy development project finance and are necessary to account for, and cover, imperfections in current legal and economic systems. Hence, governmental support appears indispensable for the achievement of sustainable energy development projects.

In this regard, China has several problems that must be addressed. First, certain governmental commitments in relation to such projects lack legal force and are not binding. Second, problems arise as to how various governmental functions should be regulated, for instance, whether local governments have the power to commit to preferential tax treatment and the transferability of foreign exchange. Existing legislation

---

[21] See J. Scriven, "Banking Perspective on Construction Risks in BOT Schemes," (1994) 11 *International Construction Law Review* 315.

[22] See http://www.com-law.net/fagui/touzi/concession.htm.

[23] See http://www.transonline.com.cn/manage/jlrxd/j20020706_01.html.

does not authorize concession authorities, for sustainable energy development project financing, to make any commitments for the reduction of government duties or powers. Therefore, local governments should not make commitments that are contrary to the fixed categories and rates of tax under Chinese law, unless special powers are granted by relevant authorities or are regulated by new legislation. The host government should also adopt different measures in relation to various commitments concerning sustainable energy development project finance. Special clauses should be included in the relevant legislative framework for commitments in relation to the land on which the relevant project is to be constructed, ancillary facilities, and preferential duties. Agreement on the supply of raw materials could be reached in relevant contracts rather than providing for such commitments in the concession agreement. Furthermore, the government does not need to guarantee risks in relation to the foreign exchange rate, but rather needs to provide certain other measures to diversify the currencies, to adjust the terms and fix rates of foreign exchange, and to establish exclusive accounts and insurance for the various kinds of financial risks.

It should be noted that government commitments for sustainable energy development project finance differ from securities provided under civil law. First, the subject of the security is different. The subject of the security in civil law is usually a third party, while under concession agreements, the government makes the relevant commitment itself. Second, the contents are different. Securities under civil law aim to guarantee certain commercial risks, however the government makes commitments in relation to its own behavior and facilities for the ongoing project, rather than in relation to operating risks. Third, the relationship between contracts is distinct. The security contract is a sub-contract in civil law, however government commitments under concession agreements have the same binding force as other contracts signed in connection with the sustainable energy development project. Fourth, the governing laws differ. The civil security is subject to civil and commercial laws, while government commitments are subject not only to civil law but also to international public law. Sixth, their characters vary. Under civil law, the security, as a matter of private law, is classified according to the terms of relevant statutes governing the behavior of each of the commercial parties. However, government commitments in relation to political risks and remedies for the violation of such commitments depend on political considerations, such as the sovereignty of the host country and relevant policies, which are relevant for the purposes of international public law.

5.3 The Host Government Guarantees Exclusivity for the Project Sponsor of the Sustainable Energy Development Project through the Exclusivity Clause

Exclusive access to relevant markets plays an important role in sustainable energy development project finance. The operating conditions of the project are regularly evaluated as the main collateral on the loan depends on the revenue stream of the project. Therefore, in order to obtain a steady cash flow and repayment to project lenders, maintaining the sound operation of the project and establishing a large market share are the main concerns for the project sponsor and project lenders.

Investors pay more attention to long-term, steady revenue streams, as sustainable energy development projects are capital intensive projects. Should relevant markets be easily accessible for many other investors in the same field, the market share of the current development project would be limited, which in turn decreases the projected revenue of the project in its feasibility proposal, and rates of return on investments would also fall. Hence, the common concern for the project sponsor and project lenders is to ensure that the project retains its exclusivity in order to protect its market share, and to ensure good operating conditions for the project and the capacity for repayment by the project company.

In most circumstances, "exclusivity clauses" are usually directly or implicitly included in relevant contracts, especially for high tech projects. Such exclusivity clauses in the context of sustainable energy development projects require the host government to make commitments in relation to the exclusivity of market access for the project company. Essentially, exclusivity clauses prevent the host government from granting similar licenses to other investors during the initial years after the completion of the project. Only several years later can the host government grant new licenses for entry by new investors or project developers into the same market, usually by inviting public bidding for such licenses after notifying the project company. At this stage, treatment of investors in relation to future sustainable energy development projects, in relation to financial, legal, and technological issues, should be equal.

5.4 The Sustainable Energy Development Project Company Enjoys Advantages in the Market through the Most Favored Treatment Clause

Guarantees concerning the rate of return for investments are usually the subject of "most favored treatment clauses." These clauses require nondiscriminatory treatment for project companies in the same market. The most favored treatment clause provides that the host government should grant nondiscriminatory treatment to all project companies rather than granting preferential treatment to a particular project company. However, under such clauses, new competitors are permitted to enter the market provided that there is a corresponding increase in market demand, and improvements in the operating conditions of project companies. The most favored treatment clause is not meant to confine or preclude the development of new or potential competitors, but rather, to ensure that existing project companies enjoy the same treatment as any future market entrants. Most favored treatment clauses are also binding in relation to host governments and thus preclude other project companies from demanding more favored treatment in relation to operating conditions in order for them to effectively access the same market.

5.5 The Project Lenders Obtain the Privilege of Appointing Substitutes through the Step-In Clause and the Substitute Clause

Project sponsors and project lenders are entitled to gain a substantial correction period following breach of contract by the project company. The host government should not immediately terminate the concession agreement and recapture the project unless the project lenders are determined to relinquish it. Typical "step-in clauses" usually read as follows:

> The government should not terminate the contracts either before the project company provides the government with written notice at the time that the relevant

financial crises occurred or during the correction period for the project company and the project lenders. The project lenders are capable of gaining another ninety days for the correction period upon written notice by the project lenders to the government, upon the expiry of the initial correction period. During this additional period, the project lenders shall evaluate the conditions of the project itself, determine whether to take over the relevant project company, and decide whether to seek remedies for the breach by the project company. If the project lenders notify the government in writing that remedies will be sought for the project company's breach of contract in accordance with the loan agreement, before the expiry of the ninety-day correction period, the project lenders will be entitled to another 120 days to seek a remedy for all relevant violations of the contracts. Hence, the concession agreement will not be terminated and the project shall not be recaptured by the government following the commencement of proceedings for appropriate remedies.[24]

Step-in clauses are always based on "substitute clauses." Under substitute clauses, the project lenders have the right to recommend that a third party take the place of, and assume all the rights and obligations of, the project company. Note that, typical step-in clauses also usually allow the project lenders to recommend a third party as substitute for the project company by giving written notice to the government, subject to the condition that the recommended company should be clearly identified. The host government and project lenders are required to negotiate for no more than sixty days following receipt of this written notice during which, or after which, the host government is capable of rejecting the recommended company as long as it considers that the company is not qualified to operate and manage the sustainable energy development project. The recommended company would not be rejected by the host government for any other reasons. The host government, the project company, and the newly recommended company would then change the original parties in the contract, and the recommended company would assume all the rights and obligations of, the project company.

The author of this chapter considers that longer periods of time are needed to seek remedies for breach of contract committed under sustainable energy development projects. Substitution rights are exclusive rights held by project lenders, under which project lenders can choose the most suitable project company on the basis of its own interests through nonpublic bidding.

6 THE HOST GOVERNMENT'S INTEREST IN INTERNATIONAL PROJECT FINANCE FOR SUSTAINABLE ENERGY DEVELOPMENT

A primary concern of host governments entering into utility related contracts is the continuity and price of services provided under such contracts. These matters have a high degree of political sensitivity, particularly when the products or services provided by the project company are a monopoly, either de jure or de facto. In most circumstances, the continuous supply of, and the rationality of prices for, the products or services fall within the scope of compulsory governmental regulation and there is no room for bargaining. Host governments should ensure, from a risk perspective, that contracts are designed to prevent the project company from withholding supply or charging monopoly prices through the following measures.

---

[24] Nassar, *supra* note 20, at 73.

6.1 Government Price Control and Review of the Project Company

Equity theory not only mandates the fair allocation of interests through bargaining, but also requires the creation of additional interests through the good faith cooperation of the parties to the contract. The parties' behavior under the contract is linked to the realization of their interests in and through the contract. Equity plays a role in reducing the uncertainty and cost of the deal through providing for a more specific and inspiring legal framework. In international project finance for sustainable energy development, exclusivity clauses confer sole rights of project development in certain markets to the project sponsors. Therefore, such clauses restrict competition for the duration of the government's promise and have the result that the price of the project's products or services are subject to the monopoly powers of the project company. To avoid the charging of monopoly prices, under the legal framework for international project finance for sustainable development, price control or price review clauses can also be provided for.

Under such clauses a special regulatory agency, constituted by both representatives from the host government and the project company, is responsible for reviewing the prices of the project products or services. This agency also has the right to veto price fixing and the charging of monopoly prices for the project's products or services. This price review system aims at restraining the project company's ability to engage in price fixing and preventing the charging of monopoly prices by such project companies.

6.2 Government Supervision of the Project Company's Ordinary Operations

As the American scholar Benjamin N. Cardozo noted, there are certain artificial mechanisms present in each legal system and, generally speaking, they exist mainly for convenience, safety, and other public interests.[25] The validity and continuing function of the relevant development project lies in its continuous provision of public services. To achieve this, the host government should supervise the operations of the relevant development project. An agreement concerning the project's operations is usually signed immediately after the signing of the main contract in international project finance for sustainable energy development. The host government's investigation and certification of the project operator are the basis upon which the main contract comes into effect. The project company has the right to operate the project company itself and achieve maximum production with minimal costs. The project company can also employ professional operations contractors to operate the project. This does not exempt the project company from its obligations under the contract, however. The project company must establish an operating committee, including a delegate from the host government. The committee is in charge of the supervision of the daily operations of the project company, to see whether these conform with the requirements under the contract and also whether the project company is in violation of the price fixing and monopoly rules. Thus, the operating committee functions as the direct pledge by the project company of the development project's appropriate and continuous operation.

The project operator's qualifications and its project manager have a significant impact on the normal operations of the project, as well as the continuous supply of the

---

[25] *Supra* note 11.

project's products or services. Further, the company undertaking the exploitation of sustainable energy development may not necessarily have professional experience in operating and managing the relevant project. Accordingly, generally the project company would employ professional operations contractors to operate the project. However, if the project company is the only or major player in providing certain products or services, then the host government has veto rights exercisable against the appointment of a professional operations contractor.

6.3 The Correction Period for Government in the Event of Default

A standard default provision in international project finance for sustainable energy development protects against any and all risks of the evaporation of funds. This provision would include not only cases of nonpayment under the revenue contract, but also instances of dissolution, winding up, bankruptcy, liquidation, or the appointment of receivers, lack of foreign reserves, as well as adverse changes of law affecting the profitability of the transaction. In addition, in the event of default, there is a catch-all provision allowing for termination buyouts, which is set out below:

> ... any material breach by the government of this agreement that is not remedied within 45 days after notice from the company identifying the material breach in question in reasonable detail, and demanding remedy thereof; provided, however, that for material breaches of this agreement that can be cured only in more than 45 days, the government may have such additional time to cure any material breach under this agreement as it estimates may be necessary to cure such material breach if, prior to the end of the 45 day period, the government provides satisfactory evidence to the company that (i) it has commenced and is diligently pursuing a cure and (ii) that more than 45 days is required in order to effect such cure and provides a good-faith estimate of when the material breach will be cured.

A catch-all provision is meant to protect the project company against any unpleasant risks affecting the performance of the government's contractual obligations. It also allows for the continuation of the project if such risks do not represent a serious threat. And if one of the party's interests is threatened by the other where no remedy is taken, then the first party can force compliance by the other party through terminating the contract. This catch-all clause is meant to create a balance among the competing interests of the parties without allowing either party greater leverage.

6.4 The Government's Right of Withdrawal in Relation to International Project Finance for Sustainable Energy Development

One of the most serious matters for the project lender is the possibility that international project financing arrangements for sustainable energy development will be terminated during the loan period. The termination of the sustainable energy development project will undoubtedly affect cash flow and repayment by the project company will become extremely difficult. Standard project finance practice requires long correction periods and step-in and substitution rights in the contract. However, the host government still cannot exercise the right of recision to withdraw the project unless it settles all repayments. These repayments cannot be set off, subtracted, counter-claimed, or taken out of any tariff. The purchase price is calculated in accordance with a special formula and irrespective of whether the loan is due or not, when the project terminates, the formula will be different. The lender bank will insist that the purchase price paid by the host government should be not less than the loan that the project company owes to the bank, even if the termination of the contract is caused by the company's default. If the government defaults, then the price the government is required to pay is an amount equal to the stock price of the project company owed by the project sponsors.

7 THE BALANCE OF INTERESTS BETWEEN THE PROJECT COMPANY OR SPONSORS AND THE PROJECT LENDER

In international project finance for sustainable energy development, equity theory not only operates in relation to interests as between the host government and the project sponsors or project lenders, but also in relation to interests as between the project company or project sponsors and the project lenders.

7.1 Limited Recourse Debt Financing Allocates the Financial Risk of the Project Company to the Project Lenders

Nonrecourse project financing for sustainable energy development, highly leveraged debt, and the reduction of the overall risk for major project participants to an acceptable level are the most salient features of project finance. In traditional corporate finance, what the project lender appreciates is the business reputation of the borrower, not the performance of the project, as the borrower has other assets offered as a guarantee for repayment. The primary source of repayment for investors and creditors is the project sponsor, backed by its entire balance sheet. Although project lenders will usually still seek to assure themselves of the economic viability of the project itself, a more important factor in their decision is the overall strength of the project sponsor's balance sheet as well as business reputation.

However, in international project finance for sustainable energy development, generally the project sponsor will set up a new company and the project lender provides the funds directly to the project company, not to the project sponsor. Compared with traditional corporate finance, the international project finance for sustainable energy development is secured solely on the basis of the project itself and its projected revenues, and involves no recourse to the project sponsor. Project finance for sustainable energy development is typically accomplished on a nonrecourse basis, which means the debt is not secured by the assets of the borrower but by the assets generated by the project itself. For example, in the case of a power plant, the debt might be paid off with the revenue stream generated by selling its output to a provincial government or with export revenues produced by a mine, with an offshore special purpose entity receiving payments in U.S. dollars.[26] That is, if the project revenues are insufficient to cover the principal and interest payments of the project debt, the project sponsors do not have any obligation to guarantee such repayment, and the project lender relies solely on the project collateral in enforcing rights and obligations in connection with the project finance loan. Thus, while in corporate finance, should a project fail, the project lender

---

[26] Miyamoto, *supra* note 4.

does not necessarily suffer as long as the project sponsor remains financially viable, in project finance, the failure of a project can inflict significant losses on both the project lender and project sponsor.

Theoretically, international project finance for sustainable energy development provides a structure that does not impose upon the project sponsor any obligation beyond its equity investment. As a practical matter however, project financing is often carried out on a limited recourse basis, especially in the case of most developing market projects. For example, during the construction period, the project lenders generally require project sponsors to provide a contingent financial commitment under the terms of a project completion agreement. Moreover, if the risks associated with a nonrecourse debt are too high, the project lender may require various types of credit enhancement in the form of guarantees, warranties, and other covenants from the project sponsor or third parties to support the risk allocation.

International project finance for sustainable energy development is generally provided in the form of limited recourse debt financing. But there are still disputes in relation to the understanding of limited recourse debt financing. The most important function of such arrangements is the isolation of the project's assets and the assets of the project sponsors. The main basis of the loan is the feasibility of the project itself, not the business reputation of the project sponsors. And the main resources for repayment are the cash flow and profitability of the project, as generated by the project company and the project assets. Apart from the investment of equity assets, the project lenders still require project sponsors to provide certain guarantees toward the loan, so that in the future if the project's assets and revenues are insufficient to cover the principal and interest of the project debt, the project lenders can exercise their right of recourse to the project sponsors. So, the object of such limited recourse refers to the project sponsors and is limited to the equity assets and the guarantees that the sponsors put into the project, rather than all the assets of the sponsors. Limited recourse should also include recourse to all credit guarantors.

8 OVERVIEW OF VARIOUS RISKS

Due to the nonrecourse, or limited recourse, nature of international project financing for sustainable energy development, the complex financial and legal structures and the project lenders' reliance on the underlying cash flow from revenue producing contracts over a long payment period, international project finance for sustainable energy development requires a complex scheme of risk identification, evaluation, and allocation. The success of a project depends on a proper allocation of each risk to the project participant who is best able to manage and mitigate the risk. In general, the risks fall into two basic categories: commercial and political.

Commercial and political risks include, but are not limited to, construction risks (construction cost overruns, delays in completion, and failure to achieve target performance), operating risks (operating cost overruns and failure to maintain target performance), fuel risks (fuel price increases, fuel supply shortfall or interruptions, and transportation delays or interruptions), market risks (inadequate market demand for power and inadequate market prices for power), currency related risks (exchange rate fluctuations and inflation), and environmental risks.

Although commercial risks are common to all types of project financing, international project finance for sustainable energy development in developing countries is more susceptible to extensive political risks, such as adverse changes in the law, currency inconvertibility or nontransferability, expropriation, and possible civil unrest. The commercial and political risks of project finance for sustainable energy development in a developing country must be carefully allocated among the participants: the project company, project sponsors, the host government, multilateral and bilateral agencies, project lenders, and other project financing participants (such as, purchasing utilities, construction contractors, operations contractors, and fuel suppliers). In accordance with the fundamental theory of allocation of risks to the parties best able to manage it, the commercial risks associated with the completion and operation of the project are usually shifted to the private sector participants and insurance companies. On the other hand, the political risks are typically allocated to the host government, its agencies, and to multilateral and bilateral agencies providing political risk insurance.

8.1 Specific Clauses under the Framework for International Project Finance for Sustainable Energy Development for the Purpose of Allocating Risks of Project Lenders

Project financing participants allocate risks through the project's contractual framework and contract terms. For example, the parties may contractually allocate the fuel pricing risk to the fuel supplier with a fixed price, long-term fuel supply agreement. Alternatively, in a "pass-through" arrangement, the fuel pricing risk can be shifted to purchasing utilities and ultimately to the retail utility consumers in the tariff. Useful clauses which are applied in the legal framework for international project finance for sustainable energy development are discussed below.

Ensuring Project Lenders' Rights through Floating Charges

Guarantees provide indispensable leverage for the development of the market economy and are the core of guaranteed properties. Once set, the project lender obtains limited rights to control the exchange value of the guaranteed properties. The guarantee in international finance for sustainable energy development is a complex but systematic arrangement. Compared with traditional corporate finance, project lenders bear much more significant risks. Accordingly, project lenders concentrate more on the allocation of risks through guarantee arrangements. The balance of interests is framed under the contract system of project risks and allocation of risks. As debt repayment is limited to the project itself, floating charges on the project company's assets are adopted to lower the project lenders' risks and balance the interests in international project finance for sustainable energy development. The objects of floating charges can be the whole or part of the relevant project's assets, including the facilities, buildings, land or the servitude of land, accounts receivable, raw materials, inventories, contract rights, and so on. When the borrower breaches the contract and cannot repay the debt, the project lenders can appoint a receiver to take over the whole project. Floating charges are very inclusive and can cover both movables and immovables, such as workshops, facilities, and stocks, or they can cover accounts receivable, patents, trademarks, and business reputation.

Floating charges have the following features. First, the charged assets can be current assets or future assets. Second, the forms of the charged assets are transferable during the course of ordinary business. Third, the borrower reserves the right to dispose of the guaranteed properties in the ordinary business course before crystallization of the floating charge. If some of the guaranteed properties are transferred to a third party, then these assets no longer belong to the charged assets and there is no need to seek removal of the charge. Newly acquired assets become charged assets automatically. Accordingly, the value of the floating charge is limited to those properties at the time of the crystallization of the charge. The floating charge will finally be changed into a fixed guarantee when certain specific events occur, for example, breach of contract or the bankruptcy of the borrower. The project lenders then have the right to take over all the charged assets.

The achievement of the security rights of the project lenders through floating charges is different from common guarantees. In common guarantees, the project lenders would sell the charged assets to acquire relief, while under the floating charges, the project lenders will appoint a receiver to take over the project, and to operate the project, in the interest of the project lender until the expiration of the relevant license, at which time the project lenders will transfer the project to the host government voluntarily. The project lenders can also sell the project assets immediately. Unless the floating charge is registered, however, it does not operate against third parties.

Floating charges are a kind of guarantee constantly used in international project finance for sustainable energy development and China already has successful cases in practice. For example, in relation to factory B of the Shenzhen Shatoujiao Electric Factory in 1985, the project lenders took a floating charge over factory B and also established fixed guarantees over all the plant assets of the Shenzhen Shatoujiao Electric Factory.[27] As a means of balancing interests as between the project company or sponsors and the project lenders, such a mixed guarantee framework is highly successful in the context of international project finance for sustainable energy development.

Protecting the Interests of Project Lenders through Negative Pledge Clause

"Negative pledge clauses" require the project company to ensure that it will not set up priorities over its assets before the repayment of all the project debt. These clauses can greatly restrict the ordinary business activities of the project company, so there are some limitations and exceptions in the application of such clauses. In international project finance for sustainable energy development, project lenders should notice that negative pledge clauses may affect the assets and cash flow of the project assets that are the guarantee and repayment resource for creditors.

The project company should represent to project lenders that it will not do anything proscribed under the negative pledge clause. Accordingly, the project company is unable to establish any mortgages, guarantees, pledges, liens, or other security rights over its assets or revenues before the repayment of all debts and there is no room for the continuity of such security rights. The function of the negative pledge is to prevent the project company from setting up other security rights over the project assets in the interest of other project lenders. This prevents a situation where the rights of the initial project lenders to repayment of the project debt are made subordinate to the rights of subsequent project lenders in circumstances of reverse compensation. Negative pledge clauses ensure that equivalent project lenders are treated equally and hold the same

---

[27] *See* http://www.h2o-china.com/report/bot/030414-15.htm.

rights to repayment of the project debt. Furthermore, a negative pledge clause can indirectly prevent the project company from incurring new debts so as to protect its solvency. In the absence of such a clause, when the project company is in financial need, it will logically try to establish new guarantees on its assets to subsequent project lenders which is highly disadvantageous to the original project lenders. Under the limitations imposed by negative pledge clauses, new project lenders are unlikely to loan money to the project company as it is unable to provide sufficient guarantees.

Moreover, a negative pledge clause provides contractual rights for project lenders that are useful only when the project company obeys the contract. If the project company breaches the contract and establishes mortgages or other guarantees over its assets, the project lenders have no rights to bring a claim in court to reverse these subsequent security rights. All the project lenders can do is to accelerate the maturity date and to withdraw the loan in advance due to the project company's breach of contract. There are no provisions in Chinese law dealing with negative pledges, however, it is most necessary to include negative pledge clauses in international project finance. At this time, the foundation in Chinese law and the Vulgate international rule of *pacta sunt servenda* can be quoted to adopt the negative pledge clause.

Ensuring Cash Flows and Solvency of the Project Company through Take-or-Pay Agreements and Take-and-Pay Agreements

"Take-or-pay agreements" and "take-and-pay agreements" are two highly important collateral measures in international project finance for sustainable energy development. While they are in the nature of a loan security, there are inevitably some differences between the two agreements. However, both are long-term marketing contracts between the operational constructor and purchaser of the products under the framework of international project finance for sustainable energy development. Such agreements are used widely in all kinds of international project finance for sustainable energy development. These agreements are also used between the project company and the raw material or fuel supplier in some international project finance for sustainable energy development.

Take-or-pay agreements and take-and-pay agreements are indirect guarantees provided by the product purchaser. There are two similarities and two differences between these two kinds of agreements. The major difference is that in take-and-pay agreements, the purchaser of the products bears the payment obligation determined by the agreement on the basis of acquiring the vested products or services, but not the absolute payment obligation. Take-and-pay agreements are closer to general long-term business purchasing contracts and are more easily accepted by project investors and purchasers of products. However, from the standpoint of the project lenders, the guarantee function of take-and-pay agreements is somewhat limited and is not as effective as the guarantee provided by take-or-pay agreements, and it is quite possible that the project sponsors would be required to provide extra guarantees by way of supplementary securities to the take-and-pay agreement. In international project finance for sustainable energy development, both take-or-pay agreements and take-and-pay agreements act as guarantees for the interests of the project lenders. To avoid the purchaser of the products canceling the agreement or reducing their contractual obligations by reason of the project company's breach of contract, the project lender usually requests that the project company establish certain provisions in the agreement to limit or eliminate its liability.

Ensuring the Rights of Project Lenders To Acquire
Through a Covenants Clause

Under international project finance agreements, the contracting parties always agree to some financial covenants. The major functions of such a covenants clause is:

1. first, it is used to supervise and instruct the financial activities of the project company; and
2. second, to act as an alarm, as once the project company breaches the covenants, it can be a timely reminder to the project lenders to take remedial action immediately.

Generally, financial covenants require the project company to regularly report on its financial conditions to the project lenders and the project company should also abide by particular standards for asset evaluation which are reflected in its financial statement. First, the project company should provide audited financial statements to the project lender and provide relevant information in relation to business and financial conditions in accordance with the reasonable requirements of the project lender. Second, the project company should abide by the already settled standards for asset evaluation. Commercial banks in common law countries employ a raft of complex financial covenants and standards for asset evaluation and these requirements are gradually being incorporated in international project finance for sustainable energy development.

Apart from these matters, there are other covenants, such as merger clauses and restrictive clauses. Merger clauses prevent the project company from merging with other companies in order to avoid the unfavorable consequences of the transfer of equity interests in the project company, and changes in the company's assets and debts. Restrictive clauses forbid the project company from selling, transferring, renting, or taking other measures to dispose of its enterprise or assets so as not to influence the solvency of the project company.

Should the project company breach these covenants, the project lender is entitled to bring a claim for damages. In addition, the project lender can also seek remedies prescribed by law, such as specific performance or an injunction.

The agreements or contracts adopted in the context of international project finance for sustainable energy development are aimed at balancing the interests of relevant contracting parties. The project's ultimate revenue determines whether a project is successful or not and this revenue itself is determined by the allocation of project risks. Through a covenants clause in relevant legal documents, it is possible to flexibly and effectively reduce all kinds of risks, so as to facilitate the success of the sustainable energy development project. In this way, legal arrangements and structures for international project finance for sustainable energy development act as a mediating influence, balancing the interests of all contracting parties. Such structures are the key to success in international project financing of sustainable energy development.

9 CONCLUSION

Obviously, the interests of each party need to be balanced in international project finance for sustainable energy development. Law is the result of the search for a mechanism to resolve conflicts in society. Different interest groups have different expectations and demands and it is possible to identify both cooperation and conflict in their legal values. Different parties face fierce conflicts between contradicting legal values during the contract negotiation period. Equity tries to resolve these conflicts and provides the ideological basis and theoretical pivot for the legal framework of international project finance for sustainable energy development. The "check and stimulate" mechanism, generated by the operation of equity theory in international project finance for sustainable energy development and relevant legal relations, is an active response to the market economy's characteristics of "check and stimulate." The goal of equity theory is to provide for an energetic, efficient, and orderly transnational civil and commercial transaction structure. In international project finance for sustainable energy development, both the interests between the host government and the project lender, and the interests between the project lender and the project sponsor, refer to equity theory.

29 Emissions Trading Systems

Cao Ming-de*

1 THE THEORETICAL BASIS OF THE "EMISSIONS TRADING" SYSTEMS

There are three major theories on "emissions trading" systems: the externality theory; transaction cost theory in economics; and property theory on environmental capacity resources.

The main proponents of the externality theory were Professors Marshall and Pigu at Cambridge University in the twentieth century. Externality theory refers to the by-products or the side effects of economic activities beyond the regulation of market mechanism, that is, the side effects of part of economic activities that cannot be reflected in the price. It can be divided into external economy and external diseconomy.[1] Pollution is the external diseconomy of economic activities, as the enterprises' business activities produce negative effects on others and its surrounding environment, but the enterprises never bring this into its cost and price of the market transaction. The enterprises gain benefits from these economic activities, while the society and others bear the burden of paying the controlling fees caused by its emissions, and become the victims of emissions, which leads to a gap between the enterprises' cost and the society's payment, thus forming the so-called external diseconomy. This is the basic theory western economics uses to explain the environmental issues. As the government pays the pollution controlling fees, and its revenue mainly comes from taxes, the enterprises gain profits from this process, which is not in keeping with social justice. If the enterprises put the pollution controlling fees into its cost of production, it would be reflected by the price, and eventually the consumers and the society would assume the pollution controlling fees. Therefore, it is believed that the enterprises' external diseconomy should be internalized, while the emissions trading system is the specific reflection that the enterprises internalize its external diseconomy produced by its operating activities. That is why western economics on externality theory is one of the economic bases of emissions trading systems.

From the economic perspective, environmental resources have the nature of public property which can easily lead to the "tragedy of the commons," as the British scholar Garllet Harding put it. The ancient Greek philosopher Aristotle once alleged:

---

[1] Huang Gui-qin, "On Emission Trading System" (2003) 3 *Hebei Science Journal* 202.

* LL.D. (CASS), Professor of Environmental Law, Associate Editor-in-Chief of Modern Law Science (law journal), Southwest University of Political Science and Law, Chongqing, China.

507

"Common things are often given the least consideration, and people care their own having while neglecting the common things. Of all the common things, he only cares the part somewhat relative to him."[2] Harding took a ranch as an illustration as to how environmental resources are used for free. The ranch is owned by the public, while the sheep are owned by the herders. In order to maximize his or her own economic benefits every herder as a rational economic soul seeks to herd more sheep, but the capacity of the ranch is limited, the competition among herders leads to the degeneration of the ranch and the destruction of the commons. The manifestation of the tragedy of the commons in the use of environmental resources is not that people take something from the commons but that they put something onto the commons, for example, they release toxic, chemical, radioactive substances into water, atmosphere, land, or space. The environmental economics research makes clear that one of the major reasons for the degeneration of environmental quality and the overconsumption of resources is that the environmental resources possess the nature of common things that lead to the popular free ride. Since environmental resources possess the nature of common things, it cannot create exclusive ownership according to traditional civil property theory. For this reason the environmental resources are universally abused. To solve the problem that many people use environmental resources without paying anything, it is necessary to redefine the ownership and use of environmental resources, and make full use of market mechanisms to allocate environmental resources in an effective way. The essence of pursuing an emissions trading system is the specific device of paying for the use of environmental resources (including environmental capacity resources), and such a practice could affirm the property nature of this right (the right of using environmental resources). This in fact confirms at law that environmental resources are private in nature. Even though scholars seldom mention this point, it is because environmental resources possess the nature of private property that we may possibly regulate it by way of private law.

Another economic theory about emissions trading systems is the transaction cost theory. R. H. Coase published "The Problem of Social Cost" in the *Journal of Law and Economics* of the University of Chicago in 1960. In this article, he applied the transaction cost theory to analyze the effect of legal institutions, and proposed the famous "Coase Theorem." If the transaction cost is zero, no matter how the law defines the right, resources could be effectively allocated by the market mechanism under the condition of free exchange, that is to say, any allocation of legal rights could produce effective results with no transaction cost. But the transaction cost is always more than zero in the real world, therefore the second Coase Theorem was put forward: if the transaction cost is positive, a different definition of legal rights could produce different resource allocation with different efficiency. Hence the law that could minimize the transaction cost is most appropriate. Property right economists believe, in essence, that economics is the study of scarce resources, the distribution of the scarce resources in a society is the arrangement of the resources' ownership and the right of use, and the institution of property affects resources' distribution and its efficiency in use. If the Coase Theorem is applied, the ownership of the environmental rights and its transfer could be made clear and protected by law, and the private law could play an important role in protecting environmental resources with moderate intervention from the government. The final

---

[2] Aristotle, *Politics*, at 30 (Chinese version from the Commercial Press, Beijing, 1983).

result could be that the owner and user of environmental resources would choose to buy the emissions quota (the right of using environmental capacity resources), or give up buying such emissions but devote more efforts to controlling pollution according to the maximum self-benefits and profit maxims. This would not only fully respect the market subjects' rights and freedoms, but also reflect the equal relation between both of the trading parties in an adequate manner.

The third theoretical basis of the emissions trading system is the property right theory of environmental capacity resources. It is believed that the environmental capacity[3] is limited, and it is this limitation that makes it a scarce "resource." The scarceness of such a capacity resource makes it possess value; thus it is in the nature of a commodity, and can be exchanged at the market. It is thought that because the environmental values cannot be reflected at the same time, the resources with some environmental values become scarce. For instance, in a certain time and space, some environmental resources cannot satisfy people's life need if they are used to meet another's production need, and if they are used to meet another's production need, the contradiction between the environmental values and the scarceness of some environmental resources appear. Such scarceness of the environmental functions and the environmental capacity resources are the economic reasons for designing an emissions trading system.[4] What is the nature of an emission from a jurisprudential perspective? On this issue, there is a difference of opinion among scholars. The author believes that emissions are the obligee's right to use the environmental capacity, i.e., release certain quantity of pollutant within a lawfully acquired environmental capacity limit; it is a kind of property right. Scholars such as Lv Zhong-mei and Liu Chang-xin believe that environmental capacity could be the object of civil relation. They proposed: "After the government determines the total environmental capacity, it can transfer it to the private sector by the form of contract and thus realize the private right of using environment under the state control; the private sector could transfer the environmental capacity it gained lawfully under the state supervision and the environmental capacity trading is realized."[5]

2 THE IMPLICATION, ORIGIN, BASIC CONTENT, PROCEDURE, AND IMPLEMENTATION BASIS OF EMISSIONS TRADING SYSTEMS

2.1 The Implication of Emissions Trading Systems

A licensing system is one of the basic institutions of environmental resources law. An emissions trading system is its major manifestation in the sector of preventing and controlling pollution. The emissions trading system is based on the premise of implementing emissions license supervision and controlling the total emissions. Enterprises are encouraged to save emission quota through technology improvement and pollution

---

[3] It is believed by some scholars that environmental capacity is the reflection of the ecological value possessed by the environmental resources, which could be defined as the amount of waste that can be assimilated by the environment in normal equilibrium process. *See* Lv Zhong-mei, Liu Chang-xing, "On Environmental Contract System" (2003) 3 *Modern Law Science* 110.

[4] Huang Gui-qin, *supra* note 1.

[5] Lv Zhong-mei, Liu Chang-xing, "On Environmental Contract System" (2003) *3 Modern Law Science* 110.

control. Such a quota is regarded as "environmental capacity resources," "valuable resources," or a "reserve" for enterprises in the need of expanding its production. The
newly built pollution source or the old ones without an emissions quota could seek
to buy it from the enterprises with surplus quota in the emission trading market.
In western countries, emissions trading systems play an important role in controlling the total emission. The main purpose of designing emissions trading is to make
clear the polluters' access to environmental capacity resources, that is, the legal emissions right under the condition of fulfilling environmental quality requirements. Such
a right can be bought and sold like commodities, thus optimizing the allocation of
resources.

2.2 The Origin and Development of the Emissions Trading System

An emissions trading system was proposed initially by the American economist Dales
in 1968. It was initially adopted by the Environmental Protection Agency (EPA) for
controlling atmosphere pollution and water pollution, and gained unprecedented success with great economic and social benefits, especially after it was used to control total
SO_2 emissions in 1990. The market price of emission license is far lower than expected,
which adequately shows the two advantages of emission trading: guaranteeing the environmental quality and lowering the cost of reaching the standard. So far, the United
States has developed a comprehensive emissions trading system with the core content of
Offset, Bubble, and Banking,[6] and Netting,[7] which has gained tangible environmental
and economic benefits in practice. Over a thirty-year period of environmental supervision, the EPA adopted three emissions trading policies successively: Offsets,[8] Bubble,[9]
and the acid rain program.

Many countries, such as Germany, Australia, and the UK, have adopted emissions
trading schemes. China has begun its pilot project of emissions trading since 1991,
and has gathered some experience. Emissions trading is now a kind of mainstream
environmental economic policy in many countries. By giving environmental capacity
resources value, this system defines the property rights, allows for the free transfer of
property rights, allocates environmental capacity resources effectively, and reduces the
social cost of controlling pollution, so it becomes an effective measure to implement
total environmental control.

---

[6] Enterprises' surplus quota is handled by "Banking," or "saved" for future use, or sold to other enterprises.
[7] By this process, an enterprise expands its production and keeps its emissions range below the emission
     right it owns by improving its producing process.
[8] Offsets is a type of emissions policy initially implemented by the United States, designed to solve the
     contradiction between environmental protection and economic growth faced by the United States in the
     1970s. Offsets allow newly built and expanding polluting sources in areas below the specified standard
     subject to the condition of buying sufficient emissions quota from the existing polluting sources to
     meet the emissions requirement of the new polluting sources. This policy aims at ensuring that the total
     emissions will not be increased in this area after polluting sources are newly built or expanded. It is
     proved that this policy is successful and effective in practice, as determined by the 1977 Clean Air Act.
[9] A factory with many polluting sources is a "bubble." Under specified circumstances, a factory is allowed
     to increase emissions of some kinds of polluting resources if it commensurately reduces other kinds
     of polluting resource at the same time. Since the bubble has a large transaction cost, this policy never
     became a major policy of the United States for controlling its air pollution, but nevertheless it formed
     the basis for other emissions trading policies and provided useful experience.

2.3 The Basic Content of Emissions Trading

Under the premise of satisfying society's requirement for environmental quality, emissions trading schemes determine the legal right of releasing pollutants (emissions), and allow emissions trading at the market, thus controlling the overall emissions. In practice, the emissions license the enterprises and institutions receive is usually issued by the government, the emissions license and the emissions it represents can be transferred freely, and therefore the enterprises and institutions could buy or sell their emissions according to their own needs. The functioning of the emissions trading system includes three basic elements: public decision making relating to the pollution that a certain area or society would be willing to accept or bear; the restriction and allocation of total emissions; and the establishment of an emissions trading market. Relative to these three elements, an emissions trading system is composed of two parts: emissions license and emissions trading.[10]

2.4 The Procedure of Emissions Trading

In some pilot areas of China, the procedure of emissions trading is as follows: first, the emissions unit applies for more emissions, whereupon the environmental protection sector examines and determines the need for additional emissions; then, the license is determined and the two trading parties sign a comprehensive assignment agreement; in the end, the environmental protection sector witnesses, examines, and approves the agreement, and alters the emissions licenses of the two trading parties.

2.5 The Implementation Basis of Emissions Trading

To ensure that emissions trading is undertaken successfully, its implementation is based on total emissions control and a system of certain market mechanisms, laws, and regulations. First, total emissions control is the basis for emission trading. In the process of undertaking emissions trading, in the beginning a certain geographical area is specified. The environmental protection administrative department in charge determines the environmental quality objective in this area, and determines the total emissions of certain pollutants according to the environmental capacity of selected area and distributes it (or sells it by auction) to the polluting sources in the form of quota. The quota is determined on the basis of the total emissions. Only after the total emissions control objective and the total actual emissions level of the area is determined can the total quota be counted. This is the premise underlying emissions trading. Total emissions control could guarantee an improvement in environmental benefits. Second, a mature market mechanism is an important condition for ensuring successful emissions trading. The United States is the most successful country in undertaking emissions trading, where emissions can be traded like stocks and bonds. With the implementation of 1990 Clean Air Act Amendment Acid Rain Program, the U.S. emissions trading developed into the second stage. The success that the United States achieved – a remarkable environmental protection performance, the emissions reduction of SO_2 being far above the fixed objective, the market price of emission license being lower than expected – is

---

[10] *See* http://www.zei.gov.cn/zjeco/0304/16.htm.

closely related to its mature market mechanism. Third, an effective and mature legal system is an important basis for implementing emissions trading. Emissions trading mainly relies on the market mechanism, while the maturity of the market mechanism depends on the efficient working of the legal system. Therefore, in addition to determining the total emissions trading quota, such a series of legal mechanisms as trading rules, quota regulations, emissions reporting system, examination system, monitoring system, supervising measures, and a quota follow-up system also need to be developed.[11]

3 THE ADVANTAGES AND DISADVANTAGES, AND COUNTERMEASURE ANALYSIS OF EMISSIONS TRADING SYSTEMS

Compared to other environmental controls, an emissions trading system has two advantages:

First, emissions trading is beneficial for ensuring environmental quality. Under the conditions of emissions fees and penalties, the government can only passively discipline the polluters. It is the responsibility of the enterprises to choose pollution control or pay fines based on the applicable economic incentives. For example, if it will cost Enterprise A a large amount of money to replace or rebuild pollution control facilities, and there exists an alternative to pay emissions penalties, A is likely to choose the latter. Under conditions of emissions trading, the government and environmental protection organizations could react timely to the environmental quality through the trading of emissions. On the other hand, the implementation of an emissions trading system is based on the premise of total emissions control. Total emissions control regards a certain controlling area (such as administrative region, drainage area, environmental functioning area) as an integral system, and measures are taken to control the total emissions of this area below a certain level; therefore the environmental quality requirement is satisfied in this area. Total emissions control is not only a type of environmental control concept, but also a way to supervise the environment, which corresponds to "density control." China proposed a total emissions control requirement in 1995, which is advantageous for ensuring the environmental quality in certain areas.

Second, emissions trading helps to lower the enterprises' cost for reaching the prescribed emissions standards. If the cost for an enterprise to control its pollution is higher than the price of emissions at the market, it would rather buy emissions rights than invest in pollution control facilities, and vice versa. If an enterprise's cost of controlling pollution is lower than the price of emission at the market, it will prefer controlling pollution to saving emissions quota and will sell the surplus emissions quota at the market. For example, say the cost of reducing one ton of SO_2 emissions for Enterprise A is ¥12, but for Enterprise B it is ¥8, and the cost of reducing SO_2 emissions for Enterprise A is ¥4 less than Enterprise B. If A buys the emissions quota from B at the price of ¥10 per ton, B could gain economic benefits through transferring its emissions quota, and A also reduces its own pollution control and reaches the emissions standard. The total emissions are not increased. Therefore, the essence of emissions trading is to redistribute the pollution control work among enterprises and thus make enterprises with lower pollution control cost assume more controlling work. This will correspondingly

[11] Lu Yuan-tang, "The Implementation Basis of Emission Trading System," *Chinese Environmental Daily*, Feb. 14, 2003.

reduce the enterprises' cost of controlling pollution and will help to increase social welfare.

In addition, emissions trading helps to promote enterprises carrying out research and development work, and aids in the adoption of advanced pollution prevention and technology control. The existence of an emissions trading market helps citizens express their own will and thus provides a democratic basis for environmental protection.[12]

However, the advantages of emissions trading should be analyzed and considered rationally. The following major issues are worthy of further research:

1. Can emissions trading completely get to the state of "unity between the enterprises' interests and the public interests" and "unity between efficiency and fairness" under the market mechanism?

It is believed that the implementation of an emissions trading system can achieve the unity between social interests and the enterprises' interests, and attain the unity between the partial interests and the whole interests. "Where the market economy and the law of value could play a role, enterprises discharging pollution would necessarily adopt advanced pollution control technologies and develop more effective technologies constantly, the surplus emission produced by the technological progress would bring enterprises benefits, thus reflecting the unity between efficiency and fairness."[13] This is where the legal value of emissions trading lies. From the theoretical perspective, this argument is tenable. Nevertheless, it still needs detailed analysis whether emissions trading could achieve a win-win result for society and enterprises. First, we should measure correctly the environmental capacity of the area where the two emissions trading parties are, and determine the rights and obligations of the assessors as well as the legal liabilities they have to assume. How can we determine the environmental capacity in one area scientifically? Can people sense the geographical difference between areas and the change of environmental capacity in one area? How can the legislature control the acts of the environmental capacity assessors? This objectively calls for new comprehensive legislation, and local legislation in particular.[14] Second, the administrative cost of emissions trading is relatively large, especially without scientifically efficient regulations.

2. How can we avoid deviations from the purpose of emissions trading?

The intention of emissions trading is to reduce the emissions and achieve the coordinated development of economics, the society, and the environment. But another problem being demonstrated by the environmental diplomacy of the environmental protectionists and the EU may appear: emissions trading can reduce the polluter's motive to control pollution, as they may rather spend money fulfilling their obligations than exert themselves to reduce pollution. Therefore, emissions should be a kind of private right with strong public right color. The government should strengthen the macroregulation and supervision of emissions trading and expand the channels of public participation.

---

[12] Li Jian, "The Undoubted Advantages of Emissions Trading," *The People's Daily*, overseas page 11, Dec. 24, 2003. *See* http://www.people.com.cn/GB/paper39/6838/666157.html.

[13] Huang Gui-qin, *supra* note 1, 203.

[14] Zhao Li, *On Emission Trading System*, 6 (unpublished).

3. How can we avoid the possible transfer of pollution between areas caused by emissions trading?

First, the underlying basis of emissions trading is total emissions control, that is, it is carried out with the emissions being steady, and it cannot improve the environmental quality. Second, some enterprises may give up the best available technology to control pollution and buy an additional emissions quota, which would increase the local emissions in seriously polluted areas though it may not be above the upper emissions limit of the region in which they are situated. Third, the emissions trading may take place between polluters (enterprises), especially between polluters of different regions, which would damage the environmental benefits of the local inhabitants where the buyers are situated. Although the trading is undertaken after carrying out an environmental impact assessment (EIA) in the region where the buyers are situated, the issue of transferring pollution between regions still exists. Therefore, when it is time to design the emissions trading system, a hearing procedure should be prescribed, in particular the holding of a hearing to consult the inhabitants where the buyers are situated. In other words, the inhabitants should participate in the decision-making process.

4 THE PRACTICE OF EMISSIONS TRADING IN CHINA AND ITS ASSESSMENT

China is active in the pilot project on emissions trading, mainly in relation to air pollution and water pollution.

In relation to air pollution, supported by the efforts of the National Environmental Protection Agency, in 1997 the Environmental Defense and Beijing Environment and Development Seminar began their theoretical study on the feasibility of carrying out emissions trading in China under the condition of total emissions control. As the preliminary research bore fruit, the research program has been expanded to the stage of a case study since the latter part of 1997. A pilot project was carried out in Benxi and Nantong. The pilot project in Nantong focused on supervising the emissions trading, and its operating procedure was based on the existing environmental protection law and regulations. The pilot project in Benxi focused on developing a local regulation involving total emission control and emission trading, that is, the Administrative Rule of Benxi Total Air Emission Control. In 1999, when Premier Zhu visited the United States, China and the United States signed a Feasibility Letter of Intent on Applying the Market Mechanism to Reduce SO_2 Emissions. This project is formally determined by the U.S. Environmental Protection Agency as a component of this letter of intent.

The Sino-America cooperation project, Applying Market Mechanism to Control SO_2 Emissions, achieved success. The signing ceremony for the sale of SO_2 emissions from Nantong Tianshenggang Power Plant Corporation Ltd. to anther large chemical Corporation Ltd. in Nantong was held in Nantong, Jangsu. This is the first Chinese SO_2 emissions trading in the real sense. According to the agreement, the seller may sell 1,800 tons of SO_2 emissions to the purchaser, and the purchaser may use the emissions in the following six years. This creates a precedent for emissions trading in China. In this transaction, the SO_2 emission was sold in yearly terms (300 tons per year), and the transaction payment was also settled in yearly terms. After the contract expired, the emissions were owned by the seller, with the purchaser getting the right of using the emissions. It was also stipulated in the contract that the remainder of the emissions that the purchaser did not use could be carried forward to the next year's account during the contracting period, and could even be transferred to a third party after fulfilling some conditions. It has also been reported that commencing in July 2003, Jiangsu Taicanggan Environmental Protection Power Plant Corporation Ltd. would buy 1,700 tons of SO_2 emissions from Nanjing Xiaguan Power Plant at a price of ¥1700,000. This is the first Chinese transregional transaction of SO_2 emissions trading. Taicanggan Environmental Protection Power Plant Corporation Ltd. decided to expand its generating and heating unit, and desulphurize its emissions. Although its desulphurization rate is as high as ninety percent, the corporation has no extra SO_2 emissions quota, and the corporation would increase its annual SO_2 emissions by 2,000 tons. Nanjing Xiaguan Power Plant introduced advanced technologies to control its pollution, and its desulphurization rate was as high as seventy-five percent. The actual annual SO_2 emissions were 3,000 tons less than the emissions quota approved by the Environmental Protection Department. One corporation would break its total emissions upper limit for its expansion, another had surplus emissions quota for its successful desulphurization. Jiangsu Environmental Protection Department acted as go-between to help the two power generating enterprises in different areas negotiate a trade. After several rounds of negotiations, an SO_2 emissions trading agreement was reached. According to the agreement, during the period from July 2003 to 2005 Taicanggang Environmental Protection Power Plant Corporation Ltd. will buy annual SO_2 emissions of 1,700 tons from Xiaguan Power Plant at a price of ¥1 per kilo, and it will pay Xiaguan Power Plant ¥1700,000 per year. The two parties will redetermine the price according to the market conditions after 2006. The experts concerned had undertaken a comprehensive assessment of the feasibility of Taicanggang Environmental Protection Power Plant Corporation Ltd. carrying out SO_2 emissions trading, and concluded that Taicang at present still had a relatively large environmental capacity after this corporation bought the emissions, and its environmental impact on the surrounding area would be very small even under the most unfavorable climate conditions. Jiangsu Province is one of the first provinces to carry out SO_2 emissions trading in China, and drafted the "Provisional Measures of Jiangsu Province for Controlling SO_2 Emissions Trading." It resolved to advance SO_2 emissions trading fully in Jiangsu province from October 1, 2002, and to try actively to develop transactions between counties or municipalities.

At present, the National Environmental Protection Agency is carrying out the model project of "Total SO_2 Emissions Control and Emission Trading Policy in Seven Provinces and Municipalities" in Shangdong, Shangxi, Jiangsu, Henan, Shanghai, Tianjin, and Liuzhou. The purpose of this project is to seek a way to apply the economic lever and stimulate the initiative of the enterprises and achieve total SO_2 emissions reductions under the socialist market oriented economy. At the same time, based on the practice in model areas, it solved some problems on technological support and controlling norms needed in implementing an emissions trading policy, and lay the foundation to establish a China-wide emissions trading system. In China coal accounts for seventy percent of primary energy consumption, and the SO_2 air pollution caused by burning coal is very large. The acid rain resulting from SO_2 emissions has caused losses amounting to ¥110 billion. China enacted legislation to control acid rain pollution in "The Law on

Preventing and Controlling Atmospheric Pollution" for the first time in 1995, and "The Tenth Five-Year Plan on National Economy and Social Development" stated: "As of 2005, the major pollutant emissions will be further reduced, the whole country's SO_2 emissions will be reduced by 10 percent compared with the level of 2000; total SO_2 emissions in the two areas of control (SO_2 and acid rain pollution) will be reduced by twenty percent compared with the level of 2000."

The Chinese emissions trading system is still in an exploratory stage, and much work remains to be done in relation to policies, law and regulations, operational measures and methods. A thorough exploration and improvement is still needed in these fields. In the author's mind, there are several major reform issues involved in building a successful Chinese emissions trading system:

First, the legal nature and ownership rights of environmental capacity resources should be made clear. The legal nature of the environmental capacity resources is the right to use environmental resources – this should be owned by the state, with enterprises and citizens having the right of using and transfer it in accordance with the law.

Second, the distribution of the environmental capacity resources should be equitable. At present unfairness exists in the original distribution of environmental capacity resources between existing and newly built polluting enterprises. If the original environmental capacity resources are distributed among the polluting enterprises free of charge, it is unfair for the newly built enterprises which will pay for the environmental capacity resources. On the other hand, the government will suffer a loss of income. If the emissions are distributed with compensation, it is worth studying whether it is sold by auction or by government pricing. The former may result in large enterprises manipulating the market and hoarding for speculation. The latter may not reflect the supply and demand of the market.

Third, the government should moderately intervene and supervise the emissions trading. As mentioned in Section 3, emissions are a private right with a strong public right color; environmental capacity resources not only have the nature of public property, but can also become the object of civil relations possessing the nature of a private right. Emissions trading involves not only public interests but also the benefits of the two parties trading emissions quotas; for this reason, the government should protect the legitimate interests of the two parties trading emissions on condition that the public interests are guaranteed. However, the government or government agencies must never trespass on the private rights and legal interests of the trading parties.

Fourth, the environmental monitoring capacity needs to be improved, and corresponding on-line monitoring devices and a quota follow-up system should be developed. The provision of accurate data is the basis of trading, so the enterprises should install on-line monitoring devices; only by so doing can we ensure the accuracy of the data, help the responsible Environmental Protection Department obtain reliable information and monitor the emissions trading more closely. A quota follow-up system is a comprehensive financial system of collecting, determining, and maintaining financial data as well as tradable quota ownership and trading records. Through an effective quota follow-up system, the transactions between accounts can be supervised to ensure their legality and to help to form an effective market mechanism.

In summary, we should undertake a more detailed and rational review of the emissions trading system, and avoid rushing headlong into ill-considered action. As part of the on going pilot projects, we should try to explore trading patterns and create an early warning mechanism suitable for Chinese conditions, make best use of the advantages of the system while avoiding the disadvantages, and bring into play the positive role and advantages of the system in allocating environmental capacity resources by way of market mechanisms. There is good reason to believe that in China there is a wide scope and promising future for emissions trading.

PART SEVEN

CIVIL SOCIETY AND THE PROCEDURAL REQUIREMENTS OF ENERGY LAW FOR SUSTAINABLE DEVELOPMENT

30 The Role of Civil Society

Svitlana Kravchencko*

1 INTRODUCTION

The role of civil society is becoming a major aspect of international law. Nongovernmental organizations (NGOs) and individuals are becoming actors in international law in general and in international environmental law in particular. The environmental rights of citizens are being recognized on the international level (globally and regionally) and the national level. The role of citizens and NGOs in decision making is helping to prevent or mitigate adverse impacts on environment. Citizens' rights to access to information and public participation are prerequisites to the successful management of sustainable energy regimes.

Why is public participation important? Some governmental officials are likely to think that public participation is an unnecessary burden. It may appear to make decision making processes more complicated and time consuming. On the other hand, the public may suggest alternative solutions that will increase the quality of the decision and save resources and money. An improved decision may decrease or prevent negative impacts on the environment. Transparency of decision making also helps to avoid corruption. Since economically powerful private interests will always find a way to participate, even without legal provisions, allowing public participation can provide a counterbalance of forces, allowing well-intentioned civil servants to carry out their responsibilities free of outside pressure.

2 ENVIRONMENTAL RIGHTS IN INTERNATIONAL LAW

One of the foremost instances of civil society becoming active partners in important government decisions is in the field of environmental rights. These rights are being recognized at the global, regional, and national levels.

2.1 Recognition of Rights at the Global Level

Civil society first tried to play a role in international environmental law at the 1972 United Nations Conference on the Human Environment in Stockholm. Its representatives

* Svitlana Kravchenko has taught environmental law for 25 years and lectured in more than 20 countries. Founder and president of Ecopravo-Lviv, the first public interest law firm in Ukraine, she is also founder of the Ukraine office of the Environmental Law Alliance Worldwide. At the international level, she is cofounder and Codirector of the Association of Environmental Law of CEE/NIS.

monitored the proceedings, published a newspaper concerning daily negotiations, and acted as observers. It is probably not a coincidence that an outcome of that meeting was that the right of each person to a favorable environment was also recognized for the first time at the international level. According to Principle 1 of Stockholm Declaration, "[m]an has the fundamental right to freedom, equality and adequate conditions of life, in an environment of a quality that permits a life of dignity and well-being."[1]

Twenty years later civil society played a more significant role. In the UN Conference on Environment and Development in Rio de Janeiro its representatives were official delegates. Further development of the environmental right and formulation of other environmental rights can be found in the 1992 Rio Declaration on Environment and Development. Principle 1 proclaims that "[h]uman beings . . . are entitled to a healthy and productive life in harmony with nature."[2]

This right to a safe environment can be considered a "substantive right." This is a right that, if implemented, would produce a better environment. Usually a right held by one person is connected to a reciprocal duty by another person not to violate that right. The duty would be on everyone (both companies and governments) to avoid taking actions that would harm the environment.

Another type of environmental right is a "procedural right" – a right that is actually related as much to democratic theory as it is to environmental protection. Principle 10 of the Rio Declaration provides that

> each individual shall have appropriate *access to information* concerning the environment that is held by public authorities, including information on hazardous materials and activities in their communities, and *the opportunity to participate* in decision-making processes. States shall facilitate and encourage public awareness and participation by making information widely available. Effective *access to judicial and administrative proceedings*, including redress and remedy, shall be provided.

These three procedural rights (information, participation, and justice) can be seen as ways of achieving the substantive environmental right or simply as part of the democratization of decision making. The Rio Declaration was signed by high-level governmental officials of 179 countries. This can be understood as a commitment of countries to develop both substantive and procedural environmental rights on the global and national levels.

At the 2002 World Summit on Sustainable Development (WSSD), the role of civil society and environmental rights were important issues. Civil society participated actively in the preparatory committees leading to the WSSD and then participated in the WSSD itself, lobbying for a strong formulation of environmental rights in its main documents. In many cases civil society failed: the Implementation Plan includes weak provisions on the "possible relationship between environment and human rights" and the necessity to "enhance partnerships between governmental and nongovernmental actors."[3] A Proposed Article 151 concerning global guidelines on access to information

---

[1] Declaration of the United Nations Conference on the Human Environment, available at www.unep.org/ Documents/Default.asp? DocumentID=97&ArticleID=1503.

[2] Rio Declaration on Environment and Development, available at www.unep.org/Documents/ Default.asp?DocumentID=78&ArticleID=1163.

[3] World Summit on Sustainable Development. Plan of Implementation, Articles 150–152, available at http://www.johannesburgsummit.org/html/documents/summit_docs/plan_final1009.doc.

and public participation in environmental decision making was deleted from the text.

Frustration of civil society with the outcome of the WSSD, however, was changed to hope a few months later when the United Nations Environment Programme's Governing Council made a decision in February 2003 to assess the possibility of promoting, at the national and international levels, the application of Principle 10 of the Rio Declaration on Environment and Development, and to determine if there is value in initiating an intergovernmental process for the preparation of global guidelines on the application of Principle 10.[4]

Environmental rights – particularly procedural environmental rights – are included in various multilateral environmental agreements (MEA) such as the Desertification Convention, the Framework Convention on Climate Change, the Convention on Biological Diversity, the Cartagena Protocol on Biosafety, and others.[5]

In the field of energy, Article 19(1)(i) of the 1994 Energy Charter Treaty between states of Western, Central, and Eastern Europe calls on parties to "promote the transparent assessment at an early stage and prior to decision, and subsequent monitoring, of Environmental Impacts of environmentally significant energy investment projects."[6] Article 20 requires parties to publish "laws, regulations, judicial decisions and administrative rulings of general application made effective by any Contracting Party, and agreements in force between Contracting Parties, which affect other matters covered by this Treaty."

International financial institutions have also started to recognize the role of civil society. Several of them make their documents publicly available and provide mechanisms for participation of civil society in decision making. For instance, the International Bank for Reconstruction and Development (IBRD) has organized an Inspection Panel to investigate claims from citizens and NGOs about harm to the environment or violation of human rights by World Bank financed projects.[7] The World Trade Organization's (WTO) Appellate Body established a procedure for NGOs to submit amicus curiae briefs in cases with environmental implications, although it later backtracked by refusing to accept the briefs that were submitted.[8]

2.2 Recognition of Rights at Regional Level – Europe

2.2.1 Aarhus Convention

Public participation in environmental decision making is becoming a reality in Europe and Central Asia – the region of the United Nation Economic Commission for Europe (UN ECE). This is partly the result of the good will of governments, who recognize the benefits of more open and participatory societies and have committed themselves to

---

[4] Decision GC.22/17-II-B, "Enhancing the application of Principle 10 of the Rio Declaration on Environment and Development."

[5] D. Shelton, Joint UNEP-OHCHR Seminar on Human Rights and Environment, 14–16 January 2002, Geneva, Background paper #1, "Human Rights and Environment Issues in Multilateral Treaties Adopted between 1991 and 2001."

[6] Available at http://www.jurisint.org/pub/01/en/doc/224_1.htm.

[7] The World Bank Group, The Inspection Panel, available at http://www.worldbank.org/html/ins-panel.

[8] P. C. Mavroidis, "Amicus Curiae Briefs before the WTO: Much Ado about Nothing," J. Monnet Working Paper 2/01, available at http://www.worldtradelaw.net/articles/mavroidisamicus.pdf.

construct them in the Aarhus Convention.[9] It is equally the result of the hard work of NGOs, which have been playing an unprecedented participatory role in the Convention's formation and implementation.

2.2.1.1 Process of Negotiations. The process leading to the Convention and occurring afterwards is itself a significant example of public participation in environmental decision making at the international level. About 200 public interest environmental experts organized as the European ECO Forum, NGO Coalition provided suggestions and comments to the draft Convention.[10] NGOs organized Round Tables in Central and Eastern countries and in some West European countries and Newly Independent States (NIS) to inform and educate the public and governments about the content, importance, and potential of the Convention for building environmental democracy. Under the umbrella of the European Environmental Bureau (ECO Forum headquarters) and the Regional Environmental Center, public interest experts from all European countries conducted research and made an assessment of trends and practices on public participation in Eastern Europe, Western Europe, and the Newly Independent States of the former Soviet Union, along with a Pan-European Assessment. REC published four volumes titled *Doors to Democracy*.[11]

Citizen's organizations participated in all UN ECE negotiation sessions. At the negotiating table, the European ECO Forum was treated by UN ECE and the governments as a partner, taking the floor, making suggestions, being heard, and having its opinion taken into consideration. At the time of signature, a special session with participation of the public was organized at the Ministerial Conference "Environment for Europe" in Aarhus, at the time of adoption of the Convention. During this session, representatives of the public discussed with the Ministers problems and obstacles for implementation of the Convention.

2.2.1.2 Impact of Aarhus. The Aarhus Convention is surely the most impressive development of Principle 10 of the Rio Declaration. It was signed by thirty-nine countries of Europe in 1998 in Aarhus, Denmark, during the Fourth Ministerial Conference "Environment for Europe" and entered into force in October 2001.

As UN Secretary General Kofi Annan said about the Aarhus Convention:

> Although regional in scope, the significance of the *Aarhus Convention* is global. It is by far the most impressive elaboration of principle 10 of the *Rio Declaration*, which stresses the need for citizens' participation in environmental issues and for access to information on the environment held by public authorities. As such it is the *most ambitious venture in the area of 'environmental democracy' so far undertaken under the auspices of the United Nations*. Its adoption is a remarkable step forward

---

[9] Convention on Access to Information, Public Participation in Decision-Making, and Access to Justice in Environmental Matters, UN ECE (1998), hereinafter Aarhus Convention, available at http://www.unece.org/env/pp/.

[10] *See* http://www.participate.org.

[11] *Doors to Democracy: Current Trends and Practices in Public Participation in Decisionmaking*, available at www.rec.org/REC/Publications/PPDoors. The author of this article made the regional assessment for NIS based on 6 country reports.

in the development of international law as it relates to participatory democracy and citizens' environmental rights.[12]

2.2.1.3 Basic Features of Aarhus. The Aarhus Convention states both kinds of fundamental environmental rights: the substantive right of every person of present and future generations to live in an environment adequate to health and well being; and the procedural rights of access to information, public participation in decision making, and access to justice in environmental matters. The procedural rights provide broad avenues for civil society to play its role. Access to information and public participation in decision making enhance the quality of decisions, give the public the opportunity to express its concerns, and enable public authorities to take due account of such concerns. It improves accountability of, and transparency in, decision making and strengthens public support for the implementation of the decisions.

(i) Information. The right to information can be said to have both a passive and an active aspect. "Passive" access to information means a duty of public authorities to answer a request of the public. The public does not have to show some special interest: any member of the public can obtain information. Information must be provided in the requested form, as soon as possible and at the latest within one month, unless the volume and the complexity of the information justify an extension of this period up to two months after the request.[13] If a public authority does not hold the environmental information requested, the public authority shall, as promptly as possible, inform the applicant of the public authority to which it is possible to apply for the information requested, or transfer the request to that authority and inform the applicant accordingly.[14]

"Active" access to information means that public authorities have to possess and update, collect and disseminate environmental information that is relevant to their functions. Parties to the Convention shall establish an adequate flow of information to public authorities about proposed and existing activities that may significantly affect the environment.[15] Each party shall ensure that environmental information progressively becomes available in electronic databases which are easily accessible to the public. Each party shall every three or four years publish and disseminate a national report on the state of the environment, including information on the quality of the environment and information on pressures on the environment.[16]

(ii) Participation. According to Article 6 of the Convention the "public concerned" shall be informed, either by public notice or individually as appropriate, about proposed activities that may affect the environment. This must happen early in an environmental decision making procedure, and in an adequate, timely, and effective manner. The notice must describe the nature of the possible decision, the relevant public authority, the commencement of the procedure, and the opportunity for the public to participate. Early notification gives the opportunity for the public to participate effectively, when

---

[12] K. Annan, "Foreword," *The Aarhus Convention: An Implementation Guide,* United Nations (New York–Geneva, 2000) at v, prepared by S. Stec and S. Casey-Lefkowitz, Regional Environmental Center for Central and Eastern Europe.

[13] Aarhus Convention Art. 4.1, 2.   [14] *Id.,* Art. 4.5.

[15] *Id.,* Art. 5.1.   [16] *Id.,* Art. 5.4.

all options are open. The Convention also provides public participation in strategic decision making – in the preparation of plans, programs, and policies[17] and in executive regulations and other legally binding norms.[18]

(iii) Access to Justice. The environmental rights to a healthy environment, to information, and participation may be mostly "promises on paper" unless citizens can take cases of their violation to the courts or other independent bodies for a remedy. Access to justice guarantees that these rights become a reality. According to Article 9 of the Aarhus Convention, a person who considers that his or her request for information has been ignored, wrongfully refused, whether in part or in full, or inadequately answered has access to a review procedure before a court of law or another independent and impartial body established by law.[19] Also members of the public concerned, having a sufficient interest or, alternatively, maintaining impairment of a right, have access to a review procedure before a court of law and/or another independent and impartial body, to challenge the substantive and procedural legality of any decision regarding public participation.[20] The terms "sufficient interest" or "impairment of a right" are required to be interpreted so as to include NGOs dedicated to environmental protection.[21] In addition, members of the public must be allowed to "challenge *acts and omissions* by private persons and public authorities which contravene provisions of its national law relating to the environment," although the class of litigants can be limited by criteria laid down in national law.[22] Article 9.4 requires parties to provide adequate and effective remedies, including injunctive relief as appropriate, and be fair, equitable, timely, and not prohibitively expensive.

2.2.1.4 Ratification. Civil society played an important role in the ratification of the Aarhus Convention, especially in Eastern Europe and the NIS of the former Soviet Union.[23] The Regional Environmental Center for Central and Eastern Europe organized round tables and seminars for ratification of the Aarhus Convention in the countries of the CEE region, putting NGO participants together with governmental officials and the news media. The TACIS Environmental Awareness Raising Program of the European Union helped create a participatory process for ratification of the Aarhus Convention in the NIS. As the Director of the Parliamentary Component of this program, the current author was responsible for organizing fifteen open parliamentary meetings in the NIS countries, bringing together all stakeholders of the society: members of the parliaments, governmental officials from the Ministry of Environment, NGO representatives, and journalists. After the introduction of the main provisions of the Aarhus Convention, the participants discussed necessary measures for ratification in the country, needed changes in national legislation, problems and obstacles, and collaboration between government and civil society. Partly as a result of this dialogue, ten of the sixteen ratifications needed for the Convention to enter into force came from NIS countries and several others came from the CEE region.

---

[17] *Id.*, Art. 7.   [18] *Id.*, Art. 8.
[19] *Id.*, Art. 9.1.   [20] *Id.*, Art. 9.2.
[21] *Id.*   [22] *Id.*, Art. 9.3.
[23] The term "NIS" is no longer used in the region, which now refers to itself as Eastern Europe, Caucasus, and Central Asia or "EECCA."

2.2.1.5 Implementation and Compliance. Now, as the Convention moves into its early implementation, NGOs are again accepted partners. Delegates from the European ECO Forum and other NGOs participate actively in all intergovernmental working groups and expert groups established by the Meetings of Parties, offering the views of civil society and attempting to influence the outcome.

In continuation of the tradition of recognizing the role of civil society, the compliance mechanism provides that NGOs can participate in nominating independent experts for election to the Compliance Committee. Furthermore, the Rules of Procedure will allow an NGO representative to have a seat as an observer in the Bureau of the Convention. The Compliance Mechanism and Rules of Procedure were adopted by the First Meeting of the Parties of the Aarhus Convention in October 2002 in Lucca, Italy.

Four experts were nominated by the European ECO Forum, NGO coalition. Two of them (including the author) were selected to the Compliance Committee that consists of eight members, and became independent members of Compliance Committee.

One important feature of the compliance mechanism under the Aarhus Convention is that it provides for members of the public to make communications to the Committee on cases of alleged noncompliance with the Convention, which the Committee is then required to deal with. In international environmental agreements, it is unusual that the public has the right to make communications claiming that a state party to the agreement is not fulfilling its obligations under that agreement. However, this could be seen as a logical consequence of the fact that the Aarhus Convention, unlike other environmental agreements, seeks to guarantee the rights of the public, not only the rights of parties.[24] The compliance mechanism, enriched by input from the public, is expected to provide an important stimulus to parties to comply with their obligations under the Convention. Civil society has its significant role to play in the implementation of the Convention.

The Aarhus Convention is regional, but it is opened for other countries of United Nations to accede the Convention.[25] UN ECE has expressed interest to expand the Convention beyond the region and support similar regional environmental governance initiatives.

2.2.2 Espoo EIA Convention

Public participation can have an international, cross-border dimension as well, when an environmental effect is not confined to a single country. The Espoo Convention on Environmental Impact Assessment in a Transboundary Context was adopted to deal with such extraterritorial environmental impacts.

> The *Espoo (EIA) Convention* stipulates the obligations of Parties to assess the environmental impact of certain activities at an early stage of planning. It also lays down the general obligation of States to notify and consult each other on all major projects under consideration that are likely to have a significant adverse environmental impact across boundaries.[26]

---

[24] Aarhus Convention Compliance Committee. Communications from members of the public, available at www.unece.org/env/pp/compliance.htm.

[25] Aarhus Convention, Art. 19.3.

[26] Convention on Environmental Impact Assessment in Transboundary Context, available at http://www.unece.org/env/eia/eia.htm.

The party of origin must provide, in accordance with Article 2.6, an opportunity to the public in the areas likely to be affected to participate in relevant environmental impact assessment procedures regarding proposed activities. The party of origin must also ensure that the opportunity provided to the public of the affected party is equivalent to that provided to the public of the party of origin. This is a remarkable commitment on the part of countries, to consider the views of even the citizens and residents of another country in their governmental decision making.

The Espoo Convention entered into force in 1997. Its Implementation Committee was created in 2001 to help ensure compliance with the Convention. The Committee has not had any cases about noncompliance so far, however. One reason may be that it does not officially accept communications from the public. However, where the Committee becomes aware of possible noncompliance by a party with its obligations, it may request the party concerned to furnish necessary information about the matter. It may also consider any information forwarded by the Secretariat concerning compliance with the Convention.[27]

In order to get information in front of the Implementation Committee, the Ukrainian NGO Ecopravo-Lviv submitted a complaint to the Secretariat in August 2003 claiming violation of the Espoo Convention by the government of Ukraine.[28] This would become the first case of noncompliance to be considered by the Implementation Committee. The Government of Ukraine is planning to build a deep navigation canal through the strictly protected zone of the Danube Biosphere Reserve – part of a designated Wetland of International Importance under the Ramsar Convention and part of a bilateral UNESCO biosphere reserve (shared with Romania). This is being done without notification to countries likely to be affected (such as those whose migratory waterbirds spend some time in the Ukrainian portion of the Danube Delta). There has been no transboundary environmental impact assessment prior to decision to authorize or undertake any proposed activity required by Article 2.3 of the Convention.

Article 2.6 of the Espoo Convention requires that a party of origin "shall provide," in accordance with the provisions of this Convention, an opportunity to the "public in the areas likely to be affected" to "participate" in relevant environmental impact assessment procedures. Furthermore, the country must "ensure that the opportunity provided to the public of the affected [p]arty is equivalent to that provided to the public of the [p]arty of origin."[29] The complaint charged that Ukraine is ignoring both of these requirements.

At its meeting on March 10–11, 2003, the Implementation Committee, decided that it would be able to seek information from the public, but on the possibility of the public to initiate a compliance procedure before the Implementation Committee, it decided to wait. It was recommended that the relevant Aarhus Convention Compliance Committee activities should be monitored first. This matter would be reviewed in the light of experience and a recommendation might be made to the parties in 2004. It was

---

[27] Decision II-4 Review of Compliance, *see* http://www.unece.org/env/eia/implementation.htm#Decision.
[28] Letter to Mr. Wiek Schrage, Secretary of the Espoo Convention, from Svitlana Kravchenko and Andriy Andrusevych, Ecopravo-Lviv, August 2003.
[29] Espoo Convention, Art. 2.6.

also agreed to consider possible future proposals amending the provisions for public participation.[30]

Despite this slow approach, the complaint submitted by Ecopravo-Lviv (EPL), in light of the imminent construction activities on the proposed Danube Delta Canal, challenged the Espoo Implementation Committee to consider whether the public would be allowed to raise issues of noncompliance. So far, the answer appears to be "No." During its meeting on October 29–30, 2003, the Implementation Committee initially decided to consider information presented by EPL, while stating that EPL had not presented enough scientific information to prove transboundary effects. Then, in December 2003, EPL presented additional information, including affidavits of leading scientists based on scientific research indicating adverse transboundary effects on migratory birds, fish, and shared water resources of the Danube and the Black Sea. Rather than consider this, and reversing their original decision by a narrow four to three vote, the states in the Implementation Committee decided on December 18–19 that they would not accept information from the public. The committee's procedures allow it to consider information when it becomes aware of a situation without a formal complaint from an affected party, but the majority decided not to act under this provision. The matter was referred to the next EIA Working Group meeting in January 2004 to consider what, if anything, they would do in such situations. At that meeting the EIA Working Group referred the matter to the Meeting of the Parties scheduled for June 2004 to decide.

2.2.3 Protocol on Strategic Environmental Assessment

Strategic Environmental Assessment is a process of evaluation of environmental effects (including health) prior to preparing policies, plans, programs, and legislation. The Protocol on Strategic Environmental Assessment[31] (SEA) was signed in Kyiv, Ukraine, on May 21, 2003, by thirty-five countries of Europe at a special meeting of the parties to the Espoo Convention. This occurred during the fifth Ministerial Conference, "Environment for Europe." Civil society participated in all negotiation sessions, lobbying for a wide scope of the Protocol and for strong public participation provisions. One observer has noted:

> Most delegations lacked . . . *Aarhus* experts. Thus, the rather pure, procedural . . . concerns . . . were defended by representatives from the NGOs. But in general, the impact from the NGOs was rather limited in the end.[32]

This judgment seems largely accurate, for the NGO representatives lost on many of their proposals for expansive public participation in strategic environmental assessments to be performed under the Protocol.

The Protocol requires its parties to evaluate the environmental consequences of their official draft plans and programs. SEA is undertaken much earlier in the decision making process than EIA, and it is therefore seen as a key tool for sustainable

---

[30] Report from the Third Meeting of Implementation Committee, available at http://www.unece.org/env/documents/2003/eia/wg.1/mp.eia.wg.1.2003.8.e.pdf.

[31] Protocol on Strategic Environmental Assessment to the Convention on Environmental Assessment in a Transboundary Context, available at http://www.unece.org/env/eia/documents/protocolenglish.pdf.

[32] J. De Mulder, "The New UNECE Protocol on Strategic Environmental Assessment" (2003) 2 *ELNI Review* 13 at 19.

development. The scope of the Protocol covers plans, programs, and, to the extent appropriate, policies and legislation. Its provisions are mandatory only for plans and programs, but recommendatory on policies and legislation. The Protocol is silent on access to justice.

Nevertheless, the Protocol guarantees a uniform minimum set of standards and procedures for the process of strategic environmental assessment and provides the basis for advancing democracy, by including good practices of public participation in the most important decisions made by governments and public authorities.

Why is public participation important in SEA? Public participation both helps to promote democratization and leads to better decisions. Of course one role for the public is to criticize mistakes and see the negative aspects of a proposal. But experience shows that the public also will often suggest alternative ways and solutions, which produce better decisions. This is even more crucial for plans, programs, policies, and legislation, than for individual projects.

The SEA Protocol in Article 3.3 explicitly calls upon its signatories to treat civil society organizations as full partners in the improvement of environmental policy. The Protocol is a new step forward in the continuing dialog between government and civil society, and a new tool for the public to make strategic decisions more transparent.

2.2.4 Protocol on Pollutant Release and Transfer Registers

Public participation provisions are an essential part in another new Protocol, the PRTR Protocol, under the auspices of the Aarhus Convention. It was signed in May 2003 at the Kyiv Ministerial Conference.

The Protocol on Pollutant Release and Transfer Registers is the first legally binding international instrument on pollutant release and transfer registers. Its objective is "to enhance public access to information through the establishment of coherent, nationwide pollutant release and transfer registers (PRTR)."[33] The Protocol requires each party to establish a PRTR that is publicly accessible through the Internet, free of charge, and user friendly in its structure. The PRTR must also provide links to other relevant registers; present standardized, timely data on a structured, computerized database; cover releases and transfers of at least 86 pollutants covered by the Protocol and allow for public participation in its development and modification.

Civil society participated actively in preparation of the PRTR Protocol, and all negotiation sessions. The Protocol gives civil society the power of access to information about sources, types, and amounts of pollution. This information empowers citizens to put direct pressure on polluters to reduce emissions or to sue them in court. The PRTR Protocol is an important tool for civil society to fight against pollution and to make polluters accountable.

2.3 Recognition of Rights at Regional Level – Other Regions

In addition to the many international efforts in Europe involving the Aarhus Convention, Espoo EIA Convention, SEA Protocol, PRTR Protocol, and other instruments, regional efforts to grant increased procedural environmental rights are taking place in other regions of the world. A few examples illustrate this.

---

[33] Protocol on Pollutant Release and Transfer Register, available at http://www.unece.org/env/pp/.

2.3.1 Americas

At the 1994 Miami Summit of Americas, the countries reiterated their commitment to Principle 10 of the Rio Declaration and the importance of participation of civil society for vigorous democracy. At the 1996 Santa Cruz Summit Conference on Sustainable Development, the heads of states emphasized legal and institutional mechanisms for access to information and consultations to ensure civil society involvement into in environmental governance. The next 1998 Santiago Summit of the Americas reaffirmed the commitment of governments to develop institutional and legal framework to encourage public participation.[34] Other efforts are going forward as well under the auspices of the Organization of American States (OAS).

2.3.2 North America

The North American Trade Agreement (NAFTA) between Canada, Mexico, and the United States did not adequately take into account environmental and labor concerns. As a result a "side agreement" – the North American Agreement on Environmental Cooperation (NAAEC) – was developed. NAAEC is promoting and developing recommendations regarding public access to environmental information held by the government and public participation in decision making (Art.10(5)(a)), transboundary EIA, and access to administrative and judicial bodies in transboundary pollution cases. The NAAEC allows citizens to file a complaint with the NACEC that any party is not enforcing its environmental laws.[35]

2.3.3 Africa

The newest development in Africa is that the revised African Convention on Conservation of Nature and Natural Resources contains Article XVI "Procedural Rights." It requires:

1. The parties shall adopt legislative and regulatory measures necessary to ensure timely and appropriate:
   a) dissemination of environmental information;
   b) access of the public to environmental information;
   c) participation of the public in decision making with a potentially significant environmental impact; and
   d) access to justice in matters related to protection of environment and natural resources.
2. Each party from which a transboundary environmental harm originates shall ensure that any person in another party affected by such harm has a right of access to administrative and judicial procedures equal to that afforded to nationals or residents of the party of origin in cases of domestic environmental harm.[36]

This is a truly dramatic development, for it commits parties to begin the process of acting on each of the three main environmental procedural rights.

---

[34] C. Bruch and R. Czebiniak, "Globalizing Environmental Governance: Making the Leap from Regional Initiatives on Transparency, Participation and Accountability in Environmental Matters" (2002) 32 *Environmental Law Reporter* 10428 at 10436.

[35] Available at http://www.cec.org/pubs_info_resources/law_treat_agree/naaec/index.cfm?varlan=english.

[36] Adopted by the Assembly of the African Union on July 11, 2003 in Maputo, Mozambique.

3 ENVIRONMENTAL RIGHTS IN NATIONAL LAW (UKRAINE)

Environmental substantive and procedural rights are being recognized and implemented not only in international law, but also on a concrete basis in national law. One example where this process is far advanced, at least on paper, is Ukraine. It is worth noting that while the recognition takes place at the level of government, the successful implementation of these rights is one of the main roles that civil society can play.

3.1 1996 Constitution of Ukraine

The Constitution of Ukraine declares the fundamental environmental right of citizens:

> Everyone has the right to an environment that is safe for life and health, and to compensation for damages inflicted through the violation of this right.

> Everyone is guaranteed the right of free access to information about the environmental situation, the quality of food and consumer goods, and also the right to disseminate such information. No one shall make such information secret.[37]

> Appeals to the court in defense of the constitutional rights and freedoms of the individual and citizen directly on the grounds of the Constitution of Ukraine are guaranteed.[38]

The Constitution of Ukraine thus explicitly protects the substantive right to a safe and healthy environment and two of the procedural rights – information and access to justice, although not the right of public participation. Furthermore, access to the Constitutional Court for citizens is limited, and protection of constitutional environmental rights has not happened in reality so far. In addition, another provision of the Constitution states:

> Human and citizens' rights and freedoms are protected by the court. Everyone is guaranteed the right to challenge in court the decisions, actions or omission of bodies of state power, bodies of local self-government, officials and officers.[39]

This provision might be used for the protection of environmental rights, both substantive and procedural.

Nobody has yet attempted to use the constitutional provision for a safe and healthful environment in court actions in Ukraine, but some cases have attempted to use the constitutional provision on access to information.

3.2 1991 Law on Protection of Natural Environment

The Law on Protection of Natural Environment is the main environmental law, and in fact was one of the first laws of independent Ukraine, adopted in 1991. The substantive right to a healthy environment and all three procedural rights of access to information, public participation, and access to justice are provided by this law. It granted environmental rights before the adoption of the Constitution of Ukraine and the Aarhus

---

[37] Constitution of Ukraine, Art. 50.   [38] *Id.*, Art. 8.
[39] *Id.*, Art. 55.

Convention. Chapter II, "Environmental Rights and Duties of Citizens," stipulates, among others, these rights of citizens:

- to an environment that is safe for life and health;
- to take part in the discussion of draft legislation, material pertaining to the location, building, and reconstructing objects that might negatively affect the condition of the environment, and to submit proposals to state bodies, institutions, and organizations on these questions;
- to take part in the development and implementation of measures on environmental protection,
- to associate in nongovernmental environmental organizations;
- to receive by established procedure complete and trustworthy information on the condition of the environment and its effect on the health of the population;
- to take part in conducting public ecological *expertisas*;[40]
- to bring action against state bodies, enterprises, institutions, organizations, and citizens on compensation for damage caused to the health and property of citizens in consequence of the negative effects of the environment.[41]

All these rights make the Ukrainian public very powerful in theory. For example, the public can participate in draft legislation when the government makes a draft law or regulation publicly available and accepts public comments. Participation of civil society representatives in environmental impact assessment and the preparation of ecological *expertisas* of concrete projects that may have negative impact on environment has become rather ordinary, if the government notifies the public at an early stage. Sometimes the public uses a right to conduct independent public *expertisa*. It has become more experienced in how to get information from governmental authorities.

But in terms of bringing actions against government or industry, civil society still prefers to use demonstrations, campaigns, or petitions instead of using legal tools and the courts in particular. Enforcement of environmental rights is therefore lacking in reality.

3.3 1992 Law on Information

Concealment of information about the Chernobyl nuclear disaster in 1986 shocked Ukrainian society and led to the consequences being worse than they had to be. Secrecy aggravated the horrible consequences. One result was that after Ukraine became independent it adopted a progressive law on access to information. This law is not restricted to environmental information. It applies broadly to all categories of information.

Securing citizens' access to information is one of the core directions and methods of state informational policy. All citizens of Ukraine have the right to information, namely the possibility of free receipt, use, distribution, and storage of any data as may be required for the implementation of their rights, freedoms, and lawful interests, as well as for carrying out their tasks and their functions.[42]

---

[40] An ecological *expertisa* is an expert review process that exists in all countries of the former Soviet Union; *see* Section 3.4 of this chapter.

[41] Law of Ukraine on the Protection of Natural Environment, Art. 9.

[42] Law of Ukraine on Information, Art. 9.

State authorities and bodies of local and regional self-government have the obligation to inform the public about their activities and decisions, setting up special information services or systems within state bodies, and to provide access to information.[43]

A citizen has the right to request (in written form) state bodies to give access to any official document, regardless of whether the document relates to that citizen, except in cases of restricted access stipulated by this Law. A request must be met within a month, unless otherwise provided by law. Ukraine is one of the few states that imposes not only disciplinary, civil, and administrative, but also criminal responsibility for violation of legislation related to information. This includes ungrounded denial of information, false information, information not provided in a timely manner, and deliberate concealment of information.[44]

3.4 1995 Law on Ecological Expertisa

The tool of ecological *expertisa* (a Soviet phenomenon, similar to the Western concept of environmental impact assessment or EIA) is potentially one of the most powerful tools of *public participation* in decision making in Ukraine and countries of the former Soviet Union. The Law on Ecological Expertisa stipulates a duty of developers to announce in the mass media the plans to conduct an *expertisa* of a planned project or activity that may have a negative impact on environment.[45]

The public can participate in ecological *expertisa* by sending written comments, proposals, and recommendations, by including public experts in expert commissions, and, of course, by expressing its opinion in the mass media. With the aim of taking public opinion into account the developer or state body responsible for ecological *expertisa* must conduct public hearings. The conclusions of the ecological *expertisa* must take into account public opinion and must be made publicly available.[46] Whether any of these actually happens is, however, a different matter.

3.5 Citizen Enforcement of Environmental Laws in Ukraine

The reality can be much less than the promise of the law. In response to what they perceive as shortcomings, citizens in Ukraine are beginning to seek the assistance of the courts to enforce their procedural rights. Public interest environmental law organizations are working throughout the region for the benefit of the public, protection of the environment, and citizens' environmental rights through citizen enforcement in the courts. One of the leaders of public interest law in Ukraine and Eastern Europe is Ecopravo-Lviv (EPL). It has brought several cases to the national courts, challenging government decisions that would harm the environment or that violate the procedural rights of information and public participation. In addition, law students in Ukraine are also playing a role.

3.5.1 Ecopravo-Lviv's *Danube Cases*
Ecopravo-Lviv (EPL) has recently launched a series of interconnected legal actions in various legal forums at both the national and international levels,[47] dedicated to the

---

[43] *Id.*, Art. 10.   [44] *Id.*, Art. 47.
[45] Law of Ukraine on Ecological Expertisa, Art. 10.   [46] *Id.*, Art. 11.
[47] *Supra* note 28.

protection of the delta of the Danube River, where the river slows down and enters the Black Sea. The Danube Delta is one of 200 most significant, internationally recognized regions of biological diversity in Europe[48] as well as a recognized Ramsar wetland site.

On June 10, 2003, the President of Ukraine issued a decree that dramatically changed the status quo in the Danube Delta. The decree removed "natural protected area" status from all inland waters (both flowing water from the Danube and inland ponds) from the Danube Biosphere Reserve. Essentially the decree tries to leave only the land in the Reserve, while allowing construction of a shipping canal through the waters.

EPL filed a lawsuit arguing that this decree violates the Law of Ukraine on Natural Reserve Fund, which established the procedure of removal of the protected area status. The procedure requires making scientific evaluation, organized by Ministry of Ecology and to come a conclusion that the area lost its scientific, ecological, cultural, and other values. Such a procedure did not take place prior to issuance of the decree. The court accepted the suit against the President of Ukraine, which has the legal effect of stopping construction for the time being. EPL also appeared in another suit to defend a regional government and the Danube Biosphere Reserve against a legal case seeking to have lands of the Reserve taken away, based on the President's decree. The judges have ruled against EPL, but EPL has appealed their decisions to higher courts.

EPL succeeded in a lawsuit arguing that the project did not have a positive conclusion of ecological expertisa, a requirement of the Law of Ukraine on Ecological Expertisa and the Law on the Protection of the Environment. Article 29 of the Law on the Protection of the Environment prohibits the implementation of programs, projects, and decisions without a positive conclusion of a state ecological examination. The ecological *expertisa* of the Ministry of Ecology and Natural Resources actually concluded that it was not possible to build the channel on the territory of a biosphere reserve. However, government officials decided to treat this conclusion as positive (based on the decree removing the waters from the Reserve), thus supporting the start of canal construction. (A final approval is awaiting approval of the Cabinet of Ministers.) In February 2004 the Commercial Court in Kyiv ruled that the Ministry had violated both national legislation and the Aarhus Convention, with respect to public participation and needed elements for an *expertisa*.[49] The Ministry has appealed that decision.

3.5.2 *Citizens v. National Nuclear Generating Energy Company*

In 2002, a group of law students of Kyiv National University, representing the Civil Committee of National Security, decided to use legal remedies to challenge a proposed energy project, namely the completion of the two nuclear powered reactors using old Soviet-era technology. They applied to the Pechersky District Court with a suit against the National Energy Company, asking the court to stop construction of the reactors on the ground that the project did not have an ecological *expertisa*, as required by law. The Ministry of Ecology and Natural Resources of Ukraine had not approved the project

---

[48] According to scientists at the World Wide Fund for Nature (WWF), the Danube Delta is "the most important wetland area in Europe," *see Waterway Transport on Europe's Lifeline, the Danube. Impacts, Threats and Opportunities*, World Wide Fund for Nature (Vienna, January 2002). It is also "the largest interconnected reed-bed in the world," the home to 325 species of birds and 75 species of fish, several of both listed in species Red Books and threatened with extinction, *id.*, and *see also* http://www.wcmc.org.uk/protected_areas/data/wh/danubed.html.

[49] *See* http://www.elaw.org/resources/text.asp?ID=2321.

and had returned materials to the National Energy Company for additional research and investigation. The law students argued that completion of the reactors without a positive conclusion would violate their constitutional right to an ecologically safe environment.[50]

The district court rejected the suit on the ground of no standing to sue. The judge relied on Articles 100, 112, and 113 of the Civil Procedure Code, which provide that citizens can apply to the court representing other citizens or "society," but they have to have a power of attorney. She ruled that plaintiffs did not have a "power of attorney" to represent "society" as a whole.[51]

The students applied to the Appellate Court of Kyiv. They argued that they were not claiming to represent "society," but that the lead plaintiff represented his own interest and the interest of his other colleagues, relying on Article 4 of the Civil Procedure Code of Ukraine. This provision stipulates that every citizen can apply to the court to defend his own rights or interests protected by law.[52]

The Appellate Court cancelled the decision of the district court on the ground that citizens do not need power of attorney to represent their own interests. The case was returned to the district court for a new hearing. At the new court hearing on July 14, 2003, the district court rejected the suit again, on the ground that the government had received the required "positive conclusion" of an ecological *expertisa* for the completion of the reactors.[53]

This case was one of the first court cases in which civil society confronted government at the highest levels. The students were threatened by different unknown persons, calling by telephone and telling them that violent methods might be used by "state patriotic forces" if the students did not stop their "antistate activity." They were told to withdraw the suit if they wanted to graduate from law school. Despite these threats, the students persevered.

Although the students did not stop completion of the reactors, they were satisfied that they had pushed the government to comply with the law using the court system. This is perhaps the most significant result of their efforts.

3.6 1995 Law on Usage of Nuclear Energy and Nuclear Safety

The Law on Usage of Nuclear Energy and Nuclear Safety declared principles of state policy in this sphere, among them: priority of protection of people and the environment; openness and accessibility of information concerning usage of nuclear energy; and public participation in the formation of state policy.[54] Chapter II concerns the rights of

---

[50] Art. 50 of the Constitution, Art. 9 of the Law on the Protection of Natural Environment.

[51] A. Kozhuhov, "Legal practice," Ukranian newspaper, July 10, 2002, available at www.ypgazeta.com.

[52] They could have, but did not, argue that NGOs had the right to sue, because Ukraine had signed in 1998, and ratified in 1999, the Aarhus Convention. Art. 9 states that "the public concerned" should have access to the courts, and Art. 2 defines as eligible "the public affected or likely to be affected by, or having an interest in, the environmental decision-making." It states further that "for the purposes of this definition, non-governmental organizations promoting environmental protection and meeting any requirements under national law shall be deemed to have an interest."

[53] Their suit was based on violation of Art. 29 of the Law on the Protection of National Environment and Art. 39 of the Law on Ecological Expertisa, which requires projects to have a positive conclusion of ecological *expertisa*.

[54] Law of Ukraine on Usage of Nuclear Energy and Nuclear Safety, Art. 5.

citizens and their associations. Citizens and NGOs have a right to require and receive information from relevant government bodies about nuclear safety of planning or existing facilities and even to visit those facilities.[55]

Citizens and their associations have rights to participate in discussions of draft legislation and programs involving nuclear energy, as well as discussions on the location, construction, and usage of nuclear facilities.

Despite these legal requirements, the reality in Ukraine has been much different. In 1996 the Parliament adopted a National Energy Program of Ukraine through the year 2010. They did so without public participation or consultation with the public, or any ecological *expertisa*. This document, the National Energy Program, was considered to be for "internal business use." It included the construction of blocks 2, 3, and 4 of the Khmelnitsky (K2, 3, and 4) and block 4 of the Rinve (R4) nuclear power stations.[56] These had been started in 1985 and 1986 and were based on an old type Soviet reactor that do not meet western safety standards.

Some international effort was devoted to emphasizing the importance of public participation. For example, the Board of Directors of the European Bank for Reconstruction and Development (EBRD) approved an investment of US$215 million for Ukraine for completion of the K2 and R4, but dependent upon certain conditions, including public participation. The European Commission approved US$585 million for Euratom (European Commission Euratom Supply Agency)[57] to invest in Ukraine. Euratom announced public hearings. However, critical analytical data were excluded from documentation by Euratom and the EBRD. Furthermore, the developer created barriers to access to necessary documents and did not provide them on time. Meanwhile, President Kuchma of Ukraine criticized demands by the EBRD to use new technology, and asked Russia to continue financial support "on any conditions [costs]." With these Russian credits, K2 will be finished in 2004 and R4 in 2006.[58]

Despite inadequacies in official public participation processes and the government's sidestepping of demands for safer nuclear designs, NGOs inside and outside of Ukraine have continued to fight against completion of K2-R4, using different methods of lobbying, public hearings, political pressure, and demonstrations. Whether they will be successful, however, is open to much doubt.

The latest development is that EBRD is planning a Euro 250 million sovereign guaranteed loan to Energoatom[59] of Ukraine. The proceeds from the loan are to be used for pre- and post-completion safety improvements to K2 and R4. Both units are nearing completion. The EBRD has previously commissioned an environmental due diligence

---

[55] *Id.*, Art. 10.

[56] After the world's worst nuclear disaster in April 1986 in Chernobyl, a strong antinuclear movement resulted in a 5-year moratorium on nuclear power development, adopted by the Parliament of Ukraine in 1990. Under the pressure of the nuclear lobby, however, the Parliament of Ukraine cancelled the moratorium in 1993. In 1995 the G-7, European Commission, and government of Ukraine signed a memorandum on the permanent closure of Chernobyl in 2000, in exchange for financial support of the development of an energy system in Ukraine based on the concept of "cheapest cost" and nuclear safety. Finalization of the construction of block 2 of Khmelnitsky NPS and block 4 of Rivne NPS (K2-R4) were among priorities in the program of foreign investment.

[57] *See* http://europa.eu.int/comm/euratom/index_en.html, and note that Euratom is one of the founding treaties of the EU that supports nuclear power development across the EU, available at http://www.eu-energy.com/euratom.html.

[58] *See* www.dovkilia.kiev.ua/ua/news.

[59] Energoatom is a Ukrainian national energy company; *see* http://www.energoatom.kiev.ua.

report for this project, including the preparation of Environmental Impact Assessments (EIA), completed in 1997, for both units. The EBRD is now considering updating the previous EIA, in accordance with the requirements set out in the EBRD Environmental Policy and Procedures, including public disclosure and consultations because (a) Ukrainian legislation has changed and (b) the EBRD environmental policy has been updated. It remains to be seen whether the new EBRD efforts at public participation will be more serious than previous ones.

3.7 The Future of Public Participation in Ukraine

The Cabinet of Ministers of Ukraine recently prepared a broad public consultation regulation. On paper it looks excellent. Its aim is to create organizational and legal mechanisms of public participation in the process of the formation and realization of state policy by executive authorities.[60] The draft regulation was made publicly available on the governmental Web site on September 30, 2003, for public comment.[61] (This commenting process itself is an implementation of the concept of public participation.)

According to the draft regulation, public discussion will be mandatory for programs of activity of the Cabinet of Ministers, and for draft legislative and normative acts concerning citizens' rights, their freedoms, and interests. Methods of public consultation will be chosen by the governmental authority. Among possible methods are the following: open public debate in mass media (radio, TV), public hearings, round tables, conferences, seminars, direct telephone "hot lines," conducting sociological surveys, and simply monitoring of mass media.

The regulation provides that public discussion and different opinions should be taken into account in decision making. Results of public discussions, the final decision, arguments on which it is based, and analysis of rejected alternatives shall all be made publicly available. Only time will tell whether this regulation will finally make public participation a reality in Ukraine.

Many of the strong and democratic provisions of Ukrainian legislation and proposals mentioned in this chapter can be, and often are, just nice words – "democracy on paper" – if there is no citizen enforcement. Citizen enforcement (or access to justice) is a relatively new concept for Ukraine and Eastern Europe, but several environmental lawyers have been working to develop it. They have the goals of promoting social change and strengthening democracy using law. The concept was brought from the United States and Western Europe a decade ago and transplanted onto very different soil[62] – a region of post-communist reality. Lessons were learned, however, and the seeds have sprouted. Their growth will depend on careful tending by Ukrainians.

---

[60] Regulation on Procedure of Conducting Consultations with Public on the Matters of Formation and Realization of State Policy by Central and Local Bodies of Executive Power with the Goals to Implement the Decrees of the President of Ukraine, "On Preparation of Proposals for Ensuring Glasnost and Openness of Activities of Governmental Authorities" (on May 21, 2001) and "On Additional Measures Ensuring Openness in Activities of Governmental Authorities" (on August 29, 2002).

[61] Available at http://www.kmu.gov.ua/control/newsnpd/projects.

[62] *Pursuing the Public Interest. A Handbook for Legal Professionals and Activists*, Columbia Law School (New York, 2001) at xix, 9.

4 CONCLUSION

The role of civil society is growing not only in Western countries, but in countries in transition and the developing world. Its recognition in international environmental law and domestic legislation in many countries is a positive trend. However, there is much to do to fill the gap between laws and real life. Civil society is learning to be a powerful force, lobbying during negotiations of international treaties and the preparation of national policies, laws, and regulations, and also during their implementation and enforcement. It is not an easy task because many obstacles exist, among them lack of environmental education and public awareness, financial barriers, and corruption. But civil society itself argues that a better environment and democracy are too important to leave in the hands of the government alone.

31 Foundations in University Education

Michael I. Jeffery*

1 INTRODUCTION

> Energy is not so much a single product as a mix of products and services, a mix upon which the welfare of individuals, the sustainable development of nations, and the life-supporting capabilities of the global ecosystem depend. In the past, this mix has been allowed to flow together haphazardly, the proportions dictated by short-term pressures on and short-term goals of governments, institutions and companies. Energy is too important for its development to continue in such a random manner. A safe, environmentally sound, and economically viable energy pathway that will sustain human progress into the distant future is clearly imperative. It is also possible. But it will require new dimensions of political will and institutional co-operation to achieve it.[1] (Brundtland Report)

In first articulating the principle of sustainable development – that form of economic transformation that ensures development meets the needs of the present without compromising the ability of future generations to meet their own needs – the 1987 Report of the World Commission on Environment and Development (the Brundtland Report), provided a powerful argument for a comprehensive, integrated, and participatory approach to the interlocking crises of environment and development, an approach that calls for profound policy, institutional, legal, and personal change. The concept of sustainable development was strongly endorsed by the United Nations and its member states at the 1992 Conference on Environment and Development (UNCED), resulting in Agenda 21, a comprehensive and detailed blueprint for implementation at both global and local levels, and has since been adopted, both internationally and domestically, in various environmental contexts.[2]

Definitions of and approaches to sustainability vary, however each emphasizes that activities be ecologically sound, socially just, economically viable, and humane, and

---

[1] Concluding paragraph of Chapter 7, "Energy Choices for Environment and Development," in *Our Common Future, Report of the World Commission on Environment and Development* (the Brundtland Report), 1987, Oxford University Press, Oxford, p. 202.

[2] United Nations, Agenda 21, A/CONF.151/26 (Vol. II) 13, Rio de Janeiro, Brazil, 1992.

* B.A., LL.B., University of Toronto, LL.M., Osgoode Hall, York University, Canada. The author is currently Professor of Law and Director, Centre for Environmental Law, Macquarie University, Sydney, Australia and former Chair of the Environmental Assessment Board of Ontario, Canada. Professor Jeffery is also Deputy Chair of the World Conservation Union's (IUCN) Commission on Environmental Law. The author gratefully acknowledges the invaluable assistance of Rachel Carey in the research and preparation of this chapter.

will continue to be so for future generations.[3] The profound policy, institutional, legal and personal change necessary to achieve this vision mandates widespread education, public awareness, and training as part of the wider capacity building project. Agenda 21 regards both formal and nonformal education to be indispensable for changing people's attitudes so that they may have the capacity to assess and address their sustainable development concerns. It states that education is critical for achieving environmental and ethical awareness, values and attitudes, skills and behavior consistent with sustainable development and for effective public participation in decision making.[4]

While basic education is the underpinning for environment and development education,[5] this chapter focuses on the role of university education within a comprehensive strategy for building capacity for a sustainable future. As universities educate the majority of those who develop and manage society's institutions, they are well situated, and bear the responsibility, to promote environmental literacy, awareness, knowledge, training, technologies, expertise and to provide the tools important for addressing sustainable development and encouraging environmentally sustainable actions and decision making.[6] By shaping ethical values, such as intragenerational and intergenerational equity, social justice, and ecocentrism, university education can enable people to make informed and ethical choices, as well as encourage a sense of individual responsibility for the preservation and enhancement of the bios.[7] This chapter therefore addresses university education for sustainable development on a broader scale before turning to the specific issue of the role of universities in the development of environmental law and energy conservation.

The Brundtland Report regarded a safe and sustainable energy pathway to be crucial to achieving sustainable development. Energy fuels economic growth and social development while existing patterns of energy production and use have led to a plethora of environmental problems including, but not limited to, local and regional pollution, desertification, and climate change.[8] The World Energy Assessment describes sustainable energy as energy produced and used in ways that support human development over the long term, in all its social, economic, and environmental dimensions. The term is not meant to refer solely to a continuing supply of energy, but to the production and use of energy resources in ways that promote, or at least are compatible with, long-term human well-being and ecological balance.[9] The key elements of sustainable energy

---

[3] R. M. Clugston and W. Calder, "Critical Dimensions of Sustainability in Higher Education" in W. Filho and P. Lang (eds.), *Sustainability and University Life* 1999 cited at http://www.ulsf.org/pdf/Critical_dimensions_SHE.pdf.

[4] Agenda 21, supra note 2, para. 36.3.

[5] *Id.*, para. 36.4. This paragraph calls for countries to endorse the recommendations arising from the World Conference on Education for All: Meeting Basic Learning Needs 2/ (Jomtien, Thailand, March 5–9, 1990) and to strive to ensure universal access to basic education, and to achieve primary education for at least 80 percent of girls and 80 percent of boys of primary school age through formal schooling or nonformal education and to reduce the adult illiteracy rate to at least half of its 1990 level.

[6] Clugston and Calder, *supra* note 3.

[7] A. Rest, "The Shift of a Paradigm: from 'Environmental Education' to 'Education for Sustainable Development,'" presentation for *Biopoltics International Organisation Bio-Environment & New Millennium Environmental Education Workshop*, Athens, March 29–April 1, 2001.

[8] The Brundtland Report, Chapter 7, *supra* note 1. *See also* UNDP/UN DESA/WEC, World Energy Assessment: Energy and the Challenge of Sustainability, An Overview, UNDP, 2001.

[9] UNDP/UN DESA/WEC, World Energy Assessment: Energy and the Challenge of Sustainability, An Overview, UNDP, 2001.

are identified by the Brundtland Report to be: sufficient growth of energy supplies to meet the needs of humanity (including an allowance for development in nondeveloped countries); increase and improvement in energy efficiency and conservation measures; shifting the current energy mix more toward renewable resources; public health, recognizing the safety risks posed by energy use and production; and protection of the biosphere and elimination of local pollution problems.[10]

Environmental law has emerged as a major pillar of sustainable development.[11] Both the World Commission on Environment and Development and UNCED believed law to be critical to any endeavor to establish the processes of sustainable development.[12] The World Commission observed that "Human laws must be reformulated to keep human activities in harmony with the unchanging and universal laws of nature,"[13] while Agenda 21 states "laws and regulations suited to country-specific conditions are among the most important instruments for transforming environment and development policies into action."[14] Certainly, environmental law is an essential tool for the governance and management of sustainable regimes, providing the foundation for government policies and actions for the conservation of the environment and ensuring that the use of natural resources is both equitable and sustainable. Development in the field of international environmental law has been rapid in recent years. Beginning with the principles set forth in the 1972 Stockholm Declaration on the Human Environment, over 700 relevant global treaties have been adopted on environmental subjects as diverse as Biological Diversity, Climate Change, Desertification, and Protection of the World's Cultural and Natural Heritage.[15] Many environmental agreements have been concluded at a regional level or on a bilateral basis. In addition, numerous international "soft law" instruments on the environment have been adopted over the last two decades, such as the 1982 World Charter for Nature and the 1992 Rio Declaration on Environment and Development.[16] The effectiveness of these agreements and instruments depends on the effectiveness of each state's system of environmental law.[17] On the national plane therefore, albeit unevenly, environmental law is emerging in different regions and is taking on characteristics specific to each nation. Certainly, environmental law is one of the fastest growing fields of law today.[18]

However, despite the significance attached to energy issues in the Brundtland Report, and the resulting recognition at every major United Nations conference in the 1990s of the importance of energy as a tool for meeting the goal of sustainable development, the legal responses of governments and the international community to sustainable energy

---

[10] *Id. See* A. Bradbrook, "Energy and Sustainable Development" (1999) 4 *Asia Pacific Journal of Environmental Law* 309.

[11] N. Robinson, "Curriculum Planning For Teaching Environmental Law (International and Comparative)," Planning document for *IUCN/ APCEL/UNEP Course on Capacity Building for Environmental Legal Education*, 1994.

[12] N. Robinson, "Comparative Environmental Law: Evaluating How Legal Systems Address Sustainable Development," presentation for the Elizabeth Haub Colloquium, April 17–19, 1997, Wiesbaden, Germany.

[13] The Brundtland Report, *supra* note 1.   [14] Agenda 21, *supra* note 2, para. 8.13.

[15] P. Birmie, and A. Boyle, *International Law and the Environment*, Oxford University Press, Oxford, 2nd ed., 2002.

[16] Rio Declaration on Environment and Development, 31 I.L.M 874 (1992), World Charter for Nature UN GA RES 37/7, 1982.

[17] Robinson, *supra* note 12.

[18] N. Robinson, "Attaining Systems for Sustainability Through Environmental Law," *Natural Resources and Environment*, Fall 1997.

can be regarded at best as patchy and inadequate.[19] Aside from a recognition of the unsustainable nature of current energy development and use, energy issues were virtually excluded from Agenda 21 and the range of activities it proposes are an inadequate basis for promoting sustainable development in the energy sector.[20] The unfortunate fact is that energy has featured only marginally in environmental law in the past decade as it has been mired by numerous political issues and vested interests that have thwarted the necessary changes in policy, institutions, law, and individuals called for by Brundtland.[21] Indeed, fourteen years after the Brundtland Report was delivered, the World Energy Assessment attests that the current energy systems are not addressing the basic needs of all people, environmental degradation as a result of conventional energy production and consumption has not abated, and the continuation of business-as-usual practices may compromise the prospects of future generations.[22]

There needs to be a global understanding of the role that environmental law is able, and ought, to play in developing sustainable energy strategies. Energy issues need to be moved from the realm of policy, and legal frameworks for sustainable energy need to be developed that address the key elements for sustainable energy identified by the Brundtland Report and itemized above. Environmental law remains a youthful and evolving field of law, and modern international approaches, in addition to national legislative efforts, reveal a discernible shift from the strict "command and control" approach to environmental issues toward an expansive approach where environmental law is able to serve as an intersectoral, dynamic, flexible, and normative tool that may encompass ecological, social, cultural, and economic factors. It is this expansive concept of environmental law that is necessary to give effect to the vision of sustainable development laid out in Brundtland. Indeed, Agenda 21 regards environmental law as an important tool for achieving sustainability "not only through 'command and control' methods, but also as a normative framework for economic planning and market instruments."[23]

Agenda 21 therefore notes the importance of environmental legal education and training, stating that "efforts to provide an effective legal framework for sustainable development should be oriented towards improving the legal institutional capacities of countries to cope with national problems of governance and effective law-making, and the application of these in the field of environment and sustainable development."[24] Endogenous capacity building for environmental law as part of a wider capacity building initiative is essential to achieving the aims of sustainable development. The challenge for university education, therefore, lies in developing curricula to disseminate the expansive interpretation of environmental law that is vital for the necessary comprehensive, integrated, and participatory approach to the interlocking crises of environment and development.

For the purposes of this chapter, environmental law needs to be understood as a combination of substantive and procedural elements. Substantive elements include laws governing natural resources, pollution abatement and control, and energy generation, transmission, and efficiency use to name a few. The subjects of procedural environmental law include the establishment of principles such as intergenerational and intragenerational equity, public participation procedures, environmental impact

---

[19] Bradbrook, *supra* note 10.
[21] *Id.*
[23] Agenda 21, supra note 2, para. 8.13.

[20] *Id.*
[22] World Energy Assessment, supra note 9.
[24] *Id.*, para. 8.26.

assessment, and compliance and enforcement systems.[25] University education must first attend to capacity building for environmental law before it can address the development of sophisticated approaches to compliance and enforcement procedures.

Legal frameworks for sustainable energy need to be considered in the wider context of interdisciplinary environmental legal education through identifying and disseminating the root causes and extent of environmental degradation and in developing mechanisms to enable processes, such as monitoring, enforcement, and compliance, and to be reflected in regimes that are likely to be effective in the context of specific states of development, cultures, and legal systems. The comparative environmental law approach within university education together with effective use of case studies drawn from the North and South are a valuable way of illustrating basic principles and methodologies to demonstrate strengths and weaknesses of current approaches to energy law.[26]

Altogether, the tertiary sector has not been traditionally designed for rapid capacity building in key areas of social need and development. This chapter provides an example of a collaborative educational effort, in which universities played a key role, to promote rapid endogenous capacity building for environmental law in the Asia Pacific region (see Section 3.2).

The need for tertiary research capacity is also a critical area in which collaboration between universities, or between universities and other important sectors such as industry, is necessary in order to develop the technologies appropriate for sustainability, such as mechanisms for increased energy efficiency or alternative energy supply.

The challenge of moving beyond mere rhetoric, to truly "think globally, act locally" and therefore adopt and implement an expansive approach for environmental legal frameworks is as much an issue for Northern countries as it is for countries in the South. Thus, while capacity building efforts need to focus on development of legal education in the South, universities in the North also need to face up to the challenge of appropriate curricula development, particularly in the context of developing legal frameworks for sustainable energy.

2 UNIVERSITY EDUCATION FOR SUSTAINABLE DEVELOPMENT

The United Nations Conference on the Human Environment held in Stockholm in 1972 recognized the importance of environmental education as essential "in order to broaden the basis for an enlightened opinion and responsible conduct by individuals, enterprises and communities in protecting and improving the environment in its full human dimension."[27] Certainly, education is very important in sensitizing people to current global realities, in developing an environmental ethic, and in building both a responsive and responsible society.[28] Education for sustainable development is an

---

[25] Robinson, *supra* note 12.

[26] The development of modern international environmental law has been dominated by deep seated differences among developed countries, primarily located in the Northern hemisphere. and developing countries located in the Southern hemisphere. This situation is often characterized as the "North South debate."

[27] Principle 19, United Nations, Declaration of the United Nations Conference on the Human Environment, (the Stockholm Declaration), Stockholm, 11 ILM 1416 (1972).

[28] K. L. Koh, "Teaching Environmental Law: Trends in the Region," paper presented at the IUCN-CEL Meeting, IUCN First World Congress, Panel on Teaching Environmental Law, Montreal, October 1996.

integral part of promoting social and economic development, alleviating poverty, managing the use of natural resources, promoting sustainable consumption and production, and controlling population growth.[29] Such education not only provides the knowledge, expertise, and tools required, it also provides the motivation, justification, and social support to pursue and apply them.[30]

It has been noted that just as the environmental threats to Earth's natural system result from the accumulations of many small acts and mistakes, so too global environmental protection can be realized only if each jurisdiction adopts an environmental ethic integrating the ecological, economic, and social dimensions.[31] Certainly, sustainability mandates a significant and widespread change in current, fundamentally unsustainable, attitudes and patterns of behavior, a change that necessitates a new set of values informed by a sense of ethical responsibility. For example, the World Energy Assessment cites as a factor impeding a shift to increased energy efficiency, the "patterns and habits of consumers, operators, and decision makers, which may be influenced by many factors, including ideas of social presage and professional norms."[32]

In the context of the role of education in building capacity for compliance and enforcement, there exists a real need for the development of institutional capacity for effective environmental management, a new paradigm for decision making and a culture of environmental awareness and concern within that true compliance and enforcement may take place. Thus, if we are to move to a truly sustainable use of our environment, then a major culture change is called for. In this sense education for sustainable development may be seen as a means of cultural renewal for facing global problems.[33]

Through the development of a holistic, interdisciplinary, multidisciplinary, and ethically oriented form of education, universities are in a position to disseminate the capacity for devising solutions for the problems linked to implementing sustainable regimes.[34] Universities are well situated to promote environmental ethics in society as they have expertise in all fields of research, both in technology as well as in the natural, human, and social sciences, and it is these institutions that train the future generations of teachers, community leaders, business leaders, policy makers, engineers, and urban and rural planners. The promotion of such ethics as part of primary and secondary school teacher training in particular allows for the dissemination of environmental awareness, literacy, and responsibility to their students.[35]

Through promoting a sense of ethical responsibility, university education can enable sustainability to be addressed at the individual level, essential at the heart of any successful move toward sustainable usage and development. In addition to being provided with a sound ethical grounding, practicing professionals, particularly those who are destined to develop and manage major institutions, must be provided with the awareness, knowledge, training, expertise, and tools important for addressing sustainable development and encouraging environmentally sustainable actions and decision making. This is critical as institutional stagnation resulting from maintaining institutional

---

[29] Rest, *supra* note 7.

[30] *Id.*

[31] Robinson, *supra* note 18.

[32] World Energy Assessment, supra note 9.

[33] Rest, *supra* note 7.

[34] "The University Charter for Sustainable Development," *Co-operation Programme in Europe for Research on Nature and Industry through Co-ordinated University Studies (COPERNICUS)*, Geneva, May 1994, cited at http://www.mls.miljo.gu.se/copernicus/copernic.htm.

[35] *Id.*

players who preside over traditional attitudes and policies acts as a major impediment to the effective operation of sustainable development policies.[36]

Tertiary programs therefore need to integrate into all disciplines the dynamics of both the physical/biological and socioeconomic environment and human (which may include spiritual) development, and should employ formal and nonformal methods and effective means of communication.[37] The challenge for universities, therefore, is for them to take an active role in educating for sustainability, in incorporating environmental and developmental issues into existing curricula and study programs, and in developing new programs and teaching methods.[38] In addition, university education for sustainable development should translate and demonstrate theoretical ideas in ways that are meaningful and practical. Because in many ways a university is a microcosm of the larger community, the manner in which a university carries out its daily activities is an important demonstration of ways to achieve sustainable living.[39] By way of example, the University of Melbourne, Australia, has contracted with an energy provider for an annual purchase of electricity of which 1,500 megawatt hours will be sourced from renewable energy generators, the equivalent of the energy used by 263 average homes each year. In addition, it has built an energy and environment building, incorporating cutting edge ecologically sustainable design principles.[40]

As Professor Rest has succinctly stated the case, university education for sustainable development has to

- Bring about the changes in values, behaviour and lifestyle that are needed to achieve sustainable development and ultimately democracy, human security and peace;
- Disseminate knowledge, know-how and skills that are needed to bring about sustainable production and consumption patterns and to improve the management of natural resources, agriculture, energy and industrial production; and
- Ensure an informed populace that is prepare to support changes towards sustainability emerging from other sectors.[41]

The Cooperation Programme in Europe for Research on Nature and Industry through Coordinated University Studies (COPERNICUS), a programme of the Association of European Universities (CRE), has developed a University Charter for Sustainable Development.[42] This sets forth ten principles of actions for the widespread propagation of environmental literacy and capacity for addressing sustainable development issues. These are as follows:

1. *Institutional commitment.* Universities shall demonstrate real commitment to the principle and practice of environmental protection and sustainable development within the academic milieu.
2. *Environmental ethics.* Universities shall promote among teaching staff, students, and the public at large sustainable consumption patterns and an ecological lifestyle,

---

[36] Robinson, *supra* note 18.   [37] Agenda 21, supra note 2, para. 36.3.
[38] R. Fincham, S. Georg, and E. Nielsen (eds.), *Beyond the Summit: The Role of Universities in the Search for Sustainable Development*, University of Natal Press.
[39] "Report And Declaration Of The Presidents Conference," *University Leaders For a Sustainable Future (ULSF)*, 1990, accessed at http://www.ulsf.org/program talloires report.html.
[40] *See* Australian for Gas and Electricity (AGL), March 6, 2000, accessed at http://www.agl.com.au/AGL/Press+Releases/Green+scheme+ takes+off+at+Melbourne+Uni.htm.
[41] Rest, *supra* note 7.   [42] *Supra* note 34.

while fostering programs to develop the capacities of the academic staff to teach environmental literacy.

3. *Education of university employees.* Universities shall provide education, training, and encouragement to their employees on environmental issues, so that they can pursue their work in an environmentally responsible manner.

4. *Programs in environmental education.* Universities shall incorporate an environmental perspective in all their work and set up environmental education programs involving both teachers and researchers as well as students, all of whom should be exposed to the global challenges of environment and development, irrespective of their field of study.

5. *Interdisciplinarity.* Universities shall encourage interdisciplinary and collaborative education and research programs related to sustainable development as part of the institution's central mission. Universities shall also seek to overcome competitive instincts between disciplines and departments.

6. *Dissemination of knowledge.* Universities shall support efforts to fill in the gaps in the present literature available for students, professionals, decision makers, and the general public by preparing information, didactic material, organizing public lectures, and establishing training programs. They should also be prepared to participate in environmental audits.

7. *Networking.* Universities shall promote interdisciplinary networks of environmental experts at the local, national, regional, and international levels, with the aim of collaborating on common environmental projects in both research and education. For this, the mobility of students and scholars should be encouraged.

8. *Partnerships.* Universities shall take the initiative in forging partnerships with other concerned sectors of society, in order to design and implement coordinated approaches, strategies, and action plans.

9. *Continuing education programs.* Universities shall devise environmental educational programs on these issues for different target groups: for example, business, governmental agencies, nongovernmental organizations, and the media.

10. *Technology transfer.* Universities shall contribute to educational programs designed to transfer educationally sound and innovative technologies and advanced management methods.

If such principles are to be achieved, governments and key community players need to be mobilized at the national level to recognize the role universities ought to play in educating for sustainable development and to put into action the necessary programs, curricula development, and training. A central issue in this context, therefore, is the necessity to change the view of many central governments in both developed and developing countries to provide much greater support for universities, through both financial means and political will. In many countries support for tertiary education is dwindling, and increasingly universities are being forced to operate as privatized institutions. It ought to be kept in mind that in many sectors, we have seen attempts to bring important sectors back into the public domain following an initial rush to privatization.[43] Sustainable development must not be seen as a fad in academic literature but a serious

---

[43] Airport security is a good example of this in the United States. Since the events of September 11, all airport security that had previously been privatized has now been brought back under government control under the authority of the Office of Homeland Security.

long-term goal that must be kept in focus, and therefore support for tertiary institutions needs to be viewed as an integral part of any move toward achieving sustainable development.[44]

3 UNIVERSITY EDUCATION AND THE DEVELOPMENT OF ENVIRONMENTAL LAW FOR SUSTAINABILITY

In addition to legislative measures at the international and regional levels, national legal frameworks that are culturally, economically, and socially appropriate are essential for the successful governance and management of sustainable energy regimes. Capacity building for environmental law and sustainable development at the national, regional, and international levels is an evolutionary and interdisciplinary task, and environmental law capacity building constitutes just one of the components of capacity building for sustainable development. The development of legal frameworks is part of a wider project involving the establishment of environmental institutions and machinery; the development of policies and strategies; the development and use of economic instruments and market based incentives; mechanisms for gathering, assimilating, and dissemination of information; the training of human resources in relevant technical disciplines; the development of new analytical tools, such as national environmental profiles, impact assessment, environmental accounting, environmental audits, environmental indicators, environmental education, community involvement, technology development, and transfer; and financing.[45]

The national development of environmental law is affected by an array of social, cultural, economic, and political factors specific to a particular country and therefore, in order to be enduring, it is essential that capacity building develops endogenous legal expertise, such as that of local people with local knowledge. With this in mind, the aim of capacity building in environmental law and institutions is to develop as appropriate, human and material resource capabilities of countries, particularly developing countries and countries with economies in transition, to achieve the following goals:

- To secure, in the light of their respective country specific conditions, the development of national policies and strategies for environment and development, and facilitate their integration through appropriate legal and regulatory policies, instruments and enforcement mechanisms at national, state, provincial, and local levels;
- To secure the effective implementation and enforcement of international and national legal and institutional regimes in the field of sustainable development; and
- To secure the effective participation of these countries in the negotiation of new international legal instruments in the field of sustainable development; and the review and, where necessary, revision of existing instruments, their international operation and effective implementation at national levels.[46]

---

[44] A. Downes, "Education And Sustainable Development: Historical Perspectives and Projections for Barbados," accessed at http://www.iacd.oas.org/La%20Educa%20120/downes.htm.

[45] D. Kaniaru and L. Kurulasuriya, "Capacity Building in Environmental Law," in Sun Lin and L. Kurukulasuriya (eds.), *UNEP's New Way Forward: Environmental Law and Sustainable Development,* UNEP, Nairobi, 1995.

[46] *Id.*

Environmental legal education is an essential component of environmental law capacity building. The IUCN/APCEL/UNEP Training the Trainers Course on Capacity Building for Environmental Legal Education, a unique, intensive, and endogenous capacity building exercise in the Asia Pacific region, recognized that a great deal of local "capacity" in this region resides in universities and other tertiary institutions. It regarded the long-term development of environmental law capacity building in Asia Pacific legal education to be one of the most enduring forms of capacity building, allowing for a multiplier effect in developing environmental law expertise and producing environmental lawyers who are local and therefore able to develop culturally, economically, and socially appropriate environmental frameworks.[47] While this project, discussed further in Section 3.2, was unique in time, scale, and focus, it serves to highlight the pivotal role of universities in the development of appropriate legal frameworks for sustainable regimes.

The success of any framework for the management of sustainable energy regimes turns on the appropriateness and effectiveness of compliance and enforcement procedures, which in turn depend on effective monitoring and reporting. Notwithstanding differences in the respective legislative development for sustainable regimes, capacity building for enforcement and compliance is both a developing and a developed country issue. Controversies continue about which approaches to regulation and enforcement work best at the international, regional, national, and local levels. Debate and discussion on compliance and enforcement, particularly in the context of education, need to be brought back to the broader context of capacity building for environmental law and implementing the true spirit of the Brundtland Report. With the foundations of environmental law, it is possible to draw lessons in terms of approaches to legal education that are relevant to capacity building for effective compliance and enforcement mechanisms and sustainable energy law.

3.1 Teaching Approaches to Environmental Law

Environmental legislation will not operate effectively unless the causes of environmental degradation are understood and legislative responses are integrated into the wider social arena.[48] In the context of sustainable energy regimes, energy use is closely linked to a range of social issues, including poverty alleviation, population growth, urbanization, and a lack of opportunities for women. The relationship is two-way, these issues affect energy demand while the quality and quantity of energy services, and how they are achieved, have an effect on social issues.[49] Existing patterns of energy production and use continue to contribute to a plethora of environmental problems such as local and regional pollution, desertification, and climate change. There are major economic and political factors involved in changing the status quo in regards to energy, and there exists a clear interface with science in this sector in terms of understanding the nature and

[47] D. Craig, A. Robinson, and K. L. Koh (eds.), *Capacity Building for Environmental Law in the Asia and Pacific Region: Approaches and Resources*, Asian Development Bank, Manila, Philippines, 2002, p. 135.

[48] D. Craig, "Role of Science, Technology, Economic Approaches and Mechanisms, Public Participation, Financial Assistance in Environmental Law and Policy," syllabus prepared for IUCN/APCEL/UNEP Training the Trainers Course on Capacity Building for Environmental Legal Education, Singapore, 1997.

[49] World Energy Assessment, *supra* note 9.

extent of the impacts of energy use, and in the development of new technologies such as those to promote energy efficiency or alternative resource use.

The World Energy Assessment recognizes the ability of markets to deliver on the economic objectives of sustainable energy, but notes that markets alone cannot be expected to meet the needs of the most vulnerable groups and to protect the environment.[50] Just as law cannot ensure that justice, responsible government, or good urban planning is achieved without simultaneous economic, social, and political strategies, market mechanisms cannot by themselves provide a solution to the pressing problems of energy issues in the absence of legal frameworks that provide normative frameworks, clear rules, criteria, and standards and, where appropriate, flexibility mechanisms for more discretionary policy decisions.[51]

Legal regimes governing energy are sorely needed but are inadequately developed because of the complexity of the area, the considerable nature of controversy involved in altering the status quo, and a lack of the political will called for by the Brundtland Report. Governments are after flexibility in dealing with energy issues, and the area has largely been relegated to the realm of policy; however, in its expansive and modern form, environmental law can offer a flexible and normative framework that is able to address the broader aims for sustainable energy.

Environmental law seeks to maintain the quality of life – for humans as well as flora and fauna – in the biosphere, so that the socioeconomic systems that depend on stable natural resources can prosper and attain an equitable distribution of well being.[52] Older forms of sectoral environmental regulation relied on the use of criminal offenses and administrative schemes to limit the worst causes of pollution, rarely addressing the real causes of pollution or monitoring the cumulative causes and effects of environmental degradation.

Modern environmental law is defined by its orientation toward achieving sustainable development that requires integrated legal approaches and institutions that transcend the normal boundaries of sectors. The ethical and interdisciplinary dimensions inherent in achieving sustainable development require profoundly different approaches to environmental law. In its new and evolving form, modern environmental law draws on a huge range of disciplines and utilizes many areas of law such as constitutional law, international law, human rights law, resources law, and local government laws as well as specific environmental protection laws. Certainly, interdisciplinary approaches are necessary to foster an understanding of the complex ecosystems and human impacts on them, in addition to social, cultural, and economic dimensions that will give lawyers access to expertise to identify environmental problems and potential legal strategies and options.[53]

To give effect to the broader aims of Brundtland, an expansive approach to environmental law needs to be embraced that addresses root causes of environmental degradation in order to achieve a reduction in environmentally exploitative and energy intensive approach to development. Concepts and principles of inter- and intragenerational

---

[50] *Id.*

[51] *See* M. Jefffery and W. Baird, "Using Market-Based Incentives to Curtail Greenhouse Gas Emissions: Factors to Consider in the Design of the Clean Development Mechanism, Joint Implementation and Emissions Trading" (2001) 6(2) *Asia Pacific Journal of Environmental Law.*

[52] Robinson, *supra* note 12.

[53] Robinson and Koh (eds.), *supra* note 47, pp. 85, 335.

equity and environmental justice that are inherent in sustainable development, in addition to fundamental issues such as North/South equity and meeting the essential needs of the world's poor by ensuring that they receive a fair share of global resources and the promotion of new technology, need to be incorporated into any understanding of environmental law.

In this context environmental law may be regarded as a combination of substantive and procedural elements within an overarching normative framework. The substantive laws for energy generation, transmission, and efficient use would relate to renewables (wood, business, hydropower, wind, solar), fossil fuels, and atomic energy. The procedures would include:

- Basic obligations including constitutional provisions, human rights aspects, establishment of the precautionary principle, polluter pays principle, intergenerational equity, and public participation procedures;
- Scientific surveys and data assembly – baseline date, monitoring, research;
- Reporting, publication, and dissemination of environmental information;
- Establishing environmental standards, both ambient for natural resources or public health, and operational or performance norms (process requirements, emission or effluent limits, etc.);
- Administration of standards and techniques appropriate for each subject sector (e.g., permits, licenses, audits, user fees, other economic incentives);
- Environmental Impact Assessment (EIA);
- Compliance and enforcement systems (administrative, civil, criminal); and
- Restoration of damaged ecosystems and resources and compensatory remedies for damages.[54]

University legal education needs to adapt and modify curricula development and teaching approaches for modern environmental law to foster an understanding of this area of law as an intersectoral, dynamic, flexible, normative tool that encompasses ecological, social, economic, and political dimensions in a national, regional, and international setting. Environmental legal education, therefore, by the very nature of the subject, necessitates a teaching method that extends past the orthodox teaching of substantive law. An intersectoral and interdisciplinary approach is required that fosters a more complete understanding of the ecological, social, economic, and political contexts within which environmental law operates. In addition, teaching methods ought to adopt a discursive and participative approach and may involve, for example, role plays, a simulation of ministerial meetings, interdisciplinary interactive seminars, and so forth.[55]

Comparative legal analysis can contribute much to an understanding of how law can further sustainable development and is essential to the study of any particular area of environmental law. In practically every nation, there is a substantial body of recent legal experience suited to comparative legal study of how different nations are addressing the comparable environmental or developmental issues.[56] Case studies are a valuable way of illustrating basic principles and approaches and fostering a deeper understanding

[54] Robinson, *supra* note 12.
[55] *See* B. Boer, "Training the Trainers Programme Teaching Methods for Environmental Law," IUCN/APCEL/UNEP Training the Trainers Course on Capacity Building For Environmental Legal Education, Singapore, 1998; and Koh, *supra* note 28.
[56] *Id.* and Robinson, *supra* note 12.

of the role of environmental law in achieving sustainable development. These allow an appreciation for what sort of approaches will be appropriate for the state of development of particular nations and are likely to be effective in the context of specific cultures and legal systems.

Sustainable development will take on an infinite variety of forms in national jurisdictions around the world, as legal approaches will be culturally and locally specific. The use of comparative approaches to environmental legal education can also assist in developing legal frameworks for new frontiers such as energy. Case studies could be drawn from the North and South to demonstrate strengths and weaknesses of current approaches to energy law.

3.2 The "Training the Trainers" Project

This project was a unique and innovative capacity building process. The Asia Pacific Centre for Environmental Law (APCEL) of the National University of Singapore (NUS), in conjunction with the Commission on Environmental Law of the World Conservation Union (IUCN-CEL) and UNEP, prepared a four-week course for university law professors in Asia and the Pacific on how to introduce, prepare, and teach courses in environmental law. The main objective of this capacity building course was to equip law graduates in the region to develop the legal aspects of sustainable development, as recommended in Chapter 8 of Agenda 21. There were two, one-month-long courses held in 1997 and 1998 for over sixty university teachers and a few government officials, in which the participants were trained to teach national, regional, sectoral, and international environmental law. Participants for the two courses were selected from the following countries: Bangladesh, Cambodia, People's Republic of China (PRC), Fiji Islands, India, Indonesia, Laos, Malaysia, Myanmar, Nepal, Pakistan, Papua New Guinea, Philippines, Sri Lanka, Thailand, and Viet Nam. The courses were funded by ADB, and supported by the National University of Singapore (NUS) and a number of other institutions including IUCN–Environmental Law Centre, United Nations Training and Research (UNITAR), Pace Center for Environmental Law and the United Nations University (UNU).[57] Over thirty resource persons taught in each of the courses, nearly all on a pro bono basis, using a curriculum developed over three years for this particular purpose.

This was a serious investment in the multiplier effect of people as trainers and environmental experts in the region and was unique in scale, time, focus, the depth of the partnerships, and the local and regional environmental capacity building. Universities and law faculties have rarely been used in the way they were in this project. First, it was a strong partnership between an NGO (IUCN) and the tertiary sector and it was the first time that the ADB had funded this kind of rapid capacity building through environmental legal education in universities. The process and outcomes were achieved over a much faster time frame than is normal in the tertiary education process and the intensive course approach involving many academics allowed for the rapid multiplication of endogenous environmental law expertise.[58]

---

[57] Robinson and Koh (eds.), *supra* note 47, p xxiii.
[58] D. Craig, "Capacity Building for Environmental Law in the Asia Pacific Region: Approaches and Resources," presentation for book launch of D. Craig, A. Robinson, and K. L. Koh (eds.), *Capacity Building*

From 1994 to 1995, a Planning Committee comprising a group of experts from ADB, IUCN, UNEP, ESCAP, and members of the Faculty of Law, NUS, held seven meetings to draft the syllabus for the training course. The syllabus focused on both the methodology of teaching environmental law at university level as well as a content suited to the needs of the Asian and Pacific region. Hitherto, environmental law teachers have had to rely on books written by Western writers, as there was almost a complete dearth of "local" textbooks and materials in the region. The group of experts carefully drafted a syllabus encompassing topics that were of relevance to the region, with case studies culled from the region, for example, PRC, India, Indonesia, Malaysia, Philippines, and Singapore.[59] The curricula adopted a broad view of sustainable development being the basis for modern environmental law with an emphasis on social justice and equity, and thus this capacity building project allowed for the multiplication of environmental legal expertise suited to develop legal frameworks that aim to implement the broader aims of sustainable development identified by the Brundtland Report.

A teaching framework for such a rapid endogenous environmental law capacity building initiative is set out in Section 3.3.[60] Its purpose was as follows:

- To acquaint lawyers and law students with the framework of international environmental law and how it depends on, and links, the national legal systems for implementation;
- To develop an understanding of the basics of the environmental sciences and how knowledge of these allied fields is essential for the effective use of environmental law;
- To introduce the jurisprudential and ethical premises for environmental law, including general principles of international law and legal ethics. The Islamic principles of environmental protection and doctrinal elements from other religious or social frameworks can be reviewed;
- To develop an understanding on how Agenda 21 provides guidance for further intersectoral national law reform and for the progressive development of international law, toward the objectives of environmentally sustainable development;
- To establish a sound working knowledge of laws and procedures for environmental impact assessment and state-of-the art evaluation techniques in use;
- To provide illustrations of the principal tools of environmental law, with exemplars of the best examples of legislative drafting or procedures for administrative implementation and enforcement;
- To provide a solid grounding in public participation procedures in environmental law, in the development of new policies and rules, in the observance of and education about environmental, health and safety, citizen enforcement rights, and customary laws;
- To explain the economic considerations in environmental law and policy, including the use of economic tools to avoid or minimize waste, encourage demand-side

---

for Environmental Law in the Asia and Pacific Region: Approaches and Resources, Asian Development Bank, Manila, Philippines, at Bonn, Germany, 2002.

[59] D. Craig, A. Robinson, and K. L. Koh (eds.), *supra* note 47, p. xxiii.

[60] This has been adapted from N. Robinson, "Curriculum Planning For Teaching Environmental Law (International and Comparative)," planning document for IUCN/APCEL/UNEP Course on Capacity Building for Environmental Legal Education, 1994.

management for energy efficiency, and establish shadow costs or compensatory systems to cope with environmental externalities;

- To introduce the state-of-the art procedures in commercial legal practices for industrial corporate environmental auditing, due diligence analysis of sites, public reporting to investors or regulators, insurance coverage and liability issues; and
- To elaborate on special applications of environmental law: (a) in times of armed conflict; (b) as a base to free trade rather than a barrier; (c) as a spur to remediate heavily contaminated industrial or other sites; and (d) in agricultural contexts.[61]

An early outcome of this capacity building project was the creation of APCEL. During the project, APCEL prepared a report and database of ASEAN environmental laws and, in a few years, was established as the preeminent source of environmental law expertise in the region. APCEL continues to undertake environmental law training courses such as their ten training courses for senior officials in the Ministry of Environment, Foreign Affairs Office, and Attorney Generals Office in Singapore. Another outcome was the development of a textbook specific to the region, "Capacity Building For Environmental Law in the Asian Pacific Region," as a resource incorporating the interdisciplinary and comparative curricula developed for the course.[62] IUCN and partner organizations are building on the "Training the Trainers" experience and similar regional capacity building initiatives are proposed for the Persian Gulf Region and South America. The textbook is intended to be the basic curriculum and resource, supplemented by case studies and legislation drawn from the region.

Four alumni of the courses have prepared a draft curriculum for introducing environmental law in Pakistan utilizing the curricula and materials from the courses. The first environmental law course in Pakistan is now being taught. Other alumni are introducing similar training courses for government officials and more intensive approaches to promoting environmental legal education within their countries. Examples are India, Indonesia, the People's Republic of China, and Kuwait. Finally, the partnership between UNEP and IUCN has been pursued in a related area of developing environmental law symposia for judges. UNEP has organized symposia for judges in South Asia, Southeast Asia, Central America, and the South Pacific, and IUCN and the Arab Regional Centre for Environmental Law (ARCEL) are assisting with the forthcoming symposia for judges in the Persian Gulf Region.

3.3 Capacity Building for Compliance and Enforcement

With the foundations of environmental law established, environmental legal education can focus on specific procedures such as the development of effective monitoring, compliance, and enforcement strategies relevant to sustainable energy law. Lessons learned from the "Training the Trainers" courses reveal comparative approaches to be a vital tool in this context. Case studies can provide a useful demonstration of socially and culturally appropriate compliance and enforcement mechanisms, and provide an

---

[61] N. Robinson, "Curriculum Planning For Teaching Environmental Law (International and Comparative)," Planning document for IUCN/APCEL/UNEP Course on Capacity Building for Environmental Legal Education, 1994.
[62] *See supra* note 47.

understanding of the relative strengths and weakness of different approaches. Such case studies ought to be drawn from both the North and the South.

The form of environmental regulation will affect the level of compliance, enforcement practices and options, and the scope of liability when environmental harm occurs. The command-and-control approach to environmental regulation has been around ever since environmental law emerged as a distinct subset of administrative law in the late 1950s and early 1960s.[63] Such an approach provides wide powers to regulators to "authorize" or "prohibit" activities or pollution. This regulatory system comprises environmental standards, permitting enforcement procedures, and liability assignment and penalties (civil or criminal) for noncompliance.[64]

The relative ineffectiveness of enforcement associated with command and control environmental regulation and ensuing damage to the environment together with the increasing costs of cleanup gave rise in the early 1970s to a "front end" planning and preventative approach through the introduction of EIA. Often described as a planning tool, EIA sought to curtail further damage to the environment by imposing a rigorous methodology of assessing the merits of proposed development in advance of allowing such development to proceed, on the basis of whether the development was likely to cause significant harm. A significant feature of EIA was, for the first time, to expand the concept of "environment" in terms of going beyond assessing impacts only to the natural environment, (i.e., impacts to air, land, and water). It required an assessment of impacts to the natural environment together with impacts to the social, economic, and cultural environment. However, because of the significant expenses associated with EIA in terms of both the time and cost to prepare EIS, many jurisdictions found it necessary to limit its application to certain generic types of development or by means of an often arbitrary monetary or sectoral threshold.[65]

It has long been recognized that the "big stick" approach emphasizing deterrence and punishment through the imposition of harsher penalties may not in the long run be as effective, efficient, or expedient as the creation of an atmosphere of cooperation and communication between industry, government, and public interest groups. Top down enforcement is not enough to ensure compliance; incentives to undertake certain activities need to be built into regimes. Properly conceived and implemented, studies have shown that economic incentives can significantly enhance a regulatory authority's ability to induce abatement of polluting activities.[66] There has thus been a marked shift in many nations toward the use of a "regulatory mix," an approach that combines environmental standards and enforcement policies with compliance incentives and strategies utilizing such economic instruments as pollution charges, tax measures, market creation, tradable permits, environmental liability insurance, subsidies, deposit–refund systems, and enforcement incentives.[67] In addition, in nations with few resources for enforcement, there is an increasing use of civil law contracts between regulatory agencies and polluters as well as the use of publicity such as naming "names"

---

[63] M. Jeffery, "Environmental Management and Market-Based Incentives," prepared for D. Craig, A. Robinson, and K. L. Koh (eds.), *supra* note 47, p. 340.

[64] D. Craig, "Enforcement of Environmental Law and Standards – Legal and Economic Mechanisms," syllabus prepared for IUCN/APCEL/UNEP Training the Trainers Course on Capacity Building for Environmental Legal Education, Singapore, 1998.

[65] Jeffery, *supra* note 63.   [66] *Id.*

[67] Craig, *supra* note 64.

of polluters who breach licenses in newspapers. In some cultures these measures are effective and cheaper than cumbersome court procedures and are more appropriate to a certain stage of development and the cultural context.

Students of environmental law need to be equipped to develop innovative financial mechanisms and innovative regulatory strategies that are appropriate to their respective jurisdictions. Through an interdisciplinary and comparative teaching approach using case studies, it is possible to provide students with a "smorgasbord" of legal and economic mechanisms to encourage compliance and enforcement that are culturally and economically appropriate; the skills to provide a framework for prioritizing, timing, and choosing a mix of regulatory measures and environmental instruments; and an understanding of the impediments to enforcement and compliance and how they might be overcome.[68]

Current legislative approaches to encourage clean energy solutions include economic and market mechanisms, government programs, utility regulatory requirements and programs, standards, government encouraged voluntary programs, and citizen suit enforcement measures.[69] Some examples are discussed below. These are not meant to be exhaustive but to provide an illustration of the variety of mechanisms that can be produced in a comparative legal teaching method.

emissions trading. In 1974 the U.S. Environmental Protection Agency (EPA) began a program whereby companies that reduced emissions below the level required by law received credits that could be used to allow greater emissions elsewhere. Under programs of "netting and bubble," companies have been allowed to trade emission reductions among emission sources within the company so long as total emissions comply with the aggregate limits applied to the combined sources. As a result of economic and other factors, the program grew to include trading emission credits between companies. The offset programs allow companies who wish to establish new sources in areas not in compliance with ambient air standards, to offset their new emissions by reducing existing emissions by a greater amount. This was initially done between different plants of the same company and rapidly expanded to include offsets between different companies. A further incentive for companies to become innovative is the ability for them under authority of the "banking" program to store emission credits for future use. The logical extension of the initial program was to establish a system of marketable emission permits. The principal advantage to participants in such a scheme was to allow individual polluters to choose their own best cost-efficient strategy for pollution control. Companies would be allowed to trade emission permits giving them a right to emit a certain quantity of pollutants or they could pursue other production or abatement strategies that reduced their emissions, whichever was felt the most cost effective. In short, each company would be left to decide whether, for that particular corporation, it was cheaper to reduce emissions or to buy additional permits on the open market. Normal market forces such as supply and demand would determine permit price.[70]

---

[68] *Id.*

[69] R. L. Ottinger and M. Jayne, "Global Climate Change Kyoto Protocol Implementation; Legal Frameworks for Implementing Clean Energy solutions" (2000) 18 *Pace Environmental Law Review* 19.

[70] Jeffery, *supra* note 63.

technology incentives. Renewable energy sources (such as biomass, solar, wind, geothermal, and hydropower) that use indigenous resources have the potential to provide energy services with zero or almost zero emissions of both air pollutants and greenhouse gases.[71] These renewable energy sources require substantial up-front capital costs, however technologies enable considerable savings from costless fuels and low maintenance requirements. Temporary subsidies to bring new technologies into the marketplace can be effective, and often essential, to accelerate their market acceptance. The Danish government provided subsidies for up to thirty percent of the investment costs of a wind turbine in 1980, reduced to fifteen percent in 1984, and repealed in 1989 as the market accepted the new technology. In addition, consumers pay less for wind power than for power generated from fossil fuels.[72]

environmental disclosure. Several countries have introduced the requirement of disclosure of the emissions and the sources of their power generation by their utilities. The information required usually requires generation sources, fuel mix, fuel emissions, kWh price, price volatility, and contract terms. The disclosure enables informed decisions to be made by consumers about the environmental impacts of their choices.[73]

standards and citizen enforcement. There are various legislated standards for pollution in relation to building codes, appliance efficiency, and vehicles. Any standards program requires substantial resources for training, inspection, and enforcement. Government enforcement can be limited by a variety of factors, and in the United States citizen enforcement such as that adopted in the Clean Air Act has proven to be effective as an enforcement mechanism. The presence of citizen suit provisions enables nongovernmental organizations to enforce standards and benefit from the award of attorney's fees for such litigation.[74]

enforcement incentives. Enforcement incentives are economic instruments designed to encourage discharges to comply with environmental standards and regulations. These include noncompliance fees or fines, performance bonds, and liability assignment in addition to denial of public subsidies and financing, and partial or total suspension of plant operations.[75]

In conclusion, different forms of the regulatory mix will be appropriate to the specific cultural and economic conditions of a country and the nature of the particular issue being addressed. A developed, fossil fuel dependent nation will have a different regulatory mix than a nation that is hydro dependent, less developed, and possesses a cultural aversion to public shaming. Comparative teaching in university legal education is thus a highly effective tool in furthering understanding of the creative combinations of mechanisms that can best achieve effective compliance and enforcement.

---

[71] World Energy Assessment, supra note 9.

[72] Ottinger and Jayne, *supra* note 69.

[73] *Id.*

[74] *Id.*

[75] J. D. Bernstein, "Alternative Approaches to Pollution Control and Waste Management: Regulatory and Economic Instruments," *UNDP/UNCHS/World Ban Urban Management Programme*, 1997.

4 THE IMPORTANCE OF COLLABORATION

An open flow of information among all universities around the world, particularly in developing countries, is crucial to the development of new knowledge, technology, tools, and skills for sustainable development.

4.1 Collaborative Agreements among Particular Universities

In recent years a number of universities in various regions of the world have negotiated specific formalized arrangements covering such things as faculty and student exchanges, collaborative research initiatives, and the joint teaching of environmental law units of study on a comparative law basis. My own university, for example, has through its Centre of Environmental Law signed Memoranda of Agreement with the Asia Pacific Center for Environmental Law of the National University of Singapore, Pace University Center for Environmental Legal Studies, The Washington College of Law of American University, WWF–India, and the University of Arizona.

These arrangements facilitate an ongoing dialogue and exchange of information among environmental law academics that encourage innovative curriculum development, teaching methodologies, and research opportunities in the area of environmental law. It is through these types of networks that the development of environmental law around the world will be enhanced.

4.2 Research Collaboration

As the principal repository for both the academic expertise and the institutional framework for conducting research, universities will remain the focal point for the development of environmental law and applied solutions through research. In the future, university research will be done increasingly in collaboration with both government and industry and many countries, including Australia, are revising their university funding models to reflect an increase in reliance on research outcomes.

Of particular importance to developing countries is the necessity of collaborating in the context of research projects with both individual academics and universities or institutions that have an established history of obtaining research funding. The ability for academics in developing countries to collaborate with and be included in such research projects often provides the basis for these academics to acquire a needed research profile.

4.3 IUCN Academy of Environmental Law

The importance of establishing a practical collaborative network among universities around the world has been significantly reinforced with the establishment of the IUCN Academy of Environmental Law. This initiative, first proposed by the IUCN's Commission on Environmental Law and announced at the fiftieth anniversary of IUCN celebrated in Fontainebleau in 1998, became a reality with the launch of the academy in Shanghai at the outset of this very colloquium. The Academy is designed to bring together a group of participating universities with established or growing expertise in environmental law.

It will be comprised of a consortium of specialized research centers in university law faculties, departments or schools dedicated to advancing the effectiveness of the field of environmental law. An Academic Collegium, whose members are selected by the universities that comprise the Academy, will direct the Academy, which will be autonomous in its governance and financing but coordinated with IUCN's environmental law program.

The initial program of the Academy will focus on three particular areas:

1. The encouragement of the teaching of environmental law, through the preparation of published references, textbooks, and curriculum development, comprising the basis for comparative law instruction in the various regions and between regions. The objective for this endeavor is to ensure that each university has the teaching and reference materials for providing core sources on (a) national environmental law, (b) comparative environmental law, and (c) international environmental law.
2. Research. The Academy, in collaboration with the IUCN's environmental law program, would identify research issues that require further study and a research agenda would be prepared in consultation with the IUCN environmental law program, in furtherance of and in cooperation with the United Nations Environment Program's "Montevideo" environmental law program and in collaboration as appropriate with other universities and institutions.
3. An annual international colloquium in environmental law with the proceedings to be published as the annals of the IUCN Academy. The colloquia would be on different topics of environmental law and hosted annually by a university that would both organize the colloquium and edit the proceedings for publication as The Annals. Shanghai Jiao Tong University has been accorded the honor of hosting the Academy's inaugural annual colloquium on the law of energy for sustainable development.

It is anticipated that the Academy will play an ever increasing and important role in promoting the role of the university as one of the essential pillars for educating for sustainable development.

5 CONCLUSION

Based on our past experience, the road to sustainable development will be both difficult and by no means assured. It will require firm resolve, political will, technological innovation, and above all the education necessary to achieve what has been clearly articulated by the international community of the past thirty years as necessary for our survival in the decades ahead. The role of university education lies at the heart of this debate and some of the recent initiatives outlined in this chapter will serve to strengthen and broaden the knowledge networks represented worldwide at the tertiary level. It is with this in mind that we now embark upon our most difficult challenge of the twenty-first century.

32 The Role of the Judiciary

Paul Stein*

In each jurisdiction where Environmental Law is strong and effective, we can see the role of the courts as an essential force. The courts serve a crucial role in ensuring that the systems recommended in Agenda 21 may become widespread. . . . Clear articulation of the basic legal principles underlying environmental law can guide society in shunning conduct that breaches the strictures of those principles. With the careful delineation of such principles in judicial opinions, the ministries of government can guide the affairs of state accordingly. . . . In short, as the courts advance the remedial objectives of Environmental Law, they advance the Rule of Law itself.[1]

1 INTRODUCTION

One may well ask, "What has sustainable development got to do with the judiciary? Of what interest is the observance and enforcement of Environmental Law to society in general or to the judicial branch of government in particular?"

Part of the answer must be that a healthy, balanced legal system, led by a knowledgeable, honest, and fair judiciary, is critical to the harmonious and successful working of any modern society. The well-being of its people and of the environment of a nation is dependent upon an acceptable and universally respected system of laws; that is, a system that is accepted by all of the institutions of society, including the executive branch of government.

2 RELEVANCE OF JUDGES TO GOOD GOVERNANCE

Good governance is dependent on accountability of all of its organs to the people. Accountability can be policed by a skilled and independent cadre of judges. Only judges can build a universal respect and adherence to the Rule of Law. Conversely, if judges fail to act honestly and impartially, then any system of law will implode. A nation cannot

---

[1] N. Robinson, *Principles of Environmental Justice: A Foundation for Dispute Prevention and Resolution* (1995). *See* D. Craig, N. Robinson, and K. L. Koh (eds.), *Capacity Building for Environmental Law in the Asian and Pacific Region: Approaches and Resources*, Asian Development Bank (Manila, Philippines, 2002) at 112–19.

* Former Judge of the NSW Court of Appeal and of the NSW Land and Environment Court; Visiting Professor of Law at Macquarie University, Sydney.

effectively trade and prosper if its legal system is nonfunctioning or corrupt. Further, environmental degradation is the result if basic environmental laws are not complied with or not enforced by the courts.

2.1 The Universal Importance of Environmental Law and the Enforcement Gap

In terms of environmental law and the impact of humankind on the environment, there is little doubt that today's greatest challenge is for countries to secure more effective implementation and enforcement of fundamental laws. Most nations, including developing ones, have basic environmental protection laws in place, but an enormous gap exists between the letter of the law and what is actually happening on the ground. The gap is the problem. The answers are manifold but include judicial capacity building in environmental law.

2.2 The Johannesburg Principles

Acknowledging the gap, judges have realized the need for a comprehensive capacity building program for judicial officers, prosecutors, legal practitioners, NGOs, and others engaged in environmental protection and enforcement. The Johannesburg Principles, proclaimed in August 2002 by 132 judges from sixty-two countries immediately before the World Summit for Sustainable Development (WSSD), emphasized the link between poverty and environmental degradation and the significance of international environmental law at a domestic level. Given the fragile state of the global environment, the judges, as guardians of the Rule of Law, emphasized the need for judges to boldly and fearlessly implement and enforce environmental laws. They also emphasized the role of the judiciary in contributing to the realization of the goals of sustainable development by implementation, development, and enforcement of the law.

2.3 Need for Judicial Capacity Building

In order to achieve these goals, the assembled judges stated that a concerted and sustained work program should be developed urgently, focusing on education, training, and dissemination of information, including at a regional and subregional level. Much was to be learned from a collaboration of judges within and across regions. Positive benefits would result from the exchange of knowledge, experience, and expertise. This collaboration should not only extend across regions but across legal systems, civil and common law, and across languages and culture, and political and trading blocks.

3 IMPLEMENTATION OF THE JOHANNESBURG PRINCIPLES

UNEP has been instrumental in developing and implementing the program. It has been assisted in this work by the input and advice of a representative group of judges, led by the Chief Justice of South Africa, The Hon. Arthur Chaskalson.

The work of UNEP has been augmented by many partnerships with international organizations, such as the IUCN. It has also been supported by many donor states.

Indeed, comprehensive judicial capacity building would be quite impossible without donor aid.

Since the WSSD, there has been a great deal of follow-up action in the implementation of the Johannesburg Principles. Well before the global meeting of judges in Johannesburg in 2002, UNEP sponsored and convened regional symposia on Sustainable Development Law and Enforcement for judges. I had the privilege of being a faculty member at Colombo and Manila in 1997 and 1999 respectively. These were high-quality symposia that exposed the developing jurisprudence of many nations in South and South East Asia, in particular India, Sri Lanka, Pakistan, and The Philippines. Importantly, these symposia enthused judges in less developed countries in the region to increase their awareness, knowledge, and training in environmental law.

These were followed by conferences in other parts of the globe, including a meeting of judges of South Pacific Island States in Brisbane in early 2002. UNEP perceived a need for worldwide judicial capacity building and to this end convened the global summit of judges later that year. It was indeed a great success.

Much could be said about the meeting, but I will merely make a small number of hopefully pertinent observations. First, although the assembled judges were from diverse backgrounds and different systems of law, culture, language, and economic development and of varying levels of sophistication of environmental law, they soon found they shared many of the same problems and aspirations. A spirit of camaraderie quickly developed. What they wanted to see was action to deter further degradation of their environments. They were acutely aware of the link between human health and a healthy environment. They agreed unanimously on the need for more effective implementation and enforcement of environmental law. The judges were also united in calling for a comprehensive program for judicial training in the enforcement of basic environmental laws.

Spurred by the success of the Johannesburg meeting, IUCN's Commission of Environmental Law (CEL), with the assistance of UNEP, organized a meeting of Western European judges in London in October 2002, chaired by the Lord Chief Justice Lord Woolf. It issued the London Bridge Statement, which, among other things, established a European Judicial Forum.

In the meantime, IUCN, in association with UNEP, developed an Internet based, online judicial portal for judges worldwide to communicate and exchange judgments. I had the pleasure of launching this initiative in Johannesburg. The portal is undergoing development and the aim is for it to fulfill its undoubted potential within the next few years.

The CEL also formed a Specialist Group on the Judiciary to assist in the implementation of the IUCN's program of work.

Also in October 2002 a highly successful symposium of fifty judges from the Arab region was held in Kuwait. This was organized by the Arab Regional Centre for Environmental Law, IUCN, UNEP, and the Kuwait Institute for Judicial and Legal Studies.

The impetus was well and truly under way. UNEP then called together a smaller ad hoc group of regionally representative judges in Nairobi, immediately prior to its Governing Council meeting in February 2003. The task of the meeting was to assist UNEP in planning how best to design and implement the required judicial capacity building program.

The meeting produced an Outcome Statement, details of which are to be found in my report Judges Active in Promoting Environmental Law Capacity Building.[2] An ad hoc advisory group of judges was appointed to assist in the development of the program. Chief Justice Chaskalson reported to the Governing Council on the progress and outcomes made by the judges. The Council called upon the Executive Director of UNEP to support the initiative.

4 REGIONAL MEETINGS OF JUDGES

Since February 2003 the impetus has been maintained and a lot has occurred. Further successful conferences were held in May in Rome and in Lviv, Ukraine, involving significant international partnerships. June saw a regional meeting for South East Asia in Bangkok. A Latin American meeting recently took place in Buenos Aires, and an Anglophone meeting is planned for Eastern, Central, and West Africa. A regional meeting for the Pacific was to take place in Auckland, New Zealand in December. Before the end of 2003 it was hoped that meetings will also take place in the Caribbean, Southern Africa, and Francophone Africa. Early 2004 should see meetings in the Arab states and in North America.

4.1 Educational Training and Materials

These regional meetings are important on a number of levels. They will, of course, help determine regional needs, which obviously differ throughout the world, as well as within regions. While these regional initiatives are taking place, UNEP has been, with the help of judges and other experts, working on educational and training materials.

An extensive Environmental Law Training Manual is being prepared by UNEP with the aid of a group of environmental law academics. It should be trialed by the end of the year. A reference book for judges is also being written. Following discussions in Rome, Judge Weeramantry produced an outline and a group of senior judges will review the manuscript. UNEP also plans to prepare a handbook on international environmental instruments and a companion handbook on examples of national legislation and its implementation.

Describing this burst of activity is not to detract from the numerous other judicial education programs carried out in many parts of the world by a large number of organizations. There is, of course, a need to prevent duplication and to explore appropriate joint ventures to maximize the use of scarce resources. By way of an example, I will briefly describe one such program in Indonesia.

5 INDONESIAN JUDICIAL TRAINING PROGRAM IN INDONESIA

Australia's foreign aid agency, AUSAID, funded a Judicial Training Program in Environmental Law Enforcement in Indonesia between 1999 and 2003. It was developed at the request of the Supreme Court of Indonesia. Judges of that court were involved in the delivery of the program, together with presenters from the Indonesian Centre for

---

[2] *See* Environmental Policy and Law, Vol. 33, Number 2, April 2003.

Environmental Law (ICEL) and the Australian Centre for Environmental Law (ACEL), University of Sydney and the University of South Australia.

5.1 The Project

The project involved two separate strands. First, training in the enforcement of environmental law was conducted for groups of judges and others in Indonesia. More than fifty courses were held in every part of Indonesia, involving more than 1300 judges from every court in the land. Each course lasted six days. In addition, eight specialized advanced training courses were held in 2002–03 for the strongest participants. At their request a special symposium was also held for judges of the Supreme and High Courts.

The second strand of the project involved more intensive training of Indonesian judges and law enforcement officers in Australia. Groups of up to twenty participants attended for a period of two to three months in Sydney and Adelaide. Seven such courses have taken place, attended by 130 judges, prosecutors, enforcement officers, and civil society. It is usually the most proficient students who have been selected to attend the Australia based courses. The program has included extensive attendance at specialist environmental and other courts.

Indonesian trainers have included senior judges, academics, NGO leaders, and practitioners. Australian trainers have included judges, environmental lawyers, academics, and enforcement officers.

It is worth mentioning that most of the training is delivered in the Bahasa Indonesian language with the aid of power point presentation and skilled interpreters. Some Australian trainers spoke Bahasa. Case studies are extensively utilized. Comparative law is stressed. The participants must prepare Action Plans. The workshops are continuously evaluated.

5.2 Course Content

Areas covered by the training, both in Indonesia and Australia, include:

- International Environmental Law, including the law of Sustainable Development
- Criminal Law and Enforcement
- Class Actions
- Civil Liability
- Civil Enforcement – injunctions and damages
- Judicial Review
- Merit Appeals
- Alternative Dispute Resolution

These areas are covered in a comparative law exercise involving similar factual case studies under Indonesian and Australian Law. The fact that Indonesia has a civil law system has not impeded the delivery of the training program. This is partly due to western style statutes and a tendency to convergence of civil law with aspects of common law systems.

Discussions with participants include a merit system of judicial appointment; permanency of judicial tenure; security of tenure; adequate judicial salaries; adequate administrative support; obedience to orders of a court; and ongoing judicial education. Also discussed are the obligations of judges to render procedural fairness; to impose appropriate penalties; to comprehend technical issues; to provide well-reasoned, public judgments; and to dispose of litigation efficiently in an effort to deliver timely, effective, and affordable justice.

Another topic dealt with the limitations on judicial power, lest judges misunderstand their proper mandate and act above or outside the law.

Early on, the Indonesian judges indicated a willingness to include others such as prosecutors, police, environmental agency officers, academics, and NGO personnel in the training program. Judges have however always predominated. The involvement of others in the training has never caused any problem. Indeed, to the contrary, they have proved a useful addition. For example, judges assisted prosecutors in describing common problems they encountered in prosecutions. At the same time, prosecutors were able to tell judges about problems in evidence gathering. NGO representatives were able to enlighten participants about issues at a village level that impacted on environmental breaches.

5.3 Outcomes

What have been the outcomes? Recently, many of the participants got together and formed an alumni association. This has the capacity to spawn ongoing training and education. Although difficult to measure, it is clear that the training has elevated and enhanced awareness and understanding of the environment and of environmental law. The mandatory action plans have made participants think creatively about environmental problems and solutions.

Feedback has often been most positive. In the advanced courses, drafting exercises have improved the quality of judicial decisions and indictments. Understanding of the receipt of evidence has been refined. In recent months, courts that included participants from the workshops have given a number of important environmental decisions. Judges are starting to appreciate and understand principles of judicial independence and impartiality.

This said, it must be acknowledged that much more progress is to be made. The will is there but the public lack of trust in the courts remains. A legacy of corruption is slowly being overcome. The Indonesian judiciary is now ably led by its Chief Justice who, together with other Indonesian judges, attended the Johannesburg Global Forum.

All in all I think that the Indonesian experiment has been an outstanding success. Much has also been learned by the trainers themselves, which will enhance the delivery of future training. The workshops have evolved and the final model points the direction of future training ventures in Indonesia. One of its mainstays has been the input of Indonesian trainers and judges. Also, comparative law exercises have been useful and instrumental in the teaching.

Delivering the program to so many judges, and other actors in the system of environmental law enforcement, has been a challenge but has undoubtedly enhanced the understanding and application of environmental law principles. The proof, no doubt, will lie in the future. The training is but the start of a major overhaul, not only of the judicial system, but also of all the organs of government. The enhancement of the legal skills and knowledge of Indonesian judges is an important aspect of good governance. It provides a useful example for many other countries.

6 CONCLUSION: HOW TO CLOSE THE ENFORCEMENT GAP

The enforcement gap, to which I have referred earlier, is the raison d'etre for environmental capacity building. Environmental laws will never be obeyed or enforced unless there exists, at all levels of society, sufficient legal and institutional capacities and a will to protect and enhance the environment. This need extends also to elected politicians, to leaders and policy makers, to public officers, to police and prosecutors, and to the private legal profession. Unless the capacities of all of these groups are expanded to a genuine understanding of the environment and sustainable development, the gap will continue to grow.

Above all, judges have a role to play in the development, upholding, and enforcement of the law. For the most part, the law is there. What is required, indeed demanded, is the capacity and the will of all to see that the Rule of Law prevails and our fragile environment is better protected.

33 Access to Justice and Citizen Enforcement

John E. Bonine*

William Shakespeare famously put in the mouth of Henry VI this prescription: "The first thing we do is kill all the lawyers."[1] Thinking about this recently led me to two questions: First, why kill all the lawyers? Second, how many would that be and how long would that take? Third, what is the problem to be addressed? Is there another solution?

In the field of environmental law, these questions are worth asking. Is the environment better off with or without environmental lawyers? How many environmental lawyers exist and what do they do? If there is an imbalance, can something be done to right it?

I will venture some answers to these questions, and then look at enforcement of environmental laws by lawyers representing citizens and civil society.

1 HOW MANY ENVIRONMENTAL LAWYERS AND WHOM DO THEY SERVE?

While the Shakespeare quotation gives rise to laughter in most audiences, the context of the quotation reveals a more serious meaning. In his play, Shakespeare has rebel leader and megalomaniac Jack Cade fantasizing about taking over England through force and becoming its King, so that the people will "worship me their lord." In order to set up such a tyranny, one of his followers exclaims, "The first thing we do is kill all the lawyers."[2] Lawyers are a bulwark that stands in the way of those who would take power in order to abuse it. Law controls not only citizens, but also government. Lawyers bring the rule of law both to society and to the process of governing.

However, lawyers can also stand against the legitimate exercise of power. Tyranny can come in many forms, including not only the tyranny of unbridled government, but also the petty tyrannies of private and public actors making decisions outside the rule of law that have substantial impacts on others. Sometimes lawyers are the ones who resist application of the law or help those outside of the law escape its punishments. Such lawyers are simply doing what they are paid to do. Their job, they might explain in a moment of frankness, is to use the law to gain advantage for their clients, even if the result is less enforcement.

---

[1] Henry VI, Part 2, Act 4, Scene 2. http://www.shakespeare-literature.com/Henry_VI,_part_2_13.html.
[2] Id.

* Professor of Law, University of Oregon, USA. This is a rewritten version of a presentation made at the opening of the IUCN Academy of Environmental Law in Shanghai, China.

While this may tempt the cynical to cast a vote on the side of Shakespeare's Jack Cade and "kill all the lawyers," it is not the solution. For one thing, the task is simply too large, at least in many countries. If Shakespeare's prescription were to be carried out, we would want to know how many lawyers there are. I looked for a few examples and found these figures:

- China: 100,000 as of 2002[3]
- United Kingdom, Germany, Italy: 110,000–150,000 each, as of 2002[4]
- USA: 1,000,000 as of 2003[5]

How many of these are environmental lawyers? More importantly, are they part of the solution, or potentially part of the problem – at least with regard to protection of the environment? My research for the United States has uncovered the following semi-reliable figures:

- Private environmental lawyers in USA: 9,000[6]
- Citizen environmental lawyers in USA: 500[7]
- Government environmental lawyers in USA: 500[8]

If these figures are reasonably close, then ninety percent of the environmental lawyers are working for businesses, five percent are representing citizen groups or individual citizens, and five percent are working for government agencies and departments.

What are the 9,000 private environmental lawyers doing? They are using their skills on behalf of their business clients, for whatever goals their clients may have. Their purpose is to help businesses navigate their way through a regulatory maze and to persuade an official to issue a permit. They seek compensation from another business for contaminating land that the client business has bought. They lobby for laws and regulations that are advantageous to a client business, and challenge in the courts the decisions, regulations, and laws that restrict the business client's freedom of economic

---

[3] Zhang Fusen, Minister of Justice, quoted in news article, "China in need of more good lawyers," People's Daily (March 24, 2004), http://english.peopledaily.com.cn/200403/23/eng20040323_138295.shtml.

[4] Council of the Bars and Law Societies of the European Union, *Number of lawyers in European countries in 2002* (January 10, 2003), http://www.ccbe.org/doc/stat_avocats.pdf. Figures by country can be misleading, however, depending on whether the legal profession is highly regulated or not, whether one is counting graduates of law schools, lawyers registered to practice (not a uniform requirement in every country), or some other aspect. *See, e.g.,* Ray August, "Mythical Kingdom of Lawyers, America Doesn't Have 70 Percent of the Earth's Lawyers," 78 *ABA Journal* 72–4 (September 1992).

[5] American Bar Association, *National Lawyer Population by State* (2003), report published at http://www.abanet.org/marketresearch/2002nbroflawyersbystate.pdf.

[6] A state-by-state search by the author of data found at Martindale-Hubbell's http://www.lawyers.com/, using the term "environment," on March 31, 2004, produced the figure 8,700. I have rounded this figure upward to 9,000 for convenience. Martindale-Hubbell's directory covers 440,000 lawyers and law firms, or about 40% of the lawyers in the United States. Most environmental lawyers are probably included because most business law firms presumably are listed in Martindale-Hubbell and most environmental lawyers work in such law firms.

[7] Data compiled by J. Bonine (on file with author). I have been compiling names for several months through a variety of sources (including asking some of them for the names of others).

[8] This figure is based on guesswork, considering lawyers at the United States Environmental Protection Agency, the U.S. Department of Justice, State Attorneys General, and state and local environmental agencies.

action. In short, ninety percent of environmental lawyers are not paid to protect the environment, but to protect and assist the business client.

On the other side of the negotiating table, legislative lobby room, or courtroom from the business client's environmental lawyer sits the government environmental lawyer. Occasionally the environmental lawyer for a citizen group (a nongovernment organization, or NGO) finds time to participate, but with 9,000 on one side and 500 on the other (eighteen times as many lawyers representing business clients as there are lawyers representing citizens), you can see that there might be some imbalance in the messages being delivered. If a government official sees a business environmental lawyer one day per week, she or he might see a citizen environmental lawyer only one day every four months.

These numbers suggest how strong the gale force business wind blows at the bureaucrat's front, while the light breeze from citizen groups is blowing at the official's back. In the courtroom it is no different. A veritable army of lawyers are at call for business clients to challenge the government or respond to a citizen group. And on the other side? A ragtag group of environmental law partisans in the forest is able to come down to the courthouse only on occasion to defend the trees before a judge.

The situation does not look much different worldwide. If anything, the imbalance is much, much worse. While I do not have comparable figures outside the United States for environmental lawyers in general, I do have some for citizens' environmental lawyers. They amount to something like this – citizen environmental lawyers outside the United States: 300 in sixty countries in the E-LAW network.[9]

Even if we guessed that E-LAW has brought only half or one-fourth of the citizen environmental lawyers in the world into its network (which seems doubtful), the numbers would still be a drop in the ocean of lawyers worldwide and a mere speck on the steering wheel of the bulldozer of development.

The solution for these grave imbalances is not to kill all the lawyers, but to increase all the lawyers who are working on the side of the public. They are the few who are developing the idea of "citizen enforcement." Furthermore, we may consider increasing the tools available to these outnumbered public interest lawyers and figuring out how to pay them.

2 REMEDIES AVAILABLE TO CITIZEN LAW ENFORCERS

Public interest environmental lawyers, as few as they are, must use leverage to accomplish their goals. Although these citizen lawyers may be few, they are undeniably both creative and brave. Their stories can inspire all of us. I have retold a few of their stories in a recent essay.[10]

---

[9] www.elaw.org. There are, of course, other environmental lawyers, teaching in universities, providing occasional help to citizens, working for government departments, and of course representing business clients. *Leading* environmental lawyers (all sides) can be estimated at 900 in 130 countries, for this is the number who are members of the IUCN Commission on Environmental Law. Commission on Environmental Law (CEL). www.iucn.org and personal discussions with Professor Nicholas Robinson, Chair, IUCN CEL.

[10] *See* John Bonine, "Public Interest Environmental Lawyers – Global Examples and Personal Reflections," *Widener L. Rev.* (2004) (in press).

For now our task is to think about some specific questions involving enforcement of environmental laws against private businesses and also judicial review against government departments for claims of violation of environmental laws. Enforcement and judicial review in the courts are needed for two reasons. The first can help ensure that private enterprises obey the law (classical "enforcement"). Such assurance can be obtained in suits brought by government authorities or in "citizen suits" filed by private citizens and NGOs. The second, judicial review, may be considered a different kind of enforcement that helps ensure that public officials obey the law. It should not be restricted to private business enterprises, but be made widely available to private citizens and NGOs. While judicial review of government actions by citizen enforcers is important, this chapter will confine itself to enforcement against private enterprises.

The main remedies available to any enforcer of the law are basically of two types: indirect remedies (primarily economic penalties) and direct remedies (injunctions or imprisonment). Each of these remedies can have some role to play in a robust enforcement regime.

Economic penalties or instruments can be found in criminal law as "fines," in civil enforcement as "civil penalties," and in civil injury suits as "damages." Each of them uses the power of money to affect behavior. (Economics can also affect pollution levels through taxes, the selling of licenses, and so on, but our focus here is simply on enforcement for violations of legal norms.) In a broad sense, every use of an indirect economic penalty or instrument may be seen as a use of the "polluter pays principle."

Direct remedies can be found in criminal law as imprisonment or in civil enforcement as "injunctions" (either "negative" injunctions to stop doing something – such as a court order preventing discharges of pollution or cutting of trees – or "positive" injunctions requiring a defendant to do something – such as a court order commanding a defendant to clean up a problem it has created). In a broad sense, every use of a direct, negative, injunctive remedy or imprisonment may be seen as a use of the "precautionary principle," in the sense that harm is prevented for the future rather than its damage being calculated later and perhaps compensated.

Indirect (Economic) Remedies for Private Citizens

The right to obtain each of these remedies can potentially be given to citizen enforcers, not only to government. For example, in terms of indirect economic penalties, in the United States the Clean Water Act allows "any citizen" to "commence a civil action on his own behalf" against "any person" who is alleged to be violating a regulatory limit on discharge of pollution. In such a civil action the court is authorized "to apply any appropriate civil penalties."[11]

Citizens may similarly recover economic sums for damages caused to them or the environment by a polluter. For example, the Supreme Court of India has stated, in a

---

[11] Clean Water Act § 505, 33 U.S.C. § 1365(a). A well-known case involving a citizen suit that obtained a civil penalties order is *Friends of the Earth v. Laidlaw Environmental Services, Inc.*, 528 U.S. 167 (2000). Readers without direct access to United States case law can find the full decision online at http://supct.law.cornell.edu/supct/html/98-822.ZS.html.

case brought by an individual citizen of India against 510 industries whose air pollution was damaging the world renowned Taj Mahal and people living nearby:

> The "Polluter Pays Principle" as interpreted by this Court means that the absolute liability for harm to the environment extends not only to compensate the victims of pollution but also the cost of restoring the environmental degradation. Remediation of the damaged environment is part of the process of "Sustainable Development" and as such the polluter is liable to pay the cost to the individual sufferers as well as the cost of reversing the damaged ecology.[12]

Citizens in China also have the power of citizen enforcement, apparently in a civil action. Chapter 1, Article 6, of the Environmental Protection Law of the People's Republic of China states:

> Article 6. All units and individuals shall have the obligation to protect the environment and shall have the right to report on or file charges against units or individuals that cause pollution or damage to the environment.[13]

An article published in *Sinosphere* in 1999 asserted:

> Citizen suits to seek remediation of environmental pollution or damages therefrom are provided for in the Chinese environmental regulatory system. [Citing Article 6.] The draft amendment to the EPL retains this provision and will provide needed details as to the statute of limitations, burden of proof, and availability of injunctions and damages.[14]

Such enforcement is apparently rare in China. It could be a fertile ground for future development.

Direct (Injunctive) Remedies for Private Citizens

Citizens may be given the power to seek direct remedies of injunction (negative or positive) against those harming the environment. Using the example of the private citizen who filed lawsuits to protect the Taj Mahal again, the Supreme Court of India ruled:

> 35. We order and direct as under :
> (1) The industries (292 listed above) *shall approach/apply* to the [Gas Authority of India Ltd.] before 15-2-1997 for grant of industrial gas connection. . . .
>
> (4) Those industries which neither apply for gas connections nor for alternative industrial plot *shall stop functioning* with the aid of coke/coal in the TTZ [Taj Trapezium zone] with effect from 30-4-1997. Supply of coke/coal to these industries *shall be stopped forthwith.*[15]

---

[12] M. C. Mehta v. Union of India, WP 13381/1984 (1996.12.30) (Taj Trapezium Case), quoting from *Vellore Citizens' Welfare Forum v. Union of India* (1996) 5 SCC 647 at 658–60, paras. 11–14. The full case is available online at http://www.elaw.org/resources/text.asp?id=1044.

[13] Translation published at http://www.netd.com.cn/english/w_zcfg/ws_zcfg_10f.html.

[14] Zhang Hongjun and Richard Ferris, Jr., "Shaping an Environmental Protection Regime for the New Century: China's Environmental Regulatory Framework," Part VI – Practical Concerns of Foreign Investors," 2 *Sinosphere* No. 3, pages 38, 40 (1999). http://www.chinaenvironment.net/sino/sino5/page40.html.

[15] *Id.*, at para. 35 (emphasis added).

The Supreme Court of India also issued positive injunctions, requiring the State government to take specific remedial action, such as:

(9) The U.P. State Government/Corporation *shall render all assistance* to the industries in the process of relocation. The allotment of plots, construction of factory buildings, etc., and issuance of any licence/permissions, etc., *shall be expedited and granted on priority basis.*

(10) In order to facilitate shifting of industries from TTZ, the State Government and all other authorities *shall set up unified single agency* consisting of all the departments concerned to act as a nodal agency to sort out all the problems of such industries.[16]

The Supreme Court of India even ordered the national government to take action:

(i) Directions have been issued to the Government of India to decide the issue, pertaining to declaration of Agra as heritage city within two months.[17]

The extraordinary breadth of relief granted by the Supreme Court of India to solve an intractable problem involving hundreds of enterprises is surely inspirational and instructive.

Direct Criminal Enforcement by Private Citizens

Injunctions are not the only tool of direct enforcement. In England, Wales, France, and elsewhere, private citizens have the power to initiate private criminal prosecutions.[18] In England, the courts have called private prosecution "a valuable constitutional safeguard against inertia or partiality on the part of authority."[19] The government even lauds them on its Web site: "Individual citizens can bring private prosecutions for most crimes, but some need the consent of the Attorney General and these cases may be taken over by the DPP."[20] Similarly, the Ontario Water Resources Act in Canada allows any person who believes an offense has been committed to initiate a prosecution that can include the penalty of imprisonment upon conviction.[21]

Private criminal prosecutions are also authorized in parts of China. The Director of Public Prosecutions in Hong Kong wrote in 2001:

Private prosecutions have been instituted with some regularity in the courts of Hong Kong both before and after reunification. In 1996, there were ten private prosecutions; in 1997, there were six; in 1998, there were six; in 1999, there were two; in 2000 there were six. These thirty prosecutions in turn generated sixty-five summonses. In one

---

[16] *Id.* (emphasis added).   [17] *Id.*, at para. 38.

[18] Sue Anna Moss Cellini, "The Proposed Victims' Rights Amendment to the Constitution of the United States: Opening the Criminal Justice System to the Victim," 14 *Ariz. J. Int'l & Comp. Law* 839, 839 (1997). *See also* Private Prosecutions, http://www.constitution.org/uslaw/pripro01.htm.

[19] *Gouriet v. Union of Post Office Workers* (HL) [1978] AC 435, [1977] 3 All ER 70 (dictum).

[20] Guide to Government: The judicial system – Other criminal justice agencies in England and Wales, http://www.ukonline.gov.uk/CitizenSpace/GuideToGovernmentArticle/fs/cy?CONTENT_ID=4000056&chk=7LJFxA.

[21] "Karyn Keenan, Environmental Tool Kit: Private Prosecutions," 25 *Canadian Environmental Law Association Intervenor* Nos. 3 & 4, page 19 (December 2000). http://www.cela.ca/Intervenor/25_3&4/25_3&etk.htm.

instance only has it been necessary for the Secretary for Justice to intervene and terminate a private prosecution.[22]

It is unknown whether private prosecutions exist elsewhere in China, but the tool might be considered quite appropriate in terms of the background and traditions of China since 1948.

Creative Combinations of Remedies by Private Citizens

One of the most interesting types of citizen enforcement is the use of a citizen civil suit for monetary civil penalties (indirect enforcement and one application of the polluter pays approach) as leverage to persuade a defendant to agree to direct enforcement that will lead directly to the prevention of pollution (which can be seen as a precautionary approach). As an example, in an early case using this tactic, Trial Lawyers for Public Justice, a law firm serving citizens, sued a company in 1991 for failing to report its discharge of toxic chemicals into the environment and, instead of proceeding through to a court decision, reached a settlement agreement with the defendant. In the settlement, "[t]he company ... agreed to spend at least $115,000 implementing the measures identified in the audit, with a goal of reducing toxic chemical usage by 90 percent."[23]

3 THE PROBLEMS OF ECONOMICS IN CITIZEN ENFORCEMENT

Despite the theoretical attractiveness of enlisting citizens in the enforcement task against those violating environmental laws, the reality is that it is expensive work and there are few resources available for it. This was recognized in a declaration of Justices of Supreme Courts and Constitutional Courts from Eastern Europe, Caucasus, and Central Asia, issued after a meeting in Ukraine in 2003:

> [The judges] Acknowledge ... the important role played by citizens and their organisations in bringing matters before the courts.... [and] Further identify the need for financial and other support for: ... lawyers to assist citizens and their organisations to apply to the courts to defend environmental rights.[24]

A similar declaration was adopted by judges meeting in Rome a few weeks earlier, the Rome Judges Statement,[25] and another a few months before that in London called the "London Bridge Statement."[26]

---

[22] Mr. I. Grenville Cross, SC, JP, Director of Public Prosecutions, Department of Justice, Government of Hong Kong Special Administrative Region, Instituting Private Prosecutions, originally published in *Hong Kong Lawyer* (October 2001), http://www.info.gov.hk/justice/new/depart/pdf/art1001e.pdf.

[23] http://www.mapcruzin.com/scruztri/docs/seek8.htm.

[24] The Lviv Judges Declaration, approved by 15 Chief Justices and senior judges from Supreme and Constitutional Courts from 11 countries of Central/Eastern Europe, Caucasus and Central Asia (the EECCA Region). http://www.iucn.org/themes/law/pdfdocuments/Lviv%20Statement%20FINAL.pdf.

[25] http://www.iucn.org/themes/law/pdfdocuments/Rome%20Statement%20FINAL.pdf (noting concerns about "the ability of citizens to obtain access to the courts to further enhance the effective implementation, compliance with, and enforcement of, environmental laws").

[26] http://www.iucn.org/themes/law/pdfdocuments/LN-290304London%20Bridge%20Statement.pdf (stating that the judges "Recognise the value to society of enhancing the ability of citizens to obtain access to the courts to further enhance the effective implementation, compliance with, and enforcement of, environmental laws").

Let us look at some of the economic obstacles and some possible solutions. The two with the biggest impact are the lack of positive funding for citizens' lawyers and the suppressive effects of a "loser pays" principle regarding attorney fees (costs).

Lawyers working for private enterprises are paid well because their work can save a company millions of dollars – for example, by delaying for several years the cost of installing pollution control devices. The lawyers can tie the government enforcers up in knots, challenging the new regulations and slowing down the implementation process. It is almost always true that "litigation costs less than compliance." Lawyers for environmental groups have almost no financial support. The interests that they protect are diffuse and the losses and benefits are spread throughout society. The victories that they achieve are not likely to put money directly into someone's pocket. As a result, few people are willing to provide money for such lawyers and their numbers are minuscule.

The loser pays principle is in effect through much of the world. Under it, the winning party in a court case is entitled to collect the costs of his attorneys' fees from the losing party. While this might seem fair on the surface, it is important to look at the assets that may be at risk of loss. A business that is earning millions of dollars or yuan per year can afford to pay the few thousands of dollars of attorney costs of an environmental group that wins an enforcement case against the business. On the other hand, if a private citizen brings an enforcement action against a business and loses, the attorney costs of the business might exceed even the value of the citizen's house and certainly will far exceed his or her income for years to come. Faced with the risk of high loss, many citizens will never authorize a lawyer to proceed in their names. In addition, some countries impose high fees on a plaintiff to initiate litigation (even including law suits that have the effect of enforcing the laws).

There are several possible solutions. In the case of funding, a number of models are of interest. In Australia most state governments support "Environmental Defenders Offices" (EDOs).[27] The lawyers in these offices are expected to represent the interests of the diffuse public in environmental matters. In the United States a solid base of private, charitable foundations provide financial support for some law firms.[28] Even without such funding, a growing number of lawyers in the United States and other countries count themselves as members of the "private public interest bar." These lawyers represent paying clients on a variety of matters, from employment discrimination to personal injury suits. If they are careful to represent little people against big institutions in their paying law practice (such as workers against businesses, or injured people against big insurance companies), they have no conflict of interest when an environmental citizen groups comes to ask for help. On the other hand, a lawyer who regularly represents business interests is unlikely to be available to take on serious challenges to economically important institutions in society. Even if there is no direct conflict of interest, the paying clients have

---

[27] See http://www.edo.org.au. The early history of the EDO movement in Australia can be found at http://www.edo.org.au/edonsw/site/background.asp.

[28] The earliest and longest running support by private charitable foundations has been that provided by the Ford Foundation, which helped launch the first public interest environmental law firms in the United States, supported anti-apartheid public interest law in South Africa, and has been responsible for a host of other initiatives. See Ford Foundation Grantees and the Pursuit of Justice, http://www.fordfound.org/publications/recent_articles/docs/lawgrantees.pdf.

a way of making it quite clear that they expect their lawyers to be probusiness in their total career.[29]

The problem of fee shifting through the loser pays principle must be attacked head on, as must the problem of high court fees. Several courts, such as the Land and Environment Court of New South Wales in Australia, have created an exception for public interest cases, in which the normal loser pays approach does not apply if a citizen group brought its litigation in good faith and with a reasonable chance of winning on its legal points. Thus, even if they lose, they may not have costs assessed against them.[30] Twenty-seven countries (at the time of writing), mostly in Europe, have committed themselves under the Aarhus Convention[31] to court procedures that are "free of charge or inexpensive."[32] Such Parties to the Aarhus Convention furthermore "shall consider the establishment of appropriate assistance mechanisms to remove or reduce financial and other barriers to access to justice."[33]

Although my focus has been on citizen enforcement against private enterprises violating environmental laws, one aspect of the loser pays approach is worth mentioning because of its large impact in the United States. In a notable decision more than thirty years ago, the U.S. Supreme Court ruled that federal courts would not follow the loser pays rule. Environmental groups were denied the recovery of attorney fees from their opponents, after having won an important case involving construction of the Trans-Alaska Oil Pipeline. The groups saw it as an economic defeat. In reality, however, it was a great victory because it meant that they would not have to pay companies in the future when the environmental groups were unsuccessful. Meanwhile, Congress had enacted a large number of laws giving citizens the right to collect fees at least against the government after victories, while denying the government the right to collect fees from groups that lost. These "one way" attorney fees ultimately led to a law titled the Equal Access to Justice Act,[34] which provides a solid basis on which citizens' lawyers can plan to recover at least some of their costs of litigation, while shielding their clients from the risks that are inherent in a loser pays jurisdiction. This may well be one of the most significant aspects of the growth in public interest lawyers in the United States. While their numbers are still small in comparison to business lawyers, the public interest lawyers have surely created one of the most vibrant legal systems in the world for citizen enforcement of environmental law.

4 CONCLUSION

The imbalance in legal forces in the environmental field is substantial. Those who identify themselves as "environmental lawyers" work mostly for private businesses and not for the environment. Just as "tax lawyers" do not have to support higher taxes,

---

[29] *See* John Bonine, "The New Private Public Interest Bar," 1 *J. of Envir. L. & Litig.* 1 (1986).

[30] *Alyeska Pipeline Service Co. v. Wilderness Society*, 421 U.S. 240, 259 (1975).

[31] Convention on Access to Information, Public Participation in Decisionmaking, and Access to Justice in Environmental Matters, signed at Aarhus, Denmark, June 25, 1988, http://www.unece.org/env/pp/ctreaty.htm.

[32] *Id.*, at Article 9, para. 1.   [33] *Id.*, at Article 9, para. 5.

[34] Public Law 96–481; 94 Stat. 2325 et seq., 28 U.S.C. § 2412. *Cf.* Civil Rights Attorney's Fees Awards Act of 1976, Pub. L. 94–559, 90 Stat. 2641, 42 U.S.C. § 1988.

environmental lawyers do not have to support a cleaner or more protected environment – and certainly do not have to favor enforcement of environmental laws against their clients.

The solution is not, however, to kill all the lawyers. Rather, it is to support broadened enforcement efforts by citizen environmental lawyers. This must include removing economic barriers to their work. With such reforms and a healthier environment, the public might even stop laughing at jokes quoting Shakespeare.

34 The Business Case and Approach to Sustainable Energy

Nick Wood*

1 INTRODUCTION

Economic growth must be socially and environmentally sustainable, fueled by sustainable energy resources. This is a challenge for all parts of society that consume energy, but energy companies have a fundamental role as problem solvers and innovators in the supply of energy. Shell companies are committed to contributing to sustainable energy, and are integrating it into the way they do their work. They are committed to transparency and engaging with people's concerns and expectations.

2 THE CHALLENGE OF SUSTAINABILITY

Energy demand has grown by eighty percent since 1970, with developing countries taking an increasing share. With the bulk of the world's people still in the full flight of development, energy consumption could grow even faster. By 2030 the world could be consuming twice as much as now – sixty percent of it in today's developing countries. Furthermore, we have an urgent need to address the needs of the almost two billion people, one-third of the world's population, who have no access at present to modern sources of energy. So we need more energy for development. What does this mean for the world in which we live and for the choices which we will have to make? How do we deliver the energy for sustainable development?

Talking to energy company customers all over the world we find that people have very much the same wants and worries. Whether in Africa, China, Europe, India, or the United States, people want to have access to reliable, clean, and economical energy at the flick of a switch or the turn of a key. Reliability, availability, and economy are all very important to them. But at the same time people worry about the consequences of this availability. They worry about the local environmental impact and they worry increasingly about the global impact on our climate.

People also want access to personal transportation. Sometimes the developed world forgets the liberation and independence that personal transportation brought to some countries in the twentieth century: the ability to reach other parts of the country, the ability to bring our produce to market. This is what many people in developing countries aspire to also. First to own a motor scooter or motorcycle and then a car. But at the same

* External Affairs Director, Shell Companies in China

time we worry about the consequences of this – the traffic jams and the local pollution. In five years time will it take three hours to drive across Beijing or Guangzhou and will we choke to death in the process? Some say it already takes three hours to get across Beijing.

People also want personal and national economic development. Those who have very little at present aspire to some security of livelihood. Some who are better off also worry about inequality. They feel uncomfortable with the inequality that they see in their own countries and, perhaps, even more by the inequality that they see in other countries on their television screens. But will it be possible to bring others up to an acceptable standard of living, let alone one equal to theirs, without blowing the global environment apart?

An energy company has to address the wants and needs of its customers. It has to meet their immediate needs, but at the same time address their concerns. This is not to claim Shell already has the solution to their concerns, or to tell them that there is no cause for concern, but to say that as energy companies we share those concerns and are prepared to work with society, using their expertise to find solutions. This is not just a matter of morality. It is a matter of good business to meet the needs of your customers and to address their concerns.

3 SHELL'S APPROACH TO SUSTAINABLE ENERGY

The technological solutions adopted by Shell include: gas use, gas to liquids, coal gasification, renewable energy, and energy efficiency. Shell is also concerned with issues relating to energy and climate change, regulatory frameworks, responsible operations, and social development. Attention to these issues is important to ensure that economic, social, and environmental aspects are balanced and demonstrate a commitment to sustainable development.

This chapter focuses on how Shell pursues sustainable energy under each of these themes with reference to China and its particular needs as a fast growing economy.

4 CHINA'S ENERGY CHALLENGES

China's per capita GDP today compared to OECD countries shows that, despite an astonishing record of economic growth averaging 9.5 percent over the last twenty years, it is just the start of the country's growth. Most of the impact that growth will have on the Chinese people and its neighbors has still to be felt.

The energy demand required by China to maintain its target of seven percent growth per year is expected to double by 2020 when the country could be consuming sixteen percent of the world's primary energy – almost half that of the entire region.

Since 1980 the Asia-Pacific region's share of global primary energy consumption has risen from eighteen to twenty-six percent. By 2020, forecasts suggest that figure will reach about forty percent, accounting for perhaps two-thirds of the world's incremental energy requirements over that period.

Meeting these needs will be a challenge, because the Asia-Pacific region contains only about four percent of the world's proved oil reserves and seven percent of the proved gas, so it has to import most of its energy.

4.1 Energy Diversification

The Chinese government's focus is to diversify supply both for security reasons and to reduce the environmental and social burden. At the same time, it wants to improve the environmental performance of coal, which has left a legacy of pollution in the country.

The increasing overseas activity of China's top three State Owned Enterprises (SOEs) in the oil and gas business, PetroChina, Sinopec, and CNOOC, reflects the drive for energy security as well as the ambitions of these SOEs to expand onto the international stage following successful initial public offerings.

4.2 Oil

China has been a net importer of oil since 1993. It now consumes five million barrels of oil a day, of which one-third is imported. Increased exploration and development of domestic oil and gas will not reduce this dependence on overseas supplies. By 2010, China is expected to be consuming seven million barrels a day of oil with imports accounting for half of this. There are major investments being made to improve the performance of refineries and develop a transportation economy. The importance of this is underlined by the rapid rise in car ownership. In Beijing alone some 650 new cars find their way onto the streets every day.

4.3 Natural Gas Development

It seems clear that natural gas is central to sustainable economic growth in China and in this region. It has environmental advantages, and its reserves have, until recently, been largely untapped in this region.

Natural gas is a key part of the government's energy development plans in the Tenth Five-Year Plan. The planned eightfold increase in natural gas consumption in China over the next twenty years will be a major undertaking, involving harnessing indigenous resources, developing the infrastructure, and securing external supplies. Above all it will require more foreign investment in upstream gas projects, as well as timely investment in downstream infrastructure.

With further developments in the longer term, the in-country pipeline infrastructures could be connected to an Asian gas grid. This could link supply and demand right across the region. This will be complex, requiring regional cooperation with multigovernment involvement and massive investment by governments and private business.

4.4 Coal

China's dependency on coal has contributed to massive pollution in the past and at a major direct and indirect financial cost. This is recognized by the government. Coal will, however, continue to be a major contributor to the economy and the challenge for the government is not just to shut down poor quality coal sources but also to find ways to encourage the cleaner use of better quality coal through supporting the development of new technologies, improving management skills, and introducing effective regulatory mechanisms.

5 SHELL IN CHINA

Shell's focus in mainland China is to provide clean energy solutions that are sustainable over the long term, and help alleviate current serious pollution problems in the country.

This supports the government's commitment to improve the environmental performance and efficiency of today's coal based industry and introduce clean energies to fuel the rapidly growing economy in a sustainable way.

Shell is concentrating on gas and renewable energy and new methods of using coal as well as providing consulting services on energy efficiency and technological solutions.

In the fuels, lubricants, bitumen, and chemicals businesses, Shell offers the latest technological and environmental solutions to contribute to sustainable development.

All five of Shell's core businesses are represented in China: Exploration and Production; Gas and Power; Oil Products; Chemicals; and Renewable Energy.

Currently Shell has sixteen wholly owned or joint venture companies employing more than 1,000 staff and joint venture staff, more than ninety-five percent of whom are citizens of the People's Republic of China.

It has partnerships with all three of China's major oil and gas companies, PetroChina (and China National Petroleum Corporation – CNPC), The China Petroleum and Chemicals Corporation (Sinopec), and the China National Offshore Oil Corporation (CNOOC).

Key business developments currently are:

- The West-East Pipeline Project;
- The USD 4.3 billion Nanhai petrochemicals project in Guangdong Province;
- Jiangsu Oil Products retail joint venture in Jiangsu Province involving 500 stations;
- Growing lubricants and bitumen business throughout China;
- Gas developments onshore and offshore in the Tarim Basin, Bohai Bay, and the East China Sea;
- Coal gasification development;
- Solar electrification project in Xinjiang Autonomous Region.

5.1 Technological Solutions

The industry has a long record of successful technological change and this continues today. Gas has great competitive advantages for heating and power generation, as a source of ultra-clean liquids to help meet rising fuel standards, and – potentially – as a source of hydrogen for fuel cells.

Emitting much less carbon than coal and negligible sulphur, gas is a vital bridging fuel for reducing greenhouse emissions, as well as for improving air quality in developing cities. Gas consumption could double – perhaps grow threefold – by 2030. Gas use will be vital to the development of India and China.

Extending gas use and developing new forms of energy such as gas to liquids, hydrogen fuel cells, and renewables – overcoming technological challenges and fierce competition – requires long-term commitment.

5.2 Gas Use

Shell uses scenarios as a way of exploring much wider possibilities – encouraging debate, challenging assumptions, raising questions, and testing strategies.

Shell produced two sets last year. One explored how people may react to forces like globalization over the next two decades. The other considered alternative ways in which a dynamic energy system could develop while halting the rise in global carbon dioxide emissions before 2050. They help us plan how we are going to pursue the business opportunities of these changes.

We have worked with the Energy Research Institute in China to help it develop similar long-term energy scenarios for China, funded by the Shell Foundation.

Both scenarios confirm the increasing importance of gas – with its competitive advantages in costs, efficiency, cleanliness, reduced carbon, and role in new energy technologies. Gas could overtake oil to become the dominant fuel.

This depends on developing the secure infrastructure for delivering it to markets. Shell has particular capabilities in this area, including the world's leading liquefied natural gas (LNG) business.

An LNG plant in Nigeria, in which Shell has a share, is now being expanded and will help reduce the flaring of gas associated with oil operations in the country, thus making more efficient use of the resource and reducing CO_2 emissions. By 2006, $21 billion will have been invested in this plant to create one of the world's largest LNG schemes. Another new plant in Oman came into operation in 2000, supplying Korea. Shell is working on new schemes, including its largest LNG project so far on Sakhalin Island.

China is developing the country's natural gas markets. The largest gas infrastructure project is the West-East Pipeline, 4,000 kilometers long and capable of carrying twelve billion cubic meters of natural gas a year from western China to consumers in the east, equivalent to half China's current gas production. If all this gas were used to generate electricity, it would provide clean power for sixty million people – ten cities the size of Beijing. Shell is part of a consortium of three international oil companies negotiating to become involved in the project.

China is planning to build its first LNG terminal in Guangdong with supplies to come from the North West Shelf gas fields in Australia, in which Shell is one of six partners. Further import terminals are being planned, including plans for a terminal in Fuijian, and LNG will be an important part of China's gas development, along with the harnessing of reserves offshore in the East China Sea and Bohai Bay.

LNG is critical to the development of all North East Asia countries. LNG has historically been concentrated in the Far East, which today accounts for seventy percent of global sales. The majority of this goes to Japan, which, along with South Korea and Taiwan, imports most of its gas as LNG. Today, more than 110 million tonnes of LNG is sold annually in Asia Pacific. This business is anticipated to grow rapidly in the coming decade with important markets emerging in China and India.

5.3 Gas to Liquids

Gas can also be turned into liquid fuels used to produce ultra-clean products to reduce engine emissions. In Thailand, Shell recently launched a diesel incorporating these products from its pioneering plant in Sarawak. The fuel has immense potential for China, especially for public transportation. It can be used in existing diesel engines without conversion.

The Shell Group is at the forefront of Gas to Liquids (GTL) and has designed the leading proven technology to convert natural gas to middle distillates.

The Shell Middle Distillate Synthesis (SMDS) process uses natural gas as feedstock to produce high-quality middle distillates, such as diesel and kerosene, that are nontoxic, easy to transport, and biodegradable.

SMDS diesel burns much more cleanly than standard fuels making it a cost effective way to reduce emissions of hydrocarbons, particulate matter, carbon monoxide, and nitrogen oxides in the exhaust from diesel engines. This makes SMDS products attractive in markets such as Japan and California that put a premium on clean fuels.

Unlike some other alternative fuels, SMDS products can be delivered using the existing oil products infrastructure to power standard diesel engines. They can also be used in dedicated engines where, for example, the fuel's uniquely high octane number can boost fuel economy and its emissions benefits can be fully leveraged.

A Shell joint venture company built the first commercial middle distillate GTL plant in the world at Bintulu, Malaysia, in 1993. The plant produces 12,000 bbl/day of oil products for distribution around the world.

Shell Gas and Power has announced a Heads of Agreement in Qatar to build the world's largest Gas to Liquids plant.

5.4 Coal Gasification

Gas can also be produced cleanly from coal, of potentially major application in China, which has one-third of the world's coal reserves. China's huge and expanding economy depends on burning coal for nearly two-thirds of its energy.

Coal gasification is a partial combustion of carbonaceous materials, such as coal and petroleum coke, which uses only twenty to thirty percent of the amount of oxygen that would normally be required to achieve complete combustion.

Shell's coal gasification process is a dry process that uses nitrogen gas to transport powdered coal to the burners. The primary product is syngas, which is a mixture of carbon monoxide and hydrogen. The syngas contains about eighty percent of the original energy in the coal. Another fifteen percent of useful energy is recovered in the form of steam. Energy losses during gasification are only around five percent.

Syngas can be used to manufacture pure hydrogen and to synthesize ammonia, methanol, oxo chemicals, and their derivatives, such as urea fertilizer and synthetic hydrocarbon fuels. It can also be used directly as a fuel to generate heat, steam, and electricity in power plants and be supplied to town gas grids.

None of the constituents in the coal are wasted in Shell's process. The sulphur is recovered as pure sulphur and sold as a feedstock to the chemical industry, and the ash is recovered as clean slag that is used to make ceramic tiles and bricks. The process consumes little water and the waste water can easily be cleaned. Another advantage is the flexibility of Shell's process to be able to operate on wide range of coal qualities, including low quality subbituminous coal and lignite.

Shell has twenty-five years experience of this technology and is applying it in China in the fertilizer industry, providing a more affordable and cleaner feedstock.

Shell has a 50:50 joint venture with Sinopec in Yueyang, Hunan, to build a 2,000 tonne a day coal gasification plant to supply synthetic gas as feedstock to the Sinopec Baling Fertiliser Plant. Construction of the plant is now in progress. Shell Research Ltd.

has also signed six new licenses for its coal gasification technology to major fertilizer plants and other businesses in China.

5.5 Developing Renewable Energy

By 2030, when the world has doubled its energy demand, fossil fuels will remain important, but people are unlikely to tolerate increased pollution, extra infrastructure, and the possible effects on the climate. The world needs low emission and low carbon energy. It will take more than a decade before alternatives with large-scale potential can compete effectively. It will take several more decades before they deliver a large share of the globe's energy.

But many companies are working actively in this area. Shell Renewables, one of the five core businesses of the Royal Dutch/Shell Group, is working to reduce the costs of solar power and expanding its wind power business. Other parts of Shell are pursuing biofuels, geothermal (underground rocks), and hydrogen.

The costs of providing solar energy have fallen by more than fifty percent over the last ten years, thanks to rising output and advances in technology. That downward cost trend continues, making solar an increasingly attractive and viable choice for businesses and consumers.

Shell Solar is one of the leading solar companies in the world and aims to develop the commercial opportunities of solar electric power also known as photovoltaics (PV).

China is Shell's largest solar market in the Asia Pacific region and will continue to grow in the short and long term, particularly its rural electrification markets where Shell was a leading supplier in 2002 and 2003.

A major Shell project to bring electricity to up to 78,000 rural households over five years in the Xinjiang Autonomous Region started to deliver in 2002. Production of the home systems started in August and some 7,000 had been sold by the middle of 2003.

In wind energy, the latest turbines, can generate ten times the power at a third of the cost of their 1990 predecessors. The wind industry is continuing its pattern of rapid expansion and Shell's activities are designed not only to keep pace, but also to grow its position in the sector toward market leadership.

Hydrogen offers one of the most challenging prospects in this century for sustainable, emission free energy. In order to generate energy, a "fuel cell" is used. A fuel cell is an electrochemical device that contains a membrane that allows hydrogen ions (protons) to pass unimpeded to combine with oxygen to form water. Electrons cannot cross the membrane and are forced to take a longer route through wiring outside the cell and produce electricity.

Many companies in the energy and automobile industries are collaborating on development. Shell Hydrogen is involved in hydrogen demonstration projects for sustainable mobility in California, the Netherlands, and Luxembourg. It is also a partner in a project developing fuel cells for stationary applications in Norway.

We have opened a hydrogen station in Reykjavik, Iceland. The station will be used to refuel three DaimlerChrysler fuel cell buses that will be run on Reykjavik's streets. Private hydrogen vehicles are expected to be driving on Iceland's streets in the future.

In addition, Showa Shell has opened the first liquid hydrogen refueling station in Tokyo and we also plan to install a hydrogen dispenser at an existing Shell retail station in Washington DC, USA.

Other forms of renewable energy being pursued include biomass, biofuels, geothermal energy, and hydroelectric power.

6 ENERGY AND CLIMATE CHANGE

But how do we ensure that energy patterns evolve in a way that delivers these desirable
results while meeting the needs of society? What can responsible businesses do?

We need to make plain the inevitability of the climate impact, but begin to take
action to ensure that the outcome remains acceptable. As energy companies, we need to
address our own emissions, work on developing energy choices that help our customers
meet theirs, and establish GHG Cap and Trade systems – both internal to our companies
and nationally and internationally, developing a market that ensures that resources are
used most effectively.

Shell has found that putting a cost of carbon into project economics is a valuable step.
Although the impact on returns is often quite small, the impact is important because
it makes engineers think about the implications at an early stage. It makes thinking of
carbon impact a part of normal business.

Improving energy efficiency and reducing flaring are central to our commitment to
cut greenhouse gas emissions by ten percent from the 1990 level. This is an absolute
reduction. Taking account of business growth, the actual reduction is in the order of
thirty percent.

This reflects Shell's belief that action is required now to lay the foundation for stabilizing atmospheric greenhouse gas levels in the atmosphere equitably and economically.
Market-based policies are important. Shell has begun to learn by becoming a leading
player in emerging international markets for emissions credits. And it takes account of
potential future carbon costs in its investment decisions.

7 REGULATORY FRAMEWORKS FOR ENERGY GENERATION

There are limits to what business can do on its own. So what can business and government do together with consumers? Can we rely on consumers making the right choices
and guiding the path of development? Experience shows that for the common good to
be achieved or protected we need collective action. Governments provide a regulatory
framework; business works in commercial markets within that framework.

To encourage development of new technologies the government needs to set a policy
framework to encourage cleaner energy either through pricing, incentives, or subsidies.

At the moment the government is subsidizing solar photovoltaic projects in China
to bring electricity to remote rural areas.

A key factor in developing a viable natural gas industry in China is ensuring that
the large markets for gas are developed in parallel with the infrastructure, encouraged
and supported by government-provided enabling policies.

China is further defining a long-term natural gas strategy and developing a clear
legislative and regulatory framework. One key area is pricing policy. Natural gas is
price competitive with most alternative fuels in China, such as manufactured gas. Thus,
natural gas pricing should be based on prices customers currently pay for alternatives –
a policy common in other markets around the world, often referred to as "competitively
based sectoral pricing."

Enabling policies are also required for the urban natural gas distribution sector, including the reform of state owned distribution companies, promotion of third party investment, provision of stable, long-term franchise periods, and appropriate fiscal and tax support.

Experience also shows that stable markets and companies must be fully developed, and infrastructure put in place, before liberalization can work.

8 RESPONSIBLE OPERATIONS

Shell companies are committed to contributing to sustainable development in their business principles, and are integrating it into the way they do their work. They are committed to transparency and engaging with people's concerns and expectations. As well as responding to present challenges – improving the way operations are carried out and projects managed – they are pursuing innovatory ways of producing, supplying, and using energy. They believe that contributing to sustainable development is essential for continued business success.

The standard definition is from *Our Common Future* (the Brundtland Report), which is that "sustainable development is development that meets the needs of the present without compromising the ability of future generations to meet their own needs." In her foreword, Gro Harlem Brundtland argued for "a new era of economic growth – growth that is forceful and at the same time socially and environmentally sustainable."

Sustainable development is a process, not a state – a journey without a defined destination. The route is difficult. There are intractable issues and tough choices – and many different perspectives on them. There is still much to learn about what is required and how best to proceed.

Contributing to sustainable development does not mean philanthropy, nor public relations. It means doing good business – managing it properly and reaping the opportunities from doing so.

As Dr. Brundtland made clear, sustainable development is about raising people's living standards. Business is fundamental to that process and can not focus exclusively on it economic role. It is inseparable from its social and environmental impact. It means balancing the economic, social, and environmental aspects of operations: action today with tomorrow in mind.

9 SHELL COMPANIES APPROACH SUSTAINABLE DEVELOPMENT

Shell adopted the principle of sustainable development (SD) in 1997 and included it and human rights in its overarching business principles that define globally the way Shell people and companies do business.

It was seen as a business driven initiative that would be a powerful differentiator for Shell and bring tangible bottom line business benefits.

The concept was progressively rolled out to Royal Dutch/Shell Group companies in succeeding years so that all companies had management systems in place incorporating the principles of sustainable development by the end of 2001.

A two-step approach was taken:

- Hardwiring: integration of SD into business processes
- Awareness: increasing staff awareness

Figure 34.1

9.1 Hardwiring

An SD Management Framework was produced to provide a step-by-step guide for its introduction. It included examples and case studies of SD in action and a full "tool kit." This became one of the key tools to help staff understand how they could implement SD and integrate it into the planning and daily conduct of business activities. The framework consists of a series of eight management processes (see Figure 34.1), and for each of these processes, a number of questions, deliverables, and suggested activities were incorporated. These acted as prompts for employees to implement SD into their business. The framework also emphasized the importance of engaging with stakeholders. Sustainable development also became part of the "scorecard" for every business so staff bonuses and pay raises were partly linked with their business's success in ensuring SD was introduced successfully.

9.2 Awareness

To succeed, the Group needed to engage the "hearts and minds" of staff in a similar way to safety which a decade earlier successfully became an integral part of the way we did business. Deadlines were set to build awareness of the sustainable development principles among staff. These included the requirement for senior managers to participate in workshops on sustainable development to understand what it meant and what part they played in developing awareness among their staff.

9.3 Reporting

We started reporting annual Group results against the triple bottom line of sustainable development in 1998 and Group companies started doing the same. Shell companies in mainland China have produced an SD annual report for three years.

Shell has developed seven principles to define sustainable development and these now guide decision making. None were new to the way Shell works, but taken together they helped us find a balance between long- and short-term goals. They are:

- Generating robust profitability;
- Delivering value to customers;
- Protecting the environment;
- Managing resources;
- Respecting and safeguarding people;
- Benefiting communities; and
- Working with stakeholders.

At the same time we redefined the way we looked at social issues, moving from an approach based on social investment – programs that brought benefits to society running in parallel to its business – to social performance that sought to understand and integrate all the ways in which our business has an effect on society, looked to mitigate the negative impacts, and take advantage of opportunities to bring benefits.

9.4 Use of Tools Like Environmental, Social, and Health Impact Assessment (ESHIA) and HSE-MS

Besides the SD management framework, other tools have been developed to help businesses introduce SD. These include business process tools, project and operations related tools, total cost assessment tools, management systems, and stakeholder engagement tools. Two critical tools used in China are ESHIA and HSE-MS.

This is the key tool for all major new projects to define and understand the social, economic, and environmental issues connected with the project and develop mitigation measures to reduce the impact and opportunities to bring benefits. Shell has guidelines and processes for this assessment, which are used routinely around the world, including China.

HSE-MS is a risk-based management system to manage HSE issues in an established or new business.

Shell has completed ESHIA work to Chinese and international standards on its two major projects to date: the USD 4.3 billion Nanhai petrochemicals project and the West–East Pipeline project, a 4000-kilometer natural gas pipeline running across the country.

The Nanhai Project

Shell is a fifty percent shareholder in the Nanhai project, which involves the construction and operation of a world scale petrochemical plant. At the heart of the complex is a world scale condensate or naphtha cracker producing 800,000 tpa ethylene and 430,000 tpa propylene.

Despite regulatory approval being received for an Environmental Impact Statement (EIS) in 1997, the board of the joint venture agreed to proceed with a new Environmental and Social Impact Assessment (ESIA) to international standards. The aim was to add the social element, which was missing in the earlier work, and also do more work on the environmental side to reflect the more detailed design work completed since 1997.

The joint venture approach to the ESIA was to form a partnership among contractor companies including international and Chinese companies. The group included:

- AD Little;
- Zhongshan University, which completed the 1997 EIS;
- the Nanjing Environmental Protection Research Institute (NEPRI), a Chinese company with growing experience of the international requirements for EIAs; and
- Environmental Risk Management;

Emphasis in the ESIA was placed on obtaining accurate and complete data of the environment using local expertise and advice. The Institute of Environmental Science at Zhongshan University is the acknowledged expert in the area and was part of the ESIA consortium. It also was responsible for gathering and coordinating other expert data available in Guangdong. Links were also established with the South China Sea Research Institute and the management of a turtle reserve close to Daya Bay. Development of social and health impacts and economic background data came from links with a range of government authorities including planning, statistics, and tourism.

Marine impact from the project will be mainly temporary from construction of a jetty, a dolphin berth for ships delivering feedstock, and two subsea pipelines carrying feedstock and effluent.

Benthic studies were completed in these areas to mitigate and minimize impacts. Dredging techniques were developed to minimize siltation and avoid sensitive habitats. The benthic survey revealed there to be more diverse and healthier coral than expected close to the causeway/marine offloading facility area. These colonies could be affected by operations so the joint venture decided to relocate approximately 400 m² of healthy ball-shaped coral to a location about ten kilometers from the construction site in an effort to assist its continued survival. The work was done in partnership with The South China Sea Fisheries Institute in May and June. A program has been set up to monitor the transplanted coral.

Hong Kong NGOs were consulted on the terms of reference for the ESIA and a workshop of NGOs, academics, and government representatives from Guangdong and Hong Kong was held to discuss the draft results. An Environmental and Social Management Plan was developed from the ESIA and is being used for construction which started this year.

West-East Pipeline Project

Shell is part of an international consortium of companies, including ExxonMobil and Gazprom, looking to take a combined forty-five percent shareholding in the project, with PetroChina (fifty percent) and Sinopec (five percent).

Negotiations toward finalizing the Joint Venture Contracts are still taking place, so we are not formally official partners in the project yet. Consequently, our role to date has been one of influence.

It is a complex integrated upstream, midstream, and downstream project, costing some US\$ 8.5 billion, to bring gas from the northwest of China to the fast developing cities in the east. It forms an important part of the Chinese government's plan to increase use of gas and develop cleaner energy resources to sustain economic growth.

Shell has worked with its prospective partners to develop strategies and tools to encourage the West-East project toward international standards and to ensure their implementation on the ground.

Prior to Shell's entry into negotiations for the project, EIAs had already been conducted for each province and approved by the Provincial Environmental Protection Bureaux (EPBs) and subsequently by the State Environmental Protection Administration (SEPA). As part of this EIA process, consultation was undertaken by PetroChina and options evaluated for rerouting, wherever considered practical and cost effective.

We had to work through and balance a myriad of arrangements, including:

- building the case to go beyond mere regulatory compliance;
- justifying broader approaches to stakeholder consultation; and
- undertaking an ESIA to build on the already government approved EIAs.

The first step was to agree on a set of health, safety, environment, and social standards and sustainable development principles that would be followed that met all potential partner needs. Shell signed this document as part of its first agreement on the pipeline.

It did this in parallel with an evaluation of the ESHIA work that had been done and agreed that more work was needed, especially for a social impact assessment, which is not required by law in China.

All parties agreed on a delay in construction and developed a fast track ESHIA process that allowed construction to start in a phased fashion as work was completed in each area.

A set of minimum criteria were quickly agreed to allow trial construction to start, essential as automated techniques new to China were being used for construction. The minimum criteria covered issues such as construction at cultural relics sites, Great Wall, nature reserves, avoidance of local communities, compensation and resettlement arrangements, health and safety, and audits/inspections.

This has been undertaken within a challenging context of negotiating a minority shareholding in a nonoperated joint venture.

But we also invest in the community – as a way of engaging with the societies in which we operate, and to make sure our neighbors share in the benefits of our operations.

9.5 Social Performance

At the same time Shell redefined the way it looked at social issues, moving from an approach based on social investment – programs that brought benefits to society running in parallel to its business – to social performance that sought to understand and integrate all the ways in which our business has an effect on society, looked to mitigate the negative impacts, and take advantage of opportunities to bring benefits.

An example for Shell in China is the West–East Pipeline project. It had been agreed with PetroChina that Shell conduct a Social Impact Assessment along the pipeline route. Managing an engagement exercise along 4,000 kilometers of the route was a major challenge for a commercial company such as Shell, legally not connected to the project and faced with legislation restricting foreign companies in sponsoring surveys.

Given the complexities involved, Shell initiated a "first of its kind" partnership in China with the United Nations Development Program (UNDP) and the China International Centre for Economic and Technology Exchange (CICETE) to conduct the social impact survey. UNDP, with its unique status in the country, its well-developed partnerships with national institutions and its experience of conducting similar surveys in China, was well placed to perform the work.

It was the first major social impact assessment survey of its kind for a major infra-structure project in China, engaging 10,000 people along the pipeline route.

UNDP hopes that the social survey will have a major impact on the way large-scale investment projects will be carried out in the future in the country and we hope to continue this partnership into developing programs to help alleviate some of the issues that were recorded in the survey.

9.6 The Shell Foundation

The Shell Foundation is an essential element of this – an independent grant making charity, dedicated to helping people help themselves. The Foundation is separated from Shell's commercial interest. But its ability to make a difference is strengthened by its relationship with Shell companies all around the world. Its programs – supporting efforts to reduce the impact of fossil fuels, to help poor communities gain access to modern energy, and to help them generate income – reflect this relationship.

The board is composed of three of Shell's most senior executives and three external trustees of international repute and with professional experience directly relevant to its work. With an endowment from Shell of US$250 million, the Foundation has long-term financial security and complete independence.

The focus of the Shell Foundation is directed toward finding sustainable solutions to social and environmental problems linked to energy production and consumption, as well as to harnessing the potential of globalization to enhance the development prospects of vulnerable communities. The decision to explicitly couple social investment with issues associated with Shell's core business and multinational character is the defining determinant of the foundation's core programs.

In China, the Shell Foundation has spent US$ 2.2 million. It is sponsoring rice straw gasification trials. The Institute for Thermal Power Engineering (ITPE) of Zhejiang University is exploring the feasibility of the gasification of rice straw in Zhejiang Province to reduce pollution and provide low cost energy. The goal of the research project is to develop, demonstrate, and commercialize an advanced biomass gasification technology that produces medium calorific gas from rice straw stubble, normally burned in the fields creating serious pollution.

It also sponsored a community biomass project in Yunnan China. The project helps farmers in a Yunnan nature reserve convert animal waste to heat and fertilizer and so reduce firewood collection while increasing their income by growing cash crops in greenhouses attached to their dwellings. The first phase of this two-year project, by the South-North Institute for Sustainable Development, finished in 2002, demonstrating that the pilot greenhouse system worked.

10 CHALLENGES IN CHINA

Most of Shell's activities are in the business development stage involving projects that are about to start, or have just started. The key tool for implementing SD in these cases is the ESHIA, which maps out the key social, health, and environmental issues surround-ing the projects and provides the data from which Environmental, Social and Health Management Plans can be developed. ESHIAs to Chinese and international standards have been developed for the company's Changbei project, the Nanhai petrochemicals project, and the West-East Pipeline project. These have all involved an integrated approach involving partners and governments to ensure experiences and learning are shared.

The key learning when developing the SD approach with partners and government departments is the need to work across skill sets and disciplines in order to integrate SD and look at the concept holistically. The concept is counter to the typical organization models in use in China and requires patience and persistence to build a common understanding, align views, and agree on approaches. This is important for Shell as nearly all of our businesses in China are joint ventures with Chinese companies.

There are differences in approach in the Chinese and international models for elements of SD. In the international model, HSE management systems are risk based on the concept of "As Low As Realistically Practicable" (ALARP), rather than the China system – driven by legislative standards. Social issues present a greater gap with social impact assessment not yet an established part of the ESHIA system in China. In many cases, typically social issues are not handled within a company but separately by the provincial or municipal government with little interaction. Building up those links is a key part of the process.

Social assessment work completed in 2002 on the West-East Pipeline project involving UNDP in tandem with Chinese institutes and organizations marks a new approach in developing major state infrastructure projects.

11 A BUSINESS CASE

We see a clear business case for sustainable development. We believe it increases our effectiveness by reducing costs through ecoefficiency, as well as the risks of doing things that might damage our business.

We think it promotes innovation – helping us to understand the business opportunities arising from changing values and lifestyles.

We think it is fundamental for our reputation, particularly with our customers, and vital for attracting and motivating the talent we need for success in an increasingly demanding business environment.

At Shell, we are committed to growing value for our shareholders by delivering robust profitability and making the best of our competitive edge. But have no doubt that doing so depends on being seen to respond to changing expectations. We don't just think that contributing to sustainable development is good business. We think it is fundamental for our future.

In such a dynamic and expanding economy as China's, sustainable development is even more important and dovetails with the government's own commitment to growing its economy is a sustainable way.

This brings me back to the point of partnership. Business is part of the solution. So are government and other parts of society. The future is shared. The future is ours.

Index

For EU product safety concerns, contact us at Calle de José Abascal, 56–1°,
28003 Madrid, Spain or eugpsr@cambridge.org.

www.ingramcontent.com/pod-product-compliance
Ingram Content Group UK Ltd.
Pitfield, Milton Keynes, MK11 3LW, UK
UKHW030806060825
461487UK00019B/1723